LAW FOR JOURNALISTS

LAW FOR JOURNALISTS

Fifth Edition

Frances Quinn

PEARSON

Harlow, England • London • New York • Boston • San Francisco • Toronto • Sydney
Auckland • Singapore • Hong Kong • Tokyo • Seoul • Taipei • New Delhi
Cape Town • São Paulo • Mexico City • Madrid • Amsterdam • Munich • Paris • Milan

PEARSON EDUCATION LIMITED
Edinburgh Gate
Harlow CM20 2JE
United Kingdom
Tel: +44 (0)1279 623623
Web: www.pearson.com/uk

First published in 2007 (print)
Second edition published 2009 (print)
Third edition published 2011 (print)
Fourth edition published 2013 (print and electronic)
Fifth edition published 2015 (print and electronic)

ISBN: 978-1-292-01775-4 (print)
978-1-292-01778-5 (PDF)
978-1-292-01776-1 (eText)

British Library Cataloguing-in-Publication Data
A catalogue record for the print edition is available from the British Library

Library of Congress Cataloging-in-Publication Data
Quinn, Frances, 1963- author.
Law for journalists / Frances Quinn. – Fifth edition.
pages cm
ISBN 978-1-292-01775-4
1. Journalists—Legal status, laws, etc.—Great Britain. 2. Press law—Great Britain. 3. Mass media—Law and legislation—Great Britain. I. Title.
KD2875.Q56 2015
349.4202'407–dc23

2015005338

10 9 8 7 6 5 4 3 2 1
19 18 17 16 15

Print edition typeset in 9.5/12 ITC Giovanni Std by 71
Printed in Malaysia, CTP-PJB

NOTE THAT ANY PAGE CROSS REFERENCES REFER TO THE PRINT EDITION

Brief contents

Acknowledgements xii

Table of cases xiii

Table of European legislation xxiv

Table of statutory instruments xxv

Table of statutes xxv

Section 1 LAW AND THE LEGAL SYSTEM 1

Chapter 1 How law is made 3

Chapter 2 The legal system 11

Chapter 3 Criminal courts and procedure 18

Chapter 4 Civil courts and procedure 43

Chapter 5 Human rights and English law 53

Section 2 WRITING ABOUT THE COURTS 61

Chapter 6 Contempt of court 63

Chapter 7 Access to the courts 97

Chapter 8 General reporting restrictions 113

Chapter 9 Reporting restrictions in criminal cases 126

Chapter 10 Reporting restrictions concerning children 149

Chapter 11 Reporting the family court 165

Chapter 12 Reporting inquests 187

Chapter 13 Reporting tribunals and inquiries 194

Chapter 14 Challenging reporting restrictions 203

Section 3 DEFAMATION AND MALICIOUS FALSEHOOD 211

Chapter 15 Defamation 213

Chapter 16 Defences and remedies for defamation 245

Chapter 17 Malicious falsehood 278

Section 4 **PRIVACY, CONFIDENTIALITY AND COPYRIGHT** 283

Chapter 18 Breach of confidence 285
Chapter 19 Privacy 299
Chapter 20 Trespass, harassment and unethical behaviour 321
Chapter 21 Protecting sources and source material 328
Chapter 22 Data protection 344
Chapter 23 Copyright 358

Section 5 **CODES OF PRACTICE AND ETHICS** 379

Chapter 24 IPSO and the Editors' Code of Practice of the Press Complaints Commission 381
Chapter 25 The Ofcom Code 389

Section 6 **REPORTING GOVERNMENT AND BUSINESS** 407

Chapter 26 Official secrets 409
Chapter 27 Reporting local government 416
Chapter 28 Reporting elections 428
Chapter 29 Freedom of information 434
Chapter 30 Writing about business 450

Section 7 **RACE, RELIGION AND PUBLIC ORDER** 461

Chapter 31 Race and religion 463

Section 8 **PHOTOGRAPHY** 469

Chapter 32 Photography 471

Appendix 1 Editors' Code of Practice of the PCC 478
Appendix 2 The Ofcom Broadcasting Code 482
Appendix 3 Defamation Act 1996 516
Glossary 523
Further reading 528
Index 530

Full contents

Acknowledgements xii
Table of cases xiii
Table of European legislation xxiv
Table of statutory instruments xxv
Table of statutes xxv

SECTION 1 LAW AND THE LEGAL SYSTEM 1

1 How law is made 3

Sources of law 3
Key points 9
Test your knowledge 10
Online resources 10

2 The legal system 11

Types of law 11
The court system 12
People in the legal system 13
Key points 15
Test your knowledge 16
Online resources 17

3 Criminal courts and procedure 18

The criminal courts 18
Magistrates' courts 18
Criminal justice procedure 19
Types of sentence 28
Appeals and retrials 31
Common crimes 35
Key points 40
Test your knowledge 41
Online resources 42

4 Civil courts and procedure 43

The civil courts 43
Civil litigation procedure 45
Appeals in civil cases 47
Common civil claims 49
Key points 51
Test your knowledge 51
Online resources 52

5 Human rights and English law 53

The European Convention and the Human Rights Act 53
Human rights and media law 55
Key points 58
Test your knowledge 59
Online resources 60

SECTION 2 WRITING ABOUT THE COURTS 61

6 Contempt of court 63

Publications prejudicial to a fair trial 64
'Strict liability' contempt 64
Intentional contempt 82
Other types of contempt 86
Sanctions for contempt 91
Key points 94
Test your knowledge 95
Online resources 96

7 Access to the courts 97

The general rule on access 97
Restrictions on court access 100

Key points 110
Test your knowledge 111
Online resources 112

8 General reporting restrictions 113

Reporting restrictions under the Contempt of Court Act 1981 113
Postponing publication: the s4(2) order 114
Preventing publication: the s11 order 119
Other general reporting restrictions 123
Key points 124
Test your knowledge 125
Online resources 125

9 Reporting restrictions in criminal cases 126

Restrictions on hearings before trial 126
Restrictions in rape and sexual offences 133
Reporting pleas in mitigation 139
Protecting vulnerable witnesses 140
Reporting restrictions in appeals against acquittal 143
Key points 146
Test your knowledge 147
Online resources 147

10 Reporting restrictions concerning children 149

Youth court cases 149
Children in adult courts 152
Provisions against anti-social behaviour 160
Provisions not yet in force 161
Key points 162
Test your knowledge 163
Online resources 164

11 Reporting the family court 165

The work of the family court 165
Access to family proceedings 166
Reporting the family courts 172
Key points 183
Test your knowledge 186
Online resources 186

12 Reporting inquests 187

Inquest procedure 187
Reporting inquests 189
Key points 192
Test your knowledge 192
Online resources 193

13 Reporting tribunals and inquiries 194

Reporting tribunals 194
Employment tribunals 196
Public inquiries 200
Key points 201
Test your knowledge 201
Online resources 202

14 Challenging reporting restrictions 203

Preventing restrictions 203
Challenging orders 204
Key points 209
Test your knowledge 209
Online resources 210

SECTION 3 DEFAMATION AND MALICIOUS FALSEHOOD 211

15 Defamation 213

The elements of defamation 214
The meaning of 'defamatory' 214
Referring to the claimant 231
Publication 236
Who can sue for defamation? 239
Slander 241
Key points 242
Test your knowledge 243
Online resources 244

16 Defences and remedies for defamation 245

Defences 245
Remedies for defamation 272

Key points 275
Test your knowledge 276
Online resources 277

17 Malicious falsehood 278

What is malicious falsehood? 278
Key points 280
Test your knowledge 281

SECTION 4 PRIVACY, CONFIDENTIALITY AND COPYRIGHT 283

18 Breach of confidence 285

Elements of a breach of confidence claim 285
Defences 292
Remedies for breach of confidence 295
Key points 296
Test your knowledge 297
Online resources 298

19 Privacy 299

Elements of a privacy claim 299
Remedies in privacy actions 311
Claims under the Protection from Harassment Act 1997 314
Key points 319
Test your knowledge 319
Online resources 320

20 Trespass, harassment and unethical behaviour 321

Trespass 321
Harassment 322
Intercepting calls, post or emails 323
Key points 326
Test your knowledge 326
Online resources 327

21 Protecting sources and source material 328

The Contempt of Court Act 1981 329
PACE – information required by the police 332
The Official Secrets Acts 336
The Terrorism Act 2000 336
Other legislation 338
Key points 341
Test your knowledge 342
Online resources 343

22 Data protection 344

Information covered by the Act 344
Media duties under the Act 346
Exemptions for the media 349
Investigation and enforcement 351
Problems with gathering information 352
Obtaining information from others 355
Key points 355
Test your knowledge 356
Online resources 357

23 Copyright 358

Works protected by copyright 358
Ownership of copyright 362
Infringing copyright 364
Defences 366
Remedies for breach of copyright 372
Moral and privacy rights 373
Key points 375
Test your knowledge 376
Online resources 377

SECTION 5 CODES OF PRACTICE AND ETHICS 379

24 IPSO and the Editors' Code of Practice of the Press Complaints Commission 381

Complaints to IPSO 381
The Editors' Code of Practice 382
Key points 387
Test your knowledge 388
Online resources 388

25 The Ofcom Code 389
The Ofcom Broadcasting Code 389
Provisions of the Code 390
Complaints under the Code 402
Key points 403
Test your knowledge 404
Online resources 405

SECTION 6
REPORTING GOVERNMENT AND BUSINESS 407

26 Official secrets 409
The Official Secrets Act 1911 409
Official Secrets Act 1989 410
Defence Advisory Notices 413
Key points 414
Test your knowledge 415
Online resources 415

27 Reporting local government 416
The basic rules on reporting local government meetings 416
Access to local government meetings 417
Access to local government records 423
Other local public bodies 425
Key points 426
Test your knowledge 427
Online resources 427

28 Reporting elections 428
Offences related to election reporting 428
Other legal considerations 431
Key points 432
Test your knowledge 433
Online resources 433

29 Freedom of information 434
The Freedom of Information Act 2000 434
Environmental information 445
Key points 447
Test your knowledge 448
Online resources 448

30 Writing about business 450
The law on business information 450
Information on limited companies 451
Insolvency proceedings 454
Other proceedings for companies in trouble 457
Key points 458
Test your knowledge 459
Online resources 460

SECTION 7
RACE, RELIGION AND PUBLIC ORDER 461

31 Race and religion 463
Incitement to racial hatred 463
Religious hatred 465
Key points 467
Test your knowledge 467
Online resources 468

SECTION 8
PHOTOGRAPHY 469

32 Photography 471
Private property 471
Public places 472
Copyright and confidentiality 475
Key points 476
Test your knowledge 476
Online resources 477

Appendices
1 Editors' Code of Practice of the PCC 478
2 The Ofcom Broadcasting Code 482
3 Defamation Act 1996 516

Glossary 523
Further reading 528
Index 530

Acknowledgements

Thanks to Pat Bond of Pearson Education, who first came up with the idea for this book – there've been times in the past few years when I've cursed you for it, Pat, but thanks anyway! Michelle Gallagher was my editor during the first stages of the book, and a constant source of support and enthusiasm – thank you. Thanks are also due to my second editor, Zoë Botterill, and her assistant, at the time of the first edition, Cheryl Cheasley, who were a mine of good ideas during the writing of the book – I really appreciate all the hard work you both did.

Thanks to all the people who generously shared their experience and knowledge, and patiently answered my questions, particularly Rod Dadak of Lewis Silkin, former magistrate John Shillum, Freedom of Information campaigner and journalist Heather Brooke, Tony Jaffa of Foot Anstey, barristers' clerk Deborah Anderson, and of course, my consultant editor, Ken Eaton. Thanks too to journalist and lecturer Janice Bhend, for introducing me to Ken.

Finally, thanks to all the friends and family who put up with me moaning about how this book would never be finished, and most of all, to my husband, Mike Jeffree, for support, advice and always knowing when to open a bottle of wine.

Acknowledgements to the second and third editions

Thanks to Steve Harris and Gill Ursell of the Broadcast Journalism Training Council, and Nick Myers of ITV Meridian, for helping me to increase the coverage of broadcast journalism, and to Gary Birch for creating the new, more user-friendly index.

Acknowledgements to the fourth edition

Thanks to my editor for this edition, Cheryl Cheasley, and to Project Editor, Liz Johnson.

Acknowledgements to the fifth edition

Thanks to my editor, Owen Knight, and copy-editor, Linda Dhondy.

Publisher's acknowledgements

We are grateful to the following for permission to reproduce copyright material:

Appendix 1 from Editors' Code of Practice and extracts on pages 145, 165, 166, 186, 331, 397, 480 and 487, reprinted by permission of the Press Standards Board of Finance Ltd.; Appendix 2 from the Ofcom Broadcasting Code and extracts from pages 145, 165, 166, 186, 332, 406, 407 and 410 © Ofcom; Appendix 3 from the Defamation Act, and various extracts from HMSO contain public sector information licensed under the Open Government Licence (OGL) v3.0. http://www.nationalarchives.gov.uk/doc/open-government-licence.

In some instances we have been unable to trace the owners of copyright material, and we would appreciate any information that would enable us to do so.

Tables

TABLE OF CASES

A *v* Independent News and Media (2010) (unreported) *184*

A *v* Times Newspapers Ltd [2002] EWHC 2444 (Fam); [2003] 1 All ER 587 *209*

AAA *v* Associated Newspapers Ltd [2012] EWHC 2224 (QB); [2012] All ER (D) 07 (Aug) ***305***

Ackroyd *v* Mersey Care NHS Trust [2006] EWHC 107 (QB); 88 BMLR 1 **333**

Adam *v* Ward [1917] AC 309; 86 LJKB 849; [1916–17] All ER Rep 157, HL *262*

Adam Sheppard *v* Daily Star (2010) 27 September (unreported) *385*

Aiken *v* Police Review Publishing Co Ltd (1995) (unreported) *238*

Aitken *v* The Guardian and Granada Television (1997) (unreported) *248*

Ajinomoto Sweeteners Europe SAS *v* Asda Stores Ltd [2010] EWCA Civ 609; [2011] QB 497; [2010] 4 All ER 1029 *281*

Al-Fagih *v* HH Saudi Research and Marketing (UK) Ltd [2001] EWCA Civ 1634; [2002] EMLR 215; [2001] All ER (D) 48 (Nov) *268*

Allan *v* Clibbery [2001] 2 FCR 577; [2001] 2 FLR 819 *187*

Allen *v* Grimsby Telegraph [2011] EWHC 406 (QB); [2011] All ER (D) 30 (Mar) *121*

Application by Guardian News and Media Ltd and others in Her Majesty's Treasury (Respondent) *v* Mohammed Jabar Ahmed and others (FC) (Appellants); Her Majesty's Treasury (Respondent) *v* Mohammed al-Ghabra (FC) (Appellant); R (on the application of Hani El Sayed Sabaei Youssef) (Respondent) *v* Her Majesty's Treasury (Appellant) [2010] UKSC 1; [2010] 2 AC 697; [2010] 2 All ER 799 *123*

Archer *v* News of the World (1987) (unreported) *250*

Archer *v* Williams [2003] EWHC 1670 (QB); [2003] EMLR 869 *289*

Armstrong *v* Times Newspapers Ltd [2006] EWHC 1614 (QB); [2006] All ER (D) 358 (Jun) *251*

Arthur Bennett *v* Newsquest (2006) (unreported) *259*

Ashdown *v* Telegraph Group Ltd [2001] EWCA Civ 1142; [2002] Ch 149; [2001] 4 All ER 666 *370, 372*

Ashworth Hospital Authority *v* MGN Ltd [2002] UKHL 29; [2002] 4 All ER 193; [2002] 1 WLR 2033 *332, 335, 345*

Aspro Travel Ltd *v* Owners Abroad Group plc [1995] 4 All ER 728; [1996] 1 WLR 132 *237*

Assistant Deputy Coroner for Inner West London *v* Channel 4 Television Corporation [2007] EWHC 2513 (QB) *333*

Attorney-General *v* Associated Newspapers (1983) *The Times*, 12 February *81*

Attorney-General *v* Associated Newspapers [1994] 2 AC 238; [1994] 1 All ER 556; [1994] 2 WLR 277 *89*

Attorney-General *v* Associated Newspapers and MGN Ltd [2012] EWHC 2029 (Admin); [2012] All ER (D) 185 (Jul) *73*

Attorney-General *v* Associated Newspapers and News Group Newspapers [2011] EWHC 418 (Admin); [2011] 1 WLR 2097 *73*

Attorney-General *v* Barker [1990] 3 All ER 257 *289*

Attorney-General *v* BBC [1981] AC 303; [1980] 3 All ER 161; [1980] 3 WLR 109 *196*

Attorney-General *v* BBC (1987) *Times;* 18 December *291*

Attorney-General *v* BBC and Hat Trick Productions [1997] EMLR 76 *70*

Attorney-General *v* English [1983] 1 AC 116; [1982] 2 All ER 903; [1982] 3 WLR 278 *80, 81*

Attorney-General *v* Evening Standard [1998] EMLR 711 *72*

Attorney-General *v* Express Newspapers Ltd [2005] EMLR 13 *74, 78*

Attorney-General *v* Guardian Newspapers Ltd (No 2) [1990] 1 AC 109; [1988] 3 All ER 545; [1988] 2 WLR 805 *291, 292, 294, 296, 315*

Attorney-General *v* Guardian Newspapers Ltd (No 3) [1992] 3 All ER 38; [1992] 1 WLR 874 *69*

Attorney-General *v* ITV Central [2008] EWHC 1984 (Admin); [2008] All ER (D) 192 (Jul) *70*

Attorney-General *v* Jonathan Cape Ltd; Attorney-General *v* Times Newspapers Ltd [1976] QB 752; [1975] 3 All ER 484; [1975] 3 WLR 606 *289*

Attorney-General *v* Leveller Magazine [1979] AC 440; [1979] 1 All ER 745; [1979] 2 WLR 247 *97, 100*

Attorney-General *v* MGN [1997] 1 All ER 456; [1997] EMLR 284 *72, 77, 78*

Attorney-General *v* MGN [2002] EWHC 907 (Admin) *70*

Attorney-General *v* MGN and Another (2011) (unreported) *75*

Attorney-General *v* Morgan (1997) *Independent,* 17 July; [1998] EMLR 294 *70*

Attorney-General *v* News Group Newspapers [1986] 2 All ER 833; [1987] QB 1; [1986] 3 WLR 365 *69*

Attorney-General *v* News Group Newspapers [1988] 2 All ER 906; [1989] QB 110; [1988] 3 WLR 163 *69, 83*

Attorney-General *v* News Group Newspapers (1999) (unreported) *71*

Attorney-General *v* Seckerson and Times Newspapers Ltd [2009] EWHC 1023 (Admin); [2009] EMLR 371; [2009] All ER (D) 106 (May) *89*

Attorney-General *v* Sport Newspapers [1992] 1 All ER 503; [1991] 1 WLR 1194 *83*

Attorney-General *v* Sunday Newspapers Ltd [1999] COD 11, QBD *71*

Attorney-General *v* The Spectator (2012) (unreported) *87*

Attorney-General *v* TVS Television Ltd (1989) *The Times,* 7 July *81*

Attorney-General *v* Unger [1998] 1 Cr App Rep 308; [1998] EMLR 280 *70, 75*

Attorney-General's Reference No 3 of 1999: Application by the British Broadcasting Corporation to set aside or vary a Reporting Restriction Order [2009] UKHL 34; [2009] All ER (D) 175 (Jun) *144*

Author of a Blog, The *v* Times Newspapers Ltd [2009] EWHC 1358 (QB); [2009] NLJR 924 *302–303, 308*

Axel Springer AG *v* Germany (Application No 39954/08) (2012) 32 BHRC 493 *308*

BBC *v* British Satellite Broadcasting Ltd [1992] Ch 141; [1991] 3 All ER 833; [1991] 3 WLR 174 *371*

BBC *v* Kelly [2001] 1 FLR 197; [2001] 1 All ER 323; [2001] 2 WLR 253 *179*

BKM Ltd *v* British Broadcasting Corp [2009] EWHC 3151 (Ch); [2009] All ER (D) 24 (Dec) *296*

Baigent *v* Random House (*Re* The Lawyer) [2006] EWHC 1131 (Ch); [2006] All ER (D) 26 (May) *91, 362*

Banier *v* News Group Newspapers Ltd [1997] FSR 812; [1997] 30 LS Gaz R 29 *370, 475*

Barot, *Re* [2006] EWCA Crim 2692; [2007] EMLR 145; [2007] UKHRR 577 *117*

Belfast Telegraph Newspapers Ltd's Application, *Re* [1997] NI 309; (1997) *Times*, 27 August *122*

Bento *v* Chief Constable of Bedfordshire Police [2012] EWCA Civ 956; [2012] All ER (D) 189 (Jul) *230*

Berkoff *v* Burchill [1996] 4 All ER 1008; [1997] EMLR 139 *217*

Bernstein of Leigh (Baron) *v* Skyviews and General Ltd [1978] QB 479; [1977] 2 All ER 902; [1977] 3 WLR 136 *324*

Birmingham Mail *v* ED [2011] EWCA Civ 1759 *115*

Blackshaw *v* Lord [1984] QB 1; [1983] 2 All ER 311; [1983] 3 WLR 283 *261*

Bonnick *v* Morris [2002] UKPC 31; [2003] 1 AC 300; [2002] 3 WLR 820 *265*

Bowman *v* MGN Ltd [2010] EWHC 895 (QB); [2010] All ER (D) 173 (Apr) *218*

Brandon Webster; *Re*; Norfolk County Council *v* Webster [2006] EWHC 2733 (Fam); [2006] All ER (D) 32 (Nov) *176*

Branson *v* Bower (No 1) [2001] EWCA Civ 791; [2001] All ER (D) 315 (May) *254*

Bright *v* Central Criminal Court, *See* R *v* Central Criminal Court, *ex p* Bright

British Chiropractic Association *v* Singh [2010] EWCA Civ 350; [2011] 1 WLR 133 *254*

British Steel Corpn *v* Granada Television Ltd [1981] AC 1096; [1981] 1 All ER 417; [1980] 3 WLR 774 *293*

Browne of Madingley (Lord) *v* Associated Newspapers Ltd [2007] EWCA Civ 295; [2008] QB 103; [2007] 3 WLR 289 *305*

Budu *v* BBC [2010] EWHC 616 (QB); [2010] All ER (D) 85 (Apr) *227*

Bunn *v* BBC [1998] 3 All ER 552 *291*

Burns *v* Associated Newspapers Ltd (1925) 89 JP 205; (1925) 42 TLR 37 *431*

Burstein *v* Associated Newspapers Ltd [2007] EWCA Civ 600; [2007] 4 All ER 319 *256*

Burstein *v* Times Newspapers Ltd [2001] 1 WLR 579; [2000] All ER (D) 2384 *223*

Byrne *v* Deane [1937] 1 KB 818; [1937] 2 All ER 204 *217*

CTB *v* News Group Newspapers, *See* Giggs (previously known as CTB) *v* News Group Newspapers

Cairns *v* Modi; KC *v* MGN Ltd [2012] EWCA Civ 1382; [2012] All ER (D) 01 (Nov) *218*

Camelot Group plc *v* Centaur Communications Ltd [1999] QB 124; [1998] 1 All ER 251; [1998] 2 WLR 379 *332*

Campbell *v* MGN [2004] UKHL 22, HL; *Reversing* [2002] EWCA Civ 1373 *288, 301–304, 307, 309, 322, 347, 352, 473, 475*

Campbell-James *v* Guardian Media Group plc [2005] EWHC 893 (QB); [2005] All ER (D) 161 (May) *270*

Capehorn *v* Independent News and Media (2006) (unreported) *243* Caron *v* BBC (2002) (unreported) *237*

Cassidy *v* Daily Mirror Newspapers Ltd [1929] 2 KB 331; [1929] All ER Rep 117 *224*

Charleston *v* News Group Newspapers Ltd [1995] 2 AC 65; [1995] 2 All ER 313; [1995] 2 WLR 450 *226*

Charman *v* Orion Publishing Group Ltd and McLagan [2007] EWCA Civ 972; [2008] 1 All ER 750 *267, 282*

Chase *v* News Group Newspapers [2002] EWCA Civ 1772; [2002] All ER (D) 20 (Dec) *229*

Chief Constable of Surrey Police *v* JHG and DHG [2002] All ER (D) 308 (May) *155*

Child X (Residence and Contact: Rights of Media Attendance) [2009] EWHC 1728

(Fam), [2009] Fam Law 930, [2009] EMLR 26 *170*

Church (Charlotte) *v* MGN Ltd [2012] EWHC 693 (QB); [2012] All ER (D) 103 (Apr) *218*

Ciaran Convery *v* Irish News [2008] NICA 14 *256*

City of Wakefield Metropolitan District Council *v* Media and others [2010] EWHC 262 (Fam) *181*

Clare Balding *v* Sunday Times (2010) 17 September (unreported) *389*

Clark *v* Associated Newspapers Ltd [1998] 1 All ER 959; [1998] 1 WLR 1558 *376*

Clayton *v* Clayton [2006] EWCA Civ 878; [2007] 1 All ER 1197 *175, 176*

Cleese *v* Clark and Associated Newspapers Ltd [2003] EWHC 137 (QB); [2004] EMLR 37; [2003] All ER (D) 63 (Feb) *271*

Cleveland Bridge UK Ltd *v* Multiplex Constructions (UK) Ltd [2006] EWHC 1341 (TCC); [2006] All ER (D) 167 (Jun) *108*

Coco *v* AN Clark (Engineers) Ltd [1968] FSR 415; [1969] RPC 41 *287, 288*

Commissioner of Police of Bermuda *v* Bermuda Broadcasting Co Ltd [2008] UKPC 5; [2008] All ER (D) 240 (Jan) *295*

Cooke and Another *v* MGN Ltd [2014] WLR(D) 379, [2014] EWHC 2831 (QB) *221*

Cooper-Hohn *v* Hohn [2014] EWHC 2314 (Fam) *177*

Cork *v* McVicar (1995) (unreported) *295*

Cornwall *v* Myskow [1987] 1 WLR 630, [1987] 2 All ER *504 253*

Crawford *v* Director of Public Prosecutions (2008) *Times,* 20 February *157*

Cream Holdings Ltd *v* Banerjee [2004] UKHL 44; [2005] 1 AC 253; [2004] 4 All ER 617 *57, 314*

Creation Records Ltd *v* News Group Newspapers (1997) *Times,* 29 April; [1997] EMLR 444 *289, 292, 361, 477*

Culnane *v* Morris [2005] EWHC 2438 (QB); [2006] 2 All ER 149; [2006] 1 WLR 2880 *433*

Curistan *v* Times Newspapers Ltd [2007] EWHC 926 (QB); [2007] 4 All ER 486 *262*

DH NHS Foundation Trust *v* PS (by her litigation friend the Official Solicitor) [2010] EWHC 1217 (Fam); [2010] All ER (D) 275 (May) *184*

Dallas McMillan (A firm) and A *v* B and Mrs F Davidson (2008) (Transcript UKEATS/0006/07/MT) (unreported) *200*

David and Carol Johnson *v* Radio City (1988) (unreported) *229*

David Hunt *v* Times Newspapers Ltd [2012] EWHC 1220 (QB) *267–268*

David Soul *v* Matthew Wright (2001) (unreported) *256*

Derbyshire County Council *v* Times Newspapers Ltd [1993] AC 534; [1993] 1 All ER 1011; [1993] 2 WLR 449 *242*

Desmond *v* Bower [2009] EWCA Civ 667; [2009] All ER (D) 276 (Jul) *251*

Distillers Co (Biochemicals) Ltd *v* Times Newspapers Ltd [1975] QB 613; [1975] 1 All ER 41 *291*

Dobson *v* Hastings [1992] Ch 394; [1992] 2 All ER 94; [1992] 2 WLR 414 *83*

Douglas *v* Hello! Ltd (No 2) [2003] EWCA Civ 139; [2003] All ER (D) 161 (Feb) *289*

Douglas *v* Hello! Ltd (No 3) [2007] UKHL 21; [2008] 1 AC 1; [2007] 4 All ER 545 *289, 297 349, 350, 352, 477*

Douglas *v* Hello! Ltd (No 6) [2005] EWCA Civ 595; [2006] QB 125; [2005] 4 All ER 128 *289, 349, 350, 352, 477*

Durant *v* Financial Services Authority (Disclosure of Information) [2003] EWCA Civ 1746; [2004] FSR 573 *347*

Dwek *v* Macmillan Publishing Ltd [2000] EMLR 284 *224*

ETK *v* News Group Newspapers Ltd [2011] EWCA Civ 439; [2011] 1 WLR 1827 *306*

Ellis *v* National Union of Conservative and Constitutional Associations; Middleton and Southall (1900) 44 SJ 750; 109 LTJ 493 *431*

Evans *v* Lloyd [1962] 2 QB 471; [1962] 1 All ER 239; [1962] 2 WLR 541*426*

Ex parte, Central Independent Television plc (1990) *Times,* 7 November *116*

Ex parte, HTV Cymru (Wales) Ltd *v* Crown Court at Cardiff [2002] EMLR 11 *92*

Ex parte, News Group Newspapers Ltd [2002] EMLR 160 *115*

Express Newspapers plc *v* News (UK) Ltd [1990] 3 All ER 376; [1990] 1 WLR 1320 *363*

Film Investors Overseas SA *v* Home Video Channel Ltd [1996] 45 LS Gaz R 30; [1997] EMLR 347 *374*

Flood *v* Times Newspapers Ltd [2012] UKSC 11; [2012] 4 All ER 913, SC; *Reversing* [2010] EWCA Civ 804; [2011] 1 WLR 153, CA; *Reversing* [2009] EWHC 2375 (QB), QBD *267, 269*

Fraser *v* Evans [1969] 1 QB 349; [1969] 1 All ER 8; [1968] 3 WLR 1172 *372*

Fraser *v* Thames Television Ltd [1984] QB 44; [1983] 2 All ER 101; [1983] 2 WLR 917 *288, 370*

GKR Karate (UK) Ltd *v* Yorkshire Post Newspapers Ltd [2000] 2 All ER 931; [2000] 1 WLR 2571; [2000] EMLR 396 *266*

Gaddafi *v* Telegraph Group plc [2000] EMLR 431; [1998] All ER (D) 504 *251*

Galloway *v* Jewish Communications Ltd (2008) (unreported) *232*

Galloway *v* Telegraph Group Ltd [2006] EWCA Civ 17; [2006] 07 LS Gaz R 23 *254*

Gecas *v* Scottish Television (1992) (unreported) *248, 249*

General Medical Council *v* British Broadcasting Corporation [1998] 3 All ER 426; [1998] 1 WLR 1573; 43 BMLR 143 *196*

Giggs (previously known as CTB) v News Group Newspapers Ltd [2012] EWHC 431 (QB), [2012] 13 LS Gaz R 24 *307, 311*

Gillick *v* BBC [1996] EMLR 267 *227*

Global Torch Ltd *v* Apex Global Management and Others [2013] EWHC 223 (Ch) *97*

Goldsmith *v* Bhoyrul [1998] QB 459; [1997] 4 All ER 268; [1998] 2 WLR 435 *242*

Grappelli *v* Derek Block (Holdings) Ltd [1981] 2 All ER 272; [1981] 1 WLR 822 *281*

Green Corns Ltd *v* Claverley Group Ltd [2005] EWHC 958 (QB); [2005] 2 FCR 309 *306–307, 311*

Greene v Associated Newspapers (2004) (unreported) *276*

Grobbelaar *v* News Group Newspapers Ltd [2001] EWCA Civ 33; [2001] 2 All ER 437 *266, 275*

Guardian Newspapers Ltd (Court Record Disclosure), *Re* [2004] EWHC 3092 (Ch); [2005] 3 All ER 155; [2005] 1 WLR 2965 *110*

H *v* Ministry of Defence [1991] 2 QB 103; [1991] 2 All ER 834; [1991] 2 WLR 1192 *121*

HRH Prince of Wales *v* Associated Newspapers Ltd [2006] EWCA Civ 1776; [2008] Ch 57; [2007] 2 All ER 139 *306, 312*

Hayward *v* Thompson [1982] QB 47; [1981] 3 All ER 450; [1981] 3 WLR 470 *230, 234*

Heather Mills *v* The Sun (unreported) *306*

Hillingdon London Borough Council *v* Paulssen [1977] JPL 518 *425*

Hodgson *v* Imperial Tobacco Ltd (No 1) [1998] 2 All ER 673; [1998] 1 WLR 1056 *99, 109*

Hubbard *v* Vosper [1972] 2 QB 84; [1972] 1 All ER 1023; [1972] 2 WLR 389 *295*

Hunt *v* Severs [1994] 2 AC 350; [1994] 2 All ER 385; [1994] 2 WLR 602 *50*

Hutcheson *v* News Group and others [2011] All ER (D) 172 (Jul); [2011] EWCA Civ 808 *308*

Hyde Park Residence Ltd *v* Yelland [2001] Ch 143; [2000] 3 WLR 215 *370–372, 374*

IPC Media Ltd *v* Highbury-SPL Publishing Ltd (No 2) [2004] EWHC 2985 (Ch); [2004] All ER (D) 342 (Dec) *362*

Independent Publishing Co Ltd *v* Attorney-General of Trinidad and Tobago; Trinidad and Tobago News Centre Ltd *v* Attorney-General of Trinidad and Tobago [2004] UKPC 26; [2005] 1 AC 190; [2005] 1 All ER 499 *210*

Independent Television Publications Ltd *v* Time Out Ltd [1984] FSR 64 *360*

Infopaq International A/S *v* Danske Dagblades Forening [2009] ECDR 16, [2012] Bus LR 102 *366*

Initial Services Ltd *v* Putterill [1968] 1 QB 396; [1967] 3 All ER 145; [1967] 3 WLR 1032 *295*

Interbrew SA *v* Financial Times and others [2002] EWCA Civ 274; [2002] All ER (D) 106 (Mar) *333*

Ivereigh *v* Associated Newspapers Ltd [2008] EWHC 339 (QBD) *217*

JC and Another *v* The Central Criminal Court [2014] EWHC 1041 (Admin), [2014] 4 All ER 319, [2014] Crim LR 902, [2014] 1 WLR 3697 *152*

JCA, *Re* (2003) (unreported) (13 November) *120*

JIH *v* News Group Newspapers Ltd [2011] EWCA Civ 42; [2011] 2 All ER 324 *316*

Jaggar *v* Darling (2005) (unreported) *303*

Jameel *v* Times Newspapers Ltd [2004] EWCA Civ 983; [2004] All ER (D) 361 (Jul) *230, 239, 277*

Jameel *v* Wall Street Journal Europe SPRL [2006] UKHL 44; [2007] 1 AC 359; [2006] 4 All ER 1279 *266–267*

Jason Donovan *v* The Face (1992) (unreported) *217*

Jean Bellfield (Mrs) *v* Daily Mirror (2009) 23 July (unreported) *388*

Jersild *v* Denmark [1994] ECHR 33; (1995) 19 EHRR 1 *466*

John *v* Associated Newspapers Ltd [2006] EWHC 1611 (QB); [2006] EMLR 772 *304*

John *v* Guardian News & Media Ltd [2008] EWHC 3066 (QB); [2008] All ER (D) 134 (Dec) *233, 334*

John *v* MGN Ltd [1997] QB 586; [1996] 2 All ER 35; [1996] 3 WLR 593 *275*

John Cleese *v* Evening Standard, *See* Cleese *v* Clark and Associated Newspapers Ltd

Johnson *v* Express Newspapers; Transcript (25 July 2005) (unreported) *224*

Joseph *v* Spiller [2010] UKSC 53; [2011] 1 AC 852; [2011] 1 All ER 947 *254*

Joyce *v* Sengupta [1993] 1 All ER 897; [1993] 1 WLR 337 *281*

Karim (Imran) *v* Newsquest Media Group Ltd [2009] EWHC 3205 (QB) *239*

Kaschke *v* Osler [2010] EWHC 1075 (QB); [2010] All ER (D) 118 (May) *271*

Kaye *v* Robertson [1991] FSR 62; (1990) *Times*, 21 March *280–282, 324*

Kearney *v* Smith New Court Securities [1997] EWCA Civ 1211 *199*

Keays *v* Guardian Newspapers Ltd [2003] EWHC 1565 (QB); [2003] All ER (D) 04 (Jul) *254*

Kennedy *v* The Charity Commission [2014] UKSC 20, [2014] 2 All ER 847 *447*

Kenrick & Co *v* Lawrence & Co (1890) 25 QBD 99; 38 WR 779 *361, 367*

Kent County Council *v* B and others [2004] EWHC 411 (Fam); [2004] 3 FCR 1; [2004] 2 FLR 142 *174*

Khashoggi *v* IPC Magazines Ltd [1986] 3 All ER 577; [1986] 1 WLR 1412 *276*

Kiam *v* MGN Ltd [2002] EWCA Civ 43; [2003] QB 281; [2002] 2 All ER 219 *274*

Kirkland *v* Wiltshire Gazette (2008) 23 April (unreported) *385*

Knightley *v* Associated Newspapers (2007) (unreported) *218*

Knupffer *v* London Express Newspaper Ltd [1944] AC 116; [1944] 1 All ER 495 *237*

Konfidence International Ltd *v* Splash About International Ltd (Transcript HQ07X02514) (unreported) *232*

LM (a child) (reporting restrictions: coroner's inquest), *Re* [2007] EWHC 1902 (Fam); [2007] 3 FCR 44; [2008] 1 FLR 1360 *191*

Ladbroke (Football) Ltd *v* William Hill (Football) Ltd [1964] 1 All ER 465; [1964] 1 WLR 273 *361*

Lakah Group *v* Al Jazeera Satellite Channel [2002] EWHC 2500 (QB); [2002] All ER (D) 383 (Nov) *209*

Laura Gaddis (Mrs) *v* Hamilton Adviser (2007) (unreported) *318*

Leicester University *v* A [1999] ICR 701; [1999] IRLR 352 *199*

Lennon *v* News Group Newspapers Ltd and Twist [1978] FSR 573 *294*

Levi *v* Bates [2009] EWHC 1495 (QB); [2009] All ER (D) 45 (Jul) *255*

Lewis *v* Daily Telegraph Ltd (No 2) [1964] 2 QB 601; [1964] 1 All ER 705; [1964] 2 WLR 736 *229*

Liberal Democrat Party *v* Daily Telegraph (2011) 10 May (unreported) *388*

Lion Laboratories Ltd *v* Evans [1985] QB 526; [1984] 2 All ER 417; [1984] 3 WLR 539 *295, 373*

Lloyd *v* David Syme & Co Ltd [1986] AC 350; [1986] 2 WLR 69 *234*

Lonhro plc and Observer Ltd, *Re* [1990] 2 AC 154; [1989] 2 All ER 1100; [1989] 3 WLR 535 *68*

Loutchansky *v* Times Newspapers Ltd (No 2) [2001] EWCA Civ 1805; [2002] QB 783; [2002] 1 All ER 652 *239*

Lowe *v* Associated Newspapers Ltd [2006] EWHC 320 (QB); [2007] QB 580; [2006] 3 All ER 357 *255*

M and N (Minors) (Wardship: Publication of Information), *Re* [1990] Fam 211; [1990] 1 All ER 205; [1989] 3 WLR 1136 *178*

MGN Pension Trustees Ltd *v* Bank of America National Trust and Savings Association and another (Serious Fraud Office intervening); Bishopsgate Investment Management Ltd *v* Crédit Suisse (Serious Fraud Office intervening) [1995] 2 All ER 355 *116*

McCartan Turkington Breen (a firm) *v* Times Newspapers Ltd [2001] 2 AC 277; [2000] 4 All ER 913; [2000] 3 WLR 1670 *260–261*

McCartney *v* Hello! (unreported) *317*

McClaren *v* News Group Newspapers Ltd [2012] EWHC 2466 (QB) 309, 310

McGrath and another *v* Dawkins, Amazon and others [2012] Lexis Citation 28 *239*

McKennitt *v* Ash and Purple Ink Press [2005] EWHC 3003 (QB); [2006] IP & T 605; [2006] EMLR 178 *305, 307, 309, 311*

McKerry *v* Teesdale and Wear Valley Justices (2000) 164 JP 355; [2001] EMLR 127; [2000] All ER (D) 140 *151, 204*

McKillen *v* Misland (Cyprus) Investments Ltd [2012] EWHC 505 (Ch); [2012] All ER (D) 150 (May) *101*

McPherson *v* McPherson [1936] AC 177; 105 LJPC 41; [1935] All ER Rep 105 *99*

Mahmood *v* Galloway [2006] EWHC 1286 (QB); [2006] EMLR 763 *293*

Major *v* New Statesman (1993) (unreported) *228*

Malik *v* Central Criminal Court; *See* R (on the application of Malik) *v* Central Criminal Court

Man, A *v* Lancashire Telegraph (2007) 31 October (unreported) *342–343*

Man, A *v* Staffordshire Newsletter (2011) 3 May (unreported) *160*

Marks & Spencer plc *v* Granada Television Ltd and another [1998] All ER (D) 40 *250*

Marshall *v* Southampton and South West Hampshire Area Health Authority (Teaching) (Case 152/84) [1986] QB 401; [1986] 2 All ER 584; [1986] ECR 723 *7*

Miller *v* Associated Newspapers Ltd (No 3) [2005] EWHC 557 (QB); [2005] All ER (D) 45 (Apr) *249*

Mitchell *v* Faber and Faber Ltd [1998] EMLR 807 *222*

Moore *v* News of the World Ltd [1972] 1 QB 441; [1972] 1 All ER 915; [1972] 2 WLR 419 *376*

Morgan *v* Odhams Press Ltd [1971] 2 All ER 1156; [1971] 1 WLR 1239 *234*

Mosley *v* News Group Newspapers Ltd [2008] EWHC 1777 (QB); [2008] EMLR 679; [2008] All ER (D) 322 (Jul) *303, 306, 309, 310*

Murray *v* Express Newspapers plc; *sub nom* Murray *v* Big Pictures (UK) Ltd [2008] EWCA Civ 446; [2009] Ch 481; [2008] 3 WLR 1360 *302, 304*

N (a Minor), Re (2014) EWHC 749 (Fam) *172*

NAB *v* Serco Ltd and another [2014] EWHC 1225 (QB) *109*

Nail *v* News Group Newspapers Ltd; Nail *v* Jones [2004] EWCA Civ 1708; [2005] 1 All ER 1040 *270*

Newspaper Licensing Agency Ltd *v* Meltwater Holding BV [2010] EWHC 3099 (Ch) *367*

Newstead *v* London Express Newspaper Ltd [1940] 1 KB 377; [1939] 4 All ER 319 *236, 269*

Norfolk County Council v Webster (2006) [2007] 1 FLR 1146, [2007] Fam Law 399, (2007) HRLR 3, [2006] EWHC 2733 (Fam) *172*

Norman *v* Future Publishing Ltd [1999] EMLR 325; [1998] All ER (D) 606 *226*

North London Central Mosque Trust *v* Policy Exchange and another [2010] EWCA Civ 526 *242*

Northampton Borough Council, *ex p* Oliver; *See* Oliver *v* Northampton Borough Council

Nottinghamshire Healthcare NHS Trust *v* News Group Newspapers Ltd [2002] EWHC 409 (Ch); [2002] RPC 962; [2002] All ER (D) 221 (Mar) *375*

Oliver *v* Manchester Evening News (1998) *386*

Oliver *v* Northampton Borough Council (1986) 151 JP 44 *426*

O'Shea *v* MGN Ltd [2001] EMLR 943; [2001] All ER (D) 65 (May) *236*

PCR Ltd *v* Dow Jones Telerate Ltd [1998] FSR 170; [1998] EMLR 407 *293, 366*

PNM *v* Times Newspaper [2014] EWCA Civ 1132 *311*

Pamplin *v* Express Newspapers Ltd (No 2) [1988] 1 All ER 282; [1988] 1 WLR 116n *275*

Parker *v* News Group Newspapers Ltd (2005) (Transcript HQ05X00736) (unreported) *218*

Peach Grey & Co (a firm) *v* Sommers [1995] 2 All ER 513; [1995] ICR 549; [1995] IRLR 363 *196*

Peck *v* United Kingdom (Application 44647/98) (2003) 36 EHRR 719; [2003] EMLR 287; [2003] All ER (D) 255 (Jan) *304*

Pickering *v* Liverpool Daily Post and Echo Newspapers plc [1991] 2 AC 370; [1990] 1 All ER 335; [1990] 2 WLR 494 *91, 196*

Pirbhai *v* DPP [1995] COD 259 *431*

Practice Direction (Attendance of Media Representatives at Hearings in Family Proceedings) April 20, 2009 *169*

Practice Direction (Contempt of Court Act: Report of Proceedings: Postponement Orders) [1983] 1 WLR 1475 *122*

Practice Direction (Crown Court: Trial of Children and Young Persons) (2000) *Times*, 17 February *153*

Practice Direction (Supreme Court: Contempt: Reporting Restrictions) [1982] 1 WLR 1475 *122*

Practice Guidance (Use of live text-based forms of communication from court) (2012) *Times*, 16 January *108*

Pro Sieben Media AG *v* Carlton UK Television Ltd [1999] 1 WLR 605; [1999] FSR 610 *369, 371*

Quigley *v* Zoo (2006) (unreported) *317–318*

R (on the application of the BBC and Dominic Casciani) *v* Secretary of State for Justice; with Babar Ahmad as interested party (2012) *Times*, 13 April *56*

R (on the application of British Sky Broadcasting Ltd (BSkyB), the BBC, Hardcash Productions Ltd and Jason Parkinson) *v* Chelmsford Crown Court [2012] All ER (D) 37 (Jun) *336–337*

R (on the application of Corner House Research, Campaign Against the Arms Trade) *v* Director of the Serious Fraud Office [2008] EWHC 714 (Admin); [2009] AC 756; [2008] 4 All ER 927 *108*

R (on the application of Guardian News and Media Ltd) *v* City of Westminster Magistrates' Court [2012] EWCA Civ 420; [2012] 3 All ER 551; [2012] 3 WLR 1343 *109*

R (on the application of Harper) and R (on the application of Johncox) *v* Aldershot Magistrates' Court with the Press Association, Surrey and Berks Media, and the CPS; Hampshire as interested parties [2010] EWHC 1319 (Admin); 174 JP 410; [2010] All ER (D) 11 (Jun) *121*

R (on the application of HTV Ltd) *v* Bristol City Council [2004] EWHC 1219 (Admin); [2004] 1 WLR 2717 *425*

R (on the application of Malik) *v* Central Criminal Court [2006] EWHC 1539 (Admin); [2006] 4 All ER 1141; [2007] 1 WLR 2455 *99, 100*

R (on the application of Middleton) *v* West Somerset Coroner [2004] UKHL 10; [2004] 2 AC 182; [2004] 2 All ER 465 *190*

R (on the application of Pelling) *v* Bow County Court [2001] EWCA Civ 122 *99*

R (on the application of The Telegraph Group plc) *v* Sherwood [2001] EWCA Crim 1075 *117, 118*

R (on the application of Trinity Mirror plc) *v* Croydon Crown Court [2008] EWCA Crim 50; [2008] QB 770; [2008] 2 All ER 1159 *118, 157*

R (on the application of Y) *v* Aylesbury Crown Court [2012] EWHC 1140 (Admin); [2012] Crim LR 893; [2012] All ER (D) 89 (May) *154*

R *v* Arundel Justices, *ex p* Westminster Press Ltd [1985] 2 All ER 390; [1985] 1 WLR 708 *119*

R *v* Beaverbrook Newspapers and Associated Newspapers [1962] NI 15 *82*

R *v* Blackpool Justices, *ex p* Beaverbrook Newspapers Ltd [1972] 1 All ER 388; [1972] 1 WLR 95 *129*

R *v* Burrell (2004) (unreported) *116*

R *v* Central Criminal Court, *ex p* Bright [2001] 2 All ER 244; [2001] 1 WLR 662 *336*

R *v* Central Criminal Court, *ex p* Crook and Godwin [1995] 1 All ER 537; [1995] 1 WLR 139; [1995] 2 FCR 153 *154, 158*

R *v* Central Criminal Court, *ex p* Simpkins (1998) *Times*, 26 October *158*

R *v* Chaytor [2010] EWCA Crim 1910; [2010] UKSC 52 *131*

R *v* Clerkenwell Metropolitan Stipendiary Magistrate, *ex p* Telegraph plc [1993] QB 462; [1993] 2 All ER 183; [1993] 2 WLR 233 *204*

R *v* Crook (1991) 93 Cr App Rep 17, CA *101*

R *v* Croydon Crown Court, *ex p* Trinity Mirror, *See* R (on the application of Trinity Mirror plc) *v* Croydon Crown Court

R *v* D (acquitted person: retrial) [2006] EWCA Crim 733; [2006] 1 WLR 1998; [2006] All ER (D) 387 (Feb) *144*

R *v* Evesham Justices, *ex p* McDonagh [1988] QB 553; [1988] 1 All ER 371; [1988] 2 WLR 227 *106, 120*

R *v* Felixstowe Justices, *ex p* Leigh [1987] QB 582; [1987] 1 All ER 551; [1987] 2 WLR 380 *104*

R *v* Horsham Justices, *ex p* Farquharson [1982] QB 762; [1982] 2 All ER 269; [1982] 2 WLR 430 *117*

R *v* Hutchinson (1985) 82 Cr App Rep 51; [1985] Crim LR 730 *136*

R *v* Lee [1993] 2 All ER 170; [1993] 1 WLR 103 *154*

R *v* Legal Aid Board, *ex p* Kaim Todner (a firm) [1999] QB 966; [1998] 3 All ER 541; [1998] 3 WLR 925 *120*

R *v* Liverpool City Council, *ex p* Liverpool Taxi Fleet Operators' Association [1975] 1 All ER 379; [1975] 1 WLR 701 *424*

R *v* Malvern Justices, *ex p* Evans: R *v* Eversham Justices, *ex p* McDonagh [1988] QB 540; [1988] 1 All ER 371; [1988] 2 WLR 218 *100*

R *v* Manchester Crown Court, *ex p* H and D [2000] 2 All ER 166; [2000] 1 WLR 760 *158*

R *v* Praiil (2004) (unreported) *138*

R *v* Reigate Justices, *ex p* Argus Newspapers and Larcombe (1983) 5 Cr App Rep (S) 181; [1983] Crim LR 564 *101*

R *v* Rhuddlan Justices, *ex p* HTV Ltd [1986] Crim LR 329 *117*

R *v* Southampton Industrial Tribunal, *ex p* INS News Group Ltd [1995] IRLR 247 *199*

R *v* Southwark Crown Court, *ex p* Godwin [1992] QB 190; [1991] 3 All ER 818; [1991] 3 WLR 689; 94 Cr App Rep 34 *157*

R *v* West [1996] 2 Cr App Rep 374 *69*

R (A Minor) (Wardship: Restrictions on Publication), *Re* [1994] Fam 254; [1994] 3 All ER 658; [1994] 3 WLR 36 *179*

RA's Application for Judicial Review, *Re* [2010] NIQB 99; [2011] NI 20 *123*

Reynolds *v* Times Newspapers Ltd [2001] 2 AC 127; [1999] 4 All ER 609; [1999] 3 WLR 1010 *263–265, 268, 279*

Rice *v* Connolly [1966] 2 QB 414; [1966] 2 All ER 649; [1966] 3 WLR 17 *335*

Riches *v* News Group Newspapers Ltd [1986] QB 256; [1985] 2 All ER 845; [1985] 3 WLR 432 *238*

Ricketts *v* Cox (1981) 74 Cr App Rep 298; [1982] Crim LR 184 *20*

Rio Ferdinand *v* MGN Newspapers Ltd [2011] EWHC 2454 (QB); [2011] NLJR 1417 *308, 309*

Robert Dee *v* Telegraph Media Group Ltd [2010] EWHC 924 (QB); [2010] All ER (D) 215 (Apr), QBD *226*

RocknRoll *v* News Group Newspapers Ltd [2013] EWHC 24 (Ch) *310*

Roberts *v* Gable [2007] EWCA Civ 721; [2008] QB 502; [2008] 2 WLR 129 *268*

Roddy (a child) (identification: restriction on publication); *Re;* Torbay Borough Council *v* News Group Newspapers [2003] EWHC 2927 (Fam); [2004] 1 FCR 481; [2004] All ER (D) 150 (Feb) *181*

Rothschild *v* Associated Newspapers Ltd [2012] EWHC 177 (QB); [2012] All ER (D) 104 (Feb) *250*

Sanoma Uitgevers BV *v* Netherlands (Application No 38224/03) (2010) 30 BHRC 318; (2009) 51 EHRR 739 *335*

Schering Chemicals Ltd *v* Falkman Ltd [1982] QB 1; [1981] 2 All ER 321; [1981] 2 WLR 848 *293*

Scott *v* Sampson (1882) LR 8 QBD 491; [1881–5] All ER Rep 628 *222*

Scott (otherwise Morgan) *v* Scott [1913] AC 417; [1911–13] All ER Rep 1 *169*

Secretary of State for Defence *v* Guardian Newspapers Ltd [1985] AC 339; [1984] 3 All ER 601; [1984] 3 WLR 986 *331*

Service Corpn International plc *v* Channel Four Television Corpn [1999] EMLR 83 *295*

Solicitor-General *v* Henry and News Group Newspapers Ltd [1990] COD 307 *80*

Spelman *v* Express Newspapers (No 2) [2-12] EWHC 355 (QB) *310*

Spiller *v* Joseph, *See* Joseph *v* Spiller

Stone *v* South East Coast Strategic Health Authority [2006] EWHC 1668 (Admin); [2006] All ER (D) 144 (Jul) *352*

Storer *v* British Gas Plc [2000] 2 All ER 440; [2000] 1 WLR 1237; [2000] IRLR 495 *99, 199*

Sun Printers Ltd *v* Westminster Press Ltd [1982] IRLR 292; 126 SJ 260 *294–295, 372*

Surrey County Council *v* Al-Hilli and the Chief Constable of Surrey (2013) [2013] EWHC 3404 (Fam) *172*

Thornton; Dr Sarah *v* Telegraph Media Group Ltd [2010] EWHC 1414 (QB); [2011] 1 WLR 1985; [2010] All ER (D) 169 (Oct) *218*

Tillack *v* Belgium (2007) (Application No 20477/05) (unreported) 27 November *342*

Tillery Valley Foods *v* Channel Four Television [2004] EWHC 1075 (Ch); [2004] All ER (D) 133 (May) *290*

Time Warner Entertainments Company LP *v* Channel Four Television plc (Clockwork Orange) [1994] EMLR 1 *369, 371, 372*

Times Newspapers Ltd and others, *Re* [2007] EWCA Crim 1925; [2008] 1 All ER 343; [2008] 1 WLR 234 *119*

Times Newspapers *v* MGN Ltd [1993] EMLR 443 *295*

Tolley *v* JS Fry & Sons Ltd [1931] AC 333; 100 LJKB 328; [1931] All ER Rep 131 *223*

Trimingham *v* Associated Newspapers Ltd [2012] EWHC 1296 (QB); [2012] 4 All ER 717 *306, 316, 317*

Turcu *v* News Group Newspapers Ltd [2005] EWHC 799 (QB); [2005] All ER (D) 34 (May) *249*

Turner *v* News Group Newspapers Ltd [2005] EWHC 892 (QB); [2005] EMLR 553; [2005] All ER (D) 175 (May) *270–271*

Taj Hargey *v* Muslim Weekly (2009) (unreported) *217*

Taylforth *v* News Group Newspapers (1994) (unreported) *248*

Terry *v* Person Unknown [2010] EWHC 119 (QB) *302, 303, 314, 315*

Tesla Motors Ltd *v* British Broadcasting Corporation [2012] EWHC 310 (QB); [2012] All ER (D) 168 (Feb) *232, 282*

Thomas *v* News Group Newspapers Ltd [2001] EWCA Civ 1233; [2002] EMLR 78; [2001] All ER (D) 246 (Jul) *316, 329*

Thomson *v* Times Newspapers Ltd [1969] 3 All ER 648; [1969] 1 WLR 1236 *93*

Veliu *v* Mazrekaj [2006] EWHC 1710 (QB); [2007] 1 WLR 495; [2006] All ER (D) 129 (Jul) *271*

Venables *v* News Group Newspapers Ltd; Thompson *v* News Group Newspapers Ltd [2001] Fam 430; [2001] 1 All ER 908; [2001] 2 WLR 1038 *56, 292, 300*

Veolia ES Nottinghamshire Ltd *v* Nottinghamshire County Council [2009] EWHC 2382 (Admin); [2010] PTSR 797; [2009] WLR (D) 273; [2009] All ER (D) 78 (Oct) *425*

Von Hanover *v* Germany [2004] EMLR 379; (2005) 40 EHRR 1 *312*

Von Hanover *v* Germany (No 2) (2012) 55 EHRR 15 *310, 312*

Von Hanover *v* Germany (No 3) [2013] ECHRR 835 *312*

Voskuil *v* The Netherlands (Application No 64752/01) [2007] ECHR 965; [2008] EMLR 14; (2010) 50 EHRR 9; 24 BHRC 306 *342*

W v M (Tolata Proccedings:Anonymity) [2012] EWHC 1679 (Fam) *177*

W (Children) (Care Proceedings: Witness Anonymity), *Re* [2002] EWCA Civ 1626; [2003] 1 FLR 329; [2003] Fam Law 83; [2002] All ER (D) 81 (Oct) *122*

Walker Wingsail Systems *v* Sheahan Bray and IPC Magazine (1994) (unreported) *232*

Walter *v* Lane [1900] AC 539; [1900–3] All ER Rep Ext 1666 *363*

Walter *v* Steinkopff [1892] 3 Ch 489; 67 LT 184; 8 TLR 633 *363*

Ward (William) (In the Matter of), Dr A, Dr B and others *v* Victoria Ward and Jake Ward [2010] EWHC 205 (Fam) *181*

Warwick Film Productions Ltd *v* Eisinger [1969] 1 Ch 508; [1967] 3 All ER 367; [1967] 3 WLR 1599 *367*

Weller *v* Associated Newspapers Ltd [2014] EWHC 1163 (QB*) 304–305*

Williams *v* Settle [1960] 2 All ER 806; [1960] 1 WLR 1072 *375*

Woman, A *v* The News (Portsmouth) (2010) 28 January (unreported) *386*

X *v* Dempster (1998) (unreported) *174*

X (A Child) (Residence and Contact: Rights of Media Attendance: FPR Rule 10.28(4)), *Re* [2009] EWHC 1728 (Fam); [2009] EMLR 489; [2009] All ER (D) 361 (Jul) *171*

X (A Woman Formerly Known as Mary Bell) *v* O'Brien [2003] EWHC 1101 (QB); [2003] EMLR 850; [2003] All ER (D) 282 (May) *292*

X (HA) *v* Y [1988] 2 All ER 648; [1988] RPC 379 *288, 295*

X Ltd *v* Morgan-Grampian (Publishers) Ltd [1991] 1 AC 1; [1990] 1 All ER 616; [1990] 2 WLR 421 *288, 331, 332, 334*

XXX *v* YYY [2004] EWCA Civ 231; [2004] IRLR 471; [2004] All ER (D) 144 (Feb) *198*

X, Y, Z (Morgan v A Local Authority), Re [2012] 1 WLR 182, [2011] EWHC 1157 (Fam) *173*

TABLE OF EUROPEAN LEGISLATION

Directive 2010/13/EU (Audiovisual Media Services Directive) *484, 504*
- Art 6 *491*
- Art 27 *484*
- Art 28 *497*

European Convention on the Protection of Human Rights and Fundamental Freedoms 1950 *3, 8, 9, 53–59, 179–80*
- Art 2 *54, 123, 190*
- Art 3 *54*
- Art 4 *54*
- Art 5 *54*
- Art 6 *54, 58, 63, 97–98*
- Art 7 *54*
- Art 8 *54, 58, 123, 171, 312*
- Art 9 *54, 491*
- Art 10 *55–58, 63, 98, 171, 298, 331, 332, 342, 466, 484, 488, 491, 492, 495, 498, 504, 513*
- Art 11 *54*
- Art 12 *54*
- Art 14 *488, 491*

European Convention on the Protection of Human Rights and Fundamental Freedoms 1950, First Protocol *54*
- Art 1 *54*
- Art 2 *54*
- Art 3 *54*

Lugano Convention *243*

TABLE OF STATUTORY INSTRUMENTS

Civil Procedure Rules 1998, SI 1998/3132 *45, 88, 98, 244*
- r 2.3 *108*
- r 5.4 *108*
- Pt 20 *108*
- r 32.13 *109*
- r 39.2 *106–107*
- PD 39 *107*

Consumer Protection from Unfair Trading Regulations 2008
- r 3(4)(d) *504*

Copyright and Related Rights Regulations 2003, SI 2003/2498 *372*

Coroners Rules 1984, SI 1984/552 *190*
- r 43 *190*

Coroners Rules 2013, SI 2013/1616 *191*
- r 23 *192*

Criminal Justice (Children) (Northern Ireland) Order 1998, SI 1998/1504 (NI 9) *102, 150*
- Art 22 *153*

Criminal Procedure Rules 2013, SI 2013/1554 *98, 100,103, 104, 204, 211*

Data Protection (Processing of Sensitive Personal Data) Order 2000, SI 2000/417 *350*

Education (School Information) (England) Regulations 1998, SI 1998/2526 *428*

Electronic Commerce (EC Directive) Regulations 2002, SI 2002/2013
- reg 19 *239*

Employment Tribunals (Constitution and Rules of Procedure) Regulations 2013, SI 2013/1237 *198*
- r 49 *200*
- r 50 *199, 200*
- r50(7) *199*

Environmental Information Regulations 2004, SI 2004/3391 *447–450*

Family Procedure Rules 2009
- r 11.4 *182*

Family Procedure Rules 2010 *167*
- r 10.28 (4) *171*
- r 11 *170*

Family Proceedings (Amendment) (No.2) Rules 2009, SI 2009/857 *182, 187*

Family Proceedings Rules 1991, SI 1991/1247 *182*
- r 10.28(4) *168*
- r 11.4 *182*

Local Authorities (Executive Arrangements) (Meetings and Access to Information) (England) Regulations 2012, SI 2012/2089 *421–442*

Local Authorities (Members' Allowances) Regulations 1991, SI 1991/351 *426*

Openness of Local Government Bodies Regulations 2014 *418–424*

Town and Country Planning General Regulations 1992
- r 3 *420*

TABLE OF STATUTES

Abortion Act 1967 *4*

Access to Justice Act 1999 *190*

Administration of Justice Act 1960 *99, 177*
- s 12 *90, 119, 173–174, 175, 177, 182, 185*
- s 12(1) *178*

Adoption and Children Act 2002 *173, 175, 177*

Anti-Social Behaviour, Crime and Policing Act 2014 *160*
- s 17 *161*

Anti-Terrorism, Crime and Security Act 2001 *338*

Audit Commission Act 1998 *426, 429*

s 15 *425*

Bail Act 1976 *22*

Bribery Act 2010 *327, 328*

Broadcasting Act 1990 *222, 360, 468*

s 164 *465*

s 202 *504*

Sch 2, Pt 1, para 3 *504, 506, 507*

Broadcasting Act 1996 *216, 501*

s 107(1) *498*

s 130 *498*

Building Societies Act 1986 *420*

Business Names Act 1983 *453*

Charities Act 2003 *447*

Charities Act 2011 *420*

Children Act 1989 *90, 164,168, 173, 186, 187*

Pt IV *185*

Pt V *185*

s 97 *174, 175*

Children and Families Act 2014 *166*

Children and Young Persons Act 1933

s 39 *141, 153, 155–156, 157, 158, 161, 162, 179, 191, 209*

s 47 *142, 149, 163*

s 49(5) *151*

Children, Schools and Families Act 2010 *183*

Civil Evidence Act 1968 *231*

Communications Act 2003 *392, 504, 506*

s 3(2)(f) *498, 500*

s 3(4)(g) *488*

s 3(4)(h) *484*

s 3(4)(j) *491*

s 3(4)(l) *488*

s 319(2)(a) *484, 488*

s 319(2)(b) *491*

s 319(2)(c) *492, 495*

s 319(2)(d) *492*

s 319(2)(e) *491*

s 319(2)(f) *484, 488, 513*

s 319(2)(i) *513*

s 319(2)(j) *513*

s 319(2)(l) *488*

s 319(6) *491*

s 320 *492*

s 326 *498, 500*

s 333 *507*

Sch 12, para 18 *495*

Companies Act 1985 *420, 454*

Companies Act 2006 *420, 454, 455*

Contempt of Court Act 1981 *61, 63–82, 89, 95, 124, 191, 196, 298, 330–334, 343, 415, 476, 483*

s 2(2) *64*

s 3 *79*

s 4 *80*

s 4(1) *80*

s 4(2) *113, 114, 115, 116, 117, 118, 122, 179, 191, 197, 207, 208, 311*

s 5 *80*

s 8 *88–89*

s 9 *86*

s 10 *331, 334*

s 11 *113, 114, 119, 120, 121, 122, 124, 179, 191, 197, 205, 207, 208*

s 19 *81–82*

Sch 1 *65*

Copyright, Designs and Patents Act 1988 *360–379*

s 3(1) *361*

s 3(2) *362*

s 31 *373*

s 58 *373*

Coroners and Justice Act 2009 *35, 36, 142–143, 188, 189*

s 76 *142*

s 86 *142*

Counter-Terrorism Act 2008 *477*

s 58a *477*

Courts Act 2003

s 93 *91–92, 128*

Crime and Disorder Act 1998 *129, 132*

s 52A *127, 128*

Crime (Sentences) Act 1997 *151*

Criminal Justice Act 1925

s 25 *87*

Criminal Justice Act 1972 *34, 104*
Criminal Justice Act 1987 *341, 344*
Criminal Justice Act 1988
s 39 *37*
s 159 *103, 205, 207, 210*
Criminal Justice Act 1991
s 53 *132*
Sch 6 *133*
Criminal Justice Act 2003 *22, 23, 29, 33, 34, 72, 144*
s 75 *33, 144*
s 82 *144*
Criminal Justice (Northern Ireland) Act 1945 *87*
Criminal Justice and Immigration Act 2008 *351, 352, 465*
Criminal Justice and Public Order Act 1994 *19, 151, 324*
Criminal Procedure and Investigations Act 1996 *33*
s 37 *131*
s 38 *131*
s 41 *130*
s 42 *130*
s 54 *68*
ss 58–61 *139*

Data Protection Act 1998 *103–104, 105, 285, 346–357, 351, 438, 448*
s 7(4) *353*
s 32 *351*
s 55 *357*
Sch 2 *349, 350*
Sch 3 *350*
Defamation Act 1952
s 5 *255*
s 10 *433*
Defamation Act 1996 *196, 259, 269, 274, 279, 456, 518–524*
s 1 *273*
Sch 1 *278, 518–524*
Sch 1, Pt I *259–260, 318*
Sch 1, Pt I, paras 1–8 *518*
Sch 1, Pt II *261, 518–524*
Sch 1, Pt II, para 9 *518–519*
Sch 1, Pt II, paras 10–13 *519–520*
Sch 1, Pt II, para 13(2)(a)–(5) *520–521*
Sch 1, Pt II, paras 14, 15 *521–523*
Sch 2 *196*
Defamation Act 2013 *215, 216, 220, 246, 259, 263, 274, 279*
s 1 *241*
s 2 *248*
s 3 *253*
s 3(5) *255*
s 3(6) *256*
s 3(7) *255*
s 4 *264*
s 4(3) *268*
s 5 *239*
s 6 *262–263*
s 8 *238*
s 8(5) *238*
s 10 *273*
Disability Discrimination Act 1995—
s 17A *199*
s 25(8) *199*
Domestic and Appellate Proceedings (Restriction of Publicity) Act 1968 *100*
Domestic Violence, Crime and Victims Act 2004 *36*

Education Act 1996 *427*
Education Act 1997 *427*
Education Act 2011 *145*
s 13 *145*
Education (No 2) Act 1986 *427*
Employment Tribunals Act 1996
s 11(6) *199*
European Parliamentary Elections Act 1978 *430*

Financial Services Act 1986 *334, 340, 344*
Financial Services and Markets Act 2000 *340*
s 21(1) *504, 513, 517*
Fraud Act 2006 *38*
Freedom of Information Act 2000 *201, 421, 424, 426, 427, 436,–450*
s 14 *438*
s 16 *444*

s 21 *439*
s 22 *440*
s 23 *439*
s 24 *440*
s 26 *440*
s 27 *440*
s 28 *441*
s 29 *441*
s 30 *441*
s 31 *441*
s 32 *439*
s 33 *441*
s 34 *439*
s 35 *441*
s 36 *439–442*
s 37 *442*
s 38 *442*
s 39 *442*
s 40 *442*
s 42 *442*
s 43 *442*
Sch 1 *437*
Friendly Societies Act 1972 *420*
Friendly Societies Act 1974 *420*

Health and Safety at Work etc Act 1974 *188*
Highways Act 1980 *324*
s 137 *476*
Homicide Act 1957 *36*
Human Rights Act 1998 *3, 8, 9, 53–59, 97–98, 100, 123, 198, 276, 297, 334, 374, 438*
s 2 *292*
s 12 *57, 275, 313*
s 12(2) *57*
Hunting Act 2004 *5*

Industrial and Provident Societies Act 1965 *420*
Industrial and Provident Societies Act 1978 *420*
Inquiries Act 2005
s 18 *201*
Investment Recommendation (Media) Regulation Act 2005 *504*
s 3 *513*

Judicial Proceedings (Regulation of Reports) Act 1926 *175, 176*
s 1(a) *175, 176*
Justice and Security Act 2013 *103, 107*

Legal Aid, Sentencing and Punishment of Offenders Act 2012 *231*
Limited Liability Act 2000 *453*
Local Government (Access to Information) Act 1985 *421*
Local Government Act 1972 *421, 428, 429, 513*
ss 100A–100D *520*
s 100E *520*
s 100J *520*
Local Government Act 2000 *421, 429, 519–520*
s 22 *513*
Local Government etc. (Scotland) Act 1994 *519–520*
Local Government (Northern Ireland) Act 1972 *519–520*
Localism Act 2011 *427*

Magistrates' Court Act 1980 *129*
s 6(5) *104*
s 8 *129*
s 8C *130*
s 69 *168*
s 69(2) *168*
s 69(3) *168*
s 71 *176*
Matrimonial Causes Act 1973 *185*
Mental Capacity Act 2005 *183*
Mental Health Act 1983 *30*

Northern Ireland Act 1998 *397, 496*

Offences Against the Person Act 1861—
s 18 *37*
s 20 *37*
s 47 *37*
Official Secrets Act 1911 *330, 343, 411–412, 416*

s 1 *423, 411*
s 1(a) *411*
s 1(b) *411*
s 1(c) *411*
s 2 *412*
s 9 *338*
Official Secrets Act 1920 *330, 343*
s 1 *338*
s 6 *338*
s 8(4) *103*
Official Secrets Act 1939 *330, 337, 343*
Official Secrets Act 1989 *330, 343, 411–417, 474, 478*
s 1 *412, 413*
s 2 *412, 413*
s 3 *412, 413*
s 4 *412, 413*
s 5 *413–414*
s 6 *412, 413*
s 8 *339*
s 11(4) *108*

Police Act 1964
s 51 *476*
Police Act 1996 *335*
Police Act 1997 *341, 344*
Police and Criminal Evidence Act 1984 *19, 21, 330, 334–339, 343, 414*
Sch 1 *336, 337*
Political Parties, Elections and Referendums Act 2000 *495, 496*
Proceeds of Crime Act 2002—
s 70 *129*
Protection from Harassment Act 1997 *316, 324, 328, 329*
s 1 *316, 325*
s 4 *316, 325*
s 7 *325*
Public Bodies (Admission to Meetings) Act 1960 *428*
Public Interest Disclosure Act 1998 *290*
Public Order Act 1986 *434, 463, 465, 477*
s 17 *465*
s 19(2) *467*
Punishment of Incest Act 1908 *139*

Racial and Religious Hatred Act 2006 *465, 467–470*
Regulation of Investigatory Powers Act 2000 *328, 329, 341–342, 344*
s 1 *325*
Rehabilitation of Offenders Act 1974 *231*
Representation of the People Act 1983 *430, 435*
S 66A *495*
s 75 *432*
s 92 *495*
s 93 *495*
s 106 *430*
s 160 *435*
Representation of the People Act 2000 *430, 432*

Sale and Supply of Goods Act 1994 *50*
Senior Courts Act 1981—
s 37 *123*
s 45(4) *157*
Serious Crime Act 2007 *31, 327, 328*
Serious Organised Crime and Police Act 2005 *19, 20, 102, 143, 337, 341, 344*
Sexual Offences Act 2003 *37, 38, 133*
Sexual Offences (Amendment) Act 1976
s 4 *104*
Sexual Offences (Amendment) Act 1992 *133, 134, 200*
s 3(a) *134*
Sexual Offences (Amendment) Act 2003 *208*

Taking of Hostages Act 1982 *8*
Terrorism Act 2000 *330, 338–340, 344, 345, 478*
s 19 *339, 340*
s 38b *338*
s 39 *339*
s 39(1) *339*
s 39(2) *339*
s 58 *339, 475*
Sch 5 *339*
Sch 5, para 5 *339*
Sch 5, para 13 *340*
Theatres Act 1968 *216*

Theft Act 1968 *39, 336*
s 23 *39*
Trade Union and Labour Relations (Consolidation) Act 1992 *242*
Tribunals and Inquiries Act 1992 *195*

Wireless Telegraphy Act 1949 *326*

Youth Justice and Criminal Evidence Act 1999 *133, 136, 140–142, 162*
s 25 *102*
s 37 *102*
s 43 *103*
s 44 *162*
s 45 *162*
s 46 *141, 164*
s 46(8) *141*
s 47 *102*
Sch 2 *133*

LAW AND THE LEGAL SYSTEM

As a journalist, there are two main reasons why you need to learn about the law. The first is that there are legal rules which affect what you can and cannot publish, and, clearly, you need to know what these are. The second is that the law and legal proceedings will often form part of the subject matter of the stories you write. This is most obviously the case on local papers, where reporting the local courts is an important part of the news coverage, but legal issues and court cases are also covered by national papers, TV and radio, women's magazines and the trade press, even if not always to the same extent. For that reason, you need to have a basic knowledge of the legal system, and how it works. That forms the subject of this section, while later sections look at how the law will affect you in your daily work.

How law is made

If you asked the average person where to find out 'the law' on a particular subject, most would probably assume that, somewhere, it must all be written down: the answer to every question from 'Can my neighbour build a shed that blocks my view?' to 'Is it legal to sneak into a celebrity's wedding and take pictures?' In fact, there is no single set of written rules that make up 'the law'; instead, there are seven different sources of law which interact with each other. For that reason, in many court cases, the courts are asked to decide not just whether someone has broken a law, but what the law actually is on a particular issue. In this chapter, we look at where law comes from and how it is made.

Note that in this book, English law refers to the courts of England and Wales, as the Scottish system is different. In addition, there are some differences in Northern Ireland, which are pointed out where relevant in the text.

SOURCES OF LAW

The seven sources of law are:

- statute;
- delegated legislation;
- case law;
- European Union (EU) law;
- international treaties;
- custom;
- equity.

In this context it is also important to know about the effect of the European Convention on Human Rights, which has now been incorporated into English law in the Human Rights Act 1998. Although not a separate source of law, it has an important effect on the way in which law is interpreted. It is important to realise that human rights law, developed under the European Convention, is not the same thing as European Union (EU) law (for more information on this, see Chapter 5).

Statute

Statutes are laws passed by Parliament, and are also known as Acts of Parliament. They take precedence over any other type of law, except EU law. Parliament can make or cancel any law it chooses, and the courts must apply that law. This is not the case in many other countries, such as the USA, where the courts can refuse to apply legislation that they consider goes against the country's constitution.

How Acts of Parliament are passed

The Bill stage: All statutes start out as a Bill, which is essentially a proposal for a new law or a change in the law. There are three types:

- **Public Bills:** These are put forward by the Government, and form the basis for most legislation. In many cases, a consultation document called a Green Paper is published beforehand (the name comes simply from the colour of the paper it is printed on). A Green Paper explains why the Government is looking at the law in a particular subject area, and gives general details of the options they are considering. The Government then invites anyone who might be affected by the plans to give their views on the proposals. Pressure groups in the relevant area will usually give a response, for example, but the paper may also ask for views from ordinary members of the public who are likely to be particularly affected by a change in the law; for example, if considering changes to particular areas of the welfare services, responses might be invited from users of those services and charities who work with people using the services. The Government can then choose which – if any – of the views expressed should influence the final content of the Bill. Usually, it will produce a White Paper which details the conclusions it has come to after the consultation process.
- **Private Members' Bills:** These are put forward by an individual Member of Parliament (MP) who is not a Cabinet member. Pressure on parliamentary time means there are only limited opportunities to do this, and around half of Private Members' Bills come from a ballot, held once each Parliamentary session, for the chance to put forward a Bill. Members who get this chance then have to persuade the Government to allow sufficient Parliamentary time to get the Bill passed; this rarely happens, and, as a result, Private Members' Bills are more useful as a way to draw attention to an issue, which may later be taken up in a Public Bill, than they are as a way to change the law straight away. Some important legislation has been made this way, however – the Abortion Act 1967, for example, started as a Private Members' Bill.
- **Private Bills:** These are put forward by individuals, local authorities or companies, and essentially concern specific local issues: for example, Railtrack, which runs the tracks for Britain's railways system, might use a Private Bill if it wanted to build a new railway line. Anyone who might be affected by the decision has to be consulted. If the Bill is passed, it only applies to the specific area cited in the Bill, and does not give any general powers applicable to the whole country. Only a handful of Private Bills come before Parliament every year, usually relating to large construction projects.

First reading: The title of the Bill is read to the House of Commons, to notify the House of the proposal.

Second reading: The proposals are debated by the House of Commons, and amendments may be suggested and voted on. MPs then vote on whether the Bill should go on to the next stage.

Committee stage: The Bill is referred to a House of Commons Committee, which will scrutinise it in detail, and may make further amendments.

Report stage: The Committee reports back to the House of Commons, and any amendments are discussed and voted on.

Third reading: The Bill goes back to the House of Commons for a vote on whether to accept or reject its proposals.

House of Lords: The Bill then passes to the House of Lords, where it goes through a similar three-reading process. If the House of Lords suggests any changes, these are passed back for the House of Commons to consider, and the Commons either accepts the suggestions, rejects them and says why, or suggests alternative amendments. If no agreement can be reached, the Commons can use special procedures to pass legislation without the Lords' approval (this is often referred to as using the Parliament Acts). In practice, the House of Lords usually gives up on changes that the Commons clearly does not want, but the Parliament Acts were used, for example, in passing the Hunting Act 2004.

Royal Assent: The final stage is for the Queen to give her consent to the new law (in practice this is never refused).

The Bill then becomes an Act of Parliament, though this does not necessarily mean that all or even any of its provisions take effect immediately: the Act may specify future dates when particular provisions take effect or allow the Government or a particular minister to decide when this should happen. In some cases, elements of an Act may never actually come into force.

Where a piece of legislation is unlikely to be objected to by any of the major political parties, a simpler process can be used, with the first three readings in the Lords followed by three in the Commons, and a final reference to the Lords only if there is disagreement.

You can find out what stage a Bill before Parliament has reached at the UK Parliament website: http://services.parliament.uk/bills.

Delegated legislation

Some types of legislation require very detailed rules, often of a technical nature; examples would be the law on health and safety at work, or the enormous number of road traffic provisions. Rather than using up Parliamentary time making these detailed rules, Acts of Parliament often create a framework for the law on a particular issue, putting general rules into place without necessarily specifying exactly how they should work in particular situations.

Acts drawn up in this way will include provisions for who should make the detailed rules – usually a government department or Secretary of State, local authorities, or public or nationalised bodies. These rules are known as delegated legislation (or sometimes secondary legislation), and there are three types:

- **Statutory Instruments** are drawn up by government departments.
- **By-laws** are made by local authorities, public bodies and nationalised bodies. For example, rules on what can and cannot be done in a specific park will usually be made in the form of by-laws drawn up by the local authority.
- **Orders in council** are regulations which are made by the Government at a time of national emergency (such as in wartime).

Delegated legislation is also used where rules may need to be changed quickly in response to circumstances, and the Parliamentary procedure is considered too slow-moving and cumbersome to cope with these demands, or where local knowledge is required to make the detailed rules (local by-laws are examples of this). Whatever the reason, delegated legislation carries as much legal force as statutes themselves.

Case law

Case law (sometimes called common law) comes from the decisions made by judges in certain legal cases. The courts are arranged in a hierarchy (see Figure 1.1 The hierarchy of the courts), and it is decisions made in the higher courts (from the High Court up) which can make law, through a system called judicial precedent (see next paragraph). Cases reach these courts through a system of appeals, which provides a route for parties who believe their case has been decided wrongly in the lower courts to take them to higher courts. In most cases permission is required for such appeals, which ensures that the higher courts mostly hear cases which raise important issues of law (the Supreme Court, for example, hears fewer than 100 cases a year).

Deciding a case involves two stages: first, establishing what actually happened (often referred to as the facts of the case); and second, deciding how the law applies to the facts. In many cases the latter will be obvious, but there are situations where the law is unclear. For example, if a statute states that 'vehicles shall not be allowed in parks', it is obvious that you cannot drive a car or van round the park – but can you ride a pushbike or use a skateboard? Where these dilemmas arise, it is up to the court deciding the case to determine what the words of the statute actually mean. When a higher court does this, the decision forms what is called a precedent. Once a higher court has set a precedent by interpreting a legal provision in a particular way, that approach should be followed in all the courts that are lower in the hierarchy, and only a higher court can authorise a different approach.

The idea behind case law is that justice requires that like cases be treated alike; once a court has decided what a statutory provision means and/or how it applies to a particular set of facts, later cases with similar facts should be treated in the same way, rather than each judge interpreting the law according to their own sense of justice. For example, if the imaginary case referred to above went to the Supreme Court, and it decided that for the purposes of the legislation, a skateboard was a vehicle, other courts faced with cases involving skateboards used in parks would be expected to take the same view. Case law accounts for a huge proportion of English law – for example, the law of negligence, which essentially creates the right to sue for loss or injury caused by someone else's carelessness, is almost exclusively a creation of case law.

EU law

Laws made by the EU are rapidly becoming one of the most important sources of law for the UK, because the terms of membership of the EU mean that they take precedence over any other source of law. However, although it is widely believed that the EU can dictate the law on anything, in fact there are only specific areas which can be affected by EU law. The EU can, for example, make legislation on transport, agriculture and many of the rules regulating how industry behaves, but it does not legislate in the areas of family or criminal law; these are still made solely by the UK Parliament and courts.

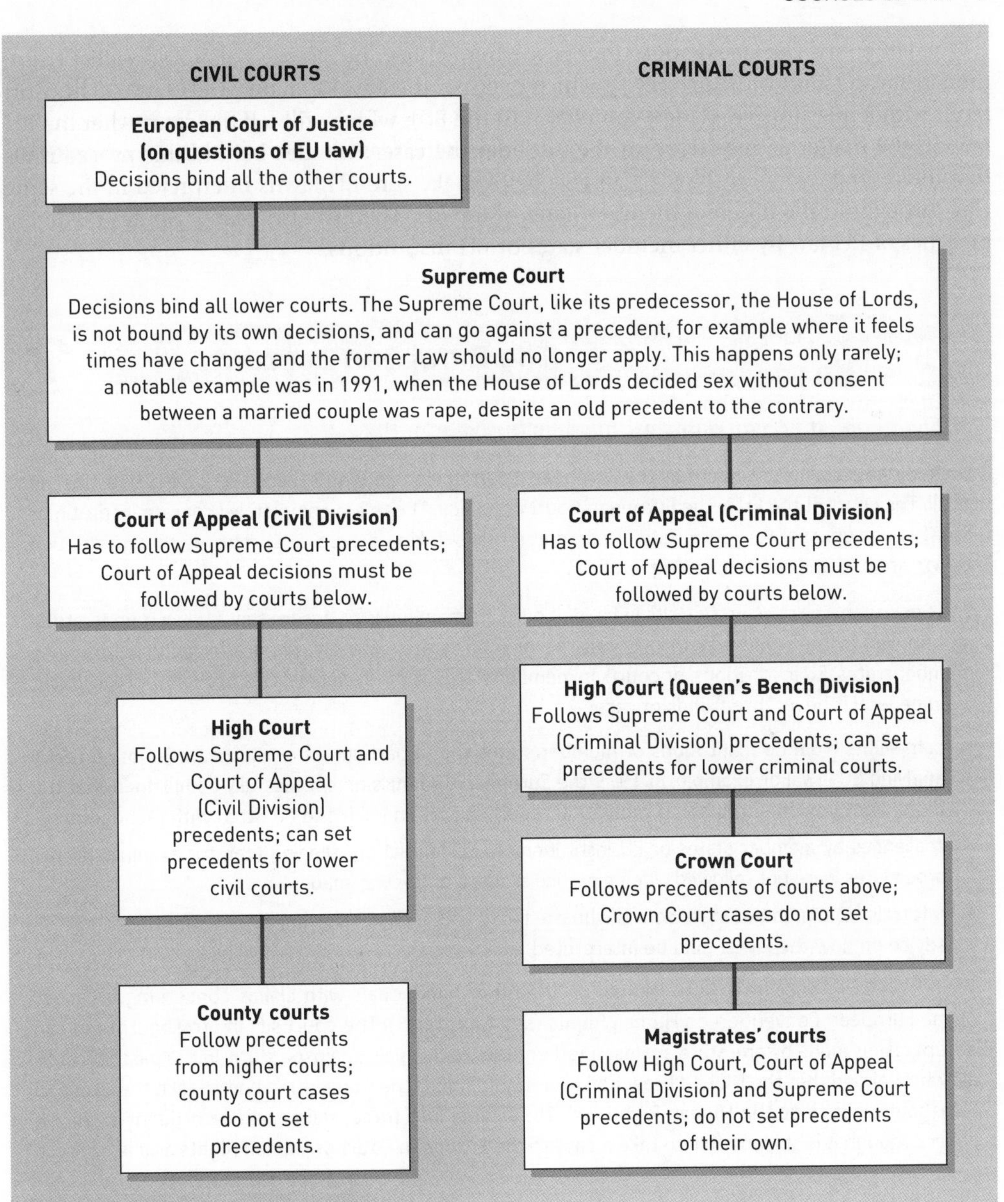

Figure 1.1 The hierarchy of the courts

As well as producing new law which must be applied here, the EU affects UK law in a second way, in that the courts must interpret and apply UK law in such a way as to avoid conflict with EU law. For example, in the case of ***Marshall* v *Southampton and South West Hampshire Area Health Authority*** (1986), an NHS dietician challenged her employer's policy of making employees retire at the state pension age, which was 60 for women but 65 for men. This was legal under the relevant UK legislation, but the House of Lords found that it conflicted with an EU law requiring equal treatment for male and female employees. Where this happens, it is expected that Parliament will amend the domestic legislation to conform with the EU law.

The UK courts can decide questions involving EU law, but there is also a specialist court, the European Court of Justice (ECJ), which oversees the development of EU law. A UK court faced with a question on EU law can refer it to the ECJ, which will tell the court what the EU law on the matter is; the UK court then decides the case. The idea behind this procedure is that the central overview the ECJ can give helps make sure EU law is interpreted in the same way throughout the different member states of the EU. The ECJ also hears disputes involving breaches of EU law by either member states or EU institutions.

Myths and misconceptions **The European courts**

✗ *Claims about human rights are heard in the court of the EU.*

Human rights claims are heard by the European Court of Human Rights, which is not an EU institution at all. The court of the EU is the European Court of Justice. These are completely separate institutions, but it is not unusual for journalists to use phrases like 'taking a case to Europe' as though the two courts are one and the same thing.

The European Court of Justice sits in Luxembourg. Its main job is to ensure that EU law is understood and applied in the same way throughout the member states. Most cases are brought before it by member states, EU institutions, or courts in member states; it rarely hears cases brought by individuals.

In general it hears three kinds of case:

- complaints from EU institutions or member states that a particular member state is not correctly applying EU law. For example, in 1979 the European Commission successfully complained that the UK had not implemented an EU regulation requiring certain lorries to be fitted with tachographs;
- challenges by member states or EU institutions to EU legislation, alleging that, for example, proper procedures were not followed when a particular piece of law was made;
- referrals from member state courts who are faced with a case involving EU law, and want the ECJ's advice on how the law should be interpreted.

The European Court of Human Rights, on the other hand, deals with claims concerning breaches of the European Convention on Human Rights **(see Chapter 5)**. The court sits in Strasbourg, and can accept claims made by one state against another, or by individuals against a state. In the past, individuals who claimed that the UK had breached their rights under the Convention had to take their case to Strasbourg, but since the Human Rights Act 1998 came into force, claims can be brought in the UK courts, though it is still possible to take a case to the European Court of Human Rights as a last resort.

International treaties

In many countries, signing an international treaty automatically incorporates the provisions of the treaty into the law within that country. In the UK, however, Parliament has to turn the provisions into legislation. The Taking of Hostages Act 1982 is an example of a statute created to put into domestic law the provisions of an international treaty signed by the UK.

Custom

When English law was in its early stages, the decision on whether something was or was not lawful would often be influenced by traditional local practice – if a landowner attempted to stop people taking firewood from his forests, for example, local people might argue that having been allowed to do so for many years effectively gave them a right to continue, even if such a right conflicted with the general law. These days custom can theoretically still play a role in such decisions, but in practice it arises extremely rarely.

Equity

Historically, equity was a system of rules which grew up in parallel to the common law, to fill perceived gaps where justice could not be achieved by using the common law. For example, at one time, the common law provided that a person who had been caused loss by someone else could only claim financial compensation, which was not always an adequate solution to a problem. Equity developed its own special remedies, which could be granted at the court's discretion: for example, the injunction, which is an order to do something or not do something, and is used where compensation would not solve the problem. Equity survives now as a specific branch of law, largely concerning the ownership of property, but equitable remedies, especially injunctions, are used in many branches of law, including defamation.

The European Convention on Human Rights

The Human Rights Act 1998 made the provisions of the European Convention on Human Rights part of English law and, for this reason, the Convention is not, strictly speaking, a separate source of law. However, to an extent, it acts like one, because it can modify the way other laws operate. As well as being applied by UK courts, human rights law under the Convention has its own court, the European Court of Human Rights, which can create case law (not to be confused with the European Court of Justice, which oversees EU law). **(This is discussed more fully in Chapter 5.)**

KEY POINTS

Sources of law

Law is not written down in one place; it comes from seven different sources of law, which interact with each other.

Statute

This means Acts of Parliament.

Delegated legislation

This comprises detailed regulations derived from a framework set out in statute.

Case law

This is made by the decisions judges take in cases which reach the higher courts.

EU law

European law must be applied by the UK courts.

International treaties

These must be incorporated before they can become law.

Custom

Traditional customs can be a source of law, but this is rare.

Equity

Equitable rules were originally created to fill gaps in case law.

The European Convention on Human Rights (ECHR)

The ECHR acts like a source of law, as its provisions, incorporated in the Human Rights Act 1998, can modify the way UK law is interpreted.

TEST YOUR KNOWLEDGE

1. What are the seven sources of law?
2. How is case law made and why?
3. What is a Green Paper?
4. What does 'using the Parliament Acts' refer to?
5. How does EU law affect the decisions of UK courts?
6. Which European court hears cases concerning EU law?

WWW ONLINE RESOURCES

The United Kingdom Parliament website has information on legislation and the legislative process, at:
www.parliament.uk

Details of current Green Papers can be found at:
www.parliament.the-stationery-office.co.uk/pa/cm/cmwib/wgp.htm

Supreme Court judgments can be read at:
www.supremecourt.uk

The European Union website is at:
europa.eu

The legal system

This chapter covers the way the English legal system is organised: the two main branches of law; the personnel of the legal system and their roles; and the courts which make up the system. As court cases very often form the basis of stories, a knowledge of the system will help you understand what is going on when you report on such stories, and will ensure that you use the right terminology when writing about court proceedings.

TYPES OF LAW

There are lots of different areas of law in terms of subject, but the most important divisions are between:

- criminal and civil law; and
- public and private law.

Criminal and civil law

Criminal law deals with wrongs that are considered so serious as to be an offence against the whole community, and for this reason they are prosecuted in the name of the state (or specifically, the Queen). It also possible to bring a private prosecution, but this happens relatively rarely (see p. 24).

Civil law covers everything else, from road accident victims suing for compensation or neighbours fighting over who owns a fence, to newspapers being sued for libel or companies disputing tax decisions by the HM Revenue & Customs.

In some cases, the same course of action can lead to both a criminal and a civil case. For example, someone who injures another as a result of dangerous driving may be prosecuted for the crime of dangerous driving, and sued in the civil courts by the person injured.

Criminal and civil law use completely different sets of terminology, and it is important to know which terms apply to which area of law. Not only does it look ill-informed if you refer to, for example, being found guilty of negligence, it could potentially even be libellous, since you would be suggesting that someone had committed a criminal offence, when in fact negligence is a civil wrong, which is generally considered less serious.

Public and private law

A second important distinction is between public and private law. Both public and private law are aspects of civil law.

Private law comprises disputes between individual parties, such as someone injured in an accident suing the person who caused it, or a celebrity suing a newspaper for libel.

Public law is the set of legal principles which governs the way public authorities, including the Government, use their powers. Public authorities cannot act just as they please, but can only exercise the powers given to them by law, and public law is designed to make sure these powers are not exceeded or misused. The main form of action in public law is the application for judicial review, which allows individuals (or organisations) to challenge the decisions or acts of public bodies (see p. 49).

Know your terms

Criminal law	Civil law
When a criminal case is brought against someone, that person is described as being charged with that offence; if the case comes to court, he/she is described as being prosecuted.	When a civil case is brought against someone, that person is described as being sued.
Someone accused of committing a crime is called a defendant; the other side (acting for the Crown) is called the prosecution.	The person bringing the case is called the claimant and the person the claim is against is called the defendant.
Criminal cases are referred to in writing as *R* v *xxxxx* (the name of the person being prosecuted), but in speech this would be read as 'The Queen against xxxxx' (R stands for Regina, Latin for queen).	Civil cases are described with the names of both parties (e.g. ***Smith*** v ***Jones***), with the defendant's name first. In speech this would be read as 'Smith and Jones'.
If the prosecution wins its case, the defendant is described as being found guilty, or convicted.	If the claimant wins the case, the defendant can be described as having lost, or being held liable for the relevant wrong (e.g. libel, negligence). He or she should never be described as being found guilty of (for example) negligence or libel.
A convicted defendant is sentenced.	If the claimant wins, he or she will usually be awarded a remedy. This is most often damages, which is a sum of money, but there are other civil remedies such as, for example, being reinstated in a job from which you have been wrongfully dismissed. You can say that the defendant had damages awarded against him or her; you should never say that he or she was sentenced or fined.

THE COURT SYSTEM

The English court system consists of:

- magistrates' courts;
- county courts;
- the Crown Court;

- the High Court;
- the Court of Appeal; and
- the Supreme Court.

The Crown Court only hears criminal cases and the county courts only civil ones, but the others hear both civil and criminal cases.

As explained earlier, the courts form a hierarchical system, in which appeals can pass up through the courts, and decisions made in the higher courts have to be followed by those lower down. Traditionally, the House of Lords was the highest appeal court in the UK, but membership of the EU has meant the European Court of Justice is effectively the highest court for cases which concern EU law. In 2009, the House of Lords was replaced by the new Supreme Court, but for the purposes of this book, its role remains the same. The Supreme Court also hears appeals from some other countries within the Commonwealth; when it sits in such a case it is known as the Privy Council. (The functions of each court, and the hierarchy of courts for appeals, are explained in Chapter 3, on criminal procedure, and Chapter 4, on civil procedure.)

PEOPLE IN THE LEGAL SYSTEM

The main legal personnel that journalists need to know about are:

- lawyers;
- judges;
- government legal officers.

In all three cases, a knowledge of what these people do, and how to refer to them, will ensure that your reports appear authoritative.

Lawyers

The English legal profession comprises two different types of lawyer: barristers and solicitors. Traditionally, the two branches did different types of work. Today, this distinction is increasingly breaking down, but the terms 'solicitor' and 'barrister' still describe two different professionals, who each undergo a different training process and set of exams in order to qualify. Barristers are also known as counsel. The term lawyer, however, covers both.

Traditionally, the major difference between the work of the two branches was that solicitors dealt directly with clients, while barristers were usually called on by a solicitor where necessary, either to give advice on a detailed area of law, or to represent the client in court. In addition, only barristers could appear in the higher courts. However, changes made in the 1990s have broken down some of the differences between the two branches. Clients can now consult barristers directly without being referred by a solicitor, and solicitors can appear in all courts, provided that they have undergone a specialist training course (solicitors who do this are often known as solicitor advocates). In fact, although it is often believed that barristers do most court work, solicitors have always done a lot of criminal court work, because 95 per cent of criminal cases are heard in the magistrates' courts, where the defendant is usually represented by a solicitor rather than a barrister.

QCs (short for Queen's Counsel) are barristers and solicitors who have been in practice for at least ten years and are considered particularly talented and experienced. Becoming a QC is not, however, automatic – lawyers must apply for the title, and some apply several times before being granted it, while others never get it at all. Becoming a QC generally means a lawyer will be offered higher-paying work.

Judges

There are six different categories of judge in the legal system, as well as magistrates, who, although they are lay people and not considered part of the judiciary, actually decide 95 per cent of all criminal cases.

Supreme Court Justices sit in the Supreme Court. There are 12 of them. They are referred to as, for example, Lord or Lady Brown.

Lord and Lady Justices of Appeal sit in the Court of Appeal. There are 38 of them. They are referred to as, for example, Lord or Lady Justice Brown. The most senior judge in the Civil Division of the Court of Appeal is called the Master of the Rolls; in the Criminal Division, the head is the Lord Chief Justice.

High Court judges sit in the High Court and also hear the most serious cases in the Crown Court; there are just over 100 of them. They spend some of their time 'on circuit', travelling around the regional courts, where they may, for example, hear Queen's Bench Division cases or Family Division cases which would otherwise have to be held at the High Court in London. In the official reports of legal cases, and in law textbooks, a High Court judge called Smith would be referred to as Smith J, but for journalists, it is more usual to write Mr or Mrs Justice Smith (not Judge Smith).

Circuit judges sit in the county court and in middle-ranking Crown Court cases. There are around 650 of them, and they are referred to as, for example, Judge Simon Smith or Judge Ann Jones. Occasionally they may also sit in the Court of Appeal.

District judges hear the majority of cases in the county courts; there are around 450 of them. There are also around 100 district judges (formerly known as stipendiary magistrates) who hear the more complex and serious cases in the magistrates' courts of larger cities. Both are usually referred to as, for example, District Judge Jane Brown.

Recorders are part-time judges who hear the least serious Crown Court cases and some county court cases. They are usually still working as barristers or solicitors, and the job is viewed as a kind of apprenticeship before becoming a full-time judge. They are referred to as the recorder or, for example, Mr John Smith or Mrs Mary Smith. The title of recorder is also used in a slightly different context: the Recorder of Manchester is the most senior circuit judge in the Manchester Crown Court, and similar titles are used for the same role in Liverpool, Belfast and some other cities. The title Recorder of London applies to one of the senior judges who sits at the Central Criminal Court (the London Crown Court which is better known as the Old Bailey).

Magistrates (also known as Justices of the Peace, or JPs) are lay people, drawn from the local community, who sit in the magistrates' courts (usually in a panel of three) hearing criminal and some kinds of civil cases. Though they receive training in court procedure, they are not required to be legally qualified or to know the law, but have a legally qualified clerk to advise them. The work is voluntary (magistrates receive expenses, but no pay) and part-time – most magistrates sit for 35–70 half-days per year. Magistrates are selected by local committees, though they are officially appointed by the Lord Chancellor. When reporting cases involving magistrates, it is usual to refer to them as 'the magistrates' rather than by name, but a magistrate's name can be used if you need to refer to one specifically. In ***R* v *Felixstowe Justices ex p Leigh* (1987) QB 582, *R* v *Evesham Justices ex p McDonagh* (1988)**, the Divisional Court of the Queen's Bench ruled that a magistrates' court could not legally withhold the name of a sitting magistrate from the press.

Government legal officers

There are four government legal officers:

- the Lord Chancellor;
- the Attorney-General;
- the Solicitor-General;
- the Director of Public Prosecutions.

The Lord Chancellor is a Cabinet Minister, and the head of the Ministry of Justice, which is responsible for the courts, prisons, probation and constitutional affairs. He or she can be a member of either the House of Commons or the House of Lords.

The Attorney-General and the Solicitor-General (together known as the Law Officers) are both Government Ministers, though not members of the Cabinet. The Attorney-General is the main legal advisor to the Government (the Attorney-General at the time of the war in Iraq, for example, gave the Government advice on whether the war was legal under international law), and is responsible for important legal cases involving the Government, whether at home or abroad. Certain types of crime (such as offences under the Contempt of Court Act – see Chapter 6) require consent from the Attorney-General before prosecutions can be brought, and if this consent is given, the prosecution is brought in the name of the Attorney-General. The Solicitor-General is effectively the Attorney-General's deputy, and may fulfil any of his or her functions where necessary.

The Director of Public Prosecutions (DPP) is the head of the Crown Prosecution Service (CPS), and is responsible for ensuring the independent review and prosecution of criminal proceedings started by the police in England and Wales. He or she makes decisions about the most complex and sensitive cases and advises the police on criminal matters, and prosecutions for certain types of cases require his or her permission. The DPP reports to the Attorney-General.

KEY POINTS

Types of law

English law can be divided into:

- Criminal law, which deals with offences that are considered severe enough to warrant investigation and punishment on behalf of the whole community, in the name of the state.
- Civil law, which covers all other areas of law.

Civil law can be divided into:

- private law, which deals with disputes between individual parties;
- public law, which regulates the way public bodies use their powers.

The court system

The courts are organised into a hierarchy, and cases decided in a lower court can, in certain circumstances, be sent on appeal to the next court up.

The Supreme Court is the highest court in the UK, except on matters of EU law, where the European Court of Justice is effectively the highest court.

People in the legal system

There are two types of lawyers in the English system: barristers and solicitors.

There are six different categories of judge:

- Supreme Court Justices
- Lords Justices of Appeal
- High Court judges
- circuit judges
- district judges
- recorders.

Cases are also heard by magistrates, who are non-legally-qualified lay people.

There are four government legal officers:

- the Lord Chancellor
- the Attorney-General
- the Solicitor-General
- the Director of Public Prosecutions.

TEST YOUR KNOWLEDGE

1 Define criminal and civil law.

2 Nuisance is a civil wrong. Which of these sentences about it are inaccurate?
  (a) John Smith was convicted of nuisance.
  (b) John Smith was found guilty of nuisance.
  (c) John Smith was charged with nuisance.
  (d) John Smith was sued for nuisance.
  (e) John Smith was fined for nuisance.

3 What term applies to someone who brings a civil case? What is the other side called?

4 What is a QC?

5 If a case is called R v Smith, will it be a civil or a criminal case?

6 You are reporting a court case, and want to mention a judge by name. How should you refer to him or her if they are:
(a) a judge in the Court of Appeal
(b) a circuit judge
(c) a recorder
(d) a magistrate?

7 What is the highest court in the English legal system?

8 Describe the roles of the Lord Chancellor, Attorney-General and Director of Public Prosecutions.

ONLINE RESOURCES

The Law Society website has information on the solicitors' profession, at:
www.lawsociety.org.uk

The Bar Council website has information on the work and training of barristers, at:
www.barcouncil.org.uk

Details about the different types of judge, their training and work can be found at the Judiciary of England and Wales website:
www.judiciary.gov.uk

Information about the selection, training and work of magistrates can be found at the Magistrates' Association website at:
www.magistrates-association.org.uk

The Ministry of Justice website contains information on the legal system, including the government legal officers:
www.justice.gov.uk

Criminal courts and procedure

A society without crime might be a very pleasant place to live in, but it would throw thousands of journalists out of work at a stroke. Reporting criminal trials is an everyday occurrence on local and national papers, but in almost every other area of journalism you are likely to come across the subject now and then. That means it is important to have a grasp of how the criminal justice system works, which is the subject covered in this chapter. Later (in Section 2), you will find details of how the law restricts the way in which you report criminal investigations and trials.

THE CRIMINAL COURTS

Criminal cases are heard by either a magistrates' court or the Crown Court, depending on the type of offence (see the box).

Types of criminal offence

Crimes fall into three categories, based on where they can be tried:

- **Indictable offences** (or offences triable only on indictment) are the most serious crimes, and can only be tried in the Crown Court, by a jury.
- **Either way offences** can be tried in either the Crown Court or the magistrates' courts. The defendant can insist on being tried in the Crown Court; if he or she does not do so, the magistrates decide whether to try the case themselves or send it to the Crown Court, taking into account the seriousness of the offence and whether they are likely to have adequate sentencing powers if the defendant is found guilty (see below).
- **Summary offences** are tried only in the magistrates' courts. They should not, however, necessarily be seen as trivial – over the years, more and more offences have been made summary, and the category includes, for example, assaulting a police officer and drink-driving.

MAGISTRATES' COURTS

All criminal cases start in the magistrates' court, where one or more initial hearings will take place before the trial itself. Around 95 per cent of criminal cases (all involving summary or either way offences) then go on to be tried in the magistrates' courts (the rest go to the Crown Court for trial).

Cases are decided by three lay magistrates or, in certain areas, by a district judge. The magistrates are advised by the clerk to the justices, who usually sits in front of them. The clerk will be legally trained, and is there to advise on the law and legal procedure, but does not take part in the actual decision in the case. The maximum sentence a magistrates' court can impose is six months' imprisonment, or 12 months if passing consecutive sentences for more than one offence. If a defendant is convicted by magistrates who feel that a longer sentence is appropriate, they can refer the case to the Crown Court for sentencing. Youth courts are a branch of the magistrates' court, and hear cases where the defendant is under 18 (for more details on criminal cases involving under-18s, see Chapter 10).

Crown Court

The Crown Court is where cases are decided by jury. Despite the impression given by films and TV, only a tiny minority of cases go through this process: 95 per cent of cases are decided by magistrates and of the 5 per cent left, most will plead guilty, so no jury is needed. Only about 1 per cent of cases is tried by a jury, though this still amounts to around 30,000 cases a year. Where a jury does decide the case, its role is to decide whether the defendant is guilty or innocent; if the jury finds that person guilty, the judge decides the sentence (this is why juries are only used if the defendant pleads not guilty).

A jury consists of 12 people who are chosen at random from the local electoral roll. They must be between 18 and 70, though anyone over 65 can choose not to serve if called. People who are on bail, have ever been sentenced to more than five years in prison, or received a prison sentence, suspended sentence, community order or probation order in the past ten years are not allowed to sit on a jury, and nor are people with mental health problems that require them to be in hospital or under regular medical treatment. In the past, members of certain professions, such as lawyers, politicians, judges and doctors were exempt from jury service but this exemption was abolished by the Criminal Justice Act 2003.

There is only one Crown Court, even though it can be sitting in different places at the same time, so it is technically correct to refer to 'the Crown Court' rather than 'crown courts' or 'a crown court'. However, it is standard practice to talk about, for example, 'Maidstone Crown Court', even though technically this is the Crown Court sitting in Maidstone.

CRIMINAL JUSTICE PROCEDURE

Stage 1: investigating crime

Most criminal cases will begin with the role of the police, who are responsible for investigating most crimes (though some are investigated by other agencies, such as the Health and Safety Executive or the Serious Fraud Office). Police procedure during criminal investigations is regulated by the Police and Criminal Evidence Act 1984 (known as PACE), the Criminal Justice and Public Order Act 1994 and the Serious Organised Crime and Police Act 2005, which between them specify the circumstances in which the police can stop, search, arrest, detain and interrogate members of the public.

A criminal case officially starts either when an arrest is made (see below), or when the police send the magistrates' court a document giving particulars of the alleged offence. This is called laying an information, and as a result of it the magistrates can issue either an arrest warrant or a summons, which is sent to the defendant and states what he or she is accused of, and the time and date at which he or she must attend court. Magistrates cannot try a summary offence unless the information is laid within six months of the offence being committed.

In some areas the laying of information process has been replaced by a simpler procedure called 'written charge and requisition', where the prosecuting authority writes to the accused, informing them that they have been charged and giving the date when they must attend at the magistrates' court.

Pre-arrest powers

Nobody is obliged to answer questions put by a police officer, or to go to or be detained at a police station, unless lawfully arrested. However, obstructing the police is an offence, and cases suggest that there is a fine line between refusing to answer questions and obstruction: in ***Ricketts* v *Cox* (1982)**, a defendant who was abusive and uncooperative when asked questions by two police officers investigating an assault was found guilty of obstruction.

Someone who goes voluntarily to a police station for questioning has the legal right to leave when they want to, unless they are arrested, so the often-used phrase 'detained for questioning' has no real legal meaning – a suspect is either under arrest and being questioned, or is undergoing questioning voluntarily.

→ **How much can you report?** See pp. 66–67 and p. 82

Powers of arrest

The main police powers of arrest are contained in the Serious Organised Crime and Police Act 2005. Arrests can be made when a police officer reasonably suspects that someone has committed, is committing or is about to commit an offence, and the police officer has reasonable grounds to believe that an arrest is necessary. This will be the case where:

- the suspect refuses to give a name or address, or the officer reasonably believes the one given is false;
- the arrest will prevent the suspect from suffering physical injury, harming themselves, someone else, or property, committing an offence against public decency, or obstructing the highway;
- the arrest is needed to protect a child or other vulnerable person;
- the arrest will allow the prompt and effective investigation of the offence or the suspect's conduct;
- arrest is needed to prevent the person from escaping.

This very broad set of circumstances means arrest is now possible in the majority of cases where the police would wish to do so. However, in the few cases where none of the criteria is fulfilled, the police can apply to a magistrate for a warrant. This is not a common process today, and is mainly used for defendants who have failed to turn up for trial.

Police questioning

PACE states that if the police arrest someone, they must tell the person why they are being arrested. The police can then detain them for up to 36 hours, and must then either release them or charge them, unless the case is an indictable offence. In that case the police can authorise a further detention of up to 12 hours, if necessary, to secure or preserve evidence. After that, the police must get permission from a magistrate to hold the suspect for further periods: the maximum is a total of 96 hours, after which the suspect must be either released or charged (except where the suspected offence concerns terrorism, in which case suspects can be detained for up to 21 days).

Where someone is held for an unreasonable time without being charged, there is an ancient form of legal action called 'habeas corpus', which allows that person's friends or family to get an order from the High Court requiring him or her to be released. In practice though, prolonged detention before charge or release happens fairly rarely: only 5 per cent of suspects are held for more than 18 hours, and 1 per cent for more than 24 hours.

Under the PACE Code of Practice, once someone is charged, police questioning should stop. The Code of Practice provisions are not legal requirements, but breach of them can lead to disciplinary action, and serious breaches can mean that a court will rule that evidence obtained by means of the breach cannot be used against the defendant.

Someone who is arrested and later released without ever being charged may be able to bring a civil claim against the police for false arrest or wrongful imprisonment, if the grounds for the arrest were unreasonable.

→ **How much can you report?** See pp. 66–67

Information from the police

In 2013 the College of Policing issued guidelines to be used by all police forces, on how to work with the media during criminal investigations. The document is called 'Guidance on Relationships with the Media' and is available at http://college.pressofficeadmin.com/repository/files/Press%20Releases/Media_Relationships_Guidance_0513.pdf.

Its main points are as follows.

- The police have a duty to safeguard the confidentiality and integrity of information, but they must balance this with the duty to be open and transparent wherever possible.
- Officers are encouraged to speak with the media about matters for which they are responsible and to be open, honest and approachable.
- Media organisations should be treated in a fair and equal manner, and once in the public domain, information should be accessible to all. It may be appropriate for the police to work with a particular media organisation on a specific issue (such as a local paper campaigning against a particular crime issue) but the opportunity to do this should be available to all equally. Where a media outlet itself generates an exclusive, its right to share information in confidence with the police should be respected.
- On some occasions it may be reasonable to delay releasing information to allow time to put resources in place to deal with public feedback.

- Where the press are taken on operations, this should be done in a manner which avoids favouritism, In this situation, the owners of private property can refuse access to the media and, if so, access is for the media to negotiate, not the police.
- Where someone is arrested, or suspected of a crime, but not yet charged, the decision on whether to release his or her name should be made on a case by case basis, but unless there are exceptional circumstances, names and/or identifying details should not be made public. Reasons for releasing names or details would include a threat to life, the prevention or detection of crime, or matters of public interest or confidence. Forces can however provide non-identifying information such as gender, age and location of arrest.
- Once someone is charged, the police should release his or her name, address, occupation and charge details, unless any legal restrictions apply.
- Information about witnesses or victims should not be disclosed except in agreement with the people concerned, unless there is a public interest reason for doing so.

Bail

At various stages in the criminal justice process, a decision has to be made on whether to keep a suspect in custody or allow them out on bail. To be allowed out on bail simply means that the suspect is allowed to go free, on condition that they turn up at a specific place and date in the future. While a case is being investigated, for example, the police may let someone out on bail after interviewing them, on condition that they come back to the police station when required, if they think they will need to speak to them again. Bail is also considered after someone is charged, and sometimes again when someone has pleaded guilty to a charge and the case is adjourned to be heard at a later stage. In both those cases, the suspect/defendant is bailed on condition they turn up for their court hearing. If someone granted bail does not turn up at the appointed date and place, that is a criminal offence, and usually an arrest warrant for them will be issued.

Bail can be granted by the police, either at the police station, or as what is called 'street bail' at the place where the person was arrested. Once a suspect is charged, if the police do not grant bail, the suspect must be brought before magistrates as soon as possible and they then take the decision on whether to grant bail or not.

There is a general presumption that unconvicted defendants should be granted bail, but under the Bail Act 1976, it can be refused where:

- there are substantial grounds to believe the defendant will abscond, commit other offences, interfere with witnesses or obstruct the course of justice;
- the defendant should be kept in custody for his/her own protection (or is already serving a prison sentence);
- there is not yet sufficient information to make the decision.

Where the defendant is already on bail for an indictable offence (see p. 18), a court is not required to grant bail even if the above requirements are not fulfilled. Under the Criminal Justice Act 2003, the same applies to a person charged with an imprisonable offence, who tests positive for a Class A drug and refuses treatment. If the defendant is charged with murder, manslaughter, rape or attempted rape or murder, and has a previous conviction for such an offence, bail should only be granted in exceptional circumstances, and the court must state its reasons. If bail is refused, the defendant has the right to apply to a judge to have the decision reversed; the prosecution also has this right where bail has been granted despite their objections.

Both the police and magistrates can impose conditions when they grant bail, such as that the person reports regularly to a police station, or lives in a bail hostel. They can also ask for a surety, which means that someone – usually a friend or relative of the accused – puts up a sum of money as a guarantee that the person will turn up for court. If they fail to appear, the surety loses their money, and can be jailed if they do not pay it, so sureties are usually only asked for in very serious cases.

During a bail hearing, the court will usually be told of any previous convictions that the defendant has, and given an outline of the police case against them. In some cases, the defendant's lawyer will also put forward reasons why they should be given bail. Some of this material could clearly be prejudicial to the eventual trial (a jury may be more likely to convict if they know the defendant has previous convictions, for example), so there are strict rules about what you can and cannot report from a bail hearing.

→ **How much can you report?** See p. 135

Myths and misconceptions **Bail**

✗ *Bail means someone pays money to get another person out of custody.*

In American films and TV dramas, you often see situations where someone who has been arrested is allowed out of jail because someone posts bail for them, meaning that they hand over a sum of money that they will get back if the person turns up for their court hearing, or lose if the person disappears. Bail in the UK has a different meaning, and simply applies to a decision by a court that a person charged with an offence should not be kept in custody for the time between being charged and appearing in court. Although the courts can require that someone guarantees the person will appear in court by pledging a sum of money if they do not appear, this is not routine and only happens where the charge is a very serious one, such as murder or a major drugs offence.

Stage 2: prosecution

Once the investigation is complete – which may happen quickly or take a long time – a decision must be made on whether to charge someone, drop the case, or issue a caution. A caution is a formal warning, and can only be given where the defendant admits guilt and there would be a realistic prospect of a successful prosecution. It is not, as popularly thought, a kind of get-out clause that can be used when the police think they cannot prove their case, or when the suspect might not be guilty of the particular offence in question but is thought to be a bad lot generally. Cautions are recorded, and if a person is later convicted of another offence, the caution can be cited as part of their criminal record. In around 75 per cent of cases, the police make this decision, but where the offence is a serious one or the case is especially complex, the decision is passed to the Crown Prosecution Service (CPS).

In deciding whether to prosecute, the CPS uses a two-stage test:

1 Is there sufficient evidence to provide a realistic prospect of conviction? This essentially means that the evidence is such that the court is more likely to convict than not to do so. If there is not sufficient evidence, the case should not go ahead, no matter how serious or important it seems. If there is sufficient evidence, the CPS goes on to ask the second question.
2 Is a prosecution in the public interest? The reasons which can be taken into account for this test are contained in the Code of Practice for Crown Prosecutors. Factors making a prosecution more likely to be in the public interest include:
   - that a conviction is likely to result in a significant sentence;
   - that the offence was committed against someone serving the public (such as a police officer);
   - where an offence is relatively minor, the fact that it happens very frequently in the relevant local area.

Circumstances which can make a prosecution less likely include:

- the defendant being very elderly or unwell;
- a long delay between the offence taking place and the potential date of the trial.

None of these factors is conclusive; the CPS will usually need to weigh a number of factors against each other in coming to a decision.

Private prosecutions

If the CPS decides not to prosecute, a victim of crime can bring a private prosecution, but because legal aid is unavailable, this happens very rarely. Where the offence is a serious one, the Director of Public Prosecutions must be informed before a case can go ahead, and the law allows the CPS to take over private prosecutions. It will only do this if there is good reason to do so. The CPS can then continue the prosecution if it passes the two-stage test described above, or end it if there is so little evidence that there is really no case to answer, or if the prosecution is not in the public interest.

Stage 3: hearings before a trial

Almost all criminal cases begin in the magistrates' courts. Around 95 per cent of them are actually tried there; the rest go on to be tried in the Crown Court, but there will be at least one pre-trial hearing in the magistrates' courts first. In some cases, particularly if the case is a high-profile one, the pre-trial hearings will be held via a video link to the prison where the defendant is being held. The defendant is addressed and treated as if they were there in the court.

Pre-trial hearings in the magistrates' courts

The type of pre-trial hearing depends on the category of offence.

Summary offences: Pre-trial hearings are optional for summary offences, but one magistrate or the magistrates' clerk may hold a hearing in which both sides can agree the main issues in the case, and identify what needs to be done in preparation for the trial itself.

Either way offences: These can be tried in the magistrates or Crown Court, and a pre-trial hearing called the allocation procedure is held to decide this. If the defendant is going to plead guilty, there will be no trial. The magistrates will be given details of the offence, and the defendant's previous convictions, if any, and if on the basis of this, they believe their sentencing powers are sufficient to deal with the offence, they will sentence the defendant then and there, or adjourn the case to do so later (remember that magistrates can only sentence offenders to up to six months for one offence and 12 months for more than one). If they believe the case may deserve a more severe sentence than they can pass, they will commit the case for sentencing to the Crown Court.

If the defendant intends to plead not guilty, the magistrates must decide whether to hear the case or send it to the Crown Court. This decision is based on whether their sentencing powers would be sufficient if the defendant was found guilty, so at this stage they hear details of the evidence, and the defendant's previous convictions, if any, so as to assess the seriousness of the case. If they decide against trying the case themselves, it is sent to the Crown Court for trial.

If the magistrates agree they can try the case, the defendant is then asked whether they want to be tried there or in the Crown Court. If the defendant chooses a Crown Court trial, the case will be sent there; if they choose trial by the magistrates, they then formally enter their plea, and the trial either goes ahead there, or more often, is adjourned so that the lawyers can make their preparations.

For either way offences involving serious fraud and certain offences against children, the allocation procedure is not used, and cases are instead sent to the Crown Court by a 'sending' hearing.

Indictable offences: For indictable offences, there is a fast-track procedure through the magistrates' court called sending for trial. The defendant usually appears just once before the magistrates' court, and at this hearing the court decides issues concerning funding from the Legal Services Commission (what used to be called Legal Aid), whether the defendant should be given bail until the Crown Court trial, and any questions about the use of particular statements or exhibits.

Pre-trial hearings of all kinds frequently hear material which could be prejudicial to the eventual trial, and, for that reason, there are strict rules on what you can report from them.

→ **How much can you report?** See pp. 130–133

Bail applications

Where a defendant is to be tried in the Crown Court, the defence lawyer may ask that the defendant be granted bail until then (there can be a long delay before cases come before the Crown Court). The prosecution will be invited to put forward any objections to bail being granted such as that the defendant is likely to abscond, interfere with witnesses or commit another offence. If bail is refused, the defendant can apply to a judge in chambers to reverse the decision.

→ **How much can you report?** See p. 133

Pre-trial hearings in the Crown Court

Once a case has been sent to the Crown Court, the next stage is a plea and case management hearing, where the defendant enters a plea of guilty or not guilty (this part of the process is known as the arraignment).

If the plea is guilty, the judge will sentence the defendant if possible, or may adjourn the case so that reports can be produced on, for example, the defendant's mental state, if it is thought this might be relevant to the sentence that should be passed.

If the plea is not guilty, the prosecution and defence will be asked to identify the key issues in the case, and provide any additional information needed to organise the trial itself, such as details of witnesses, facts that are agreed by both sides, and any questions of law that are expected to arise. The purpose of this is to encourage both sides to prepare their cases at an early stage, making it less likely that a case will fall apart at the last minute, wasting public money and court time.

For particularly serious or complex cases, there may also be a preparatory hearing which is treated as the start of the trial, even though it happens before the jury is sworn in. This hearing provides a more detailed examination of the issues in the case, to help the judge manage the trial, reduce its length and make it as easy as possible for the jury to understand.

→ **How much can you report?** See pp. 131–133

Stage 4: the trial

The procedure for trial is essentially the same in both the magistrates' and the Crown Court. The prosecution's job is to prove beyond reasonable doubt that the defendant is guilty. If the prosecution does not do this, the defendant should be acquitted; the defence is not required to prove that the defendant is innocent.

At the beginning of the trial, the charges (sometimes called counts) are read out by the clerk of the court. The details may be different from those specified in the magistrates' court during committal, so it is important that reporters do not simply repeat what it says in the report of the earlier hearing. The defendant then pleads guilty or not guilty.

Guilty pleas

If the defendant pleads guilty, the prosecution lawyer will give details of the evidence, and of the defendant's previous criminal record, if any. Social inquiry reports, which detail the defendant's circumstances and are used to help the court decide on the sentence, are read out, and defence lawyers may make pleas in mitigation. These are arguments put forward to persuade the court to be more lenient in sentencing than it otherwise would (they might, for example, draw attention to the fact that a defendant has previously been of good character, or to any evidence that the defendant is trying to make reparation for what he or she has done). The court then passes sentence.

Not guilty pleas

The trial begins (after the jury has been sworn if in the Crown Court) with an outline of the case by the prosecution lawyer, who will usually be a solicitor or barrister employed by the Crown Prosecution Service. Witnesses for the prosecution are then called, and each one is questioned by the prosecution counsel (this is called examination-in-chief). After each examination-in-chief, the witness is questioned by the defence (referred to as cross-examination). If the prosecution feels it necessary to address any points brought out in cross-examination, it can then re-examine the witness.

When the prosecution has presented all its witnesses, the defence can argue that there is no case to answer, which essentially means that there is not sufficient evidence to enable any reasonable jury or magistrate to convict. If the judge or magistrates agree, a verdict of not guilty is given straight away.

If the argument of no case to answer is unsuccessful (or, as is usually the case, the argument is not put forward), the defence then puts its case, using the same procedure as the prosecution: examination-in-chief, cross-examination and, where necessary, re-examination. The defendant may give evidence, but cannot be forced to.

Witnesses who do not wish to give evidence can be ordered to do so by the court, and anyone who then refuses to do so can be jailed for up to a month, or fined. This does not usually apply, however, where the defendant is the spouse or live-in partner of the unwilling witness; in that case the witness cannot be compelled to give evidence unless the offence was committed against them or their children.

In some cases, a witness questioned in court may deny things that they previously said in witness statements, give different evidence or refuse to give the evidence expected. In that situation, they become what is known as a hostile witness, and the side which called them as a witness may challenge the evidence given in court, and remind the witness of what was originally said.

Each side then makes a closing speech: the prosecution addresses the jury first, pointing out the reasons why it should find the defendant guilty, and then the defendant's lawyer addresses the jury, highlighting the reasons for an acquittal (in some cases, with permission, either side may address the court twice).

In the magistrates' court, the magistrates then leave the court to discuss their verdict. In the Crown Court, there is an additional stage, the judge's summing up. The judge outlines the evidence on both sides of the case and explains the law, but reminds the jury that it is its job to decide on the facts – that is, what it believed happened. The judge should also explain the concept of proof beyond reasonable doubt, and stress to the jury that it should only convict if it considers the prosecution case has been proved to this standard. However, where the judge believes that the evidence presented is clearly insufficient for the case to be proved beyond reasonable doubt, he or she should direct the jury to acquit the defendant.

The jury then retires to consider its verdict. If it does not reach a unanimous decision within what the judge considers a reasonable time (no less than two hours, and often much longer), the judge can accept a majority verdict of 11–1 or 10–2. However, a unanimous verdict is always preferred and most judges will ask juries to spend longer trying to achieve one. If the number of people on the jury has been reduced during the trial (e.g. through illness), the judge can accept a verdict of 10–1 or 9–1.

→ **How much can you report?** See pp. 68–79, 82–85, 88–90, 113–122

Myths and misconceptions **Trial procedure**

✘ *Courtroom dramas are an accurate representation of court procedure.*

In courtroom dramas on film and TV, the case often takes an unexpected twist with the appearance of a surprise witness, or an unexpected piece of evidence. In real life, this is unlikely to happen. Court rules provide that both sides are required to disclose their evidence to each other, and to state who they will be calling as witnesses. Evidence or witnesses not included in the disclosure process will only rarely be allowed.

Stage 5: sentencing

If the defendant is found guilty, the magistrates or the judge must decide the sentence. At this stage, any previous convictions can be revealed, and the defence can make pleas in mitigation. Cases are often adjourned at this stage so that reports can be prepared into issues that affect the decision on a suitable sentence, such as the defendant's mental state, or home or work situation.

→ **How much can you report?** See pp. 139–140

Previous convictions and TICs

In most cases, a defendant's previous convictions should not be mentioned in court until and unless they are found guilty. However, there are some exceptions to this rule, and previous convictions can be mentioned where:

- the defendant gives a false impression as to their character;
- the defendant attacks the character of prosecution witnesses; or
- where the court believes that the information would shed important light on the case, and would not make the trial unfair (an example might be where the facts of the case are so similar to incidents which led to previous convictions that they can be taken to show a pattern of behaviour).

Sometimes a defendant found guilty will ask for other offences to be 'taken into consideration' (often called TICs). These should not be confused with previous convictions: they are in fact offences of a similar nature and seriousness, which the defendant has not been charged with but is willing to admit to. The reason for this is that the procedure offers advantages to both sides: the police can close the relevant cases and not waste time and money investigating them, while the offender gets only a small increase in sentence, and avoids the risk of being investigated and convicted for those offences later.

TYPES OF SENTENCE

Sentences fall into seven main types:

- imprisonment;
- fines;
- community sentences;
- mental health orders;
- compensation and confiscation orders;
- binding over orders;
- absolute and conditional discharges.

Courts can also make civil injunctions to prevent nuisance and annoyance, and Criminal Behaviour Orders, which replace ASBOs (see Chapter 10).

Imprisonment

A sentence of imprisonment (also known as a custodial sentence) is viewed as the most serious punishment a court can impose. Under the Criminal Justice Act 2003, a court should only impose a prison sentence if the crime is so serious that only a custodial sentence is justified, and must impose the shortest term that is commensurate with the seriousness of the offence, though there are some exceptions to this rule, for example regarding violent crime. Where the defendant has been tried in the magistrates' court and the magistrates feel imprisonment is appropriate, they can only sentence up to six months for one offence, or 12 months for two or more. If the case requires a longer sentence, the magistrates will commit the defendant to the Crown Court for sentencing. Sentences usually run from the time they are stated in court, so a defendant who is sentenced to imprisonment will be taken there from the court. However, if they have been remanded into custody up until the trial, the time spent 'on remand' will be subtracted from their sentence; this can mean that some defendants sentenced to imprisonment walk free from the court.

Length of sentence

The length of a prison sentence may be fixed by law or decided by the judge according to a tariff system.

Fixed sentences: Only a small number of offences have fixed prison sentences, the most notable being murder, which carries a mandatory sentence of life imprisonment.

Tariff sentences: For most offences the law only lays down a maximum sentence. This gives judges and magistrates discretion to match the sentence to the seriousness of each case, but they are usually guided by what is called a tariff system. This is not a rigid scale of punishments but a guideline as to the type and seriousness of penalties that would usually be applied for a particular offence; it is informed by guidance produced from time to time by the Court of Appeal.

Life sentences

Despite the name, a life sentence does not always (or even often) mean that the offender will go to prison until they die; most are released at some point. The Criminal Justice Act 2003 requires the trial judge to put an offender sentenced to life for murder into one of three categories: those who have committed the most serious crimes (such as serial killers and terrorist murderers), who should stay in prison for the whole of their lives; those who should serve at least 30 years, a category likely to include murderers with sexual, racial or religious motives, or killers of police or prison officers; and the rest, who should serve at least 15 years. Once the specified minimum term has expired, the Parole Board can consider whether the person should be released, and can order this when the appropriate time comes.

Consecutive and concurrent sentences

Where a defendant is found guilty of more than one offence and so given more than one custodial sentence, these can be ordered to run consecutively or concurrently:

- **Concurrent sentences** all start at the same time, which effectively means that the defendant only stays in custody for the length of the longest one.
- **Consecutive sentences** run one after the other.

Suspended and deferred sentences

Custodial sentences may also be suspended for a particular period. This means that the defendant does not have to go to prison unless, during that period, they commit a further offence for which a prison sentence could be imposed. If you are reporting a court case where the sentence is suspended, you should always mention this in the story, and a defendant given a suspended sentence should not be referred to as being 'jailed'.

The courts can also defer passing a sentence for up to six months. This power is intended for use in cases where a court has reason to believe that an offender's circumstances are likely to change in the near future, with the result that no punishment will be necessary, or the appropriate punishment will become less severe; it might be used, for example, where during the deferral period the offender makes reparation to the victim, settles down to steady employment, or otherwise shows that they have changed for the better.

Fines

Fines can be imposed for almost any offence (unless there is a mandatory sentence of imprisonment, as for murder, for example). Where an offence is defined in statute, the maximum fine that can be imposed will be stated, otherwise it is for the court to decide. In that case, magistrates can only impose fines of up to £5,000, but in the Crown Court there is no limit.

Community sentences

Defendants aged 16 or over can be given a community order, which is essentially a period of supervision in the community. Depending on the offence committed, and the offender's circumstances, conditions will normally be attached to the order: the offender can be required to do community work, get treatment for problems such as drug addiction, obey a curfew, live in a particular place and/or abstain from specified activities.

Mental health orders

Under the Mental Health Act 1983, courts can order the detention in hospital of defendants convicted of an imprisonable offence, who have a mental disorder of a type and seriousness which makes detention for treatment appropriate. They can only do this if this kind of detention is the most appropriate way to deal with the offender.

Compensation and confiscation orders

An offender who has physically injured someone, or caused loss or damage, can be ordered to pay compensation of up to £1,000 by a magistrates' court, and an unlimited amount if sentenced by the Crown Court. The courts can also order stolen property to be given back to its owner, or for the offender to pay back some or all of its value. Motor vehicles used for the purposes of theft can be confiscated. These orders can be made in addition to other punishments.

Binding over orders

The binding over order has been used since the fourteenth century, and is a way of dealing with people who are charged with minor violent offences, or breach of the peace, which essentially means behaviour which is either violent or likely to provoke violence. A binding over order involves the defendant promising to 'be of a good behaviour' (in practice, this essentially means not doing anything that could get them arrested) for a certain period, usually a year. In most cases they will be bound over for a particular sum of money, and will have to pay that sum if they break the binding over order.

Binding over orders are sometimes given after a defendant has been found guilty of a minor offence but, in many cases, the offer of a binding over order may be made before the trial; if the defendant accepts, the charge may be dropped and no trial held. Where this happens, there is no criminal conviction, so it is important not to report the binding over as a sentence.

Absolute and conditional discharges

If a defendant is given a conditional discharge, they are free to go with no penalty – but if they commit another offence during the period which the court specifies, they can then be sentenced again for the original offence as well as the further one. This should not be confused with an absolute discharge, which is given when the magistrates or judge consider that, in the circumstances, the defendant's conduct, though against the law, does not deserve punishment. In this case the defendant is free to go without any conditions.

→ **How much can you report?** See p. 161–162

Serious Crime Prevention Orders

Created by the Serious Crime Act 2007, a Serious Crime Prevention Order (SCPO) is a civil order that requires the recipient to do something (such as supplying financial information) or not do something (such as travelling), and can apply for up to five years. The Crown Court can impose SCPOs on individuals or organisations that have been convicted of involvement in serious crime, where the court has reasonable grounds to believe that the order would protect the public by preventing or restricting involvement in serious crime. In addition, where there has been no conviction, the prosecution can apply to the High Court for an SCPO, even if there is not enough evidence to satisfy the criminal standard of proof. Breach of an SCPO is a criminal offence punishable by up to five years' imprisonment.

APPEALS AND RETRIALS

The end of a trial is not always the end of the case: in some circumstances, a defendant who has been acquitted may be retried, and there is also a system of appeals where one side or the other believes the court has made the wrong decision, or the case has not been properly conducted.

Appeals by the defendant

A defendant who has pleaded not guilty, and believes they have been wrongly convicted, can appeal to a higher court to re-examine the case. A convicted defendant can also appeal against a sentence which is alleged to be too harsh; this right exists whether the defendant pleaded guilty or not guilty.

The route through the appeals system depends on where the original case was heard.

From magistrates' courts

There are four routes of appeal from the magistrates' courts.

To the High Court, by way of 'case stated': If the defence believes the magistrates have made a mistake about the law, or acted outside their powers, the magistrates can be asked to 'state the case' to the Queen's Bench Division of the High Court. The Queen's Bench Division can confirm, reverse or vary the verdict, or order the case to be retried by different magistrates. Magistrates can refuse to state the case where the application is judged to be frivolous. If not satisfied with the result of the High Court hearing, the original defendant (now known as the appellant) can make a further appeal straight to the Supreme Court, if the Divisional Court agrees that the case involves a point of law that is of public importance, and either this court or the Supreme Court gives permission for a further appeal. It is important to note that the case stated procedure is only for possible mistakes about the law, or the way the magistrates handled the case; it is not used where the defendant simply believes the wrong verdict was reached.

To the Crown Court: A defendant who has pleaded not guilty can appeal to the Crown Court, on the grounds that they have been wrongly convicted, and/or too harshly sentenced. A defendant who has pleaded guilty can only appeal against the sentence, not the conviction itself. The appeal must be made within 28 days. Cases are heard by a judge and two to four magistrates, except where the appeal is against the sentence, when it will be heard by a judge alone. The Crown Court can either confirm the original verdict and/or sentence, or reverse the verdict and/or alter the sentence. The Crown Court can impose any sentence which the magistrates' court could have imposed, which can sometimes mean that an appeal results in a higher sentence. If either side believes the appeal decision is wrong on a point of law, the case can then go to the High Court, by way of case stated, as above.

Referral by the Criminal Cases Review Commission: This is an independent body set up to review cases which may involve miscarriages of justice. Where a case has failed an original appeal (or one was not made in time), and new evidence comes to light which makes it likely that the conviction was wrong, the Criminal Cases Review Commission can refer it to the Crown Court for another hearing.

Magistrates' error: Where the magistrates accept that they have made an error (e.g. in applying the law), they can reopen the case and, where it is in the interests of justice, have it reheard by a different set of magistrates. They can also use this power to vary a sentence.

From the Crown Court

There are three types of appeal from cases originally heard in the Crown Court.

To the Court of Appeal: A defendant who believes the Crown Court reached the wrong verdict on the facts, applied the law wrongly, or passed a sentence that was obviously too severe, can appeal to the Court of Appeal, but only with permission from the trial judge or the Court of Appeal. The Court of Appeal does not rehear the whole case, but reassesses the evidence that was given, and, if necessary, any new evidence. It can confirm the conviction, quash it or order a retrial, and can also reduce a sentence (but not increase it). Where a case was heard in the magistrates' court but sent to the Crown Court for sentencing, and a sentence of over six months' imprisonment is imposed, the defendant can appeal against the sentence to the Court of Appeal. If either side believes the appeal decision is wrong on a point of law, the case can be appealed to the Supreme Court, if the Court of Appeal or the Supreme Court gives permission, and the Supreme Court certifies that the case involves a point of law of public importance.

Referral by the Criminal Cases Review Commission: As for appeals from the magistrates' courts, above.

By case stated: As explained above.

Second appeals to the Court of Appeal

In exceptional cases, the Court of Appeal may hear a second appeal in the same case, or, in other words, an appeal from its own decision. This will only happen where it is likely that a significant injustice has been done in the case, the circumstances are exceptional, and there is no other remedy.

Retrials and appeals against acquittal

In the past, it was considered a general rule that once a person had been acquitted, the decision was final, and they could not be retried later for the same offence; this was known as the rule against double jeopardy. There were always some exceptions to this rule, but it has now been officially abolished under the Criminal Justice Act 2003, which allows an acquitted defendant to be retried if compelling new evidence is found. There are now several ways in which an acquittal can be reversed, a sentence increased or a retrial ordered.

Witness intimidation

Under the Criminal Procedure and Investigations Act 1996, where a defendant has been acquitted, but witnesses or jurors have been intimidated (meaning threatened or otherwise improperly persuaded to acquit), the High Court can quash the acquittal, and order the defendant to be retried. This power can only be used where someone has been convicted of interfering with a witness and/or juror, and where the court which held the original trial agrees that the acquittal would not have happened if the interference with witnesses or jurors had not taken place. (Judges can also stop a trial if, while it is taking place, it is discovered that jurors or witnesses have been interfered with, or can discharge the jury and order that the trial continues without them.)

New evidence

If, after someone has been acquitted of a serious offence, compelling new evidence comes to light, s75 of the Criminal Justice Act 2003 allows the Director of Public Prosecutions (DPP) to authorise an application to the Court of Appeal, which, after assessing the new evidence, can quash the acquittal and order a retrial. The DPP should only allow an application to the Court of Appeal where the new evidence is reliable, substantial and provides a high degree of proof, and the DPP must also consider whether a retrial would be in the interests of justice, taking into account the length of time which has elapsed since the original trial and the likelihood of a new trial being fair. This power is used extremely rarely.

Appeals by way of case stated

Where the prosecution believes an acquittal is the result of a court making a mistake about the law, it can appeal to the High Court by way of case stated (see p. 32).

Appeals from the Court of Appeal

If a case reaches the Court of Appeal, and the prosecution believes the appeal decision is wrong on a point of law, it can appeal to the Supreme Court, if the Court of Appeal or the Supreme Court gives permission, and the Supreme Court certifies that the case involves a point of law of public importance.

Sentence review

For some more serious offences, the Criminal Justice Act 2003 allows the Attorney-General to ask the Court of Appeal to review a sentence passed by the Crown Court, which they believe is unduly lenient. The Court of Appeal can quash the sentence and pass a more appropriate one.

Stopped trials

Where a judge stops a trial part-way through (e.g. if they believe there is insufficient evidence to support a conviction), the prosecution can appeal against this decision to the Court of Appeal.

In addition, where a person has been acquitted and the case involved a dispute over a point of law, the Criminal Justice Act 1972 allows the Attorney-General to refer the case to the Court of Appeal for its opinion on the legal point (in order to clarify it for future cases). However, this is not strictly speaking an appeal, as the defendant's acquittal cannot be quashed under this provision, and they are not required to appear before the court again.

The routes for criminal appeals are summarised in Figure 3.1.

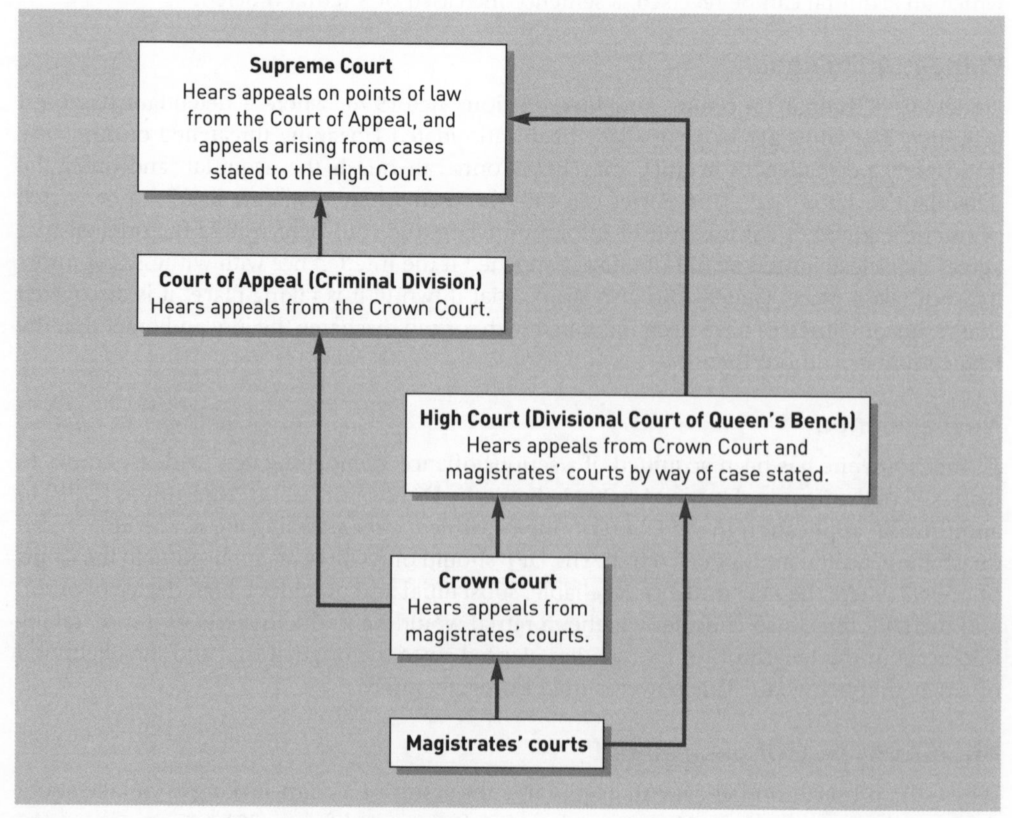

Figure 3.1 Routes for criminal appeals

COMMON CRIMES

Although a journalist does not need the same detailed knowledge of particular crimes as a lawyer would, it is important to understand the basics of the most common offences, and to be able to distinguish between them. In everyday language, for example, the terms 'robber' and 'thief' are virtually interchangeable, but in legal terms, robbery is a much more serious offence than theft, because it involves violence as well as dishonesty.

Before we look at the definitions of some common offences, it may help to know that the legal definition of a crime is made up of two parts: the criminal act, known as the *actus reus*, which is what the offender must do in order to have committed the crime; and the mental element or *mens rea*, which is the mental state with which they did that act. For example, the *actus reus* of most homicide offences is the unlawful killing of another person, but whether such killing amounts to murder or manslaughter can depend on whether the killer acted intentionally or not.

An exception to this rule is what are known as strict liability offences. For these, the defendant need only have committed the relevant criminal act; the prosecution does not have to prove that they intended to do it, or even that they were at fault in any way. Some driving offences carry strict liability, and so do many of the laws which are used to regulate industry, such as those on safety at work and food hygiene.

Homicide offences

Homicide means the killing of a human being. As well as the most serious homicide offence, murder, there are two types of manslaughter, voluntary and involuntary, and a fourth offence, infanticide. Yet another offence is causing or allowing the death of a child or vulnerable adult.

Murder is defined as the unlawful killing of another human being 'with malice aforethought'. The old-fashioned term 'malice aforethought' essentially means an intention to kill or cause very serious bodily harm. It has nothing to do with malice as we usually understand it – it is the degree of deliberateness that is legally relevant, not the reason for acting. So, in law, deliberate euthanasia performed in order to free a loved one from suffering conforms to the definition of malice aforethought as effectively as shooting someone because you hate them.

Voluntary manslaughter takes place where a defendant kills someone unlawfully, with malice aforethought, but there are mitigating circumstances which reduce their liability from murder to manslaughter. As a result it is not possible to charge someone with voluntary manslaughter; they are charged with murder, and must then put their defence at trial. If the defence succeeds, they can be convicted of manslaughter instead of murder. The three defences which can reduce murder to manslaughter are loss of control, diminished responsibility and suicide pact:

- **Loss of control** is a defence that is essentially aimed at situations where the defendant cannot be said to have acted intentionally, because they have lost control in circumstances where a reasonable person might have done the same. It is defined in the Coroners and Justice Act 2009, and applies where three conditions are satisfied:
  - the defendant's acts resulted from a loss of self-control; and
  - his or her loss of self-control was caused by a 'qualifying trigger', which the Act defines as either a fear of serious violence being used by the victim against them or someone

else, or things said or done that amount to 'extremely grave' circumstances and caused the defendant to 'have a justifiable sense of being seriously wronged'; and

- a person of the defendant's age and sex, with the normal amount of tolerance and self-restraint, might have reacted in the same way if they were in the same circumstances.

- **Diminished responsibility** is defined in the Homicide Act 1957, as amended by the Coroners and Justice Act 2009. It applies where a defendant has an 'abnormality of mental functioning', which substantially impairs their ability to understand the nature of what they are doing, form rational judgements, or exercise self-control. The abnormality must arise from a recognised medical condition, and the defence will only apply if that abnormality causes, or significantly contributes to causing, the defendant to do what they did.
- **Suicide pact** applies where two people agree they will both commit suicide, and one helps the other to die (and, obviously, survives). Without a suicide pact, helping someone to commit suicide can be murder, but if there is a suicide pact, liability is reduced to manslaughter.

(Note that the above are only defences to murder, not to any other crimes.)

Involuntary manslaughter is committed when the defendant has unlawfully killed another, but without malice aforethought. This covers cases where death has been caused by gross negligence, or where the defendant commits a dangerous crime which results in the victim's death, even if they did not intend to kill.

Note that although involuntary and voluntary manslaughter are terms used in legal textbooks, when reporting cases it is usual simply to say manslaughter, whichever type is meant (though remember that if the case is one of voluntary manslaughter, the initial charge will be murder).

Infanticide is a charge which can be used instead of murder or manslaughter in cases where a mother kills her child when it is under 12 months old, while her mind is disturbed.

Causing or allowing the death of a child or vulnerable adult is an offence, defined in the Domestic Violence, Crime and Victims Act 2004. It was created primarily to deal with the situation where children or vulnerable adults are killed by a parent or step-parent, usually after a history of physical abuse, but it is not clear which parent actually caused the death. In the past, this meant neither could be convicted. The new offence is committed where a child or vulnerable adult dies, and the following factors apply:

- the death is the result of unlawful conduct;
- a member of the household in frequent contact with the victim caused the death;
- the death occurred in anticipated circumstances;
- the defendant either caused the death or was or should have been aware that the victim was at risk of serious physical harm, and failed to take reasonable steps to prevent the death.

Assaults

There is a legal hierarchy of assault charges, depending on the degree of harm done to the victim, and the state of mind of the defendant.

Wounding with intent and causing grievous bodily harm (GBH) with intent are the most serious physical assaults, carrying a maximum sentence of life imprisonment. They are committed when a defendant causes serious harm, including psychiatric as well as physical harm, or wounds the victim, which technically covers any injury that breaks the skin. The offence is contained in s18 of the Offences Against the Person Act 1861.

Malicious wounding and inflicting GBH are committed by inflicting serious harm or wounding. They carry a maximum sentence of five years. The offence is contained in s20 of the Offences Against the Person Act 1861.

Assault occasioning actual bodily harm (ABH) is committed where an assault causes some degree of harm that is more than merely trivial. The offence is contained in s47 of the Offences Against the Person Act 1861.

Common assault is the usual charge for the least serious physical assaults. CPS guidelines say that this should usually be the charge where injuries are limited to cuts, grazes, bruising or a black eye. It is contained in s39 of the Criminal Justice Act 1988.

Sexual offences against adults

Most sexual offences are now defined by the Sexual Offences Act 2003, which updated the law on rape, and created some new offences.

Rape is now defined as being committed when a man intentionally penetrates the vagina, anus or mouth of another person, with his penis, where that person does not consent to the penetration and the defendant does not reasonably believe that the person consents. Rape can be committed against a woman or a man; only a man can be charged with committing rape, but a woman can be charged as an accomplice.

Assault by penetration is committed by penetrating the vagina, anus or mouth of another person, with a part of the body other than the penis, or with any other object, where that person does not consent to the penetration and the defendant does not reasonably believe that the person consents.

Sexual assault is committed by any intentional touching that is sexual, where the victim does not consent and the person touching them does not reasonably believe that they consent.

Causing sexual activity without consent is committed by intentionally causing someone to engage in sexual activity, where that person does not consent and the defendant does not reasonably believe they consented. It would cover, for example, forcing someone to be a prostitute.

→ How much can you report? See pp. 133–139

Sexual offences against children

The Sexual Offences Act 2003 provides that if, in the case of rape, assault by penetration or sexual assault, the victim is under 13, then doing the specified act (e.g. intentional penetration by the penis) is enough to lead to a conviction, and consent or lack of it is irrelevant. In addition, the Act defines a number of sexual offences which can only be committed against children, including the following:

- **Causing or inciting a child under 13 to commit sexual activity** is committed by inciting or causing someone under 13 to engage in a sexual activity.
- **Causing or inciting a child to commit sexual activity** is committed when someone over 18 incites or causes someone to engage in a sexual activity, and either the victim is under 13, or is under 16 and the defendant did not reasonably believe that person was at least 16.
- **Sexual activity with a child** is committed when someone over 18 touches someone who is under 13 sexually, or touches someone under 16 sexually and does not reasonably believe that that person is at least 16.

→ **How much can you report?** See pp. 159–160

Theft and fraud

This group of offences includes burglary, and a range of offences where money or other benefits are obtained by deception.

Theft is legally defined as the dishonest appropriation of property belonging to another, with the intention of permanently depriving the other of it. In most cases 'appropriation' simply means taking, but it can also cover doing anything with property that only the owner has the right to do. Theft may be described as stealing, but should not be referred to as robbery, which is a more serious offence.

Robbery is committed where a defendant commits theft, as defined above, using force or the threat of force.

Burglary is defined as entering a building as a trespasser (which essentially means without permission to be there), and stealing or attempting to steal, or inflicting or attempting to inflict GBH. Burglary can also be committed by entering as a trespasser with the intention to steal, inflict GBH, or do unlawful damage.

Aggravated burglary means committing burglary, as defined above, while armed with any kind of offensive weapon.

Blackmail is committed by making an 'unwarranted demand with menaces', with the intention of making a gain, or causing loss to another. This usually means asking for money, and threatening to do something, such as expose a secret, if the demand is refused.

Fraud essentially means using deception to obtain financial gain and/or cause financial loss to someone else. It covers a broad range of circumstances, from company directors transferring assets from one company to another to avoid paying debts, to individuals dishonestly claiming benefits they are not entitled to, making fake or exaggerated insurance claims, or using a credit card which is not theirs. The defendant's actions must have been dishonest, and they must have acted with the intention of making a gain or causing a loss (the offence can still be committed even if no gain was actually made). The offence is defined in the Fraud Act 2006, which also makes it an offence to obtain services dishonestly.

Handling covers dishonestly receiving or assisting in the disposal of stolen goods, knowing or believing them to be stolen. It is a widely drawn offence and covers not only keeping or selling stolen goods, but doing almost anything else with them.

Law in practice Offering rewards

In high-profile cases, rewards may be offered for information leading to a conviction, and there is no problem with reporting these (in fact often it is the press that puts up the reward). However, s23 of the Theft Act 1968 states that it is an offence to offer a reward for the return of stolen goods where the implication of the offer is 'no questions asked'. This has been held to cover reports of such an offer being made, even though the offer was not made by the newspaper itself.

Offences related to motor vehicles

Taking without owner's consent: This offence was created to deal with the problem of 'joyriders'. Because, as we have seen, theft requires an intention permanently to deprive the owner of their property, it was difficult to apply to joyriders, who usually abandon cars rather than keeping them. Therefore, this offence (often referred to as a 'TWOC') was created and is committed when someone takes a vehicle without the owner's consent. It applies to passengers as well as the driver. There is also a more serious version of this offence, usually called aggravated taking without consent, which applies where, for example, the defendant drives dangerously, injures someone or damages property.

Careless driving covers driving which is below the standard to be expected of a reasonable, prudent, competent driver in all the circumstances of the particular case.

Dangerous driving is committed where a driver falls considerably below the standard of driving expected of a competent and careful driver, and it would be obvious to a competent and careful driver that driving in that way would be dangerous.

Causing death by dangerous driving is committed where a defendant drives dangerously, as defined above, and as a result causes someone's death.

Being in charge of a vehicle while unfit applies when someone is unfit to drive due to drink or drugs, and though they are not actually driving a vehicle when caught, the court believes they intended to drive (an example might be where someone is sitting in the driving seat while the car is stationary). There is a defence if it can be proved they were not intending to drive.

Driving with excess alcohol is committed when a person drives with a blood alcohol level that exceeds the legal limit.

Causing death by careless driving when under the influence of drink or drugs applies when a driver is over the blood alcohol limit or unfit to drive through drink or drugs, and someone is killed as a result.

Driving under the influence of drugs is committed if a person's driving is impaired by drugs; police carry out a five-point test to check this, followed by medical tests such as blood samples.

Failure to provide a specimen is committed by refusing to be tested for alcohol when asked, either at the roadside or at the police station.

Driving without insurance is self-explanatory; it is also an offence to lend a car to someone who is not insured.

KEY POINTS

Criminal courts

Cases are heard by either the magistrates' courts or the Crown Court, depending on whether the offence is:

- indictable;
- either way; or
- summary.

Criminal procedure

A criminal case goes through the following stages:

- investigation;
- bail;
- prosecution;
- pre-trial hearings;
- trial.

Sentencing

The range of sentences includes:

- imprisonment;
- fines;
- community sentences;
- mental health orders;
- compensation and confiscation orders;
- binding over;
- absolute or conditional discharge.

Criminal behaviour orders can also be ordered in criminal cases.

Appeals

Criminal appeals can go:

- to the High Court by way of 'case stated';
- to the Criminal Cases Review Commission;
- from magistrates' court to Crown Court or Crown Court to Court of Appeal.

Magistrates can also reopen a case to correct an error.

Acquitted defendants can be retried if:

- compelling new evidence surfaces; or
- witness intimidation taints the original trial.

Common crimes

Commonly reported crimes include:

- **homicide offences:** murder, manslaughter, infanticide, offence of causing or allowing the death of a child or vulnerable adult;
- **assaults:** wounding with intent, causing GBH with intent, malicious wounding and inflicting GBH, assault occasioning ABH, common assault;
- **sexual offences against adults:** rape, assault by penetration, sexual assault, causing sexual activity without consent;
- **sexual offences against children:** causing or inciting a child under 13 to commit sexual activity, causing or inciting a child to commit sexual activity, sexual activity with a child;
- **theft and fraud offences:** theft, robbery, burglary, aggravated burglary, fraud, handling;
- **offences related to motor vehicles:** taking without owner's consent, careless driving, dangerous driving, causing death by dangerous driving, being in charge of a vehicle while unfit, driving with excess alcohol, causing death by careless driving while under the influence of drink, driving under the influence of drugs, failure to provide a specimen, driving without insurance.

TEST YOUR KNOWLEDGE

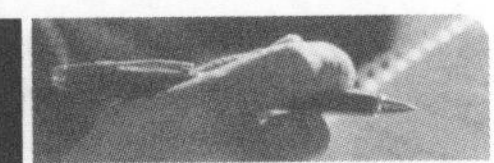

1 What is the maximum sentence a magistrates' court can impose?

2 Describe the role of the clerk to the justices.

3 Who decides the sentence for a defendant convicted in the Crown Court?

4 What are the three types of criminal offence?

5 What does 'detained for questioning' mean in legal terms?

6 What is an arrestable offence?

7 How long can the police detain suspects before charging them?

8 Who can grant bail?

9 In what circumstances should a magistrate refuse bail to a suspect with no previous convictions?

10 Who decides whether a suspect should be prosecuted?

11 Describe the course of events in a criminal trial.

12 What are the effects on a tariff sentence of mitigating and aggravating factors?

13 Which of the following could lead to a defendant ending up in prison?

(a) a suspended sentence

(b) a conditional discharge

(c) an absolute discharge.

→

14 When can evidence of previous convictions be used in court?

15 What is the legal definition of murder?

16 Which of these phrases is inaccurate?

(a) John Smith was charged with murder.

(b) John Smith was charged with manslaughter, on grounds of diminished responsibility.

(c) John Smith was charged with diminished responsibility.

(d) John Smith was charged with manslaughter.

17 What is the legal definition of rape?

18 What is the legal definition of theft?

19 John Smith is a pickpocket who has recently been convicted in your local court. Which of these terms can you use to describe him?

(a) pickpocket

(b) thief

(c) robber.

ONLINE RESOURCES

The Crown Prosecution Service website carries information about the work of the CPS, and press releases about newsworthy cases:
www.cps.gov.uk

The Home Office website has information on crime and the criminal justice system, at:
www.gov.uk/government/organisations/home-office

The Government's Sentencing Guidelines website has information on sentences and sentencing policy, at:
http://sentencingcouncil.judiciary.gov.uk/sentencing-guidelines.htm

Civil courts and procedure

The civil legal system handles all non-criminal cases, a vast category that covers everything from commercial disputes between companies to divorce cases and care proceedings, or claims for medical negligence, personal injury, libel or trespass, and much more. In this chapter we look at how the civil system works in some of the types of case that journalists are most likely to come across (three specialist types of civil case, family proceedings, inquests and insolvency proceedings, are dealt with later (in Chapters 11, 12 and 30).

At the end of this chapter, you will find definitions of some of the most common civil claims. Those which specifically affect the media, such as defamation and breach of confidence, are explained in detail in their own chapters later on.

THE CIVIL COURTS

The main civil courts are the High Court and the county courts; magistrates' courts also hear some types of civil case (e.g. family proceedings, which decide issues such as contact with children and maintenance payments when couples split up). The vast majority of civil cases are decided by judges or magistrates; juries can only be used in cases of defamation, malicious prosecution, false imprisonment and fraud, and are not always used in these cases.

The High Court

People often refer to the Royal Courts of Justice on the Strand in London as the High Court, but in fact the High Court (like the Crown Court) is not a building at all, but a single court which sits at different places. The Royal Courts of Justice are its administrative headquarters, but High Court hearings also take place in some of the larger county courts around the country. High Court cases are usually heard by High Court judges, either in London or when they go 'on circuit' around the country, but in some situations a circuit judge may hear a High Court case.

The High Court is made up of three divisions, which work separately, each with its own judges:

- **The Family Division** hears cases concerning marriage, children and families, such as divorce cases and disputes over wills.
- **The Chancery Division** deals mainly with disputes over money and property, such as tax cases, business disputes and bankruptcy.
- **The Queen's Bench Division** is the biggest division, and has the most varied caseload. It deals with specialist commercial and shipping cases, but the bulk of its work is hearing breach

of contract and tort cases. A tort is the civil law's version of a crime, but whereas a crime is a wrong against society as well as the individual victim, and is punished by the state, a tort is seen as a wrong against a specific person (or company or organisation), who can sue the wrongdoer for compensation (see the end of this chapter for definitions of some common torts). The High Court generally hears tort and contract cases involving claims of at least £15,000, or in cases where the claim is for personal injury, at least £50,000. The Queen's Bench Division also includes the Administrative Court, which deals with public law claims (see p. 12).

The county courts

There around 200 county courts spread across the country. They hear the majority of civil cases, comprising claims for debt repayment, some family cases, housing disputes and those tort and contract cases which are not heard in the High Court.

Writing about civil litigation

There are several important things to be aware of when writing about civil cases.

Terminology: The parties in civil litigation are called the claimant (who brings the case), and the defendant. The claimant sues the defendant, and if the claimant wins, the defendant is found liable (do not use 'guilty'). 'Torts' are the name given to civil wrongs for which the victim can claim damages, such as breach of contract, negligence, trespass or defamation (for more on terminology, see p. 12).

Standard of proof: In a criminal case, the prosecution must prove its case beyond reasonable doubt, but the standard of proof in the civil courts is lower. The claimant only has to prove their case 'on a balance of probabilities', which effectively means that they have to prove that there is a more than 50 per cent chance that the defendant committed the civil wrong they are claiming – or to put it another way, that it is more likely than not that the defendant is liable. This is why a person can be acquitted in a criminal case, yet be successfully sued for damages regarding exactly the same event in the civil court.

Settlements: The vast majority of civil law disputes never actually get as far as the courts. Though the claimant may start legal proceedings, in most cases the parties will agree a settlement between them before the case actually comes to court. While such settlements are legally binding on the parties themselves, they are not the same thing as a decision by the court as to which party was in the right. For this reason, it is not correct to treat a story about a settlement as though it has implications for similar cases, or as an indication of what the law is on a particular issue. If a case is settled, the result of the case is a matter between the parties concerned, and not something which changes or even clarifies the law for future cases. Nor should a claimant in a settled case be described as having won, or won damages, since the court has not actually made a decision. Sometimes a settlement includes an admission of liability by the defendant, which means that they are admitting that they did what the claimant says they did, and committed whichever wrong they are being sued for. However, this is not always the case, and you should never report – or imply – that a defendant has admitted liability unless you know for certain that they have, because this could be defamatory.

Costs: If a civil case goes to trial, the parties do not necessarily each pay their own costs. At the end of the case, the judge will make an order stating who should pay what. Traditionally, the rule is that the loser pays the winner's costs (as well as any compensation ordered), and although some costs are incurred during the pre-trial preparation, costs escalate drastically once a case goes to court. This means that the threat of having to pay costs can be used as a weapon to try to get one side or the other to settle out of court, even if the offered amount is less than they would get if they won their case. This has always been a particular problem where, for example, the claimant is an ordinary individual and the defendant a wealthy company (as is the case in many personal injury cases, where the defendant is an insurance company). However, since 1990, solicitors have been allowed to work under what are called conditional fee agreements (sometimes known as 'no win, no fee'), which mean that if the client loses, they pay no fee (or sometimes a vastly reduced one), and if they win, the lawyer is paid a percentage over what the basic fee would have been. The solicitor arranges insurance to pay the other side's costs if the case is lost.

CIVIL LITIGATION PROCEDURE

Civil litigation is the name given to most of the disputes handled by the civil legal system (others, covered in a later chapter, include family and divorce cases). Civil litigation covers all the cases where one individual (or organisation) sues another. These include, for example, businesses suing other businesses for unpaid debts or other breaches of contract; people injured in accidents or through medical negligence suing for compensation; landowners suing for trespass or nuisance; and of course, the media being sued for libel.

The processing of most types of case through the civil courts is laid down in the Civil Procedure Rules (often referred to as the CPR). Because civil cases are often lengthy and complex, they can also be very expensive. Successive governments have been keen to find ways to control costs, so the CPR give courts a duty to manage the progress of a case so that the parties are treated fairly but resources are allocated sensibly, and neither time nor costs are wasted.

Stage 1: Making the claim

The majority of civil cases begin with the claimant filling in a claim form, which will explain the basis of their claim, and the remedy that they want (this is most often damages, but the courts can also issue a range of orders, for example stating that the other party must do something or stop doing something). The court then sends the claim form to the defendant, who has 14 days to respond, either by simply acknowledging the claim, or filing a defence if they wish to fight the claim.

If the defendant does not respond in time, the claimant can ask the court to pass judgment 'in default', which means that judgment is made in their favour, without the need for a full trial (though there may still have to be a hearing in these cases to decide the amount of damages payable).

Stage 2: Allocating the case

If a defence is filed, the court will then allocate the case to one of three 'tracks':

- **The small claims track** is the usual route for claims worth less than £10,000, or £1,000 for personal injury cases. These are dealt with at the county courts, but using a faster, simplified procedure which is designed to allow claimants to represent themselves rather than using lawyers. (Cases brought in this way are often described as being heard in the small claims court, but it is not in fact a separate court, just a specific procedure.)
- **The fast track** is for claims worth £5,000–£25,000 (or for personal injury claims, up to £50,000), which are usually heard by the county courts. Once a case is allocated to this track, the court gives directions for the management of the case, and sets a timetable for the pre-trial process and a date for the trial. Cases should be heard within 30 weeks, and the hearing should normally not last more than a day.
- **The multi-track** is for cases worth more than £25,000, or which are particularly complex. When a case is allocated to the multi-track, the court will issue case management instructions, and set a timetable for the required steps to to be taken, but because these cases are usually the more complex ones, it does not usually set a trial date at this stage. This is done as early as possible but there may be a case management conference or a pre-trial review to sort out certain matters or promote a negotiated settlement in the meantime.

Stage 3: Pre-trial procedure

Whichever track a case is on, the parties will each put their claim into a statement of case: the claimant details the basis of the claim, and the defendant explains their defence to it. They will also exchange copies of documents and witness statements to be used in the case, so by the time the trial takes place, each side knows what evidence the other intends to put forward. Where a case involves technical or scientific details (e.g. medical evidence in personal injury cases), expert witnesses may be used; this can only be done with the court's permission. Expert witnesses have a legal duty to give evidence impartially, and, as part of the court's duty to manage cases so that they do not waste time or money, the court will often insist that a single expert is used for both sides, rather than one each, unless the evidence is likely to be a matter of serious dispute between the parties.

Although this work is done as preparation for an eventual trial, the majority of civil claims never actually make it that far. Typically, the defendant will make an offer of compensation, and the claimant will either accept, or try to negotiate a higher figure. If they eventually agree, this is known as settling out of court, and ends the case (see the box above, *Writing about civil litigation*). It may be done at any time before the trial starts, and it is not unknown for cases to settle on the day planned for trial – this is often described as a case being settled at the door of the court.

→ **How much can you report?** See pp. 64–83

Stage 4: The trial

Fast-track and multi-track trials follow roughly the same procedure, but small claims track procedure is different, and much less formal.

Fast-track and multi-track cases usually involve lawyers for both sides, but this is not obligatory and a small number of people choose to conduct their cases themselves. A claimant who chooses to do this can ask another lay person (known as a Mackenzie friend) to give advice and help them with things like taking notes, but this person is not usually allowed to address the court directly.

Before the trial, the judge will have been given the 'trial bundle', a package of documents which details the legal arguments being put forward by each side, and includes written statements from witnesses and any other relevant documentation. The judge reads this before the case starts, so he or she is already familiar with the issues and evidence.

The claimant's witnesses are called first, and asked to confirm that the contents of their statements are true; they are not usually required to give the evidence again verbally, though the claimant's lawyer may ask some supplementary questions. Each witness is then cross-examined by the defendant's lawyer, and sometimes the judge will ask questions too. The same process is followed with the defence witnesses, and then the lawyers for each side address the judge, arguing their case on the basis of the evidence given and how they believe the law should be applied. In the few cases where there is a jury, the judge then sums up the case for jurors, and they retire to decide their verdict.

Where there is no jury, the judge may give judgment there and then, or may reserve judgment to a later date. In this case the judgment will be a written one, which can either be read out in court or 'handed down' (issued in writing). Accredited court reporters are usually given a copy of the judgment.

Finally, the judge will make an order dictating who should pay the costs of the trial (see the box above, *Writing about civil litigation*).

Small claims track hearings take place before a district judge, often in the judge's office rather than a courtroom (though the hearing is still a public one) and the procedure is less formal than in the other courts, with less strict rules about what can and cannot be put forward in evidence. The idea is that claimants should be able to put their own case, without needing to use a lawyer, which means the procedure is less expensive. If they prefer, the claimant can ask another lay person, such as a friend, to put the case for them. The judge will often ask questions to try to establish the truth of what happened. Judgment is usually given there and then, and the judge must give reasons for his or her decision.

→ **How much can you report?** See pp. 64–83, 114–124

APPEALS IN CIVIL CASES

As with the criminal legal system, there is a system of appeals from decisions made in the county courts and the High Court. In almost all cases, a party in a civil case who wants to appeal will need permission, either from the court which heard the case first, or from the appellate court. Permission is only given where the appeal has a realistic chance of success, or where there is some other compelling reason why it should be heard (such as where the case raises an important point of law, for example). All of the appeal routes (see Figure 4.1) can be used by either party in the case (assuming they get any necessary permission).

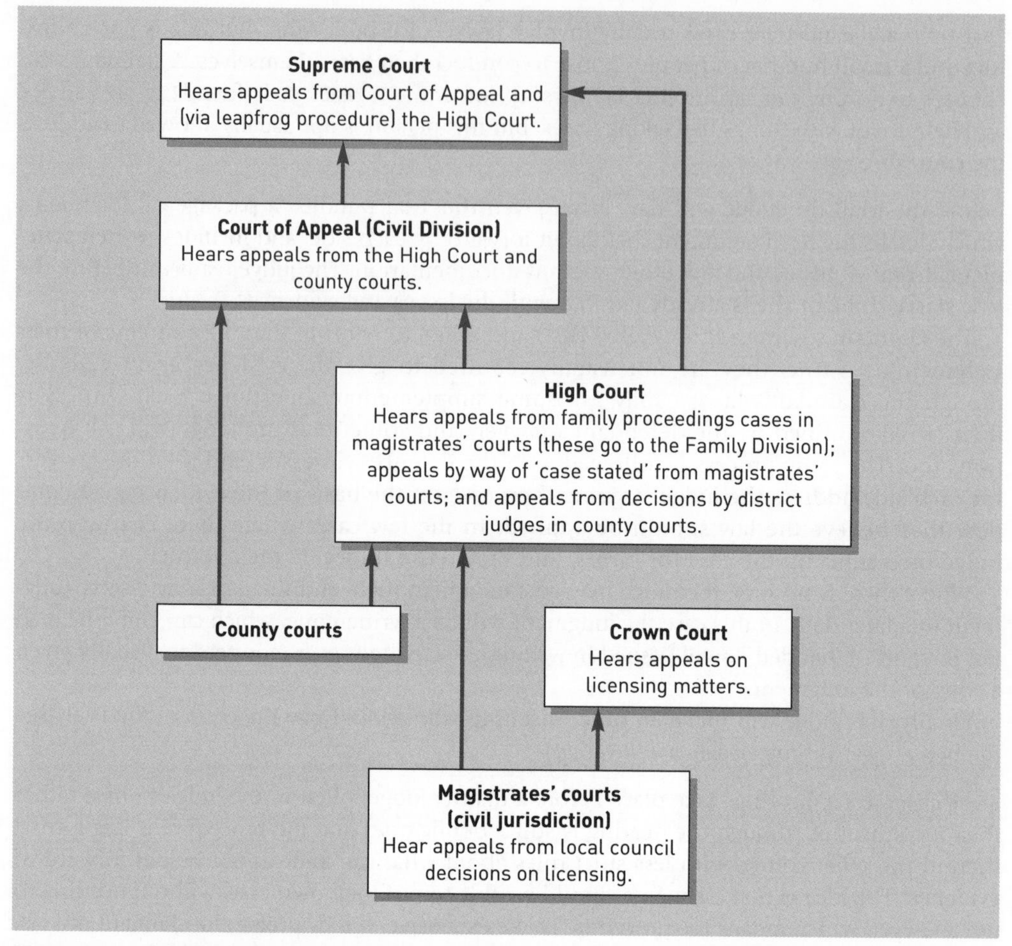

Figure 4.1 Routes of appeal in civil cases

From the county courts

If either side believes the county court has wrongly judged the facts of a case or the application of the law, they can appeal to to the Civil Division of the Court of Appeal (unless the decision was made by a district judge; in this case appeals normally go first to a circuit judge and then to the High Court). The appeal hearing does not sit through all the evidence again, but examines the notes made by the trial judge and/or any documentary evidence that was presented. The appeal court can confirm or reverse the judgment, or vary the remedy given (e.g. increasing or decreasing the level of damages awarded).

From the Court of Appeal, either side can make a further appeal to the Supreme Court, but only with permission from the Court of Appeal or (more usually) the Supreme Court. This is not often granted.

From the High Court

Cases which begin in the High Court can be appealed (by either side) to the Civil Division of the Court of Appeal, and, as with appeals from the county court, the case is usually examined on paper rather than being heard again. From there, a further appeal can be made to the Supreme Court, with permission from the Court of Appeal or the Supreme Court.

There is also an additional appeal route, known as the 'leapfrog' procedure, by which a High Court case can go straight to the Supreme Court, bypassing the Court of Appeal, where it concerns a matter on which the Court of Appeal would have to follow an earlier House of Lords precedent (which therefore makes the Court of Appeal stage a waste of time).

From the civil jurisdiction of magistrates' courts

Appeals concerning family proceedings go to a county court, and further appeals from there to the Court of Appeal and then the Supreme Court (with permission from the Supreme Court). Appeals on licensing matters are heard by the Crown Court. Appeals concerning points of law can also be appealed using the 'case stated' procedure (explained at p. 32).

Judicial review

Judicial review is a procedure which can be used to challenge decisions made or actions taken by most public bodies and officials, including the Government, local councils, the police, and the courts. Cases are heard by the Administrative Court, which is part of the Queen's Bench Division of the High Court.

Essentially, an application for judicial review alleges that the decision was unlawful, and so the focus is on the way in which the decision was made. Judicial review does not consider whether a decision was right or wrong, so it cannot be used as a form of appeal where an applicant simply believes the wrong decision was made. There are three basic ways in which a decision may be considered unlawful:

- **Illegality**: this applies, for example, where an authority has misunderstood the law, has acted in excess of its powers, or has refused to act because it (wrongly) believed it had no power to do so.
- **Irrationality**: a decision may be unlawful if it was 'so unreasonable that no reasonable authority could have made it'.
- **Unfairness**: this applies where the way in which the decision was made was unfair, for example if one side failed to get a fair hearing, or there was a possibility of prejudice for or against one side on the part of the decision maker.

If the High Court finds against the decision-making body, it can quash the decision made, and either make the decision itself, or ask the public body to consider the matter again, in the light of the court's views about the fairness of the process. This means that a successful application for judicial review does not necessarily mean the decision itself will change; the decision-making body may consider the case again, and still come to the same conclusion.

COMMON CIVIL CLAIMS

There is a vast number of possible claims under civil law, many of which are very specialised. However, there are some which come up more commonly and are often the basis of news stories, and it is worth having a basic idea of how these arise and are defined.

Breach of contract

A contract is a legal agreement between two parties; it need not be in writing. Every contract includes terms, which lay down what each of the parties is obliged to do. Sometimes these terms are agreed by the parties, but in many types of contract, the law provides that certain terms will be included, whether the parties agree to them or not. For example, when you buy something from a shop, you enter into a contract between you and the retailer, and the Sale and Supply of Goods Act 1994 states that it is a term of that contract that the thing you buy must be as described to you, and of satisfactory quality; if not, the seller is in breach of contract. Where one party breaches a contract term, the other party can sue for damages. Breach of contract cases include everything from small consumer disputes to claims worth millions of pounds concerning contracts made between companies, and also include debt recovery cases, where the claimant has performed their side of the contract but not been paid.

Negligence

Negligence is the most important tort (civil wrong) in modern law. To put it at its simplest, where someone is injured or caused loss by someone else's failure to take reasonable care, negligence law allows the injured person to sue for damages that will put them back in the position they would have enjoyed if this carelessness had not happened (this is a very much simpler definition than most lawyers would give, and it is important to know that not every instance of carelessness amounts to negligence, and not every kind of loss will be compensated in a negligence action). Typical claimants include people physically injured by substandard medical treatment or in accidents that are someone else's fault, but negligence can also, in some circumstances, compensate for psychological injury, financial loss and damage to property, and actions can be brought by companies as well as individuals.

One important thing you should know about when reporting negligence cases is the role played by insurance. If, due to your carelessness, you run someone over in your car and they sue you, it would be your insurance company who had to pay if the claim was successful; equally, if you hurt yourself at work and sue your employer, they would have insurance against this type of claim. In practice, most people or organisations sued in negligence are covered by insurance relating to the activity in question, and this can lead to what seem to be odd cases: for example, in ***Hunt* v *Severs*** (1994), the claimant was very seriously injured in a car accident caused by her fiancé, and sued him for damages, yet still married him. This seems less strange when you realise that he would have had car insurance, and so she was effectively suing the insurance company, and not her fiancé, even though he was officially the defendant.

Nuisance

This tort protects against unreasonable interference with a person's use of their land (whether they own or rent it). It covers, for example, cases where noise, dust, fumes or smells spread on to someone's land (or into their house) from neighbouring land; water leaking from one flat down into another; tree roots encroaching across a boundary; and even cricket balls escaping on to land adjacent to a sports ground.

Trespass

Most people think of trespass as meaning entering land where you are not permitted to be, and trespass does include this. However, trespass to land is wider than that, and includes any unreasonable interference with someone else's land (e.g. throwing something on to it).

KEY POINTS

Civil courts

Civil cases are handled by:

- magistrates' courts;
- county courts;
- the High Court.

Civil procedure

Civil cases go through up to four stages:

- making the claim;
- allocating the case to a track;
- pre-trial procedure (possibly leading to settlement);
- trial.

Appeals

- County court cases are appealed to the Court of Appeal.
- High Court cases go to the Court of Appeal, or by 'leapfrog' procedure straight to the Supreme Court.
- Family proceedings appeals go to the Family Division of the High Court.

Common civil claims

- Breach of contract applies when someone breaks the terms of a contract.
- Negligence allows someone to sue if they are injured or caused loss by another's failure to take care.
- Nuisance protects against unreasonable interference with a person's use of their land.
- Trespass comprises any unreasonable interference with someone else's land.

TEST YOUR KNOWLEDGE

1 Which kinds of civil cases are decided by juries?

2 Name the three divisions of the High Court.

3 What are the parties in civil litigation called?

4 Explain the different standards of proof in criminal and civil cases.

5 What is the 'leapfrog' procedure in the civil appeals system?

6 Where are claims worth less than £10,000 heard?

7 Explain the standard of proof in civil cases.

8 A local hairdresser has sued her employer after she claimed that the hairspray she used at work gave her asthma. She has settled out of court, with her employer agreeing to pay damages of £10,000. Which of these sentences can accurately be used in this story?

(a) Hairdressers can no longer be forced to use hairspray, after a local stylist who developed asthma through her work won her case against Curly Top hairdressers.

(b) Local stylist Sharon Crimper has won her case against Curly Top hairdressers.

(c) Curly Top hairdressers have been forced to pay a stylist damages of £10,000, after she developed asthma at work.

9 What is judicial review?

10 On what grounds can judicial review disturb the decision of a public body?

ONLINE RESOURCES

The Courts Service website has information on the civil courts, at:
www.hmcourts-service.gov.uk

The Community Legal Service website has information on personal injury claims, at:
www.clsdirect.org.uk

The Children and Family Court Advisory and Support Service has information about family proceedings, at:
www.cafcass.gov.uk

The Public Law Project has information on judicial review, at:
www.publiclawproject.org.uk

Human rights and English law

The European Convention on Human Rights was incorporated into English law in the Human Rights Act 1998 (see Chapter 1). Human rights is an important area of law for journalists, for two main reasons. Firstly, more and more legal cases are being brought under the provisions of human rights law, and many of these will make the news. Secondly, several of the rights protected have a direct impact on laws which govern the work of journalists, the most important being the rights to freedom of expression, privacy and a fair trial.

THE EUROPEAN CONVENTION AND THE HUMAN RIGHTS ACT

The set of human rights which is protected in the UK today was originally laid down in the European Convention for the Protection of Human Rights and Fundamental Freedoms (better known as the European Convention on Human Rights), an international treaty that was drawn up in 1950. It was a reaction to the horrors of the Second World War, and aimed to secure for the people of Europe a set of basic rights, which all countries who signed up to the treaty would respect. A special court, the European Court of Human Rights (ECHR), was set up to deal with claims that countries (or their official organisations) had breached the provisions of the Convention. (The ECHR is not the same thing as the EU court, which is called the European Court of Justice – see p. 8.)

There are now 45 countries which have signed up to the Convention. The UK has been a signatory since 1953, but the protection it offers to people in this country was greatly strengthened when the Human Rights Act 1998 was passed. This incorporated the Convention into UK law, which had several important effects.

Breaches of the Convention: The provisions of the Convention are now applicable in UK courts, so anyone whose rights have been breached can bring a case in the UK courts, instead of going to the ECHR in Strasbourg, as he or she would have had to do before the Act was passed. Individuals can still take cases to Strasbourg if they are not satisfied that the UK courts have correctly applied a Convention provision, but they must take any legal action that is available through the UK courts first.

Interpretation of legislation: The courts often have to interpret legislation in order to work out how it should apply in a particular case (see p. 6). The Human Rights Act provides that UK courts should, as far as possible, interpret all UK legislation in a way which is compatible with the rights detailed in the Convention, so if there are two ways of interpreting a particular statutory provision, courts must choose the one that conforms to the Convention. Where a statute is clearly in conflict with the Convention, the courts cannot refuse to apply the statute, but they can make a declaration that there is a conflict, and, when that happens, the Government can (but does not have to) use a fast-track procedure to amend the domestic legislation to bring it into line with the Convention.

Effect on public bodies: The Act makes it unlawful for any public body to act in a way that is incompatible with the rights provided by the Convention, and an individual whose Convention rights have been violated by a public body can bring an action against the body concerned. Public bodies definitely include national and local government, the courts, and organisations which are obviously 'public', such as the NHS and the police, but there is still some debate over how far the definition extends beyond these.

Precedent: A UK court deciding questions connected with a Convention right must take into account any decision of the ECHR on that issue. Decisions made by the higher courts form precedents that build up into the body of case law (see Chapter 1). This is equally the case for decisions involving Convention rights, so, over time, case law will increasingly come to show the influence of human rights law.

New legislation: When passing new legislation the relevant Minister has to make a statement saying whether or not the new law is compatible with the Convention (so although new law does not have to be compatible, attention will be drawn to any provisions that are not).

Protected rights

The original Convention lists 12 basic rights and freedoms which are to be protected, and three more were added in 1952 by an additional document called the First Protocol. The rights protected are:

- right to life (Article 2);
- freedom from torture, inhuman or degrading treatment (Article 3);
- freedom from slavery and forced labour (Article 4);
- right to liberty and security of the person (Article 5);
- right to a fair trial (Article 6);
- freedom from unlawful punishment (Article 7);
- right to respect for private and family life (Article 8);
- freedom of thought, conscience and religion (Article 9);
- freedom of expression (Article 10);
- freedom of assembly and association (Article 11);
- right to marry and found a family (Article 12);
- right to peaceful enjoyment of possessions (Article 1, First Protocol);
- right to education (Article 2, First Protocol);
- right to take part in free elections by secret ballot (Article 3, First Protocol).
- right to enjoy the above rights without discrimination on any ground such as sex, race, colour, language, religion, political or other opinion, national or social origin, association with a national minority, property, birth or other status.

A few of the rights are protected absolutely, which means that any breach of them, whatever the circumstances, is a breach of the Convention; an example is the right to freedom from torture, protected by Article 3. However, most of the rights are subject to what are called derogations, which means the Convention allows them to be restricted in certain important circumstances. For example, Article 8 provides that the right to respect for private and family life can be subject to such restrictions as are 'necessary in a democratic society in the interests of national security, public safety or the economic well-being of the country, for the prevention of disorder or crime, for the protection of health or morals, or for the protection of the rights and freedoms of others'. Even Article 2, the right to life, can be restricted in certain situations, for example where someone kills in self-defence.

The phrase 'necessary in a democratic society' has been interpreted by the ECHR as meaning that restrictions subject to this requirement are only allowed where there is a 'pressing social need' for them.

Applying the Convention rights

When considering human rights cases, the courts often describe themselves as performing a balancing act. This might be between two conflicting rights: for example, a journalist's right to freedom of expression might conflict with what the subject of a story feels is their right to privacy. Alternatively, the balancing act might be between a Convention right, and one of the circumstances in which restrictions on it are allowed. For example, the right to freedom of expression can be restricted 'where necessary . . . in the interests of national security', so if the Government sought to suppress publication of information in the interests of national security, the courts might be called upon to decide whether the restriction was really 'necessary in a democratic society'.

In performing this balancing act, the courts are required to follow the principle of 'proportionality'. This means that any restriction on a Convention right must be proportionate to the reason for that restriction; in other words, the restriction must not just be necessary in the first place, but must go no further than is necessary. Take, for example, a case where a court issues an order preventing the press from publishing details of a trial so as to avoid prejudice to the defendant's right to a fair trial. The principle of proportionality might allow the press to argue that, although some restriction is justified in the circumstances, the right could be adequately protected by postponing, rather than banning publication.

HUMAN RIGHTS AND MEDIA LAW

The Convention contains three rights that have a particularly important effect on the way you do your work as a journalist. They are:

- the right to freedom of expression;
- the right to a fair trial;
- the right to respect for private and family life (often called the right to privacy).

Freedom of expression

Article 10 provides that:

1 Everyone has the right to freedom of expression. This right shall include freedom to hold opinions and to receive and impart information and ideas without interference by public authority and regardless of frontiers. This Article shall not prevent States from requiring the licensing of broadcasting, television or cinema enterprises.

2 The exercise of these freedoms, since it carries with it duties and responsibilities, may be subject to such formalities, conditions, restrictions or penalties as are prescribed by law and are necessary in a democratic society, in the interests of national security, territorial integrity or public safety, for the prevention of disorder or crime, for the protection of health or morals, for the protection of the reputation or rights of others, for preventing the disclosure of information received in confidence, or for maintaining the authority or impartiality of the judiciary.

Note that the right to freedom of expression includes a right to receive information as well as to impart it. This means that when the term 'freedom of expression' is applied in a case involving the media, what is at stake is not just the journalist's freedom to write or broadcast, but the ability of the public to find out what he or she has to say.

As explained above, when applying Convention rights, the courts often have to balance competing rights and interests against each other. The ECHR has made it plain that the right to freedom of expression is considered extremely important, and should not easily lose out when this balancing act is performed, and in the earliest cases heard after the Human Rights Act came into force, the English courts confirmed this approach. However, despite being described by one judge as 'the trump card that always wins', the right to freedom of expression is not an absolute licence to print anything, and there are clearly cases where other rights will prevail. The major step forward though is that now, whenever the media's activities are threatened with restriction, the courts will bring freedom of expression into the balance.

In October 2000, orders granted to the Secretary of State preventing publication of details about the role of the security forces in Northern Ireland were overturned, when the *Sunday People* argued that the orders breached the right to freedom of expression. The judge said that the starting point was that the scales were weighted in favour of freedom of expression, and the orders could only be allowed if they were strictly necessary and proportionate to the state's aim; in this case, they were not.

In ***Venables and Thompson* v *News Group Newspapers and Others*** (2001), the courts were asked to consider whether the media could be prevented from publishing the new identities which would be given to the killers of James Bulger, who was murdered at the age of two in 1993 by two ten-year-old boys. Weighed against the media's right of freedom of expression were the killers' rights to life and freedom from torture (it was argued they might be attacked or killed if their whereabouts were publicly known), and to privacy. The Family Division of the High Court agreed that the order should be issued.

In ***R (on the application of the BBC and Dominic Casciani)* v *Secretary of State for Justice, with Babar Ahmad as interested party)*** (2012), the BBC used the Human Rights Act to overturn a ban on it filming and broadcasting an interview with a terrorism suspect who had been held for over seven years without trial, and was the subject of attempts to extradite him to the USA. The Ministry of Justice had initially granted permission for an interview to take place, but then withdrew it when the BBC insisted that they needed to film the interview. The Ministry said that there was a general policy against filming interviews in prison, and, in this case, there were compelling reasons for the ban, given the seriousness of the alleged offences. They argued that for the purposes of freedom of expression, it was sufficient for the BBC to do the interview and then report Mr Ahmad's answers, rather than broadcasting the interview itself. The Court disagreed, saying that the ban was a disproportionate interference with the right of freedom of expression. Mr Justice Singh said that the case was an exceptional one, given the length of Babar Ahmad's detention and the fact that the extradition treaty with the USA was a matter of public debate. He stressed that it should not be seen as setting a precedent for other cases.

The courts' obligation to take into account the importance of freedom of expression is likely to have an impact in any case involving the media, and is already becoming important in areas such as defamation and contempt of court, as you will see when you read the chapters on those areas of law.

Protection against injunctions

Section 12 of the Human Rights Act adds some extra provisions concerning the protection of the right to freedom of expression, which apply in cases where someone (such as the subject of a news story) is seeking an order which would restrict freedom of expression. The provisions would apply where someone applies to the court for an injunction (a form of court order) to stop the publication or broadcast of a story. An injunction can be ordered to stop the media from repeating something which has already been published, or can be ordered to prevent it from being published in the first place.

Decisions on injunctions: Section 12 provides that in deciding whether to grant an injunction, the courts must take into account the right to freedom of expression. In addition, where the material concerned is journalistic, the court has to take into account how far the information has been, or is about to be, available to the public; to what extent publication would be in the public interest; and the provisions of any relevant privacy code (such as, in the UK, the Editors' Code of Practice, used by the Independent Press Standards Organisation or the Ofcom Code of Practice).

Media representation: Section 12(2) states that orders which would restrict freedom of expression should not be granted where the potential recipient of the order is not present, unless all practical steps have been taken to notify them, or the court is satisfied there are 'compelling' reasons why they should not be notified. In the past, injunctions were sometimes granted at the last minute before publication, without the newspaper or broadcaster in question even knowing that an application had been made. This provision is designed to ensure that the media get a chance to argue their case before an injunction is granted, though, as we will see, it does not always work (see Chapter 19).

Injunctions preventing publication: Where someone is asking for an injunction which prevents the material from being published in the first place, further provisions apply. For many centuries before the Convention was drawn up, it was a fundamental principle of English law that the press should not, as a rule, be censored before publication. This was known as the 'rule against prior restraint', and meant that although pre-publication injunctions could be allowed in certain circumstances, in general, English law preferred to deal with the consequences of unlawful publication afterwards (e.g. with damages for defamation or fines for contempt of court) rather than prevent publication in advance. Section 12 preserves this approach, and provides that, where an interim injunction would restrict freedom of expression, it should only be granted where the court is satisfied that when the issue goes to trial, the party seeking the injunction is likely to be able to prove their case. In ***Cream Holdings Ltd* v *Banerjee*** (2004), the House of Lords held that this meant that, unless the party seeking the injunction could establish that it was more likely than not that it would win at trial, the courts should be 'exceedingly slow' to grant the order. However, there might be some cases where it was appropriate to grant the order even without such a strong case, such as where the consequences of publication were especially serious, or where time factors meant the court needed to impose a 'holding injunction' in order to consider the application for an interim injunction.

Section 12 does not apply to criminal proceedings, so it cannot be used in cases concerning reports of criminal cases.

The right to a fair trial

Article 6 provides that:

> In the determination of his civil rights and obligations or of any criminal charge against him, everyone is entitled to a fair and public hearing within a reasonable time by an independent and impartial tribunal established by law. Judgment shall be pronounced publicly but the press and public may be excluded from all or part of the trial in the interest of morals, public order or national security in a democratic society, where the interests of juveniles or the protection of the private life of the parties so require, or to the extent strictly necessary in the opinion of the court in special circumstances where publicity would prejudice the interests of justice.

For journalists, the area where this right has most effect is in covering the courts and police investigations. In a number of cases, lawyers have tried to use Article 6 to restrict court reporting, arguing that reports might otherwise prejudice their clients' right to a fair trial. In response, the media have put forward the right to free expression, and the courts have had to strike a balance between the two. (These cases are covered in Section 2 of this book.)

The right to respect for private and family life

Article 8 provides that:

> 1 Everyone has the right to respect for his private and family life, his home and his correspondence.
>
> 2 There shall be no interference by a public authority with the exercise of this right except such as is in accordance with the law and is necessary in a democratic society in the interests of national security, public safety or the economic well-being of the country, for the prevention of disorder or crime, for the protection of health or morals, for the protection of the reputation or the rights of others, for preventing the disclosure of information received in confidence, or for maintaining the authority and impartiality of the judiciary.

Clearly, there are many situations where the media's right to freedom of expression will clash with the right to privacy of those they write about, and Article 8 now has a profound impact on the way the British media does its job. The most obvious effect is illustrated by the stream of cases brought by celebrities who allege that their privacy has been infringed by the press, and, although as the law currently stands there is no specific claim in English law for breach of the right to privacy, the existing law on confidentiality has now been developed to such an extent that it does the same job. (This subject is covered in Chapter 18.)

KEY POINTS

The European Convention and the Human Rights Act

The Human Rights Act incorporates the Convention into UK law. As a result:

- Convention cases can be brought in English courts;
- legislation should be interpreted compatibly with the Convention;

- public bodies must act in accordance with Convention rights;
- UK courts must take into account decisions of the ECHR;
- Ministers must make a statement on compatibility of new legislation.

The European Convention on Human Rights lays down 15 basic rights, including:

- absolute rights, which cannot lawfully be breached;
- rights subject to derogations.

The European Court of Human Rights (ECtHR) deals with breaches of these rights.

Human rights and media law

Three Convention rights have particular influence on the media:

- the right to freedom of expression;
- the right to a fair trial;
- the right to privacy.

Section 12 of the Human Rights Act 1998 provides special protection against orders which restrict freedom of expression.

TEST YOUR KNOWLEDGE

1 How does the Human Rights Act 1998 affect the decisions of UK courts?

2 Which of these statements about the incorporation of the Convention into UK law through the Human Rights Act are true?

(a) Parliament must ensure that all UK laws passed since 1998 protect the rights laid down in the Convention.

(b) If a law conflicts with the Convention, UK courts do not have to apply it.

(c) Public authorities can be taken to court if they breach the Convention.

(d) Cases involving breaches of the Convention rights must be brought before the European Court.

3 What is the principle of proportionality?

4 Which three rights have the most important impact on the work of journalists?

5 You have a story on a local politician, which accuses her of embezzling party funds. When you contact her for comment on the allegations, she goes to court to get an injunction preventing you from publishing the story. What issues does s12 of the Human Rights Act require the court to take into account when deciding whether to grant the order?

6 A UK citizen believes his right to privacy has been breached by an NHS Trust. Where can he bring his case?

ONLINE RESOURCES

The Human Rights Act 1998 can be read at:
www.legislation.gov.uk/ukpga/1998/42/contents

The European Court of Human Rights website is at:
http://www.echr.coe.int/Pages/home.aspx?p=home

Cream Holdings Ltd v *Banerjee* (2004) can be read at:
www.publications.parliament.uk/pa/ld200304/ldjudgmt/jd041014/jee.pdf

WRITING ABOUT THE COURTS

One of the basic standards for a just and fair court system is that the workings and decisions of the courts should be open for the public to see. The idea behind this principle is that in order to do its job, a court system has to command the respect of the society it serves, and it is more likely to do this if the system is open and clear, than if decisions are made behind closed doors and the reasons for them not revealed. As a result, in the UK, there is a basic rule that court proceedings should be held in public, so that anyone who wishes to can go along to a court to watch and listen. Since most members of the public have neither the time nor the inclination to spend hours sitting in court, it is accepted that it is important for the media to have access to the courts, so that we can act as the public's eyes and ears.

However, neither access to the courts, nor the right to report what goes on there, are unrestricted. There are three main types of restriction, which are discussed in this section:

- **Contempt of court:** The law on contempt of court aims to prevent any publication which could adversely affect the workings of the law. For example, it is contempt to publish anything during a trial which carries a substantial risk of seriously prejudicing the result of that trial, such as details of a defendant's previous convictions. These rules are covered in Chapter 6.
- **Restrictions on access:** Most court cases are held in public, but some types of case may be held in private, in which case the media can be excluded from them. In some circumstances it is still possible to report on these cases, even though journalists have not been allowed to hear the proceedings. Chapter 7 covers the rules on when journalists may or may not attend court hearings, and whether you can report those you are not allowed to attend.
- **Reporting restrictions:** The fact that reporters are allowed to be present at a hearing does not always mean that they can report everything they hear. The Contempt of Court Act 1981 gives courts discretionary powers to postpone or ban reporting of a case, or specific details about it, and these powers are the subject of Chapter 8. In addition, particular courts and types of case may be subject to specific restrictions, some of them automatic and some discretionary; these are covered in Chapters 9–13.

The final chapter in this section covers the actions members of the press can take when they believe reporting restrictions have been wrongly imposed. This happens surprisingly often, and there are many cases where the media have been able to get restrictions either lifted or relaxed, so that they can report a case properly.

Contempt of court

The popular image of contempt of court – largely created by courtroom dramas on TV and film – is of a defendant or lawyer being rude to a judge, or someone shouting abuse from the public gallery, at which point the judge usually tells them to be quiet or 'I'll have you in contempt'. While this kind of behaviour is certainly included within the definition of contempt of court, the phrase also has a wider meaning. Essentially, contempt of court is the court system's means of punishing anyone who interferes, in any way, with the functioning of the court system.

The main way in which a journalist can become liable for contempt is by publishing something which creates a substantial risk of serious prejudice to the outcome of a particular court case (this is usually referred to as prejudicing a fair trial). Examples might include:

- publishing a defendant's previous convictions;
- publishing background information which might sway a jury's view of the defendant or witnesses;
- publishing a photograph of a defendant in a trial where the identity of the culprit is at issue.

There are also other ways in which a journalist can be liable for contempt, including:

- publishing something which puts you in breach of a court order or an undertaking given to a court;
- taking photographs in court;
- publishing, or even just asking questions about, the deliberations of a jury.

In this chapter we look first at contempt by prejudicing a fair trial, as that is the most common issue journalists face, and then consider the other forms of contempt afterwards.

However it is committed, contempt of court is an extremely serious issue, because, if a publication is judged to be in contempt, the court can order whatever punishment it sees fit. There is no limit on the fines that can be imposed and, in very serious cases, there may even be a sentence of up to two years' imprisonment.

In deciding contempt cases involving the media, the courts must take into account the right to freedom of expression under Article 10 of the European Convention on Human Rights, which has to be balanced against the Article 6 right to a fair trial. Because of the importance of this balance, most cases of contempt are referred to the Attorney-General, and he or she also maintains an overview of the law on contempt, and from time to time issues guidelines to the media on particular aspects of it, and on reporting of high-profile cases (see *Online resources* at the end of this chapter).

Although England and Scotland are both covered by the same law of contempt, the Scottish courts tend to interpret it more strictly, which means that stories written about Scottish cases can lead to a contempt action, when the same story would probably pass without comment if it concerned an English case. This means that you need to take particular care when writing about cases that are before the Scottish courts, whether or not your report is published/broadcast in Scotland (especially as the internet means that most news coverage is effectively published everywhere). For this reason, although this book mostly covers only English law, there is a section on contempt in Scotland (see p. 84).

PUBLICATIONS PREJUDICIAL TO A FAIR TRIAL

There are two offences of contempt which relate to publications prejudicial to a fair trial:

- 'strict liability' contempt, which was created by the Contempt of Court Act 1981;
- 'intentional contempt', which comes from common law.

In both cases, what the law seeks to prevent is the publication of information or opinion that could sway those deciding the case. This is because it is a principle of English law that cases should be decided on the evidence before the court, and nothing else (this is also the reason why information about a defendant's previous convictions is not usually given in court).

Given this, it is accepted that cases which are to be decided by a jury (and, to a lesser extent, by lay magistrates) are more at risk of being prejudiced by media reports than cases being decided by a judge, because judges are trained to put aside other influences and judge on the evidence alone. This means that the media is most likely to be held in contempt when reporting criminal trials in the Crown Court, which are decided by juries. Contempt actions are less of a risk in civil proceedings, which are usually heard by a judge, but it is important to remember that the law on contempt still applies in these cases, and, even if it is unlikely that a judge would be swayed by anything they read, it is possible that a court could find that a publication might influence witnesses and perhaps colour the evidence they give. A few civil actions (including certain actions against the police) are heard by juries, and these demand the same extreme care as criminal proceedings.

'STRICT LIABILITY' CONTEMPT

Defined in s2(2) of the Contempt of Court Act 1981, this is the form of contempt action which is most often used today. Actions under the Contempt of Court Act can only be brought by the Attorney-General (see p. 15), a provision which was designed to protect the media from frivolous cases being brought by people who have lost their court cases and seek to blame media coverage. If the Attorney-General decides not to bring a case, then no one else can do so. (The abbreviation A-G in the names of contempt cases stands for Attorney-General.)

The Act states that strict liability contempt applies to any publication about 'active' proceedings, which 'creates a substantial risk that the course of justice in the proceedings in question will be seriously impeded or prejudiced.'

There are therefore three elements to the rule:

- strict liability,
- 'active' proceedings,
- a substantial risk of serious prejudice.

Strict liability

Strict liability essentially means that, if you publish something about active proceedings that carries a substantial risk of prejudice, you can be liable, regardless of whether or not you intended to prejudice the proceedings, or realised you might do so. Nor will you escape liability because you can prove you did all possible checks, took legal advice, or only committed contempt because you made a mistake about something. (The one exception is if you can prove that despite taking all reasonable care, you did not know that proceedings were active; this is the defence of 'innocent publication' – see p. 79.)

A court may take some of these issues into account when deciding on a suitable punishment, but they will make no difference to whether you are found guilty or not. Motive is also irrelevant, and a publication that amounts to contempt will not escape liability just because it might be considered a public service, such as, for example, revealing the past convictions of a suspect still at large, in order to warn the public (but see p. 66 on police appeals).

Active proceedings

The Contempt of Court Act lays down the points at which cases will become active, and when they stop being active. When proceedings are not active, as defined by the Act, there is no liability for strict liability contempt (though there may be liability for intentional contempt, which is discussed later).

Schedule 1 of the Act defines when cases become active and cease to be active, as follows.

Criminal proceedings

Criminal proceedings become active when any of the following apply:

- a suspect is arrested without a warrant;
- a warrant for arrest is issued;
- a summons to appear in court is issued;
- an indictment or other document specifying the charge is issued (this would include a written charge and requisition – see p. 20); or
- a suspect is orally charged.

Often a case will feature more than one of these steps, but it will become active as soon as any one of them happens. It quite often happens that someone is arrested, but later released without being charged. In this case, proceedings cease to be active, unless the person is released on bail. If the suspect is released on bail, the proceedings remain active – even though the suspect may in fact never be charged with the offence.

It is also possible for a warrant to be issued for someone's arrest, and that person not to be arrested for months, if at all – they may, for example, have left the country. If the person is not arrested within a year of the warrant being issued, the proceedings cease to be active – but until then, they are subject to restriction, even if the prospect of a trial seems small.

Criminal proceedings stop being active when any of the following occur:

- a person arrested is released otherwise than on bail;
- 12 months have passed since the issue of a warrant and no arrest has been made;
- the charge or summons is withdrawn;

- the defendant is found to be unfit to be tried or unfit to plead;
- the defendant is acquitted;
- the defendant is sentenced; or
- any other verdict or decision brings the proceedings to an end (such as, for example, the court deciding that charges should 'lie on file', which means no further action will be taken about them).

Note that if a defendant is found (or pleads) guilty, the proceedings remain active until after they are sentenced. Where magistrates hear a case, they may decide that their sentencing powers are insufficient and refer the case to the Crown Court; it remains active until the Crown Court has passed sentence. Even where the case has originally been heard in the Crown Court, there is often a longish gap between conviction and sentence, especially if the judge asks for sentencing reports. In practice, however, if the sentence is to be passed by a judge, it is unlikely that anything published about the case at this stage would be considered to create a substantial risk of prejudice, because professional judges are considered to be able to ignore such influences. However, if the sentence is to be passed by magistrates, more care needs to be taken with anything published between conviction and sentencing.

Law in practice Investigation and arrests

Reporting investigations: It is not always clear whether someone who is being interviewed at a police station has been arrested or not, and asking the police will not always help, because if there are other suspects, the police may not want to disclose whether someone has been arrested. If someone is being held at the police station against their will, then in law they are under arrest, even if the formalities of an arrest have not taken place, which therefore makes proceedings active. If they are at the police station voluntarily (or 'helping police with their inquiries' as it is usually described), proceedings are not active, but they could of course become active at any time, so extreme care needs to be used in this situation (especially as there can also be libel risks in naming someone who is 'helping police with their inquiries' – see Chapter 15).

It is not contempt of court to name someone who has been arrested for a particular crime, nor to give general background about the suspect and the crime. However, it is absolutely essential that such stories do not contain details which could be said to link the suspect to the crime (in the sense of suggesting that they did it), even if those details are given out by the police.

Police appeals: In some cases, the police will want to appeal for the public's help in tracing a suspect, after a warrant has been issued for their arrest. Strictly speaking, publishing such an appeal puts the media at risk of committing contempt, since the warrant makes proceedings active, and the appeal would clearly suggest that the police think that person committed the crime. However, during the passing of the Contempt of Court Act, the then Attorney-General stated that in helping with such appeals, the media were performing a public service, and should not be discouraged. He said that the press 'has nothing to fear from publishing in reasoned terms anything which may assist in the apprehension of a wanted man'. This has been taken as an assurance that helping with police appeals will not result in a contempt charge, and no such charge has been brought to date.

Bear in mind, however, that publishing or repeating the same information after the person has been found and arrested would not be covered by this assurance, since to do so would not be helping to apprehend the suspect.

Reporting after an arrest: Once someone has been arrested, it is very important to take care in what you write about the case.

- You can report that 'a man' has been arrested in connection with a particular crime, but not that 'the man' who police have been looking for or suspect has been arrested.
- You can name the person who has been arrested, and give some general background, so long as none of the details given suggest that that person actually committed the crime.
- If an arrest has been made, steer clear of publishing any descriptions given by witnesses to the crime. If you say, for example, that a mugger was tall and blonde with several piercings, and the person arrested fits that description, this could be contempt.
- Never state that a person who has been arrested has previous criminal convictions.
- Be careful reporting anything that an arrested person says. Contempt can be committed by suggesting that someone is innocent as well as suggesting they are guilty, and statements made by the person arrested themselves are no less likely to lead to a contempt action than information from any other source.
- Do not assume that because information about an arrested person (or any other information, for that matter) has been issued by the police, it is safe to publish. In 1995, the BBC was found in contempt for broadcasting details of a suspect's previous convictions, even though the information was provided in a police press conference.

The Editors' Code of Practice used by IPSO and the Ofcom Code contain provisions regarding reports of pre-trial investigations into crime (see pp. 90 and 143).

New guidance issued by the College of Policing states that the police should not release the identities of suspects who have been arrested but not yet charged, other than in exceptional circumstances, such as where not doing so could involve a threat to life, or where doing so would help prevent or detect crime or is otherwise in the public interest. However, the guidelines do not have legal force, and the Director of Public Prosecutions had said there should not be a blanket rule that no suspect is identified at the point of arrest (see Chapter 3 for more on the College of Policing guidelines).

Civil proceedings

Civil proceedings become active when:

- arrangements are made for the case to be heard (this is usually when the case is 'set down for trial', which means it is put on a waiting list, which may be months long); or
- when the trial begins.

It should be possible to find out from the court where the trial is to be held whether or not a date has been fixed, and the Attorney-General has instructed courts to help journalists seeking this information.

Before a civil case is heard, there may sometimes be pre-trial proceedings. For example, in a civil court procedure called a striking-out application, the defendant argues that there is no legal case to answer. Without trying the case fully, the court asks whether, assuming the facts alleged are true, there is a legal cause of action or not; if not, the case can be 'struck out' and not continued. Similarly, in a libel action, for example, the claimant may seek an interim injunction to prevent publication or further publication, and the hearing to decide whether this should be granted takes place before the full trial. Pre-trial proceedings like these become active from the time a date for the hearing is fixed, and stop being active when the hearing is over. In practice reporting them carries a fairly low risk of contempt action, because they are always heard by judges.

Civil proceedings cease to be active when they are:

- settled by the parties;
- decided by the judge or jury;
- discontinued; or
- withdrawn.

Appeals

If either party in a case decides to appeal, the appeal proceedings become active when that party applies for leave to appeal, or when the notice of appeal is lodged. This means that anything published after the initial case is concluded, and before the appeal becomes active is not at risk of strict liability contempt (though intentional contempt can still apply – see p. 82). Often, the announcement that someone intends to appeal comes straight after the verdict, but the proceedings will still not be active until the formalities have started.

In 2000, Ulster Television was taken to court over a programme about two men who had recently been convicted of murder. The programme contained information that had not been put before the jury. The men claimed that they intended to appeal, and that this appeal might result in a retrial, which could then be prejudiced by the information in the programme. They therefore sought an injunction to prevent the programme being shown. The court refused the injunction, saying that it was by no means certain that there would be a retrial, given that the appeal might not overturn the guilty verdict.

Appeals from summary trials in the magistrates' court and from Crown Court trials to the Court of Appeal are lodged at a Crown Court office, while appeals from Crown Court trials to the Queen's Bench Division of the High Court go to the Royal Courts of Justice in London.

Appeal proceedings cease to be active when the hearing of the appeal is completed, but if a retrial is ordered, that trial becomes active from the date that the order for retrial is made. In practice, it is very unlikely that anything written about an appeal would result in a charge of contempt, simply because appeals are heard by the legal system's most experienced judges, who are considered very unlikely to be prejudiced by anything they read in the papers or see on TV. This was specifically stated in ***Re Lonhro Plc and Observer Ltd*** (1990). However, if a retrial is ordered, much more care is needed, as the retrial will be heard by a jury.

As we saw (on p. 33), s54 of the Criminal Procedure and Investigations Act 1996 gives the power to retry someone who has been acquitted, where the original trial was tainted. The person accused of tainting the trial will be tried for what is known as an 'administration of justice offence' (intimidation, perjury or attempting to pervert the course of justice), and if they are convicted, the judge can issue a certificate stating that the original trial was tainted. The retrial becomes active from that point, even though in fact the decision on whether to retry has not at that stage been made. A retrial can only go ahead if the High Court decides to quash the original conviction and this decision may not come for weeks after the certificate is issued. Once the decision is made, it will be sent to the relevant Crown Court and must be displayed there for 28 days.

Substantial risk of serious prejudice

To fall within the definition of contempt under the Contempt of Court Act, a publication must create a substantial risk of serious prejudice to a particular court case, but what does this actually mean? In *A-G v News Group Newspapers* (1986), the court said that the first question to be asked was:

- Is there is a real risk that the trial will be affected at all by what has been published?

If the answer was yes, the court should ask a second question:

- Would the potential effect of the publication amount to serious prejudice?

Summing up the test, the High Court in *A-G v Guardian Newspapers Ltd (No. 3)* (1992), stated that 'a substantial risk of serious prejudice' would exist where there was a real prospect that, as a result of the publication, the outcome of the case would be different, or the jury would have to be discharged. Having to stop the hearing or move the trial to another area would also be considered serious prejudice.

In assessing this question, the courts are likely to take into account the following factors:

- who the case is tried by;
- timing of publication;
- location of the trial;
- circulation of the publication;
- content of the report.

Who the case is tried by

For a publication to prejudice a trial, it must usually have the potential to influence the person or people who will decide that case. The risk, therefore, varies according to whether a case is being tried by judges, a jury or magistrates.

As explained at the beginning of this chapter, it is generally assumed that professional judges have the training and experience to be able to resist being influenced by anything other than the evidence before them. As a result, it is unlikely that a publication would be considered to create a substantial risk of serious prejudice to cases which are being heard by a judge or group of judges alone (though in theory it could happen). This means that most civil cases and appeals are low-risk with regard to contempt, and in fact no publisher or broadcaster has been punished for contempt of an appeal court in the past 60 years.

Cases tried by juries are the area of highest risk, as juries are considered much more likely to be influenced by outside factors than a professional judge would be. This means that Crown Court trials, and the handful of civil cases in which juries sit, demand the highest standards of care with regard to possible contempt. However, the courts do allow for the fact that juries are told in court to disregard anything but the evidence before them, and several judges have suggested that a publication would have to be quite extreme to make it impossible for them to follow that instruction.

In ***R* v *West*** (1996), the murder trial of Rosemary West, wife of the serial killer Fred West, her lawyers argued that the enormous adverse publicity about the couple when the killings were discovered meant that she could not possibly get a fair trial. This argument was roundly rejected by the then Lord Chief Justice, who said that if that were the case, then it would never be possible to try any alleged murderer where the details of the crime were especially horrifying.

As we saw earlier (in Chapter 3), the vast majority of criminal cases are tried by lay magistrates. They have some training, and often considerable experience of hearing cases, and are considered less likely to be unduly influenced than jurors, but more so than professional judges. Some magistrates' court cases are tried by district judges (formerly known as stipendiary magistrates). They are professional judges, and for contempt purposes should be viewed like any other judge.

Timing of publication

The longer the time between the publication and the start of the court proceedings, the less likely it is that a court will find a substantial risk of serious prejudice. However, it is important to note that the factors on the list above are not taken in isolation, but interact with each other: so, for example, a publication that is made six months before a trial but widely seen might be more likely to be in contempt than one made the same length of time before a trial but seen by fewer people. Equally, a story whose content is particularly strong or dramatic may be considered memorable enough to stick in people's minds over several months, as might particular details about a defendant, such as a serious criminal record.

This means that, although contempt is much more likely to arise from material published close to a trial, it is possible to be in contempt over publications made at a very early stage, if the details are particularly memorable.

In *A-G* v *Unger* (1998), the *Daily Mail* was taken to court over a story about a woman who had been charged with theft from an elderly woman who employed her as a home help. The *Mail* had video film of the thefts, and shortly after the arrest, published stills, with the headline 'The home help who helped herself'. The trial judge found this to be a clear case of 'trial by newspaper', comprising exactly the kind of assumption of guilt that the law of contempt is there to prevent. However, at the time of publication, the trial was still nine months away, and the court held that by that time, the story would have faded from potential jurors' minds so that there would be no real risk of serious prejudice to the defendant. This is often referred to as the 'fade factor'.

In *A-G* v *BBC and Hat Trick Productions* (1997), the BBC TV programme *Have I Got News for You* referred to Kevin and Ian Maxwell, sons of the newspaper proprietor Robert Maxwell, as 'heartless scheming bastards'. At the time, the Maxwell brothers were awaiting trial for fraud, with the hearing due in six months' time. Despite the time delay between the broadcast and the trial, the court pointed out that the programme was very popular, and the speakers well-known, which could increase the impact of their statements. In addition, the programme had been repeated even though the Maxwells' solicitor requested that it should not be. The BBC and the programme's production company were found to be in contempt and fined £10,000.

In *A-G* v *Morgan* (1998), the *News of the World* published an article under the headline 'We smash £100m fake cash ring'. The story concerned an investigation by the paper, which had uncovered a conspiracy to distribute counterfeit money. The paper had passed the details it discovered to the police, who had arrested two men. The story was published the day after the arrests, and clearly assumed the two men's guilt. It also mentioned the men's previous convictions, and was generally written in a very dramatic style. At this stage the trial was about eight months away, but the publishers were held to be in contempt, because the court said that the prominence and effect of the story made it likely that potential jurors would remember it, and in particular the information about previous convictions. This was made even more likely by the fact that the reporter would be called as a witness for the prosecution. The publishers were fined £50,000.

In *A-G* v *ITV Central* (2008), the TV company was fined £25,000 for contempt of court after a news report mentioned that a defendant in a trial that was about to start had previously been convicted for murder. The trial was scheduled to start later the same day, and the information was reported in two further bulletins. The court case had to be postponed to a later date, and ITV Central voluntarily agreed to pay the costs of the postponement, at £37,000.

Publications made during the course of a trial carry the greatest risk of being found in contempt, as this is the time when a jury is actively considering the evidence.

In *A-G* v *MGN* (2002), the *Sunday Mirror* published an article about a trial for assault, where the defendants included two Leeds United footballers. The piece was an interview with the father of the victim, and it alleged that the attack was racially motivated. The judge in the trial had specifically told the jury that there was no evidence of this. The timing of the article could not have been worse, in terms of the risk of contempt: it was published when the jury had begun considering its verdict, and had been sent home for the weekend. The trial collapsed, and a new one had to be held several months later. MGN was fined £75,000.

The 1999 case of ***A-G* v *News Group Newspapers*** concerned the trial of men charged in connection with a bomb attack in London. One of the accused was convicted of conspiracy to bomb, and then the jury went off overnight to consider the second charge of murder. At this point the *Sun* published a story alleging that one of the defendants was under arrest as an IRA sniper. As a result, the murder charge had to be abandoned. The *Sun* was fined £35,000 for contempt.

Location of the trial

In assessing whether a substantial risk exists, the courts will consider how likely it is that potential jurors would see or hear the publication in question. So, for example, a report published in a local paper in Kent is fairly unlikely to carry a risk of prejudicing a trial to be held in Newcastle. There is a possibility that potential jurors in Newcastle might have come across the report, but a mere possibility is not enough to amount to a substantial risk.

In ***A-G* v *Sunday Newspapers Ltd*** (1999), *Sunday Business* was acquitted of contempt after it was proved that there was only a 2000:1 chance of a copy of it being sold to someone in the jury catchment area for a trial it had written about.

This factor only applies to local publications, and can be cancelled out if the publication is available on the internet. However, if a local story is picked up and published by national media and thereby prejudices a trial, the local paper would not be held responsible unless it had in some way encouraged exposure to a wider audience (e.g. by selling the story on).

Circulation of the publication

Obviously, the smaller the circulation, the smaller the chance that a potential juror will read the report. Again, this can be cancelled out if the publication is available on the internet. A very high circulation (or viewing figure) will increase the chance of a court finding that there is a substantial risk of serious prejudice – as we saw above, this was a factor in the ***A-G* v *BBC*** case, where it was pointed out that the total audience was 6.1 million people.

Content of the report

There is no set list of the types of content that will be considered seriously prejudicial; anything that a court could consider likely to influence those deciding the case, or affect the behavior of witnesses, is a risk. However, the following are some of the obvious areas over which care must be taken.

Criticism of the decision to prosecute: The fact that the police believe a crime has been committed and know who is responsible does not necessarily mean that that person will be prosecuted. Both the police and the Crown Prosecution Service have a degree of leeway in deciding which cases should go to court, and, in making this decision, they take into account the public interest. Therefore, general criticism of a decision to prosecute (such as stating that the law in question is outdated) can legitimately be published before the trial is over. However, if this spills over into suggesting the likely result of the trial, or criticising the witnesses or the victim, contempt is a risk.

Previous convictions: In criminal trials, the defendant's previous convictions were traditionally kept from the jury, on the basis that a juror who knows the defendant has a criminal record might be unduly swayed by that knowledge when deciding whether the defendant has committed the crime in question. The Criminal Justice Act 2003 now allows disclosure of previous convictions in some circumstances (see p. 28), but there are still strict rules as to when this is permitted, and the change does not mean the press can publish details of previous convictions without risking contempt. However, if the previous convictions are already widely known about, it becomes much more difficult to prove a substantial risk of serious prejudice.

In ***A-G* v *Evening Standard*** (1998) the *Evening Standard* published a story about defendants who were on trial for attempting to escape from prison. The report was published in the middle of the trial, and mentioned that some of those accused of trying to escape were IRA terrorists. Although the court accepted that, by the nature of the charge, jurors would already know that the defendants had been convicted of something serious enough to put them in prison, it said that the revelation that some of them were terrorists posed a substantial risk of serious prejudice, and the *Standard* was fined £40,000.

In 1996, the *Sun* carried an interview with snooker player Ronnie O'Sullivan, in which he said that he was determined to win the Master's title, in order to celebrate his mother's release from prison, after serving a 12-month sentence for evading VAT. Unfortunately, at the time the interview was published, Mrs O'Sullivan was on trial again, this time for dealing in obscene publications. The *Sun* story made it possible for jurors to find out about her previous convictions, and the jury had to be discharged. The *Sun* was fined £10,000.

In ***A-G* v *MGN*** (1997), several tabloids were taken to court over stories published about Geoff Knights, boyfriend of the actress Gillian Taylforth. Mr Knights had been charged with assault, and the *Mirror, Star, Sun, Today* (now closed) and *Daily Mail* all published articles referring to his violent past and previous convictions. As a result, the criminal proceedings against Knights were dropped, with the court deciding that it was now impossible for him to receive a fair trial. The five newspapers were prosecuted for contempt, but the court held that, in the circumstances of the case, it was impossible to single out one particular report that created a substantial risk of serious prejudice, because Knights' background was already public knowledge; it had been widely written about when Ms Taylforth brought a libel action some months earlier. Therefore none of the newspapers was guilty of contempt.

The Northern Irish paper *Sunday World* and its editor were fined £60,000 in 2008 after a trial had to be moved to a different court due to a risk of prejudice caused by articles published in the paper. In November 2005 and July 2006, the paper wrote a series of articles about two men who were due to face trial for intimidation, criminal damage and malicious wounding, as part of what it claimed was a crusade against local drug dealers. The men's trial was scheduled for January 2007, but was postponed after their lawyers said that they intended to apply for a stay of proceedings (a ruling that the case should be postponed, possibly indefinitely), because of the articles published in the *Sunday World*. Shortly afterwards, the court imposed a complete ban on reporting the case, but the *Sunday World* then went on to run two further articles about the defendants in March 2007, referring to their alleged criminal activities, within days of the application to stay the proceedings. The Attorney-General's office wrote to the paper about the series of articles, but, even so, the paper then ran a further piece in July, describing one of the men as the leader of the illegal Loyalist Volunteer Force. The judge in the contempt hearing described the offence as among 'the most serious of this kind of contempt', and expressed his disapproval of the fact that the paper had not attended any of the hearings, which would have been easy to do and would have informed it about the restrictions. He also criticised the 'sensationalist and graphic language' of the articles.

Defendant's background or character: As with previous convictions, publishing details of a defendant's background which puts them in a bad light or makes them sound like the kind of person who would be likely to commit the crime in question could clearly make a juror more likely to convict, and therefore the publisher may be in contempt. But information which makes the defendant look bad is not the only danger – publishing details of a defendant's good character, or any attempt to suggest an honourable motive for the crime, could influence a juror towards an acquittal and is therefore a possible risk. It is not, however, contempt to publish the defendant's own protestations of innocence, so long as the overall publication does not go so far as to amount to a call for an acquittal.

In 1979 a Scottish newspaper was fined £20,000, after publishing an article about four people arrested for drugs offences. The story stated that three of them imported chemicals, and that a large quantity of drugs had been seized from the house where they were living, which the court believed could have led potential jurors to assume they were guilty.

In *Attorney General* v *Associated Newspapers and MGN Ltd* (2012), the *Daily Mail* and the *Daily Mirror* were found guilty of contempt over their coverage of the trial of Levi Bellfield, the murderer of schoolgirl Milly Dowler. Bellfield was convicted of the murder on 23 June, but, at that point, the jury had not reached a verdict on a second charge, of attempting to abduct schoolgirl Rachael Cowles. All the main news channels and national papers reported that Bellfield had been convicted of killing Milly Dowler, but the *Mail* and the *Mirror* included in their reports material that had been kept from the jury during the trial, and extra allegations about Bellfield's past and his personality which, among other things, suggested a perverted interest in raping schoolgirls. The trial judge said that the reporting was so prejudicial that the jury could no longer be expected to try the abduction charge, and discharged them from returning a verdict. In the contempt trial, the court found that, even though the jury would already have been well aware by that stage that Bellfield was a man with a history of savage violence against women, the key factor was that the stories included clear allegations that he had raped schoolgirls, which a jury might well think was relevant to the remaining charge of kidnapping a schoolgirl. That meant that it carried a serious risk of substantial prejudice.

In *Attorney-General* v *Associated Newspapers and News Group Newspapers* (2011), the *Daily Mail* and the *Sun* were each fined £15,000 for contempt, when pictures they used online were said to have prejudiced a murder trial. By mistake, they had included pictures of the murder suspect holding a gun, after the start of his trial. As the court pointed out, this gave a clear impression of him as a man who used and enjoyed using violence, and so was obviously prejudicial. The picture was only online for a few hours, and was not especially easy to access (to find it someone would have had to make a point of reading about the case, and then clicked through from the initial story), and after questioning the jury, the trial judge was satisfied that none of them had seen it. But it was clear that there was a substantial risk of serious prejudice, even if that risk had not materialised, and this was enough to convict the newspapers.

Circumstances of the offence: In a 2003 speech, the then Attorney-General warned against publishing detailed reports of the circumstances leading up to criminal charges in particular cases, which go into the evidence that will be presented, the defences that may be argued, and other issues which the jury will have to decide. He stated that the jury members should decide on the evidence before them and not on what they might have seen or read in the media.

Assertions of fact: Issues which are to be decided in the trial should not be presented as if they are already fact.

In 2003, the *Sunday Life* in Belfast was fined £5,000 for a report about a man who was about to be tried for drugs offences. The piece, published a month before the trial, described him as a drug dealer who had been on the run from the police, and also linked him to previous articles which said that cocaine had been found at his home, and that he had escaped and travelled back to Belfast to meet his criminal contacts.

Photographs/description: Where the identity of the culprit in a crime is in question (such as, for example, where the suspect denies being anywhere near the scene of the crime, but a witness claims to have seen them there), showing a photograph of someone who has been arrested or is the subject of a warrant can amount to contempt, as can describing their physical appearance. The previous Attorney-General has explained that, if a suspect's photograph is published, they may refuse to take part in an identification parade, which makes the police investigation more difficult, and may weaken the prosecution's case. Even if the suspect does take part in an identification parade, the defence can argue that the result should not be admitted as evidence because the court could not be sure whether the witness identified the defendant from actual memory of the event, or from their recollection of the photograph or report (the situation may be different where the police ask for a photograph to be published – see p. 66). Where identification is not in question, it is permissible to publish a photograph of someone who has been arrested, is the subject of a warrant, or is a defendant, but the Attorney-General warned that publication should not happen unless it is absolutely clear that there is no question, and will be no question, about identification.

In 1994, the *Sun* was prosecuted for contempt after publishing a photograph of a defendant, six weeks before he was to take part in an identity parade. Two witnesses who picked out the man in the ID parade had seen the picture in the *Sun*, and as a result, the defence lawyers were able to argue that their identification was unreliable, and the prosecution had to be stopped. The *Sun* was fined £80,000 and its editor £20,000.

In ***A-G* v *Express Newspapers Ltd*** (2005), the *Daily Star* was fined £60,000 for contempt after it identified two suspects in an alleged rape case. The two, who were well-known professional footballers, were among four men questioned by police about allegations of a gang rape at a London hotel. The press had been repeatedly told not to identify the suspects, because identity was an issue in the case, but the *Star* published both their names and a pixellated picture of one of them. It argued that there was a 'real possibility' that the alleged victim knew their identities, but the court said there was no evidence of this, and therefore the publication created a real risk of substantial prejudice. In the event, neither of the men was charged with the offence.

Publishing pictures of suspects is even more of a problem in Scottish cases and is rarely permissible (see p. 84).

Guilty pleas to other charges: Where a defendant is charged with several different offences, they may plead guilty to some, and not guilty to others. The jury is not in court for this part of the case, and is only brought in afterwards to try the offences to which the defendant has pleaded not guilty. Reporting the guilty pleas clearly has the potential to influence jurors' views of the other charges, so these should not be mentioned until after the trial is over, regardless of whether or not the judge points this out.

Involvement in other proceedings: The previous Attorney-General has stated that reports containing details of other proceedings in which a defendant or witness has been involved can influence jurors' views of the evidence, or the credibility of witnesses.

During a 2001 rape trial, a local radio station broadcast a short item, stating that the jury in the case was about to return its verdict, and mentioning that the defendant in the case had also been charged with a second rape, arising from an incident two years later. This was to be the subject of a separate trial, but this was not made clear in the report. At the time, the jury had already begun considering its verdict, but as jurors had not been able to agree, they had been sent home for the weekend. The judge was told about the report, and on the Monday, asked the jury whether it had heard any broadcasts about the case. One juror said she had, and further questions revealed that as a result of what she had heard, she believed that the defendant had committed a rape before. She was discharged from the jury, which went on to return a 10–1 verdict of guilty. The Attorney-General declined to prosecute after finding that the radio station had made an inadvertent mistake and taken steps to prevent it happening again, but the case was quoted by the Attorney-General as an example of the 'serious consequences' that could arise.

Proceedings without the jury: Once the trial has started, the jury is sometimes sent out of the court while the lawyers and the judge discuss certain issues – for example, if there is a question about whether certain evidence is admissible, the jury will be sent out while this is discussed, as clearly it would make no sense to let jurors hear what the evidence is and then declare it inadmissible. It is fine to state that the jury was sent out, and to report anything which was said about the discussions while the jury was still in court, or after it came back, but publishing details of anything not heard by the jury could well be considered to prejudice the trial, even if this material is already in the public domain.

Assuming guilt: In his 2003 speech, the Attorney-General said that a story which 'asserts or assumes, expressly or implicitly' that the defendant is guilty runs a clear risk of contempt. This might be done in a single headline, or in biased commentary about the evidence, either before or during a trial. The Attorney-General made it clear that this applies regardless of how obvious the facts seem to be. Even if a suspect has admitted the crime, whether to journalists, police or anyone else, it is dangerous to assume that they are guilty, or even that they will necessarily plead guilty.

In ***A-G* v *Unger*** (1998), the case of the home help accused of theft (described at p. 70), the defendant had been confronted by a newspaper with the video evidence of her thefts, and had broken down and admitted that she had taken the money. She later admitted the same to police. The papers therefore wrote the story in terms that took it as read that she was guilty, describing her as 'The home help who helped herself'; they had in fact had legal advice which suggested that as the case appeared clear-cut, there was no substantial risk of prejudice. However, they were prosecuted for contempt, and the court severely criticised their approach. It said that the media should not assume that someone was guilty just because they had confessed, or because the evidence seemed clear-cut. In this case, for example, the video evidence showed that the defendant had physically taken the money, but that alone did not make her guilty of theft as defined by the criminal law, which also requires that she had dishonestly intended to deprive the money's owner of it permanently. In addition, it had not been established that the video evidence was admissible, so making potential jurors aware of it could easily be prejudicial. In the end, the papers were acquitted of contempt because of the long period of time between publication and the likely date of the trial, but the remarks in the case still provide useful guidance about the courts' view of assuming a defendant's guilt.

Vilifying suspects: It now appears that it is dangerous – as well as obviously unethical – to publish material which assumes or suggests someone is guilty, even if in fact that person never goes on to be put on trial.

In ***Attorney-General* v *MGN and Another*** (2011), the *Daily Mirror* was fined £50,000 and the *Sun* £18,000, over the coverage of the murder of Joanna Yeates, whose body was found on Christmas Day 2010. The coverage centred on the arrest of Ms Yeates' landlord, Chris Jefferies, presenting him as a suspicious character who behaved oddly and was considered weird by those who knew him, linking him with someone he vaguely knew who had been charged with child abuse, saying he had a macabre fascination with death, and generally heavily implying that he was the kind of person who might well be guilty of the crime. Among the headlines were 'Jo Suspect is Peeping Tom', 'Jo Suspect "Scared Kids"' and 'Arrest Landlord Spied on Couple'. However, it very quickly became obvious to the police that Mr Jefferies was not involved, and he was released without charge; someone else was later convicted of the murder. There was therefore no trial that the publications could have affected. However, the court pointed out that this did not mean there was no contempt, because, they said, the risk had to be judged on the situation as it was at the time of publication, and at that time it looked very likely that Mr Jefferies would be charged. The papers argued that, had there been a trial, the judge would have warned the jurors not to take any notice of what they had read, and as we have seen, it has been accepted that this, along with the 'fade factor' can ensure a fair trial even where very prejudicial material has been published. The court agreed that this was probably the case, but pointed out that the Contempt of Court Act 1981 states that it applies to publications which create a serious risk that the course of justice will be seriously 'impeded or prejudiced'. Leaving aside the issue of prejudice, the material in the papers, the court said, was clearly capable of impeding the course of justice, because it might have prevented witnesses who could have helped in Mr Jefferies' defence from coming forward, because they would not want to be associated with him, or because the impression of guilt given was so strong, that they might start to doubt whether their own information was correct. That might prevent the trial being fair, because not all the important evidence was available. The court also said that it was possible that vilifying an innocent suspect who was then never charged could still prejudice the eventual trial, if the defendant there pleaded not guilty. By pleading not guilty, they would be suggesting that someone else committed the crime, and if there had been a lot of earlier press coverage vilifying someone else, that might well affect a jury's decision, and possibly help someone who was guilty to escape justice. That was not the situation here, as the defendant pleaded guilty, but the court's words should be seen as a warning to cover future cases.

In the Jefferies case, at the time of publication it looked very much as though there would be a trial, but the result of the case also needs to be taken into account when reporting crime stories in situations where it seems unlikely that there ever will be a trial. Even if you are writing about someone who it seems will never be tried, there can be a risk of impeding the course of justice.

Assuming the outcome of preliminary issues: The previous Attorney-General has warned that in a case where there are preliminary issues to be decided before the case begins (such as whether the defendant will be mentally fit to stand trial), the press should not publish any assertions about the outcome, or write as though the outcome was already decided.

Speculating about damages: When a jury hears a civil case (such as defamation or malicious prosecution), it decides not only who wins, but the amount of damages. Therefore, it is important not to speculate about how much a jury might award, even after the verdict has been announced. Theoretically, this principle also applies in cases heard by a judge, but as we have seen, in practice it is viewed as very unlikely that any publication would run a substantial risk of influencing a judge.

In 1999, the *Birmingham Post* reported that a jury had decided in favour of a man claiming malicious prosecution against the West Midlands Police, and said that the man was likely to get damages of £30,000. At this stage, although the verdict had been reached, damages had not been decided. As a result of the story, the judge held that the proceedings had been tainted and, rather than go through a retrial, the claimant decided to abandon his case. Contempt proceedings were not brought (though they could have been), but the judge issued a reminder to the press that civil proceedings were still active until after damages had been decided.

Protected documents/information: In civil cases, certain types of communications or documents are protected from being disclosed to the court, and publishing details of them can easily put a publication in contempt. For example, a defendant can make a 'payment into court', which is an offer to settle the case for the sum of money paid in. If the claimants refuse the offer, and go on to win the case but are awarded less than the sum paid in, they can only claim back their legal costs up to the date of the payment into court. Neither juries nor even the judge are allowed to know about a payment into court, so a newspaper revealing that such a payment has been made would run a high risk of contempt.

Interviewing witnesses: Publishing interviews with witnesses, even before a trial starts, can be problematic, as it can be argued that a witness who has seen their words reported in the media might be more likely to stick to their story, regardless of truth. Even interviewing witnesses with a view to publishing material after the trial can be risky, for much the same reason.

Paying witnesses, while not illegal, can be a breach of the Editors Code of Practice or the Ofcom Code of Practice (see p. 90).

In 1991, the Court of Appeal strongly criticised a television programme which featured interviews with three people who were to be witnesses at a drug trial, even though the programme was not shown until after the trial ended, and the programme had been made with the cooperation of Customs and Excise. The witnesses were filmed as if they were giving their evidence in court, and the Court of Appeal said that the defence should have been told that the witnesses had previously given their evidence on camera.

Undermining witnesses: The previous Attorney-General has warned that assessing the reliability of witnesses is a task for the jury to do, based on what it sees and hears in court; it is not something that should be influenced by the media. Stating or suggesting that a witness might not be telling the truth, might have an ulterior motive for what they say, or might be habitually dishonest could clearly sway a juror's view of their evidence, and therefore be contempt.

Interfering in proceedings: Any publication that could have the effect of persuading a witness not to testify, or to change their evidence, or which could intimidate them in any way, may be contempt. The same applies to a publication which could deter the claimant in a civil case from pursuing their claim.

Inaccurate reporting: A report which contains inaccuracies about critical issues in a trial could wrongly influence jurors, and can therefore be contempt.

Balancing the relevant factors

As explained earlier, the factors listed above are not taken in isolation, or in any hierarchy of importance, but interact with each other, making it quite difficult to predict which factors a court will place most importance on. In ***A-G* v *MGN*** (1997), the Geoff Knights case (referred to at p. 72), the court gave some useful guidelines on the way in which the courts should approach these factors. It said that each case must be decided on its own facts; previous cases may be helpful, but they can only be guides. In deciding whether there has been a 'substantial risk of serious prejudice', the court will look at:

- the likelihood of the publication being seen by a potential juror, bearing in mind where the publication was in circulation, and how many copies were published;
- the likely effect of the publication on an ordinary reader, given its prominence and the novelty of the content (i.e. how interesting or attention-grabbing it was);
- the residual impact at the time of the trial.

The judge in the Knights case made it clear that the third factor, 'residual impact' was the most important. It essentially asks how likely it is that a theoretical juror would be influenced by the publication when they came to try to the case. The time period between publication and trial would be relevant in assessing this, but the court should also consider how far the experience of taking part in the trial and listening to all the evidence would increase the juror's ability to set aside any outside influences and concentrate on the evidence. The court should also take into account the fact that the judge would be able to direct the jury to ignore outside influences, and allow for the effect of such directions. Only if the court, after assessing all these factors, was certain that there was a substantial risk that the trial would be, not just prejudiced, but prejudiced to a serious degree, should it convict a publisher of contempt.

In 1994, ITN, the *Daily Express, Today* (now closed), *Daily Mail* and *Northern Echo* were prosecuted for contempt over stories about two men arrested for murdering a special constable. Two days after the arrests, ITN and three of the papers carried stories naming one of the men as an IRA terrorist who had been convicted of murdering an SAS officer. The other paper also published details about the man's background. Lord Justice Leggatt said those details should not have been published before the trial, which at that stage was likely to be about nine months away. However, having weighed up the factors of time and type of publication against the content of the stories, he concluded that there was only a very remote risk of serious prejudice. The relevant factors leading to this conclusion were that the publication was a long time before the trial, that relatively few papers containing the offending material had been in circulation, and that ITN had only carried the details in one broadcast, which was unlikely to make a sufficient impression on viewers to cause a serious risk of prejudice to a trial nine months later (though the court said this might have been different had the story been repeated in later broadcasts). Although there was a possiblility that a potential juror had seen the stories, it was a very small one, and therefore not sufficient to justify a conviction for contempt.

Note that the Contempt of Court Act imposes liability for *creating* a risk of serious prejudice. If you create such a risk, you can be liable, even if the risk does not materialize because it is later decided that the trial can go ahead as planned, or the trial does not go ahead but for other reasons.

In ***A-G* v *Express Newspapers Ltd*** (2005), the *Daily Star* named two premiership footballers who were suspected of rape, despite the fact that the Attorney-General had repeatedly warned the media that identity would be an issue in any eventual trial, and so no names should be published. The newspaper was fined £60,000, even though the two men were not prosecuted (for reasons unrelated to their naming in the press), and so there was no trial to prejudice.

Multiple publications

Where a particular allegation or information has been published at different times by different publications, the court in ***A-G* v *MGN*** (1997) made it clear that each publication will be assessed separately. The fact that an earlier publication has already created a risk of prejudice does not mean that a later one cannot be judged to create a new and further risk.

Contempt and the internet

The internet poses new problems for the law of contempt. In high-profile cases, a great deal of background material may have been written and published, quite legally, before the point at which proceedings become active. From that point, the media should refrain from publishing new material which risks serious prejudice, but much of the already published material will still be available in the online archives of magazines and newspapers, and can easily be found by jury members. The problems this can cause were shown up in 2008, when a criminal trial at the Old Bailey collapsed after it came to light that one of the jurors had been searching the internet for background information about the defendant, and had shared his discoveries with the rest of the jury.

No media organisation has yet been prosecuted over online archive material, but in 2012, a High Court judge ordered the *Daily Mail* to remove from its online archives two articles about a policeman who was about to be tried for the manslaughter of a man who died during demonstrations in London. The articles had been published two years before, and detailed allegations of violent misconduct which had previously been made against the police officer. The judge had refused to allow these allegations to be mentioned in evidence, and said that leaving the articles online would be contempt of court.

Law in practice Dramatising trials on TV

The same rules on contempt of court apply to both print and broadcast journalists, but one pitfall which uniquely affects TV news reporting is that of using reconstructions to show what is alleged to have happened during the commission of a crime. Judges take a dim view of this, as the vivid portrayal of dramatic events clearly has the potential to influence juries.

In 1983, a judge trying a case at the Old Bailey criticised ITV's *News at Ten* for showing a reconstruction, played by actors, of events which had been described during a court case that day. He suggested that the programme was wrong to put forward its own interpretation of events, which it had not witnessed, and said that he had considered contempt proceedings, though in fact none was brought.

The courts have also acted against reconstructions of trials themselves, even where there is no possibility of a jury being influenced. In 1987, an injunction was granted preventing Channel 4 from showing a reconstruction of the appeal hearing for the men convicted of the Birmingham pub bombings (who were eventually found to have been wrongly convicted). The broadcast was to have taken place while the proceedings were still going on, but as appeal hearings are heard by judges, not juries, it would not usually be considered that anything broadcast or published could influence the outcome of the case. However, the Lord Chief Justice, who issued the injunction, said that using actors to play witnesses would allow viewers to make judgements based on what seemed to be the real thing, but was not. This might then affect the public's view of the court's eventual judgment.

Currently, it does not appear that the media is expected to search its archives for possibly prejudicial material and remove it (which would obviously be a huge and constant task). However, if a publisher is told that material may be prejudicial, for example by a judge, it would clearly be a good idea to remove it, at least until the case is no longer active.

Defences

The Contempt of Court Act 1981 provides for three defences against a charge of strict liability contempt:

- innocent publication;
- fair and accurate contemporary reports;
- discussion of public affairs.

Innocent publication

Although the name of this defence suggests it might cover publication of details by mistake, this is not the case. As explained earlier, strict liability means that you can be liable regardless of whether you intended to prejudice a trial, or simply made a mistake that caused a risk of prejudice. 'Innocent publication' in fact covers only one very specific (and in practice rare) situation, detailed in s3 of the Act. It provides that a publisher is not guilty of strict liability contempt if:

> at the time of publication (having taken all reasonable care) he does not know and has no reason to suspect that proceedings are active.

Anyone who seeks to put forward this defence must prove that:

- they took all reasonable care; and
- they had no reason to suspect that proceedings were active.

This is not an easy test to pass. Usually, a call to the police, the court or the defendant's lawyer will establish whether proceedings are active, and if you have not done this, you cannot be said to have taken all reasonable care. It is therefore essential that anyone making such calls takes, and keeps, notes of whom they spoke to, date and time, and what was said. Similarly, the requirement that the publisher of the material must have 'no reason to suspect' that proceedings were active is a tough one, when the mere fact of knowing that someone is 'helping police with their enquiries' naturally gives reason to suspect that that person might at some point be arrested.

In *Solicitor-General* v *Henry and News Group Newspapers Ltd* (1990), the *News of the World* published a news story about the disappearance of a woman called Shirley Banks. It reported that a man had been arrested for armed robbery, and, after the arrest, Mrs Banks' car had been found in his garage. He was described as a 'sex beast' and the story gave details about his previous conviction for a sex offence. The man was rearrested, while still in custody, for the murder of Mrs Banks, which made the proceedings with regard to her murder active. The newspaper said it did not know this but, nevertheless, was found in contempt and fined £15,000.

In practice, the main situation in which this defence is likely to be of use to the press is where proceedings become active just as the presses are rolling or the programme is being transmitted, but, even in this situation, the responsibility is on the publisher to prove that it took all reasonable care to avoid the situation occurring.

Fair and accurate contemporary reports

Section 4(1) of the Contempt of Court Act 1981 provides that:

> a person is not guilty of contempt of court under the strict liability rule in respect of a fair and accurate report of legal proceedings held in public, published contemporaneously and in good faith.

To successfully use this defence, therefore, you need to show that the report was:

- fair and accurate;
- published contemporaneously (both this and the 'fair and accurate' requirement are essentially the same as for the defence of absolute privilege in libel – see p. 257);
- published in good faith (meaning honestly and without any ulterior motive);

and that the legal proceedings in question were held in public (which means that the public must be freely entitled to attend).

Discussion of public affairs

Section 5 of the Contempt of Court Act provides that:

> a publication made as, or as part of, a discussion in good faith of public affairs or other matters of general public interest is not to be treated as contempt of court under the strict liability rule if the risk of impediment or prejudice to particular legal proceedings is merely incidental to the discussion.

Essentially, this defence means that discussion of important public issues does not have to stop merely because a case which raises those issues becomes active.

In *A-G* v *English* (1983) the case concerned an article in the *Daily Mail*, arguing for a Pro-Life election candidate, and strongly criticising an alleged practice among doctors of allowing severely handicapped babies to die of starvation. At the time the article was published, a doctor was on trial for murder, after allegedly allowing a baby with Down's Syndrome to starve. The article did not specifically mention the case. The *Mail* was prosecuted for contempt, but the prosecution failed. The House of Lords held that, although the article was likely to prejudice the trial, it met the requirements of s5 of the Act, and therefore there was no contempt. The point of the article was a serious discussion of a matter of public interest, and the prejudice was merely a side-effect of that discussion.

In ***A-G* v *Associated Newspapers*** (1983), the *Mail on Sunday* published prejudicial information about the character of Michael Fagin, who was accused of burglary after breaking into Buckingham Palace and making his way to the Queen's bedroom. The paper was able to rely on the s5 defence, because the details were part of a report on the security precautions around the Queen, and the court held that the Queen's safety was a matter of public interest.

In ***A-G* v *English*** the House of Lords spelt out the test to be applied in judging whether prejudice is 'merely incidental'. It said that the court did not need to ask whether the story could have been written just as effectively without the potentially prejudicial parts, or whether the piece could have been worded differently in order to reduce the risk. Instead, the question to be asked was whether the risk of prejudice actually created by the words was no more than an incidental consequence of the author getting their message across.

The fact that an article discusses a matter of public interest will not, however, always save it from the danger of contempt. Essentially, the closer the subject matter comes to the specific facts of a case, the higher the chances that the prejudice will not be considered merely incidental, and the defence will fail. Actually mentioning the defendant(s) clearly increases the risk.

In ***A-G* v *TVS Television Ltd*** (1989), TVS had shown a programme called *The New Rachmans*. Rachman was a landlord who was infamous during the 1960s for bullying and harassing tenants, and the programme alleged that certain landlords in Reading were behaving in a similar way, and were also obtaining money by deception from the Department of Health and Social Security (DHSS). One of the landlords featured in the programme was on trial for conspiracy to defraud the DHSS, and, as a result of the programme his trial had to be stopped, at a cost of £215,000. He had been shown on the programme, and although his face was blacked out, he was still identifiable. When TVS was prosecuted for contempt, it sought to use the s5 defence, arguing that the programme was an examination of the general shortage of rental accommodation in the south-east of England, which was an issue of public interest; the situation with the landlords in Reading was an example of the problem. The details of the Reading situation, it said, were merely incidental to this discussion. The court did not agree; the prejudice was not merely incidental and TVS was guilty of contempt.

At around the same time as the *Daily Mail* published the article referred to in ***A-G* v *English***, above, the *Express* printed a piece specifically about the murder case involving the doctor and the Down's Syndrome baby. It criticised the fact that the trial was taking five weeks, and stated that if the baby had been allowed to live for that long, 'he might have found someone other than God to love him'. This was judged to amount to contempt. Express Newspapers was fined £10,000 and the editor, who wrote the piece, £1,000.

If you are writing about a topical issue which you know is the subject of a court case, the safest option is to make sure that you do not refer to the case at all, or at the very least, that you make sure nothing you say suggests whether the defendant is guilty or not guilty (or liable or not liable if it is a civil case). You should then be covered by the s5 defence.

Scope of strict liability contempt

Section 19 of the Contempt of Court Act 1981 provides that strict liability contempt applies to proceedings of 'any tribunal or body exercising the judicial power of the state'.

This clearly includes all cases heard in the criminal and civil courts, and in employment tribunals, coroner's courts, mental health tribunals and courts martial. However, not every kind of tribunal is covered by the statute – for example, in ***General Medical Council* v *British Broadcasting Corporation*** (1998), it was held that the General Medical Council was not a body exercising the judicial power of the state (see Chapter 13 for more on contempt and tribunals).

INTENTIONAL CONTEMPT

Intentional contempt is a common law offence which existed before the Contempt of Court Act 1981 was passed. Although it overlaps with the contempt offence defined by the Act, there are differences, which means there are situations where someone who is not guilty of contempt under the Act may nevertheless be guilty of the common law offence. For example, if the proceedings you write about are not active, there is no liability for contempt under the Act, regardless of what you write – but there may be liability at common law. Because the offence requires proof beyond reasonable doubt that the publisher intended to prejudice a trial, common law contempt is harder to prove than strict liability contempt, and prosecutions are rarer, but do still happen.

A person (or company) will be guilty of intentional contempt if they publish material with the intention of prejudicing or interfering with proceedings which are 'imminent or pending'. There are therefore two important differences between intentional contempt and strict liability contempt:

- proceedings must be 'pending or imminent', rather than 'active' (though there is some overlap – see below);
- the publisher must intend to prejudice the trial.

Proceedings pending or imminent

It is generally understood that once someone has been arrested, proceedings can be considered to be 'pending'. The issue of when proceedings are 'imminent' is less clear, but it seems that proceedings can be considered 'imminent' even before someone is arrested, which means that the period in which proceedings are pending or imminent may begin before the period in which they would be 'active' under the Contempt of Court Act.

In ***R* v *Beaverbrook Newspapers and Associated Newspapers*** (1962), the *Daily Express* was fined for publishing prejudicial material about a man who had not been arrested at the time of publication, but was obviously about to be.

Intention

The prosecution must prove, beyond reasonable doubt, that the publisher of the material intended to prejudice the trial. In everyday speech, to 'intend' to do something means to act with that purpose in mind, and anyone who deliberately set out to prejudice a trial would certainly be covered by the offence. However, given the possible punishment for contempt, such cases will clearly be rare, and for the purposes of contempt, intention also has a wider meaning than its everyday one. Intention can be assumed if the publisher was:

- aware that proceedings were imminent; and
- aware of the nature of the material they were publishing.

In other words, someone who publishes material that is obviously likely to cause prejudice can be assumed to have intended such prejudice, even if they say they did not mean for or wish that to happen. It was made clear in ***A-G* v *Sport Newspapers*** (below), however, that intention should only be assumed where the probability of prejudicing the trial was 'little short of overwhelming'.

In ***A-G* v *News Group Newspapers*** (1988), the *Sun* announced that it was funding a private prosecution against a doctor who was alleged to have raped a little girl. There was medical evidence that the child had been raped, but because she was only nine, the Director of Public Prosecutions decided not to prosecute. The *Sun* expressed its outrage at the decision with the headline 'Rape Case Doc: Sun Acts', and the offer to pay for the private prosecution. It called the doctor 'a beast and a swine', clearly assumed he was guilty, and accused him of other sexual crimes. The prosecution took place, and the doctor was acquitted. The *Sun* was prosecuted for contempt. It maintained that it had not intended to prejudice the trial, but the judge said that, in the circumstances, the editor must have realised that talking about the doctor as a rapist and offering to fund the prosecution were potentially seriously prejudicial. The paper was found guilty and fined £75,000.

In ***A-G* v *Sport Newspapers*** (1992), the *Daily Sport* published a story about the rape and murder of a 15-year-old schoolgirl, which said that police suspected a man called David Evans of the crime, and gave details of Evans' considerable criminal record. The story called him a 'vicious, evil rapist' with a 'horrific history of sex attacks'. At the time, Evans was on the run, and five days before the article was published, the police had held a press conference to ask for the public's help to find him, though no warrant had been issued for his arrest at this stage. At the conference, the police spokesman specifically stated that publishing details of Evans' criminal background was likely to prejudice a future trial. The *Sport* did not have a reporter at the conference, but was told about the police's wish to keep Evans' record out of the media at least two days before it published the article. Five days after publication, Evans was arrested, and was tried and convicted of the murder in the following year. The *Sport* was prosecuted for contempt but the Court of Appeal said the case did not have the necessary intent, because at the time of publication, it was uncertain whether Evans would actually be caught, let alone charged and tried.

In ***Dobson* v *Hastings*** (1992), a finance writer from the *Daily Telegraph* was writing a story about some company directors who were facing proceedings for disqualification. She went to the court to look at the relevant file, and was told that she had to have the court's permission to do so. She was given the file to take to the registrar in order to get this permission, and while she waited to do so, she took notes from documents in the report. This was a breach of court rules, but she did not know this, having never dealt with court documents before. When she told the registrar what she had done, he complained to her editor, but her story was still published. The company directors tried to bring an action for contempt, but it was dismissed on the grounds that she had made an honest mistake and there was nothing on which to base an assumption of intention.

Myths and misconceptions *Sub judice*

✘ *You can't report things which are 'sub judice'.*

The Latin phrase *sub judice* means 'under judicial consideration', and is often used to describe the situation where legal proceedings are under way, such as where someone has been arrested, or someone has begun proceedings to sue someone else. It is widely believed that matters which are *sub judice* cannot be mentioned or discussed at all in the media, but this is not the case. As long as you follow the law as described in this chapter (and any other reporting restrictions, as detailed in the following chapters), it is perfectly legal to discuss or report on legal cases. The *sub judice* argument is sometimes used by people (often politicians, who should know better) to avoid having to make a comment on an issue, so it is useful to know that it is not the all-encompassing rule that it is often thought to be.

Contempt in Scottish cases

Scotland is covered by exactly the same contempt laws as the rest of the UK, but the Scottish courts interpret the law in a much stricter way, and the media has been fined for contempt there in cases which would not have led to prosecution in England. And unlike in England, where the Attorney-General's consent is needed for a contempt prosecution, in Scotland cases can be brought by an accused person, which clearly increases the risk. This means you need to be especially careful in reporting Scottish cases, whether or not your coverage is published/broadcast in Scotland (and of course if your story goes online, it will be published in Scotland, regardless of where the original was published or broadcast). A case is considered to be Scottish if it is under the jurisdiction of the Scottish courts (regardless of whether the defendant is Scottish or not). In addition, there are some differences in Scottish criminal procedure, which will affect the way you can report cases.

Active proceedings: Scottish criminal proceedings become active when a suspect is arrested or charged, or when a warrant for arrest is granted, or when a warrant to cite (the equivalent to a summons) is granted. As in England and Wales, there is no danger of contempt before this stage. Civil actions become active when the parties' pleadings (the equivalent of the statement of case) are finalised and the Record (the written case) is closed.

Pictures: Identification of the person in the dock is considered more important in the Scottish system, and the Scottish courts will almost always consider publication of a picture or film of a suspect to be contempt. Therefore, pictures or film of a suspect cannot usually be used once proceedings become active. In exceptional cases, where the defendant is very well-known, it may be possible to use a picture, but you should always check with a lawyer first. In some cases, an accused person may voluntarily talk to reporters, knowing that they are being photographed or filmed, and in some cases it will be possible to use these pictures, but you should always take legal advice first.

In 1992, the BBC was found guilty of contempt for showing a man accused of murder emerging from a police van and being led into court by police officers. The court said that the man was clearly identifiable from the film.

Hearings in chambers: In Scotland pre-trial hearings, including bail hearings, are usually held in the judge's chambers, and reporters are not admitted. You can report some details of these hearings if the defence lawyer or the Procurator Fiscal (the Scottish equivalent of a Crown prosecutor) is willing to give you the information about them, but neither is obliged to do so. You may not report what questions were asked or answers given, even if you get this information from the defence lawyer or the Procurator Fiscal.

Initial reports: Be careful when reporting the early stages of Scottish trials, when the court has been told the charge and the circumstances of the offence but no actual evidence has yet been given. In English cases it is routine to use phrases such as 'The court heard that' or 'The court was told that' when referring to the indictment being read out, but the Scottish courts take a dim view of this practice, because it can give the impression that what was said is part of the evidence. In a Scottish case, it is safer to use phrases such as 'The Crown's allegation is that' or 'The indictment stated that' until you are reporting actual evidence.

Background information: The Scottish courts have taken a noticeably harder line on publication of details about a defendant's background, even where this information is already widely known.

In 1997, the *Daily Record* and the *Sun* were both prosecuted for contempt over stories about a case involving a man called John Cronin. He was charged with making nuisance phone calls to women and, during his trial, the papers both carried stories about the fact that he had previously been jailed for six years for a sex attack. Normally any mention of previous convictions would be an obvious contempt but, in this case, the previous conviction had been so widely publicised at the time that most readers would already be aware of his background. The papers' lawyers advised that in those circumstances, it was safe to print the information, basing their decision on the recent decision in the English case of ***A-G* v *MGN*** (1997), where it was held that there was no contempt in publishing information about the violent background of a defendant, because that background had already been widely publicised during an earlier libel case brought by his girlfriend, the actress Gillian Taylforth (see p. 72). However, the Scottish courts took a different view and, after admitting contempt, the papers were each fined £5,000, and the editors £500.

The Public Information Officer of the Scottish Judiciary has produced a very useful guide for journalists reporting the Scottish courts, which details who should be approached for information at each stage of a case, what information they can provide, and contact details. It is available at the Society of Editors website (see *Online resources* at the end of this chapter).

Law in practice Are contempt laws really enforced?

By this point in the chapter, trainee and student journalists may well be struggling to reconcile the rules laid down here with what they read, see and hear in the news every day. Over the past decade it has become increasingly common for the press to report high-profile criminal cases, and the investigations that lead up to them, in ways that would seem very clearly to flout the contempt laws, by offering a mass of prejudicial detail about the suspect/defendant's past and the circumstances of the crime, and/or very heavily implying that they are guilty. Yet it has been rare for prosecutions to be brought. There have also been suggestions that, now that the internet makes it so easy for potential jurors to find out about, for example, previous convictions, the contempt laws are becoming almost irrelevant.

However, the approach may be changing. The previous Attorney-General, Dominic Grieve, made it clear that he expected the contempt laws to be obeyed, and in his first two years as Attorney-General, he brought more contempt cases than his predecessors did over a decade. In a speech to the City University School of Journalism, he said he had become concerned at the tendency of the media to 'test the boundaries' of contempt law, and that at times he felt they had 'lost any sense of internal constraint' and felt entitled to print whatever they liked about criminal cases.

He stressed that proceedings are 'active' from the time of arrest, so the press should be cautious about what they report on cases involving an arrested suspect. At the pre-charge stage, he suggested, there was much to be said for the approach that the media used to take, of simply reporting that 'a man is helping police with their inquiries'. This avoided publication of unnecessary detail which could seriously damage the reputation of someone who later turned out to be innocent (as happened in the Chris Jefferies case, discussed on p. 75). He also emphasised that online publication was subject to the laws of contempt just like any other form of publication.

Dominic Grieve has now been replaced as Attorney-General by Jeremy Wright, who at the time of going to press had not given any indication of his views on the subject.

OTHER TYPES OF CONTEMPT

So far, we have looked at the issue of publications which are in contempt because they may prejudice the outcome of a particular court case. But these are not the only way that a journalist or publisher can commit contempt of court. Other ways include:

- contempt in the face of the court;
- scandalising a judge;
- using a tape recorder or taking photographs in court;
- failing to comply with a court order;
- frustrating court orders addressed to others;
- using documents disclosed during proceedings;
- investigating or publishing jury deliberations;
- identifying jurors;
- interfering with witnesses;
- reporting hearings heard in private;
- breaking embargoes on court judgments.

Contempt in the face of the court

This covers the kind of behaviour so beloved of courtroom dramas: loud demonstrations, insulting the judge to their face, and generally anything done in the courtroom which undermines the authority of the court. A journalist will only be liable in this way if they themselves behave in a way that amounts to contempt; it is not contempt to report that someone else has done so (unless, for example, what is said in the report amounts to contempt in some other way, such as by prejudicing the trial).

Scandalising a judge

This is committed by making a statement (written or spoken) which is designed to bring the court or a judge into public contempt, or lower their authority. Examples would include accusing a judge of being biased, taking bribes, or falling asleep in court, and the criticism need not refer to particular proceedings. Until very recently, it was considered that the offence had fallen into disuse, as there had not been a prosecution for decades, and it was thought likely that to prosecute someone for criticising a judge would now be considered a breach of the right to freedom of expression. However, in 2012, the MP Peter Hain was charged with contempt by 'scandalising a judge' after he criticised a High Court judge in a book. The case was later dropped, after Mr Hain wrote a letter to the judge, clarifying the comments he had made in the book. The Law Commission is now considering whether the offence should formally be abolished.

Tape recording and photographs

Section 9 of the Contempt of Court Act 1981 provides that it is contempt to use, or even take into court, a tape recorder. However, under Part 1.2 of the Consolidated Criminal

Practice Direction, a criminal court can give permission for use of a tape recorder for note-taking purposes, including to journalists. In deciding whether to give permission, the court should consider whether the person requesting it has 'any reasonable need', and whether use of a tape recorder would distract or worry witnesses, or disturb the proceedings. There is also a possibility that permission may be granted for making sound recordings for broadcast (see p. 108).

Section 25 of the Criminal Justice Act 1925 makes it contempt to take any photograph, make or attempt to make any portrait or sketch of a judge or witness in, or a party to, any proceedings before the court, either in the courtroom or its precinct. (In Northern Ireland a similar rule applies under the Criminal Justice (Northern Ireland) Act 1945.) It is, however, permissible for an artist to sit in on a trial and make notes, from which they produce sketches afterwards, away from the court. This is how the drawings which often accompany reports of a high-profile trial are produced.

The ban on filming court proceedings was lifted in October 2013, and cameras are now able to broadcast from the Court of Appeal. The Government has said it will now consider allowing certain elements of Crown Court trials to be broadcast.

Law in practice **Filming outside the court**

It is accepted practice for broadcasters to show the arrival and departure each day of key players in a high-profile trial, but it is important to take care to not to show anything here that could cause a serious risk of prejudice. In trials involving suspected terrorists, for example, heavy security precautions may be visible outside the court, and showing these could potentially be viewed as indications that the accused are dangerous, which clearly has the potential to prejudice the jury. You should also edit out accusations made by angry onlookers, or anything said or done by the accused outside the court, which could prejudice the jurors for or against them.

Failing to comply with a court order

If a court makes an order, disobeying that order will be contempt. An example would be if a court granted an injunction preventing a paper from publishing a particular story, and the paper went ahead and printed anyway.

In ***Attorney-General* v *The Spectator*** (2012), the publisher of the *Spectator* magazine was fined £3,000 and ordered to pay £2,000 to the parents of the murdered teenager Stephen Lawrence, after publishing an article which jeopardised the trial of his killers. The defendants in the case had been charged with the murder years before and acquitted, and in the intervening years, much had been written about their criminal connections and convictions. For the second trial, the court put in place an order banning publication of that material, but it was used in the *Spectator* article, along with descriptions of the defendants as 'white trash' and 'racists'. The writer, Rod Liddle, acknowledged in the piece that they risked a contempt charge but suggested that there was no way to find a jury that was not already prejudiced against the defendants because so much had been written about them over the years since the murder. The article was published in the middle of the trial, and there was a serious risk of the trial collapsing, though in the event the judge was able to establish that none of the jurors had read the piece, and the trial went ahead. The court warned that if the trial had ended as a result of the piece, the consequences would have been more serious.

It is possible to disobey a court order unintentionally, but even here, the courts may be severe.

In 1997, the *Daily Mail* and its columnist Nigel Dempster were fined £25,000 and £10,000 respectively for non-intentional breach of an injunction not to repeat an allegation that the claimant in a libel trial against them was mean. The judge said that if he had thought the disobedience was deliberate, he would have sentenced Dempster to prison.

A publisher can only be liable for this form of contempt if there has been a court order; the fact that a judge has requested the media not to behave in a particular way, or publish certain material, is not enough to create liability if the request is not complied with. There must also be proof that the publisher was given notice of the order. (If it is an order not to publish something and is delivered in court, the fact that someone from the publisher was in court at the time will be sufficient notice.)

Frustrating court orders addressed to others

It is not only court orders directed specifically against them that can cause problems for publishers. It can also be contempt to breach a court order directed against another publication.

In 1987, a former MI5 officer, Peter Wright, published *Spycatcher*, his memoirs of his time in the Secret Service. The book was banned in the UK, but was published in America. The *Guardian* and *Observer* sought to publish extracts from the book, but were prevented from doing so when the Attorney-General successfully sought an injunction against them. A little later, four other papers printed details from the book, and were then taken to court. None of them had been named in the injunction, and the House of Lords agreed that they could not be said to have disobeyed the court order as it was not addressed to them. However, by publishing the details, they had effectively destroyed the purpose of the injunction, which was to keep the book's contents secret; once they were made public, there was no point in the injunction. The House of Lords held that this was contempt.

Using documents disclosed during proceedings

Care needs to be taken if you get hold of documents from one party to a case which belong to the other party and have been disclosed as part of the court proceedings (disclosure here refers to the pre-trial exchange of information between the two parties, not necessarily disclosure in court). Publishing the information in such a document is a breach of the Civil Procedure Rules, and could easily lead to a contempt charge. The exception is if the document was read to or by the court, or referred to at a public hearing.

Investigating or publishing jury deliberations

In some countries (notably the USA), it is very common for jurors to be interviewed by the media after a trial about why they reached the decision they did. In this country, however, the law states that jury deliberations should be secret, and jurors are not allowed to tell anyone at all what was said in the jury room.

For this reason, s8 of the Contempt of Court Act 1981 states that it is contempt of court to obtain, disclose or solicit any particulars of statements made, opinions expressed, arguments advanced or votes cast by members of a jury in the course of their deliberations in any legal proceedings.

Contempt proceedings under s8 can only be brought by the Attorney-General. Note that it is not only publishing details of jury deliberations that will get you into trouble: it is also an offence to 'solicit' such information, so even just asking a juror questions about how the verdict was reached can be contempt.

Section 8 only applies to jury deliberations, in other words the process of reaching a verdict. It is not contempt under s8 to ask for, or publish, a juror's view of, for example, whether the prosecution should have been brought in the first place, how the trial was conducted, or whether the eventual sentence was appropriate, as long as no questions are asked and no information published about anything said or done during the jury's deliberation on the verdict, or what led it to reach that verdict.

In *A-G* v ***Associated Newspapers*** (1994), the *Mail on Sunday* published an article about the 'Blue Arrow' trial, a long-running, high-profile fraud case. The piece contained quotes from several jurors, detailing what they thought of the evidence in the trial, and mentioning that one juror had only agreed on a verdict because he wanted to get home. The paper was prosecuted for contempt, but argued that it could not be said to be disclosing the jurors' deliberations, because they had already been disclosed to an American researcher, and it was the research that the paper had published. The House of Lords rejected this view, saying that publication itself could amount to disclosure, and in this case it did. Publication could only be distinguished from disclosure where it was merely repetition of known facts.

In *A-G* v ***Seckerson and Times Newspapers Ltd*** (2009), *The Times* was fined £15,000 for publishing articles reporting that two jurors in a manslaughter case were questioning the verdict, and explaining the role that medical evidence had played in the jury's decision. The stories did not name individual jurors, nor disclose the opinions of any individual juror. The paper argued that they were written in good faith, to create debate on a matter of public interest, namely the heavy reliance placed on expert medical evidence in cases of the kind mentioned, which involved a baby said to have been shaken to death. There has been controversy over whether incorrect diagnoses may have been made in some of these cases. The court acknowledged these as mitigating factors, but said that it nevertheless had to impose penalties severe enough to mark the seriousness of breaching s8, and to deter others from breaching the Act. The jury member who spoke to *The Times*, Mr Seckerson, was also convicted and fined £500.

Identifying jurors

Although not specifically prohibited by the Contempt of Court Act, identifying an individual juror during the trial could potentially be a contempt, if it made the juror fear harm from the defendant or their associates. However, in cases where a juror is discharged from a case because of some misdemeanour, such as being late, or researching the case on the internet, and is named in court, it will be safe to report that, as the juror will no longer be involved in the case.

Interfering with witnesses

In high-profile cases, the media will sometimes pay a key witness for the exclusive rights to their story (to be published after the trial). Theoretically, this could prejudice the trial, since the witness might be tempted to embellish the story to make it more saleable, or to stick to it even if cross-examination suggested it was wrong. This is even more likely if the amount payable is dependent on the result of the case. In his speech to the 2003 Law for Journalists conference, the then Attorney-General said that he regarded this as 'a serious matter', pointing out that it can undermine the credibility of witnesses, and could lead to the acquittal of the guilty, as well as the conviction of the innocent. However, no contempt action has so far been brought for paying a witness, and in the discussion paper published when the then

Government considered making paying witnesses a specific offence in 2002, it concluded that the current law on contempt probably did not cover witness payments. A new offence was not introduced, however, and it appears that the only current rules against paying a witness are in the Editors' Code of Practice used by IPSO and the Ofcom Broadcasting Code (see the box below).

Where a newspaper has paid a witness for their story, it may insist that the witness does not speak to other publications, or even hide the witness away so that other publications cannot get to them. According to the media law experts, Geoffrey Robertson QC and Andrew Nicol QC, this is not in itself contempt, but a contempt charge could result if the witness's evidence is tampered with, or the witness is concealed from the police or prosecuting authorities.

What the codes say **Paying witnesses**

The Editors' Code of Practice used by Independent Press Standards Organisation (IPSO) states that once proceedings become active, payment should not be offered to anyone who might reasonably be expected to be called as a witness. This ban lasts until any one of the following happens:

- the suspect is freed unconditionally or proceedings are otherwise discontinued;
- the defendant pleads guilty; or
- the court gives its verdict.

Where proceedings are not yet active, but are likely and foreseeable, payment to potential witnesses should not be offered, unless it can be shown the publication of the information concerned is in the public interest, and there is an overriding need to make or promise payment in order to get access to the information. In that case, all reasonable steps should be taken to make sure the payment does not affect the outcome of the trial; it is never permissible to make payment conditional on the outcome of the trial (e.g. by promising a witness more money if the defendant is convicted).

Any person who has been paid for their story should be warned that they must disclose this to the defence and the prosecution if they are called as a witness.

The Ofcom Code says that where criminal proceedings are likely and foreseeable, payments should not be made to people who might reasonably be expected to be witnesses, unless there is a clear public interest, such as investigating crime or serious wrongdoing, and the payment is necessary to elicit the information. Any payments should be disclosed to the defence and prosecution if the person later becomes a trial witness. Once criminal proceedings are active, payment should not be made or promised to anyone who may reasonably be expected to be called as a witness, and no payment should be made dependent on the outcome of the trial.

Reporting hearings heard in private

Section 12 of the Administration of Justice Act 1960 provides that it is not automatically a contempt to publish details of a hearing heard in private. However, the Act provides that it is contempt to report 'information relating to the proceedings' of a hearing in private where that hearing concerns any of the following:

- the Children Act 1989;
- wardship of court;

- other matters relating to the maintenance or upbringing of children;
- mental health proceedings (such as a patient applying to a mental health tribunal for discharge from a secure mental hospital);
- national security;
- a secret process, discovery or invention which forms part of the issues in the case.

As with any other hearing, it is also contempt to report information disclosed in a private hearing where the court has made an order prohibiting or postponing such disclosure.

Although it is contempt to publish anything said during a private hearing which falls into one of the above categories, it is not contempt to publish the fact that the hearing was held, when and where, or the fact that it was held in private. It is also permissible to report the verdict, any order made, any comments from the parties or details from documents they hold, so long as the court does not make an order prohibiting such disclosures (and of course anything written about a hearing in private is subject to the normal rules on contempt if it creates a risk of prejudice).

In *Pickering* v *Liverpool Daily Post* (1991), a man who had been detained in a secure mental hospital after being convicted of sexual attacks was applying to a mental health tribunal for discharge from the hospital. He wanted to stop the press from reporting his application, but the House of Lords said that the media were free to report that a named person had applied to a tribunal, and the result, because that was not 'information related to the proceedings'. It was not, however, permissible to report the reasons the tribunal gave for its decision because doing so would reveal the evidence given in the hearing.

Where a private hearing does not fall within any of the categories listed above, and no reporting restrictions are imposed, reporting the hearing will not in itself be contempt, provided the usual rules on contempt are followed.

Breaking embargoes on court judgments

Judgments from the higher courts are routinely supplied to lawyers and their clients before they are officially handed down, subject to an embargo. Publication of the result or any details before the judgment is officially handed down will be contempt.

In 2006, the magazine *The Lawyer* broke a court embargo by publishing details of the judgment in *Baigent* v *Random House* (2006), the case involving the book *The Da Vinci Code* (see p. 362), on its website, 90 minutes before the judgment was handed down. The judge in the case accepted that the magazine had not known of the embargo rules on judgments, and, in view of the fact that it agreed to print a front-page apology, there was no prosecution for contempt. However, the magazine was ordered to pay costs, and the judge warned that, in future, any other publications which breached a court embargo could face 'severe consequences'.

SANCTIONS FOR CONTEMPT

As explained at the beginning of this chapter, being found in contempt of court can have serious implications for the media. The court may order a fine and, as some of the cases in this chapter show, these can amount to thousands of pounds. In serious cases, an editor can even be sent to prison for contempt.

In addition, regulations made under s93 of the Courts Act 2003 give magistrates' courts, the Crown Court and the Court of Appeal power to order that where a trial is delayed or stopped as a result of 'serious misconduct' by a third party (meaning someone other than the people involved in the case), the third party can be ordered to pay costs. Serious misconduct is not defined in the legislation, but in a press release issued when the change was announced, one of the examples given was of prejudicial reporting of a criminal case, and it seems clear that the provisions could well be applied to the media. When you consider that a case which collapses due to prejudicial reporting can waste a million pounds or more of public money, this is a formidable threat, though when the regulations were introduced, the Lord Chief Justice said they would need to be used 'with discretion'. A further concern is that, unlike a prosecution of contempt, a costs order does not require the consent of the Attorney-General; the decision is made by the magistrates or judge in the relevant case.

Preventing publication

Court actions for contempt are not limited to situations where the contempt has already taken place; where it is known that material about to be published may be in contempt, an injunction can be sought to prevent publication, or even research into a story (as in the ***HTV Cymru*** case below). However, as with all injunctions preventing initial publication, the standard of proof is very high. The applicant must prove beyond reasonable doubt that there is a real risk of prejudice, and that, without an injunction, the publishers will go ahead and publish the material.

In ***Ex parte HTV Cymru (Wales) Ltd, Crown Court at Cardiff*** (2002), the High Court agreed to an injunction against HTV, preventing it from interviewing witnesses in a murder trial for a documentary, even though the programme would not have been shown until after the end of the trial. The judge held that being interviewed for the programme might change the witnesses' views on the evidence they had given, and given that at least one of them was likely to be recalled before the end of the trial, there was a serious risk of substantial prejudice. The injunction was only to last until all the witnesses had given their evidence.

In 2005, Channel 5 defeated an attempt to prevent broadcast of a programme just two hours before it was due on air. The programme covered the activities of the Noonan brothers, described as well-known underworld figures in Manchester. Two days before it was due to be shown, one of the brothers, Desmond, was fatally stabbed. The killing was widely covered by the press that weekend, and the stories included details of Desmond's criminal activities. On the day the programme was due to go out, the police applied for an injunction to prevent it, arguing that it would seriously hinder the investigation into Desmond's murder, and stop people coming forward as witnesses because they would be intimidated by the picture given of the Noonans as powerful underworld figures. Channel 5 argued that much of the information had already been reported, and the Noonans were already known to the public, but the injunction was granted. With just two hours to spare, Channel 5 secured a late sitting with the Court of Appeal, which lifted the injunction. It said that there had to be clear and significant evidence of substantial prejudice to the police investigation, and this had not been identified.

Applications for injunctions can be made by the Attorney-General, or if the alleged contempt is intentional contempt under common law, by the person affected by the contemptuous statement, without the consent of the Attorney-General. It is not clear whether persons affected can apply for an injunction in cases where the allegation is one of strict liability contempt under the Contempt of Court Act (this was considered in a 1991 House of Lords case, but no rule was stated).

Law in practice Common problems with contempt

Defences for contempt and defamation: Many media law students get confused about two apparently similar defences, which apply to contempt of court and defamation.

- Fair, accurate and contemporary reporting is a defence to strict liability contempt of court. It applies where the material published is a fair, accurate report of court proceedings held in public, published in good faith and contemporaneously (i.e. at the time of the trial).
- Privilege is a defence to defamation, which allows the media to report statements which would otherwise be defamatory, where they are made in court and reported fairly, accurately and (for absolute privilege) contemporaneously (for more about this defence, see p. 257).

Both these defences spring from the same principle, that there should be open reporting of court cases, but in legal terms, they do different jobs and are not actually related to each other. Fair, accurate and contemporary reporting is a defence that is specific to a prosecution for contempt, and should not be referred to, as it often is by media law students, as 'privilege for contempt'. Similarly, if you are talking about a defamation case involving reports of court proceedings, the name of the defence is 'Absolute privilege' or 'Qualified privilege' (depending on circumstances), and not 'Fair, accurate and contemporary reporting'.

Contempt and libel: When reporting anything to do with criminal investigations and court cases, it is easy to focus on contempt of court provisions and forget about libel. It is important always to remember that they are two separate actions, and you can be as careful as possible about one and yet still leave yourself open to the other. For example, take the situation where you write that someone is being investigated for fraud. If the proceedings are not active, you will not be in danger of strict liability contempt, and if you can show that you did not intend to prejudice the trial, you will not be guilty of intentional contempt either. None of this, however, prevents you from being sued for libel if your words can be shown to have a defamatory meaning.

Gagging orders: As stated earlier in this chapter, there is a widespread belief that any case which is sub judice cannot be reported. This myth is sometimes used to try to stifle criticism, by issuing a writ for libel against one publication, and then threatening the others with contempt if they write about the matters that are the subject of the libel case. This is known as a 'gagging order'.

Such threats can sound very plausible, but in ***Thomson v Times Newspapers*** (1969), Lord Salmon stated that: 'There is no authority that I know of to support the view that further comment would amount to contempt of court.' As long as what is written about a libel case does not pose a substantial risk of seriously prejudicing that case (and it is unlikely to now that juries are rarely used), nor suggest that the publisher intended to prejudice it, there should be no risk of contempt (though clearly there may be a risk of libel if the defamatory allegations are repeated).

Police information: Prejudicing a trial can, in extreme cases, lead to the cost and hassle of a retrial, and even to suspects being allowed to evade justice. For that reason, it is tempting to assume that information provided on the record by the police must be safe to use, since they are unlikely to want this to happen, and, you might assume, they know the rules. This is not a safe assumption, however, and there have been prosecutions for contempt based on publication of information supplied by the police. Regardless of where information comes from, it should only be used within the rules of contempt.

KEY POINTS

Publications prejudicial to a fair trial

There are two different contempt offences which can be committed by publishing prejudicial material; both can be punished with a fine or imprisonment.

Strict liability contempt

This is committed by publishing any material which

- concerns 'active' proceedings, and
- 'creates a substantial risk that the course of justice in the proceedings in question will be seriously impeded or prejudiced'.

Whether there is 'substantial risk of serious prejudice' depends on:

- who the case is tried by;
- how close to the hearing the report was published;
- where the trial is being held;
- the circulation of the publication;
- the content of the report.

There are three defences:

- innocent publication;
- fair and accurate contemporary reports;
- discussion of public affairs.

Intentional contempt

This is committed by publishing material with the intention of prejudicing or interfering with proceedings which are 'imminent or pending'.

Intention covers both:

- material deliberately published with the purpose of interfering with legal proceedings; and
- material published when the publisher knew proceedings were imminent or pending and knew the nature of the material it was publishing.

Contempt in Scotland

The Scottish courts take a stricter view of contempt than the English ones, and more care must be taken. Key issues are:

- when proceedings become active;
- use of pictures;
- hearings in chambers;
- initial reports;
- background information.

Other types of contempt

Journalists can also be found guilty of contempt if they:

- cause a disturbance in court;
- use a tape recorder or take photographs in court;

- fail to comply with a court order;
- frustrate court orders addressed to others;
- use documents disclosed during proceedings;
- investigate or publish details of jury deliberations;
- interfere with witnesses;
- report hearings heard in private.

TEST YOUR KNOWLEDGE

1 When do proceedings become active, and cease to be active, under the Contempt of Court Act 1981?

2 Which of the following statements could leave you open to a charge of contempt?

(a) Jack Smith was arrested yesterday for the murder of Jane Jones.

(b) After a month-long search for the killer of Jane Jones, the man sought by police was arrested yesterday.

(c) After a month-long search, police yesterday arrested a man for the murder of Jane Jones.

(d) A man who spent five years in prison for assault was arrested yesterday in connection with the murder of Jane Jones.

(e) Jack Smith, a convicted rapist, was yesterday arrested for the murder of Jane Jones.

(f) After a nationwide manhunt, police said yesterday that they had arrested the killer of Jane Jones.

3 Police find the body of a young woman at her boyfriend's home. Her boyfriend has disappeared. The police hold a press conference at which they reveal that the boyfriend has previous convictions for violence against women. They describe the boyfriend as 'a very dangerous man' and ask for anyone who knows where he is to come forward. The local TV channels that evening name the boyfriend, and report what was said at the press conference. The following day, the boyfriend is found and arrested. Four days later, the local weekly paper reports the arrest, stating that the suspect was described as 'very dangerous' by the police, and mentioning the previous convictions that the police listed at the press conference. Do the TV stations run the risk of being found in contempt? Does the newspaper?

4 In what circumstances can it be contempt to publish a photograph of someone suspected of a crime?

5 You have been researching a feature about women who steal other people's babies. You have spoken to a number of experts, and the feature puts forward the idea that, rather than punishing such women, society should be sympathetic to them, because they are usually suffering from some kind of trauma or mental problem. A few days before the piece is due to be published, a baby is snatched from the local maternity unit; it is found within 24 hours, and the woman who took it is arrested. Can you safely publish your feature? Would your answer differ (and if so, why) if:

(a) the woman was already on trial;

(b) your feature focused on the trauma that baby snatching causes the victims, rather than being sympathetic to those who take babies.

6 Can you be found in contempt of court for writing about someone suspected of a crime, before the proceedings become active?

7 A fraud trial has just ended at your local Crown Court. It has been going on for almost six months, and there was a huge amount of very convincing evidence against the defendants. However, the jury found them not guilty, by a majority of 10–2. Afterwards, you interview one of the fraudster's victims, who says the whole case has been a miscarriage of justice, and the defendants were clearly guilty. She is willing to give you an on-the-record interview about how the fraud has wrecked her life. Back at the office, you get a call from one of the jurors. He says that ten of his fellow jury members admitted in the jury room that they were scared of the fraudsters, and were not willing to take the risk of finding them guilty. He is willing to give you a full interview so long as you do not name him in print. Can you safely use either or both of these stories?

8 A woman convicted of assault appeals against her sentence. The court quashes her conviction, and orders a retrial. When do the retrial proceedings become active?

9 Information about legal proceedings can come from many different sources. Which of these is it always safe to quote, as far as contempt is concerned?

(a) details given in police press conferences;

(b) off-the-record comment from police sources;

(c) information from the victim;

(d) comments from the lawyers in the case;

(e) anything the defendant says.

10 What does it mean to say that particular legal proceedings are sub judice?

ONLINE RESOURCES

Guidance notes issued by the Attorney-General can be read at:
https://www.gov.uk/government/organisations/attorney-generals-office

The Crown Prosecution Service website has information on prosecuting contempt of court, at:
www.cps.gov.uk

The Scottish Judiciary Public Information Office's Guide for Journalists can be found at:
http://www.societyofeditors.co.uk/userfiles/file/Guide%20for%20Journalists%20Sept08.pdf

Access to the courts

As explained in the introduction to this section, as a general rule, the English courts are open to the public, and that means to the media as well. There are circumstances in which both the public and the media can be excluded from a court hearing, but this can only be done where the law specifically allows it; a judge cannot simply decide to hear a case in private, nor can either of the parties simply demand this.

There are, however, situations where a judge or magistrates may try to exclude the press even though they do not have a lawful justification to do so, and in such cases journalists can often get the decision changed if you can show that the law does not allow it. To be able to recognise those situations, and know what action to take, you need to have a firm grasp of the law in this area.

THE GENERAL RULE ON ACCESS

Support for the general principle that courts should be open to the public and the media can be found in case law, in statute, and in the rules and guidelines to which the court system works, all of which can be helpful if you have to challenge exclusion from a court.

Case law: The basic rules about media access to the courts were summed up by the House of Lords in ***A-G* v *Leveller Magazine*** (1979). There, Lord Diplock said that it was a fundamental principle of justice that proceedings should be held in open court, and that nothing should be done to discourage publication of a fair and accurate report of those proceedings. The courts should only depart from this principle where not doing so would 'frustrate or render impracticable the administration of justice'. Other cases, such as ***Scott* v *Scott*** (1913), have specifically stated that preventing embarrassment to the parties in the case is not by itself a lawful reason for excluding the press from a court.

The Court of Appeal has recently reiterated that court hearings should be held in public unless a private hearing is strictly necessary in the interests of justice, and that potential damage to the reputations of the parties is not a valid reason to hold a hearing in private. In ***Global Torch Ltd* v *Apex Global Management and Others, with Guardian News and Media and The Financial Times Ltd as interested parties*** (2013), two companies who were fighting a commercial case between themselves tried to have the hearings held in private, and secure a ban on the media seeing court documents. They claimed that this was necessary to uphold their right to reputation under Article 8 of the European Convention on Human Rights. However, the Court of Appeal said this right did not outweigh the fundamental principle of open justice.

Statute: The Human Rights Act 1998, which brings into English law Article 6 of the European Convention on Human Rights, details the right to a fair hearing before the courts, and confirms that a fair hearing should be one held in public. It also lays down certain circumstances in which the media can be excluded from all or part of a trial. These are:

- in the interest of morals, public order, or national security;
- where required in order to protect the interests of juveniles;
- where required in order to protect the private life of the parties;
- where publicity would prejudice the interests of justice.

This does not, however, mean that a court can restrict press access merely because, for example, a case contains details about the parties' private lives. Where one of these factors is present, the court can consider whether it would be appropriate to exclude the press, but it still has to balance the relevant factor against the right to freedom of expression contained in Article 10 of the Convention. So if, for example, it is suggested that allowing press access to a hearing would harm national security, the court must consider whether it is more important to prevent that harm, or to uphold the principle of freedom of expression, which requires that the media should be able to report court proceedings. As usual when considering two competing human rights issues, the court must also respect the principle of proportionality (see p. 55), so if it can avoid the problem by, for example, imposing reporting restrictions rather than preventing access to the court, it may be possible to argue that course instead.

Court rules and guidelines: The Civil Procedure Rules reiterate the principle that hearings should usually be in open court, as do guidelines issued by the Judicial College to magistrates' courts and the Crown Court. These guidelines can be useful ammunition if you need to challenge a ruling on court access (see p. 101 for a summary of them).

The Criminal Procedure Rules 2013 now state courts must not make orders restricting access to court proceedings, or imposing restrictions on reporting them, unless any person 'directly affected' (which includes the press) is present or has had the opportunity to attend or make representations. This effectively means that courts must notify the press in advance of applications to restrict reporting, and where that is not possible, allow them to make representations as soon as possible afterwards.

Types of hearing

In terms of access, there are three types of hearing:

- in open court;
- in private;
- in chambers.

In open court means that the hearing is in a courtroom, and both the public and the press are admitted. However, the fact that a hearing is in open court does not necessarily mean you can report everything said or done there, and in some circumstances reporting restrictions will apply, either automatically or by order of the court. (These restrictions are examined in later chapters of this section.)

In private means that the hearing is closed to the press and public. Often, there will be reporting restrictions on private hearings, but where reporting restrictions do not apply, proceedings held in private can be reported, assuming someone present is willing to tell the press what happened, but note that a report based on such information is not considered to be a report of court proceedings for the purposes of the privilege defence in defamation (see p. 257). The Administration of Justice Act 1960 makes it a contempt of court to publish details of certain types of hearing held in private (see p. 173).

In some cases, a judge may not specifically state that a hearing is to be held in private, but may take deliberate steps that effectively ensure the press is excluded. In ***R (on the application of Pelling)* v *Bow County Court*** (2001), it was held that such measures could amount to holding a hearing in private, and if there is no legal right for that hearing to be held in private, the exclusion of the press (and public) will be unlawful. In the ***Bow County Court*** case, the court said the test was whether the arrangements, taken as a whole, inhibit public access to such an extent that the hearing is in reality a private one.

In ***McPherson* v *McPherson*** (1936), the case was the divorce hearing of a Government minister. He was keen to avoid publicity, and so the judge held a hearing at lunchtime, in his library, which was accessed by a door marked 'Private'. Although the door was left ajar, and the judge stated before proceedings started that the hearing was open, the Privy Council stated that the openness was a sham and in reality the hearing was held in private. At the time there was no lawful reason for such hearings to be private, and so the order made at the end of the proceedings was invalid.

In ***Storer* v *British Gas*** (2000), an employment tribunal which held a hearing in a room whose door could only be opened with a key code was held to have sat in private.

In chambers usually refers to a hearing held behind closed doors, usually in a room which is not open to the public in the way that an ordinary courtroom usually is, such as an office (though unfortunately 'in chambers' is also sometimes used, incorrectly, to refer to a secret hearing). Many types of hearing are conducted in chambers, usually for reasons of convenience rather than secrecy; bail hearings are a common example, while in civil cases, hearings in chambers are often held to discuss technical issues relating to trial procedure. Unless the hearing is of a type where there is a legal power to exclude the press and public, media representatives should be allowed to attend.

In most cases, hearings in chambers are of no interest to the press, but there are some types of cases heard this way which the media may want to report. However, this can obviously create problems if the hearing is being held in a small office, and this issue was addressed in ***Hodgson* v *Imperial Tobacco*** (1998). In that case, Lord Woolf stated that judges should usually make arrangements to ensure that holding a hearing in chambers did not materially interfere with the right of the public, including the media, to know and observe what happens in legal proceedings. If the media want to report a particular hearing in chambers, but there are practical problems (e.g. lack of space), Lord Woolf advised that judges should use their discretion to make this possible, for example by allowing one representative of the press to attend, or giving judgment and an account of the proceedings in open court.

Even where reporters are not allowed to sit in on a hearing in chambers, the fact that the case was held in chambers does not in itself mean they cannot report what was said, if one of the parties wishes to tell them about it. Whether the hearing can be reported will depend on whether there is a specific legal provision which prevents reports; this was confirmed in ***Malik* v *Central Criminal Court*** (2006) (see p. 100).

If you are not sure whether reporters are allowed into a hearing, ask for an enquiry to be sent to the judge.

RESTRICTIONS ON COURT ACCESS

There are three main types of power that the courts can use to exclude the press: common law powers; powers derived from statute; and powers detailed in court rules (which are delegated legislation). The common law powers apply in all courts, but the statutory powers and court rules are specific to particular areas of the court system. The Human Rights Act 1998 also provides for certain circumstances in which the press and/or public can be excluded from court proceedings. Where a lower court was legally entitled to hear a case in private, the Domestic and Appellate Proceedings (Restriction of Publicity) Act 1968 provides that a court hearing an appeal from such a case can also sit in private.

In a few cases, the courts are required to exclude the public from a hearing, but in the majority of cases, the powers are discretionary. This means that, if the required circumstances apply, the court can choose to sit in private, or can choose not to; the existence of powers to exclude does not mean that a court should always do so.

In *Malik* v *Central Criminal Court* (2006), the Divisional Court considered the Criminal Procedure Rules which allow that bail applications 'may' be dealt with by a judge in chambers. The defendant wanted his application heard in public, but the Crown Prosecution Service (CPS) had argued that it was 'normal practice' for bail applications to be held in chambers, and there was nothing about this case that meant normal practice should not be followed. The court held that 'may' meant only that bail hearings could be dealt with in chambers where it was necessary to do so; it did not mean that there was a presumption that bail hearings should be held in private. While it was fine to hold hearings in private, if there was an application to hold one in public, it should be accepted, unless there was a sound reason for excluding the public. The court stated that such applications could legitimately come from the media, as well as parties to the case.

In 2008, a reporter from the *Warrington Guardian* successfully challenged her exclusion from a bail hearing at Warrington Crown Court. After court staff denied her access to the hearing, and then refused to tell her what had been decided, she took a letter to the judge, arguing that bail applications should be held in public unless there is a real reason not to do so. She was given the results of the hearing a few hours later.

General powers to restrict access

All courts have a general common law power to control their own proceedings (often referred to as an 'inherent jurisdiction'), and this power can be used to exclude the public and/or press from a trial where it would be impossible or impracticable for justice to be done if the trial (or part of it) were held in open court. An example might be where evidence concerned a secret commercial process (such as the formula for a food or drink), and giving the evidence in public would reveal that secret and therefore make the proceedings pointless.

In practice, magistrates and judges these days are more likely to use the statutory powers which are specific to their courts (and described further on in this chapter). The inherent jurisdiction still exists, but in A-G v *Leveller Magazine* (1979), the House of Lords stressed that this power should only be used in exceptional circumstances, where it is clear that justice would be frustrated if the hearing was in public. Similarly in ***R* v *Malvern Justices, ex p Evans; R* v *Evesham Justices, ex p McDonagh*** (1988), the Court of Appeal explained that exclusion was not justified merely to save parties, witnesses or others from embarrassment or to conceal facts which might, on more general grounds, be desirable to keep secret.

In *R* v *Reigate Justices ex p Argus Newspapers* (1983), the case concerned a criminal trial where the defendant had helped the police. His lawyer intended to mention this help as part of the pleas in mitigation **(see p. 26)**, but the defendant did not want it to be publicly known that he had helped the police, and persuaded the magistrates to exclude the press and public from the court while the pleas in mitigation were made. Their decision was strongly criticised by the Queen's Bench Divisional Court, because it was not necessary in order to do justice in the case.

In *McKillen* v *Misland* (2012), a property developer involved in a high-profile business dispute with co-investors in a hotel company sought to have part of the evidence heard in private, because it related to 'personal financial matters'. After hearing objections from a number of media organisations, Mr Justice Richards ruled that Mr McKillen's reasons for wanting a private hearing came 'nowhere near' overcoming the basic requirements of open justice. The judge reiterated that hearings could be held in private for reasons of necessity, but not for reasons of convenience.

In general, if the public are excluded from a hearing using these powers, the press can be too. However, in *R* v *Crook* (1991), the Court of Appeal stated that there might be cases where the press should be allowed to remain even though the public were excluded. They gave the example of a prosecution for offences related to pornography, where they said the public might have to be excluded while a pornographic film was shown to the jury, because laughing and giggling from the public gallery would make it harder for jurors to do their job. This would not require the removal of the press as well.

Access to the criminal courts

Both the magistrates' courts and the Crown Court come under the general rule that cases should be heard in public, but in both cases there are circumstances where a case can be held in private.

The 2014 Judicial College guidelines on media access to the criminal courts emphasise the importance of the basic principle that cases should be held in open court. The guidelines, which are a useful weapon if you ever need to challenge a refusal to allow you into a court hearing, state that:

- The only principle that justifies a criminal court sitting in private is that it is necessary to avoid frustrating or rendering impracticable the administration of justice.
- The test is one of 'necessity'; the fact that sitting in private would spare witnesses embarrassment does not meet this test. Circumstances where the test of necessity might be met include where the nature of the evidence is such that revealing it could threaten national security, or identify someone whose identity there are strong public interest reasons for protecting, such as an undercover police officer.
- The application to hear the case in private must be supported by relevant evidence.
- If the court can achieve the necessary aim by a less restrictive measure, such as ordering a reporting restriction, it should do that rather than exclude the press.
- Other possible alternative measures include referring to witnesses by a pseudonym (or an initial) and banning their identification in the press, or allowing sensitive parts of the evidence to be written down and not shown to the public or press. But these are still exceptional and strict tests should be applied before they are used.

- If the court does believe the situation justifies excluding the press, it should consider whether exclusion for only part of a case could achieve the necessary aim, and allow the press back into the court as soon as possible after exclusion becomes unnecessary.
- Where the court decides there is a need to remove the public because of disorder in the court, the media should usually be allowed to remain.

In 2008, a judge rejected attempts to have part of a blackmail trial held in secret, after representations were made by members of the media. The case involved a blackmail plot against a member of the Royal family, and the Crown Prosecution Service requested that parts of the trial were closed to press and public, even though reporting restrictions were in place, to avoid the risk of the victim being named on the internet by foreign reporters. Representatives of the media argued that a ban on access to the court was disproportionate to the risk, which could be handled by reporting restrictions under the Contempt of Court Act 1981, and other measures available to the court. The judge agreed, and ruled that the press should be allowed to cover parts of the trial from which the public were excluded, and that the CPS could select four journalists to stay in court for those parts of the trial.

Restrictions on access to the criminal courts

In addition to the common law powers of exclusion explained above, the situations in which criminal courts are permitted to exclude the public and/or the press from the court (subject to the guidelines detailed above) include the following.

Child witnesses in sex offences: Under s37 of the Youth Justice and Criminal Evidence Act 1999, the public can be sent out of court while evidence is given by witnesses under 18 in cases involving offences against decency and morality (which effectively means sex offences). However, bona fide representatives of newspapers, broadcasters and news agencies cannot be excluded under this provision. The law on this point is different, however, in Northern Ireland, where the Criminal Justice (Children) (Northern Ireland) Order 1988 allows a court to exclude anyone not concerned in the case, where a witness who is under 18 is giving evidence likely to be of an indecent or immoral nature.

Special measures directions: Section 25 of the Youth Justice and Criminal Evidence Act 1999 allows magistrates to make what is called a 'special measures' direction to exclude anyone from the court while a child or vulnerable witness gives evidence in a case concerning a sexual offence, or where there are grounds for believing that the witness has been, or could be, intimidated. This can include the press, but the s25(3) states that one nominated member of te press should be allowed to remain in court. The Act also bans the media from reporting, before the end of the trial, that a special measures direction has been made, unless the jury is told of it.

Defendants assisting the police: The Serious Organised Crime and Police Act 2005 provides that where a court is reviewing the sentence of someone who has helped the police, or who secured a reduced sentence by promising assistance but then reneged on the agreement, the court can exclude the public and media, where it is necessary to do so to protect any person, and is in the interests of justice.

Youth court proceedings: Section 47 of the Children and Young Persons Act 1933 states that the public is not entitled to attend youth court proceedings, except at the court's discretion. The press, however, may attend.

Cases under the Official Secrets Act: Section 8(4) of the Official Secrets Act 1920 and s11(4) of the Official Secrets Act 1989 provide that a court can order the public or a section of it to leave the court during any part of a hearing concerning an offence under the Act, if publication of the evidence to be given would be prejudicial to the safety of the country.

Evidence of sexual history: In cases of rape and other sexual offences, the defendant will sometimes want to introduce evidence of the victim's sexual history. They have to get the court's permission to do this, and s43 of the Youth Justice and Criminal Evidence Act requires that applications for such permission are held in private. However, the court must give its decision, and any reasons for it, in open court, though the jury will be excluded while this happens.

Closed material procedure: The Justice and Security Act 2013 allows courts dealing with civil claims to hear evidence in private, without even the claimant hearing it, if disclosing that evidence to the public and the claimant would damage national security. The provision was enacted to allow the Government to fight claims from alleged terrorists without having to reveal the evidence against them in open court.

Rules for excluding the press from criminal courts

The 2013 edition of the Criminal Procedure Rules, which sets out how the criminal courts should operate, lays down rules for excluding the public (including the press) from a trial, where the court has power to do so. If the prosecution or defence wish to hold all or part of a trial in public, they should apply to the court in writing, at least five working days from the start of the trial (though there is some discretion to hear later applications). The court officer should display a notice of the application, and give the media notice of it. The media must be allowed to make representations against it, and if the application is granted, the trial should be adjourned to allow time for an appeal under s159 of the Criminal Justice Act 1988 (see Chapter 14).

Law in practice Defendants in multiple trials

A common reason for excluding the press from the criminal courts is where the defendant is involved in multiple trials, and the court fears that reporting the current trial may prejudice later ones. Tony Jaffa, Head of Media at solicitors Foot Anstey, advises that in these cases, it can be worth challenging the exclusion on the basis that there are less restrictive ways to avoid that prejudice, for example by making a s4(2) order postponing reporting of the current trial until the others are over (see p. 114).

Obtaining information from the criminal courts

Crown Court lists may be accessed over the internet from CourtServe.net. Magistrates' courts lists are available from the court offices of the court concerned and are the subject of a 1989 Home Office circular that encourages justices' clerks to meet reasonable requests by the media for copies of court lists and the register of decisions in magistrates' courts. The circular states that court lists should be made available in court on the day of the hearings and, where provisional lists are prepared in advance, copies should be available on request. At a minimum the lists should contain each defendant's name, age, address and, where known, his or her profession and the alleged offence. The 2014 Judicial College guidelines state that courts will not breach the Data Protection Act 1998 by providing journalists with such information. It is also now standard practice that any reporting restriction is shown on the Crown Court list under the name of the relevant case.

Court of Appeal Criminal Division daily cause lists are available at **www.justice.gov.uk** and similarly indicate where reporting restrictions are or may be engaged.

In 2009, HM Courts Service issued the Protocol for Sharing Court Registers and Court Lists with Local Newspapers, which provides that, where possible, copies of magistrates' court registers and lists should be supplied by email, at no charge, and should contain details of any reporting restrictions when they are first made. If the material is not available by email, it can be collected, or the press can pay for it to be posted. The Protocol also encourages Crown Courts to put similar systems in place.

Section s6(5) of the Magistrates' Courts Act 1980 provides that, following committal proceedings – either on the same day or on the day after – the court should display a public notice detailing the name, address and age of the defendant, the offence with which they were charged, and whether they were discharged or committed for trial. If the person was committed, the notice should include the charges, and the court to which the defendant has been committed. Such notices are subject to s4 of the Sexual Offences (Amendment) Act 1976, and so must not identify complainants of sexual offences (see Chapter 9). The name and address of any person under 17 years old should not be included in the notice, unless the justices have stated that, but for this prohibition, such information would have been included, and the name needs to be mentioned in order to avoid injustice to the person aged under 17.

The Judicial Studies Board guidelines on reporting restrictions make it clear that the identity of magistrates presiding over particular proceedings should be made public, in accordance with the decision in ***R* v *Felixstowe Justices ex p Leigh*** (1987), ***R* v *Evesham Justices ex p McDonagh*** (1988), which stated that a court could not legally withhold the name of a sitting magistrate from the press.

The Criminal Procedure Rules state that certain information should be available to the public, including the press, where the court officer has the details and the case is either ongoing or finished no more than six months before, and no reporting restrictions prevent disclosure. The information covered is:

- the date of any public hearing, unless any party to the case has not yet been notified of it;
- the alleged offence(s) and the plea(s) entered;
- the court's decision at any public hearing, including decisions about bail or sending the case to another court;
- whether the case is to be appealed;
- the outcome of any trial or appeal;
- the identity and addresses of the prosecutor, the defendant, and the parties' lawyers;
- the name of the judge, magistrate(s) or justices' legal advisor who made a decision at a public hearing in the case;
- any reporting restrictions imposed by the court.

This information can be requested in person or by phone (the request need not be in writing), and no reason for wanting it has to be given. However, a fee may be charged.

If a case is older than six months, the same information should still be supplied, but the court can require the request to be in writing, and you would need to explain why the information is required. If you want other information, the court has the power to decide whether to provide it, and can do this with or without a hearing.

New rules issued by the Lord Chief Justice should make it easier for reporters to get access to court documents, including opening notes, written submissions and skeleton arguments. The new Criminal Practice Directions say that where journalists request such documents, the general principle is that they should be supplied, unless there is a good reason not to in order to protect the rights or legitimate interests of others, and the request does not put an undue burden on the court. However, the media should be aware of the limitations on use of such material, such as not publishing details of evidence discussed in the absence of the jury.

The judgements in criminal appeal cases are available online (see *Online resources*, at the end of this chapter).

Law in practice Court information and the Data Protection Act

It has been known for court staff to refuse to reveal information about defendants, such as their address or occupation, on the grounds that doing so would breach the Data Protection Act. The 2014 Judicial College guidelines make it clear that court lists should contain defendants' names, addresses, ages, occupations where known, and the alleged offence, and that giving this information to journalists is not a breach of the Data Protection Act.

Information from the prosecution

In 2005, the Director of Public Prosecutions (DPP) announced a new Protocol covering the type and amount of information which the media can generally expect to be provided by the prosecution in criminal cases. It states that the aim is to ensure greater openness in reporting legal proceedings, by making sure that the media has access to as much relevant material as possible, and 'at the earliest appropriate opportunity'. The Protocol divides information into two categories:

1. Information which the prosecution used when making their case in court. This category of information should automatically be released to the media and includes:
   - CCTV footage of the defendant (provided that copyright issues do not prevent its release);
   - photos or video footage of crime reconstructions;
   - maps, photos, diagrams or drawings used in court;
   - video footage of the crime scene, or seized property, stolen goods or weapons, recorded by the police;
   - transcripts of interviews and/or statements (or part of them) as read out in court.
2. Other material which may be released after consideration by the CPS, in consultation with the police, victims, witnesses and/or relatives. This includes:
   - statements made by victims and/or witnesses;
   - video and audio recordings of police interviews with defendants, witnesses and victims;
   - photos or CCTV footage of the defendant and the victim, or the victim alone, which has been seen in court by the jury and the public (as long as release is not prevented by copyright).

The above rules apply both where the accused pleads not guilty and the matter proceeds to a full trial, and to cases where the accused pleads guilty. However, in the case of guilty pleas, the Protocol provides that only material which informs the court's decision on sentencing will be released; this must be material which reflects the prosecution case and was read out, shown in court or placed before the sentencing judge.

The Protocol provides that, where the criminal justice agencies decide not to release a particular item, the media can make representations to the Crown Prosecution Service Head of Strategic Communications, who will review the decision.

Names and addresses

Home Office Circular 78/1967 makes it clear that courts should ensure that the names and addresses of defendants are read out in open court. This is to help the press ensure that it identifies the right person, and to avoid confusion with other people who may share the same name.

In *R v Evesham Justices ex p McDonagh* (1988), a newspaper brought an action for judicial review against a decision by magistrates to allow a defendant not to have his address stated in court, because he feared harassment by his ex-wife. The Queen's Bench Divisional Court upheld the newspaper's argument, and confirmed that addresses should, as a rule, be read out in open court.

The names of witnesses, whether for the prosecution or the defence, should usually be stated in open court, but in exceptional cases (such as where a witness may be in danger if they are identified), a court can allow a witness to write down their name, rather than having it stated out loud.

Law in practice The press bench

Traditionally criminal courts have always had a dedicated place for the press to sit, but in 2008, *Media Lawyer* reported that courts are increasingly reserving this space for police and probation officers. This leaves reporters forced to sit in the public gallery instead, where you can be open to intimidation from friends and relatives of the defendants. Court officials have also suggested that reporters have to ring in advance of a trial if they want press seating.

The issue was raised with the Courts Service by the Press Association, and, in response the Court Service stated that court staff would be reminded that journalists should normally be allocated proper seating within the body of the court, and not expected to report from the public gallery, though in cases where there is a high demand for press seats, using some seats in the public gallery could be an option. It also said that in high-profile cases, where there were insufficient press seats, the court service would try, where practical, to arrange a media annex with an audio-visual link. It confirmed that there is no rule that journalists have to ring in advance if they want to use the press seats.

Access to the civil courts

The principle of open justice is equally important in the civil courts, and rule 39.2 of the Civil Procedure Rules, which cover the county courts and the High Court, confirms that, as a general rule, proceedings should be held in public. However, the Rules state that a hearing may be held in private if:

- publicity would effectively make the proceedings pointless;
- the case involves information relating to national security;

- the case involves confidential information, which would no longer be confidential if the case was heard in public (this can include personal financial information);
- the case involves uncontentious matters concerning the administration of a trust, or the estate of someone who has died;
- privacy is necessary to protect the interests of a child or a patient;
- the case is an application without notice (which means in the absence of the person against whom the application is sought), and a public hearing would be unjust to the other side;
- the court considers privacy necessary to protect the interests of justice.

The Civil Procedure Rules are delegated legislation and, as such, the courts are obliged to interpret them, as far as possible, in a way compatible with the Human Rights Act 1998, which means they must give due weight to the importance of freedom of expression.

The rules on access to family proceedings, inquests, tribunals and divorce proceedings are dealt with in the relevant later chapters.

Housing cases

Practice Direction 39, which supplements the Civil Procedure Rules, provides that where a landlord is claiming possession of a house or flat due to non-payment of rent, or where a mortgage lender is repossessing a house, the hearing is normally listed as a private one. However, the judge can decide to hold such hearings in open court, after hearing representations on the matter (this presumably includes arguments from the press, though the Practice Direction is not specific about who can make representations).

Applications for injunctions

In the county courts, applications for injunctions must be held in open court if the person the injunction would be against is represented by a lawyer (this does not apply to injunctions concerning domestic violence). Applications for injunctions in the Queen's Bench Division are usually heard in private, but in the Chancery Division, they usually take place in open court.

Closed material procedures

The Justice and Security Act 2013 introduces new provisions for some types of civil cases, such as those involving deportation, where what is called a 'closed material procedure' can be used. This means that evidence that relates to sensitive national security issues can be given in private, with not just the press and public, but also the litigants and their lawyers, excluded from the court.

Law in practice Taking notes in court

Where there is no press bench and you have to sit in the public gallery at a criminal court, you may find that court ushers try to stop you from taking notes. As *Media Lawyer* reported in its November 2009 issue, the reasoning behind this is that witnesses who are not allowed into court before they give their evidence may send someone else into court to take notes on what has happened, so they can work out in advance their answers to any tricky questions. However, there is no legal restriction on taking notes in court, and if you explain that you are a member of the press, you should be allowed to continue. Having your press card as identification will help here.

Texting, emailing, tweeting and broadcasting from a court

In January 2012, the Lord Chief Justice issued a Practice Guidance note on sending texts, emails or tweets from inside a court (Practice Guidance (Use of live text-based forms of communication from court, 16 January 2012). The guidance states that journalists are free to send emails, texts and Twitter messages from 'an unobtrusive, hand held, silent piece of modern equipment' during court proceedings, for the purposes of fair and accurate reporting. However, it is very important to remember that anything you tweet, or anything you email or text, is subject to the same rules as any other material published as a result of a court visit. That means that you must still abide by any reporting restrictions, and anything you send will only be covered by the defence of absolute privilege for court reports if it is a fair, accurate and contemporaneous account.

Subject to these conditions, journalists are free to tweet, text or email and do not need to ask court permission to do so. A judge does, however, have the right to limit these types of communication in certain circumstances, such as where simultaneous reporting might put pressure on witnesses.

Obtaining information from the civil courts

The Civil Procedure Rules, which set down the procedure in the civil courts, provide that both the public and the media have a right to see certain documents relating to civil court cases. Rule 5.4 provides that there is an automatic right, on payment of a fee, to see what is called the 'statement of case', and rule 2.3 defines this as including:

- the claim form, which details the claim, and the parties' names;
- particulars of the claim, which gives further details where these are not in the claim form;
- the defence, put forward by the other side;
- any Part 20 claim, which covers any related claim brought by someone other than the claimant, such as a counter-claim by the defendant, or a claim which links a third party to the case;
- reply to the defence, from the claimant;
- any other information voluntarily given in relation to these documents.

Until recently it was believed that these rules did not apply to court documents for cases of judicial review (see p. 49). However, the High Court's decision in ***R (Corner House Research, Campaign Against the Arms Trade)* v *The Director of the Serious Fraud Office*** (2008) now makes it clear that the same rules cover the equivalent documents in judicial review proceedings. Similarly, in ***Cleveland Bridge UK* v *Multiplex Constructions*** (2006), it was stated that the rules also cover interlocutory hearings (these are held before the main trial, usually to discuss points of law).

Anyone named in a claim form can apply to the court to have the form's availability to the public and press restricted, or for the form to be edited before being made available to anyone not involved in the case. The Court of Appeal has ruled that where a party objects to a particular document or documents being made available, they have to give specific reasons why this would cause them damage; it is not enough just to say that the information is confidential, even if the other side agrees. In family proceedings under the Children Acts, only a record of the order made is available to the press and public; other documents can only be issued with the judge's permission.

The High Court has ruled that a document lodged with a witness statement in litigation is public and can be disclosed to the media. In ***NAB* v *Serco Ltd and another*** [2014], the court allowed the *Guardian* to see an internal document from a company involved in a court case which it was covering, The case involved an employee who was suing the company for sexual assault by one of its employees, and the court found that releasing the document was in the public interest as it showed how the woman's complaint was handled.

County court judgments, some High Court and Court of Appeal judgments, and all Supreme Court judgments are available on the internet (see *Online resources*, at the end of this chapter).

If a hearing was held in private, you will need to apply to the judge for leave to obtain a copy of the order or judgment made. The Court of Appeal in ***Hodgson* v *Imperial Tobacco*** (1998) stated that such documents should usually be made available.

Material referred to in court

In order to speed up hearings, the courts may streamline their proceedings by having both sides submit papers detailing their case to the judge beforehand. The judge is then familiar with the arguments and, rather than hearing all the evidence again verbally, the lawyers will simply refer to the papers which have been submitted. These might include witness statements, and 'skeleton arguments' or 'skellies', which explain the arguments the barristers are planning to make, and may include material such as the previous decisions they are basing their arguments on, or details of the case. This can make it quite difficult for journalists to follow what is going on, especially, as is often the case, if it has not been possible to attend court on every day of a hearing. In the past, reporters have had problems getting hold of copies of these materials, but the Court of Appeal has now ruled that the general rule should be that papers referred to in court are made available to the press. The ruling came in ***R (on the application of Guardian News and Media Ltd)* v *City of Westminster Magistrates' Court*, with the Government of the United States of America as an interested party and Article 19 as an intervener** (2012), where the *Guardian* successfully challenged a ruling in an extradition case which said that they could not have access to skeleton arguments, opening notes and witness statements, which had been referred to but not read out. The Court of Appeal said that, as a general rule, the principle of open justice suggested that documents referred to in court but not read out should be made available to journalists, unless there was a strong argument against doing so. Lord Justice Toulson made it clear that this did not mean papers would always be made available – in each case, a court would have to undertake a balancing exercise, weighing the potential value to the principle of open justice of making the material available, against any risk of harm to the legitimate interests of others that access to the documents might pose.

In addition to the decision above, rule 32.13 of the Civil Procedure Rules states that witness statements which are used in evidence must be open to inspection during the course of a trial, unless the court directs otherwise. A court should only make a statement unavailable on the grounds of one of the following:

- the interests of justice;
- the public interest;
- the nature of medical evidence contained in the statement;
- the nature of confidential information, including personal financial information, contained in the statement;
- the need to protect a child or other vulnerable person.

Information after a case is over

There are many situations where you might want to find out the details of a case after it is over, for example as background to a later story. The issue was addressed in the 2004 case of ***Re Guardian Newspapers Ltd*** (Court record; Disclosure), where the *Guardian* applied to a court for witness statements concerning payments made by a British arms firms to the daughter of the then President of Indonesia. The material was needed for research into a story about bribery by the arms industry. The documents had been disclosed during a court hearing, but the case had been settled before it could be reported. The judge hearing the paper's application for the documents confirmed that statements referred to in court should usually be made available to the press and public, and said that the fact that the case had ended did not change this. However, a party in the case can object to the documents being released and, if they do, the court may hold a hearing to decide the question. If the court decides against releasing the material, costs could be awarded against the media organisation making the request, so most publishers will want to weigh up the importance of a story before allowing a hearing to go ahead.

Records of judgments are held by individual courts, and many can also be accessed online (see *Online resources*, at the end of this chapter).

KEY POINTS

The general rule on access

Hearings should be held in public; a court can only exclude the public if it has a legal power to do so.

Restrictions on access

All courts have a common law power to restrict public access where it would frustrate the administration of justice.

Statute and court rules allow exclusion in specific circumstances:

- child witnesses in sex offences;
- special measures directions;
- hearings in camera for reasons of national security, or protection of identity;
- youth court proceedings;
- applications for further detention;
- cases under the Official Secrets Act.

Information from the criminal courts

- Daily lists should be available to the press.
- Details of committal proceedings should be displayed within a day.
- Prosecution material should be given to the press where possible.
- Names and addresses of defendants should be read in open court.

Access restrictions in the civil courts

- The Civil Procedure Rules state when hearings can be held in private.
- Repossession cases are normally held in private, but can be held in open court.
- Applications for injunctions may be public or private, depending on the court.

Information from the civil courts

- Claim forms are open to inspection.
- Judgments are published online.
- Witness statements should be available for public inspection.;
- Documents disclosed during a case should be available to the press.

TEST YOUR KNOWLEDGE

1 What is the difference between 'in private' and 'in chambers'?

2 List the four circumstances in which the Human Rights Act 1998 allows the media to be excluded from all or part of a trial.

3 You arrive at your local court to report a case, only to be told that the judge has decided to exclude the press from the court room. What is the first thing you should do?

4 Name the four situations in which a court could use its common law power to exclude the press from a trial.

5 You are in court to report the trial of a man for the rape of a teenage girl. The judge states that she will exclude the press and the public while the victim gives her evidence. What arguments could you put forward to enable you to stay in court?

6 Can the press attend proceedings of youth courts?

7 You are assigned to report a Crown Court trial, but on the first day, the judge announces that the whole of the proceedings will be held in private, for reasons of national security. What arguments can you use to get access to some or all of the proceedings?

8 You are reporting cases in the magistrates' court. Can you refer to the magistrates hearing the cases by name?

9 What information can a reporter working on criminal cases expect to get from the prosecution side?

10 You are reporting a case involving a well-known local businessman who is charged with shoplifting. He asks the court not to allow his address to be read out, as it would be embarrassing given his high profile in the community. The magistrates agree but can you provide any arguments to change their minds?

11 List the seven circumstances in which a civil hearing may be held in private.

ONLINE RESOURCES

The Judicial Studies Board guidelines on reporting restrictions are available at:
www.societyofeditors.co.uk

The Civil Procedure Rules can be read at:
www.justice.gov.uk

Crown Court lists are available at:
www.courtserve.net

County court judgments and High Court judgments since 2006 are available at:
www.registry-trust.org.uk

(The site only shows the name and address of the defendant, the amount owing, the date of judgment and the name of the court; other information is held by the court itself.) Court of Appeal judgments are available at:
www.courtservice.gov.uk

Supreme Court judgments are available at:
www.supremecourt.uk

Recent Home Office Circulars (and details of how to obtain older ones) can be found at:
https://www.gov.uk/government/collections/home-office-circulars-2014

General reporting restrictions

We looked at the rules on when reporters are allowed to attend court hearings in the previous chapter. Being allowed to attend a hearing, however, does not necessarily mean that you can report everything you see and hear. Parliament has put in place a number of statutes which restrict what you can publish about court proceedings and the people involved in them. Some of these restrictions apply generally, across the different areas of law, and these are discussed in this chapter. Others are specific to particular kinds of hearing, such as criminal cases, family proceedings and cases involving children, and these are covered in later chapters.

However, as we saw in the previous chapter, there is a basic principle of English law, underpinned by the Human Rights Act 1998, that justice should be seen to be done. Since most of the general public cannot be in court to see this, the media is viewed as the public's eyes and ears, and the principle of open justice requires that they should be able to report fully on proceedings in the courts, and the people involved in them. This means that courts should never restrict reporting without a sound legal basis for doing so. However, as you will see in this and later chapters, there are all too many examples of courts trying to do this, often at the request of someone involved in the trial who wants to avoid publicity. Journalists reporting the courts therefore need to be aware of when the courts can and cannot impose reporting restrictions, and be ready to challenge orders for which there does not seem to be a sound legal basis. It is easier to do this when you have advance knowledge of attempts to impose reporting restrictions, and the Criminal Procedure Rules 2013 now state courts must not make orders imposing restrictions on reporting, unless any person 'directly affected' (which includes the press) is present or has had the opportunity to attend or make representations. This effectively means that courts must notify the press in advance of applications to restrict reporting.

REPORTING RESTRICTIONS UNDER THE CONTEMPT OF COURT ACT 1981

As we saw earlier (in Chapter 6), the laws on contempt of court aim to prevent the publication of anything which could seriously prejudice a trial. In many cases, the press is allowed to make its own decisions on which cases to report, and how, provided that it does not publish material that breaches the law on contempt. However, the Contempt of Court Act 1981 also gives courts a general power to make orders which ban the reporting of particular court hearings, or aspects of them, where it is necessary to avoid a substantial risk of prejudice.

There are two types of reporting restriction allowed under the Act:

- orders under s4(2) allow a court to postpone publication of reports of a trial, or of any specific detail from the trial;
- orders under s11 allow a court to ban publication of a name, or any other information related to a trial.

The main difference between the two is that s4 orders are temporary, and s11 orders are permanent. The media can challenge either type of order, either on the grounds that the judge was wrong to make it at all, or that its terms are too restrictive. This chapter gives the detailed grounds on which a challenge can be made – see Chapter 14 for how to do it.

Where orders may be used

The Act provides that s4(2) and s11 orders may be made in any court, defined in s19 as 'any tribunal or body exercising the judicial power of the State'. This means that these orders can be made in any of the civil or criminal courts, in the coroners' court and in some, but not all, tribunals (see p. 203 for guidance on which tribunals are covered).

POSTPONING PUBLICATION: THE S4(2) ORDER

Section 4(2) provides that a court may, where it seems necessary to avoid a substantial risk of prejudice in any proceedings (whether already started, pending or imminent), order the postponement of any report of the whole proceedings, or any part of them.

There is no type of case in which a court has to make a s4(2) order; in each case, it should decide whether such an order is necessary. In practice, however, there are three situations in which s4(2) orders are almost always made:

- **Where matters are discussed in the absence of the jury**, such as when one side asks the judge to exclude a certain piece of evidence on legal grounds. Clearly, exclusion would be pointless if the jury heard the discussion about whether the evidence should be allowed or not, so jurors are sent out, but the press and public are usually allowed to remain. However, a s4(2) order is usually made so that the jury cannot find out about the discussion through the media.
- **Where material arising during the trial carries a substantial risk of prejudice to other pending or imminent trials.** This might be, for example, because the defendant is being tried for several offences in separate trials, or because someone else in the case is facing trial on a separate issue. In these situations, reporting the current trial, or particular details of it, could cause prejudice to those which are due to take place afterwards. Section 4(2) only allows postponement where the trial which could be prejudiced is imminent or pending, which effectively means where the defendant has already been charged, or where it is known that a charge is about to be brought. The 2014 Judicial College guidelines say a s4(2) order is rarely appropriate to postpone reporting of evidence which will be given in both trials, because in that case prejudice is unlikely to arise; the jury in the second trial will be hearing the evidence anyway.
- **Where a defendant has been acquitted, but the court believes there may be a new trial as a result of witness intimidation in the current one** (see p. 33). In this situation, publication is usually postponed until after the new trial.

Under s4(2), a court can also make an order preventing the disclosure of a person's name in open court.

Although these are the most common situations in which a s4(2) order is used, a court has discretion to make such orders wherever it believes it is necessary to avoid a substantial risk of prejudice. Unfortunately, this discretion in some cases leads the courts to believe their powers are wider than they actually are. This problem was recognised by the then Lord Chief Justice, Lord Bingham, in the 2002 case of ***Ex p News Group Newspapers***, where he commented that there was a 'serious problem' in some areas of the country with courts making orders restricting publication 'in situations where they should not be made'. It is important, therefore, to know what a court can and cannot do with s4(2) orders, and from the words of the statute, decided cases and Judicial College guidelines, the following principles emerge.

There must be a substantial risk of prejudice

The purpose of s4(2) orders is to prevent prejudice to court proceedings which are either ongoing or set to happen in the future. They are only available to postpone publication of material which poses a substantial risk of prejudicing court proceedings, and should not be used to restrict reporting of anything which does not pose such a risk. The 2014 Judicial College guidelines state that a court considering a s4(2) order should first ask whether there is a substantial risk or prejudice to the administration of justice – and if there is not, 'that is the end of the matter' and no other factors need be considered.

In *Birmingham Mail v ED* (2011), the case concerned a report which named defendants in a criminal case, who were accused of neglecting their child. The child had died while in their care, but there was a surviving sibling. The judge in the criminal case had imposed a s4(2) order, banning publication of the names and address of the parents, but only in circumstances where this could lead to the surviving child being identified as the sibling of the child that died, or being associated with the parents or the court case. The order contained a clause, which is standard in this type of order, saying that it did not prevent publication of information relating to a court hearing held in public, where that court had not made any order restricting reporting. The *Birmingham Mail* reported that the case had ended, and named the parents, but did not mention the surviving sibling.

The paper was found to be in breach of the s4(2) order, and appealed. Their lawyer argued that the s4(2) order was invalid because such an order could only be used to avoid the risk of prejudice in the court proceedings or associated proceedings, and reporting the end of the case carried no such risk. In addition, the order had specified that criminal proceedings could be reported. The Court of Appeal agreed that the paper had not breached the terms of the order, because there was no specific ban on identifying the parents and there was permission to report the outcome of criminal proceedings.

The order must be necessary

The Act states that an order can be made where the court deems it 'necessary', and the courts have pointed out, in the cases below and others, that this means an order should not be made purely because someone involved in the case has a good reason to want one. This is an issue which has been examined more often in cases involving s11 orders (see below), where it has been made clear that sparing embarrassment is not a good enough reason for such an order; however in several s11 cases, the courts have said or implied that the same reasoning applies to s4(2) orders.

In 2004, Southwark Crown Court refused to issue a s4(2) order postponing publication of the address of Marvin Dawkins, better known as Romeo of the rap group So Solid Crew, who was on trial for wounding with intent to cause GBH and violent disorder. His lawyer had initially won a s11 order banning publication of his client's address, on the grounds that his client already suffered harassment from female fans turning up at his home, and this would increase if the address was published. The Press Association pointed out that s11 orders should not be granted merely to spare the feelings of defendants, referring to the case of *R v Evesham Justices ex p McDonagh* (1988) (see p. 120), and the court overturned the order. It then refused to issue a s4(2) order postponing publication of the address until after the hearing was over.

8

General reporting restrictions

In *R* v ***Burrell*** (2004), an official in the Department for Constitutional Affairs, Michael Burrell, was accused of raping a senior civil servant. As we will see later (in Chapter 9), the press is banned from publishing the identity of rape complainants, but this does not prevent reporting of the case itself and the evidence given. The complainant asked for a s4(2) order preventing publication of large sections of her evidence, on the grounds that some of her colleagues knew she was the complainant, and that if the evidence was published, she would feel unable to return to her job. She suggested that without such an order, she might not give evidence at all. The judge refused the order, for three reasons. Firstly, Parliament had granted rape victims anonymity under the Sexual Offences (Amendment) Act 1992, and the fact that it had chosen not to provide for reporting restrictions in the same Act must mean it accepted the need for such evidence to be given in public, as a part of the general principle of open justice. Secondly, the defendant wished to exercise his right to a public trial, and the court was obliged to take this into account, and weigh it against the complainant's right to privacy. Thirdly, in several cases involving s11 orders, the courts had refused to grant orders which were requested in order to spare embarrassment or damage to career or business. The same principles applied with regard to s4(2) orders. In the event, the trial collapsed after the complainant became ill, and the judge entered a formal verdict of not guilty.

One of the most common reasons for imposing s4 orders is where a defendant in the trial is also going to appear in a later trial, the idea being that jury members in the later trial may be prejudiced if they remember reading that the defendant was previously accused (and perhaps convicted) in another case. However, the 2014 Judicial College guidelines make it clear that s4 orders will not always be necessary in this situation, and should not be made if unnecessary. The guidelines reiterate that the judge must be satisfied that there is a substantial risk of prejudice in the second trial that is sufficient to outweigh the strong public interest in full and contemporaneous reporting of the current one. They should bear in mind that the staying power of news reports is limited, and that juries can be trusted to follow instructions to judge only on the evidence.

An order will not be considered necessary where the same effect could be achieved by less restrictive means.

In ***Ex p Central Independent Television Plc*** (1990), it was held to be unnecessary to ban reports of a trial while the jury was considering its decision overnight, because any risk of prejudice could have been avoided by the court telling jurors not to switch on televisions or radios.

The risk must be substantial

This is clearly stated in s4(2), and means that a s4(2) order should not be made merely because some risk of prejudice exists; it must be a substantial risk.

In ***MGN Pension Trustees Ltd*** v ***Bank of America National Trust and Saving Association and Credit Suisse*** (1995), the judge was asked to make an order postponing publication of reports of civil trials concerning the pension funds of companies owned by the tycoon Robert Maxwell, to avoid prejudice to future fraud proceedings related to the same funds. The judge stated that, in deciding whether postponement orders should be allowed or refused, there were three questions to be asked:

- Was there a substantial risk of prejudice to the administration of justice if publication was not postponed? If yes,
- Did it appear necessary that a postponement order be made in order to avoid that risk? If yes,
- Should the court use its discretion to make the order, and if so, what should its terms be? Even if there was a risk of substantial prejudice, it did not automatically follow that an order should be made.

In this case, he said, the risk of prejudice was not substantial, and the words of the statute made it clear that an insubstantial risk was not enough to displace the importance of a free press.

In *R* v *Horsham Justices, ex p Farquharson* (1982), the Court of Appeal considered whether it was justified to use a s4 order to postpone reports of a trial, on the basis that reading them each night could prejudice the jury in the trial. It held that the risk of a jury being prejudiced, during a trial, by daily reports of it was insubstantial. Lord Denning, the Master of the Rolls, pointed out that jurors are instructed by the trial judge to decide the case only on the evidence before them, and are perfectly capable of ignoring newspaper stories. Therefore the risk of prejudice was not substantial and did not justify a s4 order.

In 2004, the Fathers4Justice campaigner David Chick was tried for causing public nuisance, after dressing up as Spider-Man and climbing a crane near Tower Bridge, where he stayed for six days, causing massive traffic disruption in the local area. Not surprisingly, the protest was widely reported at the time it happened, and when the case came to court, the trial judge imposed a s4(2) order postponing reports of the hearing until it was over, on the grounds that they might remind jurors of the previous publicity and thus prejudice the case. The Press Association was able to get the order lifted, by pointing out to the judge that press reports of the daily proceedings were no more likely to prejudice the jury than hearing the same details in court each day.

The case of *Re Barot* (2006) establishes that even in high-profile cases the courts should not not be too ready to impose prior restrictions on reporting. The case concerned the trial of Dhiren Barot, one of eight people charged with terrorist offences related to the failed suicide bomb attacks in London on 21 July 2005. It was decided that Barot should be tried separately from the other defendants, and he then pleaded guilty. His sentencing hearing was set for February 2007, whereas the trial of the other defendants would not take place until two months later, and lawyers for the others argued that if details of the bomb plot were reported in connection with the Barot hearing, their clients could not then get a fair trial. They successfully argued for a s4(2) order imposing a complete ban on reporting of the Barot hearing. This was challenged by the BBC and *The Times*, who pointed out that juries in the April trial would hear Barot's admissions then anyway. The Court of Appeal agreed to lift the order and said that, in cases like this, s4(2) orders should be the exception, not the rule.

The order must remove the risk

In ***R (on application of Telegraph Group PLC)* v *Sherwood*** (2001), the Court of Appeal pointed out that after deciding whether there is a substantial risk of prejudice, a court should ask whether a s4 order would actually remove that risk; in some cases, it would not, and therefore no order should be made. Even if an order would remove the risk, before granting it, the court should consider whether there are other, less restrictive ways of achieving the same result. This approach is backed up in the 2014 Judicial College guidelines.

Proceedings must be current, imminent or pending

Section 4(2) orders can only be made where there is a risk of prejudice to the proceedings before the court, or to other court cases which are already under way. Details of events which do not take place in a court cannot be covered by a s4(2) order.

In *R* v *Rhuddlan Justices ex p HTV Ltd* (1986), magistrates had made a s4(2) order purporting to prevent HTV from broadcasting a programme which showed a man being arrested. On appeal, it was found that they had acted outside their powers, and the order was invalid.

Postponement must be for a specific time

Typically, a s4(2) postponement order runs until the end of the trial in question, or where it is made to avoid prejudice to later trials, until the end of those. However, it is up to the court to decide the length of the order, and in some cases, courts will try to use s4(2) to impose what really amounts to a permanent ban. In ***R* v *Horsham Justices ex p Farquharson*** (1982), the court stated that this was not an appropriate use of s4(2), and confirmed that orders should last for no longer than was necessary to avoid the risk of substantial prejudice. This was confirmed by the Court of Appeal in ***Re Times Newspapers Ltd and Others*** (2007), which said that a s4(2) order that was imposed to ensure the fairness of proceedings before the court, or proceedings that were pending, could only last until the end of the proceedings in question. The 2014 Judicial College guidelines on criminal cases also make it clear that s4(2) orders can only be used to postpone reporting, and not to ban it indefinitely.

The public interest must be considered

The 2014 Judicial College guidelines make it plain that even where a court considers a s4(2) order is necessary, it still has a discretion on whether to impose one. The judge must seek to strike a balance between the public interest in fair trials against the public interest in full reporting of criminal trials. This approach was backed up in ***R (on application of Telegraph Group PLC)* v *Sherwood*** (2001), where the Court of Appeal pointed out that there may be cases where the public interest in open justice means a s4 order should be refused, even if that means a trial could be prejudiced as a result.

In 2006, a determined reporter from the *Plymouth Evening Herald* persuaded a court to lift a s4(2) order, on his third attempt. The case concerned three men involved in supplying cocaine, as part of a supply chain that stretched from the local area to South America. The judge imposed a s4(2) order because the men were also involved in other legal proceedings. However, reporter Matt Fleming argued that the seriousness of the case meant that the public were entitled to know about it, and the s4(2) order meant that it could be as long as a year before it could be reported. His first two attempts to challenge the order were rejected, but finally, with help from the prosecution lawyer, he managed to persuade the judge to lift most of the restrictions, so that the ban only covered reporting of any material which might prejudice the later trial.

In 2007, a Press Association reporter managed to get a s4(2) order lifted in the trial of a police officer accused of holding a press photographer at gunpoint after chasing the photographer in his car. The reporter argued that the fact that the defendant was a police officer, and the accusations were very serious, meant there was a public interest in the details of the case being made known. The order had been made in order to prevent prejudice in a second trial involving the defendant, but the reporter successfully argued that the second case was a long time away, and jurors could be warned to judge it on the evidence alone.

Orders made for other purposes

The law only permits s4(2) orders to be made for the purpose of avoiding a substantial risk of prejudice to a current or future hearing. Courts have occasionally tried to make them for other purposes, such as encouraging a witness to give evidence, or protecting the general welfare or safety of someone involved in the case. The Court of Appeal has stated, in ***R* v *Croydon Crown Court ex p Trinity Mirror*** (2008), and ***Re Times Newspapers*** (2007), that such orders will be invalid.

Scope of s4(2) orders

The 2014 Judicial College guidelines make it clear that s4(2) orders can only be used to postpone reports of the proceedings in question. Section 4 does not give the courts power to postpone reports of material not admitted into evidence, and not prejudicial to the proceedings, nor publication of material that is already in the public domain. They point out, however, that the media still need to take care that publication of other material does not breach the strict liability rule on contempt.

PREVENTING PUBLICATION: THE S11 ORDER

Section 11 of the Contempt of Court Act 1981 gives a court power to restrict or ban publication of details given in court proceedings. The section provides that:

> In any case where a court (having power to do so) allows a name or other matter to be withheld from the public in proceedings before the court, the court may give such directions prohibiting the publication of that name or matter in connection with the proceedings as appear to the court to be necessary for the purpose for which it was so withheld.

The phrase 'having power to do so' means that this section only applies where the court already has powers to withhold the relevant information from the public under statute or common law (e.g. s12 of the Administration of Justice Act 1960 allows a court to withhold information in certain cases involving children). If there is no legal provision which allows the court to withhold the information in the first place, a s11 order will be invalid. A court cannot use a s11 order itself to authorise withholding of information.

The name or matter must be withheld in court

Section 11 orders can only be made to prevent publication of details which have not already been revealed in open court (for this reason, applications for a s11 order may be, and often are, heard in private).

In ***R* v *Arundel Justices ex p Westminster Press*** (1985), s11 reporting restrictions banning publication of a person's name were quashed, because the name had already been mentioned in open court. The Divisional Court confirmed that a court had no power to make a s11 order in those circumstances.

In a 2004 case, a s11 order banning publication of the addresses of a couple on trial for sexual offences involving children was lifted after representations from the *Kent Messenger*. The defendants' lawyer had argued for the order because his clients' home had been fire-bombed after their address and the charges had appeared in the press. The trial judge agreed to lift it, on the grounds that the defendants' address had already been given in public at the magistrates' court hearing, and so could not be covered by a s11 order.

An exception to this rule is where information is given in open court by mistake, when it should have been given in the absence of the jury.

In ***Re Times Newspapers*** (2007), the Court of Appeal ruled that a s11 order could stand, even though it related to information stated in open court, where that information should in fact have been given in camera. The case in which the order was made was the prosecution of two defendants under the Official Secrets Act, for leaking a letter concerning details of a meeting between the then Prime Minister Tony Blair and the US President. The judge had ruled that information about the content of the letter should not be divulged in open court, but, by mistake, a question put to a witness, and the answer to that question, revealed information that should have been given in camera.

The judge made a s11 order banning disclosure of the information that should have been covered by the in-camera order, and banning publication of any material which 'might' reveal the content of the letter or the alleged damage that would result from its disclosure (in other words, any speculation about the contents of the letter). The order was challenged by *The Times*, on the grounds that s11 orders can only apply to information that has not been stated in open court.

The Court of Appeal held that the judge was entitled to make the s11 order concerning the evidence that should have been given in camera, even though it had by mistake been given in public. Section 11 could not be used to ban speculation about the contents of the letter, and so the Court of Appeal said the word 'might' should be deleted. However, publication of speculation about the contents of the letter could amount to a contempt of court, as it would be an attempt to frustrate the in-camera order.

The ban must be necessary in the interests of justice

Section 11 is a severe restriction on the principle of open justice, and both the higher courts and the Judicial College have made it clear that it should only be used where absolutely necessary, which essentially means where the interests of justice would be seriously harmed by publication. The 2014 Judicial College guidelines on criminal cases make it clear that s11 orders should not be used merely to prevent embarrassment to defendants or witnesses, to prevent damages to business interests or professional reputations, or to protect the privacy of the defendant's children, and may only be used to prevent disclosure of the defendant's name in very rare circumstances.

In *R* v *Evesham Justices ex p McDonagh* (1988), an ex-MP was being tried on a motoring offence, and asked for his address to be kept secret because he feared harassment from his ex-wife. The magistrates agreed, but, on appeal, the Divisional Court ruled that the order was not necessary in the interests of justice. It pointed out that there were many defendants who, for various reasons, would prefer not to have their addresses published, but s11 orders were not designed to be used to protect 'the comfort and feelings of defendants'.

In *R* v *Legal Aid Board, ex p Kaim Todner* (1999), a London solicitors' firm had had its legal aid franchise taken away, and sought judicial review of the Legal Aid Board's decision. It asked for a s11 order banning the press from publishing the name of the firm, but the judge refused. The Court of Appeal upheld the refusal, stating that the principle that justice should be done in public should only be compromised where justice demanded it, and protecting a firm's reputation was not such a situation.

In the 2004 case involving rapper Romeo (see p. 115), the Press Association was able to get a s11 order banning publication of the star's address overturned. It had been requested to protect him from the attentions of female fans, but the Press Association pointed out the ruling in *R* v *Evesham Justices* that s11 orders should not be made for the 'comfort and feelings' of defendants. In addition, it pointed out that as the star already had a problem with fans turning up at his house, his address must already be known. The judge overturned the order.

The courts will, however, allow s11 orders in a situation where sparing someone embarrassment is itself in the interests of justice. In ***R* v *Legal Aid Board, ex p Kaim*** (see below), Lord Woolf pointed out that, for example, a witness who was needed for a hearing but had no personal interest in the proceedings might have a good claim to anonymity, because the courts would be dependent on their cooperation. Similarly, s11 orders are commonly used to conceal the identity of victims in blackmail cases, on the grounds that such victims would be much less likely to report the crime if they thought that their secrets would be exposed in court, and clearly the interests of justice would be damaged if, as a result, fewer blackmailers were brought to justice.

Equally, where the effect of a person's identity being published goes beyond embarrassment and becomes possible mental harm, the courts may allow anonymity under s11, on the grounds that the interests of justice give that person the right of access to a court, and without anonymity, they will be unwilling to take up that right, or be unable to do so, without harming themselves. The courts have therefore allowed s11 orders for very vulnerable defendants, and some who are required to give medical evidence of a very personal nature.

In *Re JCA* (13 November 2003, unreported), a man who had mental problems was appealing against his conviction for manslaughter. The Court of Appeal found that a s11 order granting anonymity was justified because he was particularly vulnerable and might suffer mental harm from publicity. The Court stressed, however, that this was a different situation from cases where s11 orders were sought in order to spare embarrassment or distress, and confirmed that those were not appropriate grounds for an order.

In *H* v *Ministry of Defence* (1991), the Divisional Court allowed a s11 order granting anonymity to a defendant in a personal injury case, which involved embarrassing medical evidence. The Master of the Rolls, Lord Donaldson, said that in some such cases a s11 order might be necessary to protect defendants, because public knowledge of the evidence given would be more than merely embarrassing, and might cause genuine harm to the defendant. Without such protection, defendants would be put off seeking justice.

In connection with the proceedings

Section 11 orders only apply to publication of someone's name 'in connection with the proceedings' in which the order was made. This means that where an s11 order is in place, you can still write about the person concerned, provided you do not mention the court proceedings.

In ***Allen* v *Grimsby Telegraph*** (2011), the *Telegraph* was able to report a story about a man who had moved to the Grimsby area after being given a Sexual Offences Prevention Order (SOPO), despite an s11 order banning publication of his address in connection with the proceedings where the SOPO was made. The man, Gary Allen, had been charged with but acquitted of the murder of a prostitute in the Hull area, and had later been convicted of assaulting two prostitutes in Plymouth. When he moved to Grimsby, the police successfully requested that the local court make a SOPO against him, and an s11 order was made in connection with those proceedings. The *Grimsby Telegraph* reported that he had moved to the area, and his previous offences, and expressed the view that he was a danger to women. It also reported his later arrest in a nearby red light area. Neither of the stories stated his address, nor mentioned the SOPO proceedings. The High Court confirmed that they were not in contempt of court.

Risks to the person claiming anonymity

In some cases, a s11 order will be requested in order to protect someone (usually a witness) who fears for their own personal safety if their identity or address is revealed. Orders requested for this reason will only be granted in very exceptional cases. The Judicial College 2014 guidelines on criminal cases state that where a s11 order is sought on the grounds that identification would pose a threat to the witness's life, and therefore involve consideration of Article 2 of the Human Rights Act, the court should consider the extent to which the person's fears are objectively justified, and the person requiring the order should provide clear evidence that being identified would create or materially increase a risk of death or serious injury.

In ***R (Harper) and R (Johncox)* v *Aldershot Magistrates' Court with the Press Association, Surrey and Berks Media, and the CPS, Hampshire as interested parties*** (2010), the High Court supported a decision by magistrates to allow the home addresses of two police officers to be stated in open court and published by the media, despite the police officers' argument that publicity could affect their safety and/or deter them or other officers from doing their jobs. The police officers were before the court on charges of misconduct relating to speeding offences. They had both worked undercover during their careers, and one of them had, with his family, been put in a witness protection scheme for 18 months, after being involved in a serious crime investigation. They asked for a s11 order, preventing their addresses being disclosed. Lord Justice Pill said that the officers had to prove that there was a justification for interfering with the principle of open justice, and they had not done so. There was no evidence of a specific threat to them, and any threat which might occur because of their previous work was likely to be a targeted one which would not be prevented by the need to find out their addresses. (The Press Association had pointed out that keeping the addresses secret would not have any real effect, since both men were on the electoral roll, making it possible to find their addresses very easily.) Nor did he accept that publishing their addresses would be likely to deter them from doing their jobs.

In ***Re W (Children) (Care Proceedings: Witness Anonymity)*** (2002), a s11 order was used to protect the identity of a social worker in care proceedings. The case involved a woman whose children were under threat of being taken into care, but who had been told she might be allowed to keep them if she broke off contact with her husband, who had a history of extreme violence. She agreed, but before the care proceedings took place, a social worker happened to see her with her husband. The social worker agreed to give evidence in the proceedings, but given the possible risk to her from the husband (who had threatened that if he lost the children he would kill himself and, among others, the social workers), she asked to do so anonymously; the judge agreed and made a s11 order. The mother, however, appealed, and the Court of Appeal upheld her claim, stating that it was generally recognised that social workers were routinely threatened with, and actually experienced, violence in their work, and had to regard this as part of their job. This was not an exceptional case, and so the s11 order could not be said to be necessary in the interests of justice.

In ***Re Belfast Telegraph Newspapers Application** (1997)*, a man charged with indecent assault was granted a s11 order by magistrates, on the grounds that he feared attack if his address was published. The Queen's Bench Divisional Court overturned the order, stating that, while such a risk might well exist, it was not something that could prejudice the trial and therefore a s11 order was not appropriate.

In 2006, the *Oxford Mail* managed to overturn a s11 order banning identification of a man convicted of attempting to have sex with a 12-year-old girl. The order had been put in place at the request of the man's lawyer, because he was said to be a vulnerable individual who would be at risk of bullying in prison, and might even be a suicide risk. The *Oxford Mail* objected, arguing that the man had been sent to a normal prison, and his name was already in the public domain because it had been said in open court, and shown in court listings on the internet. The judge agreed that this was not an appropriate use of s11 powers.

Notice of s4(2) and s11 orders

Practice Directions issued in 1982 and 1983 make it clear that both types of order should be put into writing, stating the purpose for which the order is being made, precisely what it covers and, if not permanent, when it ceases to apply. Courts should notify the press when such orders are made, and court staff should be willing to answer queries about such orders (Practice Direction (Sup Ct: Contempt: Reporting Restrictions) [1982] and Practice Direction (Contempt of Court Act: Report of Proceedings: Postponement Orders) (1983)).

Challenging s11 orders

The 2014 Judicial College guidelines say a court considering whether to apply a s11 order must invite representations from the media. If the case is urgent, it should make a temporary order and invite the media to attend on the next convenient date.

Law in practice Is an order in place?

If an order imposing reporting restrictions of any kind is in place, a notice will usually be posted up in the court complex. However, Tony Jaffa, Head of Media at solicitors Foot Anstey, points out that some courts are more careful about doing this than others. If this is not done, the responsibility for finding out whether an order exists and following it remains with the press, so the fact that a notice has not been put up will not help you if you break it because you did not know it existed. If you are reporting a case where you would expect that an order might be made, but there is no notice to that effect, always check with the court staff.

OTHER GENERAL REPORTING RESTRICTIONS

In addition to the restrictions on reporting court cases detailed so far, there are some miscellaneous statutory provisions which apply either generally or to specific types of case.

Anonymity orders in the High Court

Section 37 of the Senior Courts Act 1981 gives the High Court the power to order any injunction 'in all cases in which it appears to the court to be just and convenient to do so'. These orders then remain in place if the case goes to the Court of Appeal or Supreme Court, unless one of those courts decides to lift them. In recent years, this power has increasingly been used to grant anonymity to parties in a case, where they have claimed that to be identified would breach their rights under the Human Rights Act 1998, most often the Article 8 right to privacy or the right to life under Article 2, where revealing the person's identity could put them in serious danger. However, in 2010, the Supreme Court took a stand against overuse of these powers.

In ***Application by Guardian News and Media Ltd and others in HM Treasury (Respondent) v Mohammed Jabar Ahmed and others (FC) (Appellants); HM Treasury (Respondent) v Mohammed Jabar Ahmed and others and another (FC); R (on the application of Hani El Sayed Sabaei Youssef (Respondent) v HM Treasury (Appellant))*** (2010), the *Guardian* and other media organisations challenged anonymity orders imposed to protect the identity of five men who were suspected of being involved in terrorism. The men had not been charged with terrorist offences, but because of the suspicions against them, the Treasury had got court orders denying them access to their financial assets. The court case in which the anonymity orders were imposed were brought by the five men to try to get the asset-freezing orders lifted. The men argued that they should be allowed anonymity because naming them in the press as terrorism suspects would have a serious impact on their private lives and their families. The Supreme Court rejected this argument. It confirmed the principle that, where possible, court proceedings should be published and those involved in them named, saying that anonymity orders should only be imposed in 'an extreme case', such as where identification posed a genuine threat to someone's life or safety. Even though identification of the men might well lead to 'outrageously hostile' reporting against them, that was not a strong enough reason to restrict press freedom. The court criticised the increase in anonymity orders and said that the courts appeared to be granting them without much consideration.

The High Court has also stated, in ***Re RA's Application for Judicial Review*** (2010), that magistrates' courts also have the power to make an anonymity order where necessary to protect someone's rights under Article 2, if they were under a 'real and immediate risk' of violence.

The High Court's inherent jurisdiction

The High Court has the power, known as its inherent jurisdiction, to order reporting restrictions in a particular case, where the court believes that the person's interests or welfare would be damaged by them being named in the press. The Court can also ban media organisations from even attempting to gather news about the case. This power can be used on behalf of both adults and children, whether or not they are wards of court, and applies to cases heard in the county courts as well as the High Court. The Court of Appeal and House of Lords can also make these orders.

In 2008, a man was convicted of repeatedly raping his daughters throughout their childhood. By the time he was prosecuted, he had fathered several children with them, and the daughters were grown up. The automatic statutory ban on identifying victims of sex offences meant that the women could not, and had not been, named in the press, but there was concern that if the press were seen to be reporting from the area around their home, this might lead to the local community being able to identify the women and their children. At the request of their lawyers, the High Court imposed an order banning reporters from approaching the women, or being in the vicinity of any address where they lived or had lived.

In 2005, the Family Division issued a Practice Direction stating that where a party to a case wants the High Court to use its inherent jurisdiction to impose reporting restrictions, that party should notify the media about the application in advance, through the Press Association Copy Direct service.

KEY POINTS

Reporting restrictions under the Contempt of Court Act 1981

Courts can order reporting restrictions where necessary to avoid a substantial risk of prejudice, in any type of case.

The s4(2) order

This order can be used to postpone publication, under these conditions:

- the order must be necessary;
- the risk of prejudice must be substantial;
- the order must remove the risk;
- proceedings must be current, imminent or pending;
- postponement must be for a specific time;
- the public interest must be considered.

The s11 order

This allows courts to ban publication of any matter that has been withheld from the public during court proceedings.

Section 11 orders can only be used where:

- the information has not been given in court;
- an order is necessary in the interests of justice.

Neither order should be given merely to spare defendants' embarrassment.

Notice of s4(2) and s11 orders

Both orders must be put into writing, stating the purpose, scope and duration.

Other reporting restrictions

The High Court can make anonymity orders under s37 of the Senior Courts Act 1981, but the Supreme Court has warned that this power should only be used in extreme cases.

The High Court has inherent jurisdiction to restrict reporting and news-gathering where a party's interests or welfare would be damaged by publicity.

TEST YOUR KNOWLEDGE

1 Explain the difference between a s4(2) order and a s11 order.

2 In which courts can these orders be made?

3 In what situations will a court be justified in granting a s11 order to spare embarrassment to someone involved in a case?

4 A local restaurant owner is on trial for fraud offences involving customers' credit cards. He asks the court for a s4(2) order banning publication of the name of his restaurant, on the grounds that publicity about the case could damage his business. What argument(s) could you use to persuade the court not to make such an order?

5 A police officer is on trial for fraud. Her lawyer asks for a s11 order, banning publication of her home address, on the grounds that she has previously appeared as a witness in trials of very dangerous criminals, and fears for her safety if her address is made public. What argument(s) could you put forward to convince the court not to grant the order?

6 You have been attending a shoplifting case in the magistrates' court, which has followed standard court procedure. After the defendant is convicted and given a community sentence, his lawyer asks the court for a s11 order, banning the press from mentioning his client's name in reports of the case. He says that his client is unemployed, and the publicity would affect his chances of getting a job. What argument(s) would you use to dissuade the court from making the order?

ONLINE RESOURCES

Useful guidelines on reporting restrictions, produced by the Judicial College, the Newspaper Society, the Society of Editors and the Media Lawyers Association are available at:
www.societyofeditors.co.uk

Useful reports of cases where reporting restrictions have been imposed or overturned can be found at the Hold the Front Page website:
www.holdthefrontpage.co.uk

The Society of Editors website also reports current cases on reporting restrictions, at:
www.societyofeditors.co.uk

Chapter 9 Reporting restrictions in criminal cases

Of all the work done in the courts, criminal cases probably hold the most interest for journalists, and no local paper would be complete without its coverage of the magistrates' and Crown Court. This coverage not only sells papers, but also has a social value, in that the thought of being featured in the press is, in a sense, part of an offender's punishment (as any reporter who has been begged to keep a case out of the paper will know). One result of this, however, is that defence lawyers will often do their very best to persuade magistrates and judges to restrict reporting, so journalists need a good grasp of the reporting restrictions in order to challenge them where this is possible. It is also, of course, essential to know about those reporting restrictions which are mandatory in certain types of cases, particularly those involving sex offences, where publishing certain types of information is a criminal offence.

Most criminal cases involving adults can be freely reported (within the provisions of the law on contempt, explained in Chapter 6), but some types of case, or parts of a case, attract specific reporting restrictions. They fall into three main groups:

- restrictions on hearings which take place before a trial;
- restrictions on cases involving rape and sexual offences;
- restrictions on pleas in mitigation.

There are also reporting restrictions designed to protect witnesses in certain circumstances.

(Criminal cases involving children and young people are subject to separate rules, which are discussed in Chapter 10.)

RESTRICTIONS ON HEARINGS BEFORE TRIAL

Before a criminal trial begins, there are one or more hearings, depending on the type of case, the main ones being sending for trial, where the magistrates' court sends the case to the Crown Court, and the allocation procedure, where the decision is made on whether an either way case should be tried by magistrates or in the Crown Court (see Chapter 3 for more details). In these hearings, there will often be discussion of the evidence, which may include details that, when the trial happens, cannot be put before the jury for legal reasons. The defendant's previous convictions may also be referred to, for example, where magistrates are deciding whether a case is too serious for them to try. If the case could then go on to be tried by a jury, publishing these details could prejudice them, so these hearings are subject to special restrictions on what can be reported. These restrictions support the general principle that when the trial begins, the jury members should be able to judge on what they hear and see during the trial, and not anything that may have happened before it.

Sending for trial and allocation hearings in a magistrates' court

These hearings can be quite newsworthy, especially in high-profile cases, because they are often the first time that precise details of the case are revealed. However, because of the risk of prejudice referred to above, both types of hearing, and any other pre-trial hearing which occurs before them in a magistrates' court, are covered by strict reporting restrictions under s 52a of the Crime and Disorder Act 1998. This provides that the only details you can report from these hearings are:

- the names of the court and of the magistrates;
- the name, age, home address and occupation of the defendant (this can include their address at the time of the offence, as well as their current one, but you must make it clear that they no longer live there, or you could face a libel claim from the person who does);
- the charges, either in full or summarised;
- the names of the barristers and/or solicitors representing the parties;
- if the proceedings are adjourned, the date and place they are adjourned to (including whether the case was sent to the Crown Court);
- any arrangements as to bail (but not details of why bail was opposed or refused, because these could be prejudicial);
- whether legal aid was granted;
- where the defendant is charged with a serious or complex fraud, 'relevant business information', which is defined as the following:
  - the address of any business the defendant runs or ran 'on his own account'
  - the name of any business carried on at the relevant time;
  - the name and address of any firm they were engaged by or a partner in at a relevant time;
  - the name and registered address of any company of which they were the director or otherwise engaged at any relevant time;
  - any working address they used in their capacity as a person engaged by that company.
  - These restrictions effectively mean that no details of what either side alleges, beyond the actual charges, can be reported at this stage.

Mentioning other details

Although the details listed above are the only ones which the Act specifically permits to be mentioned in a report of a committal or sending for trial hearing, it has become standard practice to also report that reporting restrictions prevent publication of further details, that the defendant denies the charges, and that the defendant has chosen a jury trial. None of these details carry a risk of prejudicing a jury in the trial. The press also routinely gives a description of the court room scene, and what went on during the hearing, mentioning such details as what the defendant wore, the fact that the only time the defendant spoke was to confirm their name and address, or whether other family members were present at the hearing. Again, none of this material could prejudice a future trial.

Background material

In most cases, you will want to include some background material about the accused and the crime in a report of a committal or a sending for trial, as the fact that you are reporting the hearing will usually mean that the case is a high-profile one, and you will want to let your readers know that this hearing relates to the crime they have been reading about. The reporting restrictions under the Crime and Disorder Act do not prevent this, because they apply to a report of the proceedings, and background material is not actually a report of the proceedings.

However, you do need to be careful that any background material you report does not pose a risk of prejudicing the eventual trial, and leaving you open to a contempt charge. In particular, make sure you do not give the impression that any of the background details were mentioned in the hearing, which could make a potential juror think they were part of the evidence. Where the crime itself has only just happened, and you want to report on that as well as the hearing, it can be safer to run two separate stories, one about the crime, taking care to avoid any risk of prejudice, and one about the hearing, conforming to the s52a reporting restrictions. Where the crime happened some time ago and has already been reported, this is not really feasible, but as long as you make sure that, even with the background information, the story falls within the law on contempt (described in Chapter 6), and within the s52a reporting restrictions, there should be no problem.

Factors which should never be mentioned

Exactly what information from a pre-trial hearing could be prejudicial will vary from case to case, but the following clearly pose a risk of prejudice and should never be mentioned:

- any reasons given by the police or prosecution for opposing bail;
- any reasons given by the magistrates for refusing bail;
- any previous convictions of any of the defendants;
- details of any evidence against the defendant (this is because some evidence mentioned in a pre-trial hearing might later be ruled inadmissible and not put before the jury);
- any suggestion that the defendant might be responsible for other crimes which they are not being charged with (for example, if the police are looking into other unsolved cases of a similar kind, with the suspicion that the defendant might have been involved, this might be mentioned during the discussion on bail).

In 1996, the owners and editor of the *Gloucester Citizen* were fined £4,500 for publishing a report of murderer Fred West's first appearance in the magistrates' court. The story was an accurate account of the hearing, but, in addition to the permitted details, it included a statement that West had admitted killing his daughter. Even though the case had already been widely discussed in the media before the hearing, the paper was guilty of contempt.

In 2012, the *Sun* was fined £3,350 over a report of a pre-trial hearing in a manslaughter case. The story's headline used a quote which was said in court to have come from the defendant: 'Gas pipe's cut, boom . . . you bitch'. It also contained details of texts in which the defendant threatened his girlfriend.

A breach of the s52a restrictions becomes even more serious if the publication happens after the trial has begun and is serious enough to get the trial aborted. In that case, the publisher can be liable to pay extremely high costs under s93 of the Courts Act 2003 (see Chapter 6).

Lifting the restrictions

The reporting restrictions can be lifted by the magistrates' court. This most commonly happens if the defence requests it because they want to encourage witnesses to come forward, which is more likely to happen if fuller details of what happened and when are published. If there is more than one defendant, and they disagree about whether restrictions should be lifted, the magistrates can lift them where they believe it is in the interests of justice to do so, and if they do so, the restrictions no longer apply to any of the defendants. Once they are lifted, they cannot be re-imposed (***R* v *Blackpool Justices ex p Beaverbrook Newspapers Ltd*** (1972)).

It is important to remember that, even if restrictions are lifted, reports of the hearing should not include details of previous convictions or any other information that carries a substantial risk of serious prejudice to the Crown Court trial, as this would be contempt of court.

When do restrictions end?

The reporting restrictions come to an end when one of the events below occurs:

- **The decision is made to hear the case in the magistrates' court.** However, any further pre-trial hearings in the magistrates' court will be covered by similar restrictions under the Magistrates Court Act 1980 (see below, *Pre-trial hearings in the magistrates' court*).
- **All the defendants have been tried at the Crown Court.** Once the trial is over, there is no risk of prejudice, so it is safe to report anything that was said in the committal or sending for trial, even if that includes evidence that was not put before the jury. You might want to report this in order to give a clearer picture of the background to the case, for example, or to show exactly what kind of person the defendant was. A fair and accurate report of a committal or sending for trial hearing published as soon as possible after restrictions cease to apply is treated as a contemporaneous report for the purposes of defamation law, which means it is covered by absolute privilege and you cannot be sued for defamation for anything in it (see p. 257).

Note that there is a form of committal hearing where reporting restrictions do not apply. Section 70 of the Proceeds of Crime Act 2002 allows magistrates to make an order committing a convicted defendant to the Crown Court, where a hearing will decide whether a confiscation order should be made against the defendant, to deprive them of any property gained by their crimes. In this case, the usual reporting restrictions do not apply.

Law in practice Committals for sentencing

As explained earlier (in Chapter 3), there are limits on the sentences which magistrates can impose. Mostly, magistrates send cases which appear too serious for their sentencing powers to be tried at the Crown Court, but it can happen that they decide to try a case, and only decide at the end that the offence justifies a more serious sentence than they can order. They can then send the defendant to the Crown Court for sentencing. Although this is usually described as 'committing' the defendant to the Crown Court, it is not a preliminary hearing like those described on this page, because the defendant has already been tried, and so restrictions under s8 of the Magistrates' Courts Act 1980 and s52a of the Crime and Disorder Act do not apply.

Bail applications

Section 8 of the Magistrates' Courts Act 1980 limits reporting of bail hearings to 'arrangements as to bail on committal or adjournment'. This means you can report whether bail was granted, and any bail conditions, but should not include arguments about whether bail should be granted, nor any reasons given if bail was refused.

Pre-trial hearings

In both the magistrates' courts and the Crown Court, where a defendant has pleaded guilty and is going to be tried, there may be a pre-trial hearing to pinpoint the key issues in the case, and deal with any disputes about the admissibility of evidence. In both cases, there are strict restrictions on what you can report, because of the danger of prejudicing the eventual trial.

Pre-trial hearings in the magistrates' court

These are covered by s8C of the Magistrates Court Act 1980, which defines a pre-trial hearing as any proceedings which take place after the defendant has pleaded not guilty, but before the magistrates start to hear evidence from the prosecution at the trial. When covering this type of hearing, you can only report:

- the name of the court and the magistrates;
- the names, ages, home addresses and occupations of the defendant(s) and witnesses(s);
- the charges, or a summary of them;
- the names of the lawyers involved in the proceedings;
- if the case is adjourned, the date and place to which it is adjourned;
- arrangements as to bail (but not the reasons why bail was opposed or refused – see p. 129);
- whether legal aid was granted.

You can also publish the fact that reporting restrictions were in force and, as with sending for trial and allocation hearings, you can publish descriptions of the court scene, and background to the case, as long as none of it could prejudice the trial (see p. 127). You cannot, however, publish details of the evidence on either side, except in as far as it is contained in the charges.

The Act specifically bans reporting of:

- any rulings the magistrates make on the admissibility of evidence or points of law, or any order they make to alter or discharge such a ruling; and/or
- details of the proceedings regarding applications for rulings on the admissibility of evidence or points of law, including legal arguments put forward and discussion about these issues.

This is because there is obviously no point in a court ruling certain evidence inadmissible, if potential jurors can read about it in a report of the pre-trial hearing.

Pre-trial hearings in the Crown Court

These are covered by the Criminal Procedure and Investigations Act 1996, which defines a pre-trial hearing as any hearing held after the defendant has been sent to the Crown Court for trial, but before a guilty plea is made and accepted, or where the defendant pleads not guilty, any hearing which takes place before the jury is sworn in, or before the preparatory hearing which takes place in very serious or complex cases (see below).

Sections 41 and 42 of the Act prevent reporting of anything said in a pre-trial hearing during:

- applications for rulings on the admissibility of evidence or points of law, including any rulings that the judge makes;
- applications for rulings on the admissibility of evidence or points of law to be discharged or varied, including any order that the judge makes.

As with all types of pre-trial hearings, you also need to make sure you do not report any other material which, while not specified above, might cause a serious risk of substantial prejudice in the trial.

When pre-trial hearing restrictions end

The restrictions can be lifted by the relevant court, either fully or partially, and this may be done at the request of reporters, if they can make a case showing why it is important to be able to report the hearing fully.

In *R v Chaytor and Others* (2010), representatives of the press managed to get reporting restrictions lifted on a pre-trial hearing involving three MPs and a peer, who were charged with fiddling their parliamentary expenses. The hearing had discussed whether parliamentary privilege prevented the defendants from being prosecuted, and after ruling that it did not, the judge allowed this ruling to be published. The defendants appealed against that decision, and the Court of Appeal agreed to media requests to lift the restrictions, because the ruling was on an important issue of constitutional law, and did not pose a risk of prejudice in the trial.

If the defendant objects to the restrictions being lifted, the court can only lift them if satisfied that it would be in the interests of justice to do so, and you cannot report any argument in court about whether the restrictions should be lifted until after the entire trial is over, even if the result of the arguments is that the restrictions are lifted.

The restrictions come to an end when the case is disposed of, which means either when all the defendants have been acquitted or convicted of all the charges, or when the case is dismissed by the court (for example, because of lack of evidence), or when the prosecution decides to drop the case. You can, therefore, report on anything discussed in the hearing once one of the above situations has happened.

Preparatory hearings

Preparatory hearings are also defined in the Criminal Procedure and Investigations Act 1996, and are often confused with pre-trial hearings, though they are in fact a separate type of proceedings. They are held in the Crown Court, in cases which are likely to be long and/or complicated, and in all terrorism cases, and are designed to help both sides make the issues and evidence in the case as easy to understand as possible for the jury. These hearings are held at the start of the trial, but before the jury has been sworn in.

Sections 37 and 38 of the Criminal Procedure and Investigations Act 1996 provide that reports of such hearings may **only** contain:

- the name of the court and the judge;
- the names, ages, home addresses and occupations of the accused and witnesses;
- the offence or offences charged or a summary of them;
- the names of the lawyers in the proceedings;
- where the proceedings are adjourned, the date and place to which they are adjourned;
- any arrangements as to bail;
- whether legal aid was granted.

The Crown Court, Court of Appeal and House of Lords can lift the restrictions, either completely or partially. If any of the defendants object, the court has to be satisfied that it is in the interests of justice to lift the restrictions, after hearing the representations of each accused. If the restrictions are lifted, the ban continues to apply to the accused's objections to their being lifted, which cannot be reported. Otherwise, the restrictions end on conclusion of the trial of the accused or the last of the accused to be tried.

Applications to dismiss

Where a defendant has been committed to the Crown Court for trial on an either way offence (see p. 18), or on a summary offence (this usually happens where they are also charged with a related offence triable in the Crown Court), they can apply to the court to dismiss the case on the grounds of insufficient evidence. Under the Crime and Disorder Act 1998, reports of applications to dismiss can **only** include:

- the names of the court and of the judge;
- the names, addresses and occupations of the parties and the witnesses, and the ages of the defendant(s) and witnesses;
- the offences with which the defendant is charged;
- the names of the barristers and/or solicitors representing the parties;
- if the proceedings are adjourned, the date and court to which they are adjourned;
- any arrangements concerning bail on committal or adjournment;
- whether legal aid was granted to any of the defendants.

If the application to dismiss is successful, the restrictions no longer apply and a full report can be published. If it is not successful, details of the application to dismiss (other than those listed above) can only be published after the trial is over. If there are two or more defendants and they all make an application to dismiss, restrictions only end when all of them have succeeded in their dismissal applications or been tried.

A judge hearing an application to dismiss can lift reporting restrictions if it is in the interests of justice to do so; if one or more of the defendants objects, the judge must hear their arguments and can only lift restrictions if, having heard them, they still believe it is in the interests of justice.

Transfer of sexual offence cases involving children

Where a case involves a sexual offence, s53 of the Criminal Justice Act 1991 provides a procedure by which the normal rules on committal for trial can be bypassed, and the case transferred directly to the Crown Court without any examination by magistrates. This procedure is used where the Director of Public Prosecutions is satisfied that the following three conditions apply:

- The nature of the offence makes it suitable for trial in the Crown Court.
- A child who is either the victim or a witness will be called to give evidence.
- The case should be moved to the Crown Court without delay, in order to avoid any prejudice to the welfare of the child.

In such a case, the defendant can apply to the Crown Court to dismiss the transfer on the grounds of insufficient evidence. If a defendant makes such an application, reporting restrictions apply, and reports must be limited to the same details as specified for committal proceedings, above.

Schedule 6 of the Criminal Justice Act 1991 provides that the judge can lift reporting restrictions in such cases, but if the defendant objects, the restrictions can only be lifted where it would be in the interests of justice to do so.

Law in practice Reporting pre-trial hearings

As you will have gathered by now, reporting pre-trial hearings can be a bit of a minefield. The law covering reporting restrictions in these types of hearing is spread across a number of different statutes, and often differs only slightly between different types of hearing, but, because it does differ, there is a lot to remember. What's more, the courts do not always use the same names for different types of pre-trial hearing (you may come across names not even mentioned here, even though the type of hearing is one covered in this chapter), so it can be difficult to work out which kind you are looking at and therefore which law applies. However, if you follow these rules, you should be safe:

- When reporting the hearing itself, only mention the following:
  - the name of the court and the judge or magistrates;
  - the names, ages, home addresses and occupations of the defendant(s) and witnesses (if given);
  - the charges or a summary of them;
  - the names of the lawyers in the case;
  - the date and place to which proceedings are adjourned (if they are);
  - arrangements as to bail;
  - whether legal aid was granted.
- Include a description of the court scene if you want to, but make sure no details you give could be prejudicial;
- Include background material if you want to, but make sure it is not prejudicial;
- Never mention:
  - previous convictions;
  - reasons put forward for opposing or refusing bail;
  - arguments or rulings about admissibility of evidence or points of law (unless restrictions are lifted specifically to allow a ruling to be reported);
  - details of any evidence put forward by either side.

RESTRICTIONS IN RAPE AND SEXUAL OFFENCES

In order to encourage the victims of sexual offences to report them to the police, reporting restrictions usually prevent the media from identifying such victims, not just during the trial but also for the whole of their lifetimes. These restrictions are covered by the Sexual Offences (Amendment) Act 1992, as amended by the Sexual Offences Act 2003, and by Schedule 2 of the Youth Justice and Criminal Evidence Act 1999.

The combined effect of these Acts is that once someone (man or woman) has made an allegation of a sexual offence, then 'no matter relating to that person shall, during the person's lifetime, be included in any publication if it is likely to lead members of the public to identify that person as the person against whom the offence is alleged to have been committed'. The legislation does not define 'allegation'; in practice this has been treated as meaning making a complaint to the police, but some lawyers believe it may apply earlier than this. Once someone has been accused of the sexual offence, a reporting restriction expressed in slightly different words applies, though the effect would appear to be the same: 'no matter likely to lead members of the public to identify a person as the person against whom the offence is alleged to have been committed shall, during the complainant's lifetime, be included in any publication'.

What will amount to 'matter' that could lead to identification? A new sub-section 3(a) in the amended 1992 Act states that this category includes:

- the person's name;
- their address;
- their school or any other educational establishment they attend;
- their place of work;
- any still or moving pictures of them.

However, publishing information which is not on this list can also be an offence, if it is likely to lead to identification of the person concerned. An obvious example would be stating the name of the defendant and saying that he is charged with raping his niece, since that would allow the public to identify the victim.

In 2006, the *Sunderland Echo* was fined £2,500 and ordered to pay the same amount as compensation to a rape victim after it published a description of her which allowed people who knew her to realise who she was. The paper had been told that there was no relationship between the victim and the defendant, but in fact she was his stepdaughter. This meant that when people who knew the family read the description, they could easily identify the victim.

In 2007, the Kent Messenger Group was fined £1,000 and ordered to pay £2,500 as compensation to the victim of a sex offence after information it published allowed someone she knew to identify her. The paper had reported that a 69-year-old man had pleaded guilty to a series of sex offences against a girl during the 1980s, and in putting together its report it had followed Press Complaints Commission guidelines completely. However, a friend of the victim read the story and, after doing what was described as 'detective work', put the information in the paper together with her own knowledge about the woman concerned. She concluded that her friend was the victim and began questioning her about it. The paper pleaded guilty in order to spare the victim the ordeal of having to appear as a witness.

The Court of Appeal has held that courts cannot use the Sexual Offences (Amendment) Act 1992 to give defendants in rape cases anonymity. The appeal was the result of a case in which a judge accepted arguments that naming the defendant might lead to the victim being identifiable, and so made an order banning identification of the defendant. The Court of Appeal said that the Act did not give courts power to make such an order, and that responsibility for ensuring rape claimants were not identified rested with the press.

Offences covered by the restrictions

The restrictions described apply not just to rape, but also to most other offences which contain a sexual element (including offences which do not involve any physical contact, such as indecent exposure). These include:

- rape (see p. 37 for the definition of this offence, which is now wider than often believed);
- attempted rape;

- aiding, abetting, counselling and procuring rape;
- incitement to rape;
- conspiracy to rape;
- burglary with intent to rape;
- indecent assault;
- offences involving indecency or sexual activity with children;
- indecent exposure;
- internet 'grooming';
- trafficking for sexual exploitation; controlling a prostitute for gain;
- voyeurism.

Note that these are examples and not the complete list; essentially, if there is a sexual element to an offence, it is likely to be covered by the reporting restrictions. The restrictions also apply to cases where someone is charged with attempting to commit any sexual offence, or conspiring, aiding or inciting someone else to commit one.

In 2007, the *Lancashire Evening Post* was fined £3,000 and ordered to pay £4,000 in compensation after naming two victims of trafficking for sexual exploitation. The women were named as witnesses in reports of a series of trials involving a local brothel. However, the paper's staff were unaware that the people who ran the brothel had earlier been tried for trafficking women to the UK for sexual exploitation, and that the two women were the victims of this offence.

Scope of the restrictions

The same restrictions apply to both female and male complainants, and children as well as adults. Unless lifted by a court, the restrictions last for the whole of the complainant's lifetime, even if the complaint is withdrawn or the defendant is acquitted.

The provisions apply to all proceedings which involve allegations of a sexual offence, and not just those held in the criminal courts. They would also apply, for example, in civil cases where there are allegations of a sexual offence (sex discrimination cases in the employment tribunal, for example, may involve allegations of indecent assault). They also apply to any other kind of story which could identify someone as the victim of a sexual offence, and not just reports of court cases. For example, if you were interviewing someone who said that they had been sexually abused as a child, you would need their written consent to mention that if you were naming them in the article. A child under 16 is considered too young to give consent, and a parent cannot give consent on their behalf.

In 2005, the editor of *Marie Claire* magazine was fined £2,500 after the magazine named the victim of a sex offence. In a feature reviewing stories that had hit the news over the previous year, the magazine mentioned a teenage girl who had run away from home to be with a 31-year-old former US marine. The piece included her name and a photograph. After the girl came home, the man was charged and convicted of incitement to commit gross indecency. The girl had been widely named during the period while she was missing, but at that stage, no complaint of a sex offence had been made so the ban on identification did not apply; by the time *Marie Claire* published its story, it did. The editor argued that she had no reason to suspect that the girl might be the victim of a sex offence, but the judge found that, in the circumstances, this was not a realistic argument.

The restrictions apply once an allegation has been made, even if the sex case does not actually go to court.

In 2014, the *Northern Echo* was fined after naming the victim of an alleged sexual offence, though the offence did not end up forming part of the court case it was reporting. The paper was covering a court case where the charge was physical (not sexual) assault. The defendant's barrister referred in court to a rape charge, which in the end was dropped, and did not form part of the case against his client. The newspaper reported both the allegation and the fact that it was dropped. The newspaper believed that it was safe (if arguably unethical) to name the victim, because the case did not then involve a sexual crime, and many lawyers would have agreed this was correct. However, detailed legal research into the origins of the anonymity legislation showed that this was incorrect, and it was intended for the anonymity to last through later court proceedings, even if the sex charge was dropped. The paper then pleaded guilty.

Lifting the restrictions

A judge can make an order lifting the restrictions, in two circumstances:

- Where, before a trial, the person accused of rape asks for restrictions to be lifted, in order to encourage people who may be needed as witnesses to come forward, and that person's defence is likely to be substantially prejudiced if the reporting restrictions are not lifted.
- At the trial, where the judge is satisfied that retaining the reporting restrictions would impose 'a substantial and unreasonable restraint' on the reporting of proceedings, and that it would be in the public interest to remove the restrictions.

With regard to the second of the above reasons, judges are most likely to lift restrictions in cases where the case being tried includes other, very serious offences.

In *R* v *Hutchinson* (1986) the case involved the murder of three members of a family and the rape of a fourth member, who survived the attack. The rape victim was the main witness in the murder trial, and as she had the same surname as the rest of the family, mentioning their names would have identified her. The press pointed out that this made it impossible to report the murder case adequately, and the judge agreed that it was in the public interest to lift the victim's anonymity.

In 2007, a Press Association reporter successfully applied for reporting restrictions to be lifted in a murder trial, where the defendant's defence centred on a claim that someone had tried to rape his wife. The police investigated the claim of attempted rape and no charges were brought, but once a claim is made, it is covered by the reporting restrictions under the Sexual Offences (Amendment) Act 1992. This meant that the press faced a choice of reporting the case without naming the defendant, or naming him and being unable to properly report the circumstances of the offence. After representations from the Press Association, the judge agreed that it was in the public interest to remove the reporting restriction so that the case could be reported accurately and fairly.

Restrictions can also be lifted at the request of the victim, but only if they are over 15 when consent is given. The victim must give written consent to each publication that will identify them, and the decision must have been made freely, and not under pressure from anyone. Proof of the victim's consent is a defence for a newspaper or broadcaster prosecuted under the Act. The anonymity automatically comes to an end when someone dies, which means that if a murder victim was raped, you can report that.

It is also a defence for a publisher to prove that it was not aware, and neither suspected nor had reason to suspect, that the material published was likely to lead to the complainant's identification as an alleged victim of the sexual offence. A further defence, introduced in the Youth Justice and Criminal Evidence Act 1999, applies if the publisher can show that it neither knew nor suspected that an allegation of a sexual offence had been made.

Rape complainants in later proceedings

An exception to the anonymity rule applies if someone who has made an accusation of rape appears in subsequent criminal proceedings other than appeals in the rape case – for example, in the rare cases where someone who claims to have been raped is thought to have lied, and charged with perjury. In this situation, the press can, in reports of the perjury proceedings, reveal that they were the complainant in the previous case or cases.

Jigsaw identification

The term 'jigsaw identification' refers to a problem than can occur when a variety of details about someone who has legal anonymity are published, which mean that, although the person's name has not been mentioned, it is possible for people to put the details together and work out who the story refers to. Although it comes up most often in cases involving victims of sex offences, and particularly children, it can be an issue in any story where someone is granted anonymity by the law.

Jigsaw identification can happen in three main ways. The first is that a story might contain a number of different details about the victim which, on their own, seem insignificant, but put together, could allow the victim to be identified (see p. 134 for an example of this). The second is that one publication or broadcaster might publish different details in successive editions, so that someone reading from the beginning of the coverage to the end would be able put the information together and identify the victim. This can be a particular problem with rolling news broadcasts and online updates, where new information that comes to light is added to the story over a period. The third way – and perhaps the most difficult to guard against – is that different media organisations covering a story might choose to reveal different details so that, while no single story identifies the victim, someone reading more than one could put them together and realise who the person is. For example, let's say a local businessman has been accused of raping his children's nanny. If one paper chooses to name the man, and say that he has been accused of raping a 19-year-old woman, and another does not name the man, but reports that a local man has been accused of raping his children's nanny, it would not be very difficult for someone who knows the family to work out who the victim is.

Jigsaw identification is a particular problem where the person accused or convicted of a sexual offence is a member of the victim's family or household (such as the mother's partner). If you say who the offender is, you clearly cannot then say that they raped or assaulted their wife/daughter/niece/stepdaughter/granddaughter, as that would identify the victim. In fact, it may even be a problem to mention other details such as the age of the child, because if you report that a named person has raped a 13-year-old girl, and the person concerned has a 13-year-old daughter or stepdaughter, most people know that the sexual abuse of children occurs most often within families, so it does not take much to work out who the victim is. In these cases, then, you have two choices: you can report the name of the offender, but not the circumstances of the case, or any details about the victim, or report the circumstances, including details like the age of the child, and not name the offender (or provide any other details that could identify them). Either is fine, but there may still be a problem if other publications make a different choice. For this reason, the best practice in these kinds of cases is for all newsrooms involved to take the same approach.

Other restrictions in sexual offence cases

It is important to realise that the above provisions are quite specific and protect only the victim. They do not create a general power to impose restrictions on publication of any other details, such as the defendant's name or any potentially embarrassing details given in evidence. There are, however, clearly cases where naming the defendant would mean identifying the victim (e.g. if you report that John Smith of Anytown raped his daughter, you identify her even though you do not give her name). In those cases, you would commit a criminal offence if you published the name of the defendant, because it would be material that could lead the victim to be identified.

A court can in some cases use its other powers to impose reporting restrictions in a sexual offence case (e.g. a s39 order where the defendant is a juvenile), but it has to follow the rules relating to those powers; the fact that the case involves a sexual offence is not enough in itself to justify restrictions other than those on identifying the victim.

In *R v Praiil* (2004), a judge at Maidstone Crown Court lifted an order banning the media from naming the chief executive of a charity, who had been charged with rape and indecent assault. The order had been made on the grounds that mentioning his place of work and other details would identify the complainants, but Mr Justice Aikens found that their identity could be protected without imposing such severe restrictions.

In 2004, a district judge in Cardiff refused to grant an order protecting the identity of a teacher charged with sexual offences, which was claimed to be necessary because naming the teacher would effectively identify the girls involved. The judge said that he had no power to make such an order, and deciding whether to publish the defendant's name had to be a matter of judgement for the press; if it did so in such a way as to identify the victims, there were criminal penalties to deal with that.

What the codes say **Sex cases**

The Editors' Code of Practice used by IPSO provides that:

- The press must not identify victims of sexual assault or publish material likely to contribute to such identification unless there is adequate justification and they are legally free to do so (sexual assault here really means any sexual offence, including rape).
- The press must not, even if legally free to do so, identify children under 16 who are victims or witnesses in cases involving sex offences.
- In any press report of a case involving a sexual offence against a child:
  - The child must not be identified.
  - The adult may be identified.
  - The word 'incest' must not be used where a child victim might be identified.
  - Care must be taken that nothing in the report implies the relationship between the accused and the child.

The Ofcom Broadcasting Code provides that:

- Broadcasters reporting sex cases should be especially careful not to provide clues which could lead to the identification of someone who is not yet adult, and is or might be a victim, witness or perpetrator. The provision includes providing limited information which could be pieced together with information reported elsewhere (the 'jigsaw effect'; see p. 137), or inadvertently identifying someone, for example by using the word incest, or in 'any other indirect way'.

Special rules on incest cases

In Northern Ireland, sexual offence cases involving incest may be prosecuted under the Punishment of Incest Act 1908, which no longer applies in England and Wales. The Act allows both press and public to be excluded from court proceedings, and the victim has anonymity, but the court case can be reported unless an order restricting reporting is made.

REPORTING PLEAS IN MITIGATION

When a defendant has pleaded or been found guilty, their lawyers can make pleas of mitigation on their behalf, which essentially means putting forward reasons why the court should deal with the defendant more leniently than it might otherwise do (such as that the defendant has never committed an offence before, or was provoked into acting as they did). In some cases, such pleas will involve derogatory accusations against another person. For example, take a case where the defendant has attacked the victim because the victim made a particularly unpleasant racist remark. If the defendant has pleaded guilty, they might wish to use this as part of their pleas in mitigation.

Usually, such matters can be reported, but ss58–61 of the Criminal Procedure and Investigations Act 1996 provide that reporting restrictions may be applied where there are 'substantial grounds' for believing that:

- something said in the pleas in mitigation is derogatory to someone's character (e.g. because it suggests that their conduct is or has been improper, immoral or criminal); and
- those allegations are untrue, or that the facts stated are irrelevant to the defendant's sentence.

The court can order that the allegations may not be reported for up to a year after the trial.

It is important to note that the Act requires 'substantial grounds'; restrictions should not be ordered where there is merely a chance that the allegations may be derogatory and untrue or irrelevant.

In 2006, a reporter on the *Scarborough Evening News* was able to get a reporting restriction on pleas in mitigation overturned in an assault case. The defendant was convicted of assaulting another man, and as part of the pleas in mitigation, his lawyer explained that the defendant had believed the victim was having an affair with his wife, and that she was pregnant with the victim's baby. The court was going to impose reporting restrictions on the grounds that this was a derogatory statement about the victim, but the reporter pointed out that it had to have 'substantial grounds' for believing the statement was untrue, and it did not have such grounds. The reporter also pointed out that the claim was not irrelevant to the sentence, as the magistrates had said it was grounds for giving the defendant a lighter sentence. The magistrates agreed not to make the order.

In 2007, a judge at Lincoln Crown Court rejected a prosecution application for a s58 order in a case where a defendant's pleas in mitigation included a claim that she had been the victim of domestic violence. The woman was convicted of affray, aggravated vehicle taking and having an offensive weapon, and said in mitigation that she had acted as she did because she was 'at the end of her tether' due to her former partner's violence. The prosecution applied for a s58 order on the grounds that proceedings against the ex-partner had been dropped, but the judge refused, saying that it would be impossible for the press to publish a balanced report without referring to the domestic violence allegations.

The order can be made at any time before the sentence is decided, or as soon as reasonably practical after that, and can be cancelled at any time. The 2014 Judicial College guidelines say that such an order cannot be made, however, if the allegations concerned have already been made during the trial (because in that case there would have been a chance to challenge them during the trial).

If such an order is made, it is an offence to publish the allegations while it lasts, even if the report does not name the person who the allegations are about, so long as it contains material which would make it likely that a member of the public could identify that person. The order can be revoked at any time, and the media may make representations to have it revoked. If not, it automatically lapses after 12 months.

PROTECTING VULNERABLE WITNESSES

There are a number of statutes which give courts the power to protect vulnerable witnesses in criminal cases. These can give rise to reporting restrictions, or simply make it impossible to report a victim's identity because it is not given in court. The powers arise under three different Acts:

- the Youth Justice and Criminal Evidence Act 1999;
- the Coroners and Justice Act 2009;
- the Serious Organised Crime and Police Act 2005.

The Youth Justice and Criminal Evidence Act 1999

Section 46 of the Youth Justice and Criminal Evidence Act 1999 gives the courts power to prevent identification of vulnerable adult witnesses where the witness is eligible for protection (see below) and reporting restrictions are likely to improve:

- the quality of evidence given by the witness; or
- the level of cooperation the witness gives to any party in the case, during the preparation of their case.

A witness is eligible for protection if the court is satisfied that the quality of their evidence, or the level of their cooperation is likely to be diminished by fear or distress about being identified by members of the public as a witness in the proceedings. The 'quality' of evidence is defined by the Act as relating to completeness, accuracy and coherence.

In assessing this, the court must take into account:

- the nature and circumstances of the alleged offence;
- the age of the witness and, if relevant, their social and cultural background, religious and political beliefs, and domestic and employment circumstances;
- any behaviour towards the witness by the defendant, the defendant's family or associates, or anyone else who is likely to be defendant or witness in the proceedings;
- the witness's own views on the matter.

Despite the name of the Act, this provision only applies to adult witnesses; children are covered by separate rules (see Chapter 10).

If a court decides to make a s46 order, the order bans publication of any material relating to the witness, which could lead to them being identified as a witness in the case, for the whole of their lifetime (not just the duration of the case). The Act does not specify that particular details about the person are banned from publication (though their name obviously is), only that it covers any material which could lead to their identification as a witness. The Act suggests that relevant details might include their address, any educational establishment they attend, their workplace or any still or moving picture of them, but this does not mean you cannot mention these details, only that you must not mention them if to do so could lead to the person being identified as a witness in the case. Equally, other details not listed in the Act may not be published if to do so could lead to the witness's identification.

In 1999, the Home Office issued explanatory notes which made it clear that the provisions are intended to be used in cases of real fear or distress, and not merely embarrassment about possible publicity. The guidelines also pointed out that the fact that a witness exhibits sufficient fear or distress to make use of video evidence or a screen desirable (see below) did not necessarily mean that it was also necessary to ban the press from revealing the witness's identity.

In 2005, the *Sunday Express* successfully challenged a s46 order, covering the trial of a convicted paedophile who had sent sexually explicit letters containing death threats to the family of Milly Dowler, who was murdered in 2002. The man, Paul Hughes, was in prison when he began to send letters to the family; most of them were stopped by the prison's security system, but one slipped through the net, and was opened by Milly's sister, Gemma. Hughes was charged with threatening to kill Mrs Dowler, and the judge in the case made a s46 order prohibiting the press from identifying Gemma Dowler. However, the *Sunday Express* argued that as the defendant had pleaded guilty, no witnesses were called, and if Gemma Dowler was not a witness, she could not be protected by a s46 order. The court lifted the order.

Section 46(8) of the Act provides that in judging whether to grant an order, the court must decide whether an order would be in the interests of justice, and take into account the importance of not putting unreasonable restrictions on the reporting of court proceedings. The Act also gives the courts power to lift or amend an order once made. A witness who is over 16 can waive their rights under a s46 order, in writing, so long as nobody interfered with their 'peace or comfort' in order to obtain that waiver.

Witnesses in adult courts who are under 18 have similar protection provided by s39 of the Children and Young Persons Act 1933. However, these orders come to an end when the young person turns 18.

The Youth Justice and Criminal Evidence Act 1999 also gives courts in criminal cases powers to issue a 'special measures direction', under which the public is excluded from the court while a vulnerable or intimidated witness gives evidence. Such a direction can also be used to allow a witness to give evidence by live video link from elsewhere, or from behind a screen. Section 47 of the Act makes it an offence to report before the end of a trial that such an order was made, though the evidence the witness gives can be reported, as can their identity (unless an order concerning identity has been made). Witnesses who may qualify for this protection include:

- anyone under 18;
- any witness whose evidence is likely to be diminished because of mental disorder, significant impairment of intelligence or social functioning, physical disability or physical disorder;
- alleged victims in a sex case;
- any other witness whose evidence, in the court's view, is likely to be diminished by reason of fear or distress in connection with the proceedings.

The fact that a witness falls into one of these categories does not mean that a special measures order will be made automatically, only where the court believes it is necessary.

The Coroners and Justice Act 2009

The Coroners and Justice Act 2009 introduces two new sets of provisions protecting witnesses. The first, contained in s76, allows magistrates' courts to make an 'investigation anonymity order', covering witnesses to investigations into murders or manslaughters caused by shooting or injury with a knife. The orders will usually be granted at the request of the police or another investigating body, and are largely aimed at investigations involving gangs. They prohibit disclosure of information which identifies the person specified as someone who is or was able to assist in an investigation covered by the Act, or might allow them to be identified as such a person. The orders can only be made where:

- the suspect was aged between 11 and 30 at the time the offence was committed;
- the suspect was a member of a group which can be identified from the criminal activities its members appear to engage in, and in which the members are mostly 11–30 years old;
- the person covered by the order has reasonable grounds for fearing intimidation or harm if identified as assisting the investigation;
- the person covered by the order is able to provide information which would assist the investigation, and is more likely than not to provide it if the order is made.

However, there will be no breach of an order if someone disclosing banned information does not know or has no reason to suspect that the order existed, or that the information disclosed could enable the person to be identified as helping with the investigation.

The second new provision applies to court hearings, and is contained in s86. It provides that courts may make a 'witness anonymity order' requiring such measures as considered appropriate to ensure that the witness's identity is not disclosed in, or in connection with, the court proceedings. Measures can include:

- withholding the witness's name and identifying details in the proceedings and court documents;
- allowing the witness to use a pseudonym;
- allowing evidence to be given behind a screen;

- disguising the witness's voice;
- banning questions which might identify them.

Orders can only be made where the court is satisfied that:

- the order is necessary to protect the safety of the witness or another person, to prevent serious damage to property, or to prevent serious harm to the public interest;
- the effect of the order is consistent with the defendant's right to a fair trial;
- the importance of the witness's evidence is such that:
  - they ought to testify, and
  - they would not testify without an order, or
  - there would be real harm to the public interest if they testified without an order.

A court can lift or amend the order either during the proceedings or after they have finished.

The Serious Organised Crime and Police Act 2005

The Serious Organised Crime and Police Act 2005 provides that where a court is reviewing the sentence of someone who has helped the police, or failed to help them after having agreed to do so, it can make an order banning reporting of any matter relating to the proceedings. However, any order should only go so far as is necessary to protect any person, and must be in the interests of justice.

What the codes say Reporting crime

As well as the provisions on sex cases, detailed at p. 138, the Editors' Code of Practice used by IPSO states that:

- Relatives or friends of persons convicted or accused of crime should not generally be identified without their consent, unless they are genuinely relevant to the story.
- Particular regard should be paid to the potentially vulnerable position of children who witness, or are victims of, crime. This should not restrict the right to report legal proceedings.

The Ofcom Broadcasting Code provides that:

- Broadcasters should not take or broadcast footage or audio of people caught up in emergencies, victims of accidents or those suffering a personal tragedy, even in a public place, where that results in an infringement of privacy, unless it is warranted or the people concerned have given consent.

REPORTING RESTRICTIONS IN APPEALS AGAINST ACQUITTAL

As we saw earlier (in Chapter 3), there are now several ways in which the prosecution can appeal against an acquittal, and specific reporting restrictions may apply to these procedures.

Tainted trials

Where the prosecution seeks to quash an acquittal because the original trial was tainted (see p. 33), the court can order any report of the original case to be postponed until after the new trial is finished.

Stopped trials

A judge can stop a trial if it becomes apparent that there is insufficient evidence to support a conviction. Where this happens, the Criminal Justice Act 2003 allows the prosecution to appeal against the decision. The Act provides that reports of the appeal hearing can only contain:

- the name of the court and the judge;
- the names, ages, home addresses and occupations of the defendants and witnesses;
- the offences or a summary of them;
- the names of the lawyers involved;
- if proceedings are adjourned, the place and time to which they are adjourned;
- arrangements for bail;
- whether the defendant was granted representation by the Legal Services Commission (what used to be called legal aid).

It is a criminal offence to break these provisions.

Appeals on new evidence

Where an appeal is brought under s75 of the Criminal Justice Act 2003, because compelling new evidence has come to light, s82 of the Act provides that the Court of Appeal can make an order banning publication of any material which would create a substantial risk of prejudice to the administration of justice in the retrial. It should only make such an order where it is necessary in the interests of justice to do so. The order can cover information which has already been published, but would only apply to publication of that same material again, after the order has been made. In ***R* v *D (Acquitted Person)*** (2006), the Court of Appeal said that the media should be given 14 days' notice when an order for reporting restrictions under the Act was made.

Referrals on points of law

Where the Attorney-General refers a case to the Court of Appeal for its opinion on the point of law raised, under the Criminal Justice Act 1972 (see p. 34) the Court of Appeal can make an order banning publication of the identity of the defendant.

In ***Attorney-General's Reference No. 3 of 1999: Application by the British Broadcasting Corporation to set aside or vary a Reporting Restriction Order*** (2009), the BBC successfully challenged an anonymity order imposed on a reference under the Criminal Justice Act 1972. The order banned identification of a man who was acquitted of rape in controversial circumstances. The rape occurred in 1997, and DNA samples from the scene were taken and placed on the DNA database. A year later, a man, X, was charged with an unrelated case of burglary, and had a DNA sample taken. He was acquitted, but three months later, a match was made between his DNA and that found at the rape scene. He was tried for rape, but the trial judge ruled that the DNA evidence was inadmissible, because the law required that the sample should have been removed from the database after X was acquitted of the burglary. He was acquitted of the rape. The trial was widely reported and X was named at the time. The Attorney-General referred the issue of whether the DNA evidence should have been allowed to the Court of Appeal. This procedure is designed simply to clarify the law, and does not affect the outcome of the original case. The matter was then referred to the House of Lords. In both cases, anonymity orders were in place, preventing identification of X. The BBC wanted to feature the case in a series about controversial acquittals, and applied to have the latest order removed. The House of Lords agreed, stating that there was a clear public interest in the subject matter of the programme, and that it would make a lesser impact if it could not name X. Lord Hope said it was clear that X's right to privacy would be breached, but this was outweighed by the importance of the subject.

Anonymity for teachers accused of crime

Under the Education Act 2011, which came into force in 2012, teachers accused of criminal offences against children at their schools must be given anonymity. Section 13 of the Act makes it an offence to publish any matter which is likely to lead the public to identify a teacher who has been accused of a criminal offence against a child at the school where they work. This applies even if the accusation has been referred to in public (for example, if it was part of an unfair dismissal case at an Employment Tribunal).

The anonymity only covers the period up to a teacher being charged with an offence; once they are charged, they can be named (subject to any other reporting restrictions). The anonymity also ends if the Education Secretary publishes information about the teacher concerned, in connection with an investigation or decision relating to the allegation, or if the General Teaching Council for Wales publishes information about the teacher in connection with an investigation, hearing or decision on the allegation. If none of the above happens, and the teacher is never charged, the anonymity with regard to the accusation lasts for their entire life. The teacher themselves can waive their anonymity, but they must give written consent before it is safe to publish their name, and that consent will be invalid if 'unreasonable interference with their peace or comfort' was used to obtain it.

The press can apply to a magistrates' court to remove the anonymity, and the magistrates can agree to this if satisfied that it is in the interests of justice, having regard to the welfare of both the person accused, and the alleged victim. If the application is refused, an appeal can be made to the Crown Court.

There is a defence under the Act, where the person publishing the information was not aware, and did not suspect or have reason to suspect that the publication included the information identifying the teacher, and did not suspect or have reason to suspect that the allegation had been made.

The restrictions only apply to teachers, not to other school staff, and they only apply when the child concerned goes to the same school that the teacher works at.

Extradition hearings

Extradition hearings are held when someone is wanted for a crime, or has been convicted of one, by another country. The hearing decides whether the person should be sent to that country. These are not criminal hearings in themselves, and they are not covered by any automatic reporting restrictions.

KEY POINTS

Restrictions on hearings before a trial

Special reporting restrictions apply to:

- preliminary hearings in the magistrates' court;
- bail applications;
- pre-trial hearings;
- preparatory hearings at the start of long and/or complex trials;
- applications to dismiss a case for lack of evidence;
- transfer of serious fraud cases;
- transfer of sexual offences involving children.

Restrictions on rape and sexual offence cases

- Once a complaint is made, it is an offence to publish anything relating to the complainant that might identify them as the person making the allegation.
- Once someone has been accused, no material at all which might identify the complainant as the alleged victim can be published.

These restrictions last for the complainant's lifetime, and apply to most sexual offences.

Restrictions on pleas in mitigation

Publication of arguments which are derogatory to someone else can be restricted for up to a year if they are untrue and/or irrelevant, and have not been made in open court during the trial.

Protecting vulnerable witnesses

Courts can take steps to protect vulnerable witnesses under:

- the Youth Justice and Criminal Evidence Act 1999;
- the Coroners and Justice Act 2009;
- the Serious Organised Crime and Police Act 2005.

Reporting restrictions on appeals against acquittal

- In appeals after tainted trials, courts can order reports to be postponed until a second trial is finished.
- Where the prosecution appeals against a stopped trial, reports are limited to seven specific points of information.
- In appeals on compelling new evidence, the Court of Appeal can ban publication of any material which bears a substantial risk of prejudicing a retrial.
- Where the Attorney-General refers an acquittal on a point of law, the Court of Appeal can ban publication of the identity of the defendant.

Anonymity for teachers

It is an offence to identify a teacher accused of assault or sexual assault on a child at their school, unless or until they are charged.

TEST YOUR KNOWLEDGE

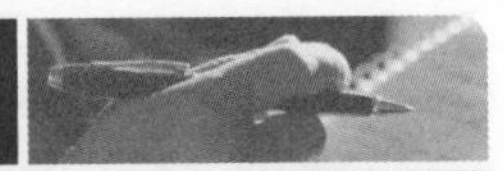

1 A report of committal proceedings in the Crown Court reads: 'James Jones, 36, appeared before magistrates this morning, charged with burglary. Ms Jane Smith, prosecuting, told the court that the defendant had been caught red-handed leaving a luxury flat in King Street; he later admitted burgling ten other apartments in the same block. The magistrates refused bail, with the Chairman, Jake Pake, explaining that there was a clear risk that the defendant would offend again before the trial.'
Which bits of the report should be removed before publishing?

2 You are reporting a bail application. The prosecution opposes bail on the grounds that the defendant is likely to try to leave the country before the trial, but the magistrates grant bail, provided the defendant surrenders his passport. What can you put in your report?

3 What details can you include in a report of an application to dismiss?

4 What restrictions apply to rape cases when a complaint is first made? How do they differ once someone has been accused?

5 When can the restrictions on reporting rape cases be lifted?

6 Which of these sentences is permissible in a report of a rape trial?
(a) John Smith is charged with the rape of his niece.
(b) John Smith is charged with the rape of his niece, Jane.
(c) A Birmingham man has been charged with the rape of his niece.
(d) A plumber of Hope Street, Birmingham, has been charged with raping his niece.
(e) A care assistant from Birmingham told the court how she was raped by her uncle.

7 John Smith has been charged with assault after punching a man whom he claims made indecent suggestions to his wife. His solicitor's pleas in mitigation include information about the victim's relationships with women. In what circumstances does the Criminal Procedure and Investigations Act 1996 allow the court to prevent the press from reporting these remarks?

8 What powers does the Youth Justice and Criminal Evidence Act 1999 give courts to protect vulnerable witnesses? What must the court consider when deciding whether to use these powers?

WWW ONLINE RESOURCES

The Youth Justice and Criminal Evidence Act 1999 can be read at:
www.legislation.gov.uk/ukpga/1999/23/contents

The Sexual Offences (Amendment) Act 1992 can be read at:
www.legislation.gov.uk/ukpga/1992/34/contents

The Criminal Procedure and Investigations Act 1996 can be read at:
www.legislation.gov.uk/ukpga/1996/25/contents

The Coroners and Justice Act 2009 can be read at:
www.legislation.gov.uk/ukpga/2009/25/contents

Useful guidelines on reporting restrictions, produced by the Judicial College, the Newspaper Society, the Society of Editors and the Media Lawyers Association are available at:
www.societyofeditors.co.uk

Useful reports of cases where reporting restrictions have been imposed or overturned can be found at the Hold the Front Page website:
www.holdthefrontpage.co.uk

The Society of Editors website also reports on the use of reporting restrictions, at:
www.societyofeditors.co.uk

Reporting restrictions concerning children

It is often believed – by magistrates as well as journalists – that the law imposes a blanket ban on identifying juveniles involved in criminal proceedings, but this is not the case. However, there are rules which can restrict the press from identifying children and young people who are involved in court cases, whether as victims, witnesses or defendants. Some restrictions are automatic, though most of these can be lifted by the courts in certain circumstances; others are applied at the court's discretion.

When considering whether to lift or apply restrictions in cases involving children, the higher courts have made it plain that the courts must give sufficient weight to the Human Rights Act 1998 and, in particular, the Article 10 right to freedom of expression on the one hand and, on the other, the rights under Articles 6 and 8 to a fair trial and respect for private and family life respectively.

As far as the law discussed in this chapter is concerned, 'child', 'young person' and 'juvenile' are all used to mean a person under 18. However, under English law, a child who is under ten cannot be charged with a criminal offence.

Until a criminal case comes to court, the media is free to publish the names of any juvenile involved, just as for adults, provided that doing so does not create a risk of prejudicing any trial, under the normal rules on contempt of court (explained in Chapter 6). The one exception is where the offence is a sexual one, in which case the complainant may not be identified (see p. 137).

YOUTH COURT CASES

In most cases where someone accused of a crime is under 18, the case is heard by a youth court. The youth court is not a building, but a type of proceedings held in a magistrates' court, usually in a smaller court room, so that the proceedings are less intimidating for the defendant(s). The first point to note here is that many magistrates, and magistrates' clerks, believe that youth courts are closed courts. This is incorrect: although these courts are not open to the public, s47 of the Children and Young Persons Act 1933 provides that bona fide journalists from newspapers and news agencies have a right to attend youth Court proceedings. Youth courts also have a power under the same section to allow in 'other persons' which presumably could apply to other types of journalists.

Where a young person is being prosecuted in a youth court, the media cannot identify them unless the court or the Home Secretary lifts reporting restrictions. Section 49 of the Children and Young Persons Act 1933 bans the media from publishing or broadcasting:

- the name, address or school of any child or young person who is involved in the proceedings (as well as defendants, this includes witnesses and victims who are under 18);
- any details that are likely to lead to a young person involved in the proceedings being identified;
- any photograph of a young person involved in the proceedings.

(In Northern Ireland, similar provisions apply, but under the Criminal Justice (Children) (Northern Ireland) Order 1998.)

If the ban is breached, the proprietor, editor or publisher of the newspaper (and those who have corresponding functions in a broadcasting company) may be prosecuted for a breach of the Act. They will have a defence if they can prove that they were unaware and did not suspect that the material published breached s49.

Note that s49 does not apply until court proceedings begin: you can legally report the name of a child who has been arrested for or charged with an offence. However, the PCC Code discourages the naming of under-16s involved in crime, except where there is 'exceptional public interest' in doing so.

The effect of s49

Section 49 makes it clear that the ban goes beyond merely mentioning the name of a youth court defendant, witness or victim: you cannot publish anything at all which is likely to identify them. It is not sufficient to make sure that no ordinary member of the public can recognise the young person from the details or images shown; the offence can be committed even if only those who know the young person would be able to identify them from the story. For this reason, merely concealing the face in a photo, for example, may not be enough to avoid prosecution.

In 2003, the *Plymouth Evening Herald* was fined £2,500 for publishing a photo of a 15-year-old boy who had been convicted at a youth court after stabbing another child. The paper had partially concealed the boy's face in the photo they used, but his friends and family gave evidence that they could still tell that it was him.

However, it appears that the restriction only applies to reports of the court proceedings themselves.

In 2010, the former editor of the *Croydon Advertiser* was cleared of breaching s49, after publishing a story about the 15-year-old victim of a knife attack, which both named the teenager and included a picture of him. Eight days before the story was published, someone had appeared at a youth court, charged with the attack, and so s49 applied to anyone under 18 who was involved in the case, including the victim. However, the judge said that the story could not be a breach of s49, because it was not a report of the youth court proceedings, and ordered that the journalist should not be liable for court costs. She nevertheless criticised the decision to run the story without checking whether a court hearing had taken place. The story had been legalled and the newspaper's solicitor, Tony Jaffa of Foot Anstey, told *Press Gazette* that he was surprised when the journalist was prosecuted, because the legal team were confident that a story which only reported the victim's experiences and opinions, without referring to any court hearing, could not be a breach of s49.

Law in practice Adults in youth court proceedings

Take care with naming adults who are involved in youth court proceedings (such as witnesses). Although there is no ban on naming anyone aged over 18, naming an adult could accidentally provide information which could identify someone under 18 in the case (e.g. if they are related or known to each other). Essentially, if someone who did not already know the details of the case could name the child as a result of reading the report, there is a risk of committing an offence under the Act.

Lifting the s49 restrictions

There are three situations in which the youth court reporting restrictions can be lifted.

1 **Avoiding injustice:** Section 49(5) of the Children and Young Persons Act 1933 allows the Home Secretary, or the court concerned, to waive the ban on identifying a child involved in youth court proceedings, 'if satisfied that it is appropriate to do so for the purpose of avoiding injustice to a child or young person'. An example of the way in which this provision might be used is where a young witness has been publicly confused with a young defendant, and naming the defendant would avoid injustice to the witness. This provision is not designed to be used as a means of 'naming and shaming' defendants.

2 **Tracing suspects:** The Criminal Justice and Public Order Act 1994 provides that the Director of Public Prosecutions can apply to a youth court to remove reporting restrictions where this could help trace a juvenile charged with or convicted of a violent or sexual offence, or any offence for which an adult could receive a sentence of 14 years or more in prison. The court can decide the extent to which restrictions are lifted, so may, for example, put a time limit on the order.

3 **After conviction:** Once a child has been convicted in a youth court, the Crime (Sentences) Act 1997 allows the court to waive the ban on identifying them, where it is in the public interest to do so. Before doing so, it should take into account any arguments for or against lifting the ban put forward by either side in the case. In 1998, the Lord Chancellor's Department and the Home Office circulated jointly produced advice on the kinds of circumstances in which waiving restrictions would be justified in the public interest. These include:

   - where the young person was a persistent or very serious offender;
   - where the offending had affected a large number of people;
   - where publicity could help prevent further criminal activity.

   The advice also identified circumstances where it would generally not be in the interests of justice for reporting restrictions to be lifted. These include:

   - where publicity might put the young person or their family in danger of harassment or harm;
   - where the offender was especially young or particularly vulnerable;
   - where the offender was sorry for their actions, and prepared to take responsibility for them;
   - where naming the offender would mean identifying the victim, and this would lead to unwelcome publicity about the victim.

Unless the court chooses to exercise one of these three options, the ban applies automatically; the court does not need to make an order imposing it. Where the media feels that the ban should be lifted, they can make representations to the magistrates.

In ***McKerry* v *Teesdale & Wear Valley Justices*** (2001), the case concerned a 15-year-old who had pleaded guilty to taking a car without consent. The magistrates sought to lift the reporting ban, on the grounds that the offender had shown a complete disregard for the law and was a danger to the public, and that if he was identified, the public would find it easier to protect themselves from his activities. The Divisional Court of the Queen's Bench stated that the power to lift reporting restrictions on youth court cases had to be used with care, and should not, for example, be used as an additional punishment to 'name and shame' the offender. However, the court agreed that this was an example of a situation in which there was a legitimate public interest in identifying the defendant.

Where the young person turns 18 during the proceedings, it has always been considered that the s49 restriction is automatically lifted, and this was confirmed by the by the Court of Appeal in R (JC and Another) v ***The Central Criminal Court*** (2014). The Court said that the restrictions were not designed to protect adults.

Section 49 restrictions do not apply to anyone who is dead.

Other courts where s49 restrictions apply

The reporting restrictions described above also apply to reports of appeals from the youth courts, either to the Crown Court, or to the Divisional Court of the Queen's Bench on a point of law. They also apply where proceedings are held in any court to vary or withdraw a supervision order against someone under 18, as long as the reporting restrictions are stated in open court.

Youth court cases being sent to the Crown Court

Where a young person has committed a serious offence, the case may (and in some cases must) be sent to the Crown Court for trial. The youth court will hold a sending for trial hearing to do this, and these are covered by the same reporting restrictions as when sending for trial happens to adult defendants in the magistrates' court (see p. 126). Remember, though, that these hearings will also be covered by the youth court reporting restrictions under s49, described above, so you cannot mention the name or address of any young person involved, even though the rules on sending for trial hearings usually permit you to mention names and addresses of witnesses and defendants.

The sending for trial restrictions do not apply where a young person has been convicted of a serious crime in the youth court, and is committed to the Crown Court for sentencing, because this is not a pre-trial hearing. The Crown Court trial itself will not be covered by the restrictions applicable to youth courts unless a specific order to that effect is made (see Children in adult courts, below).

Law in practice Youth court anonymity after 18

Youth court anonymity lasts only until the defendant's 18th birthday, so if a defendant is soon to turn 18, you may not need to bother asking the court to lift anonymity, as you will be able to write about the case after their birthday anyway, advises Tony Jaffa of solicitors Foot Anstey. This also means that once an offender turns 18, you are free to write about their youth court history, so if they are convicted again as an adult, it is permissible to use this as background after a trial is over.

CHILDREN IN ADULT COURTS

Child defendants must be tried in the Crown Court if they are charged with a homicide offence, or certain firearms offences. They may also be tried in the adult courts if there is an adult co-defendant. Some serious crimes, including causing death by dangerous driving and some sex offences are classified as 'grave', and if a person under 18 is accused of one of these, the magistrates will consider whether their sentencing powers are likely to be sufficient if the defendant is found guilty. If not, the defendant will be tried at the Crown Court. Magistrates can also send a defendant who is under 18 for Crown Court trial if they are considered 'dangerous', which essentially means that there is a significant risk of them committing further offences which might cause serious harm to the public.

Where an adult court is hearing a case that involves a defendant under 18, the rule that the court should sit in public still applies, but a Practice Direction issued in 2000 states that in some cases, it may be appropriate to take steps to make the courtroom less intimidating for a very young defendant. Where this would include restricting press access to the courtroom, arrangements should be made to relay the proceedings to another room within the same building, preferably by video but at least via an audio link (Practice Direction (Crown Court: trial of children and young persons) 2001).

Where a juvenile is involved in proceedings before any court except a youth court, their age does not automatically create any reporting restrictions. However, s39 of the Children and Young Persons Act 1933 allows the court to order that:

- newspaper or broadcast reports of the proceedings may not reveal the name, address or school of the young person, or include any details designed to lead to the young person being identified; and
- no pictures of the young person can be published or broadcast.

These orders are most commonly used in criminal cases (because they are most likely to be reported), but they can be made in any kind of court proceedings, including civil cases and inquests. Such orders can cover any person under 18 who is 'concerned in the proceedings', including witnesses and victims as well as defendants (but not victims who are dead; see below). In Northern Ireland, broadly similar provisions apply, but under Article 22 of the Criminal Justice (Children) (Northern Ireland) Order 1998. The 2014 Judicial College guidelines point out that a s39 order cannot be made until the person is charged, so cannot be used to prevent the naming of a suspect under 18 who has been arrested but not yet charged.

The court is not obliged to make a s39 order, but they commonly do. However, the 2014 guidelines issued by the Judicial College make it clear that these orders should not be made as a matter of routine. They state that:

- There must be a good reason, apart from age alone, for imposing a s39 order.
- The onus lies on the party requesting the order to show that there are good reasons for it.
- The court must give weight to the welfare of the child, but must also balance the public interest in full reporting of criminal proceedings against the desirability of not causing harm to the child.
- The court should take into account the age of the child, and the effect of labelling them as a criminal before they are an adult.
- The weight to be given to the child's interest may change if they are convicted. Where an under-18 is convicted of a serious crime, the public interest in knowing the outcome of trials, and in the deterrent effect of public disgrace will usually favour lifting the order.
- Any order must comply with Article 10 of the Human Rights Act, which means it must be necessary and proportionate, and there must be a pressing social need for it.

Where a judge is considering making an order, the press can put forward arguments against it. The basis for such arguments would generally be that in the case concerned, the importance of press freedom outweighs the possible effects of publicity on the child. The judge then has to weigh up the competing interests of press freedom and protection of the child.

In *R (on the application of Y)* v *Aylesbury Crown Court* (2012), Lord Justice Hooper said that where the competing interests were very finely balanced, the court should usually make an order restricting reporting, though it could decide to allow publication of some details and not others.

The following cases indicate some of the ways in which the courts have juggled these issues.

In *R* v *Central Criminal Court ex p Crook and ex p Goodwin* (1995), the case concerned a s39 order made in the trial of a couple for the manslaughter of their son, and cruelty to their other three children. Not being able to identify the children made it very difficult to report anything meaningful about the case, and the order was challenged by the press. However, the court held that in the circumstances of this case, the importance of protecting the children outweighed the public interest in knowing about the case.

In *R* v *Lee* (1993), the Court of Appeal approved the refusal of a judge to issue a s39 order for a 14-year-old boy who had taken part in a robbery, while he was on bail after being charged with rape. The judge had said that identifying the boy would have a strong deterrent effect on others, and the public interest in knowing who he was was greater than any potential risk of harm to the boy himself. The Court of Appeal approved this reasoning.

In 2005, two reporters from Yeovil's *Western Gazette* were able to persuade magistrates to lift a s39 order banning identification of twin boys aged 14, whose mother was charged with failing to send them to school. The order effectively meant that the mother could not be named either, and the journalists were able to argue that this was in breach of the principle of open justice.

In 2006, a s39 order protecting a teenager who killed her mother's boyfriend was lifted after a reporter from the *Lancashire Evening Telegraph* pointed out to the court that the ban made it virtually impossible to report the case at all. The victim had been a well-known figure in the area, and the reporter pointed out that the ban meant that if he was named, his relationship to the defendant, and the place where the murder happened, could not be mentioned, as these details would identify the defendant. The murder had received a lot of publicity and the restrictions would mean that readers would not even realise that it was the event referred to in the court report. In addition, it was pointed out that the ban would make it impossible to report the mitigating circumstances put forward for the defendant, so she would appear to have killed in cold blood. The order was lifted despite opposition from defence lawyers.

In 2006, a judge at Liverpool Crown Court agreed not to make a s39 order banning identification of a victim, after representations from the press. The 13-year-old victim was viciously attacked at school by another teenager, resulting in national press coverage, and the *Liverpool Echo* argued that her name had already been used in reports of the attack, and that her family did not object to her being named.

In 2006, a trainee reporter from the *Dorset Echo* persuaded a court not to impose a s39 order banning identification of a 17-year-old who had pleaded guilty to burglary. The reporter pointed out that the youth had already been named in a plea and directions hearing, and also repeated the judge's comments about the distress that burglary causes to its victims as evidence of the public interest in hearing about the case fully.

In 2007, reporters from the *Richmond and Twickenham Times* were able to persuade a court to lift s39 restrictions banning the press from identifying the teenage victims of an attempted armed robbery. The order was designed to protect the victims, but reporters pointed out that the victims and defendants already knew each other, and the victims' names had already been given in open court. In addition, the paper had earlier run a front-page story on the incident, which had attracted a lot of attention because it happened in an area where such crime was rare. This meant that a s39 order would not protect the victims, and so was pointless from that point of view, yet would prevent the paper from fully reporting the case. The judge agreed to lift the restrictions.

In 2010, a trainee reporter from the *Epsom Guardian* successfully challenged a s39 order covering two youths who viciously attacked a man who they wrongly believed was a paedophile. She argued that the seriousness of the attack meant it was in the public interest to know the identity of the defendants.

As a rule, the courts should not impose s39 orders merely for the purpose of protecting the defendant's family from publicity. In ***Chief Constable of Surrey* v *JHG and DHG*** (2002), the Queen's Bench Division held that the effect of publicity on the family should only be taken into account in very exceptional cases, where the impact on the relatives would affect the rehabilitation of the offender themselves, or where a member of the family might suffer a degree of emotional or psychological trauma that went beyond the normal effects of being connected with someone publicly known to have committed crime.

Very young children

The Judicial Studies Board (JSB) guidelines acknowledge that where a child is very young they are much less likely to be damaged by publicity, and so s39 orders are less likely to be appropriate. The JSB does not specifically define 'very young', but explains that the risk is smaller because the child will not be aware of the publicity, which suggests the principle is confined to children young enough not to be aware. In a number of cases, the press has been able to get restrictions lifted on this basis.

In 2000, the *Banbury Guardian* convinced local magistrates to lift a s39 order preventing identification of an 18-month-old child, whose father had pleaded guilty to being drunk in charge of a child. The magistrates agreed that a child of this age could not be affected by any publicity about the case.

In 2004, a reporter on the *Worcester Evening News* successfully challenged a s39 order banning identification of a two-year-old, in a child neglect case. The reporter cited the *Banbury Guardian* case above, and the court agreed that this was a similar case where the child was too young to be affected and the ban would unreasonably restrict reporting.

In 2006, the *Eastern Daily* Press persuaded a court to lift a s39 order which applied to a 11-month-old baby, whose stepfather was accused of child cruelty. The paper pointed out that a ban on identifying the child meant it could not name the defendant either, and the judge agreed that as the child was so young, there was no real chance of it being affected by the proceedings.

Naming dead children

There have been cases where judges have attempted to use s39 orders to ban publication of the names of dead children, even though the names have already been made public, for example in inquest reports or news stories about the deaths. The JSB guidelines state that the powers under s39 cannot be used in this way. However, it is important to make sure that mentioning a dead child does not mean that other children who are subject to a s39 order (such as siblings) are effectively identified as well.

Children not 'concerned in the proceedings'

As explained earlier, s39 permits orders to be made in respect of children 'concerned in' court proceedings. The 2014 Judicial College guidelines make it clear that in a criminal case, the only children considered to be 'concerned in the proceedings' are defendants, victims and witnesses (though other children may be considered to be 'concerned in' other types of proceedings, such as family cases).

A s39 order should not be applied to children who are not actually part of the proceedings, but merely related to someone who is.

In 1998, the local press in Bingley, West Yorkshire, were able to convince magistrates to lift a s39 order banning identification of a 14-year-old boy whose mother was assaulted by his father's girlfriend during a row about the boy.

In 2008, the Press Association successfully challenged an order banning publication of the address of a couple charged with running a brothel, and a picture of the wife. The order had been imposed to protect their children from publicity, and also to protect the wife from her abusive former husband, who she feared might track her down. Press Association legal editor, Mike Dodd, pointed out to the judge at Canterbury Crown Court that the couple's children were not 'concerned in the proceedings', and a s39 order could not be used to protect an adult.

In 2010, the Press Association was able to get a s39 order lifted in a case involving a mother convicted of child neglect. Rebecca Mary Ireland was jailed for 12 weeks for neglecting her six-week-old daughter. The child died, though the cause of her death was not proved. The judge made a s39 order banning identification of the defendant's younger child, but the Press Association legal editor, Mike Dodd, pointed out that this child could not be said to be involved in the proceedings, as it was not even born until after the events which led to the neglect charge.

In March 2012, a Press Association reporter successfully overturned an s39 order banning the press from naming Kai Rooney, son of Wayne and Coleen Rooney. The case in question involved a plot to blackmail Coleen Rooney into handing over £5,000 to get back some stolen family photos, and the judge at Manchester Crown Court imposed an order banning the press from naming the couple's son. The ban was successfully overturned when a Press Association reporter argued that Kai was not involved in the proceedings and, in addition, that his name and photograph had been widely used in the media before the case and, in fact, his mother had tweeted photos of him to the public.

Orders attempting to cover other proceedings

It seems that the child must be concerned in the actual proceedings before the court making the order; a court cannot make a s39 order banning identification of a child because the child is concerned in another court case (though, of course, the court in that case can).

In *R* v *Lee* (1993), the Court of Appeal held that a s39 order covering a hearing in a magistrates' court could not apply when the same case reached the Crown Court. If anonymity was necessary, the Crown Court judge would have to make their own order.

Other coverage of children subject to s39 orders

The purpose of s39 orders is to prevent the child in question being identified as being involved in the court proceedings where the order was made, and the 2014 Judicial College guidelines make it clear that the fact that a child is the subject of a s39 order does not mean that you cannot identify them in other contexts. So if a child to whom a s39 order applies wins a prize at school, or saves a drowning dog, there is no problem with reporting that and naming them in the story, so long as you do not also mention that they are involved in the court case.

Protecting adult defendants

There may be cases where to name an adult involved in a trial inevitably means identifying a child who is the subject of a s39 order. Where this is the case, naming the adult will breach the order. However, the Judicial College's 2014 guidelines state that it is not lawful for a court specifically to ban publication of an adult's identity in a s39 order. The courts may offer guidelines where identifying an adult could identify a child, but their suggestions are not binding, and it is open to the press to find other ways of staying within the law and still naming the relevant adult. The guidelines give the example of incest cases, where if the word incest is used, then naming the defendant may identify the child, suggesting that the press may be able to avoid the problem by using the term 'a sexual offence' instead. This approach was confirmed in ***R* v *Southwark Crown Court ex p Godwin*** (1992), where the Court of Appeal said that there were cases where publishing the name of an adult would breach an order because it would mean the child was identified, and that in these cases, judges could advise on whether publication of certain names or details would breach the order, but they could not use the order to ban publication of those names.

Where a child is not covered by s39 (because they are not involved in the proceedings, for example), there is no jurisdiction for the criminal courts to ban identification of an adult defendant in order to protect the identity of their children.

In ***R* v *Croydon Crown Court ex p Trinity Mirror Plc and Others*** (2008), several newspapers challenged an injunction issued by the Croydon court preventing the press from naming the children of a man convicted of possessing indecent images of children. This meant that the press were also unable to name the man himself. The children were not involved in the criminal proceedings and the order was made purely to protect them from the effects of their father's conviction being publicised. The Court of Appeal decided that the Crown Court had no jurisdiction to issue an injunction for such a reason. It could not issue a s11 order, because s11 orders cannot be used to prevent publication of evidence that has been given in open court. The Court of Appeal said that the High Court has a jurisdiction, under s45(4) of the Senior Courts Act 1981, to issue injunctions preventing publication of evidence given publicly to the Crown Court, but this could only be used in matters that related to the way in which the case itself was handled. In this case, the children were not victims or witnesses, so the injunction granted had nothing to do with the court proceedings themselves. Therefore, there was no legal basis for the injunction. The Court of Appeal also considered whether, if the Crown Court had had the power to issue the injunction, it should have done so. The argument had been that the children's right to privacy, under the Human Rights Act 1998, justified the injunction. The Court of Appeal rejected this argument, saying that it was impossible to overemphasise the importance of the media's right to report criminal trials, and that while the children of a defendant could clearly suffer prejudice and damage in this situation, there was nothing to distinguish the harm to these particular children from that caused to all the other children of people convicted of offences related to child pornography.

Despite the clear decision in ***R* v *Croydon Crown Court***, just a few months later magistrates at Chichester made an order banning identification of a man convicted of possessing almost 700 pornographic pictures of children, on the grounds that naming him could cause problems for his children. Using the authority of ***R* v *Croydon***, representatives of the press were able to get the order lifted.

In 2008, the news agency INS Group successfully argued against a s39 order banning publication of a picture of a teacher facing charges of sexual activity with children. The teacher's barrister had claimed that publishing the picture would mean that the victims could be identified. The agency pointed out that a s39 order could not be used to ban publication of an adult's identity, and in any case he had already been named in court, so that if anyone was going to be able to identify the victims from knowing his identity, it was too late to prevent that. In addition, the agency pointed out that the victims were entitled to anonymity as sex offence victims, and any child witnesses could be given anonymity via a s39 order.

In ***Crawford* v *Director of Public Prosecutions*** (2008), representatives of the press finally managed to get an invalid s39 order lifted after it had been in place for two years. The order banned publication of details of a case in which a barrister, who also sat as a judge, was convicted of harassing his ex-wife and her partner. The order had been granted because the defendant claimed publicity about the case would harm his children, but the court lifted it, finding that there was no evidence of any particular potential harm to the children, other than the obvious embarrassment of their father being convicted of a criminal offence, and this was not enough to justify the ban. The court said that the defendant's public profile was neither a reason to impose a ban, nor a reason not to; everyone should be considered equal under the law. However, the fact that the case was a criminal one was relevant, because the decision to prosecute brought the matter into the public domain. The court stressed that courts should take great care when imposing orders restricting publication of details of criminal proceedings. Such orders should not be made routinely, and, before an order is made, members of the press should be asked whether they wish to put forward arguments against it.

Issuing the s39 order

Section 39 orders should be clear and unambiguous. In ***R* v *Central Criminal Court, ex p Godwin and Crook*** (1995). Lord Justice Glidewell said that a court issuing a s39 order should:

- make the terms completely clear, and if there is any room for doubt over which child or children the order covers, this should be spelt out clearly;
- draw up a written copy of the order as soon as possible after it has been made orally, and keep a copy in the court office so that journalists can have access to it;
- include in the court lists a reference to the order, so that its existence is clear even to those who were not in court when it was made.

Lord Justice Glidewell confirmed that a court considering making a s39 order can hear representations from anyone with a legitimate interest in opposing the order, which includes the press.

There have been cases where magistrates challenged over a s39 order claim they have no power to lift or relax it, but this is not the case. The power to do so has been recognised in several cases before the Divisional Court of the Queen's Bench, including ***R* v *Central Criminal Court ex p Simpkins*** (1998), and ***R* v *Manchester Crown Court, ex p H*** (A Juvenile) (2000).

When s39 orders end

The anonymity granted under an s39 order expires automatically when the person concerned becomes 18. This also means that an s39 order cannot be made when a person is 18 or over when a case comes to court, but was under 18 when the events that gave rise to the case took place.

Law in practice Challenging s39 orders

According to Tony Jaffa, Head of Media at solicitors Foot Anstey, s39 orders are the single most common type of reporting restrictions to be wrongly imposed by the courts:

> We deal with several cases every month of courts trying to impose s39 orders banning identification of adults, or dead children, or children who are not involved in the proceedings. The legislation makes it absolutely clear that it does not cover adults or children who are not involved in the proceedings, so I would advise court reporters always to have a copy of the relevant section with them, so they can quote from it. The legislation itself doesn't specify that dead children are not covered, but that is well-established now, so it may also be useful to be able to refer to the Judicial Studies Board guidelines on this.

What the codes say Children and crime

The Ofcom Broadcasting Code provides that:

- When covering any pre-trial investigation into an alleged criminal offence in the UK, broadcasters should pay particular regard to the potentially vulnerable position of any witness or victim who is not yet adult, before broadcasting their name, address, identity of school or other educational establishment, place of work, or any still or moving picture of them.
- Particular justification is required for broadcasting the same information where the young person is a defendant or potential defendant.

The Editors' Code of Practice used by IPSO requires that:

- Particular regard should be paid to the potentially vulnerable position of children who witness, or are victims of, crime. This should not restrict the right to report legal proceedings.

Child victims of sex offences

A child who is the victim of any sexual offence has the same protection from identification as adult victims (see p. 133). This essentially means that from the time the allegation is made you cannot publish any material which might lead to them being identified and, as with adults, this protection lasts for the whole of their lives, unless it is lifted by a court. Remember that this protection applies not just to reports of criminal cases involving sexual offences, but also any case involving that victim where a report could identify them as the victim of a sexual offence. This would include, for example, family proceedings where there are allegations of sexual abuse.

With sex cases involving children, the biggest danger for the media is that of jigsaw identification, where information from a range of different reports can be pieced together to identify the child involved. Many cases involve abuse within the family, so, for example, if one publication calls the offence incest, and another names the defendant, it is instantly obvious who the victim is likely to be. For this reason, it is important to be especially careful with the information you use in this kind of story, and both the Ofcom and Editors' Codes contain provisions on reporting sex cases where children are involved (see p. 137 for more advice on avoiding jigsaw identification).

What the codes say Children in sex cases

The Editors' Code of Practice used by IPSO states that:

- The press must not, even if legally free to do so, identify children under 16 who are victims or witnesses in cases involving sex offences.
- In any press report of a case involving a sexual offence against a child –
  - The child must not be identified.
  - The adult may be identified.

- The word 'incest' must not be used where a child victim might be identified.
- Care must be taken that nothing in the report implies the relationship between the accused and the child.

The guidance on using the Code states that in sex cases involving children, editors should 'err on the side of caution', and the following adjudication shows why; even apparently insignificant details can, in certain circumstances, cause a problem.

In ***A Man* v *Staffordshire Newsletter***, May 3, 2011, the PCC upheld a complaint about a report into a case of sexual activity with a child, because it contained details that could allow people to work out who the victim was. The report gave the name of the offender, and stated the age of the child when the abuse began, how long it had gone on for, and the child's gender. These details were enough, in the context of the case, to allow local people to work out who the child was, and as a result the identity of the child had become widely known in the local community. The PCC said that the paper had been justified in naming the offender, but should have taken more care with the other details it published.

The Ofcom Code provides that:

Where statutory or other legal restrictions apply preventing personal identification, broadcasters should also be particularly careful not to provide clues which may lead to the identification of those who are not yet adult (the defining age may differ in different parts of the UK) and who are, or might be, involved as a victim, witness, defendant or other perpetrator in the case of sexual offences featured in criminal, civil or family court proceedings:

- by reporting limited information which may be pieced together with other information available elsewhere, for example in newspaper reports (the 'jigsaw effect');
- inadvertently, for example by describing an offence as 'incest'; or
- in any other indirect way.

When covering any pre-trial investigation into an alleged criminal offence in the UK, broadcasters should pay particular regard to the potentially vulnerable position of any person who is not yet adult who is involved as a witness or victim, before broadcasting their name, address, identity of school or other educational establishment, place of work, or any still or moving picture of them. Particular justification is also required for the broadcast of such material relating to the identity of any person who is not yet adult who is involved in the defence as a defendant or potential defendant.

PROVISIONS AGAINST ANTI-SOCIAL BEHAVIOUR

Anti-Social Behaviour Orders (ASBOs), are designed to prevent behaviour that causes harassment, alarm or distress. Previously ASBOs could be stand-alone, or imposed after a criminal conviction, to prevent further similar behaviour. In the latter situation, ASBOs are replaced by Criminal Behaviour Orders, under the Anti-Social Behaviour, Crime and

Policing Act 2014. This Act is also intended to replace stand-alone ASBOs but the relevant provisions were not in force when this book went to press; see the website for updates.

Criminal Behaviour Orders (CBOs)

Criminal Behaviour Orders (CBOs) can be imposed on any defendant, adult or child, after they have been convicted of an offence. They are designed to prevent further criminal behaviour so, for example, someone convicted of shoplifting might get a CBO banning them from going into certain shops. Breaching a CBO is a criminal offence.

Reporting CBOs

CBOs can be imposed by a youth court, magistrates' court, or the Crown Court. No special reporting restrictions apply to them, and where a CBO is imposed in a youth court, the normal anonymity given to the defendant does not apply to the CBO (though remember that any witnesses under 18 will still have anonymity).

However, anonymity will still apply to the youth court hearing in which the defendant was convicted of the original criminal offence, unless the court decides to lift it **(see earlier in this chapter)**. If the anonymity is not lifted, you can only include details of the original criminal act in a report naming the defendant if these details are given in the CBO hearing. In such a situation, it may be worth having a word with the court clerk before the CBO hearing, and reminding them that the Justices Clerks Society issued guidance stating than when an ASBO is drawn up, it should include details of the behaviour which led to the order being made; common sense suggests the same approach should apply to CBOs. It is also possible to argue that the s49 anonymity should be lifted in the public interest **(see Lifting the s49 restrictions earlier in this chapter for advice on this)**.

Although anonymity does not apply automatically to youth court CBO hearings, the magistrates can decide to impose it via a s39 order.

Reporting breaches of ASBOs and CBOs

Breach of an ASBO or CBO is a criminal offence. Where the defendant is an adult, there are no special reporting restrictions beyond those that generally apply to criminal cases. Where the defendant is a child and the case comes before the youth court, the usual youth court anonymity does not apply to the breach proceedings themselves, but the court has discretion to make an anonymity order. The court can make an order imposing anonymity. If an order is not made, you can report the proceedings and name the defendant, but you cannot name witnesses under 18, who will still have youth court anonymity, nor refer to separate youth court proceedings regarding criminal offences where the defendant had anonymity. If the court does propose to make an anonymity order, you can argue against it on public interest grounds (see earlier).

PROVISIONS NOT YET IN FORCE

The Youth Justice and Criminal Evidence Act 1999 contains important new provisions on reporting cases involving people under 18. However, these provisions represent a severe restriction on the ability of the press to report such cases, and were opposed by the media. Although no official statement has been made, it is now thought unlikely that they will ever come into force. However, they are worth including here, because there have been cases of judges assuming that they are in force, and trying to impose reporting restrictions which are not yet legal; in one case this was at the suggestion of a QC, who was also unaware that the provisions were not in force. If you know about the provisions that are not in force, you will be in a better position to make a challenge in such circumstances.

The two controversial provisions are contained in s44 and s45 of the Act, and if implemented would replace s39 of the Children and Young Persons Act 1933 (see p. 153) in criminal proceedings, so that s39 orders would only apply to civil cases. Section 44 of the 1999 Act provides that as soon as the police begin a criminal investigation, the media would automatically be banned from identifying any person under 18 who is involved in the case, whether as a suspect, witness or victim. (This would have meant, for example, that in the 2003 Soham murder case, the press would have been unable to publish the names of the two girls involved, once the investigation had started.) The ban would prevent publication of the juvenile's name, address, school or workplace, or any picture of them. The ban could be lifted by a court if it was in the interests of justice to do so, and the juvenile's welfare would not be adversely affected.

The automatic s44 ban would come to an end once court proceedings begin, but at this point, the court would have discretion under s45 to ban the media from identifying any juvenile involved in the case, where it is in the interests of justice and will not impose a substantial and unreasonable restriction on reporting of the proceedings.

KEY POINTS

Youth court cases

- Section 47 of the Children and Young Persons Act 1933 gives the press a right to attend youth court proceedings.
- Unless restrictions are lifted, the press may not publish anything that could identify a defendant, victim or witness under 18.

Children in adult criminal courts

No automatic restrictions apply, but courts can ban publication of anything that would identify a witness, defendant or victim under 18.

Jigsaw identification

The Press Complaints Commission requires precautions against identification via more than one publication.

ASBOs and CBOs

- No automatic restrictions apply to proceedings involving adults.
- Proceedings in youth courts do not attract the usual automatic anonymity, but an order can be made. Youth court anonymity does still cover the original criminal case.

Provisions not in force

Sections 44 and 45 of the Youth Justice and Criminal Evidence Act 1999 severely restrict reporting of juveniles in criminal cases, but are not in force and may never be.

TEST YOUR KNOWLEDGE

1 You have been sent to report a youth court case, but the court clerk refuses to let you in, stating that youth courts are closed to the public. Which statute gives you the right to be there?

2 You are reporting a youth court case, for which restrictions have not been lifted. Which of these statements can you make in your report?

(a) A 17-year-old from Birmingham has appeared in court, accused of shoplifting.

(b) John Green, 17, of Tower Road, Birmingham has appeared in court, accused of shoplifting.

(c) A 17-year-old from Tower Road, Birmingham has appeared in court, accused of shoplifting.

(d) A boy from Green Gates school has appeared in court, accused of shoplifting.

(e) The Birmingham schoolboy who last year hit the news when he saved a dog from drowning has appeared in court, accused of shoplifting.

(f) Mrs Jane Green, from Birmingham, cried in court as her son was accused of shoplifting this week.

3 You are reporting a youth court case, and the magistrates make no order regarding reporting restrictions. Can you safely name the defendant?

4 A youth court case you have been following is appealed to the Crown Court. The defendant is still under 18. What reporting restrictions apply?

5 You are reporting a case where a 16-year-old girl has been given an IPNA. What reporting restrictions apply?

6 A teenager known as a local tearaway has been convicted of criminal damage in the youth court, and has been given an CBO in the same proceedings. Which of these statements can you make?

(a) John Brown, 14, has been convicted of criminal damage and given a CBO, banning him from going near the Roundish Estate.

(b) A teenager who was convicted of eight counts of criminal damage has been given a CBO, banning him from going near the Roundish Estate.

(c) John Brown, 14, of Oxford Road, has been given a CBO, banning him from going near the Roundish Estate.

7 You are reporting a case where a man is accused of murdering his 18-month-old daughter. The judge imposes a s39 order, banning the press from identifying the little girl. What arguments could you use to get the order lifted? What arguments would you use if the charge was not murder but assault?

8 What is jigsaw identification?

9 What precautions does the Editors Code of Practice require the media to take in order to prevent 'jigsaw identification' of children in sex cases?

10 You are reporting a case involving a defendant who is under 18. The magistrates announce that they are making an order under s46 of the Youth Justice and Criminal Evidence Act 1999, banning publication of the defendant's name. What argument could you use to get this restriction lifted?

ONLINE RESOURCES

The Children Act 1989 can be read at:
www.legislation.gov.uk/ukpga/1989/41/contents

Useful guidelines on reporting restrictions, produced by the Judicial College, the Newspaper Society, the Society of Editors and the Media Lawyers Association are available at:
www.societyofeditors.co.uk

Useful reports of cases where reporting restrictions have been imposed or overturned can be found at the Hold the Front Page website:
www.holdthefrontpage.co.uk

The Society of Editors website also reports on the use of reporting restrictions, at:
www.societyofeditors.co.uk

Practice Direction (Crown Court: trial of children and young persons) 2001 can be viewed at:
www.hmcourts-service.gov.uk/cms/926.htm

The Home Office guidance document Publicising Anti-Social Behaviour Orders can be read at:
http://webarchive.nationalarchives.gov.uk/20100405140447/http:/asb.homeoffice.gov.uk/uploadedFiles/Members_site/Documents_and_images/Enforcement_tools_and_powers/ASBOs_PublicisingGuidance_0031.pdf

Reporting the Family Court

The Family Court deals with a variety of matters concerning couples and their children, including divorce, adoption, and proceedings to take children into care. Because family proceedings often deal with matters that are very personal to the people involved, they are usually heard in private, with the public not allowed to attend. In the past, the press were also excluded from most private hearings, and in recent years this has led to criticism that the workings and decisions of the family courts were too secretive, and that the public should be entitled to know, through the press, how the system worked. This criticism came against a background of growing public anxiety about cases involving children who had been removed from their parents and taken into care on apparently weak grounds, and the fact that restrictions on the press made it impossible to fully report these cases.

As a result of these concerns, in 2009, the Government announced new plans to make family courts more open to the media, including a right for the press to attend most types of family hearings, even if the public are excluded. However, despite increased access to the hearings themselves, family proceedings are still covered by strict reporting restrictions, so, although there will often be a right to attend the proceedings, what you can write about them is still limited, and it will often be the case that the parties cannot be named, which can tend to make a story much less interesting to readers. Even so, the increased access is to be welcomed as at least allowing more open discussion of the way in which the system works.

THE WORK OF THE FAMILY COURT

The term 'Family Court' was introduced in the Children and Families Act 2014, but, like youth court, refers to a type of case, rather than a specific court building (previously hearings were referred to as family courts, but the new legislation aims to create a more unified system). Family Court proceedings can take place in a magistrates' court, a county court or the Family Division of the High Court.

A wide range of different types of case fall under the heading of family proceedings, including:

- divorce, judicial separations, annulments and proceedings to end civil partnerships;
- cases concerning financial arrangements when a couple split up;
- disputes between parents who have split up about arrangements for their children;
- applications for orders to return children who have been abducted (primarily by one of their parents);
- applications, usually from local authorities, to take children into care or otherwise intervene to protect them;

- adoption cases, including those where a local authority applies for an adoption to be allowed against the parents' wishes;
- disputes about paternity;
- applications for non-molestation orders in domestic violence cases;
- applications to prevent a forced marriage.

Wardship and the High Court's inherent jurisdiction

In addition to all the types of family proceedings referred to above, there is a further type of case involving children and young people, which happens in the High Court. These are known as hearings under the High Court's inherent jurisdiction with regard to minors. The origins of this type of proceeding come from the traditional principle that the Crown had a responsibility to protect subjects who were not in a position to care for themselves, and children were traditionally considered to be in this category. Applications under the inherent jurisdiction therefore usually involve situations where a child is thought to need protection. High-profile examples have included a teenager who ran away from home to join a religious cult, an HIV positive three-year-old, whose father refused to allow him to have medical treatment, and a severely disabled child where the parents and the hospital treating him could not agree on whether he should be allowed to die or kept alive on a ventilator.

The High Court can make the child a ward of court, which means that from then on, no important step or change in the child's life can be taken without the court's permission. Where a child is made a ward of court, special restrictions apply to publication of information about them (see p. 178).

Alternatively, the High Court can make an order to resolve the dispute: for example, in a case where doctors want a child to have medical treatment but the parents do not think it is in the child's best interests (as in the HIV case above), the court can decide whether the treatment should go ahead. In doing this, they are required to make the decision based on what is best for the child.

ACCESS TO FAMILY PROCEEDINGS

Most family proceedings take place in private, with the public excluded. However, the changes made in 2009 establish that the media may attend most types of family proceedings, even though the public are not allowed in (though there are still some exceptions, which we will look at below). The rules are now contained in the Family Procedure Rules 2010. Advice on how the provisions should be applied has been provided in a guide for journalists, The Family Courts: Media Access and Reporting, published under the authority of the President of the Family Division of the High Court, the Judicial College and the Society of Editors (see *Online resources* at the end of this chapter).

The rules provide that 'duly accredited' media representatives (see *Law in Practice: Accreditation,* later in this chapter) have the right to attend 'hearings of family proceedings which take place in private'. The courts have a discretion to exclude the press from all or part of a hearing, but only for specified reasons (see below, *Exclusion from the courts*), and not merely because the judge thinks it would be a good idea, or the parties do not want the press there. The court's starting point should be that the press is allowed in.

As well as the types of hearing listed above, there are some other types of family proceedings which already allowed press access before the new rules were made, and continue to do so:

- Where family proceedings are held in public (meaning that the public are allowed to attend, even though in practice often no one does), journalists will also be allowed in.
- The press are allowed to attend family proceedings (except for adoption hearings) held in the magistrates' courts, under s69 of the Magistrates' Courts Act 1980, even though the public are not admitted. However, magistrates have discretion to exclude the press while any indecent evidence is being given, if satisfied that this is necessary in the interests of the administration of justice or public decency, and can also exclude the press from cases brought under the Children Act 1989, if such an exclusion would be 'expedient in the interests of the child'.
- Appeals to the Court of Appeal and Supreme Court on family matters are usually held in open court, and journalists can attend.

Journalists may also be allowed to attend placement hearings. These are proceedings brought by local authorities who want to put a child up for adoption, but do not have the parents' consent. Before the 2009 changes, the courts had a discretion to allow the press into this type of hearing in the High Court and county courts, but it was often refused. However, these cases were precisely the type which were causing public concern prior to the 2009 changes, and so, as part of the shift towards greater openness, the president of the family division issued a guidance note for the courts, which encourages use of the discretion to allow the press to attend placement hearings (President's Guidance Note: Care Proceedings Involving Placement Order Applications). Placement hearings are often heard in conjunction with care proceedings (i.e. where a local authority is seeking to take a child into care and then put them up for adoption), and in the guidance note the President of the Family Division said that the fact that care proceedings included a placement hearing was not by itself a reason to exclude the media. In fact, he said, where a placement hearing is heard in conjunction with care proceedings 'it would normally be appropriate for the court to allow the media to be present' unless there are grounds for exclusion under FPR 1991 rule 10.28(4) (this details the standard grounds for excluding the press; see p. 170), or there is some feature of the case that means the media should not be present, such as the need to preserve confidentiality, or where the interests of a prospective adopter might be adversely affected by the media's presence.

However, the above only applies to placement hearings in the county courts or the High Court. Where a placement hearing takes place in the Family Proceedings (magistrates') court, media representatives may not be present (s 69(2) and (3), Magistrates' Courts Act 1980).

Law in practice **Accreditation**

The accreditation required for the family courts is the Press Card issued under the UK Press Card scheme. To get one of these, the UK Press Card Authority requires you to be working professionally in the media and have a need to identify yourself in public. This covers both staff and freelance reporters and writers, but not students. The cards are issued to members/employees by a number of different organisations, including the NUJ, the Chartered Institute of Journalists, the British Association of Journalists and major employers such as the BBC and Reuters. (See **www.presscard.uk.com** for more information.)

To be admitted to the courts under the normal rules, you need to have the card with you, and most courts prefer you to wear it so that it is clear to everyone who the press are. Some courts have apparently asked journalists to provide further proof of identification, but the Practice Direction issued by the President of the Family Division on 20 April 2009 (Attendance of Media Representatives at Hearings in Family Proceedings) makes it clear that this is not required. It states that a Press Card issued under the UK Press Card scheme 'will be both necessary and sufficient to demonstrate accreditation'. The Practice Direction also states that if you do not have a card, the court can use its discretion to allow you in, but may refuse.

Which proceedings are not open to the press?

The following types of hearing are not open to the press:

Adoption hearings: The courts have a discretion to allow the press into both adoption and placement hearings, but adoption is considered to be a personal and confidential matter, and this discretion is unlikely to be used to allow the press to attend an adoption hearing.

Conciliation and mediation proceedings which are led by a judge: For example, in cases under the Children Act, the first part of the court process is a First Hearing Dispute Resolution appointment, at which the court tries to help the parties work out whether their dispute can be settled by mediation and agreement. The media would not be allowed into this type of hearing while the mediation part of proceedings is taking place. Once that part of the hearing is over the restriction is lifted.

Financial dispute resolution hearings: This is a hearing in divorce cases, in which a judge helps the couple work out an agreed financial settlement between them. The media is not allowed to attend these hearings. However, if the couple cannot agree a settlement, the case then goes to court, at what is called an ancillary relief hearing, and here the standard rules on press access apply (i.e. the press has a right to attend unless there are grounds that make it necessary to exclude them; see p. 170).

Hearings 'in camera'

In rare cases, family proceedings may be heard 'in camera', which means in secret, so that neither the public nor the media may attend. The types of proceedings which can be heard this way are:

- proceedings, or part of proceedings, for a declaration of legitimacy;
- any part of proceedings to annul a marriage where evidence of sexual capacity is given;
- proceedings where a public hearing frustrates the administration of justice, or makes it impossible (an example would be where a court is discussing how to locate an abducted child, where a public hearing might alert the abductor);
- proceedings where evidence given would cause harm to national security.

In ***Scott*** v ***Scott*** (1913), the House of Lords stated that a court had no power to choose to sit in camera merely because hearing the case in public was likely to be painful, humiliating or a deterrent to parties or witnesses, or because the evidence was 'of an unsavoury character'.

Law in practice Attending court

If you have a valid Press Card (see above), you can simply turn up at any of the types of hearing covered by the new rules, and unless the court is using its discretion to exclude the press, you should be admitted. It is not necessary to give the court prior notice that you want to attend a hearing.

Exclusion from the courts

Although the general principle now is that the press can attend family proceedings held in private, the courts can still use their discretion to exclude the press from all or part of a hearing in the following circumstances, listed in Rule 11 of the FPR 2010:

- it is necessary in the interests of any child concerned in or connected with the proceedings; or
- it is necessary for the safety or protection of a party to or witness in the proceedings, or someone connected with a party of witness. In ***Re Child X (Residence and Contact: Rights of Media Attendance)*** (2009), the court stated that this would include where exclusion was necessary to protect the parties' rights to privacy, where 'outrageous or intimate' allegations were being made; or
- it is necessary for the orderly conduct of proceedings. This provision relates to situations where media presence may cause practical problems, such as where it proves impossible to find room for all or any of the journalists who want to attend. In this situation, the 2009 Practice Direction states that the court should try to move the hearing to a bigger room, where possible, but need not adjourn the hearing for this purpose if it would involve significant disruption or delay; or
- where justice would otherwise be impeded or prejudiced.

Note that the criteria are quite strict. In the first three, exclusion must be 'necessary' for the reason given. The fact that one or both of the parties might want exclusion for one of these reasons is not, by itself, enough, and any party wishing to exclude the media will need to satisfy the court of the necessity to do so; it is not for the press to justify their attendance. Similarly, a 2009 Practice Direction makes it clear that the provision for exclusion 'where justice would otherwise be impeded or prejudiced' cannot be used merely for 'reasons of administrative convenience'. Examples of situations where it could be used, according to the Practice Direction, are:

- hearings about the parties' finances, where information to be given is price sensitive (such as confidential information which could affect the share price of a public company);
- hearings where a witness (not one of the parties) states for credible reasons that they will not give evidence in front of the press;
- hearings where there appears to the court to be a significant risk that a witness will not give full and frank evidence if journalists are present.

The Practice Direction says that when considering exclusion, the court should balance the competing rights of privacy and freedom of expression, and consider whether the risk alleged demands complete media exclusion, or whether it could be dealt with by excluding the press from a part of the hearing. It should also consider whether adequate protection against the alleged risk could be achieved by means of reporting restrictions, either those which apply automatically, or those which the court has power to order. If the relevant aim is achievable by another route, such as not reporting names (which will usually not be allowed anyway), it can be argued that there is no need to exclude the press.

If the court decides to exclude the press from all or part of a hearing, the Practice Direction says that it should give brief reasons for its decision.

In 2009, Earl Spencer, brother of the late Diana Princess of Wales, and his former wife applied for the media to be banned from hearings about their divorce settlement, arguing that the press was only interested because the couple were well-known figures. Mr Justice Munby refused, stating that to ban the press from a hearing because one or both parties were publicly known 'potentially gives privilege to one group over another'. The couple reached an agreement out of court rather than have the case heard in front of the press.

In *Re X (a child) (Residence and Contact – Rights of Media Attendance – FPR Rule 10.28(4))* (2009), the case involved a hearing regarding residency proceedings, where the father was a well-known celebrity. Sir Mark Potter, President of the Family Division, considered the principles to be applied to media access in cases involving children, and especially the children of celebrities. He stated that there was no rule that entitled the child of a celebrity to more protection than anyone else. However, he pointed out that the child's interests and welfare were always a key factor, and, given that the media interest in such cases would be more intense, the need for protection of the child from intrusion or publicity might be greater. However, the press should not be excluded from cases in which matters of public interest were raised, or which were of particular importance from the point of view of the watchdog role of the press. A court had to consider whether the interference with either the media's rights to freedom of expression under Article 10 of the European Convention on Human Rights, or the child's right to respect for privacy and family life under Article 8, corresponded to a pressing social need, was proportionate to the legitimate aim pursued, and whether the reasons given to justify it were relevant and sufficient under Article 10. In doing this, it had to consider the nature of the evidence, and distinguish between matters which were of genuine public interest, and those which were merely of interest to the public.

Where someone applied to have the media excluded, it was up to them to show that there was no other way to deal with the problem raised by media access. It would usually be easier to show this where they were asking for temporary exclusion from certain parts of a hearing, than where they wanted the press excluded from the whole proceedings.

In terms of procedure, the party wishing to exclude the media from the whole of a hearing should raise the matter with the court in advance, so that the media could be notified. Where a party sought to exclude the media temporarily from part of the proceedings, the judge should balance the competing rights to privacy and freedom of expression, and invite media representations as necessary.

In this case, he granted the father's application and excluded the press, because the hearing involved matters that were very personal and sensitive to the child, and experts in the case might be unwilling to give evidence in front of the media. There was also a risk that the child might lose trust in those experts if they gave evidence in front of journalists.

Notice of proposed press exclusion

A court is not obliged to notify the press that an application for exclusion has been made, but the applicant should, where possible, notify the relevant media organisations. This is so that the press are able to make sure they are present to make representations against the exclusion.

In ***Surrey County Council* v *Al-Hilli and the Chief Constable of Surrey*** (2013), Baker J gave a useful summary of the current principles on media access to the family courts. He said that:

- The starting point was that media representatives have a right to attend family proceedings, and should only be excluded if one of the exceptions listed in the Family Procedure Rules was fulfilled (see above).
- Any party seeking to exclude the media has to justify that exclusion, rather than the media having to justify their attendance. A party seeking exclusion has to show that it is 'necessary', and while 'necessary' did not mean the same as 'indispensable', it was not the same as 'useful', 'reasonable' or 'desirable' either. In other words, exclusion need not be absolutely essential but the reason for it must be more than simply meeting the wishes of one or more parties.
- The right of the media to attend proceedings does not always mean they have a right to report the case, but in some circumstances, their watchdog role might be even more important in a case that cannot be reported, because they have the duty of scrutinising the court's procedures as well as its decisions.
- Generally speaking, it will be harder for a party to persuade a court to exclude the press from the whole of a hearing than from part of it. Circumstances in which the media should be excluded from all of a hearing were 'likely to be rare'.
- Judges should take care not to let their natural wish to protect children and vulnerable people allow them to underestimate the importance of the right to freedom of expression under Article 10.
- In deciding whether to exclude the media, the court should analyse and balance the competing rights which arose from the question, and there must be a proper factual basis for concerns said to amount to an infringement of such rights.

Opposing press exclusion

Where a court is proposing to exclude the press, any media representative present has the right to make representations, and put forward their reasons why the press should not be excluded, or should be excluded from part rather than all of a hearing.

Representations should be made orally, rather than in writing, unless the court requests otherwise, and the court should be adjourned in order to allow this. The court is not required to adjourn in order to allow time for journalists not present to make representations, and should only do so if it is satisfied that there is a need to do so, taking into account the time and cost involved.

If, despite representations, the court decides to exclude the press, there is no route of appeal against the decision. The only opportunity to challenge it is by way of judicial review, which is expensive and takes time, so is unlikely to be used in many cases (see p. 206 for an explanation of this route).

Access to court documents

The media do not have an automatic right to see documents that are referred to in family proceedings, but the court can give permission for this. In ***Norfolk County Council* v *Webster*** (2006), the High Court said that judges faced with requests for documents should consider how difficult it might be for journalists to follow the proceedings without them, and in ***Re N (a Minor)*** (2014), a High Court judge stated that journalists should be given copies of skeleton arguments when hearings are held in open court, unless the papers contain 'very confidential material'.

A key part of the evidence in family proceedings concerning children can be reports by, for example, medical professionals and social workers. In ***Re X, Y, Z (Morgan* v *A Local Authority)*** (2011), the judge said he would like to see it become standard practice for expert reports to be given to the media. In the past, the names of experts were usually kept secret if reports were given to the press, but new guidance from England's most senior family court judge, published in January 2014, states that local authorities and expert witnesses in care cases should be named, unless there are 'compelling reasons' not to.

The guidance also states that judgments in the family courts should, as a general rule, be published. They will usually be anonymised so that the names of the parties and others do not appear, but the guidance states that there are some cases where anonymity will not be appropriate, such as where parents have been exonerated in care cases and wish to discuss their experience, or where findings have been made against a person and it is in the public interest to identify them. The guidance covers judgments delivered in the family courts by High Court judges and in some cases Circuit judges, and can be read at http://www.judiciary.gov.uk/wp-content/uploads/JCO/Documents/Guidance/transparency-in-the-family-courts-jan2014.pdf.

Divorce decrees can be read at the Principal Registry of the Family Division in London, on the same day that the information is requested.

REPORTING THE FAMILY COURTS

Although the new rules have considerably widened access to the family courts, the fact that you are allowed to attend a hearing does not mean you can report everything you hear. When making the changes to the rules on media attendance, the Ministry of Justice made it clear that the purpose of the change was to promote discussion and public awareness of the workings of the family courts, rather than to allow the media better access to the human interest stories behind many of the cases they hear. As a result, there are still strict restrictions on what can be reported in family cases, and it will rarely be possible to report these cases in much detail, or to name any children involved or mention anything else that could lead to them being identified (which in practice means it is usually impossible to name the parents as well).

General reporting restrictions

Section 12 of the Administration of Justice Act 1960 makes it a contempt of court to publish information relating to any court proceedings held in private, where the proceedings:

- relate to the exercise of the inherent jurisdiction of the High Court with regard to minors (see p. 167);
- are brought under the Children Act 1989 (this includes hearings about the arrangements for children after divorce or separation, and applications to take children into care) or the Adoption and Children Act 2002; or
- relate wholly or mainly to the maintenance or upbringing of a minor.

This last provision means that cases which are not usually considered 'children' cases may be covered if the welfare of a child is at issue in them; an example would be proceedings to obtain an occupation order to exclude a violent spouse from the family home.

For these purposes, a hearing in the county court or the High Court is considered private if the public is excluded from it, even though journalists may be allowed to attend. It is currently unclear whether this also applies to hearings in magistrates' courts. If you are reporting a case there, and the public is excluded, the safest option is to ask the magistrates whether they consider that the s12 reporting restrictions apply.

Section 12 does not ban reporting of the fact that a hearing has taken place or who was involved, and you can in fact report a number of details about the case (see below). What is prohibited is reporting the nature of the dispute, anything that went on during the hearing itself, even if you leave out the names of the people involved, any material from documents used in the case, or any summary of those documents. These restrictions continue to apply after the proceedings are finished.

In ***X*** v ***Dempster*** (1998), the *Daily Mail* and one of its journalists were fined £10,000 and £1,000 for a story which stated that evidence given in a private family hearing had suggested that the woman involved was a bad mother.

In ***Kent County Council*** v ***B and Others*** (2004), Munby J gave a useful rundown of the elements which the Act does and does not prohibit. It is permissible to report:

- the fact that a particular child is a ward of court;
- the fact that a particular child was the subject of wardship proceedings, proceedings under the Children Act, or proceedings relating wholly or mainly to their maintenance or upbringing;
- the name, address and/or photo of the child;
- the name, address and/or photo of the parties to the proceedings;
- the name, address and/or photo of any witnesses;
- the date, time or place of a past or future hearing of such proceedings;
- the nature of the dispute in the proceedings;
- anything seen or heard by a person acting lawfully in the public areas outside the court room;
- the text of any order made, or an extract from or summary of it.

Remember though that publication of some of these details may be banned under other legislation or a court order. If the case is brought under the Children Act, for example, s97 of that Act prohibits you from publishing anything likely to identify the child (see below). That means that you cannot name the child, and if one or both of the parties are the parents, you cannot name them either. Nor can you name any witnesses where to do so would lead to the child being identified.

Although the Administration of Justice Act allows publication of 'the nature of the dispute', unfortunately there will be many cases where it is difficult to distinguish between material that can be considered 'the nature of the dispute', and material which is actually evidence in the proceedings and so cannot be published.

In ***Kent County Council*** v ***B*** (2004), the Council was seeking to take a little girl into care, because, they alleged, her mother suffered from Munchausen's Syndrome by Proxy (an illness which makes mothers harm their children in an effort to make them appear ill), and had attempted to kill her children by smothering or poisoning them. The mother strenuously denied either having the illness or trying to harm her child. A *Daily Mail* story on the case contained the following text:

> A paediatrician called as an expert witness at an initial family court hearing suggested, out of the blue, that Sheila might have deliberately injected her child with the water from a flower bowl or lavatory. It was a claim considered ludicrous by one of the country's leading forensic toxicologists . . . He told the court it was a medical impossibility for Sheila to have done such a thing.

Munby J said that this copy was 'almost certainly on the wrong side of the line'. On the other hand, he said, it would not be a breach of s12 to report that the issue in the case was whether the mother had Munchausen's

Syndrome by Proxy, and whether she had attempted to kill her children by smothering or poisoning them. It was also permissible to report the names of the medical experts who gave evidence on these issues (but not the evidence that they gave). Going beyond that, he said, 'might well' be a breach of s12.

A court can disapply s12 where the public interest in reporting the case fully outweighs the arguments for confidentiality. This is most likely to be done where the parties themselves want to publicise the case.

Section 1(a) of the Judicial Proceedings (Regulation of Reports) Act 1926 forbids publication in court reports of any indecent medical, surgical or physiological details which would be calculated to injure public morals. In practice, however, it has been many years since a successful prosecution was brought under this provision, and it seems likely that these days a report would have to be extremely distasteful in order to break the law.

Where a party in a case has been compelled to supply certain information to the court (such as the financial details that divorcing couples have to provide if they want their financial settlement to be decided by a court) that information is considered confidential. If that information is given to you by the other party, you cannot publish it, unless it comes into the public domain.

Cases under the Children Act 1989

Where a case is brought under the Children Act 1989, s97 of that Act makes it a criminal offence to publish anything which is intended or likely to identify any person under 18 'as being involved' in court proceedings involving the Act before magistrates, or to state that any address or school is that of a child involved in such proceedings. A similar provision applies to proceedings under the Adoption and Children Act 2002.

Children Act cases include:

- disputes about children after divorce or separation;
- applications for social services to intervene in the care of a child, or take children into care;
- applications for parental responsibility by a father;
- applications for the appointment of a guardian;
- applications to enforce a residence order (for example, where the parent without residence has refused to bring the child back);
- applications for child maintenance.

If you are not sure whether a case involves the Children Act, you should check with the Court Clerk.

This provision means that not only can you not identify the child in reports of the proceedings, but also you cannot identify them in any story which mentions that the child is involved in such a case. This will generally mean that if you are writing about the child being involved in the case, you cannot name anyone else in the family either, and you must also be careful of the danger of jigsaw identification (see p. 137).

A publisher charged with publishing material that could identify a child in a Children Act case will have a defence if they can prove they did not know, and had no reason to suspect, that the material was likely to make it possible to identify the child.

In *Clayton* v *Clayton* (2006), the Court of Appeal said that this automatic restriction only applies while the proceedings are taking place, and not to material published after that. If a court wants to make sure that children involved in such proceedings are not identified after the proceedings, the Court of Appeal said, it had to issue an injunction to that effect, and before doing so, should weigh up the Article 8 right of the child to privacy, against the Article 10 right to freedom of expression, both of the parents and the press.

The ban on identification can be lifted or relaxed by the court, or by the Home Secretary. This is usually done where the welfare of the child requires such an action, for example, where a child is missing and publicity might help trace them. In addition, in ***Re Brandon Webster, Norfolk County Council* v *Webster*** (2006), the Family Division of the High Court ruled that the ban on identification could be lifted for reasons other than the welfare of the child, if necessary to protect the rights of others under the European Convention, including the Article 10 right to freedom of expression.

Family proceedings before magistrates

Section 71 of the Magistrates' Courts Act covers family proceedings heard by magistrates, which include hearings concerning maintenance after divorce or separation, applications for permission to marry from people under 18, declarations of parentage, applications for non-molestation orders in domestic violence cases, applications to exclude someone from the family home after domestic violence, and applications made under the Children Act to allow social workers to intervene in the care of children. Reports of these hearings may **only** contain:

- the names, addresses and occupations of the parties and any witnesses (other than children, or adults whose names could identify children in the case);
- the grounds for the application, and a brief statement of the charges, defences and counter-charges in support of which evidence has been given (charge in this context really means the reason for the application, not a criminal charge);
- submissions on any points of law that arise in the proceedings, and the decisions of the court on those points;
- the decision of the court, and any remarks made in connection with the decision.

In effect, this means that the media can only report evidence given in the case if it is referred to by the magistrates when giving their decision. In practice, this will often be the case as the Children Act requires them to give reasons for their decisions. However, you can only mention such evidence in terms of what the magistrates say about it (so if the decision merely mentions a piece of evidence in passing, you cannot elaborate on that by giving extra information that you heard in court).

Note that the second point states that you can only mention charges, defences and counter-charges for which evidence has been given. In many cases, charges, defences, counter-charges and the evidence for them may be put forward and then withdrawn, which means you cannot report them. For this reason it is safest to wait until all the evidence has been given before reporting a charge, counter-charge or defence.

Divorce cases

The Judicial Proceedings (Regulation of Reports) Act 1926 provides that reports of divorce, nullity or judicial separation proceedings must **only** contain:

- the names, addresses and occupations of the parties and any witnesses;
- a concise statement of the charges, the defence, and any counter-charges for which evidence has been given, but not abandoned charges or counter-charges (this provision means that reports cannot be published until all the evidence has been given);

- submissions made on any point of law, and the court's decision on them;
- the court's judgment, and the judge's comments on it. Other remarks made by the judge during the hearing cannot be included.

These rules also apply to proceedings to dissolve a civil partnership.

It is unclear what the current position is on reporting proceedings for ancillary relief, which deal with the division of assets between a divorcing couple. The Administration of Justice Act 1960 makes it contempt of court to publish information about hearings which relate wholly or mainly to the maintenance or upbringing of a minor (see below), but most ancillary relief hearings are not about arrangements for the children, but about how the financial assets are shared out. These may be covered by the same reporting restrictions as those detailed above for divorce hearings, but as ancillary relief hearings as they are today did not exist when the 1926 Act was passed, the situation is unclear.

This issue was addressed in ***Cooper-Hohn* v *Hohn*** (2014), widely described as Britain's most expensive divorce case, which involved the division of over a billion pounds worth of assets. Not surprisingly, the case attracted media attention, and the press applied for the usual reporting restrictions to be lifted. Rather than tackle the question of whether the Administration of Justice Act should apply to ancillary relief proceedings, the court addressed the issue as one of balance between the competing rights of privacy and freedom of expression. The judge accepted that there was a legitimate public interest in reporting the case, because of the legal issue it raised. (Mr Hohn was claiming that the usual 50:50 split of assets was unjustified because it was his exceptional talent that had made the couple so rich.) However, she also recognised that Mr Hohn, who wanted reporting restrictions, was justified in wanted to keep his financial and business information private. She therefore made an order allowing the press to report the proceedings themselves, but not any commercially sensitive details about his business.

The ***Cooper-Hohn*** case does not set a precedent, and a similar approach has already been rejected by a judge in at least one case, but it may signal a more nuanced approach to the issue of reporting restrictions in cases involving the division of assets after divorce.

Note that automatic restrictions do not apply to hearings regarding financial arrangements when a couple who have not been married split up. In ***W* v *M (Tolata Proceedings: Anonymity)*** (2012), Mostyn J said that the general rule was that the press could attend such hearings and report the proceedings, without anonymising the parties. This rule could only be displaced for 'good reason' and where a party sought exclusion or reporting restrictions, the court had to balance their rights against the rights of the press to freedom of expression. In doing so, it should 'guard against extending the best interests of children beyond their proper limitations, or making any value judgements about journalistic merit'.

Adoption cases

Because adoption hearings are held in private, they are covered by s12 of the Administration of Justice Act 1960, making it a contempt of court to publish any report of the hearing. Journalists are of course not admitted to adoption hearings, but the publication ban would also apply if you were given details of the hearing by someone involved in it.

The Adoption and Children Act 2002 makes it an offence to publish an advertisement or other information stating that a particular child is available for adoption, that a parent or guardian wants a child to be adopted, that a person wants to adopt a child, or that a person other than an adoption agency is willing to receive a child given to them with a view to he or she being adopted, or that a person is willing to take a child outside the UK with a view to them being adopted. None of this applies, however, where the information is published by or on behalf of an adoption agency.

Wardship cases

As we saw earlier, where a child is at risk of serious danger, the High Court has the power to make him or her a ward of court, which means that the court becomes responsible for the child. The Administration of Justice Act 1960, s12(1) prevents the press from reporting the proceedings in which a child is made a ward of court, and also prevents publication of certain types of story about the child once they have been made a ward. It does not, however, as commonly believed, mean that nothing can ever be written about a child who is a ward of court.

If no specific injunction has been made regarding the child, the position is as follows:

- It is permitted to state that a child involved in a story is a ward of court, but if this is stated, the child must not be identified, and details of the wardship proceedings (such as why they were brought) may not be given.
- If a story concerning a child who is a ward of court names the child, the press may not say that he or she is a ward of court, or connect him or her with the wardship proceedings. This means that if, for example, a child who is a ward of court happened to be the subject of a story which had nothing to do with being a ward of court, it would be fine to name them in that story, so long as you do not mention that they are a ward of court, or link them to wardship proceedings.
- A story which both names the child and says that he or she is a ward of court can only be published with the court's permission. Once this permission has been given and a child has already been named as a ward of court, this information can continue to be published unless an injunction is ordered.

These restrictions can be lifted by a court, either completely or partially. This tends to happen in cases where a child's whereabouts are not known, and there is a possibility that he or she may be taken out of the country; clearly in these cases publicity can be helpful.

A publisher who did not know or have reason to suspect that they were publishing information concerning wardship proceedings will have a defence.

Injunctions affecting wards of court

In many cases concerning wards of court, the courts will put in place an injunction concerning publication of information about the child concerned. These injunctions can be very wide, and may, for example, prohibit the press from speaking not just to the child, but also to their parents, carers, social workers or teachers. This can make it impossible to print anything about the child, even if you do not name them, and as penalties for breaking an injunction can be severe, you should always check whether there is an injunction in force before writing anything about a person who is a ward of court. It is safest to confirm this with the relevant court or the child's lawyers, rather than relying on information from the family, who may not necessarily understand the far-reaching nature of some injunctions.

Injunctions which place unreasonable restrictions on reporting cases of public interest can and have been challenged. In ***Re M and N (Minors) (Wardship) (Publication of Information)*** (1990), the Court of Appeal laid down guidelines for courts making such injunctions, and reminded them that the public interest in freedom of expression had to be considered in such cases. The court said that an injunction should be no wider than was necessary to achieve the purpose for which it was made, and that its scope should be clear. When deciding this scope, the courts should take account of the public interest in a free press, and recognise the distinction between articles on matters of public interest, and those which were merely satisfying public curiosity.

In ***BBC* v *Kelly*** (2001), the BBC challenged an injunction preventing it from broadcasting an interview with a teenager who had been made a ward of court at the request of his family, because he had run away from home to join a religious cult. In response to publicity about his grandmother's fears for his welfare with the group, the teenager had telephoned the BBC's *Today* programme, wanting to give his side of the story. The court imposed an injunction preventing the programme from broadcasting the interview, on the grounds that the boy was a ward of court, but the injunction was overturned. Munby J said that it was too wide a restriction on press freedom to require that no interview with a ward of court could be published without permission. He stated that permission would only be required where the media activity represented a major step in the ward's life, or where the media involvement was related directly to, or interfered with, the child's upbringing. The interview in question did not fit into these criteria and therefore could be broadcast.

In a 1989 case, Kensington and Chelsea Borough Council had obtained an injunction which banned a local paper from publishing an interview with a foster mother who had had two foster children taken from her without explanation, after having looked after them almost all their lives. The Court of Appeal held that the story the paper wanted to print covered a matter of public interest, namely the way in which a local authority had exercised its powers, and ordered that the injunction should be altered, so that the interview could be used, as long as the children, their school and the family were not identified.

In ***Re R (Wardship: Restrictions on Publication)*** (1994), the case concerned a child whose parents had separated; the courts had ordered that she should live with her mother, and gave her father only contact rights. The father then abducted the child, and took her to Israel. She was eventually brought back and her father was extradited to stand trial in the UK. The little girl had been made a ward of court, and so the Family Division issued an injunction banning reports of the criminal proceedings against her father. He challenged the order, because he wanted to publicise his case, which he felt was an example of the unfair treatment of fathers by the family courts. The court agreed to vary the order, to allow reporting of his trial, on the grounds that reporting of criminal trials should only be restricted where necessary to protect 'the proper administration of justice'. The wardship court did not have discretion to make an order prohibiting identification of the child, where such reporting had nothing to do with the exercise of the court's wardship jurisdiction; essentially, it could not give wards of courts rights that other children did not have.

Discretionary reporting restrictions

As we saw earlier (in Chapter 10), all courts, including family courts, have discretion to make an order under s39 of the Children and Young Persons Act 1933, banning publication of the name, address, school or any other details 'calculated to lead to the identification of a child involved in the proceedings, including child witnesses, or any picture of such a child'. There are limits on how this power can be used, which courts are not always fully aware of (see p. 154 for details).

Courts hearing family cases can also make orders under s11 and s4(2) of the Contempt of Court Act, to postpone or ban publication of particular information. These orders are discussed in Chapter 8.

In addition, the High Court can use its inherent jurisdiction (see p. 123), to order reporting restrictions in a particular case, to give effect to a party's rights under the European Convention on Human Rights (usually their right to privacy). This might happen, for example, where the circumstances of the case are that no automatic reporting restrictions apply, but the court believes that the person's interests or welfare would be damaged by them being named in the press (see p. 123 for more details on this power).

What the codes say **Stories involving children**

The Editor's Code of Practice used by IPSO contains the following provisions regarding stories involving children:

- Young people should be free to complete their time at school without unnecessary intrusion.
- A child under 16 must not be interviewed or photographed on issues involving their own or another child's welfare unless a custodial parent or similarly responsible adult consents.
- Pupils must not be approached or photographed at school without the permission of the school authorities.
- Minors must not be paid for material involving children's welfare, nor parents or guardians for material about their children or wards, unless it is clearly in the child's interest.
- Editors must not use the fame, notoriety or position of a parent or guardian as sole justification for publishing details of a child's private life.

The Ofcom Broadcasting Code states that:

- Due care must be taken over the physical and emotional welfare and the dignity of people under eighteen who take part or are otherwise involved in programmes. This is irrespective of any consent given by the participant or by a parent, guardian or other person over the age of 18 in *loco parentis.*
- People under 18 must not be caused unnecessary distress or anxiety by their involvement in programmes or by the broadcast of those programmes.
- Broadcasters should pay particular attention to the privacy of people under 16. They do not lose their rights to privacy because, for example, of the fame or notoriety of their parents or because of events in their schools.
- Where a programme features an individual under 16 or a vulnerable person in a way that infringes privacy, consent must be obtained from:
  - a parent, guardian or other person of 18 or over in *loco parentis;* and
  - wherever possible, the individual concerned;
  - unless the subject matter is trivial or uncontroversial and the participation minor, or it is warranted to proceed without consent.
- Persons under 16 and vulnerable people should not be questioned about private matters without the consent of a parent, guardian or other person of 18 or over in *loco parentis* (in the case of persons under sixteen), or a person with primary responsibility for their care (in the case of a vulnerable person), unless it is warranted to proceed without consent.

Family proceedings not involving children

The reporting restrictions described above do not apply to family proceedings which do not involve children.

In *Allan* v *Clibbery* (2001), the Court of Appeal was asked to consider the competing claims of privacy and freedom of expression in a case arising from the breakdown of a relationship between a wealthy businessman and his girlfriend. The woman had been living in a flat owned (but not lived in) by the man, and when the relationship broke down and he asked her to move out, she went to court to try to get a legal order allowing her to stay there. When the court found that she had no legal right to do so, she went to the *Daily Mail* and told her story, in part, she said, to warn other women about how few rights they have when an unmarried relationship breaks down. Previously, it had been assumed that family proceedings held in chambers (as this case was) were not to be reported, and the businessman got a court order banning the ex-girlfriend from giving details of the legal proceedings to any other publication. However, the Court of Appeal said a blanket ban on reporting family proceedings that did not concern children was not 'necessary in a democratic society' (in other words, there was no pressing social need for it), and the order was not proportionate to the Article 8 aim of protecting the man's privacy.

Lifting reporting restrictions

In many cases the courts will have a discretion to lift statutory reporting restrictions, and in some cases this will be requested by one of the parties, who may wish to publicise their case. Reporting restrictions imposed by injunctions can also be lifted. However, reporting restrictions will not be removed merely because the party wishes it; the courts will balance the interests of the parties, the child and the right of the press to freedom of expression.

In *City of Wakefield Metropolitan District Council* v *The Media and Others* (2010), a couple alleged that they had been treated unjustly by social workers who took their three children into care, and had two of them adopted. The local authority had obtained an injunction banning publication of any details about the case, and the couple applied to have this lifted, so that they could publicise their story in the media. The judge ruled that they could tell their story, but only if they were not named or identified, and nor were the children; they were banned from mentioning the dates of birth or even the gender of the children. The judge said that the possible disturbance and disruption any identification could cause to the children outweighed the rights to freedom of expression of both the parents and the press. However, they were allowed to identify the local authority, and those of its staff who were involved in the process.

In *In the Matter of William Ward, Dr A, Dr B* v *Victoria Ward and Jake Ward* (2010), Mr and Mrs Ward sought the removal of reporting restrictions on care hearings regarding their son, William. The proceedings were brought against them by their local authority, who alleged that the couple had injured their son, but were dropped when the court found there was no evidence to support the claim. Mr and Mrs Ward wanted reporting restrictions lifted so that they could publicise the case, and in response, two doctors involved in the case, the local authority and the NHS Trusts involved applied for injunctions banning publication of the identities of all the medical staff who had treated William, social workers involved in the case and expert witnesses who gave evidence. The court refused to grant this injunction. It said that in a care case, where the consequences for the family were so serious, there was a strong public interest in knowing who were the experts whose judgements could have led to a child being taken away from his parents.

In *Re Roddy (A Child); Torbay Borough Council* v *Newsgroup Newspapers* (2003), the High Court lifted an injunction preventing reporting of a case in which a teenage mother had tried and failed to stop her baby being adopted. The injunction had been imposed at the request of the local authority which brought the adoption proceedings, but the court stated that it was in the public interest for the mother to tell her story.

In 2002, a woman whose children were taken into care after she was wrongly accused of harming them applied to have reporting restrictions under s97 of the Children Act lifted, so that she could tell her story to the *Daily Express*. She had been able to prove that she had not harmed the children, and had got them back from foster care, and the court agreed that she should be given the opportunity to publicly clear her name.

Incidental prevention of identifying adults

In some cases, an injunction made to protect a child's identity may effectively prevent identification of an adult as well, and therefore provide a severe restriction on the ability of the press to report a story. In some cases, the press have been able to challenge such injunctions on these grounds, and have them modified to allow the story to run.

In 2003, an injunction was passed preventing the press from publishing the identities of the children of a woman who had had a relationship with Ian Huntley, the notorious murderer of two schoolgirls in the Cambridgeshire village of Soham. The ban effectively meant that the press could not report the identity of the woman either, since this would clearly make it possible to identify her children. Several newspapers challenged the injunction, and the court agreed to change its terms, allowing publication of the mother's identity but preventing publication of pictures of the children or details of which schools they attended.

Using information about family cases

In the past, there was a complete ban on parties involved in certain types of family case disclosing details of the proceedings to other people. This meant that where a party had a grievance about the way in which their case was conducted, it was very difficult for them to publicise the problem in the media, or to seek support from, for example, their MP.

This situation was changed when the Family Proceedings Rules 1991 were altered in 2009 and now a new rule 11.4 provides that parties or their legal representatives can disclose information about the proceedings, where necessary to allow the party concerned to 'obtain support, advice or assistance in the conduct of proceedings' or 'make and pursue a complaint regarding the law, policy or procedure' relating to that type of proceedings. It is possible (though not clear yet), that disclosure to a journalist could be deemed to fall within one of these categories, but if you were to be given such information, you could only use it as background to help you understand the story; you would still not be able to publish any information about what happened during the proceedings.

Where a hearing is heard in private, and therefore subject to reporting restrictions under s12 of the Administration of Justice Act, it will also be contempt to report any information taken from documents prepared for their hearing, such as witness statements or expert reports, even if they are anonymised. This applies even if you are given this information by someone who is involved in the case.

In 1994, the *Sun* and its then editor were fined £5,000 and £1,000 for publishing extracts from a medical report which had been used in a family case where the hearing was held in private.

Myths and misconceptions **Reporting family cases**

✗ *You can write about a family case if the parents agree to be interviewed.*

As we have seen in this chapter, there is a vast array of reporting restrictions which apply to family cases, and together they mean that very little can be written about these proceedings. While reporters who cover the actual court hearings generally know this, the rules can cause problems for journalists who do not cover the courts, and might be seeking to write, for example, a human interest feature for a woman's magazine. If, for example, a couple whose child has been taken into care against their wishes come to you, wanting to publicise their story, it might not even occur to you that, regardless of their wishes, there may be legal restrictions on publishing the story. If the subject matter of a feature relates to any form of family proceedings – even if the feature itself is not primarily about the court case – it is sensible to remind yourself of the restrictions or check with your legal advisor.

Rules not yet in force

The Children, Schools and Families Act 2010 introduces new provisions regarding the reporting of family cases. These were supposed to have been designed to allow more detailed reporting, but the provisions have been widely criticised as being too complex, and in March 2010, *Media Lawyer* reported that media organisations had told the then Justice Secretary that this complexity was likely to put the press off even trying to report family cases, rather than increasing reporting, which was the stated intention of the change.

At the time of going to press, the changes were not yet in force, and a date had not been set for them to come into force. Given the opposition from within the family court and child protection system to more open reporting, it is quite possible that some or all of them may never come into force. For this reason, they are not covered in this edition, but if changes are made before the next edition, there will be an update on this book's website.

The Court of Protection

Although not classified as a family court, the Court of Protection is another court which deals with related matters, and which has traditionally operated behind closed doors. It was created under the Mental Capacity Act 2005, to deal with the affairs of people who lack the capacity to make their own decisions because, for example, of some form of mental illness or serious mental or physical disability. It hears around 23,000 cases a year, and can take decisions on behalf of the person concerned regarding their finances and welfare. It can, for example, decide whether someone should have medical treatment where they are not capable of giving consent to it (including, for example, abortion or sterilisation), and where someone becomes incapacitated, it will decide who should have control of the person's finances. The court has been the subject of some criticism since it was created, with the families of people incapacitated alleging unfair and incompetent treatment.

The court's rules specify that hearings are generally held in private, but that the court can allow the press to attend and proceedings to be reported. No doubt influenced by the moves towards greater openness in the wider family courts, the Court of Protection has over the past year or so become more willing to allow access to and reporting (although restricted) of its cases.

In *A v Independent News and Media* (2010), the case concerned a blind and seriously disabled man who has become internationally known for his musical ability, and earned a substantial amount of money from it. He lives in residential care and is not able to make his own decisions about financial matters, so the Court of Protection was called upon to decide whether his family should be allowed to look after his financial affairs, or whether an independent advisor should be appointed. A group of media organisations applied to be allowed to attend and report on the hearing, and the Court of Appeal ruled that they could do so. It said that A's situation and his remarkable talent were already in the public domain, and so the media had a legitimate interest in the case. It was also relevant that the workings of the Court of Protection had been the subject of some public concern and interest. The judgment allowed a small group of journalists to attend the hearing, and then make submissions to the court on what they should be allowed to report. They were allowed to name A, and give details of his situation and the issues before the court.

In *DH NHS Foundation Trust* v *PS* (2010), the case concerned a woman who had severe learning disabilities, and was suffering from cancer. She urgently needed surgery for the cancer, and had consented to this previously, but because of her extreme fear of doctors and needles, her doctors felt that she might refuse to come to the hospital. They wanted to be able to sedate her, but without consent or a court order, this would have been an assault, so they sought the court's permission to carry out the sedation. Unusually, the judge gave the judgment in open court and gave permission for it to be reported, provided that no one involved was identified, because, he said, the outcome of this kind of case should be in the public domain.

The 2014 guidance on publishing judgments in family cases, referred to earlier in this chapter, also applies to proceedings in the Court of Protection, so it should become much easier to find out about cases, even though the judgment may still often be anonymised.

KEY POINTS

Family courts

The work of the family courts includes:

- divorce and dissolution of civil partnerships;
- financial disputes between couples splitting up;
- disputes between couples about the care of their children;
- child abduction cases;
- adoption;
- applications for social services to intervene in the care of a child;
- orders concerning domestic violence;
- orders preventing forced marriage;
- wardship and the High Court's inherent jurisdiction.

Access to family proceedings

Most family proceedings take place in private, but the media have a new right to attend:

- hearings under the Children Act 1989, Parts IV and V (care orders, supervision orders, child protection orders, orders for the emergency protection of children, and orders for the recovery of abducted children);
- cases under the Children Act 1989 involving private law (disputes between parents over residency and contact, and over financial arrangements);
- proceedings for non-molestation and occupation orders;
- proceedings for forced marriage protection orders;
- proceedings under the Matrimonial Causes Act (divorce, judicial separation, annulment proceedings, dissolution of civil partnerships).

The court has discretion to exclude the press where:

- necessary for the safety or protection of a party to or witness in the proceedings, or someone connected with a party or witness;
- necessary for the orderly conduct of proceedings;
- justice would otherwise be impeded or prejudiced.

The press have the right to argue against exclusion.

Journalists may also attend:

- family proceedings held in public;
- family proceedings (except for adoption hearings) held in the magistrates' courts;
- appeals to the Court of Appeal and Supreme Court held in open court;
- placement hearings in county courts or High Court (at the court's discretion).

Journalists may not attend:

- adoption hearings;
- conciliation and mediation proceedings led by a judge;
- financial dispute resolution appointments.

Access to court documents

The media have no automatic right to see court documents but the court can give permission for this.

Reporting the family courts

There are wide automatic restrictions on reporting the family courts:

- Section 12 of the Administration of Justice Act 1960 bans publication of information on court proceedings held in private which:
  - concern the inherent jurisdiction of the High Court regarding minors;
  - are brought under the Children Act 1989;
  - relate to the maintenance or upbringing of a minor.

- Children involved in proceedings under the Children Act 1989 must not be identified.
- Reports of Family Proceedings before magistrates must only contain:
  - names, addresses and occupations of parties and witnesses;
  - grounds for the application, and a brief statement of the charges, defences and counter-charges in support of which evidence has been given;
  - submissions and decisions on points of law;
  - the court's decision and its remarks on the decision.
- Reports of divorce, nullity, separation or civil partnership dissolution proceedings must only contain:
  - names, addresses and occupations of parties and witnesses;
  - a concise statement of charges, defence, and counter-charges for which evidence has been given;
  - submissions and decisions on points of law;
  - the judgment and the judge's comments on it.
- No report of an adoption hearing can be published.
- Wardship proceedings cannot be reported, and children cannot be identified as a ward of court, without the court's permission.

There are also discretionary reporting restrictions:

- Any court can ban identification of a child involved in proceedings under s39 of the Children and Young Persons Act 1933.
- The High Court can use its inherent jurisdiction to order reporting restrictions or ban news-gathering.

It is not contempt to report family proceedings not involving children if:

- no specific statutory reporting restrictions apply;
- the court has not issued an order restricting reporting;
- the party disclosing the information has not undertaken not to make use of material that was compulsorily disclosed in the hearing;
- there are no restrictions imposed by the law of confidentiality.

Using information about family cases

Where the law prohibits reporting of proceedings, information obtained from documents or parties to the case cannot be published either.

The Court of Protection

- This court deals with the affairs of people who lack capacity to make decisions.
- Hearings are private but the court may allow the press to attend.
- Recent judgments have shown more willingness to allow reporting of the proceedings, but this is not automatically allowed.

TEST YOUR KNOWLEDGE

1 Under what circumstances can a court use its discretion to exclude the press from family proceedings?

2 You are attending the hearing of a divorce case between two very well-known TV presenters. What can you write in your story?

3 You are contacted by a couple whose child has been taken into care by social services, because the couple are alleged to have abused them. They deny this and want to tell their side of the story. The court case was a year ago. Do any reporting restrictions apply?

4 You are contacted by a teenager who you know is a ward of court. She wants to give you an interview about the circumstances which led to her being made a ward of court. Can you use her name in the story?

5 A local teenager saves a dog from drowning, and you are sent to interview him (the teenager, not the dog!). At the end of the interview, he mentions that he is a ward of court. Can you still run the story? What checks should you make?

ONLINE RESOURCES

The Children Act 1989 can be read at:
www.legislation.gov.uk/ukpga/1989/41/contents

The Practice Directions concerning media attendance at family proceedings can be read at:
https://www.justice.gov.uk/courts/procedure-rules/family/practice_directions/pd_part_27b
The Family Proceedings (Amendment) (No. 2) Rules 2009 can be read at:
www.legislation.gov.uk

The Family Courts – media access and reporting is available at:
http://www.judiciary.gov.uk/publications/the-family-courts-media-access-and-reporting/

Chapter 12 Reporting inquests

An inquest is a special type of court hearing, which is held to look into sudden or suspicious deaths. Unlike a criminal hearing or a civil claim concerning a death, an inquest is not about attributing blame for the death: instead, its aim is to find out who the dead person is (if not known), and how and why the death occurred. The nature of the deaths investigated by inquests mean that there is often press interest in the proceedings, both local and sometimes national. A number of changes to the system were made in the Coroners and Justice Act 2009, which came fully into force in 2013.

INQUEST PROCEDURE

An inquest must be held where:

- the cause of death is unknown;
- the death is 'violent or unnatural' (this would include, for example, deaths caused by crime, accidents, suicide, neglect, drug abuse, excessive alcohol consumption or poisoning);
- the death has happened in state detention (as well as prison, this includes detention in a police station, a mental hospital or an immigration detention centre).

In practice, less than half of all deaths are the subject of an inquest.

The hearing

Some cities have specific coroner's courts, but most inquests are held in the local magistrates' courts. Apart from a small number of cases where evidence involves national security, hearings are held in public. The hearing is presided over by a coroner who will be qualified either as a doctor or a lawyer.

The vast majority of inquests are heard by a coroner sitting alone, but in some circumstances, a jury must be used. These are where the coroner has reason to suspect that:

- the death happened in state custody, and either the death was violent or unnatural, or the cause is unknown;
- the death resulted from something that a police office or member of a service police force did, or failed to do, in the execution of their duty;
- the death was caused by a notifiable accident, poisoning or disease. An accident, poisoning or disease is notifiable if any Act requires it to be reported to a government department, inspector or officer, or an inspector appointed under the Health and Safety at Work Act 1974. Some contagious diseases, for example, must be notified.

A coroner can also decide to hold an inquest with a jury if he or she believes there is sufficient reason to do so.

Where there is a jury, it decides what happened; otherwise, it is the coroner who decides. Traditionally, a jury is usually described as having 'returned a verdict' at the end of an inquest, but if a coroner decides the case, he or she is usually said to have 'recorded a verdict'. The Coroners Act 2009 decrees that the result of an inquest should now be referred to as a conclusion rather than a verdict, but it remains to be seen whether this will affect popular usage of the term.

Whether heard by a coroner alone, or with a jury, most inquests take place in two or three stages:

- There may be a pre-inquest review to look at the issues in the case.
- The inquest is opened with a brief hearing, where the coroner establishes the identity of the dead person. It is then usually adjourned while the coroner conducts investigations, and draws up a list of witnesses to be called.
- At the second hearing, the coroner questions each witness, and leads them through their evidence; the style of questioning is aimed at finding out the truth, and is often quite different from that used in a criminal trial, where the opposing barristers are trying to prove or defend a case. Close relatives and anyone potentially implicated in the death (or their lawyers) are entitled to ask questions and make statements, and the coroner has discretion to allow others to do so. This does not, however, usually extend to reporters.

Inquest verdicts

There is no set list of the verdicts that an inquest can return (it is technically up to the coroner to decide the most accurate way of describing the death), but in practice, there are standard terms, of which these are the most common:

- natural causes;
- lawful killing;
- unlawful killing;
- dependence on drugs;
- want of attention at birth;
- suicide;
- accident or misadventure;
- industrial disease;
- open verdict (this is the verdict given when there is not enough evidence to produce any other verdict).

Alternatively, a jury or coroner can return what is called a 'narrative verdict', which rather than attaching a one-word label to the death, is a short statement detailing the circumstances in which, on the evidence, they believe the person died.

It is not the job of an inquest to find out (or even suggest) who is to blame for a death. The inquest can reach a verdict which states that the death was caused by someone else (such as unlawful killing) but by law it is prohibited from suggesting who that person might be, and in 1994 the Court of Appeal found that it should not even express an opinion as to blame. However, in the landmark House of Lords case of ***R (on the application of Middleton) v HM Coroner for Western Somerset*** (2004), it was held that a jury deciding an inquest into prisoners who had committed suicide could include as part of its findings that the way the prison system was run had contributed to the deaths, though it could not blame a named person. This was to conform with Article 2 of the European Convention on Human Rights 1998, which requires a thorough investigation of deaths in state custody, so is unlikely to be applied to inquests into other types of deaths.

Under rule 43 of the Coroners Rules, where an organisation is involved in a death (for example, an employer in a workplace accident, or a hospital in the death of a patient), the coroner can send that organisation a report on the circumstances of the death, pointing out any failings within the organisation which have contributed to it, with the aim of helping them to prevent any further deaths. The organisation must send a response within 56 days, explaining what action has been or is to be taken, or if no changes are to be made, why not. The Ministry of Justice has started to post these reports, and the responses to them, online (see *Online resources* at the end of this chapter), and they can be a very useful source of news stories.

Criminal proceedings and public inquiries

Where a death is already known to be the subject of criminal proceedings, an inquest is usually opened just to take evidence of identity and cause of death, and then adjourned until after the criminal proceedings are finished. If the criminal proceedings answer all questions about the death, the coroner can formally close the inquest, but if there are good reasons to continue with the inquest (if, for example, the criminal proceedings were unsuccessful), it can be reopened.

Where a number of people have died in a major disaster – such as a fire on public transport or a boat sinking – the government will often put in place a public inquiry, headed by a judge. In this situation, the Access to Justice Act 1999 allows the Lord Chancellor to direct that any inquest into one of the deaths should be adjourned, and where this happens, the inquest is not usually reopened unless there are special reasons to do so.

REPORTING INQUESTS

Inquests must usually be held in open court, which means the press may attend. However, the Coroners Rules 2013 allow a coroner to exclude the public, including the press, from all or part of an inquest hearing on grounds of national security. The public and press can also be excluded from a pre-inquest hearing on the grounds of national security or in the interests of justice.

The date of an inquest should be made public in advance. The media has no statutory right to be informed that an inquest is to be held, but a Home Office circular published in 1980 states the coroners are encouraged to make suitable arrangements to ensure that the media, and especially local papers, are given the date, time and place of forthcoming inquests, and the resumption of any inquests which have been adjourned (Circular No. 53/1980).

Inquests and contempt of court

The Contempt of Court Act 1981 applies to inquests, and, for the purposes of this Act (see Chapter 6), an inquest is deemed to be 'active' from the time it is opened, even if the opening is only a formality and the inquest is then adjourned indefinitely. The active period ends only when the proceedings are formally closed, and so continues during any adjournment.

Where a death is suspected to be the result of a crime, and the inquest takes place before the criminal proceedings, it is not contempt of court to report the inquest (unless the coroner makes an order restricting reporting and the report breaches this order). However, if the report of an inquest has an important effect on the trial (e.g. if it has to be moved to another area), it is possible that the publisher responsible could be ordered to pay the wasted costs (see p. 91).

Inquests and defamation

For the purposes of defamation, inquests are covered by absolute privilege, which means you cannot be sued for reporting anything said during the proceedings (see Chapter 15), so long as your report is fair, accurate and contemporaneous.

Access to documents

The Coroners Rules 2013 state that coroners must disclose any document from the case, or a copy of it, to any 'interested person'. This clearly includes close relatives of the dead person but it is unclear so far whether it would include a journalist. The coroner can redact details in the document, and can refuse to reveal it in certain circumstances, such as where it relates to criminal proceedings that have started. He or she can also order that it should not be published.

Reporting restrictions

Because inquests are subject to the provisions of the Contempt of Court Act 1981, coroners can make s4(2) and s11 orders postponing or banning reports of particular details, just as in any other court. They can also impose orders banning the identification of children who are 'involved in the proceedings', under s39 of the Children and Young Persons Act 1933. (The rules for imposing these orders are explained in Chapters 8 and 10.)

In ***Re LM (Reporting restrictions: Coroner's inquest)*** (2007), the Family Division of the High Court stated that the general principle that court proceedings should be reported applied equally to inquests. The case concerned an inquest which found that a mother's ill-treatment had caused the death of her daughter. The dead child had a sister, who was five years old, and was in local authority care, awaiting possible adoption. The local authority, backed by the parents, applied for an injunction preventing identification of any member of the family, on the grounds that it could affect the child's chances of being adopted. A group of media organisations opposed the order, and the judge agreed that while the sister should not be named, the rest of the family could be. He said that leaving out the name of the person whose actions might lead to a verdict of unlawful killing made the story less interesting to readers, which could reduce the level of informed debate about criminal justice generally, and in this case the suggestion that the child's adoption chances could be harmed was purely speculative. The situation might, he said, be different where there was a real risk of harm to the child's interests.

In 2007, a police officer witness who had asked a coroner for a s11 order to ban publication of his identity was persuaded to withdraw the request after the Press Association and bereaved families objected. The objectors argued that his name was already well known as he was being sued in connection with the deaths, and so his name was in public documents filed at the court. In addition, there was no evidence that his safety was at risk.

Rule 23 of the Coroners Rules 2013 allows a coroner to take evidence in written form, rather than orally, where the evidence is unlikely to be disputed and there is good reason for the person giving it not to attend the hearing. The rule provides that where this is done the coroner must announce publicly the name of the person who the evidence has come from, and should read it aloud; however, they can direct that the evidence should not be read aloud, and this can be used as a way of preventing the press from reporting that evidence. Usually, suicide notes and psychiatric reports are not read out, though there is no legal provision to prevent this.

Law in practice Getting to know the coroner's officer

Despite the fact that the Home Office encourages coroners to keep the press informed about forthcoming inquests, this does not always happen automatically, even where a case is of obvious interest to the press. In 2003, for example, the inquest into the sudden death of Laura Sadler, a popular actress in the hospital soap *Holby City*, was not attended by any members of the press, because no one in the media had known it was taking place. With this in mind, it is worth calling the coroner's office from time to time, to check what is coming up. Information for the media about when and where inquests are to be held or reopened usually comes via the coroner's officer, who is a police officer attached to the coroner's office (sometimes only part-time). Getting to know the coroner's officer can be very useful if you want information about inquests that might be of interest to your readers.

What the codes say Inquests

The Editors' Code of Practice used by IPSO states that:

- In cases involving personal grief or shock, enquiries and approaches must be made with sympathy and discretion and publication handled sensitively. This should not restrict the right to report legal proceedings, such as inquests.
- When reporting suicide, care should be taken to avoid excessive detail about the method used.

The Ofcom Broadcasting Code includes the following provisions which, while not limited to reports of inquests, will often be relevant to such reports:

- People in a state of distress should not be put under pressure to take part in a programme or provide interviews, unless it is warranted.

- Broadcasters should try to reduce the potential distress to victims and/or relatives when making or broadcasting programmes intended to examine past events that involve trauma to individuals (including crime) unless it is warranted to do otherwise.
- As far as reasonably practicable, surviving victims and/or the immediate families should be told that the coverage is planned, even if the events or material to be broadcast have been in the public domain in the past.

KEY POINTS

Inquest procedure

Inquests are held when:

- a death is sudden and the cause is unknown;
- the death is 'violent or unnatural';
- the death has happened in state detention.

Inquests seek to find out the facts of death; they do not attribute blame.

Juries are used in cases of public interest.

Reporting inquests

Inquests must be in open court, unless there are issues of national security.

The Contempt of Court Act 1981 applies to inquests.

Absolute privilege in defamation covers fair, accurate and contemporaneous reports.

TEST YOUR KNOWLEDGE

1. What types of death are likely to be the subject of an inquest?
2. When are juries used to decide inquests?
3. In what circumstances can reporters be excluded from an inquest?
4. When does an inquest become active for the purposes of the Contempt of Court Act 1981? When does it stop being active?
5. A teenager has died at a pop concert, after being squashed against barriers at the front of the crowd. An inquest into her death has been opened and adjourned. A security guard at the concert venue comes to you with evidence that his boss has been ignoring safety rules in order to save money. Can you report this evidence?
6. During an inquest, a witness alleges that the dead person was killed by his sister. Can you report this?
7. What reporting restrictions apply to inquests?

ONLINE RESOURCES

The pressure group Inquest campaigns for improvements in the inquest system. Its website has useful background information on the inquest process and problems with the system:
www.inquest.org.uk

Copies of coroners' reports sent to organisations involved in deaths they have investigated, and the responses, can be read at:
http://www.judiciary.gov.uk/related-offices-and-bodies/office-chief-coroner/pfd-reports/

Reporting tribunals and inquiries

Around half a million cases each year are decided not by the court system, but by tribunals. These are similar to courts, but tend to have more informal procedures. Each tribunal specialises in a particular area of law: the best-known is the Employment Tribunal, which hears cases concerning employees' treatment at work, but there are around 80 others, covering areas including access to welfare benefits, housing, school admissions and complaints against professionals such as lawyers and doctors. Which tribunals are of interest to journalists depends on what kind of publication they work for. Trade and professional magazines will often have an interest in the more specialist tribunals which deal with their particular subject area, whereas tribunals dealing with subjects such as housing, welfare or education can be a source of stories for the local and sometimes national press. The most commonly reported tribunal proceedings, however, tend to be those of the Employment Tribunal and, for that reason, this chapter gives a detailed explanation of its proceedings, after looking at tribunals in general.

This chapter also looks at public inquiries, which may be required under statute (e.g. planning inquiries) or may be one-off tribunals set up to look into an issue of public concern.

REPORTING TRIBUNALS

Because there are so many different types of tribunal, their personnel and procedures vary, but most tribunals are presided over by a panel, rather than a single judge. The panel is usually chosen to represent the different interests associated with that area of law – employment tribunal panels, for example, will usually include members from organisations representing employers, and those representing employees. Most, though not all, tribunal panels also have a legally qualified chairperson.

Tribunals are designed to decide disputes more quickly and inexpensively than the court system, so procedures are less rule-bound and more informal, and often the parties will make their own case, rather than using a lawyer. However, tribunals are still expected to behave like courts in that they have to give a fair hearing to both sides, and make an open and impartial decision on the case. Under the Tribunals and Inquiries Act 1992, tribunals must, if requested, state their reasons for a particular decision. Some tribunals, notably the Employment Tribunal, have in fact become more formal over the years, and now operate very much like a normal court, with both sides often represented by lawyers.

The decisions made by tribunals can usually be challenged by some form of appeals procedure, and for the most important tribunals, appeals on points of law can be made to the High Court, and ultimately to the Supreme Court. Tribunal decisions can also be challenged under the judicial review procedure (see p. 206).

Press access to tribunal proceedings varies according to the rules of the tribunal. In the majority of cases, hearings are held in public unless the parties or the court choose otherwise, but the law on when and why they can do this differs. If you need to find out the situation for a particular tribunal, the detailed information will be contained either in the legislation under which the tribunal was set up, or its rules of procedure (in many cases these rules are published on tribunal websites).

Contempt of court

As we saw earlier **(in Chapter 6)**, the Contempt of Court Act 1981 lays down rules about what can and cannot be published about court cases. The Act defines 'court' as 'any tribunal or body exercising the judicial power of the state', which means that its provisions apply to reports of some types of tribunal proceedings. However, the Act does not define 'the judicial power of the state', so the courts have had to decide in individual cases which tribunals fit this definition. For example, in ***Pickering* v *Liverpool Daily Post*** (1991), the Mental Health Review Tribunal was said to 'exercise the power of the state' because it has the power to restore a person's liberty, and in ***Peach Grey & Co* v *Sommers*** (1995), Employment Tribunals were also deemed to 'exercise the power of the state' because they exercise a 'judicial function'. These two, therefore, are defined as courts for the purposes of the Contempt of Court Act, and covered by its provisions. On the other hand, in ***General Medical Council* v *BBC*** (1998), the professional conduct committee of the General Medical Council was deemed not to be a court for the purposes of the Act, because it does not exercise a power of the state, and in ***A-G* v *BBC*** (1981), the local valuation court was held not to be covered by the Contempt of Court Act because its functions were essentially administrative, rather than judicial.

Unfortunately, with many other tribunals, it is difficult to know whether they are covered by the law on contempt. If your company has an in-house or retained lawyer, they will be able to tell you whether the type of tribunal you want to write about has already been recognised as 'exercising the judicial power of the state' or not, but there are some tribunals for which the question has never been addressed by a court, so the answer is not known. However, during the Parliamentary debate on the Contempt of Court Act, the Attorney-General's office said that it would be willing to give assistance to members of the press who needed to know whether a particular tribunal was covered by the Act, so a call to its Press Office may get you the information you need.

Defamation

The rules of defamation (explained in Chapter 15) must always be borne in mind when reporting tribunal proceedings. Because most tribunals are relatively informal, and the parties will often represent themselves rather than using lawyers, things are often said that would not be allowed in a court, and some of these comments will be potentially defamatory. However, the law does offer some protection for tribunal reports:

- The Defamation Act 1996 provides that fair, accurate and contemporaneous reports of tribunals 'exercising the judicial power of the state' are covered by absolute privilege **(see p. 268)**, so you cannot be sued for a fair, accurate and contemporaneous report of anything said during those proceedings. However, as we saw above, it is not always clear which tribunals this covers.
- Schedule II of the Act provides that fair and accurate reports of any public meeting of a 'tribunal . . . constituted by or under, or exercising functions under, any statutory provision' are covered by qualified privilege, 'subject to explanation or contradiction' (see p. 259).

This covers any tribunal which has been set up by an Act of Parliament or delegated legislation (which is most of them). Remember though that statutory qualified privilege only applies to material which is of public concern and published 'for the public benefit'.

Reporting restrictions

A few tribunals (such as the Employment Tribunal – see below) have powers to make specific reporting restrictions relating to their proceedings; again, these powers will be contained in the legislation or procedural rules. Orders under s4(2) and s11 of the Contempt of Court Act 1981 can also be made in any tribunal 'exercising the power of the state' (see above). Remember that the ban on identifying victims of sexual offences will also cover any tribunal case where material used in a report could identify someone as the victim of a sexual offence.

EMPLOYMENT TRIBUNALS

Probably the best-known tribunals, these deal with cases involving unfair dismissal, sexual or racial discrimination in employment, redundancy and disputes over employment contracts. They are presided over by a legally qualified chairman, and two other members, one of whom is drawn from organisations representing employers, the other employees (though naturally they are all required to judge the case independently, rather than as a representative of the relevant organisation). The person bringing a claim is called the claimant, and the other side, the respondent.

Procedure

Employment Tribunals usually sit in public, but some cases may be heard privately (see below). Before the hearing, both sides will have received notice of any documents that the other side intends to use in evidence, and there will often be a pre-hearing to clarify the issues. Just as with a court, witnesses can be compelled to attend an Employment Tribunal, and give their evidence on oath (which means that lying to the tribunal can be prosecuted as perjury).

In most cases, the employer will be represented by a lawyer. Employees may also use a lawyer, and where their case is supported by their union, they will usually be represented by the union lawyer or a union official. Unlike in a court case, there are no set rules for who gives evidence first; usually, in a discrimination case, the person claiming discrimination gives their evidence first, while in unfair dismissal cases, the respondent's evidence is taken first, but this can vary. After a witness has given evidence, they can be cross-examined by the other side, and then may give further evidence to clarify any issues that were raised during cross-examination. The chairperson and/or the other members of the panel may also put direct questions to witnesses.

After all the evidence has been given, both sides will sum up their case, and then the panel retires to consider a judgment. The decision may be given in full at the end of the hearing, but often employment tribunals either give their basic decision and publish the full reasons later, or postpone the decision completely and publish it later. If the decision is given at the end of the hearing, and the claimant wins, compensation will be decided there and then.

In most cases, each side pays its own legal costs, but in a handful of cases (less than 1 per cent), the tribunal may order one side to pay the other's costs. This is only done where either the party concerned is thought to have behaved very unreasonably, or where their case was so weak the tribunal does not believe it should have been brought at all. So if costs are awarded in a tribunal decision you report on, that is a story in itself.

Appeals

Either side in an employment case can appeal to the Employment Appeal Tribunal (EAT), if they believe the decision reflects a legal error. The EAT sits in London, presided over by a High Court judge and two lay members, again from both sides of industry. Appeals can only be made on the grounds that there was an error of law, or the decision was completely unreasonable.

Reporting employment tribunals

Employment tribunals must usually sit in public and admit the press, but there are a few situations in which they can sit in private. The Employment Tribunals (Constitution and Rules of Procedure) Regulations 2013 provide that employment tribunals (and the EAT) may hold hearings in private where:

- it considers this is in the interests of justice; or
- to protect a person's rights under the European Convention on Human Rights (for example the right to privacy); or
- the evidence is likely to:
  - include information which a witness could not reveal without breaching a prohibition imposed by an Act of Parliament;
  - include information communicated to a witness in confidence, or obtained as a result of the confidence placed in the witness by someone else;
  - be such that disclosure would cause substantial injury to their employer's interests, for reasons other than its effect on negotiations over pay and conditions.

The Regulations provide that where a tribunal makes an order to sit in private, anyone with a legitimate interest (which includes the press), who has not had a chance to argue against the order, can make written representations against it.

A Minister can also direct an employment tribunal to hear a case in private in the interests of national security.

Aside from these reasons, employment tribunals should sit in public.

In *XXX* v *YYY* (2004) a nanny bringing an unfair dismissal case alleged that the father of the family she worked for had made sexual advances to her. She secretly filmed this one morning, and wanted to use the tape (on which the child could also be seen) in evidence. The Employment Tribunal agreed that it should be played during the hearing. The case was appealed to the EAT, which ruled that playing the tape was a breach of the child's right to privacy under the Human Rights Act 1998 because its contents could be described in newspapers and the images circulated. This would be severely damaging to the child as he grew older. The EAT therefore held that the tribunal could have sat in private, because the video could be categorised as evidence which could not be disclosed without breaching a prohibition imposed by an Act of Parliament. (At the time of the case, the 2000 version of the rules applied, but contained a similar provision to that in the 2004 rules.) The actual decision in the case was later overturned by the Court of Appeal, but the Court of Appeal stated that this did not affect the decision on the child's privacy.

In *Storer* v *British Gas* (2000), a tribunal hearing was held in an office, which was inside an area that could only be entered by a door marked 'Private'. The Court of Appeal held that this could not be considered a public hearing, because a member of the public would not have been able to enter if they had wanted to, and the chairman had acted wrongly in not holding the hearing in public.

In *R* v *Southampton Industrial Tribunal, ex p INS News Group* (1995), a tribunal had sat in private because it was hearing sensitive evidence in a sexual harassment case, but the Divisional Court of the Queen's Bench held that this was unlawful, and a tribunal could only sit in private in the situations listed in the Regulations.

Witnesses will usually be asked to give their names and addresses before giving evidence, but the full names, ages and addresses of the parties may not always be read out as a matter of course; they should, however, be available from tribunal officials.

Reporting restrictions

Employment tribunals have a number of powers to restrict reporting of their proceedings. Rule 50 of the Employment Tribunals (Constitution and Rules of Procedure) Regulations 2004 allows them to impose restricted reporting orders where:

- a case involves sexual misconduct; or
- a claim is being brought under s17A or s25(8) of the Disability Discrimination Act 1995, and some of the evidence is of a personal nature.

'Sexual misconduct' is defined by s11(6) of the Employment Tribunals Act 1996 as 'the commission of a sexual offence, sexual harassment or other adverse conduct (of whatever nature) related to sex, and conduct is related to sex whether the relationship with sex lies in the character of the conduct or in its having reference to the sex or sexual orientation of the person at whom the conduct is directed.' In effect this means that any case involving allegations of sexual harassment can be made the subject of a restricted reporting order, as well as any case involving allegations of a sexual offence.

The order can be requested by the claimant or, in cases of alleged sexual misconduct (but not disability discrimination), by the respondent. Alternatively, the tribunal itself can choose to make an order. It is not, however, obliged to make an order just because the case fits one of the two categories listed above, and one or both of the parties wants an order. The tribunal must take into account the public interest in the case being reported when deciding whether to issue an order, and in ***Kearney* v *Smith New Court Securities*** (1997), the Court of Appeal stressed that full consideration should be given to this question, and tribunals should not merely accede to requests for orders 'on the nod'.

The restricted reporting order prevents the press from naming anyone specified in the order, which may include the victim, or anyone else affected by the allegations (including the person alleged to be the perpetrator). However, in ***Leicester University* v *A*** (1999), it was established that, for these purposes, a company is a not a person, so such an order cannot state that a company should not be named. A notice that a restricted reporting order is in force will be put on the tribunal notice board and on the door of the hearing room.

Restricted reporting orders can only be made at a pre-hearing review, or the hearing itself, and rule 50(7) of the Employment Tribunal Rules 2004 provides that any person can make an application to the tribunal to put forward arguments about why an order should or should not be made (though whether the application is accepted is up to the tribunal). This provision has been used successfully by the press in preventing such orders.

In some cases, a tribunal may make a temporary order, which it can do without holding a hearing. The parties then have 14 days to apply for the temporary order to be converted into a full one, or revoked, otherwise it lapses. If either side applies for it to be revoked or converted to a full order, both sides must be given a chance to argue for or against this, and the press can also apply to make representations.

A full restricted reporting order usually remains in force until the tribunal has made its decision, including determining any compensation to be paid, and issued written judgments to the parties (which may be months afterwards). In some cases, though, an order may state that it only remains in force until the court has decided which party wins. Tribunals can also revoke an order before a case is decided. Where a case to which an order applies is settled before the full hearing (as often happens), the order remains in force unless the tribunal revokes it.

A potentially severe restriction on the media's ability to get reporting restrictions lifted has been put in place by the decision in ***Dallas McMillan and A v B and Ms F Davidson*** (2008). The case arose after tribunal proceedings where the claimant alleged sexual misconduct, and so the tribunal imposed a restricted reporting order. After a series of hearings, the claimant withdrew her case, so a freelance journalist covering the proceedings asked if restrictions could now be lifted, or if the tribunal could issue a written judgment so that the parties could be identified. The tribunal chairman agreed but the claimant's former employers appealed, and the Employment Appeal Tribunal held that the restrictions could not be lifted by the tribunal once proceedings were over. They could have been lifted during the proceedings, but only at the request of a party to the proceedings, so journalists would have to apply to the tribunal chair to be made a party before they could apply for the restrictions to be lifted. The only other way that restrictions could be lifted was automatically when the court had decided the case and the remedy and if, as in this case, that did not happen, the restrictions would last indefinitely.

Breaching a restricted reporting order is a criminal offence, punishable with a fine of up to £5,000.

Rule 49 of the Employment Tribunals (Constitution and Rules of Procedure) Regulations 2004 states that in cases involving allegations of a sexual offence (not just sexual misconduct) a tribunal must remove from any documents available to the public (including the judgment), anything which could lead the public to identify the victim or anyone else affected by the allegations. This includes the alleged perpetrator.

When reporting tribunal cases involving sexual misconduct, it is important to remember that the Sexual Offences (Amendment) Act 1992 also applies to Employment Tribunal proceedings and prevents identification of the victim of a sexual offence during his or her lifetime, unless the victim gives written consent to being named (see Chapter 9). This means that even once a restricted reporting order has lapsed, it will still not always be possible to name the claimant.

In addition to the restrictions on cases involving sexual misconduct, Employment Tribunals have been given new powers to restrict reporting of their proceedings, under rule 50 of the Employment Tribunal Rules 2013. The rule provides that, at any stage of the proceedings, a tribunal may make an order that prevents or restricts reporting of those proceedings, as far as it considers necessary in the interests of justice, or in order to protect the rights under the European Convention on Human Rights of any person, or in the circumstances stated in s10a of the Employment Tribunals Act (s10a deals with the circumstances in which a tribunal can sit in private when dealing with certain types of confidential information). The new rule 50 also allows tribunals to hold all or part of a hearing in private, or give anonymity to parties to the case, witnesses or other people mentioned in the proceedings.

When considering whether to impose restrictions under rule 50, the rule states that a tribunal 'shall give full weight to the principle of open justice and the Convention right to freedom of expression'. Tribunals are not obliged to ask for representations from the media before imposing restrictions, but the rule states that anyone who has a legitimate interest and has not been given a reasonable chance to make representation can apply for the order to be revoked or discharged.

The new rules also provide, in rule 44, that any members of the public attending the hearing (which would seem to include the press) can inspect any witness statement used as evidence in chief.

PUBLIC INQUIRIES

Some Acts of Parliament require that a public inquiry be held before a decision is made on any action affecting the rights of individuals or other public authorities. Such inquiries are often held, for example, in connection with major building projects such as airports or roads, which may require compulsory purchase of land, and will also have a significant effect on life in the area. The idea of the inquiry is to allow people who might be affected to put forward arguments for or against a proposal.

The inquiry is conducted by an inspector, on behalf of the relevant minister. Depending on the requirements of the statute, the final decision may be made by the inspector, or they may report to the minister, who then takes the decision.

Reporting inquiries

Some inquiries have to be held in public, and, where this is the case, it will be stated in the statute under which the inquiry has been set up. In other cases, it is up to the person hearing the inquiry whether the proceedings are open to the public or not. There are also instances where proceedings that would normally be public can be heard in private: for example, one of the most commonly reported types of hearing, the planning inquiry, is usually open to the public but the Secretary of State can direct that certain evidence is heard in private, if it relates to national security and measures taken to ensure the security of property, and if disclosing this information would be against the national interest. The findings of these kinds of public inquiries are usually made available to the public.

One-off inquiries

In addition to statutory inquiries, governments sometimes order one-off public enquiries to investigate high-profile events which have caused public concern (such as those into Bloody Sunday or the murder of Stephen Lawrence). Most of these are now governed by the Inquiries Act 2005. Section 18 of the Act provides that an inquiry chairman must take reasonable steps to ensure that reporters can attend or see a simultaneous transmission of proceedings, and see the evidence and documents given. Restrictions on this access can only be imposed by the relevant minister or the inquiry chairman when they are required by law, are in the public interest or are conducive to the inquiry fulfilling its terms of reference. Even if enquiries are held in private, their reports must be published, but material can be withheld where it is in the public interest or required by law. However, the Department of Constitutional Affairs website states that powers to withhold information will not be used to prevent disclosure under the Freedom of Information Act (see Chapter 29).

KEY POINTS

Reporting tribunals

Tribunals decide cases in specialist areas such as mental health, employment and social security.

Rules on press access are found in the statute under which a tribunal was set up, or its rules of procedure.

Contempt of court

Tribunals which exercise 'the judicial functions of the state' are subject to the Contempt of Court Act 1981.

Defamation

- Tribunals which exercise 'the judicial functions of the state' are covered by absolute privilege in defamation.
- Tribunals set up by statute are covered by qualified privilege subject to explanation or contradiction.

Public inquiries

Some statutes require public inquiries on decisions which affect a large number of people.

Press access to these inquiries varies; conclusions are usually made public.

One-off inquiries look into issues of public concern.

The press can attend these unless restrictions are needed because they:

- are required by law;
- are in the public interest; or
- are conducive to the inquiry fulfilling its terms of reference.

TEST YOUR KNOWLEDGE

1 What are the main differences between courts and tribunals?

2 On what grounds can an Employment Appeal Tribunal sit in private?

3 Name two tribunals which are definitely subject to the Contempt of Court Act 1981.

4 What legal protection is there against defamation actions for reports of tribunal proceedings?

ONLINE RESOURCES

The Tribunals Service website has links to the websites of 17 key tribunals, which details their functions and procedure:
www.justice.gov.uk/about/hmcts

The Employment Tribunal website explains the work and procedure of the tribunal:
www.justice.gov.uk/tribunals/employment

The Planning Inspectorate website lists forthcoming planning inquiries, at:
www.Planningportal.gov.uk

The Inquiries Act 2005 can be read at:
www.legislation.gov.uk/ukpga/2005/12/contents#18

Challenging reporting restrictions

There are two reasons why journalists need to know about the restrictions on reporting the courts. The first is, obviously, so that you do not break the law when publishing details about a court case. The second is so that you can spot when a court has ordered restrictions that can be challenged.

As we saw in previous chapters, a court can only impose reporting restrictions where there is a specific legal provision that allows it to do so, and, where such a provision exists, it may only order such restrictions as the provision allows. For example, s4(2) of the Contempt of Court Act 1981 allows a court to impose restrictions where it is necessary to avoid a risk of prejudice, so the restrictions ordered under this provision should only go so far as is necessary to avoid that risk (see Chapter 8). Yet courts will surprisingly often impose restrictions that are wider than the law allows, or that the law does not allow at all, particularly if defence lawyers press for this. Where this happens, the press can challenge those restrictions and may be able to get them lifted (or even prevent them being applied in the first place). This chapter details the practical steps you can take to challenge reporting restrictions.

PREVENTING RESTRICTIONS

In some cases, it may be possible for the media to persuade a court not to impose restrictions in the first place. The Criminal Procedure Rules 2014 (see *Online resources* at the end of this chapter) state that courts considering imposing reporting restrictions must take into account the importance of hearing criminal cases in public and letting them be reported. Part 16 states that courts dealing with an application for reporting restrictions should ensure that all the parties involved and 'any other person directly affected', which includes the press, is either present or has had a chance to make representations, before any restrictions are imposed. Part 16 also obliges anyone applying to remove or vary reporting restrictions to give the court and parties advance notice, and contains provisions for the press to be notified about orders for reporting restrictions or for a trial or part of a trial to be held in private.

The senior judiciary accepts that the media often have a good knowledge of the law on reporting restrictions, and where a court is considering making a discretionary order imposing reporting restrictions, the higher courts have encouraged lower courts to listen to, or even ask for, the views of the press.

In ***McKerry* v *Teasdale and Wear Valley Justices*** (2000) the Lord Chief Justice, Lord Bingham, commented that where a Youth Court was considering whether to lift anonymity from a defendant, it would be appropriate for the magistrates to ask the reporter present in court whether they wanted to argue against restrictions, and that in such cases, members of the press might well have arguments to make which could stop the court from making a mistake.

In ***R* v *Clerkenwell Metropolitan Stipendiary Magistrates, ex p Telegraph plc*** (1993), the Queen's Bench Divisional Court confirmed that all courts have discretion to hear arguments from the media about whether or not a s4(2) order (see p. 114) should be made. The court commented that the decision involves balancing the risk of prejudice against the public interest in open justice, and it made sense to consult the media, as they were in the best position to represent that public interest.

This approach is backed up by advice given by the Judicial College. In its 2014 guidance document – Reporting Restrictions in the Criminal Courts – it states that:

- The general rule is that the administration of justice should be done in public, evidence should be communicated publicly and fair, accurate and contemporaneous reporting of court proceedings should not be prevented unless strictly necessary.
- Courts should consider whether departing from the principle is actually necessary and, in particular, consider whether there are any automatic reporting restrictions or restrictions under media codes of practice, which might make a further order unnecessary.
- If is necessary to restrict access and/or reporting, the court should find the least restrictive way of achieving the aim, making sure the restrictions imposed are proportionate to the reason for them.
- If the courts are asked to restrict press access to a hearing, or reporting of it, they should invite the media to submit their arguments against this, either orally or in writing, and hear such arguments as soon as possible.
- If an order is imposed, the courts should also be ready to hear media arguments for it being lifted or varied.
- As soon as possible after an order is made, it should be put in writing, stating its terms precisely, and it may be helpful at the same time to point out that the court will be willing to listen to arguments from the media about the order.
- Every court should have procedures for notifying the media about restrictions on access or reporting, copies of the order should be available to the media, and court staff should be briefed to deal with media enquiries, including outside court hours.

This document is available online (see *Online resources* at the end of this chapter), and it can be useful to have a copy with you if you think you might need to make a challenge.

CHALLENGING ORDERS

If you are not able to convince a court not to impose restrictions in the first place, there are three ways of challenging an order:

- application to the original court;
- judicial review;
- appeals under s159 of the Criminal Justice Act 1988.

Applying to the original court

If you think that a court may have made an order which it is not legally entitled to make, or which may be wider than it needs to be, the first step is to make sure you know the legal basis on which the court believes it is acting (e.g. whether it is making a s4(2) order or a s11 one). If this is not stated at the time the restrictions are imposed, you can ask the clerk of the court, or the judge's clerk, for the information. In some cases, this alone will be enough to prompt the court to reconsider the case for restrictions and, as a result, to lift or relax them.

If not, once you know the legal provision being used, you can draw the court's attention to the reason why you believe the restrictions imposed are outside those provisions – for example, if a court has made a s11 order banning identification of a witness, but that person's name has already been stated in open court. The usual way to do this is by asking the clerk to pass a note to the magistrates or judge. Again, this simple (and, unlike all the other options, free) approach will often prompt a re-examination of the relevant law, which, if you are right, should see the restrictions lifted or relaxed accordingly.

If this strategy fails, your publisher can instruct its lawyers to make representations to the court, usually within 24 hours if necessary. The court does not have to hear these representations, but is unlikely to refuse. Of course, a drawback to this option is that unless you have an in-house lawyer who can make the case, it will involve a cost, which means the publisher may have to weigh up the importance of the story against the expense.

Law in practice Challenging restrictions

Tony Jaffa, Head of Media at solicitors Foot Anstey, represents newspapers throughout the country in challenges to exclusions from court and reporting restrictions. He has this advice for reporters faced with exclusion from a court hearing, or reporting restrictions that they believe may be unlawful:

- If possible, make your challenge as soon as the order is made, or if that is not possible, make it known that you want to challenge. If you want time to speak to your news editor and/or your legal advisors, you can say that you would like to make representations in writing, or ask if you can come back and discuss the order later. Quick action is especially important where the case is likely to finish on the same day, as once it is over, the magistrates or judge may refuse to lift the order on the grounds that they no longer have jurisdiction over the case.
- Always be polite, and show respect for the judge or magistrates, and the court. It helps to know the correct terminology to use, but your challenge will not fail because you call the judge My Lord instead of Your Honour, so long as you are respectful. Show that you know what you are talking about, for example by quoting the relevant section of the legislation, but do not be tempted to act like Rumpole of the Bailey. You can be persuasive, and even forceful in your arguments, but do not try to make your case sound stronger than it is – and know when to shut up!
- If you are reporting a particular court regularly, it makes sense to develop a good relationship with the clerks there. Once they know and trust you, and the judges begin to do the same, you are more likely to be listened to when you make a challenge.
- Do not challenge orders as a matter of routine – go for the ones where you know you have a good case. If you challenge every order a court makes, human nature means that eventually you will become irritating, and the court is less likely to listen sympathetically. You are more likely to get results if the court recognises you usually do not challenge without good reason.

Judicial review

If a court refuses to change its decision on reporting restrictions, and the press is convinced that the restrictions are not legally justified, judicial review is a way of challenging the decision in court. Essentially, the procedure asks a higher court to look at the decision of the lower court, and judge whether it was properly made; if the lower court acted outside its powers, or if the decision was clearly irrational, it can be quashed, or the lower court may be asked to look at the question again.

Judicial review has two major drawbacks. Firstly, the process can be slow, which means that by the time the court comes to a decision, the original story may no longer have much news value.

Secondly, it is usually expensive, and publishers may not get their costs paid, even if they win. In a 1995 case, for example, Express Newspapers and the INS news agency had to pay estimated costs of £10,000, after successfully challenging the right of an Industrial Tribunal (the old name for Employment Tribunals) to exclude journalists from a case involving sexual harassment.

As a result, judicial review tends only to be used by big publishers in important cases. Judicial review is not available to challenge orders made by the Crown Court with regard to trials on indictment.

Section 159 appeals

Section 159 of the Criminal Justice Act 1988 creates a right of appeal against decisions on access or reporting restrictions in the Crown Court (but not in any other court). Appeals go to the Court of Appeal and can be brought by 'any person aggrieved' by the decision, which can include the press, as well as anyone involved in the case. They may relate to:

- orders made under s4 or s11 of the Contempt of Court Act 1981 (see Chapter 8), with reference to a criminal trial in the Crown Court;
- any order restricting public access to a Crown Court trial, or part of one, or to any proceedings ancillary to such a trial;
- any order restricting the publication of reports on a Crown Court trial, or part of one, or any ancillary proceedings to that trial;
- any order from the Crown Court restricting reporting of derogatory statements made as part of pleas in mitigation.

However, there are some procedural issues which mean that these provisions are not as useful in practice as they may sound. Firstly, the right of appeal is not automatic; publishers have to apply to the Court of Appeal for permission to appeal. Notice also has to be given to the trial judge, their clerk, both parties in the case to which restrictions apply, and 'any other interested person'. Secondly, the case must be made in writing, and the press has no right to appear before the court and state its case. Perhaps the most significant drawback though is that the appeal can take time. The Court of Appeal does have the power to stop the original case while the appeal is decided, but if it chooses not to do this, and, by the time the appeal is decided, the original court case is finished, the news value of being able to report it fully may be much lower. During the appeal itself, the Court of Appeal can rule that witnesses, or anyone else in the case, may not be identified. If the appeal is successful, the Court of Appeal can lift or alter the order.

Checklists: grounds for a challenge

To get reporting restrictions lifted, or persuade a court not to impose them in the first place, you will need to show a good reason – the fact that they prevent you from reporting the case is not enough on its own. This checklist covering some of the most commonly challenged restrictions will help you judge whether you may have a case for a challenge – for more detailed information on the arguments to be made, see the chapters referred to.

As a back-up to these specific reasons for challenge, you can also point out the commitment to open justice expressed in the Judicial Studies Board guidelines (see *Online resources* at the end of this chapter).

Section 4(2) orders, used to postpone reports of any trial or specific details about a trial (see Chapter 8), can be challenged if:

- the order is not necessary to avoid a substantial risk of prejudice. Orders should not be given to spare embarrassment;
- the risk of prejudice could be dealt with by other means;
- the risk of prejudice is not substantial;
- an order would not remove the risk anyway;
- the order does not cover proceedings which are current, imminent or pending;
- the order amounts to a permanent ban. Section 4(2) orders can only impose a temporary ban;
- the order does not take sufficient account of the public interest in open justice. If there is a strong public interest in a trial being reported, that may outweigh a risk of prejudice.

Section 11 orders, used to ban publication of details about any court case (see Chapter 8), can be challenged if:

- the banned details have already been revealed in open court (unless by mistake);
- the banned details were withheld from the public, but the court did not have a legal power to do this;
- a ban is not necessary in the interests of justice. Section 11 orders should not be made to spare embarrassment (except in rare cases such as blackmail trials), or to protect business interests or professional reputations, and only rarely to protect personal safety.

Reporting restrictions on sexual offence cases under the Sexual Offences (Amendment) Act 2003 (see Chapter 9) can be challenged if:

- the restrictions impose a 'substantial and unreasonable restraint' on reporting, and it would be in the public interest to remove them. This is most likely to mean cases where other very serious offences are involved and the restrictions make it impossible to report them.

Restrictions on reporting pleas in mitigation (see Chapter 9) can be challenged if:

- there are not 'substantial grounds' for believing that the allegations concerned are untrue;
- the facts stated are relevant to the sentence.

Section 46 orders preventing identification of vulnerable witnesses (see Chapter 9) can be challenged if:

- the subject of the order is not a witness;
- the order was not issued to prevent fear or distress – preventing embarrassment is not sufficient grounds for a s49 order;
- the court has not taken into account the importance of avoiding unreasonable restrictions on reporting.

Section 49 restrictions on reporting youth court proceedings (see Chapter 10) can be challenged if:

- the defendant has been convicted and it is in the public interest to identify them. This is more likely to apply if:
  - the young person is a serious or persistent offender;
  - the offending has affected a large number of people;
  - publicity could help prevent further criminal activity.

Section 39 orders banning identification of a child in an adult court (see Chapter 10) can be challenged if:

- the court has not balanced the importance of open justice against the need to protect the child (or it can be argued that they have struck the wrong balance);
- the child is very young;
- the child is dead;
- the child is not 'concerned in the proceedings'. Merely being related to a defendant, victim or witness does not usually mean a child is involved in the proceedings;
- the order specifically bans publication of an adult's identity.

The risk of incurring costs

One thing to be aware of when considering a challenge to reporting restrictions is that in some circumstances, such a challenge could result in your publication being asked to pay costs. In ***A* v *Times Newspapers*** (2002), the Family Division of the High Court said that where the press knew that restrictions were likely to be imposed on a particular hearing, but did not apply to have them lifted until after the proceedings had begun, the publishers concerned risked having an order for costs made against them, even if the application to lift the restrictions was successful. By contrast, if the publishers made the application in good time, the courts were unlikely to impose costs, even if the challenge was unsuccessful, provided that the media at least had an arguable case. Costs are not routinely ordered against the media, however, and if such an order is made, the press can put forward arguments against it.

In 2006, a reporter from *The Argus* in Brighton persuaded a court not to impose a costs order which the defence lawyers in the case had asked for. The paper had challenged a s39 order banning the press from naming some children who had had ASBOs imposed on them. When the challenge was unsuccessful, the children's lawyers asked the court for an order requiring the newspaper to pay the costs involved in the challenge, which ran to thousands of pounds. The *Argus* reporter argued that it was in the public interest for newspapers to be able to challenge orders, and that imposing costs would make this impossible for most papers; she used the Human Rights Act 1998 and Judicial Studies Board Guidelines to back up her arguments. The court agreed not to impose the costs order.

Must invalid orders be followed?

The short answer is yes: no matter how sure you are that an order is invalid, simply ignoring it is not a sensible option. This was made plain in ***Lakah Group* v *Al Jazeera Satallite Channel*** (2002), where Mr Justice Eady stated that while an order exists, everyone who it applies to, and who knows it exists, is under an obligation to obey it, even if they believe it to be invalid, and even if that belief is actually correct. In such circumstances, he said, the answer is to put the issue before a court, not to decide it yourself. Similarly, in ***Independent Publishing Co Ltd*** v ***Attorney General of Trinidad and Tobago*** (2004), the Judicial Committee of the Privy Council stated that publishing material that was likely to prejudice the administration of justice could still be contempt, even if the order banning such publication was itself illegal.

KEY POINTS

Preventing restrictions

The higher courts and Judicial Studies Board guidelines encourage courts to listen to press arguments before ordering reporting restrictions.

Challenging restrictions

There are three ways to challenge a court order which is too wide, or unlawful:

- applying to the original court;
- judicial review;
- appeal under s159 of the Criminal Justice Act 1988, for cases heard in the Crown Court.

Costs

Challenging restrictions could result in a costs order against the press.

Invalid orders

Orders imposing reporting restrictions should be followed, even if apparently invalid.

TEST YOUR KNOWLEDGE

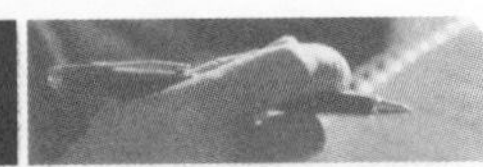

1. You are reporting a case in which the defence solicitor has asked for reporting restrictions to be imposed. You think there are good reasons for not imposing restrictions, but the magistrates say that they are not allowed to take your views into account. What arguments could you use to try to change their minds?
2. What do you need to find out before you can argue that an order imposing reporting restrictions is invalid?
3. Name the three ways in which reporting restrictions can be challenged.
4. To which courts does the s159 appeal against reporting restrictions apply?
5. Why is it risky to delay asking a court to lift reporting restrictions?
6. On what grounds can you challenge the following?
   (a) a s4(2) order;
   (b) a s11 order;
   (c) a s39 order.

ONLINE RESOURCES

The new Criminal Procedure Rules 2012, which set down rules for applications to impose reporting restrictions, can be found at:
www.justice.gov.uk/courts/procedure-rules/criminal.

'Reporting Restrictions in the Criminal Courts', containing guidelines from the Judicial Studies Board, can be found at:
http://www.judiciary.gov.uk/publications/reporting-restrictions-in-the-criminal-courts/

Useful reports of cases where reporting restrictions have been imposed or overturned can be found at the Hold the Front Page website:
www.holdthefrontpage.co.uk

The Society of Editors website also reports on the use of, and challenges to, reporting restrictions:
www.societyofeditors.co.uk

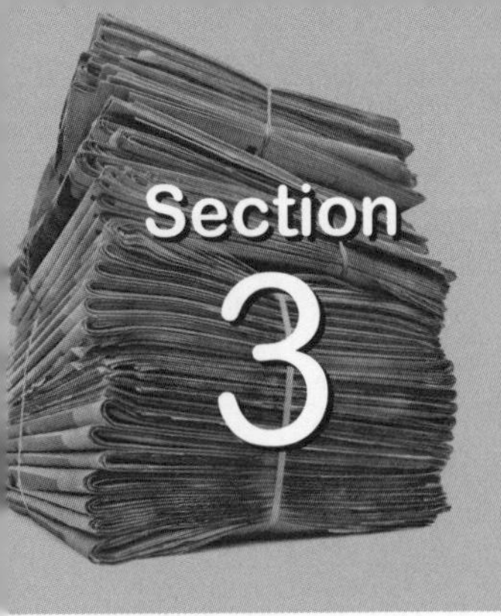

Section 3

DEFAMATION AND MALICIOUS FALSEHOOD

As far back as the eleventh century, English law has provided a legal claim for people whose reputations have been damaged by lies told about them. Over the centuries, this action developed into the modern law of defamation, and its main (though not only) use is now in cases where damaging statements are published by the media. Most legal systems have a form of defamation law, but the rules vary widely throughout the world, and England's have long been considered to make life more difficult for the media than the laws in many other countries.

Defamation is one of the most important areas of law for a journalist to know about and, for that reason, it is considered in more depth than most other subjects in this book. To keep chapters at a readable length, the coverage of defamation has been split into two. Chapter 15 explains how defamation is committed and thus how to avoid committing it. Chapter 16 explains the defences which can be used in defamation, and also details the remedies which may be ordered against publishers and broadcasters if found liable for defamation.

The final chapter in this section covers a related, but different action, called malicious falsehood. Like defamation, it is concerned with protecting people from lies published about them, but it applies to statements which cause financial damage, rather than damage to reputation.

Defamation

The law of defamation protects people against untrue statements that could damage their reputation, and is probably the single most important area of law for any journalist to know about. One of the reasons for this is that defamation can affect journalists in any field of work. If you work, for example, for a trade magazine or in the women's press, it's quite possible that you will never need to think about court reporting or official secrets after you've passed your law exams. But almost every kind of journalist, on almost every kind of publication, has the potential to defame someone, and some of the most high-profile defamation cases have involved quite small publications.

The second reason why defamation is such an important part of the law for journalists is that being successfully sued for it can be very expensive. One careless piece of research or unchecked statement could end up costing a publisher tens of thousands of pounds in damages – sometimes even hundreds of thousands – and as much again, sometimes more, in legal fees. Big national papers can absorb such losses (though decreasing circulations mean even they find it difficult), but for smaller magazines, losing a libel case can be disastrous. The magazine *Living Marxism* was actually forced into liquidation after being ordered to pay damages of £375,000 in a libel case in 2000.

Because of this, most publishers are very nervous of libel actions. One result of this is that, faced with a threat of libel, even where the journalist believes that the story is legally sound, many publishers will choose not to run it, or to water it down. In this way the threat of a libel action can be used to prevent publication of stories that really ought to be brought to the public's attention. Similarly, many publishers, faced with a complaint about a story that has already been published, will back down, print an apology and, if necessary, agree to pay some compensation, rather than allow the case to go to court and risk huge legal costs and possibly damages. In fact, most libel claims are settled out of court, and court hearings are rare.

None of this means that journalists should be so scared of being sued that we never write anything that upsets anyone, but it does mean that every journalist needs to understand thoroughly the basic rules of this area of the law – not just so that you know what not to write or say, but because defamation law does give some protection to press freedom, and by knowing the rules, you can often safely say more than you might imagine. Many newspapers and magazines publish potentially defamatory material every day, but, by making sure that what they print is covered by one of several defences to defamation, they can do so safely.

For many years, English defamation law was considered to be among the least press-friendly in the world, tipping the balance too far in favour of protecting reputation, and not far enough towards protecting press freedom. In response to this criticism, the Government passed the Defamation Act 2013, which makes significant changes to the law. The effect of the reforms in practice has yet to be seen as the Act only came into force in January 2014, and few cases had come before the courts by the time this edition went to press. The changes do not apply in Northern Ireland, which has retained the previous law.

THE ELEMENTS OF DEFAMATION

To succeed in an action for defamation, the claimant must prove three things:

- the statement complained of was defamatory;
- the statement referred to the claimant;
- the statement was published

Even if all these things are proved, a case may fail if the defendant can establish one of a number of possible defences. Defences for defamation are covered elsewhere (in the next chapter), but one thing worth knowing at this stage (because it will help explain some of the cases in this chapter) is that if you can prove that what you say issubstantially true, you will be covered by the defence of truth. and cannot be successfully sued for defamation, however serious the allegation.

Forms of defamation

There are two forms of defamation: libel and slander. Libel is committed by publishing a defamatory statement in permanent form, while slander covers defamatory statements in transient forms, such as unrecorded speech. Defamation actions against the media usually concern libel, which covers defamatory statements made in any of the following ways:

- printed;
- broadcast on TV or radio (Broadcasting Act 1990);
- in films and videos;
- on the internet;
- made during public performances of a play (Theatres Act 1968).

For this reason, the terms 'libel' and 'defamation' can be viewed as interchangeable for the purposes of this chapter. There are rare circumstances in which members of the media can face a slander claim through their work (these are covered on p. 243).

THE MEANING OF 'DEFAMATORY'

Most of the original law on defamation comes from case law (see p. 6), rather than statute, so there is no single definition of what defamatory means. Old cases have suggested that a statement will be defamatory if it 'tends to lower the person in the estimation of right-thinking members of society', or exposes the person to 'hatred, contempt or ridicule'. Both of these are still accurate, but a more comprehensive definition, in line with modern legal thinking, is given by the legal academics McBride and Bagshaw in their textbook *Tort Law*, 3rd edn (Longman, 2008). They say that a statement is defamatory if reading or hearing it would make an ordinary, reasonable person tend to:

- think less well as a person of the individual referred to;
- think that the person referred to lacked the ability to do their job effectively;

- shun or avoid the person referred to; or
- treat the person referred to as a figure of fun or an object of ridicule.

Their definition makes it clear that the important issue is not how the defamatory statement makes the person referred to feel, but the impression it is likely to make on those reading it. The person defamed does not have to prove that the words actually had any of these effects on any particular people or the public in general, only that the statement could *tend* to have that effect on an ordinary, reasonable listener or reader. Nor does the claimant need to prove that they have lost money, or suffered any other kind of loss or damage, unless they are a commercial organization (see later in this chapter). As the following cases indicate, a wide range of allegations have been found to be defamatory by the courts.

In ***Byrne*** v ***Deane*** (1937), the claimant was a member of a golf club, whose owners illegally kept gambling machines on the premises. Someone reported them to the police and afterwards a poem was posted up in the club, implying that the claimant had been the informant. He sued, and won the original case, but on appeal the courts held that the suggestion was not defamatory, because a right-thinking member of society (or as it might be expressed today, an ordinary, reasonable person) would not think less well of someone for telling the police about a crime.

In ***Jason Donovan*** v ***The Face*** (1992), the singer Jason Donovan successfully sued *The Face* magazine for saying he was gay. He based his argument on the fact that he had always presented himself as being heterosexual, and that *The Face* was therefore defaming him by suggesting he had deceived the public about his sexuality. The case did not, therefore, test whether it is defamatory merely to say someone is gay. It is unlikely that a jury today would find that it was defamatory to say someone was gay, but if someone is suing over such allegations, they are likely to have presented themselves as heterosexual, and therefore will be able to sue on the basis that saying they are gay implies they are lying and hypocritical.

In ***Berkoff*** v ***Burchill*** (1996), the journalist Julie Burchill described actor Steven Berkoff as 'hideous-looking' and compared him with Frankenstein's monster. The court argued that, although the kind of remarks made would not usually be defamatory, they become so because the claimant earned his living as an actor, and therefore the words made him an object of ridicule. The result of this case surprised many people, because, as stated above, a statement usually has to go further than being simply unpleasant and rude before it will be considered defamatory. It suggests that if rude personal remarks are judged to be excessively offensive, they may be considered to have crossed the line into defamation.

In 1997, a columnist on the *Express on Sunday's* magazine mentioned a newspaper story which had stated that the film star Nicole Kidman had insisted that builders working on her house should face the wall whenever she walked past. A judge initially found that the story, though unpleasant, was not capable of being defamatory, but Ms Kidman appealed. The Court of Appeal agreed with her that the statement was capable of being defamatory. In the event the case was settled out of court.

In ***Ivereigh*** v ***Associated Newspapers*** (2009) a former spokesman for the Roman Catholic Church won £30,000 in damages over a story claiming he had encouraged two women who he had been romantically involved with, at different times in his life, to have abortions when they became pregnant. Abortion is seen as a sin by the Catholic Church, and Mr Ivereigh had publicly spoken out against it, so the story made him look like a hypocrite and a bad Catholic. Although it was true that one of the women had had an abortion and the other had booked one but then miscarried before it could take place, Mr Ivereigh said that he had not encouraged either woman to have a termination, and the jury found in his favour.

In ***Taj Hargey*** v ***Muslim Weekly*** (2009), the claimant was a Muslim leader who is known for his liberal views about issues such as the role of women in Islam. *Muslim Weekly,* which tends to take a more conservative line, claimed his views meant he was not a proper Muslim. Mr Hargey won his case and was awarded damages described as a substantial five-figure sum.

In ***Bowman* v *MGN Ltd*** (2010) a West End actor called Simon Bowman won damages of £4,250, after the *Daily Mirror*'s website described him as former EastEnders actress Hannah Waterman's 'new man'. While the words in themselves would not be considered defamatory, Mr Bowman had been in a serious relationship with someone else for 20 years, and so the words could be taken to imply that he was being unfaithful to that person.

In ***Dr Sarah Thornton* v *Telegraph Media Group*** (2010), Mr Justice Tugendhat said that for a claim to be defamatory, it had to reach a certain level of seriousness, in terms of the effect that reading it would have on other people's attitude to the claimant. The claimant was suing the *Telegraph* over an interview it had published with her that said, among other things, that she gave copy approval to people she had interviewed for her book. She alleged that as giving copy approval was generally frowned on by professional journalists, this implied that she lacked credibility and trustworthiness as a writer. The judge said that the statement had to be judged by the standards of ordinary members of society, and, in ordinary language, to say that she gave copy approval was not capable of meaning that she had done anything reprehensible, that would affect people's attitude to her.

In ***Cairns* v *Modi*** (2012), former New Zealand cricket captain Chris Cairns won £90,000 damages over suggestions made on Twitter that he had been involved in match-fixing. Mr Justice Bean said that to make such an allegation about a sportsman was extremely serious and could destroy someone's reputation for integrity.

In ***Church* v *MGN Ltd*** (2012), singer Charlotte Church sued over a story alleging that she had proposed to her boyfriend during a 'boozy pub karoke night'. The paper claimed that it could not be defamatory to say that someone had affectionately proposed to their long-term partner, but Ms Church argued that the story implied she had 'made an embarrassingly drunken spectacle of herself', and suggested that she had demeaned the serious act of proposing marriage. Mr Justice Tugendhat agreed that the words were capable of a defamatory meaning.

Settlements in defamation cases

Most defamation cases do not go to court, but are settled between the parties, often including payment of damages. In these cases we cannot be sure that a court would find the statements complained of defamatory, but as the settlements will have been made on expert legal advice, we can assume that they are at least potentially defamatory.

In ***Parker* v *News Group Newspapers Ltd*** (2005), the former EastEnders actor Chris Parker was paid £50,000 damages by the *Sun*, after a story falsely claimed that he had been sacked from the soap after refusing to see a psychiatrist.

In 2005, actress Lisa Maxwell accepted an out-of-court settlement with the *Daily Star Sunday*, over a story which falsely claimed that, many years earlier, she had had a one-night stand with a man she had only just met.

In 2006, TV presenter Noel Edmonds accepted 'substantial' damages from the *Mail on Sunday*, after it falsely claimed that he had seduced a woman in order to make her leave her husband.

In 2007, singer Victoria Beckham accepted substantial damages from *Star* magazine, after it published a story claiming that the crew of a TV show disliked her, describing her as 'picky, demanding and rude'.

In ***Knightley* v *Associated Newspapers*** (2007), the actress Keira Knightley accepted a public apology and undisclosed damages from the *Daily Mail* after it published a picture of her in a bikini with the headline carrying a quote from the mother of a girl who died of an eating disorder: 'If pictures like this one of Keira carried a health warning, my darling daughter might have lived.' Ms Knightley alleged that the article falsely suggested she had wanted to be unnaturally thin, and set out to lose an excessive amount of weight by eating poorly and exercising inappropriately.

In 2008, Mia Amor Mottley, the former deputy prime minister of Barbados, accepted damages from *Country Life* magazine over a feature which referred to a calypso song whose lyrics included a suggestion that Ms Mottley has assaulted another woman.

In 2008, football agent Anthony McGill accepted an out-of-court settlement from the publisher of a football website which alleged that he had been 'tapping up' a professional footballer ('tapping up' means encouraging a player to break his contract and join another team, and is heavily criticised in the football world).

Former England footballer Andrew Cole accepted libel damages from the *Daily Star* in 2008 over a story concerning his arrest on suspicion of assault. He was released the following day and charges were withdrawn two days later, but the *Star* published a front-page story alleging there were strong grounds to suspect that he had been beating his wife. Mr Cole sued after the paper refused to apologise.

Former pop star Yusuf Islam (formerly known as Cat Stevens) accepted an out-of-court settlement from news agency WENN in 2008, over a story claiming that he was sexist and bigoted. Mr Islam is a Muslim and the story claimed that he refused to speak to any woman who was not wearing a veil. The story was said to have caused distress in painting him as sexist, and presenting a distorted picture of his religious views.

Italian footballer Marco Materazzi accepted substantial damages from the *Daily Mail* in 2008 after it claimed he had used racist abuse against another player.

Actor Will Smith sued the news agency WENN over claims that he had described Hitler as 'a good person'. The case was settled and the agency paid an undisclosed sum in damages.

Model Katie Price and her then husband Peter Andre accepted damages from the *News of the World* in 2008 over a story in which their former nanny alleged that they were uncaring parents.

Singer Ozzy Osbourne sued the *Daily Star* in 2008 after it claimed that he had suffered a health scare while co-hosting a music awards show. The story alleged that he had fallen over twice, had to sit down frequently and was driven around in an electric buggy. The paper accepted that the allegations were entirely untrue, and paid undisclosed damages.

TV presenter Kate Garraway sued the *Sunday Mirror* in 2008 after it suggested that she was having an affair with the dancer Anton du Beke, whom she was appearing with on the BBC show *Strictly Come Dancing.* While the stories did not specifically state that an affair was taking place, the paper used photographs, taken covertly, of Ms Garraway going about her daily life, which were presented in such a way as to imply that something was going on between her and her dance partner. The series of stories also included headlines such as 'Kate denies marriage is in trouble over dance partner pics' and 'Strictly no crisis . . . GMTV's Kate's show of unity after kiss with dancer star'. Ms Garraway sued, asking for aggravated damages **(see p. 274)** on the grounds that the newspaper had been told there was no truth in the claims but had gone ahead anyway. The case was settled out of court, with the paper paying damages said to be in six figures.

In March 2008, Kate and Gerry McCann, parents of Madeleine, who disappeared during a family holiday in Portugal in 2007, accepted a settlement of £550,000, and a public apology, from Express Newspapers after suing for defamation over stories suggesting they were responsible for their daughter's death. In the same year, Robert Murat, a property consultant based in the resort where Madeleine disappeared, accepted damages said to amount to at least £800,000 from four national newspaper publishers and British Sky Broadcasting, over a number of stories which alleged or implied that he was involved in the little girl's disappearance.

In 2010, Barry George, who was accused and later cleared of murdering the TV presenter Jill Dando, accepted damages from Mirror Group Newspapers over claims that he was obsessed with TV journalist Kay Burley and singer Cheryl Cole.

In 2010, the ex-wife of former England footballer Paul Gascoigne accepted five-figure damages from the *News of the World*, over an article that accused her of lying about the repeated violence she had suffered from her ex-husband. The article quoted Paul Gascoigne's reaction to claims made about him in his ex-wife's book, and was headlined 'You lying bitch'.

In 2010, the trustees of a charity accepted damages over a story claiming that an al-Qaida commander was one of its 'favourite speakers' at its events. In fact the trustees had never met the man named nor invited him to speak at any event.

In 2010, TV interviewer Michael Parkinson was paid damages by Associated Newspapers, over a story claiming that he had lied about his family background. The story, in the *Daily Mail*, carried claims by a cousin that Mr Parkinson had painted a false picture of his father, who he had described as honest, upstanding and well-liked. The cousin alleged that this was untrue and that his uncle was 'hateful' and disliked by most people. As Mr Parkinson's father was dead by this time, it was not possible to sue for defamation of him, but the action was brought on the basis that it was defamatory to say that Mr Parkinson had lied.

In 2010, *Take a Break* magazine paid damages to a man over a 'true life' feature about his wife. The feature was a triumph over tragedy-type piece, detailing Mrs Dionne Heneghen's battle to beat cocaine addiction, and how she had used her experience to help others. Within it, she claimed that it was her husband's treatment of her that led to her becoming addicted to cocaine, and that he abducted their child and kept him hidden from social services and the police. In fact she had been addicted before they met, and he had made efforts to try to help her overcome it. He had not abducted their son, but had taken the boy to live with him at Mrs Heneghen's request, and social services and the police knew the child's whereabouts.

In 2010, footballer Cristiano Ronaldo was paid substantial damages by the *Daily Mirror*, over a story which claimed he went 'on a bender' at a Hollywood nightclub. The story alleged that, while he was recovering from a serious foot injury, he went to the club, drank wine, champagne and vodka, and tried to dance on his injured foot. Cristiano Ronaldo does not drink alcohol, and although he had been at the club on the night alleged, the newspaper accepted that he neither drank nor put his recovery at risk by trying to dance.

The requirement for serious harm

The Defamation Act 2013 adds a new factor to the definition of 'defamatory'. Section 1 states that a statement is not defamatory unless its publication has caused or is likely to cause 'serious harm' to the claimant's reputation. This has several important implications, and means that some cases which would have succeeded under the old law will be thrown out now.

Most obviously, the requirement for serious harm means that statements that say something trivial or relatively harmless about a person cannot form the basis of a claim; in practice this was also the case under the previous law, but the Act makes it plain. Secondly, the Act makes it clear that what the court must look at is the damage to reputation, not the impact on the claimant's feelings; however hurtful or insulting a statement might be, there will be no claim if it lacks the potential to seriously damage their reputation. Thirdly, it means that statements which are clearly meant as jokes, and not to be taken seriously as factual claims, cannot form the basis of a claim; if the context means that a reasonable reader would never believe they were true, they cannot serious damage the subject's reputation. And finally – and in practice perhaps most importantly – any steps the media take to limit damage to someone's reputation, such as quickly issuing a correction and apology, may have an impact on whether a claim can be brought at all, because they can mean that in the long run there was no serious damage to reputation.

In *Cooke and Another* v *MGN Ltd* (2014) the *Mirror* ran a story about a millionaire landlord, who it said was making a lot of money renting out dilapidated properties in a road that became known as 'Benefits Street' when it was featured on a Channel 4 series. The piece also briefly mentioned a housing association which rented properties out on the same street, stating that its Chief Executive, Ruth Cooke, earned £179,000 a year. Ms Cooke and the association sued, arguing that mentioning them in this context suggested they were also disreputable landlords who were 'raking it in' from housing benefit. The judge agreed that the article could have this meaning. However, he then went on to consider whether the article had caused serious damage to reputation. The *Mirror* published a complete apology in its next edition, and the judge pointed out that although it was not as prominent as the original three-page article, it was more prominent than the single paragraph that had mentioned the claimants, and the wording was sufficient to eradicate or at least minimize the unfavourable impression given of them. The paper had also made sure that it was easier to find the apology online than the original article. The judge therefore concluded that the article had not caused, and was not likely to cause, serious harm to reputation.

Bear in mind as you read through this and the next chapter that it is quite possible that some of the cases which claimants won under the old law would be decided differently today, because of the requirement for serious harm.

There is an additional hurdle regarding serious harm where the defendant is a commercial organisation; see later in this chapter under the section *Who can be sued?*

Defamation and truth

As explained above, if you make a statement that is defamatory, but you can prove it to be true, you will be covered by the defence of truth. Equally, if you publish a statement that is not true, but is not defamatory either, you cannot be sued for defamation. For example, if you were to write that two single film stars were dating, when in fact they were not, the celebrities would not be able to sue for libel unless there was something in the story which would have a bad effect on their reputation. If one of them were married, or known to be in a serious relationship, they might have a case in defamation, because the story would be implying that they had been unfaithful, but if they were both single and the story was merely untrue but not libellous, they would not.

Obviously, the fact that there is no legal obligation to be truthful does not mean there is no moral obligation. The Codes of Practice used by the IPSO, the National Union of Journalists (NUJ) and Ofcom all recognise that journalists have a duty to ensure that the information they publish is accurate.

Myths and misconceptions **Untrue statements**

✗ ***The claimant has to prove your statement is untrue.***

A defamation claimant has to prove that the relevant statement is defamatory, but he or she does not have to prove that it was a lie. If a statement is defamatory, the court will simply assume that it was untrue. If a statement can be proved to be true, you will have the defence of truth, but it is up to you to prove that; the claimant does not have to prove it was false.

Changes over time

In deciding whether a statement could lower its subject in the eyes of others, the jury is asked to consider how an ordinary, reasonable person (referred to in some cases as a 'right-thinking person') would read and understand it. This person is often referred to by judges as 'the reasonable man', and one of the things that makes defamation claims so unpredictable is that, clearly, the views of the 'reasonable man' will change over time. At one time, for example, it would certainly have been defamatory to say of an unmarried woman that she spent the night with her boyfriend; this would not be the case today, unless, for example, that particular woman had presented herself as being against extra-marital sex, in which case she might be able to argue that the claim made her appear to be a liar and a hypocrite. In fact things have changed so much that it could now be defamatory to say a woman did not have sex with a man, as the following case shows.

In 2004, the celebrity magazine *Heat* agreed to publish an apology to a woman called Amy Barker, for saying that she had not had sex with pop star Bryan McFadden on his stag night. Ms Barker had originally sold the story of the incident to the *Sunday People*, but in an interview with *Heat*, Mr McFadden suggested that she had made the story up. Ms Barker's legal advisor sought an apology on the grounds that the *Heat* article called Ms Barker's integrity into question; neither side would say whether any damages were paid.

In ***Mitchell* v *Faber& Faber*** (1998), the claimant was a musician who had worked with the rock star Jimi Hendrix during the 1960s. The defendant was the publisher of a book about Hendrix, in which the author said that the claimant had a 'strange contempt' for Hendrix and routinely used words like 'nigger' and 'coon' in everyday conversation. However, he said that the claimant had no idea that what he said might offend anyone, and did not intend any harm. The claimant sued on the basis that the book made him appear to be racist. The defendant argued that the book was not defamatory, in that it made clear that the claimant had not intended to offend Hendrix, and that his attitude was simply typical of many people in the UK 30 years ago. The Court of Appeal said that, although it was true that those attitudes were widely held at that time, it was necessary to consider what impression the book would have on people reading it now, and therefore the words could be defamatory.

Effect of the claimant's existing reputation

What if the person you write about already has a bad reputation? Journalists often assume that if someone already has a low standing in the eyes of the public, then nothing they write about that person could be said to lower them further in the estimation of right-thinking people. This is not the case. For example, if someone was a convicted bank robber, and you wrote, wrongly, that he had been involved in the kidnap of a child, or of a sexual offence, he might well be able to sue successfully for libel. Despite his already bad reputation, it could be argued that your words have lowered his reputation even further.

However, if a person has an extremely bad reputation in one particular respect, and your false allegation is in the same vein and does not make that reputation worse, that person might well have difficulty proving that you have lowered them in the estimation of right-thinking people, or that you have caused serious harm to their reputation. For example, if an actor had serious drug problems, and this was well known to the public, he would have difficulties successfully suing for libel if you falsely claimed that he had taken drugs on a particular occasion, even if this was not true (see the Kate Moss case, p. 250).

The law, however, restricts the use which libel defendants can make of background information on a claimant. Evidence can be given to establish the fact that the claimant already has a bad reputation, but the old case of ***Scott* v *Sampson*** (1882) establishes that a defendant cannot put forward in evidence examples of the claimant's previous misconduct, unless the jury has already been told about these as part of a defence of truth. For example, take the case where a newspaper is sued over a story that claimed an actor had had an affair with his co-star, and cannot prove that particular story, but does have evidence of previous affairs. You might assume that if someone can be proved to have had serial affairs, their reputation cannot be lowered by suggesting that they had one with a particular person, but the effect of ***Scott* v *Sampson*** is that the evidence of the previous affairs could not be put before the jury. However, the situation is different where it is established that a libel has been committed, and the court has only to decide what damages should be awarded. In that situation, the case of ***Burstein* v *Times Newspapers*** (2000) establishes that background evidence which is relevant to the publication of the defamatory statement can be used to argue that the damages should be reduced.

Innuendoes

A statement does need not make a direct criticism in order to be defamatory – a defamatory implication or innuendo can be just as dangerous. This is fairly obvious when it comes to deliberate hints: if you want to say that John Jones MP has taken bribes, you cannot escape the risk of being defamatory by saying something like 'John Jones MP said he had not taken bribes, and we all know that politicians never lie, don't we?' In these types of cases, the courts will look at what the ordinary, reasonable reader would think that the words implied.

In 1986 the *Star* published a gossip column story about Lord Gowrie, an ex-Cabinet Minister, who had stepped down from his post the year before. Questioning why he had resigned, the story referred to 'expensive habits', and said that Lord Gowrie would 'snort' at the idea that he had been 'born with a silver spoon round his neck'. Lord Gowrie sued, arguing that references to expensive habits, snorting and a silver spoon implied that he habitually took cocaine. He won his case.

In 2008, Lisa Jeynes, a contestant on 'Big Brother', sued the magazine *Love it!* and the *News of the World* over a coverline on the magazine and a headline in the paper, which said: 'BB's Lisa "the geezer". My fake boobs fell out on date with James Hewitt!' Ms Jeynes said that these words, along with the fact that there were rumours at the time that 'Big Brother' was to feature a transsexual contestant, suggested she was a transsexual, a transvestite, or a man posing as a woman. Mr Justice Eady dismissed the claim, saying that no reasonable reader would assume that the words carried the implication that she alleged they did.

A second type of innuendo is where words seem innocent on the surface (and may actually have been meant quite innocently) but can be read as defamatory in the particular circumstances, or because of special knowledge possessed by some readers. For example, take a situation where you interview a celebrity over lunch. To add colour to the feature, you want to describe the meal, but you are unable to remember precisely what the celebrity ate. Assuming that it is unlikely to matter, you write that she 'tucked into a juicy steak'. In most cases, though untrue, this would not be defamatory, but if the celebrity in question was actually an ardent vegetarian, the situation would be different. Your words could then, arguably, be defamatory, since they would suggest to those who know she is a vegetarian that she has betrayed her principles, or that she was a hypocrite in only pretending to be a vegetarian. If that seems extreme, consider the following real-life cases.

In ***Tolley* v *JS Fry & Sons Ltd*** (1931), the claimant was an amateur golfer, whose picture was used, without his consent, to advertise Fry's chocolate. He argued that anyone seeing the advert would assume he had both consented to and been paid for it, and that this would suggest that he had compromised his amateur status. He won his case.

In *Cassidy* v *Daily Mirror Newspapers* (1929), the *Mirror* published a picture of a man described as Mr Corrigan, with a lady who it said was his fiancée. The man had given these details to the paper, but in fact his name was Mr Cassidy, and he was married to someone else, though they lived apart. Mrs Cassidy sued on the basis that anyone reading the article, who knew her, would assume that if Mr Cassidy had a fiancée, he must be free to marry, and therefore could not have been married to her when they were living together (remember that this case took place at a time when both living together and divorce were uncommon). She won her case, and her victory was upheld on appeal.

A claimant who argues that they have been defamed by innuendo must show not only that the facts or circumstances giving rise to the innuendo exist, but also that the statement was published to people who knew of those facts. So, in the example of the vegetarian celebrity above, the claimant would not only have to be a vegetarian, but would have to show that at least one of the readers of your publication would know this. Clearly this is easier in some cases than others.

Myths and misconceptions **Innuendo and implication**

✗ *'I didn't mean it that way' is a defence.*

In general, in defamation the important issue is not what you meant to say, but what a jury believes a reader would think you meant. So it is no defence to say that you did not mean to defame the claimant, or did not realise what your words implied.

Pictures

Defamation is not necessarily committed by words alone. It is possible to use quite harmless words, but still defame someone in print, thanks to the pictures used with those words.

In *Dwek* v *Macmillan Publishers Ltd* (2000), a book published by Macmillan included a picture, taken 20 years earlier, which showed the claimant sitting next to a woman who was (correctly) described as a prostitute. The claimant himself was not the subject of the book, and was not mentioned anywhere in it. He sued, arguing that readers would assume from the picture and caption that he was a client of the prostitute. The Court of Appeal stated that this could be defamatory.

The now-defunct magazine *Titbits* illustrated a feature on stealing at Christmas with a photograph of a meat porter winning a meat-carrying race at London's Smithfield market. The porter sued, on the basis that the use of the picture suggested he was a thief, and won his case.

In 2005, footballer Andy Johnson forced an apology and damages from Express Newspapers, after they used a picture of him alongside a feature on footballers with drink and drug problems. Although not named in the article, he claimed it implied he took drugs, which was untrue.

In 2007, the BBC was sued by Waseem Yaquib, formerly manager of an Islamic charity, after it showed a picture of him in a programme about a different charity's alleged links to the extremist group Hamas. The picture showed Mr Yaquib standing next to Dr Essam Yusuf, whose charity Interpal was the subject of the programme. Mr Yaquib was not mentioned in the programme, but he said that the photograph would mean that viewers who knew him would assume there were grounds to suspect that he was an associate of Dr Yusuf, in connection with the funding of terrorist activity. The BBC settled the case and paid damages.

Juxtaposition

A statement that by itself might be quite innocent can become defamatory as a result of the material it is placed next to.

In 1988 the business magazine *Stationery Trade News* carried an article about counterfeit stationery products which were being imported into the UK. Towards the end of the story, it mentioned a different problem, involving envelopes which were not made in the UK being marketed under a brand name which sounded British. The makers of these envelopes sued the magazine, claiming that the story implied that they were selling counterfeit envelopes. They won their case.

Juxtaposition and broadcasting

Juxtaposition can be a particular problem for broadcasters, and it is vital to think carefully about the combined impression of words and film. If, for example, you illustrate a story about drug smuggling with film of holidaymakers coming through customs, an individual who is identifiable on screen could very well sue on the basis that you have implied they are a drug smuggler, as could a shopper who is shown in a film about credit card fraud.

Make sure you check what is in the background as well as the foreground: if, for example, your commentary is about a company accused of health and safety offences, and your presenter happens to stroll past a sign for a different company in the same field, you could find yourself sued on the grounds that viewers would assume that was the company mentioned.

In 2007, Sky and Channel 5 were sued by a family after they broadcast film of the family's house which, by juxtaposition, implied that the family were involved in terrorism offences. The film showed police officers in forensics overalls going in and out of the family's house, and had been taken on a much earlier occasion which had nothing to do with any terrorism investigations. It was shown as part of a story about five men being charged with terrorist offences, and accompanied by a voiceover explaining that thousands of items had been seized as part of the investigation. The family claimed that the combination of the film and the voiceover suggested that they were suspected of involvement in the terrorist plot. The broadcasters settled out of court and paid damages.

In 2008, a quiz show participant sued the BBC over a news report which he claimed implied that he was involved in a scam. Leigh Petters was a contestant on the Channel 5 show 'Brainteaser', and footage of him taking part was broadcast as part of a BBC report about irregularities in the way the quiz show was run. The story stated that on several occasions when viewers had not rung in to enter, the programme had given fictitious names of winners, and a member of the production team had pretended to be a winner. Mr Petters claimed that the juxtaposition of this commentary with the film of him suggested that he was involved in the scam, and was posing as a winner, when in fact he had taken part and won fairly. The BBC settled and paid damages.

Law in practice Subbing errors

It's important to be aware that libel can creep it at almost any stage of a story, not just in the initial writing. Rod Dadak, Head of Defamation at solicitors Lewis Silkin, advises that all journalists should keep a copy of the unsubbed version of their story:

> Mistakes can be introduced during the subbing process, and a headline or caption can make a piece defamatory even if the original text was not. In practice it is unusual for a journalist to be sued personally, as most claimants sue publishers because they are more likely to have the money to pay damages, but if you were sued personally, you would be able to mitigate your liability by showing that you did not write the offending caption or headline, or that your original words were altered during subbing.

The importance of context

Words alleged to be defamatory must be read in their full context, rather than taken in isolation, and context can potentially include everything else on the page. As a result, an article taken as a whole may be judged to carry a defamatory implication which is not specifically stated anywhere in it. On the other hand, the context may rescue particular words from being defamatory.

Norman* v *Future Publishing Ltd (1999) concerned an article on the opera singer Jessie Norman, in which the interviewer referred to her 'statuesque' size, and quoted an anecdote in which Ms Norman got trapped in a revolving door and, on being advised to get out sideways, responded, 'Honey, I ain't got no sideways.' She sued, claiming that the quote suggested she had spoken in a vulgar, undignified way, which conformed to a degrading racist stereotype. The Court of Appeal, however, looked at the whole of the article, which it found portrayed Ms Norman as a respected professional and a person of high standing. In that context, it held, the words could not be read as defamatory.

In ***Robert Dee* v *Telegraph Media Group Ltd*** (2010), the claimant was a professional tennis player who had finally won a match after losing 54 in a row, during which time he had not won a single set. The *Telegraph* reported the victory, starting the story on their front page, with the headline 'World's worst tennis pro wins at last'. Three paragraphs on the front page described Mr Dee's losing run, with a line directing readers to the 'full story' in the sports section. Mr Dee claimed that the front page story implied that the 54 matches were the only professional ones he had ever played, and therefore that he had only ever won one game. However, the story in the sports section made it clear that this was not the case. The judge said that the front page story should not be treated in isolation: the reference to the 'full story' made it clear that the two pieces were meant to be read together, and a reader who did this would see that the paper was not claiming Mr Dee had lost every match he had ever played except one.

In ***Charleston* v *News Group Newspapers*** (1995), the *News of the World* carried a story about a computer game which superimposed the faces of well-known actors onto other people's bodies, so that they appeared to be engaged in sexual acts. The piece was illustrated with a picture showing a man and woman having sex, with the faces of the actors Ian Smith and Ann Charleston, who played Harold and Madge in the TV soap *Neighbours*, superimposed on their bodies. The headline was 'Strewth! What's Harold up to with our Madge?' Although the article made it clear that the people in the picture were not Smith and Charleston, they sued on the basis that anyone who just read the headline and looked at the pictures might think that they had been involved in pornography. The House of Lords said that using defamatory headlines could be 'playing with fire', but the defamatory effect had to be judged against the article as a whole. In this case, although the headline looked defamatory, a reader only had to glance through the first paragraph to see that in fact the paper was not making any defamatory allegation. The situation might, they said, be different if, for example, the headline was potentially defamatory and the words which explained it and removed the defamatory meaning were not found until well into the article, so that casual readers might not see them.

Cases like ***Charleston*** are often referred to in terms of 'bane and antidote', the bane being the potentially defamatory allegation, and the antidote those words which show the reader that it is untrue, or take away the defamatory meaning. A jury will be told to take the two together and decide whether the antidote does actually take away the bane.

Context and broadcasting

Part of the context of a defamatory remark is of course the medium it is presented in; someone reading a newspaper may well give more attention to that than they would to a TV or radio programme on in the background. Unlike a TV viewer, a reader can also easily go back over parts of the newspaper if a meaning seems unclear. The courts have therefore suggested that words which might not be defamatory in print, where a reader could be expected to see them in the context of a whole article, may be defamatory if they are part of a TV programme, where viewers might not be giving their whole attention and therefore might be more likely to pick up on the defamatory meaning without taking in other material that could have removed the 'sting'.

In *Gillick* v *BBC* (1996), a live TV progamme was broadcast to mark the 25th anniversary of the Brook Advisory Centres, set up to give young people advice about contraception. A guest on the programme was Victoria Gillick, well known at the time for her campaigns against under-age sex. She had won a court case in which she sought to restrict access to contraceptives for teenage girls, and the programme's presenter said to her, 'But after you won that battle . . . there were at least two reported cases of suicide by girls who were pregnant.' Mrs Gillick sued the BBC for libel, claiming that the words meant she was morally responsible for the deaths of at least two girls. The Court of Appeal held that the words should be judged on the meaning that they would imply to an ordinary person who had watched the programme once, and was neither unusually suspicious or unusually naïve. On this basis the words could carry the meaning Mrs Gillick alleged.

Defamatory remarks made during a broadcast may also be the subject of complaints to Ofcom **(see Chapter 21)**. There is, however, nothing to stop a person who goes to Ofcom from suing for defamation afterwards.

Context and the internet

Context is also important with regard to online articles, and the way in which they are accessed. If an online story would be read in conjunction with others and, as a whole, they remove a defamatory meaning, that can defeat a libel claim.

In *Budu* v *BBC* (2010), Mr Budu attempted to sue the BBC over three reports it published on its website. The first article said that Cambridgeshire Police had withdrawn a job offer from someone after discovering that he was an illegal immigrant. This was Mr Budu, but the article did not name him or identify him in any way. The second and third articles made it clear that he was not in fact an illegal immigrant at all. The articles were all archived shortly after initial publication, and could then only be accessed by someone who searched for them on the BBC site. The only thing identifying Mr Budu as the subject of the first article was the fact that the story was linked to the two later ones. Therefore, the defamatory allegation in the first story could only be published to someone who had seen the other two articles. Reading the three articles together removed the defamatory meaning, so there was no possible claim.

Other people's words

If someone makes a defamatory statement, and you report it, you are publishing that statement and you may be liable, even though the words belong to someone else (the maker of the statement may or may not be sued as well but that does not affect your liability). Journalists often believe that if they write 'Joe Brown says that Joe Bloggs is corrupt', or quote him directly, they only have to prove that Joe Brown said what they say he said, but that is absolutely not the case. Unless you can prove that the words are true (or covered by another defence), you cannot safely print the allegations whether as a direct quote or paraphrased. Repeating statements made by interviewees without being able to prove them is in fact one of the commonest causes of libel actions.

The same principle applies in broadcasting. If someone makes a defamatory statement on a TV or radio programme, the broadcaster may be liable, regardless of whether the speaker is sued. Where a programme is live, broadcasters can sometimes use the live broadcast defence **(see p. 272)**, but even here, they will have to prove they have taken reasonable care to avoid the risk of libel.

In 1993 and 1994 the *Sunday Telegraph* and the *Sun* both paid damages to the Birmingham Six, who were falsely accused and later cleared of terrorism offences. Former police officers were accused of fabricating evidence but a prosecution against them was dropped. Afterwards, the *Telegraph* reported one of the officers as saying 'In our eyes, their guilt is beyond doubt'. The matter was settled out of court, with the claimants reported to have received £25,000 from the *Telegraph*, and £1 million from the *Sun*, which had published an article based on the *Telegraph*'s interviews.

The only exception to this rule is where what you publish is an accurate and impartial report on a dispute which is a matter of public interest. In this circumstance, you may be covered by the defence of publication on a matter of public interest (see the next chapter).

Reporting rumours

Can you report defamatory rumours if you make it clear that that is all they are, or even state that you do not believe them? Many journalists believe that if they report rumours in this way, they can argue that the story is true, because they are reporting that there are rumours, and they can prove that the rumours did exist. This is not the case. The law takes the view that readers will assume there is no smoke without fire, and if you cannot prove the rumour to be true (or cover yourself with another defence), you will be taking the risk of liability for defamation.

In 1999 Belfast's *Sunday Life* was successfully sued by the actors Natasha Richardson and her husband Liam Neeson over a story about rumours that their marriage was in trouble. The story focused on the fact that people who knew the couple well had said that the rumours were untrue, but the court held that this would not necessarily convince readers, and therefore the 'antidote' did not cure the 'bane'.

In *Major* v *New Statesman* (1993), the *New Statesman* was sued by the then Prime Minister John Major, for an article which repeated rumours that he was having an affair. The magazine said that it was merely reporting that the rumours were in circulation, and had not intended to imply that they were true, but this did not protect them. Ironically, years later it was revealed that Mr Major had been having an affair at the time, but not with the person the rumours alleged.

Myths and misconceptions 'Allegedly'

✗ *You are safe from a defamation claim if you use the word 'allegedly'.*

Comedians and satirical journalists, especially on TV and radio, often use the word 'Allegedly' when making remarks that could be defamatory, in a humorous context. It is possible that using the word within a comical context could mean that a judge or jury might find that no reasonable person would believe the statement was intended to be taken as true, in which case it would not pass the 'serious harm' test, though this has not yet been tested in court. However, in any kind of serious context, merely using the word 'Allegedly' has no special protective effect – if the words are defamatory, it is only safe to use them if you are covered by a specific defence.

Implying habitual conduct

Even if you are sure you can prove that a specific allegation of bad behaviour is true, you must be careful that your description of that behaviour does not imply that the defendant behaved that way habitually (unless you can prove that as well). For example, if you were to describe someone convicted of shoplifting as 'a thief', that might be strictly true, since they would have a conviction for theft, and it would be unlikely to be a problem if the person concerned had a string of similar convictions. However, if you use the term 'thief' of someone who has just been convicted for shoplifting a packet of chewing gum, but otherwise has a completely clean record, they could argue that you were implying they were a habitual criminal who could not be trusted, and clearly you would not be able to prove that implication was true. It is not always clear where the line between these two extremes lie, so you should always be careful about using terms or making allegations that could imply habitual conduct, unless you can prove that implication.

In ***David and Carol Johnson* v *Radio City*** (1988), the radio station was sued by a couple who ran a company offering caravan holidays. The station had featured complaints about the company's holidays, and Mr Johnson was interviewed on air to give the couple's side of the story. However, during the interview, the presenter referred to Mr Johnson as a 'con man'. He sued, claiming that this implied that he was habitually dishonest. The radio station produced 20 former customers who were unhappy with the holidays they had bought, but the company produced an equal number who said they were satisfied. The judge instructed the jury that it had to decide whether the broadcast was only suggesting that some customers had been mistreated, or whether it was implying 'habitual' conduct. The jury found that the latter meaning was implied, and the Johnsons won damages of £350,000.

Reporting investigations

Obviously, saying that someone is guilty of an offence when they are not is defamatory, whether you say it yourself or report someone's else allegation (with the exception of reporting allegations made in court, which are covered by privilege – see p. 257). But what about saying that someone is being investigated in connection with a crime or other wrongdoing, or is under suspicion? Such allegations can easily lead to a claim for libel if the story is written in such a way as to suggest that they have done something that gives grounds for the suspicion. In the 1964 case of ***Lewis* v *Daily Telegraph*** (see below), the Court of Appeal stated that, depending on the way it was phrased, a claim that someone was being investigated for a crime could potentially mean any one of three different things:

1 that the person mentioned was guilty of the crime;

2 that there were reasonable grounds for suspecting the person was guilty of the crime; or

3 that there were reasonable grounds for an investigation into whether the person had committed the crime.

Clearly, meaning (1) is more seriously defamatory (and more difficult to prove) than (2), and (2) is more serious and difficult to prove than (3). As a result, a publisher who means and can prove meaning (3), may still be in trouble if the court decides that the words as written are capable of carrying meaning (2) or even (1), and the publisher cannot prove that meaning to be true.

In ***Chase* v *News Group Newspapers Ltd*** (2002) the *Sun* was sued by a nurse, over a story which implied she was involved in the deaths of a number of terminally ill children. The nurse had worked

with the children, and the newspaper based its story on the fact that allegations had been made against her to the hospital and the police. The headline ran 'Nurse is probed over 18 deaths' and the story made reference to the GP Harold Shipman, and a nurse called Beverly Allitt, both of whom had been convicted of murdering patients in high-profile cases. After the story was published, the police said that they had no grounds to suspect Ms Chase. When the nurse sued, the paper tried to justify its story by claiming that there were reasonable grounds for suspicion, but the Court of Appeal held that such grounds had to be based on evidence of the claimant's behaviour, not just allegations against her. The *Sun* paid Ms Chase £100,000 damages.

The case of ***Hayward* v *Thompson*** (1981) took place against the background of the 'Scott affair', a very high-profile case in which a man called Norman Scott alleged he was the subject of a murder plot, because of an affair he had had with the former Liberal Party leader Jeremy Thorpe. Mr Thorpe and his alleged conspirators were eventually all acquitted, but while the allegations were still being investigated, the *Telegraph* published a story headed 'Two more in Scott affair'. It said: 'The names of two more people connected with the Norman Scott affair have been given to police. One is a wealthy benefactor of the Liberal Party . . . Both men, police have been told, arranged for a leading liberal supporter to be "reimbursed" £5,000, the same amount Mr Andrew Newton alleges he was paid to murder Scott.' Since the Liberal Party had few wealthy benefactors at the time, it was not difficult to spot that the man meant was a Mr Jack Hayward, and he sued. The *Telegraph* argued that its story meant only that Mr Hayward might be able to help with the investigation, but Mr Hayward claimed that it implied he was guilty of taking part in, or at least condoning, the alleged murder plot. The jury agreed, and the Court of Appeal upheld its verdict, saying that the headline placed Mr Hayward 'in' the Scott affair, and this was backed up by the words 'connected with' in the first sentence. Nothing else in the story counteracted the impression these words gave.

In ***Jameel* v *Times Newspapers*** (2004), a wealthy Saudi Arabian businessman sued the *Sunday Times* after it published a story headlined 'Car tycoon linked to Bin Laden'. The story stated that Mr Jameel had been named as a defendant in a case brought by the relatives of victims of the September 11 bombings in the USA against over 200 defendants accused of helping to fund terrorist activity. The paper claimed that it was merely reporting the fact of Mr Jameel being named as one of the defendants, which amounted to the level (3) meaning in the list above. It pleaded justification for this meaning. Mr Jameel, however, said the story implied that there were reasonable grounds for suspecting him of being associated with Osama Bin Laden (the level (2) meaning), an allegation which the *Sunday Times* could not justify (and said it did not seek to make). He pointed particularly to the phrase 'linked with Bin Laden' in the headline, and the fact that a picture of the burning towers of the World Trade Center was used to illustrate the story. The Court of Appeal agreed with Mr Jameel that the story could be read as meaning that there were grounds for suspicion, and said that the case could be tried on this basis. Mr Jameel then applied to have the *Sunday Times'* justification (the previous name for truth) defence for the level (3) meaning struck out, on the grounds that there was not enough evidence for the paper to plead justification; he was successful. The case was then settled out of court, with the *Sunday Times* publishing a statement that it had not intended to suggest, and did not believe, that Mr Jameel had any connection with terrorism.

In ***Bento* v *Chief Constable of Bedfordshire Police*** (2012), the police were sued over a press release issued when the Crown Prosecution Service decided not to have a murder case retried. The claimant in the defamation case, Mr Bento, had been convicted of murdering his girlfriend, but he appealed and Court of Appeal quashed his conviction on the grounds that key evidence used in the case was unsatisfactory. The CPS had planned to retry the case, but then decided to drop it. The police then issued a press release saying that they were very disappointed by the decision, pointing out that in the original trial the jury had reached a unanimous verdict, and that the verdict had been set aside because of 'confusion' over the disputed evidence, and saying that they had done their best to get justice for the family. Mr Bento claimed the press release was defamatory of him, because it implied he was guilty and had wrongly escaped justice. He was awarded £125,000 in damages.

Previous convictions

Clearly, saying falsely that someone has been convicted of a criminal offence will be defamatory. But if it is true that they have been convicted, the journalist will be protected by the defence of truth. This protection also applies if a person has been convicted of an offence, and you say that they did it. Under the Civil Evidence Act 1968, the fact that someone has been convicted of a criminal offence can be taken as conclusive proof of the fact that they committed that offence, so a convicted burglar, for example, who maintains they are innocent cannot successfully sue a newspaper which says otherwise (though this would change if the burglar appealed and had the conviction quashed).

However, there is an exception to the above rules: the idea of the 'spent conviction'. This comes from the Rehabilitation of Offenders Act 1974, which was designed to help offenders reintegrate into society. Under the Act, convictions for all but the most serious crimes become 'spent' after a certain period of time, known as the rehabilitation period. The effect of this is that the offender can, to an extent, wipe the slate clean. Once an offence is spent they do not have to, for example, mention it in most job applications, it should not be mentioned in civil court proceedings, and in criminal proceedings only if absolutely necessary. The length of the rehabilitation period depends on the sentence given; this has recently been changed and can now be found in s139 of the Legal Aid, Sentencing and Punishment Act 2012.

You might expect then that the media would be forbidden to mention spent convictions, but this is not the case. Most publishers do respect the provisions of the Act and avoid mentioning spent convictions, but in strict legal terms, if you publish details of someone's spent convictions, and they sue you for libel, in most cases you will be covered by the defences of privilege, truth or honest opinion (see Chapter 16). However, the Act provides that if the claimant can show that the publication of a spent conviction was motivated by malice (see p. 263), any of these defences should fail. In addition, if a journalist claims the defence of privilege (see Chapter 16) for reporting a reference to a spent conviction that was made in court, that defence will fail if the conviction is held to be inadmissible in evidence.

Product stories

Product tests are an important feature of many consumer magazines and newspapers, because readers like them and – in many cases – they are cheap and easy to put together. It is often assumed that these features are as safe as they are simple, but that is not necessarily the case. If you look back at the definition of defamatory (on p. 216), you'll see that one of the factors which can make a statement defamatory is an allegation that a person is no good at their job or business. If, in criticising a product, you imply that the person or firm producing the product is at fault, you may be at risk of a defamation action.

That does not, of course, mean that every criticism of a product is defamatory of the manufacturer. Simply saying that a particular lipstick did not last well in your tests, or you did not like the way a car handled, are unlikely in themselves to be defamatory. Where they can become so is if they imply that the manufacturer (or possibly the seller) has acted discreditably, or is in some way unfit or unqualified to carry on their business.

In 1985, the manufacturers of Bovril successfully sued the publishers of a book which claimed (wrongly) that the product contained sugar. They were able to base their case on the claim that the book had libelled them by suggesting they lied about the product's ingredients.

In *Tesla* v *BBC* (2012), the manufacturers of an electric car sought to sue the BBC over a *Top Gear* programme which, among other things, said that the car had a range of about 55 miles, rather than the 200 miles which the manufacturer's publicity material claimed. They said that this was libellous, because it suggested that there were reasonable grounds to suspect that they had intentionally made a statement that was the equivalent of a false trade description. Mr Justice Tugendhat said such an allegation was not capable of being defamatory, and was merely an attempt to turn a statement about the product into a defamatory statement about the manufacturer.

In ***Walker Wingsail Systems*** v ***Sheahan Bray and IPC Magazines*** (1994), a case which sent shivers around the magazine publishing world, a jury awarded £1.4 million to the maker of a yacht who claimed he had been libelled in a product test by *Yachting World.* The manufacturers, Walker Wingsail, had made dramatic claims about the performance of their yacht, but when tested by the magazine, it failed to live up to those promises. There was some dispute about whether the statements made in the magazine could be considered true or not, because even the claimant's own expert witness found that the yacht did not perform as well as the manufacturers had claimed. However, the main thrust of the claim was that the article had implied that Walker Wingsail was deliberately misleading potential buyers. The firm was owned and run by a husband and wife team, and in court the wife claimed that the magazine had effectively called her and her husband liars. The magazine denied this, arguing that they had not suggested dishonesty, only that the firm had made its promises carelessly and irresponsibly, which the magazine still claimed was true. The jury, however, found for Walker Wingsail.

Frightening as the *Yachting World* case may appear, it is not a reason to be scared of criticising products. Recent developments in the law on the defence of honest comment, which should also apply to its replacement, honest opinion **(see p. 262)** mean that as long as you test fairly (e.g. treating all the products in the same way, and presenting a balanced picture of the results), make sure that any facts in the piece are accurate and state your views honestly, you should be protected, no matter how rude you are about the products.

Remember that you can be sued for defamation even if you are only repeating what someone else has said. This means that if a company criticises a rival's products or services, you should not publish those criticisms unless you are sure you are covered by a defence.

In ***Konfidence International Ltd*** v ***Splash About International*** (2007), a nappy manufacturer sued another nappy manufacturer over a press release which suggested that the claimant company's nappies were poor quality and if used in swimming pools could damage babies' health. The case was settled and the defendant company paid damages (note that, although this case was between the two companies, anyone who published the press release could potentially have been liable).

Spoofs and jokes

It is often thought that if a defamatory allegation is clearly presented as part of a joke, there will be no liability, but this is not necessarily the case. Remember that in defamation, what is important is not what the speaker or writer meant, but the effect the statement would have on a listener or reader. If an ordinary, reasonable person would assume there was some truth behind the words, then there may be liability for defamation. The fact that satirical programmes and articles regularly take this risk does not mean that the risk does not exist.

In ***Galloway v Jewish Communications Ltd*** (2008), MP George Galloway won £15,000 in damages from the Jewish community radio station Jcom. He sued over a programme which featured a fictitious Middle Eastern reporter called 'Georgie Galloway', whose only phrase was 'Kill the Jews!' Mr Galloway said that it implied he held anti-semitic views. Mr Justice Eady said that although the character was clearly intended to be a joke, the defamatory implication it carried was a serious one. Damages would have been higher had it not been for the fact that the radio station had relatively few listeners, and had apologised on its website.

If, however, it would be clear to any reasonable person that the words were not meant to be taken seriously, and that the writer is not alleging there is any truth behind the joke, there will be no defamatory meaning. This was already the case, and is now even clearer, because of the requirement under the Defamation Act 2013 for the statement to cause or have the potential to cause serious harm to reputation.

In *Elton John* v *The Guardian* (2008), Elton John sued over a spoof piece in the *Guardian*'s Weekend magazine, which mocked him. It was written in the style of a diary by Elton John, and began: 'What a few days it's been. First I sang Happy Birthday to my dear, dear friend Nelson Mandela . . . at a party specially organised to provide white celebrities with a chance to be photo-graphed cuddling him, wearing that patronisingly awestruck smile they all have.' The 'diary' went on to talk about a ball which Elton John arranges every year to raise money for his AIDS charity: 'Naturally [the guests] could afford just to hand over the money if they gave that much of a toss about Aids research – as could the sponsors. But we like to give guests a preposterously lavish evening, because they're the kind of people who wouldn't turn up for anything less. They fork out small fortunes for new dresses and so on, the sponsors blow hundreds of thousands on creating what convention demands we call a "magical world", and everyone wears immensely smug "My diamonds are by Chopard" grins in the newspapers and *OK*. Once we've subtracted all these costs, the leftovers go to my foundation. I call this care-o-nomics.' It was headed 'A peek at the diary of Elton John', but at the end included the words 'As seen by Marina Hyde'. Elton John said it was defamatory because it implied that he was insincere in his support for the charity, and that after costs, the ball made little money for the charity and he knew that. The claim was struck out, after the judge held that no reasonable reader could believe that the words were really written by Elton John. It was clear that the diary was not written by him, and was 'an attempt at humour'. Nor would a reasonable reader believe that the piece was really suggesting as a fact that the costs of the ball meant it raised little money for charity, and Elton John knew that. If the paper had wanted to make such serious allegations, it would have made them in the news section, and the fact that this article appeared in Weekend, among articles on homes and food, made it clear that it was not intended to be taken seriously.

Law in practice **Readers' letters**

A newspaper or magazine that publishes a defamatory statement in a reader's letter can be liable in just the same way as if the same statement appeared in a news story. 'Letters which make potentially defamatory allegations should always be checked', advises Rod Dadak, Head of Defamation at solicitors Lewis Silkin. 'People often use letters pages to further their own grudges, so check who the writer is, and check whether any defamatory allegations are true, or covered by another defence, before publishing. It is also sensible to check whether the person or organisation criticised in the letter is known to be likely to sue for libel.' The defence of honest opinion will often apply to letters **(see p. 253).**

REFERRING TO THE CLAIMANT

As well as proving that the statement in question is defamatory, the claimant has to show that an ordinary, reasonable reader or listener, including acquaintances of the claimant, would take the statement as referring to him or her (or it, in the case of organisations and companies).

That means that if people who know the claimant would assume that the statement referred to him or her, the statement can be said to refer to the claimant; it does not matter that the public at large might not make the same assumption.

In many cases, identification is not in question, since the claimant will be named or pictured (and of course, leaving out the name but using a clearly identifiable title, such as 'the MP for Dover' or 'the head of the Timber Trades Association' is usually the equivalent of mentioning that person by name). However, there are numerous situations where a statement can be taken to refer to a claimant even where that person is not expressly identified, and the courts have in some cases been quite relaxed about what they will accept as identification.

In ***Morgan* v *Odhams Press*** (1971), the case arose from a story about a dog-doping gang. The journalist writing the story was being helped by a kennel girl, and during the investigation, she stayed with the claimant for a few days. The dog doping story was then published, with a photo of the kennel girl, and the following day, the *Sun* published another story, saying that she had been kidnapped by the dog-doping gang. The claimant argued that while she was staying with him, they had been seen out together, and anyone who had seen him with her would assume that he was a member of the gang. The article did not mention his name, and several of the details it mentioned about the gang members did not apply to him. The court said that ordinary readers often skim-read articles and would not necessarily notice the inconsistent details; if, on reading the article they came to the conclusion that the claimant was the person meant, then identification was proved. The jury found for the claimant.

Dropping hints

Journalists often assume that if they have a potentially libellous allegation to make, it is safest to avoid naming the person, but this is not necessarily the case. You are unlikely to describe the subject of your story merely as 'a man' or 'a woman'; instead, you will hope you can drop hints that will enable readers – or at least some of them – to spot who you mean, but which will still be sufficiently vague to prevent the story forming the basis of a libel action. This is potentially dangerous, because as soon as you provide enough detail to give any meaning to the story, you give the claimant grounds to say that some readers would know who you were referring to.

The ***Burton Mail*** was sued by the Police Federation (the equivalent of a trade union for police officers) for a story about a complaint against a woman police officer. She was not named, but gave evidence that people she knew had taken the story to refer to her. The paper paid £17,500 compensation. The case was one of 95 similar actions brought by the Police Federation on behalf of its members during the late 1980s and 1990s, all of which it won.

In ***Hayward* v *Thompson*** (1981), the case concerning the Norman Scott affair (see p. 230), the *Daily Telegraph* had not referred to Mr Hayward by name, but only as 'a wealthy benefactor of the Liberal Party'. They argued that this description was not sufficient to allow readers to identify him. However, the Liberal Party had very few wealthy benefactors, and there was clear evidence that both Mr Hayward's friends, and the rest of the national media, had realised immediately who was meant.

In ***Lloyd* v *David Syme & Co Ltd*** (1986), a newspaper falsely alleged that the Australian media tycoon Kerry Packer had fixed the result of a cricket match involving the West Indian team. The team captain, Clive Lloyd, was not mentioned in the story, and had not played in the match referred to, but he successfully sued for libel on the grounds that the allegation of match fixing necessarily implied that the team had been involved, and that as captain, he must have taken part.

A publication which carries a defamatory story without naming the individual concerned can also be caught out if another publication runs the same story, but does include the name;

this clearly makes it possible for readers of the first paper to identify the person meant. The first paper will not be able to evade liability on the grounds that such identification was not its fault.

In fact, not naming your subject may not only fail to protect you from being sued by them, but could expose you to claims from other people. If, for example, you were to write that one of the directors of a particular firm was embezzling the company's money, not only could the person you meant drum up friends or relatives to say that they thought he was the person referred to, but the other directors might do so as well.

Pixellating and bleeping

As explained above, showing a picture or film of someone alongside a story means that the words of that story can be taken to refer to them. Pixellating the images will only protect against liability if it makes certain that the person could not be identified, even by someone who knows them. Similarly, bleeping out the name of a person or company in a broadcast can remove the risk, but only if they are not identifiable from the context or other details. It is sensible to take legal advice before relying on either of these devices.

In 2006, radio DJ Ian Thompson accepted what were said to be 'substantial' damages from the *News of the World*, after it published a story claiming that a 'well-known DJ' and two Premiership footballers took part in same-sex orgies. None of the subjects was named, but the story was accompanied by a picture of Mr Thompson, and footballer Ashley Cole, which had been pixellated to conceal their identities. However, thanks to the pictures and hints in the story, many readers recognised whom the piece referred to, and they were named on internet sites. The allegations were untrue, and the paper made an offer of amends to both of them. It was reported that Mr Cole had also been paid damages of £100,000.

Implied references

Be careful too of statements that imply blame on individuals even though you do not name them. For example, saying that a school is badly run is effectively the same as saying the head-teacher is running it badly, and several newspapers have had to pay damages to headteachers as a result of similar stories. That is not to say that you should never publish stories about badly run schools, but if you are aware of the risk of libel, you can take steps to make sure you are covered by a defence, usually truth or honest opinion.

Unintended references

It is quite possible to be liable for defamation if you write a story that is true about the person you intended it to refer to, but untrue of someone else who could be identified as its subject, even if you did not know the latter existed. So, for example, if you write that 'Blonde Susan Briggs, 42, of Tunbridge Wells robbed a bank', and this is true of the Susan Briggs you mean, you may still be sued by another blonde 42-year-old Susan Briggs from Tunbridge Wells, if she can make out a case that readers would have taken the article to have referred to her. The same could apply if, for example, you report that the Managing Director of Bloggs Ltd has been embezzling, and though this is true of the man you mean, he has since stepped down and the new MD is someone else.

Clearly, without an encyclopaedic knowledge of every person on the planet, this is quite difficult to guard against with certainty, and more recent cases suggest that the courts will take into account the practicality of protecting against unintentional references. They are not likely to be so understanding if the mix-up is obviously the result of careless research, or failure to check facts which would be easy to confirm.

In ***Newstead* v *London Express Newspapers*** (1940), the *Daily Express* reported that a Harold Newstead, described as a 30-year-old Camberwell man, had been convicted of bigamy. This was true of the Harold Newstead that the paper had intended to refer to, but unknown to them, there was another Harold Newstead living in Camberwell, who was not a bigamist. He sued, claiming that the article could be taken to refer to him, and won his case. In fact the newspaper had known the occupation and exact address of the bigamous Mr Newstead, but had left these out, a fact that was made much of in court and may have influenced the decision. Had the paper published those extra details, it might well have avoided being sued, and it is worth remembering that the more details you include, the less likely it is that someone else out there will fit the same description.

In 1973, the BBC paid £15,000 in damages to the owner of a company called House of Floris, after a programme criticising another company with a similar name referred to it simply as 'Floris'. The owner of House of Floris successfully claimed that viewers might think that the programme was referring to his company.

In ***O'Shea* v *MGN Ltd***, MGN published an advert for a pornographic website, containing a picture of a woman who looked very like the claimant. There were also certain details in the advert which the claimant said might lead those who knew her to think that she was the woman in the picture. She claimed the advert was defamatory because it suggested that she had allowed her picture to be used. The court agreed that the 'reasonable person' might take her to be the person in the picture, and they said that if a 'lookalike' had been used deliberately, the claimant could have a case in malicious falsehood (see Chapter 17). In this case, however, where the resemblance was totally innocent, it would be an unreasonable restriction on freedom of expression to expect a publisher to check whether every picture it published happened to resemble someone else. The claimant therefore lost her case.

The BBC was successfully sued by a London police officer, who happened to be walking out of a police station just as it was being filmed for a programme on police corruption. The programme featured general allegations and did not name anyone, but the officer was obviously identifiable from the film and could therefore make out a case that viewers might think he was one of the people to whom the corruption allegations referred.

It is always important to take care with the use of pictures, and the captions to them. If, for example, you are writing a story about Joe Bloggs, who has been found guilty of rape, and you use a picture of a completely different Joe Bloggs, who has not, the man pictured will have a clear claim in defamation, even if details in the story might make it clear that he is not the person meant.

In 2007, the *Daily Mail* paid damages to a man who was pictured alongside a story covering a robbery trial. The man who was accused of the robbery was a martial arts champion, and the man pictured had the same name, and was also a martial arts champion, which was how the mistake happened.

In 2005, the *Sunday Mirror* paid £100,000 in an out-of-court settlement with a man they had mistakenly labelled as a rapist. The paper ran a story about the convicted rapist Iorworth Hoare, who won £7 million on the National Lottery while serving a prison sentence, but the man whose photograph they showed was someone completely different. The story quoted a woman who was said to have seen him coming out of a bail hostel, who said he looked 'evil' and had a 'distinctive swagger'; in fact the man shown had not come out of the hostel and walked the way he did owing to hip surgery. The paper recalled its first edition and pulped 140,000 copies after it realised the mistake, but the man's lawyer was able to show that at least one copy was on sale near where he lived.

It is especially important to take care when using 'file' or 'stock' photographs to illustrate a story or feature. If, for example, you write a feature on the problem of binge drinking, and illustrate it with a picture you happen to have in the files of a group of girls at a party, you could be liable for defamation if the girls are identifiable, because they can claim that the story implies they are binge drinkers. If you want a shot to illustrate a general point, it is safer to use one from a picture agency, because the models they use will usually have granted permission to use the picture for any purpose (and the agency should tell you if they have not).

In ***Capehorn* v *Independent News and Media*** (2006), the *Independent on Sunday* paid undisclosed damages to actor Harry Capehorn, after it used his photo to illustrate a feature on ASBOs. The photo had been taken six years earlier for a publicity campaign for a charity, and Mr Capehorn, who was then 16, appeared in the shots as a model, and not as himself. The photo was supplied on condition that it would be captioned 'Posed by models', but this was not done. Mr Capehorn had since appeared in several TV series, and said readers would recognise him and assume he had been the subject of an ASBO, which he had not.

Because the courts have always recognised that it is very difficult to guard completely against the danger of unintentionally referring to someone, the offer of amends defence provides publishers with a way of minimising the harm done, both to the claimant and to their own pockets (see p. 269).

Defaming a group

Where a defamatory statement refers to a class or group of people (such as 'All footballers are greedy' or 'British politicians are corrupt'), it is not usually possible for that group of people to sue for defamation as a group, nor for one member of a group to sue on the grounds that the remark libels them personally. So, for example, if you were to say that plumber John Bloggs was useless at his job, he might be able to sue, but if you were to say that all plumbers are useless, neither John Bloggs alone nor the whole plumbing trade could sue.

In ***Knupffer* v *London Express Newspapers Ltd*** (1944), the defendants published an article describing the Young Russia party, a group of Russian émigrés, as a Fascist organisation. The group had approximately 2,000 members, 24 of whom were based in the UK. The claimant, a Russian emigrant living in London, sued on the basis that, as a member of the group, the statement defamed him personally. The House of Lords refused his claim, on the grounds that the statement was aimed at a large class of people and nothing in it singled him out.

However, where the group referred to is so small that the statement could be taken to refer to each and every one of them, one or all of them may be able to sue successfully. So while it is not dangerous to say 'All lawyers are useless', it may be a different story if you say 'All lawyers employed at Bodgit, Snatch and Run are useless'. Unfortunately, there is no set number above which a class of people will be considered too big for one of the members to be able to sue for a remark aimed at all of them. Each case will depend on the facts and, in particular, how large the potential group is, and how closely the individuals in that group were associated with the defamatory statement.

In ***Aspro Travel* v *Owners Abroad Group*** (1996), the defendants made a defamatory statement about the claimants' business, which was a family firm run by four members of the same family. They successfully argued that the statement could be taken to refer to any or all of them, and so were each able to sue.

In *Riches v News Group* (1986), the *News of the World* published a letter from a man who was holding his own children hostage at gunpoint, which made serious allegations against the 'Banbury CID', though without mentioning specific officers by name. Ten members of the Banbury CID successfully sued the paper for damages.

In *Aiken v Police Review Publishing Co Ltd* (1995), the *Police Review* magazine published a story headlined 'Nazi "humour" forces Jewish PC to quit', alleging that a police dog handler had been forced to leave his job because of the anti-semitic behaviour of some of his colleagues. There were 60 police officers working at the same station, 35 of them dog handlers. Ten of the dog handlers sued for libel, claiming that readers might think the allegations referred to them. The magazine applied to have the action struck out on the basis that readers would not be able to identify the claimants as the individuals whose behaviour was covered in the story. The judge refused the striking out action, saying that it was at least possible that readers might understand the story to be referring to each or any of the claimants.

Certain types of group, such as political parties, are also unable to sue for defamation whatever their size (see p. 241), and special requirements apply to defamation claims by companies (see Chapter 16).

PUBLICATION

The final element of defamation is that the statement must be published, which simply means that it is communicated to a person other than the claimant or the defendant's spouse. In media cases, of course, publication is usually in print, broadcast or online.

Traditionally, every repetition of a libel counted as a fresh publication and created a new claim. This meant that, although there are time limits within which claims for defamation must be made (see p. 274), these time limits started to run again when a defamatory statement was repeated. This caused particular problems for online publication, as the courts held that each time an article was accessed by a reader, that counted as a fresh publication. This situation has now changed, with the Defamation Act 2013 creating what is called a 'single publication rule'. Section 8 states that where someone publishes a statement and then later publishes substantially the same statement again, the time limit for a claim regarding the later publication begins at the point of the first publication, and the later publication no longer begins a new time limit. The single publication rule will not apply, however, where the manner of the later publication is 'materially different' from the first publication.

Whether the manner of publication is 'materially different' is a matter for the judge to assess, and s8(5) provides that in deciding this the court may take into account, among other things, the level of prominence that the defamatory statement is given, and the extent of the subsequent publication. The explanatory notes to the Act state that a possible example of the manner of publication being 'materially different' might be where a story was initially published in a section of a website where a reader would have to click through several links to get to it, and was later moved to a position where it could be directly accessed through the home page, which would almost certainly increase the number of hits it receives. If the manner of publication is 'materially different', it creates a new cause of action.

Note that the single publication rule only applies where the re-publication is by the same publisher. If you were to repeat defamatory allegations that someone else published long ago, you would create a fresh claim, whether or not those allegations were challenged before.

Publication and the internet

Publication online is subject to the law of defamation in just the same way as print and broadcasting. However, an online publisher may be able to avoid liability if it can show that the material has only been read by a very small number of people, though as the ***Loutchansky*** case shows, this can be difficult.

In ***Jameel* v *Wall Street Journal*** (2006), the *Wall Street Journal*, which is published in America and has a US-based website, was able to prove that an article had only been downloaded by five people in the UK, and one of those was the claimant's lawyer. The Court of Appeal held that there had not been 'substantial publication' in the UK and therefore rejected the case.

In ***Loutchansky* v *Times Newspapers Ltd*** (No. 2) (2001), *The Times* published articles suggesting that the claimant, a Russian businessman, was involved in crime. His claim included publication on the newspaper's website. *The Times* argued that it was not possible to prove that anyone had read the material online, but the judge said it was reasonable to infer that they had, given that the website had 12.5 million visits every month.

As well as content generated by journalists, most media websites also invite content from users, in the form of message boards, chatrooms, forums and bulletin boards. If any of this content is defamatory, the organisation which runs the website can be liable (just as a newspaper would be for a defamatory reader's letter).

However, in some circumstances, there will be a defence under Regulation 19 of the Electronic Commerce (EC Directive) Regulations 2002. This states that where a website provider stores material provided by users of the site, they will not be liable for damages if they did not know that material posted was defamatory, were not aware of any circumstances or facts which would have told them it was defamatory, and acted quickly to remove access to the material once they did know.

In ***Karim* v *Newsquest*** (2009), the claimant was a solicitor who sued the Newsquest group over its report of a Law Society hearing in which he was struck off. The report itself was covered by absolute privilege under s14 of the Defamation Act 1996 (see p. 257), but the website had a comments box under the story, and Mr Karim claimed that many of the readers' comments posted there were defamatory. He sought to sue Newsquest as the publisher of the comments. The court held that Newsquest were covered by the Regulation 19 defence: the comments were posted without any intervention by Newsquest, and they were not aware of any defamatory content at the time, but as soon as Mr Karim complained about them, they had removed them.

The Defamation Act 2013 will add a further way in which companies can avoid liability for material posted by members of the public on their websites. Section 5 is a provision designed to deal with the problem of readers leaving defamatory comments under online stories, known as trolling. It provides that a website operator will not be liable for defamatory statements posted on their site where they can show that they did not post the statement, or in other words that they were hosting the content rather than putting it out themselves. However, this defence will not apply where the claimant can show that:

- it is not possible for the claimant to identify the person who posted the statement;
- the claimant gave the operator a notice of complaint about the statement; and
- the operator has failed to respond to the complaint.

If a story is not defamatory in itself, but the page carries links to material that is, it is possible that the publisher and author of the original story could be liable. Whether this is the case has not been tested in the courts yet, but in ***McGrath* v *Dawkins, Amazon and Others*** (2012), a High Court judge accepted that it might be. The result of the case, if it goes to trial, will be published on this book's website.

Archive material after a libel claim

If you are successfully sued for a story that has appeared in print or been broadcast, it is important to make sure that it is removed from any online archives or amended so as to remove any libellous content.

In 2006, the father of comedian Jimmy Carr got two sets of damages from the *Sunday Telegraph* after settling a libel case regarding a story in the paper. *The Telegraph* mistakenly left the online version on its website. He got £12,000 in the first settlement and a further £5,000 in the second.

In 2009, Times Newspapers brought a case in the European Court of Human Rights (ECHR), arguing that this rule was an unjustified restriction on the right to freedom of expression, because it meant that publishers could potentially be liable for ever. The ECHR disagreed, saying it was not a disproportionate restriction on freedom of expression to expect publishers to amend their own archives. However, the ECHR said that if a libel action based on internet publication was brought too long after the original story, that might be a disproportionate restriction on press freedom. Unfortunately the decision did not specify how long 'too long' might be.

Who is the publisher?

Traditionally, the party sued for defamation could be the journalist who wrote the piece, their editor, or the publishing company, broadcaster or website that employed them, or anyone involved in getting the material out to the public, such as distributors and retailers. The Defamation Act 2013 changes this. Section 10 states that it is no longer possible to sue anyone who is not the author, editor or publisher of the statement unless the court is satisfied that it is not reasonably practicable for a claim to be brought against the author, editor or publisher. The author of a statement is defined as the originator of it, unless they did not intend that it should be published; the editor is someone who has editorial or equivalent responsibility for the content of the statement or the decision to publish it; and publisher means a commercial publisher, whose business is issuing material to the public, and who issues the material in the course of that business.

In practice, though individual journalists are occasionally sued, claimants usually target those with the deepest pockets, namely the company which employs the journalist, whether as staff or freelance.

If you are freelance, you may find that the terms and conditions you work under include an indemnity clause, under which you agree to repay the publishers any damages they have to pay as a result of libels in your work. In practice these are rarely enforced, but legally they could be.

Libels in more than one publication or broadcast

If a defamatory statement appears in more than one publication, the subject of the statement can sue all or any of them, and not necessarily at the same time (though there are restrictions on the overall amount of damages that can be awarded when this happens). This means that the fact that a claimant has not chosen to sue over defamatory allegations in another publication does not mean they are prevented from suing you if you repeat them. It is therefore not safe to assume that because an allegation or rumour has been widely reported, it becomes safe to repeat it. There is nothing to stop a claimant from deciding to sue your publication even if they have chosen not to sue others, and this has happened, especially where the claimant has a dislike of a particular newspaper, or where the initial allegations were published to a relatively small circulation and then picked up by a larger publication.

Broadcasters whose programmes feature reviews of the newspapers should be aware that if they show a libellous story in a paper, they could be sued, regardless of whether the claimant also sues the paper.

An uncle of footballer Wayne Rooney sued the BBC in 2008 over a *BBC Breakfast* item which implied he had been involved in violent behaviour at a birthday party for his nephew's then fiancée, Coleen McLoughlin. The programme's review of the day's newspapers talked about a *Daily Mail* story which said that Ms McLoughlin had banned members of her fiancé's family from their wedding because of the way they had behaved at her birthday party. The story was (wrongly) illustrated with a picture of John Morrey, an uncle who had not been at the birthday party, and the presenter showed the relevant page on camera. The case was settled and the BBC paid damages.

WHO CAN SUE FOR DEFAMATION?

Individuals: Any living person can sue for defamation. However, there is no action for libelling the dead, so it is not possible to sue for damage to the reputation of a dead relative, for example, unless a claimant can establish that defamation of the dead relative affects the claimant's own reputation as well.

In 2010, TV interviewer Michael Parkinson was paid damages by Associated Newspapers, over a story claiming that he had lied about his family background. The story, in the *Daily Mail*, carried claims by a cousin that Mr Parkinson had painted a false picture of his father, who he had described as honest, upstanding and well-liked. The cousin alleged that this was untrue and that his uncle was 'hateful' and disliked by most people. As Mr Parkinson's father was dead by this time, it was not possible to sue for defamation of him, but the action was brought on the basis that it was defamatory to say that Mr Parkinson had lied.

Corporations: 'Corporation' is a legal term, which covers not only commercial companies, but also, for example, organisations such as schools and universities which have a legal existence separate from that of the individuals who manage them. Corporations can sue, but the Defamation Act 2013 introduces a restriction on claims by commercial companies. As we saw earlier, a statement will no longer be considered defamatory unless it has caused or is likely to cause serious harm to the claimant's reputation. Section 1(2) of the Act provides that where the claimant is a body which 'trades for profit', the harm caused by a published statement will not be considered serious unless it has caused or is likely to cause it serious financial loss. This might mean, for example, lost sales, or a reduced share price, but in practice, it seems likely to be very difficult to prove that a statement alone could have this effect, since you would have to be able to strip out the effects of the many other factors that can affect sales and share prices. Some experts have suggested that this will make it much less likely that commercial companies will be able to sue for defamation.

Associations: Some associations, such as clubs, are legally incorporated and can sue like any other corporation. If not, an association cannot itself bring a claim, but often defamatory allegations about a club will reflect sufficiently clearly on its officials to allow them to bring a claim on their own behalf.

Trade unions: Although trade unions have sued in the past, the Trade Union and Labour Relations (Consolidation) Act 1992 states that unions are not incorporated bodies. According to the leading academic lawyers McBride and Bagshaw, this means that unions can no longer sue for libel. However, suggestions that, for example, a union is badly run would clearly reflect on the leaders, and they could sue in their own right.

Local authorities and central government: Elected authorities cannot sue for defamation. This was established in the landmark case of ***Derbyshire County Council* v *Times Newspapers*** (1993), where the House of Lords held that it was important for freedom of speech that there should be free and open discussion of the work of elected authorities, and therefore they should not be able to sue for defamation regarding their 'governmental and administrative functions'. (They can still sue for defamatory statements regarding their property, and also, in some circumstances, for malicious falsehood – see Chapter 17.) However, once again, individual officers of, for example, a local council, could sue if criticism of the council reflects sufficiently on their personal reputations.

Political parties: In ***Goldsmith* v *Bhoyrul*** (1998), it was stated that political parties cannot sue for defamation, for similar reasons to those advanced in *Derbyshire County Council*, above. However, it is possible for individuals who are members of or work for a political party to sue for libel over defamatory statements about the party which reflect on their personal reputations.

Unincorporated organisations: In ***North London Central Mosque Trust* v *Policy Exchange*** (2010), it was held that organisations which do not have the legal status of a corporation (in this case the charitable trust that runs a mosque) cannot sue for defamation.

Myths and misconceptions **Stories about ordinary people**

✗ *You can say what you like about ordinary people, because they can't afford to sue.*

Until recently, this was close to the truth; libel actions are extremely expensive, requiring specialist knowledge beyond most high street solicitors, and with no legal aid available for libel claims, very few ordinary people would have been able to sue, unless they were backed by a wealthy organisation such as a trade union. This has changed with the advent of conditional fee agreements (often known as 'no win, no fee' actions). These allow solicitors to take on cases on the basis that they receive nothing if the claimant loses, but boost their fees if they win. This means that someone who seems to have a good case can now sue, at no financial risk to themselves. The amount of 'uplift' lawyers can take has recently been limited, but the existence of conditional fee agreements still means it is no longer safe to assume libelling ordinary people is risk-free (to say nothing of it being ethically wrong).

Claimants from abroad and 'libel tourism'

If your work goes online – whether in its original form or as an online edition of a print publication or broadcast programme – it is worth remembering that it can be accessed from almost anywhere in the world, and if you say something defamatory about someone who is based in another country, they can sue in England. However, in response to problems with 'libel tourism', where foreign claimants took advantage of the UK's claimant-friendly libel laws to sue in the UK even for statements that were barely published in the UK, the Defamation

Act 2013 has tightened the rules for foreign claimants. Section 9 provides that cases brought by claimants not domiciled in the UK, another member state, or a state which is a contracting party to the Lugano Convention (these are Iceland, Norway and Switzerland) may not be heard in the UK, unless the court is satisfied that, of all the places where the defamatory statement has been published, England and Wales is 'clearly the most appropriate place in which to bring an action'. This is quite a wide and flexible test, so how far it restricts libel tourism will depend very much on how the courts interpret the test: there might be difficult judgements to make where, for example, a defamatory statement was published more widely abroad than in the UK, but the claimant lives here for much of the time, or has important business interests here.

SLANDER

As explained at the beginning of this chapter, there is a second type of defamation, in addition to libel, called slander. It covers defamatory words that are published in transient forms, such as speech. Obviously, in most cases, journalists are concerned with libel, and cases against the media for slander are rare. Even so, it is worth being conscious of the risk of making a slanderous statement, especially for those involved in investigative journalism. If, for example, you were to confront the subject of a story and put defamatory allegations to them in the hearing of a third party, or to repeat those allegations to someone else in the process of checking them, you could potentially be liable for slander.

People attempting to sue for slander are subject to a restriction that does not apply to libel cases. You can only be successfully sued for damages for slander if the claimant can prove that you making the slanderous statement caused them some loss (such as loss of business, for example), or if the statement you made contained or implied one of the following allegations:

- that the claimant had committed a crime that potentially carries a prison sentence;
- that the claimant is incompetent at their job or business.

Law in practice **Handling complaints**

If you are threatened with a libel action, or receive a complaint that could possibly lead to legal action, handling it correctly could save your publication from a nasty legal bill – while handling it badly can turn what would have been a simple complaint into an expensive court case, or, as the ***Campbell-James*** and ***Turner*** cases (see p. 270) show, increase the damages your publication has to pay. Rod Dadak, of solicitors Lewis Silkin, offers this advice:

- If you get a telephone call complaining about a story, it is always safer to say less than more; remember that you may be being taped. Be polite, make a detailed note of what the complaint is, and tell the caller that you need to refer the matter to your editor. Do not get involved in a debate about the story, and never offer an off-the-cuff apology. In most cases, journalists are indemnified by their employers if there is a claim for libel, which means you do not have to pay damages yourself, but if you go out on a limb and make an apology which exposes them to liability, you may lose this protection.
- Never ignore a letter of complaint; reply promptly, acknowledging the letter. Say that you will investigate the complaint, and give a date when you expect to be able to reply.

- Always tell your editor about a complaint, whether or not it seems serious, even if that means bringing to their attention a mistake they might not otherwise have noticed. Ignoring a request for a correction, or trying to hide one in a follow-up story, can very easily result in a complainant who would have accepted a proper apology suing instead. If your publication has insurance against defamation claims (as, for example, most local papers do), it is also essential that the insurers are informed at an early stage if a complaint appears to be serious.
- The Civil Procedure Rules 1998 contain a Pre-Action Protocol for dealing with complaints of defamation, which sets out a code of good practice and aims to promote early resolution of complaints, where possible without going to court. All journalists need to be aware of this procedure, and to follow it. (In 2006, the *Sun* was ordered to pay extra costs to the actor Chris Parker, because it ignored the Protocol – **see p. 218.**) The complete Protocol can be read online (see *Online resources* at the end of this chapter), but in summary, the steps are:
  - The complainant should notify the defendant of the claim, in writing, as soon as possible. The Protocol details the information which should be provided, and if a letter of complaint does not contain the information required by the Protocol, you should mention the Protocol to the complainant and ask for them to follow it.
  - The defendant should provide a full written response as soon as possible, and if this cannot be done within 14 days, should notify the claimant of the date they intend to respond.
  - Throughout the Protocol process, both parties should act reasonably to keep costs proportionate to the nature and seriousness of the case.
  - The parties should consider whether they can use an alternative to court action to settle the dispute, such as reference to ISPO, or discussion and negotiation between them.

KEY POINTS

The meaning of 'defamatory'

Defamation is the publication of an untrue statement which tends to lower the person it refers to in the eyes of reasonable people, and which has caused or is likely to cause serious harm to reputation.

Defamation can occur in:

- direct criticism;
- hints and innuendoes;
- the effect of words and pictures together;
- the effect of context and juxtaposition;
- reporting of rumours;
- untrue implications drawn from true facts.

Referring to the claimant

It must be clear to an ordinary, reasonable reader that the statement refers to the claimant, but a hint or implication may be enough.

Who can sue?

Individuals and corporations can sue for libel; elected authorities and political parties cannot.

Slander

Publication of defamatory words in transient form is slander.

TEST YOUR KNOWLEDGE

1 Which of these statements is potentially defamatory?
   (a) Jake Black is a cowboy builder.
   (b) Jake Black claims to be an honest builder, and we all know builders never do anything dodgy, don't we?
   (c) Customer Mrs Smith said, 'I'm disgusted with the mess Jake Black left behind when he converted my loft. He is a complete cowboy.'

2 A well-known businessman has recently died. In his obituary, a newspaper states that he was a well-known womaniser, who was thought to have links with the mafia. Is the newspaper at risk of a libel action from his family?

3 You are a reporter on the business magazine *Construction and Building.* At an industry function, you hear a rumour that the finance director of a major building company, who recently took early retirement, was forced to do so after being discovered stealing company funds. You are sure that your source is reliable, but the company refuses to confirm the story. Which of these is safe to write?
   (a) According to a reliable source, Bloggs Building's ex-Finance Director, John Smith, was forced to leave the company after being discovered stealing.
   (b) Bloggs Building has denied that its ex-Finance Director, John Smith, was sacked for stealing company funds.
   (c) Bloggs Building has denied that a senior member of staff has been sacked for stealing company funds.
   (d) A well-known building company this week refused to confirm that a recently retired director was sacked for dishonest conduct.

4 Which of these could sue for libel if you published a defamatory statement about them?
   (a) Thomson Holidays.
   (b) The Conservative Party.
   (c) The mayor of Tunbridge Wells.
   (d) The managing director of Marks and Spencer.
   (e) The Prime Minister.
   (f) Bromley Borough Council.
   (g) The National Union of Teachers.

5 You work for a woman's magazine, and write a feature about women who have set up their own companies. One of them mentions in passing that she had to start her own business because her husband left her penniless with three small children to bring up. You then get a letter from the husband, who is very angry, because, he says, he did not leave her penniless but in fact signed the family home over to her. His letter goes on to say that the marriage only broke up because she had an affair with his best friend. He says he doesn't want to sue, as long as you publish the letter and an apology. Should you publish it?

ONLINE RESOURCES

The Civil Procedure Rules Pre-Action Protocol for Defamation is available at:
http://www.justice.gov.uk/courts/procedure-rules/civil/protocol/prot_def

The Defamation Act 1996 can be read in full at:
www.legislation.gov.uk/ukpga/1996/31/contents

The Defamation Act 2013 can be read in full at:
http://www.legislation.gov.uk/ukpga/2013/26/contents/enacted

The explanatory notes to the Defamation Bill give useful background to the new law (but bear in mind that they refer to the original bill and some provisions changed during its journey through Parliament). They can be read at:
http://www.legislation.gov.uk/ukpga/2013/26/notes/contents

Defences and remedies for defamation

In the previous chapter, we saw that publishing a statement which lowers someone in the eyes of reasonable people can make a publisher or broadcaster liable for defamation. However, there are some circumstances in which the law will allow the publication of a defamatory statement, and a publication which falls within one of these circumstances is described as having a defence. There are a number of potential defences for defamation, which are discussed in this chapter. Having a good knowledge of them will help you to get stories published and still remain on the right side of the law.

This chapter also looks at the remedies available if a claimant in defamation wins their case, and the time limits which apply to defamation claims.

Significant changes have been made to the defences available for defamation, in the Defamation Act 2013. However, the Act does not apply to Northern Ireland, where defamation cases are still covered by the previous law, so the relevant chapters of the last edition of this book have been placed on the book's website.

DEFENCES

A defence can help you in two ways. Firstly, if it is obvious that what you publish would be covered by a defence, you (or your employer) are less likely to be sued in the first place. Secondly, if you are sued, but you can prove you have a defence, you will win the case.

The seven defences which apply to defamation are:

- consent
- truth;
- honest opinion;
- absolute privilege;
- qualified privilege;
- publication on a matter of public interest;
- offer of amends;
- the 'section 5 defence' which protects distributors and others not directly involved in publication.

A defendant can also avoid liability if the claimant does not bring their action within a specified time (see p. 274).

Consent

If the subject of a story consents to it being published, they cannot successfully sue for libel. However, in order to plead this defence successfully, the publisher would have to show that consent was given to the content of the article, including any potentially defamatory allegations, and not just consent to be interviewed for or featured in the publication. A refusal to deny something will not amount to consent, so you cannot obtain consent by telling someone that if they do not confirm or deny your story, you will publish it. In most cases the defence will be used where someone has granted and perhaps even been paid for an interview.

Consent is also known as 'leave and licence'.

Truth

If you can prove that what you have written is substantially true, you have a complete defence against a claim of defamation. This is now contained in s2 of the Defamation Act 2013, which replaces the old defence of justification (which is what you will see referred to in case law arising before the 2013 Act). However, the rules are essentially the same as for the old defence., so old case law is still likely to be influential.

In *Taylforth* v ***News Group Newspapers*** (1994), the *Sun* successfully used the defence of justification in its 1994 case against actress Gillian Taylforth. The paper had claimed that Ms Taylforth and her boyfriend had been caught by police having oral sex in a parked car. The claim was undoubtedly defamatory, but the *Sun* presented evidence that it was true, including a police witness. The couple denied it, claiming that Ms Taylforth had merely been massaging her boyfriend's stomach because he felt ill, which led to a bizarre reconstruction in court, where *Sun* journalists played the parts of the couple in the position they said they had been discovered in, in order to demonstrate to the jury how unlikely the massage claim was. The jury found for the newspaper.

It is important to remember that it is not enough simply for you to know that your story is true; you also have to be able to prove it in court. Journalists should always make sure that they have the evidence to support a story, but as the following cases show, this can be extremely difficult.

In ***Gecas* v *Scottish Television*** (1992), Scottish Television (STV) was sued over a programme about war crimes. It accused Antony Gecas, a Lithuanian man who ran a bed and breakfast in Edinburgh, of being involved in the murder of thousands of Jews in Lithuania and Belarus, during the Second World War, when he was head of a special police battalion. He sued, and STV pleaded justification, which meant finding witnesses to events that had taken place over 50 years earlier, many of whom had since moved to other countries. Not surprisingly, the case cost around £1.5 million. Had STV lost, it would have had to pay this, as well as damages, but the research paid off and STV won its case.

The *Guardian* famously won its 1997 case against the former Conservative Cabinet Minister, Jonathan Aitken, when vital evidence was found at the very last minute. The paper had claimed, among other things, that Mr Aitken had breached ministerial guidelines by accepting a stay at the Paris Ritz, paid for by a business associate. He sued, and despite four years of research, it was only the last-minute discovery of a hotel bill, during the trial, that proved the *Guardian*'s case. Mr Aitken dropped his claim, and was later jailed for perjury. The complexity of the case meant that costs had by then spiralled to £2 million, a bill that the paper would have had to pay if it had lost.

A further complication with the use of the truth defence is that if you attempt to use it, and then fail to prove your case, that can look to judges and juries as though you are persisting in a lie, and they could look less favourably on you than they would if you had never sought to use the defence at all.

Proving truth

The defence of truth can only be applied to statements of fact, not opinion (for opinions, the usual defence is honest comment, see p. 253). The statement must be proved to be substantially true, on a balance of probabilities. 'Balance of probabilities' is simply the term used for the standard of proof that applies in civil cases, and means that you have to convince the jury that the statement is more likely to be true than not to be true (as opposed to the criminal standard of proof, which is proof beyond reasonable doubt).

Substantially true

It is not necessary to prove that every single aspect of a statement is absolutely true, so long as, taken as a whole, it is accurate. Section 2 provides that there will be a defence if defamatory material is 'substantially true', so small inaccuracies will not prevent the defence applying. It also states that where an allegation contains two or more elements, and one or more of them cannot be proved substantially true, the defence can still apply if the things that were not shown to be substantially true do not seriously harm the claimant's reputation, given those things that were proved to be true. The position was the same with the old defence of justification, so again, the old cases still provide a good guide to how the law applies.

In ***Gecas* v *Scottish Television*** the case concerning STV and the Lithuanian police commander, Antony Gecas (see opposite), the programme's allegations about Mr Gecas' involvement in the killing of Jews included a claim that he personally 'finished off' Jews who had been thrown into burial pits but were still alive. Though STV was able to prove Mr Gecas' overall involvement in the murders, it could not prove this particular claim, but successfully relied on the section 5 defence. The judge said that this claim did not itself materially injure Mr Gecas' reputation, given the crimes that he had been proved to have committed.

The case of ***Miller* v *Associated Newspapers Ltd (No. 3)*** (2005) concerned the fallout from false allegations of sexual assault made against the ex-MP Neil Hamilton and his wife Christine. The allegations had been concocted by the alleged victim with a view to selling her story to the press, and the investigation into them wasted an enormous amount of time and public money, as well as causing distress to Mr and Mrs Hamilton. At the time, Mr Miller was Detective Chief Inspector of the relevant area, and the *Daily Mail* and the *Evening Standard* both ran stories blaming him for what they called the 'shambles'. Mr Miller had in fact not been the investigating officer in the Hamilton case, and had been opposed to any action being taken against them, and the judge emphasised that he had 'acted in good faith throughout'. He also pointed out that the story had been based on leaked information that was not entirely accurate. Nevertheless, it had been shown that Mr Miller was amongst those responsible for important failures that led to the Hamiltons being arrested when they should not have been, and though 'by no means solely to blame', Mr Miller did bear a share of the responsibility. The newspaper might, the judge pointed out, have 'got it right more by luck than judgement', but even so, it had proved that its allegations were substantially true, and so won the case.

In ***Turcu* v *News Group Newspapers*** (2005), the *News of the World* was sued over a story about an alleged plot to kidnap Victoria Beckham. The story claimed that, following an undercover investigation, the paper had discovered that an international gang was 'on the brink' of putting into action the planned kidnap. The claimant, Alin Turcu, was said to be part of this gang, and to have a major role in surveillance. He was arrested the day after the story was published, but when the Crown Prosecution Service decided not to prosecute him, he sued the paper for libel. The court found that there was no gang in the sense that the story suggested, just a loose group of people who were willing to get involved in criminal activity, and the claimant did not have the alleged surveillance role. There was no specific plan to kidnap Mrs Beckham either. However, it was true that the claimant was a petty criminal with a long list of charges and convictions in four different countries, and it was true that he was willing to take part in criminal activities with the others, and that he had taken part in discussions about the possibility of kidnapping Victoria Beckham. Therefore, the judge said, the paper was able to back up the 'sting' of the libel, and prove that the allegations were 'substantially, if not wholly, accurate'.

In 2001 Channel 5 broadcast a programme about the model Kate Moss, which alleged that, at a charity fashion event in Barcelona, she had taken so much cocaine, she had fallen into a coma. Ms Moss sued, but in the period between the programme being shown and the case coming to a pre-trial hearing, a national newspaper published photographs of Ms Moss taking cocaine, and she later made a public apology for 'letting people down'. In a pre-trial hearing for the libel case, her lawyers tried to prevent Channel 5 from using the allegations and her apology as evidence for its claim of justification. Channel 5 lawyers however claimed that the point the programme had made was that she was 'a serious cocaine abuser' and that was the issue, not where and when she did it. The High Court agreed to admit the evidence, but shortly before the trial was due to start, Ms Moss dropped her claim.

In ***Rothschild*** v ***Associated Newspapers*** (2012), a wealthy banker lost a libel case against the *Daily Mail*, over a story which suggested he brought together Lord Mandelson, the then European Commissioner for Trade, and Oleg Deripaska, a Russian oligarch, in order to help Mr Deripaska make a business deal. The deal in question was said to have cost 300 British jobs. The story centred around a trip made by Mr Mandelson and some friends to Russia on Mr Rothschild's private jet. Mr Rothschild said the trip was purely recreational and business was not discussed. The *Mail* admitted that some of the details they had published about the trip were inaccurate, but argued that the 'sting' of the story, which was that Mr Rothschild had brought Lord Mandelson together with Mr Deripaska in a way that endangered the dignity and reputation of Lord Mandelson's office, was true. Mr Justice Tugendhat agreed, saying that there were 'at the very least reasonable grounds to believe' that Mr Deripaska's hospitality was motivated by the reasons the *Mail* had alleged, and that Mr Rothschild knew that.

Defamation judgments often refer to the 'sting' of a libel. This is essentially the main part of a libel, the allegation that damages the claimant's reputation, in contrast to minor details of the story which do not seriously damage the person's reputation. For example, if you were to write that a man hit his wife last Thursday, and he had in fact done so not on Thursday but on Wednesday, the 'sting' would be the allegation that he had hit his wife, and if you could prove that, you would have a defence even if the incidental matter of when the incident happened was untrue.

Proving implications

A defendant who pleads truth must not only prove the factual truth of their statements, but also that any reasonable interpretation of those words, or any innuendo implied by them, is true as well. In many cases, there will be dispute over what a statement means, and, in this situation, a defendant may plead truth for a meaning which is different and less serious than that which the claimant alleges. (This is often referred to as the lesser or lower meaning.)

In ***Marks & Spencer Plc*** v ***Granada Television Ltd*** (1988), Granada was sued over a *World in Action* programme which said that M&S clothing marked 'Made in England' was in fact being made by child workers in factories in Morocco. M&S claimed that the programme implied that it was 'knowingly and deliberately' exploiting child labour to increase profits. This, they said, was not true: it had not known about the child labour and had stopped using the supplier as soon as it discovered what the supplier was doing. Granada pleaded a lesser meaning, arguing that its implication went no further than suggesting that M&S was not making adequate checks on its suppliers. There was no problem with proving that this allegation was true, as Granada had film of the factories concerned. The jury found for M&S.

In ***Archer*** v ***News of the World*** (1987), the newspaper was successfully sued by Jeffrey Archer after it claimed that he paid £2,000 to a prostitute. While it was true – and could be proved – that the payment was made, Jeffrey Archer claimed that the article implied that he had had sex with her, which he said was not true. The paper could not prove this implication and ended up paying £500,000 damages.

Where an article links the claimant with some kind of wrongdoing, the claimant will often argue that the article implies they are guilty of that wrongdoing. If the publisher cannot prove this, it may claim that the piece does not suggest guilt, but merely states that there are grounds for suspicion. It can then seek to plead this lower meaning, rather than the one alleged by the claimant, and it is for the judge or the jury to decide which is the natural meaning of the piece, and whether that meaning is true.

In ***Armstrong* v *Times Newspapers Ltd*** (2006) the champion cyclist Lance Armstrong sued *The Times* over a story which said that his performance in the Tour de France suggested that he must have taken drugs. He claimed that the story implied that he had taken drugs, but *The Times* said that it was merely repeating questions that had been raised in a book, and that the meaning of the article was no more than that there were grounds to suspect that he had taken drugs. *The Times* sought to justify that lesser meaning. In a preliminary hearing, the judge decided that the words bore the meaning that Mr Armstrong claimed; an ordinary reader, looking at the headline and the text, would have understood the article to mean that he had taken drugs to improve his performance. The case was settled shortly afterwards.

Identifying sources

When pleading justification, and most of the other defences, you may need evidence from sources to prove your case. It is a fundamental principle of journalistic ethics that a source who has been promised confidentiality should not be identified, and this principle is – to an extent – upheld by the law (see Chapter 21). This means that the fact that you cannot identify your source will not necessarily mean you cannot prove your defence.

In ***Gaddafi* v *Telegraph Group*** (2000), the *Telegraph* was sued by the eldest son of the Libyan dictator Colonel Gaddafi, over an article which claimed he was involved in attempts to break the economic sanctions that had been imposed on Libya after the Lockerbie bombing. The *Telegraph* pleaded qualified privilege (see p. 259), but said it could not identify its sources because they were members of a 'western government security agency', and might be put in serious danger if their names were revealed. The court upheld the paper's right to protect its sources, and said it could still successfully plead qualified privilege, as long as it disclosed enough information to allow the court to judge the reliability of the information provided.

New evidence

A defence of truth need not only be based on such facts as were known at the time of publication; if other facts come to light during the (sometimes very long) period between a claim and the case coming to court, they can be used to back up the defence. This happened rather spectacularly when Jonathan Aitken sued the *Guardian* in 1997, and the final piece of evidence that caused Mr Aitken's claim to fall apart was found, almost literally, at the last minute (see p. 248). Similarly, evidence that does not relate to actual events described in the story, but which does help to show that the claims were true, may be allowed.

In ***Desmond* v *Bower*** (2009), Richard Desmond, who owns a publishing company which includes the *Daily Express*, sued the author of a book which, among other things, claimed he had ordered the *Express* editor to publish certain material about a rival publisher, because he wanted to get revenge on him. The author was pleading justification, and wanted to include evidence about an incident which happened after the book was written. In this incident, Mr Desmond was recorded speaking to a man who owed money to

Mr Desmond's son, and threatening to have a damaging article published in the *Express* if the money was not paid. The Court of Appeal said that the evidence should be allowed, because the question the jury would need to ask was whether Mr Desmond was the kind of man who would behave as Mr Bower had suggested.

Journalists are often unaware of a procedural factor which can help libel defendants who plead truth: court rules state that claimants must make available to the defence any documents that are relevant to the issues in the case. This is called disclosure, and can mean that the defendants themselves have to hand over the memo, contract or email that contains proof of the story. Not surprisingly, perhaps, some claimants decide to discontinue their claim when the order for disclosure is made.

Law in practice Using the truth defence

If you are working on a story that could lead to a defamation claim, and you want to make sure you can plead truth, you need to ensure not just that the story is true, but also that you can prove it. Rod Dadak, Head of Defamation at solicitors Lewis Silkin, has this advice:

- Make sure that you have clear, admissible evidence for your allegations before you publish them. It is very much harder to find witnesses, for example, after you have published, and when a court case may already be threatened, than before you go to press.
- If you can, tape your interviews. If you prefer to take notes, always date them, use the pages of your notebook in sequence, and number the pages; this means you can prove that you have not tampered with or added to your notes. If for some reason you can't take a contemporaneous note (i.e. one while the subject is speaking), do it as soon as possible afterwards.
- If you use shorthand (or your handwriting is illegible), transcribe your notes as soon as possible; with shorthand, what you write may be susceptible to two or more different meanings, and that can make it difficult to rely on shorthand notes in court. Ideally, transcribe onto a computer, as this allows you to prove the date on which you did the transcription.
- Keep all your notes for as long as possible, and for a minimum of a year after publication.
- Do not rely on just one source. There is always the possibility that you may be dealing with someone who has a grudge, so try to get corroborating evidence from other sources.
- If your story contains allegations made by someone else, consider whether that person would give evidence for you in court, and how they would be viewed by a jury. How old are they? Do they speak English? Is there anything about them that might make a jury mistrust them? If you think there are reasons why your source might not be believed, it becomes even more important to find corroborating evidence or other witnesses.
- If you are going to publish serious allegations, for which you have a witness, ask them to sign a written statement; this means that if you are sued, and your source decides that they do not want to back you up by giving evidence, the court can issue a subpoena, which is a legal demand for them to attend court and be questioned. You can also use a signed statement as evidence if the source dies or goes abroad before the trial. In some cases, it may be worth asking your witness for an affidavit, which is a statement sworn on oath, and therefore carries considerable legal weight.
- If you haven't got enough material to prove your story is true, don't take the risk. If it's a really good story, it's better to wait, get more evidence and publish it when you can stand it up properly.
- Don't assume that because another paper is publishing a story, it would be safe for you to do it too. If you lift a story from another publication, make sure that you check for yourself whether any defamatory allegations are true.

- The level of precautions you need to take will depend on the story; not every story, for example, would require you to get an affidavit. In deciding how far you need to go, the two key things to consider are the subject of the story and the gravity of the allegations. The more high-profile the person you are writing about, the more likely it is that they will have the means to sue, though bear in mind that the availability of conditional fee agreements has made it possible for people of modest means to sue for defamation. The more serious the allegations, the stronger the precautions you need to take, regardless of who the subject is.

Honest opinion

Honest opinion is a defence which applies to opinions and comments. It replaces the old defence of honest comment (previously called fair comment), though the rules are different in several important ways. The new defence is contained in s3 of the Defamation Act 2013, and applies where:

- the statement complained of was a statement of opinion;
- the statement complained of indicated, whether in general or specific terms, the basis of the opinion

An honest person could have held the opinion on the basis of:

- any fact which existed at the time the statement complained of was published; or
- anything claimed to be a fact in a privileged statement that was published before the statement complained of.

The statement must be a statement of opinion

This is not always as simple a distinction as it seems. Obviously, if a statement includes words like 'I think' or 'It seems to me that', they are more likely to be viewed as a comment (though this should not be relied on). But take the situation where, for example, there has been debate about whether a particular public figure has misled the public, and you express your opinion on the question using the words 'The Chief Constable is a liar'. This might look like an opinion, and might have been intended to be an opinion, but in law it could be taken as an expression of fact, in which case you will not be able to use the defence of fair comment.

The explanatory notes to the Act make it clear that this requirement simply restates the former law under the honest comment/fair comment defence, so the old cases on this issue will still be a useful guideline as to what kind of material will be considered to be comment rather than fact.

In 1985 the actress Charlotte Cornwell sued the *News of the World* over an article written by its television critic Nina Myskow. The article said that Ms Cornwell could not sing or act, and had 'the kind of stage presence that jams lavatories'. The *News of the World* argued that this was comment on Ms Cornwell's performance, rather than assertions of fact, but the jury disagreed and found for Ms Cornwell.

In 1995, Jonathan Aitken was sued over a story he wrote in a Kent newspaper, about a wealthy local couple of Conservative supporters called the Pinder-Whites. He described them as being 'dreadful enough' to play JR and Sue-Ellen Ewing in the American soap *Dallas*. For those too young to remember, JR was a ruthless womaniser, and Sue-Ellen an alcoholic with a number of lovers. Mr Aitken said the story was meant to be ironic and was not intended to be taken literally. In court, evidence was given about the Pinder-Whites' glitzy lifestyle, including riding around in a white Rolls-Royce during a recent election campaign. The jury found that the story could be considered fair comment.

In ***Keays* v *Guardian Newspapers*** (2003), the *Guardian* published a story about Sarah Keays, who was known as the former mistress of a Cabinet Minister and mother of his child. After long refusing to talk to the press, Ms Keays had recently decided to publish her story, and the *Guardian* article speculated about her motives. The judge held that the article could only be read as comment, since the writer could not know as a fact what was in Ms Keays' mind.

In ***Branson* v *Bower (No. 1)*** (2001), Richard Branson sued the writer of a book for saying, about Mr Branson's bid to run the National Lottery, that some people might think he was doing it for 'self-glorification'. The writer claimed that this was comment, but Mr Branson argued that it was a statement of fact, the statement meaning that he had less than noble reasons for wanting to run the Lottery. The Court of Appeal disagreed. It said that while a suggestion about someone's motives could in some cases be an assertion of fact, in this case it was clear that the phrase was an opinion held by the writer on the basis of facts referred to in the article.

In ***Galloway* v *Telegraph Group Ltd*** (2006), the Court of Appeal upheld Labour MP George Galloway's victory over the *Daily Telegraph*, regarding a story which claimed that he had received money from Saddam Hussein's regime. The *Telegraph* pleaded fair comment, but the court said that the stories were allegations of fact, not comment. A headline, for example, stated 'damning new evidence', and the court said that the use of the word 'damning' was not a comment, but a statement that the evidence suggested Mr Galloway was guilty.

In ***British Chiropractic Association* v *Singh*** (2010), the British Chiropractic Association (BCA) sued science journalist Simon Singh over a story in the *Guardian*, which said that BCA members' claims about the medical problems their treatments could treat were made 'without a jot of evidence', and that the BCA 'happily promotes bogus treatments'. The BCA argued that the words were intended as statement of fact, and therefore could not be covered by the fair comment defence. The Court of Appeal disagreed. They pointed out that in the evidence supplied to the court, Mr Singh had set out his reasons for believing that there was no reliable evidence that the treatments worked, while the BCA in their evidence had been able to make an equally detailed case arguing that there was evidence that the treatments worked. This showed, they said, that the original article had not been intended as a statement of fact, but as an evaluation of the available evidence about the treatments. The word 'bogus' was used to emphasise Mr Singh's opinion of the evidence, rather than a factual assertion. That made the article a statement of opinion, not fact, and so the defence was available. The Court of Appeal case was purely to decide whether fair comment was available (not to try the libel claim itself) and the effect of the decision was that, had the case gone to trial, Mr Singh would have been able to argue the fair comment defence. Whether it would have succeeded must remain a mystery, as the BCA dropped their claim after the Court of Appeal decision on fair comment.

The statement must indicate what the opinion was based on

It must be clear to a reader what facts have led the defendant to make the comment. One reason for this requirement is that including some reference to the facts helps make it clear to a reader what is actually being said about the claimant. If, for example, an article says that someone is a liar, it is impossible to judge quite how serious a claim that is unless you are also given some idea of what they have lied about, and perhaps who they have lied to. To give an extreme example, it is not defamatory to say 'My mother told me my Christmas presents came from Santa. She is a liar', but it would be to say 'MP John Crooked says he has never cheated on his expenses. He is a liar'.

Again, this is a restatement of the previous law under the fair comment defence, and the explanatory notes to the Act state that it is designed to reflect the rule explained by the Supreme Court in ***Joseph* v *Spiller*** (2010), where the Supreme Court said that it is only necessary to identify 'in general terms what it is that has led the commentator to make the comment, so that the reader can understand what the comment is about'. It is not necessary, the Court said, to specify the facts in such a degree of detail that the reader could judge whether the comment was accurate.

The facts do not necessarily even have to be stated in the article; if the matter is something that the public generally know about, the background context will ensure that readers know what the comment refers to.

In *Lowe* v *Associated Newspapers* (2006), the *Evening Standard* published allegations about the Chairman of Southampton Football Club, concerning his acquisition of the club, and his sacking of the then manager. These events had happened some years earlier. The facts on which the comments were based were not stated in the article, but Mr Justice Eady said that they were known to the public and football fans would certainly have been aware of them, so it was not necessary for them to be stated alongside the comment. It was enough that readers could tell what was being said was a comment; they did not need to have enough information to judge whether the comment was accurate.

An honest person could hold the opinion on existing facts or privileged material

This effectively means the opinion must be a reasonable one; if the jury come to the conclusion that no one could honestly hold the opinion expressed, the defence will fail, even if in fact the defendant did honestly hold that opinion.

In addition to this provision, s3(5) states that the defence will not apply where the claimant can show that the defendant did not honestly hold the opinion they expressed (even if it was an opinion that an honest person could have come to). If you are wondering how the claimant could possibly prove that the defendant did not hold a particular opinion, the answer is that they will simply bring evidence that suggests this. For example, if someone publishes a very bad review of a restaurant, and there is evidence that the journalist and the restaurant owner have a history of falling out, that might suggest that the journalist did not honestly think the food was terrible, but simply wanted to annoy the restaurant owner and damage their reputation. It is then up to the jury to decide whether, despite that evidence, they believe the defendant's claim that he or she did hold the opinion that was published, or whether the claimant's evidence leads the jury to believe that that is a lie.

Note that the comment need not necessarily be based on facts; it can also be based on 'a privileged statement' that was already published. The Act defines 'a privileged statement' in s3(7) as a statement which would be covered by any one of four defences listed in the Act:

- responsible publication on a matter of public interest;
- peer-reviewed statement in a scientific or academic journal;
- absolute privilege applying to a report of court proceedings; or
- qualified privilege under s15 of the Defamation Act 1952.

We will look at all these defences later in this chapter, but the key thing to note at this stage is that all of them can apply to material which is not factually true or accurate. This means that the honest opinion defence can apply where someone makes a comment or states an opinion, even where that opinion turns out to be based on an untruth.

If you are basing your comment on facts, however, those facts must be true. So, if you say 'Millionaire actor Joe Dollars has abandoned his sick old father in a seedy nursing home. He is cold, hard and unfeeling', and the claim about abandoning his father is true, then your view that he is 'cold, hard and unfeeling' should be covered by the defence of fair comment.

However, if in fact Mr Dollars is paying to have his father looked after in the lap of luxury (regardless of whether or not you knew that), you will not be covered.

In 2006, chef Gordon Ramsey sued the *Evening Standard* over a TV review which criticised his television programme, *Ramsey's Kitchen Nightmares*. On the programme, the chef works with the owners of failing restaurants to help them turn their businesses around, and the review alleged that some of the scenes were faked to give a misleading impression of the state of the business. Reviews will usually be covered by fair comment, but, because in this case the factual allegations were untrue, the newspaper lost the case and had to pay £75,000 in damages.

In ***Levi*** v ***Bates*** (2009), the chairman of Leeds United, Ken Bates, tried to use fair comment as a defence when he was sued by a former director of the club. Mr Bates had written a series of articles in the Leeds United matchday programme about Mr Levi's role in Mr Bates' attempts to buy the club, which essentially accused Mr Levi of being dishonourable and dishonest. The court found that, although much of the defamatory material was comment rather than fact, the articles as a whole were 'riddled' with serious factual inaccuracies, and those facts that were true were not sufficient to form a factual basis for the comments. The defence therefore failed.

The defence can only be based on facts that existed at the time of publication

The 2013 Act also adds a new provision applying to anyone who has published the comment, but was not the author of it. Under s3(6), someone in this position is unable to use the defence if the claimant can show that they knew or ought to have known that the author did not hold the opinion they expressed. This might apply, for example, if a newspaper published an interview with someone who said that a particular restaurant's food was terrible, but who in fact did not genuinely believe that but had a grudge against the chef. If the newspaper was aware of that, it could not successfully use the defence. Similarly, if you publish a comment by an interviewee that you know or ought to have known was not their real opinion, you would not be covered. The jury cannot know, of course, what you or the person expressing the opinion believed, but they will draw a conclusion on this from the evidence.

Types of statement covered by honest opinion

The previous defence, honest comment/fair comment, only covered comments on matters of public interest. This is no longer the case, and honest opinion can apply to comments about any subject. Because it deals with opinion, it is the usual defence to use for claims about reviews of anything from restaurants to plays, but it can be used anywhere where the material published was in the nature of an opinion, a point of view or a comment, rather than an allegation of fact.

The previous case law makes it clear that even very rude and critical reviews could be covered by the previous defence; this should still be the case, but bear in mind that it is now necessary to show that an honest person could have held the opinion on the facts.

In ***Ciarnan Convery*** v ***Irish News*** (2008), the *Irish News* published a damning review of Goodfellas, a restaurant in Belfast, which among other things, described the cola as 'warm and watery', and a main course of chicken marsala as 'inedible'. The restaurant sued, and the newspaper put forward the defence of fair comment, but lost. On appeal, however, the Northern Ireland Court of Appeal said comment does not have to be moderate in order to be protected: it can be strong, or even grossly exaggerated, so long as it reflects an opinion that is honestly held. The Court said that it was likely that a properly directed jury would have accepted the defence of fair comment (as it was called then), but as it could not be certain, the case should be retried. Mr Convery was refused permission to appeal to the House of Lords and it appears that the case is not going to be retried.

In ***Burstein* v *Associated Newspapers*** (2007), the case concerned a review in the *London Evening Standard* of an opera about suicide bombers. The reviewer described the opera as 'horribly leaden and un-musical' and concluded, 'I found the tone depressingly anti-American, and the idea that there is anything heroic about suicide bombers is, frankly, a grievous insult'. The composer sued for defamation, claiming that the review implied that he sympathised with terrorist causes, and considered suicide bombers to be heroes. The Court of Appeal threw the case out, saying that it was very clear that the facts referred to in the review were accurate, and the opinions the reviewer formed on the basis of those facts were ones which could be honestly held.

In ***David Soul* v *Matthew Wright*** (2001), Mr Wright reviewed a play that David Soul was acting in, and called it 'without doubt the worst West End show'. He was unable to plead fair comment (as it was called then) as he had not actually been to see the play, and therefore had no facts to base his comment on. He paid damages of £20,000.

Absolute privilege

The defence of absolute privilege exists because there are some circumstances where freedom of speech is considered more important than protection of reputation. Where absolute privilege applies to the occasion on which words were spoken, no claim for defamation can be made against the person who says them, no matter how defamatory the words, whether they were true or false, or what motivated the speaker to say what they did. For example, proceedings in Parliament are subject to absolute privilege, so during a Parliamentary session, an MP can say anything at all, about anyone (not just other MPs), and even if it is completely untrue, they cannot be sued for defamation. The remarks can also be repeated in the official daily reports of Parliament, known as Hansard, and in reports published by order of Parliament (such as White Papers). However, that does not mean that you have quite the same freedom in reporting what MPs say in Parliament, as *reports* of Parliamentary proceedings are only covered by qualified privilege, which is subject to certain conditions (see p. 259).

There is, however, one circumstance where journalist's reports are covered by absolute privilege, and that is court reports. The reason for this is fairly obvious: by their nature, court proceedings tend to involve people making serious allegations against others, some of which may be untrue. It would not be possible for papers to report court proceedings if they could be sued for repeating those allegations, and since there is clearly a public interest in people knowing what goes on in the courts, absolute privilege makes this possible. It means that the media can, within the rules of the defence, safely publish defamatory statements made in any court established under the law of a country or territory outside the UK, and any international court or tribunal established by the Security Council of the United Nations or by an international agreement (the UK is not required to be a party).

Not every report of a case in these courts is covered by absolute privilege. To qualify for absolute privilege, reports must be:

- fair,
- accurate, and
- contemporaneous.

Fairness

To be considered fair, a court report must present both sides of the case, and avoid appearing to endorse or give extra weight to the arguments of one party or the other. A court case can last for days, or even months, so separate reports of each day may be carried during the progress of the case. This can mean that if, for example, a whole day (or longer) is spent by the prosecution examining its key witness, the report of that day is likely to reflect largely the prosecution's case. This is not a problem, so long as what you write fairly reflects what is said in court that day. Equally, an evening paper may report what was said in court that day up until the paper went to press, and report evidence given later in the following day's edition.

What you should not do is give a one-sided presentation of what was said in court, for example, by leaving out sections of the evidence presented. Such a report will not be considered fair, so the newspaper or broadcaster carrying it risks losing the protection of privilege, and in many cases no other defence will be available. Equally, if you have previously reported potentially defamatory allegations, and later in the trial those allegations are rebutted, you should report the evidence rebutting the allegations.

Accuracy

Court reports need not be word-for-word accounts of what was said in court, and you will usually need to summarise evidence, but it is essential that your summary accurately reflects what was said. For key or controversial points, it is often better to quote the witness directly.

There are certain areas of court reporting which can be a minefield for the unwary:

- **Allegations:** Make sure you do not report allegations as facts – in other words, if a witness, Jeannie Brown, says she saw the defendant, Joe Bloggs, running from the scene, you should write 'Jeannie Brown said she saw Bloggs running away', rather than 'Jeannie Brown saw Bloggs running away'. This is especially important in headlines, where it is tempting to choose the shorter, snappier version.
- **Names:** Unless you are reporting a high-profile case where everyone knows who the characters involved are, it is surprisingly easy to slip up and call the defendant by the name of one of the witnesses, or someone else involved in the case, especially if the names are similar. Doing this could put you at serious risk of being sued by the person you name. The same could apply if, in a civil case, you mix up the names of the claimant and the defendant, so always double-check you have used the right names. Addresses are also important – give the wrong one and you could face a claim from the person living there.
- **Verdicts:** Reporting that someone has been convicted when they have been acquitted, or that a defendant has lost a civil case when in fact they have won it obviously lays you open to a defamation claim. As well as guarding against this simple but dangerous factual mistake, you should also avoid any statement that tends to suggest that a person should have been convicted, or was guilty and got away with it.
- **Offences:** It can be defamatory to suggest that someone was convicted of a more serious offence than they actually were. In some cases a defendant will be charged with more than one offence, and convicted of some but acquitted of others; it is essential to get the details right.
- **Sentences:** It can be defamatory to suggest someone has received a more severe sentence than they actually have.

Contemporaneous

The requirement that reports must be contemporaneous essentially means that they should be published in the first issue or broadcast following the proceedings, so the exact time scale will depend on the frequency of publication. Broadcasters would be expected to cover court proceedings the same evening, and daily papers the following day, while an evening paper might start reporting a case in its first edition and add to the story in later ones, carrying the remainder of the events in court the following day. What about court reports which are published on the internet, and may therefore remain accessible for a long time after a trial is over? In ***Arthur Bennett* v *Newsquest*** (2006), it was stated that, although absolute privilege could not apply, qualified privilege (see p. 259) would, as long as the initial publication was contemporaneous.

In some cases the court may place restrictions on reporting a particular trial. The Defamation Act 1996 provides that once these restrictions are lifted, court reports should be published as soon as practically possible, in order to be viewed as contemporaneous.

Limits of the defence

Privilege only covers reports of the court proceedings themselves. If someone from the public gallery shouts out a defamatory remark, or if someone involved makes comments on the way into or out of court, these are not part of the court proceedings and you will not be protected by privilege if you report them. Nor does absolute privilege cover reports of the contents of documents seen by the judge or magistrate but not read in open court. However, the Defamation Act 1996 extends qualified privilege (see below) to fair and accurate copies of or extracts from documents 'made available by a court'.

Qualified privilege

Like absolute privilege, qualified privilege protects statements made in certain circumstances where free speech is considered to be in the public interest. It applies to a broader range of situations than absolute privilege does, but is subject to one important restriction: it will only cover statements made without malice. (For the meaning of malice as regards qualified privilege, see p. 259.) As with absolute privilege, it also requires that reports are fair and accurate.

The occasions to which qualified privilege applies are:

- a set list of official and public proceedings, decisions and documents, detailed in Schedule 1 of the Defamation Act 1996 (see Appendix 3);
- judicial proceedings in the UK;
- the proceedings of Parliament;
- occasions where someone is defending themselves against a previous attack on their character or conduct;
- publication of scientific and academic material, within certain rules.

The first of the above occasions is often called statutory qualified privilege, because it was defined in the Defamation Act 1996, while the rest are qualified privilege under common law (because the rules were made through cases decided in the courts, not by Parliament – see p. 6).

Qualified privilege under the Defamation Act 1996

Schedule 1 of the Defamation Act 1996, as amended by the Defamation Act 2013, lists the types of statement which are covered by statutory qualified privilege. These fall into two groups, one of which has slightly more restrictions on its protection than the other. The first group, listed in Part I of Schedule 1 to the Act (see Appendix 3), are statements which have qualified privilege without explanation or contradiction. These include:

- fair and accurate reports of proceedings in public of any legislature anywhere in the world (including the UK Parliament);
- fair and accurate reports of proceedings held in public in any court in the world (this provision protects non-contemporaneous reports which would not be covered by absolute privilege, and that includes mention of any spent convictions (see p. 231);
- fair and accurate reports of public enquiries set up by a legislature or government anywhere in the world;
- fair and accurate reports of proceedings in public held by an international organisation or international conference.
- fair and accurate copies or extracts from material published by a government or legislature anywhere in the world.

The second group, listed in Part II of Schedule 1, are described as 'privileged subject to explanation or contradiction'. This means that statements in the categories on this list are covered by qualified privilege, but that privilege can be lost if a person defamed by a statement supplies a reasonable explanation or contradiction of the statement, and requests its publication, and that request is refused. The list includes:

- fair and accurate reports of any public meeting or sitting held in the UK by
  - a local authority or local authority committee,
  - a magistrate or magistrates acting otherwise than as a court,
  - a commission, tribunal, committee or person appointed for the purposes of any enquiry by statutory provision or by Her Majesty or by a Minister of the Crown or a Northern Ireland Department,
  - a local inquiry held under statutory provisions,
  - any other tribunal, board, committee or body set up by and exercising functions under statutory provisions;
- fair and accurate reports of any general meeting of a UK listed company;
- fair and accurate copies extracts or summaries of documents made available by a court anywhere in the world, or a court officer or judge;
- fair and accurate copies or extracts or summaries of 'matter issued for the information of the public' by
  - the EU Parliament or any EU legislature (including the UK Parliament),
  - the government of any member state, or any authority exercising governmental functions in any member state (this includes local councils and the police),
  - any international organisation or international conference;
- fair and accurate reports of any public meeting held anywhere in the world: the Act defines a public meeting quite widely, as 'a meeting bona fide and lawfully held for a lawful purpose and for the furtherance or discussion of a matter of public interest, whether admission to the meeting is general or restricted'.
- fair and accurate reports of a press conference held anywhere in the world to discuss a matter of public interest. In the case of ***McCartan Turkington Breen* v *Times Newspapers***

(2001), the court stated that press releases given out at a press conference are also covered, even if they were not read out at the time, and as the change made by the 2013 Act was intended to put the *McCartan* decision in statutory form, it would seem this still applies.

This is an edited version of Part II of Schedule 1, and there are other important categories – you can read the full list in Appendix 3.

Contradictions and explanation: If you publish a story covered by qualified privilege 'subject to contradiction or explanation', and someone asks you to publish a contradiction or explanation, it must be published 'in a suitable manner'. The Act defines this as either in the same manner as the original story or in a manner that is 'adequate and reasonable in the circumstances'. In other words, if you splash a story over the front page, and then carry the denial or explanation in a tiny para tucked away at the bottom of page 8, you are unlikely to keep the protection of the defence.

Watch out, however, for any possibility of defamation in the explanation or contradiction itself. Take, for example, a situation where, in a general meeting of a public company, one of the directors, John Green, makes a defamatory comment about the boss of a rival company, Sarah Black. Provided that you act without malice and publish a fair and accurate report of the meeting, you are covered by qualified privilege for repeating his statement. Sarah Black then demands to have a letter published, refuting the allegations made, and making a defamatory allegation of her own about John Green. If you do not publish her contradiction of John Green's statement, you will lose the protection of qualified privilege, but if you publish her statement and include the defamatory allegation, John Green may be able to sue you for libel. In some cases like this you may be covered by qualified privilege at common law, but if you find yourself in this situation, it is worth taking legal advice to make sure you cover yourself either way.

Official information: Note that the type of material covered without explanation or contradiction is limited to material issued by the relevant body, reports, copies or extracts. Summaries are not covered in this section, though they are in some cases in Part II. Material must also be 'matter issued for the information of the public' so leaked information would not be covered.

What counts as 'matter? Clearly, published documents, consultation papers, speeches and press releases will count, but what about answers to questions you put to government officials? In ***Blackshaw* v *Lord*** (1984), the courts said these could in some circumstances be considered to be 'matter issued for the information of the public', but would not always be so. You may therefore want to seek advice before relying on this defence when publishing defamatory statements made by government officials (including the police) which are not published in writing.

Reporting proceedings: A number of the statutory provisions relate to reports of 'proceedings' of various types of official and public organisations. When reporting these, it is important to remember that (as with court reporting) only the proceedings themselves are covered by privilege. Anything said before or after proceedings by anyone involved in them, even if this is merely to expand on or explain what is said during the proceedings, or said during proceedings by anyone not officially involved (such as protestors or spectators) is not covered by the provisions of the Defamation Act (though of course there may be another defence available, including qualified privilege from common law). Similarly, if reporting on an official document, bear in mind that qualified privilege will only cover the actual words of the document and not, for example, anything said about it, even by someone involved in producing it.

Judicial proceedings

As we have seen, fair, accurate and contemporaneous court reports carry absolute privilege. Qualified privilege applies to fair and accurate court reports which do not have absolute privilege because they are not published contemporaneously.

Proceedings of Parliament

As explained earlier, MPs have absolute privilege for anything they say during Parliamentary sessions. Under common law, there is qualified privilege for fair and accurate reports of those statements.

Where a report mixes material said on any of the privileged occasions listed above with other comment, qualified privilege may still apply to the material said on the privileged occasion, but will be lost if the piece taken as a whole lacks the necessary qualities of fairness and accuracy that the privilege protects.

In *Curistan* v *Times Newspapers* (2007), the case involved a newspaper story about an MP's speech in Parliament, which said that the claimant had been involved in laundering money for the IRA. These remarks were clearly privileged but the newspaper story mixed them with other allegations, stating that there were irregularities in his business accounts. If qualified privilege had not applied, the effect would be that the paper was liable for repeating the MP's allegation that Mr Curistan was money laundering for the IRA. However, the Court of Appeal held that the defence could still apply. The story as a whole was a mixture of a privileged report and additional material produced by the newspaper's own investigation and, in principle, such a mixture was legitimate. The privilege that would ordinarily apply to the report element would not be lost simply because the newspaper had published additional material, but only if the report as a whole was materially inaccurate, 'intermingled extraneous material', or amounted to the paper putting forward the allegations made in Parliament as true. The court was satisfied that the report was sufficiently accurate and Mr Robinson's claims had not been 'adopted' as true by the newspaper. Therefore, the report element of the article was still privileged.

Reply to character attacks

If someone has been the subject of allegations which attack their character or conduct, and in response to that attack, they make a defamatory statement, they will be covered by qualified privilege, and so will a publication or broadcast which carries their reply. However, privilege only applies to such words as are necessary to address the specific allegations that have been made against them.

In *Adam* v *Ward* (1917), the claimant was an MP who, in Parliament, made a vindictive statement about a general in his former regiment. Although the statement was defamatory, the general could not sue, because the statement was covered by absolute privilege. The Secretary to the Army Council issued a statement defending the general against the attack, which was published by several newspapers. The statement was defamatory of the MP, and he sued. The House of Lords held that the secretary was protected by qualified privilege, because he had a duty to defend the general's reputation.

Peer-reviewed statements in scientific or academic journals

Section 6 of the Defamation Act 2013 introduces new protection for certain types of academic and scientific material. This provision was introduced in response to controversy about a number of defamation claims brought in recent years against scientists and science writers, which were seen as attempts by business and large organisations to silence criticism of their products and services, which the writers argued were part of legitimate academic and scientific debate.

The new defence applies to statements published in scientific or academic journals, where:

- the statement relates to a scientific or academic matter; and
- before it was published, an independent review of the statement's scientific or academic merit was carried out by the editor of the journal, and at least one person with expertise in the subject concerned. This is a process known as 'peer review' which is used by all serious academic and scientific journals, and is designed to make sure that any research has been done properly and conclusions reached are valid.

The defence not only protects the original statement published in a scientific or academic journal, but also offers the same protection to two further types of publication related to it:

- an assessment of the statement's scientific or academic merit, if written by one or more of the people who carried out the independent review of it, and written in the course of that review; and
- publication of a fair and accurate copy of extract from or summary of the statement, or the above-mentioned assessment of it.

Malice and qualified privilege

Qualified privilege, whether statutory or common law, will only be available if the publication is made without malice. A journalist will be said to have acted with malice if they were motivated to write what they did by spite or ill feeling towards their subject, or with any other improper motive. Evidence that the journalist did not believe what they were writing was true may be evidence of malice, but, equally, a journalist who writes a defamatory statement for improper motives may be judged to have acted with malice even if they believed that what they wrote was true. This is because the purpose of the defence of qualified privilege is to help the media do its traditional duty of informing the public about important issues. A journalist who says something defamatory for reasons other than doing that duty cannot be covered by the defence.

Publication on a matter of public interest

The Defamation Act 2013 introduces a new defence of publication on a matter of public interest, which is based on and replaces a previous common law defence, the ***Reynolds*** defence. It has the same purpose as the ***Reynolds*** defence, which is to protect the media when they report matters of public interest in a responsible way, even if what is said actually turns out to be untrue. You might wonder why there should be protection for reports that are untrue; the reason is that it can be very difficult, especially when dealing with powerful people and organisations, to prove than an allegation is true, especially as a story will often only be newsworthy for a short length of time, so there will be time pressures on journalists to get it out. Requiring the media to be able to prove, to the satisfaction of a court, that every allegation is true before they publish would invariably mean that some important – and true – stories would never get published at all, as well as that some false ones would be prevented from being published. The defence tips the balance in favour of freedom of expression, by allowing that it is better for the law to allow some untrue stories be published, if that means that important true stories are not suppressed because they cannot be proved. This is in turn balanced by the fact that the media will only be protected if they have behaved responsibly in the circumstances.

The new defence is contained in s4 of the Act, and applies where a defendant can show that:

- the statement complained of was, or was part of, a statement on a matter of public interest, and
- the defendant reasonably believed that publication was in the public interest.

In assessing these two issues, the court must 'have regard to all the circumstances of the case', and in determining whether it was reasonable to believe that publication was in the public interest, it must make 'such allowance for editorial judgement as it considers appropriate.'

The Explanatory Notes to the Defamation Bill state that, as the new statutory defence is based on the old ***Reynolds*** defence, the courts will be expected to take previous case law on the ***Reynolds*** defence into consideration when applying it. In ***Reynolds*** itself, the House of Lords established a set of criteria against which articles could be judged, and it seems likely that similar criteria will be used when the court considers 'all the circumstances of the case'. The ***Reynolds*** criteria are:

1. **The seriousness of the allegation.** This issue can be a double-edged sword: the more serious the allegation, the greater the care the press must show in handling it but, on the other hand, if an allegation is not especially serious, it may be of insufficient public interest to be covered by the defence.
2. **The nature of the information, and the extent to which it is the subject of public concern.**
3. **The source of the information.** Important issues here will include whether the informants had direct knowledge of the events or not, whether they were being paid for their stories, and whether they had their own 'axes to grind'. Of course, many sources do divulge information out of personal spite or to get revenge, and this alone will not mean the defence cannot apply, but it does mean that the journalist has to work harder to check the information through other channels. Similarly, if a source has been paid, they cannot be seen as entirely unbiased, and it would be sensible not to use them as a sole source if you want to claim the public interest defence.
4. **The steps taken by the journalist to check the information.**
5. **The status of the information.** This factor concerns how authoritative the source of the information is. If an allegation has already been the subject of an authoritative investigation, for example, there would seem to be good reason why the public should be told about it. The Court of Appeal also mentioned government press releases, reports by the chairmen of public companies and the speeches of university vice-chancellors as examples of sources with authority. In effect, if someone in some kind of authority puts about a defamatory allegation, there is likely to be a public interest in it being published, so that it can be either acted on, or refuted if it is not true.
6. **The urgency of the matter.** This factor takes account of the fact that, as the Court of Appeal puts it, 'news is a perishable commodity'. Although the need to publish quickly will not excuse publishers from failing to make basic checks or attempt to get the other side of the story, the courts should take into account the fact that waiting too long can make it pointless to publish at all.
7. **Whether the claimant was asked to comment on the story.** To have any weight in supporting the defence, the claimant must have been given a fair chance to give a reasoned answer to the allegations. Pouncing on them in public and demanding an instant reply, or door-stepping

them, may not be considered to qualify as a fair chance. On the other hand, a claimant who makes themselves unavailable for comment, or who genuinely could not be contacted in time will not be able to argue that the defence does not apply for this reason. The fact that comment was refused or unattainable should be mentioned in the story.

8 **Whether the article included the claimant's side of the story, at least in general terms.** Again, the press will not be disadvantaged by this factor if the reason for not putting the other side of the story is that the claimant refused to give it. The way in which the claimant's side of the story is presented will be important; there is obviously a big difference in the protection the press can expect to get for stating the claimant's view and allowing claimants to speak for themselves and, for example, quoting the view in a context which suggests it is not to be believed.

9 **The tone of the article.** A story raising queries or suggesting an investigation may, the House of Lords implied, be more likely to be protected than one which presents all the allegations as a matter of fact, or sensationalises them.

10 **The circumstances of publication, including the timing.** This last factor allows the court to take into account other factors which seem relevant to the issue of whether the publisher has behaved responsibly.

The court said in ***Reynolds*** that this list was not necessarily exclusive and other factors might also be taken into account; the weight given to different factors would also vary from case to case. It also stated that in weighing up these factors, the courts should have regard to the importance of freedom of expression, and should be slow to conclude that a publication was not in the public interest, especially where information was already in the field of public discussion. In later cases the courts made it clear that the 10 steps detailed in ***Reynolds*** were a guideline to help the courts decide whether a publisher has behaved responsibly in reporting a matter of public interest. They were not intended to be a series of hurdles which publishers have to jump in order to use the defence, and the defence could apply where not all the ***Reynolds*** criteria have been fulfilled. The same will be true of the new statutory defence.

The following are some of the cases in which the ***Reynolds*** defence was applied, and which are likely to be a good guide to how the new defence will also be used.

In ***Reynolds*** v ***Times Newspapers*** (1999), the case in which the defence was established, the claim arose from a news story published by *The Times* about the former Taoiseach (Irish Prime Minister), Albert Reynolds, and the circumstances leading up to his resignation. Mr Reynolds claimed that the article suggested that he had deliberately misled the Irish parliament. The House of Lords agreed that the subject was one of legitimate public concern. On the other hand, the allegation made was a serious one yet the paper had not mentioned Mr Reynolds' explanation for the events concerned, even though this was available to it. As a result, the Lords found that the story was not covered by the defence.

In ***Bonnick*** v ***Morris*** (2002), a newspaper published a story about a state-owned Jamaican company, JCTC, entering into two contracts with another company, Prolacto. The claimant was employed by JCTC, but had left just after the second contract was agreed. The newspaper reported that the contracts were unusually advantageous to Prolacto, and that the claimant had left JCTC just after making the second contract. The claimant argued that this was defamatory, because it implied that he had acted improperly in arranging the contract, and that was why he had had to leave. The newspaper pointed out that it had approached JCTC for comments, but it had refused to say anything, and it had also spoken to the claimant, who had explained that there was nothing suspicious about the contracts and that they had no connection with his leaving the company. The court agreed that the article was defamatory, but said it was covered by the defence because the subject was a matter of public interest, and the paper had acted responsibly, particularly given that the story was not one which was obviously defamatory.

In *Grobbelaar* v *News Group Newspapers* (2001), the footballer Bruce Grobbelaar sued the *Sun* over reports that he had been paid to fix the results of matches he played in. The paper had been given a tip-off that Mr Grobbelaar had been involved in match-fixing, and had arranged for the source to tape a conversation in which he accepted money to fix a match, and admitted to doing so in the past. The resulting story took up several pages, with headlines screaming 'World exclusive – Grobbelaar took bribes to fix games' and 'I saved goal by mistake and lost £125,000'. Before the case came to court, Mr Grobbelaar was charged with two criminal offences related to match fixing, but was acquitted. The *Sun* pleaded qualified privilege, but the Court of Appeal held that qualified privilege did not apply. Among the factors which the Court said led to this decision included the facts that the main witness against the claimant was thoroughly unreliable, the newspaper had evidence from a world-class goalkeeper that suggested Mr Grobbelaar's performance on the pitch showed no signs of match-fixing, and that there was no real urgency for the paper to publish when it did. But the main factor was the tone and weight of the story, which appeared over several pages, for seven days, and asserted Mr Grobbelaar's guilt as a fact, rather than, for example, raising questions or asking for an investigation. (However, the result of the case was less of a disappointment for the paper; although Mr Grobbelaar won, the House of Lords reduced the £85,000 damages ordered by the jury to £1, in recognition of the fact that although it could not be proved that he fixed matches, he had admitted that he took bribes.)

In *Loutchansky* v *Times Newspapers Ltd (No. 2)* (2001), where *The Times* accused Russian businessman Grigori Loutchansky of being involved in serious crime, the paper claimed qualified privilege because, it said, the subject was one of public concern, and the story was based on authoritative sources, including reports by the CIA and British intelligence services. *The Times* initially lost and appealed, and the resulting series of appeals culminated in the Court of Appeal sending the case back to the original judge to reconsider in the light of the clarifications of the ***Reynolds*** defence. Second time round, the judge still found against the newspaper. Summarising the ***Reynolds*** defence, he said the question was whether the paper had behaved responsibly in publishing the articles. He agreed that the matter was one of public concern, but said that that the allegations made were very serious and potentially very damaging to Mr Loutchansky's reputation, and therefore demanded a high degree of care on the paper's part before publishing them. This standard had not been met: some of the sources were unsafe, while the allegations were vague and the paper had not made enough effort to check them. The paper had tried to contact Mr Loutchansky, but, the judge said, it should have tried harder, and, although the story stated that Mr Loutchansky had repeatedly denied the allegations, this bare statement did not amount to giving his side of the story.

In *GKR Karate (UK) Ltd* v *Yorkshire Post Newspapers* (2000), the free paper *Leeds Weekly News* was sued for a story which warned readers about doorstep salesmen pushing karate lessons. The story alleged that the firm used unqualified instructors, overcharged and, according to one of the people quoted, 'They just take people's money and then disappear.' Despite the seriousness of the allegations, the reporter's only attempt to get the company's side of the story was to leave a message with its answering service, and when it did not reply, the story was published without a company comment. In addition, she had contacted the local Trading Standards Office and been told that it had not had any complaints against the firm; she did not report this fact in the story. The judge said that there were legitimate concerns about the way the story was investigated, but overall, the subject was one of public concern in the area which the paper served, and that the reporter had based her story on what she honestly believed was reliable evidence. Therefore, the defence could apply.

In *Jameel* v *Wall Street Journal* (2006), the claimant sued over a story which claimed that the Saudi Arabian authorities were monitoring the bank accounts of prominent businesses (including his) for evidence of links to terrorism. The paper claimed the ***Reynolds*** defence, but although they had checked the information thoroughly, they had not sought comment from the claimant. The House of Lords held that this did not mean the defence failed; the ***Reynolds*** criteria were pointers, not a series of hurdles which all had to be jumped. The key question was whether the subject was one of public interest, and the defendant had acted fairly and responsibly in gathering and publishing the information, and in this case they had. Where the complaint of defamation referred to a particular element of the story, rather than the whole thing, the inclusion of an inaccurate fact in a story which was responsibly researched and in the public interest would not mean that the defence could not apply.

In ***Charman* v *Orion and McLagan*** (2007), Mr McLagan was the author of a book called *Bent Coppers*, which suggested that there were grounds for suspecting Mr Charman, a former police officer, of corruption. Mr Charman had been charged with discreditable conduct and dismissed from the Metropolitan Police in 2004, but always denied any wrongdoing, and claimed that the book was libellous. In the High Court, the ***Reynolds*** defence was dismissed, on the grounds that Mr McLagan's personal opinion of Chapman had led him to present a distorted view of some of the evidence. However, in the Court of Appeal, the decision was reversed, and it was held that the ***Reynolds*** defence protected the allegations made in the book. Lord Justice Ward accepted that the book was 'hardly a neutral, disinterested report', but said that it was responsible journalism on a matter of clear public interest, and so fell under the ***Reynolds*** defence. Quoting comments made by the judges in ***Jameel,*** he went on to say that 'We need more such serious journalism in this country and our defamation law should encourage rather than discourage it' and 'The fact that the judge, with the advantage of leisure and hindsight, might have made a different editorial decision should not destroy the defence. That would make the publication of articles which are, *ex hypothesi,* in the public interest, too risky and would discourage investigative reporting.' The case also established that the ***Reynolds*** defence applies to books, as well as news coverage.

In ***Flood* v *Times Newspapers*** (2012), the claimant was a police officer who, *The Times* reported, was being investigated over allegations that he had taken bribes from suspected Russian criminals, in exchange for information about Home Office attempts to extradite them. The background to the story was that an informant had reported the allegations to the paper, and to the police, and when the journalists looked into the claims, they found reason to believe that the police were not investigating them. They then approached the claimant and others with the allegations, which caused a police investigation to begin. The paper reported both the allegations and the investigation. The investigation eventually found that there was no evidence for the allegations. *The Times* claimed the ***Reynolds*** defence, arguing that it was in the public interest to publish the fact that a senior police officer was being investigated for corruption. The claimant argued that although the subject matter of the story was of public interest, publishing details of the actual allegations against him, without checking whether they were true, took the story outside the defence, because those matters were not in the public interest. The Supreme Court rejected this argument. They said that the story was of serious public importance, and the allegations were an essential part of the story. They were published with the legitimate aim of getting the allegations investigated, where there was good reason to believe this was not happening. Lord Philips said that as the police officer was not a public figure, it could be argued that it was not in the public interest to name him but, on the facts, it would not have been possible to report the story without doing so, so the defence was not lost for that part.

Note that when assessing whether a newspaper behaved responsibly in publishing a story, the approach of the courts has been to consider only the information that was available up to the point of publication. In ***Loutchansky,*** new evidence came to light after publication which *The Times* said helped its case, but the courts said this evidence could not be taken into account. This seems likely to continue, and means that the courts are not looking at whether publication was reasonable in the light of all the facts about the story, but whether, on the information it had at the time, the newspaper acted responsibly.

In ***David Hunt* v *Times Newspapers*** (2013), which was decided shortly before the 2013 Act came into force, the story which gave rise to the case exposed the claimant as a 'crime lord', with a vast criminal network involved in drugs, murder and fraud, even though he had not been convicted of these offences. In deciding that the defence applied, the judge said that key factors were that the information on which the story was based came from sources that the journalist was entitled to consider to be reliable and knowledgeable, that the journalist honestly believed the allegations to be true, and that he behaved fairly and responsibly in gathering the information and ensuring that what was published was accurate and fair. It was also important that the story was 'a serious piece of investigative journalism which was expressed in forthright but not extravagant terms, and without tangential additions in order to liven up the story'. The judge also commented that the journalist's decision to ask for the claimant's reaction just before publication and through his solicitor was 'not ideal', but said that it was however clear that the claimant actually knew quite a lot about what was about to be published and had made a deliberate decision not to offer any comment.

Neutral reports of disputes

The old ***Reynolds*** defence also gave rise to what was referred to as a 'sub-species' of itself, which came to be called neutral reportage. It applied to reports on matters of public interest, where defamatory allegations were presented in a completely neutral manner, so that the report was essentially reporting the fact that the allegations had been made, rather than suggesting that they were or might be true. As a form of the ***Reynolds*** defence, neutral reportage has been abolished by the Defamation Act 2013, but the Act retains a provision which will have broadly the same effect. Section 4 (3) provides that where a defamatory statement was, or formed part of, an accurate and impartial account of a dispute involving the claimant, a court has to disregard any failure by the defendant to take steps to verify the truth of the allegations contained in the statement. The Explanatory Notes to the Act state that this means that, where a report fits within the category of neutral reportage, in that it gives a balanced picture and reports allegations without suggesting that they are definitely true, the defence can apply even if the defendant did not attempt to check that the information was true.

The following two cases are examples of the kind of situation where this form of the defence applies.

In ***Al-Fagih* v *HH Saudi Research Marketing (UK) Ltd*** (2001), a Saudi Arabian politician, Saad Al-Fagih, sued an Arabic newspaper over a story in which it reported a defamatory allegation that one of his political opponents had made about him. The newspaper had made no attempt to check whether the allegation was true, but had simply reported neutrally what the other man said; it had not suggested that the words were true. The Court of Appeal said that, although the media would normally have to make efforts to verify information reported if they wanted to claim qualified privilege, there were cases where the public interest in publication outweighed that requirement. In this case it was in the public interest that disputes between politicians were made public and, in addition, the newspaper had acted responsibly in making it clear where the allegation came from, and in presenting it as neutral 'reportage' rather than allegations of fact.

In ***Roberts* v *Gable*** (2007), the anti-fascist magazine *Searchlight* published a story about a dispute between factions within the British National Party (BNP). It reported that the BNP newsletter had alleged that three members stole money from a BNP organiser, and that an open letter published by a faction within the BNP newsletter had claimed that one of the claimants had returned this money, and both claimants, who were BNP candidates, had threatened violence against various other BNP members. The claimants were not given a chance to comment on the story, and no steps were taken to verify the allegations, and so they applied for a ruling that the magazine could not plead qualified privilege. The Court of Appeal refused, stating that the BNP was a political party and therefore the 'goings-on' within it were a matter of public interest. The magazine did not endorse or adopt the allegations, and the fact that the piece was written in a sarcastic tone and there was an element of delight at the BNP's problems did not mean that the reportage defence could not apply.

The public interest defence and archive material

Sometimes a story will be covered by the public interest defence at the time it is published, but later events may change the position. In this situation, archive material available online should be amended to reflect the change. The purpose of the defence is to protect responsible journalism on matters of public interest, and for that reason, it can cover statements which the publisher cannot prove to be true. However, this protection will not be extended to stories which are left online after the situation changes and the publisher knows that the accusations in them are false.

In *Flood* v *Times Newspapers Ltd* (2009), the case referred to above about a police officer said to have been investigated for corruption, the story was left on *The Times* website after the investigation had cleared the complainant. The Court of Appeal upheld the High Court decision that the online publication was not covered by the ***Reynolds*** defence, because leaving the story there without amending it could not be described as responsible journalism.

Offer of amends

The Defamation Act 1996 provides a special defence of 'offer of amends', which is available only where the publisher of defamatory words:

- did not know or have reason to believe that the words could be taken to refer to the claimant; and
- did not know that the words were false and defamatory of that person.

In other words, the defence is intended to be used in cases where the publisher has simply made a mistake. However, the court will assume that the above conditions apply, unless the claimant proves that they do not (which is why some of the cases below do not seem to fit into this category; if a claimant is happy to accept an offer of amends, they will not seek to prove that the above circumstances do not apply). However, if a claimant does choose to challenge use of the defence, and can prove that you did know or have reason to believe the words referred to them, and you did know the words were false and defamatory, the defence is unavailable.

An offer of amends can be in relation to a statement generally, or to a specific defamatory meaning, in which case it is called a qualified offer. A qualified offer might be used, for example, where the statement made is true, but it carries an implication that is not true and is defamatory.

This defence is particularly useful for cases like ***Newstead* v *London Express Newspapers*** and ***O'Shea* v *MGN Ltd*** **(see p. 236)**, where stories have been published that are true of the person the publication intends them to refer to, but could be taken to refer to someone else (and are not true of that person).

In 2001, Channel 4 used the offer of amends defence in a case involving the comedy programme *Phoenix Nights*. It contained a character called Keith Lard, a Bolton fire safety officer, with a bushy moustache, who habitually wore a bright yellow safety jacket. Unknown to the writers of the programme, there was a real-life fire safety officer living in Bolton, called Keith Laird, who also had a bushy moustache and wore a yellow jacket. In itself this might not have been a problem, but the programme character also had a sexual interest in dogs, and so Mr Laird sued on the grounds that the programme referred to him and was defamatory. Channel 4 broadcast an apology and paid Mr Laird £10,000.

Using the defence

To use the defence of offer of amends, the publisher must offer to publish a suitable correction and apology, and to pay compensation. If a publisher wishes to choose this defence, it must make the offer before officially putting forward any other defence – it is not possible, for example, to enter another defence and then decide to make an offer of amends later if you think that your original defence might not succeed after all. The offer of amends procedure is designed to be a way for defendants to put right the damage they have done at an early stage, rather than a 'get out of jail card' to have up their sleeves if the case starts to look shaky.

The parties can either come to an agreement on a suitable amount of compensation, or the court can decide it for them. As a recognition of the publisher offering to make amends (rather than being forced to), the court will considerably reduce the amount of damages it would have ordered had the claimant sued and won.

If the offer is accepted, the defamation proceedings come to an end. If a publisher makes an offer of amends, but the claimant refuses it and continues with their claim, the publisher can use the offer of amends as a defence, provided the court accepts that it did not know or have reason to believe that the words published were untrue and defamatory of the claimant. If the publisher does this, it cannot put forward any other defence in addition. However, if it chooses to put forward a different defence, and loses the case, the offer of amends may still reduce the amount of damages awarded.

In ***Nail*** v ***News Group Newspapers Ltd*** (2004), HarperCollins had published an unauthorised biography of the actor Jimmy Nail, which made lurid allegations about his sexual behaviour. Mr Nail claimed damages of £70,000–£100,000, and rejected an offer of amends, which included damages of £37,500. Although he won his case, the judge awarded only £30,000, and said that defendants who tried to make amends were entitled to expect that the court would acknowledge that gesture by reducing the damages payable.

Importance of good conduct

Because the principle of the offer of amends is to allow publishers voluntarily to put right the damage done by defamatory remarks, the courts expect publishers who want to use this defence to behave courteously towards claimants, and to take action swiftly to put matters right, in a way which reflects the seriousness of the allegations. They do not look kindly on publishers whose behaviour suggests they are not actually sorry, and they may well show their displeasure in the damages ordered.

In ***Campbell-James*** v ***Guardian Media*** (2005), the claimant was a distinguished soldier who had spent many years serving in the Intelligence Corps. An article published in the *Guardian* falsely linked him to the much publicised abuse of prisoners in Iraq's Abu Ghraib prison, even though he was not in Iraq at the time. In addition to the obvious damage to his personal reputation, the allegations put the claimant and his family at serious risk of harm. When his lawyers contacted the *Guardian*, the paper initially claimed that its story was covered by fair comment and qualified privilege. It only made an offer of amends over two months after the article was published, and the published apology was less than generous. When the case went before the court to decide on suitable compensation, the judge was clearly disgusted by the paper's behaviour, saying that this was a case where the allegations should have been corrected immediately, not just as a matter of good journalistic practice, but of 'elementary human decency'. Although there is no set 'discount' for using the offer of amends procedure, previous cases have suggested that around 50 per cent is normal. In this case, in view of the circumstances, the judge allowed only 35 per cent off. This meant that the *Guardian* had to pay £58,500 instead of the £45,000 it might have expected if it had behaved more quickly and considerately.

In ***Turner*** v ***News Group Newspapers*** (2005), the claimant was featured in a ***News of the World*** story about wife-swapping, in which his ex-wife alleged that he had put pressure on her to have sex with other men. He twice wrote and complained to the editor, but received no reply, and an offer of amends was not offered until six months after the article was published; even then, the brief apology was, as the judge put it, 'tucked away' on page 36. The court held that in view of the dismissive way in which the complaint had been treated, the damages should only be discounted by 40 per cent. (The claimant, however, still believed this was unfair, as the damages ordered were only £9,000, but on appeal the award was allowed to stand.)

In *John Cleese* v *Evening Standard* (2004), the *Evening Standard* had published an apology to the actor and comedian John Cleese, over a story which claimed his career was in decline. They also offered £10,000 in damages. However, when the apology was printed, it was, Mr Cleese claimed, deliberately positioned in such a way that few readers would notice it, and out of proportion to the prominence given to the original story. In addition, the terms of the apology did not, he claimed, make it clear what had been wrong with the story. He went to court and was awarded £13,500.

In ***Veliu*** v ***Mazrekaj*** (2006), Mr Veliu was the subject of a story in an Albanian-language newspaper called *Bota Sot*, which is published from Switzerland but widely read in the UK. The article claimed he was involved in the bomb attacks in London on 7 July 2005 and was a friend of one of the bombers. In fact he did not know the bomber and had no connection with the attacks. The paper initially ignored Mr Veliu's complaints, and when an apology was finally published, it was brief and somewhat flippant, stating that the article 'does not have anything to do with the reality, but it's a pure fantasy'. The publisher made an offer of amends, and the case went to court to decide the issue of damages. The judge commented on the paper's mishandling of the complaint, and the misleading nature of the apology, especially in view of the fact that the allegations made were so serious and caused the claimant great distress. As a result, he allowed a discount of just 30 per cent and awarded damages of £175,000.

Accord and satisfaction

It is of course possible to print an apology even if the case is outside the rules of an offer of amends. Printing an apology or correction is not by itself a defence, but it can become one if the claimant accepts it and, in return, agrees not to sue. This is known as 'accord and satisfaction' or waiver of claim. It will only provide a defence if the person defamed expressly or by implication accepts it as putting an end to their claim.

In *Kaschke* v *Osler* (2010), an attempt to use the accord and satisfaction defence failed for lack of evidence that there was a binding agreement to end the claim. The claimant had complained about comments made about her on the defendant's blog, and he had offered her the right to put her side of the story on the blog. He claimed that her acceptance of this offer meant she had agreed not to pursue a legal claim, but the judge said there was nothing in the email correspondence between them that suggested she was giving up her right to sue.

Although written evidence of this acceptance is not required by law, clearly if someone tries to sue after they have accepted an apology, the publisher is on stronger ground if it can present a written statement by the claimant that they are accepting the apology in full and final settlement and waiving their rights to sue. However, if the complaint comes from the person who is the subject of the story, and not through a lawyer, it may well be the case that they had not considered suing and did not even realise that they could. In that situation, if you ask them to sign a waiver, they may well realise the potential seriousness of the case and consult a lawyer.

If you print a prompt and adequate apology and the claimant does not accept it as accord and satisfaction, but goes on to sue you and wins, the court may reduce the damages it orders in recognition of the apology, typically by as much as 50 per cent. It is important to know, however, that a badly handled apology can actually end up making things worse, so it is often worth getting legal advice at this stage.

Law in practice Problems with apologies and corrections

An inappropriate or carelessly worded apology can make things much worse. The following are some of the problems that you need to watch out for when printing apologies.

Defamatory apologies: It is very easy to defame someone else in the course of making an apology. Take, for example, a situation where you have quoted defamatory remarks made by someone else. If the subject of the remarks complains, and you print an apology saying that the words were untrue, you may be calling the source a liar, and if the original words are in fact true, that could be defamatory of them.

Making things worse: Be careful that the wording of your apology does not repeat the libel, or even worsen the impression given by the original article. In the *Stationery Trade* case, where the magazine was accused of suggesting that a company was selling counterfeit envelopes, the publication ran an apology which, the court said, made things worse. It repeated the previous headline 'Counterfeits – retailers warned' and said that the claimant company had told them their envelopes were 'now origin marked' so there was no chance of customers being misled. The court said this gave the impression that the company were not selling counterfeit envelopes now, but had been previously.

Damaging admissions: If you make an apology without the claimant agreeing to waive their claim as a result, you take the risk that, if you are sued for libel, the apology will be seen as an admission that what you published was untrue and/or defamatory.

Court report corrections: If an inaccurate remark is made in court proceedings and reported by the media, the publisher may be asked to correct it in print. However, the correction will not carry the same privilege as the original report, so if it is defamatory, the publication can be sued. In this situation the safest option is to ask the complainant to arrange to make a statement of correction in open court (their solicitor can arrange this), which the newspaper can then report.

Insufficient prominence: It can be tempting to tuck away an apology at the bottom of a column, well back in the paper, but this strategy may backfire, causing a complainant who might have taken things no further to decide to sue anyway. In 2010, TV presenter Peaches Geldof complained to the PCC about a story in the *Daily Star*, with the headline 'Peaches: spend the night with me for £5k'. The story was about the fee that Ms Geldof charges for public appearances, but she claimed that the headline implied she offered sexual services for money. The paper agreed to publish an apology, but not on the front page, as Ms Geldof wanted, but on page 2. The PCC held that the apology's size and position was proportionate to the story originally published, but Ms Geldof disagreed, and sued, so that she could make a statement in open court to clear her reputation. The paper ended up settling the case and paying substantial damages.

Your own reputation: If you do write a story which results in a libel claim, and your publishers decide to apologise, keep a close eye on the wording of it, since it could very easily damage your professional reputation if it suggests, for example, that you were careless. In such cases you may want to take legal advice yourself, and your union should be able to help with this.

Innocent dissemination and the live broadcast defence

As we saw earlier, a claimant in defamation can sue not only the writer of the defamatory words, but also almost anyone involved in the process of publishing them, right down to the distributors. The Defamation Act 1996, however, provides a defence for many of the parties in the publishing chain. Section 1 of the Act provides a defence known as innocent dissemination for anyone who:

- was not the author, editor or publisher of the defamatory statement; and
- took reasonable care in relation to its publication; and
- did not know or have reason to know that whatever part they played in the publication caused or contributed to the publication of a defamatory statement.

The Act lists people who, for the purposes of this defence, are not considered to be the publisher of a defamatory statement, including printers, distributors, sellers and internet service providers (the last only applies to the services that host websites, and not those who post content online). The defence has been strengthened by a provision in s10 of the Defamation Act 2013, which states that the courts cannot hear claims against 'a person who was not the author, editor or publisher', unless it is not reasonably practicable to bring an action against the author, editor or publisher.

The innocent dissemination defence also applies in broadcasting, where it is more often known as the defence of live broadcast. It will apply where a programme is broadcast live, and a defamatory remark is made by someone over whom the broadcaster cannot effectively have control, such as an interviewee, or a viewer phoning in. However, broadcasters, like publishers, can only plead this defence if they have taken all reasonable care to avoid the risk of defamation (see the *Law in practice* box, below). It will not usually be available where a defamatory remark is made by a presenter, because a presenter would be regarded as being under the control of the broadcaster.

In 1999 the market research organisation MORI sued the BBC over a live radio interview by politician Sir James Goldsmith in which he claimed MORI was 'inefficient or dishonest', used out-of-date polls, and used its work to pursue a political agenda. It was argued in court that Sir James had a reputation for plain speaking that should have made the BBC realise he might well say something defamatory, and therefore it should have used a delay button. The case was settled out of court.

Law in practice Defamation in live broadcasts

As explained above, the defence of innocent dissemination, more often known as live broadcast, can protect a broadcaster where defamatory remarks are made live on air by someone who does not work for the broadcasting company. To make sure that you can take advantage of this defence, you need to be able to show that you took all reasonable care to avoid the risk of libel.

- Choose interviewees carefully. If you do include someone whose reputation, personality or views on the subject under discussion suggest they might be a risk, the MORI case suggests that it would be wise to use a delay button, which provides a few seconds between the words being said and being broadcast, so the offending remark can be bleeped.
- Talk to guests beforehand about any contentious subjects, so you know their views and are aware of where problems could arise. Brief interviewees about any areas they should avoid discussing, and, if there is a subject to be discussed that could lead to defamatory remarks, ask that they stick to known facts, and avoid speculating about things that may or may not have happened, or other people's motives.
- Be careful when reading out texts or emails from listeners. If a presenter reads these out, or they are shown on screen, the broadcaster can be liable for any defamatory content in them.

If an interviewee does say something potentially defamatory, move the conversation on to a different subject immediately, without drawing attention to the defamatory remark, and make sure that the rest of the conversation stays away from the risky area. Don't repeat or refer back to the statement (even to say that it isn't true). When a defamatory remark has been made on air, it is sensible to get legal advice as soon as possible after the programme, as swift action at that point could avoid a legal action.

Time limits and repeat actions

Under the Defamation Act 1996, defamation claims must be brought within a year of publication; a claim brought after this limitation period is said to be out of time, which gives the publisher a complete defence. However, the courts have discretion to extend the limitation period, and have proved to be more ready to do this for defamation claims than in many other types of case. If a claimant applies for an extension of the limitation period, the court will balance the reasons for their delay against any disadvantage the delay will cause the defendant (e.g. difficulties in finding witnesses).

REMEDIES FOR DEFAMATION

There are two main remedies for defamation:

- damages;
- injunctions.

Damages

As we have seen, the most common remedy for libel is damages. In cases which are heard by juries, they decide the damages as well as the verdict (in contrast to criminal cases, where juries decide the verdict but not the sentence). However, the Defamation Act 2013 provides that defamation cases should no longer routinely be held with juries, so although the court can decide to use a jury, this is likely to be rare.

Damages for libel fall into five categories; a single award may include damages from more than one of these.

1 Compensatory damages

These are supposed to be calculated to repair the damage done by the defamatory statement.

2 Aggravated damages

These are awarded, in addition to compensatory damages, in cases where the defendant has behaved particularly badly, so that the claimant has suffered more than would normally be expected in such a case. Typical cases might be where a paper has conducted a campaign against a particular person, or where it has repeated a libel even after being told it was untrue.

In *Kiam* v *MGN* (2002), businessman Victor Kiam was awarded £105,000 after a story questioned his business judgement. Part of the award comprised aggravated damages because the article was completely untrue, there was ample evidence that the writer had made no real effort to check it, and further defamatory articles were printed just before the trial, again without checking the facts with Mr Kiam.

3 Exemplary damages

These are reserved for cases where a publisher's behaviour is seen as so bad as to be deserving of punishment (like aggravated damages, they are awarded in addition to compensatory damages). They are generally used in cases where it appears that defamatory material has been published deliberately, for example to increase profits.

In *John* v *Mirror Group Newspapers* (1996), Elton John was awarded £350,000 for a story which suggested he had an eating disorder. The award included exemplary damages, because it was clear that the defamatory story was published deliberately, with an eye to its effect on sales. The overall amount was later reduced by the Court of Appeal (see below), but still included an amount for exemplary damages.

4 Nominal damages

These are ordered where the claimant's rights have technically been infringed, but the court feels no real damage has been done. They are usually less than £20.

In *Grobbelaar* v *News Group* (see p. 266), the case involving goalkeeper Bruce Grobbelaar, the House of Lords substituted an award of £1 for the £85,000 originally awarded by the jury, in recognition of the fact that he had admitted taking bribes.

5 Contemptuous damages

These are ordered where a jury (or judge) recognises that the claimant has been defamed, but in the circumstances, considers that the action should not have been brought. The damages (which are instead of compensatory damages) amount to the value of the least valuable coin in circulation (currently 1p). A claimant who is awarded contemptuous damages often has to pay their own costs as well.

In *Pamplin* v *Express Newspapers (No. 2)* (1988), the claimant registered his car and television set in the name of his five-year-old son, who because of his age could not be prosecuted for non-payment of licence fees and parking fines. The *Express* published a story describing him as a 'slippery, unscrupulous spiv' and a jury found that he had been defamed, but awarded him only ½p in damages. He appealed, but unsuccessfully.

Injunctions

An injunction is an order preventing publication. If a claimant wins their case, they will often ask for an injunction against the libel being repeated in future, and such injunctions are commonly awarded along with damages. However, a more controversial remedy is the interim injunction, which is ordered before publication. Typically, the claimant finds out that a story they claim is defamatory is about to be published, and goes to court for an order preventing publication. The order can be granted without a trial. Although this is technically a temporary measure, designed to 'hold the ring' until a full trial can be held, in practice a story published months or even years later is really no story at all, so by securing an interim injunction, the claimant can effectively silence the media.

Fortunately, the courts accept that injunctions which prevent initial publication can be a serious restriction on free speech, and will only grant them in exceptional cases. This is known as the rule against prior restraint. This traditional principle has been further strengthened by s12 of the Human Rights Act 1998, which provides that interim injunctions in cases affecting freedom of expression should not be granted unless the court is satisfied that, if the case does go to trial, the claimant is likely to be able to establish that publication should not be allowed.

The Human Rights Act further provides that when considering requests for injunctions on journalistic material, the courts must take into account:

- the importance of freedom of expression;
- the extent to which the material is already, or is about to be, available to the public;
- the extent to which publication would be in the public interest;
- any relevant privacy code.

The result is that interim injunctions in libel cases are only likely to be granted where the claimant can convince the court that the defendant is planning to publish defamatory stories which are obviously untrue, and there is no arguable defence, or a defence put forward is certain to fail.

In *Khashoggi* v *IPC Magazines* (1986), *Woman's Own* published a feature which claimed that Soraya Kashoggi, who was a famous 'society beauty', was having an extramarital affair with a Head of State. Mrs Khashoggi sought an injunction to prevent the article being published. The magazine could not prove this particular allegation was true, but said that it could prove justification for the 'sting' of the libel, which it argued was the suggestion that she was a person who was happy to engage in affairs. A number of other affairs had been mentioned in the article, without any complaint from Mrs Kashoggi. The Court of Appeal said that the rule against prior restraint had to apply in such a case; it was possible that the defence could succeed at trial, and if it did not, in the circumstances, the claimant could be adequately compensated by damages.

In 2005, London restaurateur Martha Greene attempted to get an injunction preventing *The Mail on Sunday* from publishing allegations that she was a business contact of Peter Foster, a convicted fraudster who had become well-known in the press over a number of years, most recently for his relationship with Carole Caplin, a friend of Tony and Cherie Blair. *The Mail on Sunday* had already printed a story linking Ms Greene to Mr Foster, which she claimed was 'littered with inaccuracies'. Ms Greene then sought an injunction to prevent publication of a further story, based on the content of emails which the paper said she had sent to Mr Foster. Ms Greene stated that the emails were faked, and the judge admitted that expert computer evidence suggested that she was more likely than not to be able to prove this at trial. Even so, he said, there was no absolute, unquestionable 'knockout' evidence that the emails were forgeries. Unless it was obvious that no defence could succeed at trial, the rule against prior restraint meant no injunction should be ordered.

A further limit on the use of interim injunctions is that a claimant applying for one may be asked to promise to pay the cost to the defendant of complying with the injunction, if the matter goes to trial and it is found that the injunction was wrongly granted (e.g. if the allegations are proved to be true). Failure to agree to such an undertaking, or doubts about the claimant's ability to pay, makes it even less likely that an injunction will be granted.

Law in practice **Protecting against libel claims**

Having read this far, you will have seen that libel can be a complex and unpredictable area of law. Because there is no set definition of a libellous statement, it is often very difficult to forecast with any kind of certainty whether a jury would find for or against a claimant. Even judges can, and do, disagree on whether a statement has the potential to be libellous. An example is the case involving Nicole Kidman (reported on p. 217). The case was brought before a judge as a striking out application, which meant that the judge was essentially being asked whether, in law, the words published could amount to defamation. He said that while the story was unpleasant, it could not be considered defamatory. The Court of Appeal, however, disagreed; it said it was not clear that there was no defamation, and the issue should be put before a jury. Similarly, in ***Jameel* v *Times Newspapers,*** the case about the Saudi businessman (see p. 230), the High Court said that the article in question was not capable of carrying the meaning that the claimant alleged, and the Court of Appeal then ruled that it was.

Since judges cannot always predict what will and will not be deemed defamatory, clearly no one expects a reporter to be able to do that with absolute certainty either. But while you are not expected to know all the answers, you are expected to know when there is a question to be asked. You should be able to spot when you are making a statement that could be considered defamatory, you should know what you need to do to make sure you are covered by a defence if you decide to go ahead and publish that statement – and, most importantly, you should know when to take further advice, whether from your editor or a lawyer.

If you are lucky enough to have an in-house lawyer, use them. On some publications, the whole of each issue is 'legalled' (read by a lawyer) as a matter of course, but if you're working in an area such as women's or trade magazines, where libel problems crop up less frequently, it may be up to individual staff to flag up when a feature needs legalling. If you have got a good story, but you are not certain you can back it up and you think the lawyer might advise against running it, it can be tempting just to 'forget' or 'not realise' that you should get it legalled. But if you don't think that you can stand it up to the in-house lawyer's satisfaction, imagine how you are going to feel being questioned in court – or, possibly worse, by your publishing director after the company has had to pay to settle out of court. The best resource in these circumstances is not to ignore the risk, but get advice on what you would need to do in order to run the story safely.

Rod Dadak, Head of Defamation at solicitors Lewis Silkin, advises that the best protection is to research your stories on the basis that, if the subject sued, you would have to defend your words in court:

> Although in practice very few libel cases now go to court, if you make sure that you have enough evidence to defend your story if it did go to trial, you will always be in a stronger position. If a potential claimant knows that you have your house in order, they will be less likely to sue in the first place, and more likely to settle if they do make a claim.

KEY POINTS

There are seven defences regarding defamation.

1 Consent

Applies where the subject of a statement agreed to its publication.

2 Truth

Applies where the statement can be proved to be substantially true.

3 Honest opinion

Applies to comments which are based on true facts or privileged material, where an honest person could hold the opinion expressed.

4 Absolute privilege

Applies to fair, accurate and contemporaneous court reports.

5 Qualified privilege

Applies to statements made without malice, regarding the following:

- proceedings, decisions and documents listed in Schedule 1 of the Defamation Act 1996;
- judicial proceedings in the UK;
- the proceedings of Parliament;
- replies to attacks on someone's character or conduct;
- balanced, responsibly researched reports on matters of public interest.
- reports of scientific and academic research.

6 Offer of amends

Applies where a publisher did not realise that a defamatory statement could apply to the claimant, and is willing to apologise and pay compensation.

7 Innocent dissemination

Applies to distributors, printers and so on who have taken reasonable care and did not know of the defamatory statement, and to live broadcasts.

Time limits

Claims must usually be brought within a year of publication; there is some discretion to extend the limitation period.

Remedies

Remedies for defamation are damages and/or injunctions.

TEST YOUR KNOWLEDGE

1 What does it mean to say that, in order to successfully plead truth, you have to prove your statement was true 'on the balance of probabilities'?

2 What is the meaning of 'malice', as used in the defence of qualified privilege?

3 Benny, Agnetha and Frida are trainee journalists on the *Waterloo Gazette*. Their editor sends them to review three plays which are on locally.

- Benny goes to see a production of *Les Miserables*, and reports (accurately) that the leading actor, a famous TV star called Terry Lovey, collapsed halfway through the first act, and that the theatre says he is suffering from food poisoning. He goes on to say, 'The *Sun* recently claimed that Terry had sought help for drug problems, but I saw no evidence that Saturday's collapse was anything more suspect than a dodgy curry.'
- Agnetha goes to see an amateur production of *Macbeth*, and is surprised to discover that the lead role is taken by Björn, an ex-boyfriend of hers, from whom she parted on very bad terms some years before. She writes: 'The actor playing Macbeth forgot his lines nine times. He was

so pathetically bad that he was an embarrassment to watch. A donkey would have played the part better.'

- Frida is sent to review a production of *My Fair Lady*, and writes: 'What a fantastic show: wonderful singing, fabulous dancing, and even the youngest performers remembered every line. What a shame that the second act was spoilt for me – and most of the audience – by the unruly behaviour of pupils from St Cedric's School. They showed the complete lack of discipline that people in this town have come to expect from this appalling comprehensive, where it is clear that no one takes the slightest interest in standards of behaviour.'

Could any of the three be liable for defamation? What defences might they be able to use, and what factors will decide whether they are covered or not?

ONLINE RESOURCES

The Defamation Act 1996 can be read in full at:
www.legislation.gov.uk/ukpga/1996/31/contents

The Defamation Act 2013 can be read at:
http://www.legislation.gov.uk/ukpga/2013/26/contents

The explanatory notes to the Defamation Bill give useful background to the new law (but bear in mind that they refer to the original bill and some provisions changed during its journey through Parliament). They can be read at:
http://www.legislation.gov.uk/ukpga/2013/26/notes/contents

Reynolds v *Times Newspapers* (2001) can be read at:
www.parliament.the-stationery-office.co.uk/pa/ld199899/ldjudgmt/jd991028/rey01.htm

A useful examination of liability for online defamation can be found in the Law Commission report, Defamation and the Internet, at:
www.lawcom.gov.uk/docs/defamation2.pdf#search=%22defamation%22

Malicious falsehood

As we saw earlier (in Chapter 15), false statements only give rise to a libel action where they lead to a lowering of the claimant in the eyes of right-thinking people. However, some untrue statements which do not fit the definition of libel can give rise to a different legal action, called malicious falsehood (and, potentially, some untrue statements could give rise to both actions).

WHAT IS MALICIOUS FALSEHOOD?

Malicious falsehood is not concerned with protecting reputation, but protecting against financial damage caused by the publication of false statements. A statement may be a malicious falsehood if it satisfies all the following:

- it is untrue;
- it is published maliciously; and
- as a direct and natural result of publication, the subject of the statement was caused financial loss, or was likely to be caused financial loss related to their business or job, or (but only where the words complained of are published in some permanent form) they were likely to cause financial damage in any other way.

The difference between this action and libel can be seen if we take the example of a local paper writing that a builder in the town is retiring. This would clearly not be defamatory, since no one would think less of the builder for retiring. However, it could (if untrue and published maliciously) be a malicious publication, because clearly if local people believe the builder is no longer taking on work, they will be unlikely to contact him when they need work done, and he is likely to suffer financially.

An untrue statement

In libel actions, the courts assume that the statement complained of is untrue, and it is for the defendant to give themselves a defence by proving it true, if they can. However, in an action for malicious prosecution, the claimant must prove that the statement is untrue. The statement need not be a direct one; as with libel, an implication can be enough.

In *Kaye* v *Robertson* (1991), the claimant was the actor Gorden Kaye, who at the time was starring in a very popular TV comedy called *Allo, Allo.* He was seriously injured in an accident, and while he lay semi-conscious in hospital, a reporter from the *Sunday Sport* got into his room, and 'interviewed' and photographed him. Mr Kaye sought an injunction to prevent publication of the resulting story and pictures, arguing that by publishing the story, the paper would be implying that he had consented to the interview, which he had not. The judge agreed that this amounted to a false statement.

In some cases, the words used may be capable of carrying a damaging meaning, or an innocent one. In ***Ajinimoto Sweeteners Europe SAS* v *Asda Stores Ltd*** (2010), the Court of Appeal said that the correct approach was to consider the potentially damaging meaning, and assess whether it was published maliciously (see next section). It was not correct to simply prefer the innocent meaning because one existed. The statement complained of must refer, directly or indirectly, to the claimant's business, property or other economic interests.

Malicious publication

For the purposes of malicious falsehood, to publish a statement maliciously means to publish it without reasonable cause or excuse, and with some kind of indirect, dishonest or improper motive. It is not necessary that the defendant was motivated by what we would understand as malice in the normal sense of the word, meaning spite or nastiness.

In ***Kaye* v *Robertson*** (1991) malice was found in the fact that the reporter must, in the circumstances, have realised that Mr Kaye was in no fit state to consent to giving an interview.

In ***Joyce* v *Sengupta*** (1993), the (now defunct) *Today* newspaper published a front-page story about a woman called Linda Joyce, who worked as a maid to Princess Anne. The story, which was based on police suspicions, claimed that Ms Joyce had stolen personal letters from the Princess and given them to a national newspaper. Ms Joyce sued for malicious falsehood and, in an interim hearing, the Court of Appeal held that the publication was malicious because the paper went ahead and published the story on the basis of what the police had told them they suspected, without making any checks as to whether the suspicions were true. Malice, the court said, could be inferred from 'the grossness and falseness of the allegations and the cavalier way they were published'. The case was later settled out of court.

Law in practice Malicious falsehood claims

The requirement for malice means that honest mistakes should not result in a successful claim for malicious publication, as long as the publisher concerned puts things right as soon as possible. If a publication is threatened with a claim for malicious prosecution, the first thing to do is check whether the facts are wrong. If they are, and the mistake was an honest one (and the statement is not defamatory), printing a correction and apology quickly will make it difficult for a court to find malice.

Financial loss

In most cases, the claimant has to prove that publication of the false statement caused (or has the potential to cause) 'special damage', which means actual financial loss.

In ***Grapelli* v *Derek Block (Holdings) Ltd*** (1981) the claimant was the famous jazz musician Stephane Grapelli. The defendants were his managing agents, who had arranged a series of concerts by him in the UK. These had to be cancelled and the defendants falsely claimed that the reason for the cancellation was that Mr Grapelli was seriously ill; so ill, in fact, that he might never be able to tour again. Mr Grapelli sued for both defamation and malicious falsehood. The first claim failed because it was not defamatory to say that someone was ill, but the second succeeded, as clearly the statement could damage his career and therefore his income.

In *Kaye* v *Robertson* (1991) the potential financial damage was held to arise from the fact that, if he chose to, Mr Kaye could have sold his story to a paper of his choice, for a large amount of money. If the story had already been published by the *Sunday Sport*, this right would be much less valuable because the story would no longer be exclusive.

In *Caron* v *BBC* (2002), the case concerned a radio programme about the singer Alma Cogan, who was very famous in the 1950s. The programme portrayed her as a drunk and her mother as domineering, and her sister wanted to stop it being broadcast. As both Ms Cogan and her mother were dead, an action in defamation was impossible, so Ms Cogan's sister (Ms Caron) sued for malicious falsehood, claiming that the programme would damage the assets of Ms Cogan's estate (the money and property left after she died, which would include the continuing income from her records). The court rejected the claim, stating that there was no proof that the programme could do such financial damage.

In *Tesla Motors* v *BBC* (2012), a car manufacturer lost a malicious publication claim over a feature on the BBC's *Top Gear* programme. The programme raced Tesla's Roadster electric car against a Lotus Elise sports car, and showed the Tesla car slowing down and then having to be pushed into a garage to be recharged. The company had admitted that some of the unfavourable statements made in the programme were true, and Mr Justice Tugendhat held that as a result of these it was impossible for Tesla to show that those parts of the item were untrue were calculated to cause, or had caused, financial damage, since buyers were as likely to be put off by the true statements as by the untrue ones.

Libel and malicious falsehood: know the differences

	Libel	Malicious falsehood
Statement must be false	Yes	Yes
Must cause financial loss	No*	Yes
Must damage reputation	Yes	No
Subject must be alive	Yes	No
Publication must be malicious	No	Yes

*But note that the Defamation Act brings in a requirement for financial damage where the claimant is a commercial organisation **(see Chapter 15)**

KEY POINTS

What is malicious falsehood?

A malicious falsehood is a statement that is:

- false;
- published maliciously; and
- causes or is likely to cause financial loss.

'Malicious'

- Malicious means published without good reason, for an improper or dishonest motive.
- Malicious falsehoods can apply to people who are dead.

TEST YOUR KNOWLEDGE

1. What are the three elements of malicious falsehood?
2. What are the main differences between malicious falsehood and libel?
3. Which of these statements, if untrue and published maliciously, could amount to malicious falsehoods:
   (a) Popular dentist Joe Brown is to retire after 30 years in practice.
   (b) Health inspectors found hundreds of cockroaches in the Happy Loaf bakery.
   (c) Local vet Alan Williams has seriously damaged his hand in a tragic accident; doctors say he may never work again.
   (d) Careless builder Jack Black set a 300-year-old cottage on fire.
4. What does 'maliciously' mean in the context of malicious falsehood?

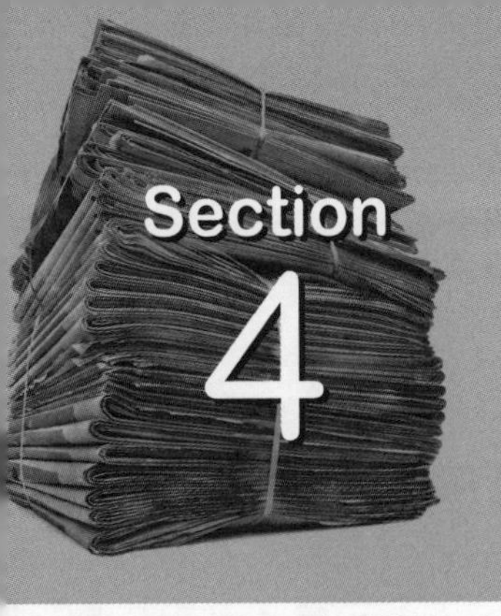

PRIVACY, CONFIDENTIALITY AND COPYRIGHT

This section brings together several different areas of law, but what the chapters have in common is that they largely concern laws which regulate the ways in which the media can use information about others or material owned by others.

Chapter 18 deals with breach of confidence, a form of civil claim that can be used to prevent publication of confidential information, such as business secrets and government matters, and Chapter 19 with privacy, a form of claim that has grown out of breach of confidence, and is now most often used by celebrities and public figures who want to stop the media discussing their private lives. Chapter 20 looks at the law on journalists and photographers invading people's privacy in the course of putting together a story.

There are many situations in which people who give information to the media may want to keep their identities secret, and it is a basic principle of journalistic ethics that a promise to keep a source confidential should be kept. Chapter 21 details the legal protection which the law provides for this principle, and the situations in which journalists can be ordered to reveal sources or hand over research material.

Chapter 22 deals with a relatively recent addition to the law, in the form of the Data Protection Act. The chapter explains both the media's responsibilities under the Act, and the ways in which journalists can deal with attempts to use the Act to keep information from the press.

The final chapter, on copyright, is about the rules which govern who owns the rights to words, pictures and other forms of expression, and how far the media can make use of such material.

Breach of confidence

The law on breach of confidence is designed to protect against the publication of material that someone – usually the owner of the material or someone referred to in it – wants to keep secret. However, it does not apply to every kind of material that someone would prefer not to be published, but only to material that has been obtained in circumstances where it is clear that it is confidential: typical examples would be business secrets that an employee finds out about while working for a company, information with a commercial value that has not been made public, and secret Government information obtained by Government employees through their work.

Before we look at the elements of confidentiality, one important thing to note (because it will help you understand the cases) is that claimants for breach of confidence will usually be looking to prevent information or pictures being published, rather than seeking to get damages after publication. This is because, in many of these cases, once confidential information is published, the damage is done: whereas with defamation, a trial can be used to clear a defendant's name, a trial for breach of confidence obviously cannot make the information secret again. For this reason, the courts are generally more willing to grant such injunctions in confidentiality cases than they would be in defamation actions.

An interim injunction is designed to be temporary and merely to 'hold the ring' until the issue can go to a full trial. However, it can take months for the trial to come on and, in many cases, by that time the information would be too old to make a decent news story or the story would have been overtaken by events. As a result, where an interim injunction is served, the media often does not bother taking the issue to trial, which means that, in practice, the interim injunction actually has the same effect as a permanent one (there are, however, still limits on when the courts should give an interim injunction, which are covered on p. 314). On the other hand, if an interim injunction is not ordered, the claimant will often not bother going to a full trial, since the secret is out and a court case would only give it more publicity. The interim stage is therefore a very important one in this area.

ELEMENTS OF A BREACH OF CONFIDENCE CLAIM

To succeed in a claim for breach of confidence, the claimant has to prove three things, which were listed in the case of ***Coco* v *A.N. Clark*** (1969) (the case did not involve the media, so the facts are not really relevant here):

- the information disclosed or about to be disclosed 'has the necessary quality of confidence' (or in other words, is information that would be considered private rather than public);
- the information was obtained in circumstances which imposed 'an obligation of confidence'; and
- the defendant has made or intends to make unauthorised use of the information.

If all three elements are satisfied, there will be a breach of confidence, unless the defendant can claim a defence. The available defences are discussed later in this chapter but essentially there are three, which arise where the defendant can show that the information was published with the claimant's consent, or was already known to the public or there was a public interest reason for the publication.

Confidential information

What type of information will be considered confidential? The latest test for this was defined by the House of Lords in ***Campbell* v *MGN*** (2004), the case where model Naomi Campbell sued the *Mirror* over stories about her attending meetings of Narcotics Anonymous (see p. 301). Although this case was actually treated as a privacy case rather than as breach of confidence, Lord Hope was talking about breach of confidence generally when he said that:

> The underlying question in all cases where it is alleged that there has been a breach of the duty of confidence is whether the information that was disclosed was private and not public . . . If the information is obviously private, the situation will be one where the person to whom it relates can reasonably expect his privacy to be respected.

In other words, if a reasonable person would think the information was confidential or private, then for the purposes of the law, it probably is. It was also stated in ***Coco* v *A.N. Clark*** that the information must have some degree of importance; the law will not protect the confidentiality of trivial material.

Examples of information which the courts have held to be 'obviously private' include ideas for commercial products, trade secrets, people's sex lives, health and medical treatment, diaries, company finances and personal photographs.

In 2005, author J.K. Rowling won an injunction preventing publication of details of the plot of her forthcoming book, *Harry Potter and the Half-Blood Prince.* The injunction was extremely wide, preventing anyone who came into possession of the book or part of it from disclosing any information about it to anyone.

In ***Fraser* v *Thames TV*** (1984), the claimant had developed a proposal for a TV drama series, based on the experiences of a pop group he had managed, comprising three female singers. The idea was discussed with the Thames' management, producers and writers, but was ultimately rejected. A little later, however, the company made a series, called 'Rock Follies', which was clearly based on the characters and stories in Fraser's proposal. He sued for breach of confidence, and evidence was given in court that the discussions he had had with the company, in which both sides were aiming to use the idea commercially, would be regarded in the industry as creating an obligation of confidentiality. His action was successful.

In ***X (HA)* v *Y*** (1988), the *News of the World* discovered that two doctors working for the same health authority had been diagnosed with AIDS. The paper got its information from an employee at the hospital where they were being treated. They published the facts of the story and intended to do a follow-up naming the doctors, but the health authority was granted a permanent injunction preventing publication of the doctors' names or the places where they worked.

In ***X Ltd* v *Morgan Grampian*** (1991), an unidentified source leaked information about a company called Tetra to the trade magazine *The Engineer.* The source said that the company was having financial problems and had prepared a business plan in order to seek a large bank loan. Tetra said that the information could only have come from the business plan, a copy of which had gone missing. It was granted an injunction preventing publication of the information.

Old information

In some cases the courts have found that information that would once have been considered confidential can stop being so after time has passed.

In ***A-G* v *Jonathan Cape*** (1976) the then Government requested an injunction to prevent publication of diaries written by a former Cabinet minister, Richard Crossman. Cabinet discussions are usually considered confidential, but the court refused an injunction, because the information related to discussions that had taken place at least ten years before and could no longer be considered confidential.

Photographs

The courts have always accepted that pictures can count as confidential information for the purposes of breach of confidence.

In ***Creation Records* v *News Group Newspapers*** (1997), a photo shoot was arranged for the cover of an Oasis album, involving a white Rolls-Royce in an empty swimming pool. There was heavy security around the set, but a photographer for the *Sun* managed to get unauthorised access to the area, and took some shots which were similar to the one eventually chosen for the album cover. The *Sun* published the picture and offered glossy posters of the shot to readers for £1.99. It was taken to court by the record company and the court found that publication was a breach of confidence.

In ***Douglas and Others* v *Hello! Ltd and Others*** (2003) the film stars Catherine Zeta-Jones and Michael Douglas sued *Hello!* magazine for publishing photographs of their wedding, taken secretly by a photographer who had sneaked in. The couple had sold exclusive rights to pictures of the wedding to *OK!* magazine, and so banned all their guests from taking photographs at the wedding, and put security provisions in place to prevent the press from getting in. Bearing this in mind, as well as the fact that it was a wedding, the Court of Appeal held that the photographs were plainly taken on a private occasion and disclosed information that was private, and 'the intrusion [by the photographer] into the private domain was itself objectionable'. *Hello!* argued that the pictures could not be considered confidential material since, rather than keeping them private, the couple had sold the rights to *OK!* However, the Court of Appeal said that the right of celebrities to sell pictures of themselves was comparable to a trade secret (such as the formula for a drink or the design of a machine), and was therefore protected by the law of confidentiality in the same way. The same protection might well not have been given to an unauthorised report of the wedding, even if it described exactly what would have been seen in the photos. In ***Douglas and Another* v *Hello!*** (2007), the House of Lords held that *OK!* also had a claim against *Hello!* The court stated that where information has a commercial value, and competitors are aware that a publisher has paid for exclusive rights to it, unauthorised use of that information may be a breach of confidence. *Hello!* was ordered to pay damages of over £1 million.

The obligation of confidence

As we have seen, the information concerned must be of a kind that might reasonably be thought of as private or confidential. In addition, it must have been obtained in circumstances where the person obtaining it realised that it was intended to be kept confidential. Classic examples of these kinds of circumstances would be where confidential information is passed between lawyer and client, doctor and patient, priest and parishioner, and the following are some of the other situations where the courts have held that an obligation of confidentiality may arise. Information passed on in personal relationships has also given rise to breach of confidence claim, but today these are more likely to be treated as privacy claims (covered in the next chapter).

Employer–employee relationships

Some employment contracts contain a specific provision, banning the employee from revealing information obtained as a result of their work. Most celebrities, for example, would include such a clause in the contracts of anyone working closely with them, such as nannies or personal assistants, and such clauses are also common in industries where trade secrets are important. In these cases, divulging information gained through work would be a breach of confidence.

In ***Archer* v *Williams*** (2003), Lady Archer, wife of the novelist Lord Archer, obtained an injunction against her former PA, who had attempted to sell stories about her to the national papers. There was a confidentiality clause in her contract.

In ***A-G* v *Barker*** (1990), a former servant of the royal family wrote a book, *Courting Disaster*, about his work. His employment contract contained a confidentiality clause, and because of this, the Court of Appeal granted an injunction preventing publication anywhere in the world, at any time.

However, the fact that an employment contract does not contain a confidentiality clause does not mean there will be no breach of confidence if information is disclosed. By accepting an employment contract, all employees take on an implied duty of 'fidelity' to their employer, which means they have an obligation not to do anything which would damage the employer's interest. This duty means that information gained through work is usually obtained in circumstances where an obligation of confidence exists. Leaking it can therefore be a breach of confidence, even after the person has left the job.

In one recent case, the High Court has held that information obtained through employment is not necessarily obtained under an obligation of confidence, although the situation was quite unusual.

In ***Tillery Valley Foods* v *Channel 4*** (2004), an investigative journalist took a job at a Tillery factory where food was prepared for hospitals and other public organisations. She secretly filmed various procedures, which suggested that the company's hygiene standards were in doubt, for a Channel 4 programme. Allegations based on the film were put to Tillery for its comment, and it responded by seeking an injunction, on the grounds that the information was obtained in breach of confidence. Tillery's lawyer agreed that the disclosure of the information might be in the public interest, but said that the court would need to balance that against the company's interest in not having it made public, and part of that balancing act would involve giving the company an effective right to reply, for which it would need both time and access to the material in the film. The court refused to entertain this idea at all. Mr Justice Mann said this was not a case of breach of confidence, but of potential defamation. The claimants had tried to 'squash' it into the law of confidence, because they were unlikely to get an injunction for defamation owing to the fact that the defendants believed they could prove justification **(see p. 256)**. He said that the fact that the information was obtained through an employment relationship did not necessarily mean it was confidential.

In 1998, the Public Interest Disclosure Act was passed to protect 'whistleblowers', employees who disclose their employer's secrets in order to expose wrongdoing (examples would be an employee who reveals that safety procedures are not being followed or one who discloses information about insider dealing). However, the protection of the Act only applies to the employee and not to the media who report their disclosures. The media's role in publishing such reports would be covered by the usual law on breach of confidence (though in many such cases the public interest defence would apply).

Government employees

Civil servants and members of the armed forces and secret services do not have written employment contracts, but the courts have accepted that they have a duty of confidence with regard to information obtained through their work. The Official Secrets Act 1989 provides for government employees who leak information to be prosecuted, but, over the years, juries have proved to be rather reluctant to convict, unless the leaks concerned real threats to national security. As a result, successive governments have turned to the law of confidence to protect their secrets instead, and the courts have been, on the whole, very willing to help them do so.

In 1986, Peter Wright, a former senior MI5 officer, wrote a book, *Spycatcher*, about his work, which contained allegations of misconduct by the service, and even treason (though the allegations were actually a small part of the book). The book was published in Australia, but the *Guardian* published details of the allegations. The Government was able to get an injunction against further publication, by the *Guardian* or any other UK media, on the grounds that members of the security services owed a lifelong duty of confidentiality. It took two years, during which the book was published in several other countries and read by many people in the UK, before the injunction against the press was eventually lifted because the information had become public knowledge (see below). Even then, the House of Lords reiterated its view that Mr Wright owed a duty of confidentiality, which he had breached.

In *A-G* v *BBC* (1987), the Government secured an injunction preventing broadcast of a series of radio programmes called *My Country, Right or Wrong*, because they featured interviews with ex-members of the security services, even though no secrets were revealed. The injunction was only lifted when the Attorney-General read transcripts of the programmes and realised that they were a completely harmless discussion of the moral issues associated with the work of a security service.

In some cases, the Government has successfully used the law of confidence to help them 'manage' news, even where the information concerned was always going to be made public at a later date (though this may now become more difficult as the Human Rights Act requires courts to take into account the extent to which information is about to be made public – see p. 314).

In 1999, the *Sunday Telegraph* obtained leaked information from a report on a public inquiry examining the unsuccessful police investigation into the racist murder of a black teenager, Stephen Lawrence. The report was due to be published a few days later, but the then Home Secretary successfully obtained an injunction preventing publication of any information from it.

In addition to the general obligations of confidence on government employees, discussions between Cabinet Ministers are protected by confidentiality.

Documents relating to court cases

During a court case, the two sides exchange documents which are to be used in evidence. Disclosure of these documents to anyone else is a breach of confidence (and may be contempt of court as well). The same applies to statements made by suspects to prosecuting authorities.

In ***Distillers Co*** v ***Times Newspapers*** (1975), the *Sunday Times* was researching a story about a drug called Thalidomide, which was later revealed to cause serious birth defects. The paper bought documents which had been disclosed by Distillers to an expert witness. Although there was a clear public interest in the issue, the court granted an injunction against publication of details from the documents, because there was an even greater public interest in protecting confidentiality during the exchange of documents before a trial.

In ***Bunn*** v ***BBC*** (1998), the BBC made a documentary about the Serious Fraud Office (SFO), which the SFO cooperated with. The SFO gave the programme makers a statement by Robert Bunn, a defendant in a fraud trial. The court held that disclosure of such statements could be a breach of confidence (though in this case, there was no breach because the judge in the case had read the statement in open court and therefore it was in the public domain – see p. 294).

Confidential circumstances

An obligation of confidentiality can also be created by the circumstances in which the information is obtained, regardless of whether there is a relationship between the person the information is from or about, and the person obtaining it. In ***A-G* v *Guardian Newspapers (No. 2)*** (1990), Lord Goff said that a duty of confidence could arise when confidential information comes to someone's attention 'in circumstances where he has notice . . . that the information is confidential, with the effect that it would be just in all the circumstances that he should be precluded from disclosing the information to others'.

Lord Goff cited the examples of an obviously confidential document being wafted by an electric fan out of an office window into the street, or a private diary being dropped in a public place. In both cases, anyone picking up the item would be under an obligation of confidence with regard to its contents, because it would be obvious that the information is private.

In ***Creation Records* v *News Group Newspapers*** (1997), the case involving a photo shoot for the cover of an Oasis album (see p. 303), the court pointed out that the fact that the record company had taken security precautions to keep people away from the shoot clearly indicated that the way the scene had been set up for the pictures was confidential.

People at risk of harm

In a handful of cases, the courts have used the law of confidentiality to protect the identities of people involved in particularly notorious crimes, where it was believed that those people could be under serious threat of harm. The cases do not fit very comfortably within the rules of the law on confidentiality, but it appears that the courts have used that law, in combination with the right to life under s2 of the Human Rights Act, to fill a loophole, where there is evidence that publishing the identity or whereabouts of the individuals could put them at real risk, and there is no other way to prevent such publication.

In ***Venables and Thompson* v *News Group Newspapers and Others*** (2001), a permanent injunction was granted, preventing publication of any information which might lead to the identification of the two young men who, ten years earlier, had killed a toddler, James Bulger. The two were about to be released from prison, and were being given new identities. The injunction lasts for the whole of their lives.

In ***X (formerly known as Mary Bell)* v *SO*** (2003), the court considered the case of Mary Bell, who in 1968, when she was 11, was convicted of murdering two younger children. She was released from prison in 1980 and given a new identity, but over the years the press had tracked her down, and she had had to change identities several more times. During that time she had also cooperated with a book about herself. When her daughter was born, the child was made a ward of court, which meant that the press could be prevented from identifying her but, even so, when parents where they lived found out who her mother was, the child was hounded out of school. The wardship ended when she was 18, so her mother applied for an injunction guaranteeing both her and her daughter lifelong anonymity. It was granted, on the grounds that she was in a fragile mental state and press intrusion could have serious consequences for both herself and her daughter.

In 2004, the High Court issued an order banning the media from publishing any information about Maxine Carr, who was the girlfriend of Ian Huntley, who murdered two schoolgirls in the Cambridgeshire village of Soham in 2002. Carr gave him a false alibi for the time of the murder and was sent to prison for 42 months. She received death threats and after her release from prison was given a new identity in a different area. Reporters tracked her down nevertheless and she went to court to get an injunction; the hearing was held within hours of her being found by the press. The injunction forbids the press not only from publishing any information about her new identity, appearance or whereabouts, but also from even trying to find out such information.

In *Mahmood* v *Galloway* (2006), the *News of the World* tried to get an injunction preventing the MP George Galloway from publishing a picture of one of its undercover reporters, Mazher Mahmood. Using various disguises and fake personas, Mr Mahmood had broken a number of high-profile stories, some of which exposed drugs dealers, arms dealers and other serious criminals, and the paper said that he had received death threats and would be in danger if his photograph was published. The judge rejected the application and said that, in his view, the injunction was not needed to protect Mr Mahmood's life, but to protect his earning capacity.

The position of the media

In many cases, the media will be a third party in breach of confidence cases. For example, if the nanny to a famous singer's children decides to reveal secrets of the family's life to a newspaper, it is the relationship between the nanny and the singer which creates the obligation of confidence. However, once that obligation exists, it covers not only the nanny, but also anyone else who makes unauthorised use of the information, if they know it was obtained as a result of a breach of confidence.

Therefore, if the media publish confidential information obtained under an obligation of confidence, they can be liable, unless they did not know it was obtained in breach of confidence. Usually this will be obvious from the nature of the information and its source, but, where the media are genuinely unaware of the obligation of confidence, there is no breach.

In *British Steel Corp* v *Granada TV* (1981), Granada journalists obtained secret documents from an employee at British Steel. It was pointed out in court that, as they were labelled 'confidential' and 'restricted', the journalists must have known they were not intended to be seen by anyone other than top management at the company. They were ordered to return them.

In *PCR Ltd* v *Dow Jones* (1998), PCR published a newsletter which was circulated to a small number of its clients, and contained confidential information about the international cocoa market. A journalist, researching this market, talked to a number of people who happened to have seen this newsletter, and who gave her information they had obtained from it, even though they were under an obligation not to disclose the information. The journalist used some of the information in her report, and PCR sued for breach of confidence. The court found that as the journalist did not know the information she was given was confidential neither she nor her employer could be in breach of confidence.

Unauthorised use

In media cases, this element is usually straightforward: publishing confidential information without consent is clearly unauthorised use of it. A more unusual situation is where a defendant has authorisation to use information for one purpose, but uses it for another; the courts have held that this can be considered unauthorised use.

In *Schering Chemicals* v *Falkman* (1982), the chemical company employed David Elstein, a TV programme-maker, to give media training to some of its employees. As part of this relationship with the company, he obtained information about its work, and decided that there was a TV programme to be made about allegations that the company's drugs could cause birth defects. Mr Elstein did not use any material he had gained as a result of his work with the company, gathering material instead from publicly available sources but, even so, the Court of Appeal held that he had acted in breach of confidence. The main argument for this result was that Mr Elstein had unfairly exploited his confidential relationship with Schering: he had been paid to help improve its image and, as a result of that job, had gone on to make a programme (for which he had also been paid) which did exactly the opposite. The court issued an injunction preventing the programme from being broadcast. The decision has been criticised, given that there was a clear public interest in the subject of the programme.

DEFENCES

There are three defences to a claim for breach of confidence:

- consent;
- information in the public domain;
- public interest.

Consent is self-explanatory; if the person confidential information belongs to or is about agrees to its publication, there can be no breach of confidence. The other two defences are explained below.

Information in the public domain

If information is already known to the public – regardless of whether or not it was divulged by the claimant – it cannot be considered confidential, and so there can be no breach of confidence.

In ***Lennon* v *News Group Newspapers*** (1978), John Lennon tried to prevent his ex-wife Cynthia from selling stories about their marriage to the *News of the World*. He was refused an injunction, because both of them had already talked to the press about their relationship in the past, so the information could not be considered confidential.

In ***AG* v *Guardian Newspapers Ltd (No. 2)*** (1990), the House of Lords reconsidered the interim injunction forbidding publication of information contained in the book *Spycatcher* (see above). The interim injunction had been imposed in 1986, but in the intervening years, the book had been published in the USA, and the allegations in it reported worldwide. The House of Lords found that the information was in the public domain, and refused to impose a permanent injunction.

In 1982, the *Watford Observer* put together a story about a local company, Sun Printers. It was based on a document which had been leaked to the paper, which said that the company was losing money and its owner, the media magnate Robert Maxwell, wanted to cut staff. Mr Maxwell was able to get an interim injunction preventing publication, but the paper challenged the order. It pointed out that, although the document had originally been distributed only to a small number of company managers, it was later circulated to many more people, including officials of the relevant trade unions and, the paper argued, could no longer be considered confidential. The Court of Appeal agreed, and for this and other reasons (see below) discharged the injunction.

However, if information has only been disclosed in a limited way, the courts will sometimes find that it is not in the public domain. The test used in ***Lennon*** (see above) was whether the information was known to 'a substantial number of people', and has usually been taken to mean that information will not be in the public domain if it is only known to a few friends or acquaintances of the person concerned. However, there are cases where information in wider circulation has still been held not to be in the public domain.

In 2000, Prime Minister Tony Blair and his wife applied for an injunction against publication of details of their family life, disclosed by their former nanny. By the time the application was heard, over a million copies of *The Mail on Sunday*, containing the story, were already in the process of being distributed. Nevertheless, the court allowed an injunction preventing further publication.

The public interest

To succeed in this defence, the media must prove that the public interest in receiving the confidential information is greater than the public interest in protection for confidential material. In cases where this arises, the courts have been very clear that there is a distinction between 'the public interest' and 'things the public are interested in'. In general, there will be a public interest in stories which, for example, expose serious wrongdoing, reveal information which affects people's daily lives, health or safety, or which relate to important issues of public debate. There will not, as a rule, be a public interest in stories about the sex lives, eating habits or other activities of celebrities, except in very limited circumstances.

In ***Initial Services*** v ***Putterill*** (1968), an ex-employee of a laundry company gave a newspaper company documents which suggested that they had been evading tax. The Court of Appeal refused the company an injunction, on the grounds that this was the kind of misconduct which it was in the public interest to know about.

In *X* v *Y*, the case concerning two doctors with AIDS (see above), the paper argued that there was a public interest in publishing the information. The court agreed that if there was any danger to patients, it would be in the public interest for the general issue to be discussed, but revealing the doctors' names might have the effect of dissuading people who might have AIDS from seeking help, in case their condition was made public, and that would be against the public interest.

In the case involving the *Watford Observer* and Sun Printers (see above), the judge accepted that it was in the public interest for people in the Watford area to know that a major local employer was considering cutting staff.

In ***Cork*** v ***McVicar*** (1995), a journalist interviewed a former police officer about allegations of police corruption. Parts of the interview were stated by the officer to be 'off the record', but the journalist was secretly taping the whole conversation, and used the 'off the record' parts in the story. A court refused to issue an injunction suppressing publication, because the information clearly revealed matters that were of great public interest.

In ***Hubbard*** v ***Vosper*** (1972), a court refused to suppress a book which detailed various courses run by Scientologists, on the grounds that there was 'good ground for thinking that these courses contain such dangerous material that it is in the public interest that it should be made known.'

In ***Times Newspapers Ltd*** v ***MGN*** (1993), the *Mirror* obtained an early copy of the former Prime Minister Margaret Thatcher's autobiography. The book was not yet published, and the publishers had arranged an exclusive serialisation deal with the *Sunday Times*. Both the publishers and the *Sunday Times* tried to prevent the *Mirror* from publishing extracts, which revealed Baroness Thatcher's not very complimentary opinions of her successor, John Major, and his colleagues. The newspaper said that these matters were of public interest, given that at the time the story was published the Conservative Party was holding its annual conference, at which they were trying to put across the impression that the party was harmonious and united. The Court of Appeal agreed, and no injunction was granted.

In 2000, the Labour fundraiser Lord Levy was refused an injunction against *The Times*, which had a story about his tax affairs, obtained via confidential information. The court said that Lord Levy was known as a high-profile supporter of the Labour Party, and the party's manifesto contained a promise to close loopholes in the tax system. It was therefore in the public interest to find out whether Lord Levy's attitude to his own taxes was in line with the aims the Party had expressed.

In ***Lion Laboratories*** v ***Evans*** (1985), an employee of a company which made breathalysers used by the police leaked information to the press which showed that the devices were not as accurate as claimed. Even though there was no suggestion that the company had done anything wrong, they were refused an injunction, because this was clearly information that the public had a right to know, given that an inaccurate reading could lead to a wrongful conviction.

In ***Service Corp International plc*** v ***Channel 4*** (1999), Channel 4 successfully used the public interest defence to protect a report into malpractice at a funeral home, using film taken by a reporter who had gone undercover and got a job at the home.

In ***Commissioner of Police of Bermuda*** v ***Bermuda Broadcasting Co*** (2008), the Privy Council (see p. 13), found that the public interest in press freedom to report on alleged wrong-doing by politicians outweighed the confidentiality which would normally attach to documents relating to a police investigation. The Bermuda police had investigated alleged corruption concerning the Bermuda Housing Corporation, a body created by statute, but the Director of Public Prosecutions found there was insufficient evidence to prosecute anyone except a junior officer of the corporation. Three years later, files relating to the investigation came into the hands of the press, which revealed that the subjects of the corruption investigation had included government ministers and other MPs. The police sought an injunction to prevent publication of any further material from the leaked documents, but the Privy Council refused. It said that there was a public interest in revealing allegations of wrongdoing among elected officials; this was what the material so far published had revealed, and as further material was likely to be of a similar character, the public interest in publishing it outweighed the claim of confidentiality by the police.

In *BKM* v *BBC* (2009), Mr Justice Mann considered the issue of film obtained using secret cameras. The case concerned a programme about poor standards in a care home run by BKM, and the film was obtained by an undercover reporter who got a job there. Mr Justice Mann said that as the programme was covered by both the Ofcom Code and the BBC's own code of practice, he had to look at the provisions of the codes, as well as the law. He pointed out that both codes say that secret filming should not be undertaken lightly, and should only be used where there is no other way to achieve the same result, and where the matter is 'sufficiently serious to justify it'. He said it was firmly arguable that the programme covered matters of public interest, which were serious enough to justify secret filming. BKM had argued that the BBC could simply have used material that was available in official inspection reports, and narration by the reporter of what she saw. The judge rejected this argument, saying it was not at all clear that this would have made the point as well as the secret filming did and, in any case, this was an editorial judgement that should not be made by a judge. BKM also argued that they should be shown the programme before broadcast, but the judge rejected this argument, saying that the courts usually respected the media practice of not showing material before publication unless they want to.

Where a story is claimed to be in the public interest because it exposes wrongdoing, the courts have held that it is not necessary to prove that wrongdoing actually took place, before a public interest defence can succeed.

In ***Attorney-General*** v ***Guardian Newspapers (No. 2)*** (1988) (part of the *Spycatcher* litigation), the Court of Appeal said that before using confidential information alleging wrongdoing, the media should assess the reliability of the source, do their own investigations into the allegations, and give due weight to the findings of any investigations that had already taken place, but they did not need to be able to prove the allegations true. In other words, as long as the media has acted responsibly, publication of allegations of serious wrongdoing will usually be in the public interest.

Public interest in Government stories

Where the claimant is the Government or another public body, the courts have said that a stricter public interest test should be imposed. In all other areas, the media must show that disclosure is in the public interest, but for disclosures of government information, the government has to show that disclosure would cause harm to the public interest.

In ***A-G*** v ***Guardian Newspapers (No. 2)*** (see above), the House of Lords approved the approach of the Australian High Court in a case about government secrecy, which had said that in a democratic society disclosure of information that sheds light on the workings on government will usually be in the public interest, and should be allowed. It should only be restrained if disclosure would cause harm to the public interest. That could not be the case here, because the information the Government sought to suppress was already available to the public from so many sources that further disclosure could not make any difference.

The injunction against publication was lifted. However, the *Sunday Times* had published material from the book before it was even published, so the same argument could not be used for them, and they were ordered to pay the Government an account of profits (see below).

The same approach may be applied to private companies when they are carrying out functions which might usually be fulfilled by a public body.

In 1994, the accountancy firm KPMG Peat Marwick sought an injunction preventing the *Liverpool Echo* from publishing information from a report they had prepared for Liverpool City Council. The report concerned a cable-laying contract which had lost the council a lot of money. The judge held that, as the report might just as well have been prepared by the council's own people, it had to satisfy the same public interest test as for government information, and it was clear that this test was satisfied.

What the codes say **Breach of confidence**

The Editors' Code of Practice used by IPSO includes the following provision:

- The press must not seek to obtain or publish material acquired by using hidden cameras or clandestine listening devices; or by intercepting private or mobile telephone calls, messages or emails; or by the unauthorised removal of documents or photographs; or by accessing digitally held private information without consent.

Breach of this rule may be allowed under the Code where it can be demonstrated that the action is in the public interest (see Appendix 1).

REMEDIES FOR BREACH OF CONFIDENCE

As explained at the beginning of this chapter, the main remedy for breach of confidence is an injunction, as the claimant will ideally want to prevent the material being published in the first place. The Human Rights Act 1998 sets down special rules about the use of injunctions in this way, which oblige the courts to take account of the effect on press freedom; these are discussed elsewhere (at p. 314), because most of the key cases about them come from privacy claims, but the rules apply equally to breach of confidence cases.

If confidential material has already been published, the claimant can seek damages and an injunction to prevent further publication. The damages ordered will take into account the commercial value of the information; in the **Douglas** case (see p. 289), *Hello!* had to pay £1m to *OK!* for its use of photographs of the wedding of Catherine Zeta-Jones and Michael Douglas.

Two other remedies may be available in breach of confidence cases: an order for delivery up, and an account of profits.

Order for delivery up

If the confidential information is in physical form (such as a document), a court can order it to be handed back to the owners. This can cause problems for the media, because in some cases, the documentation will identify who leaked it to the press – this might be the case if, for example, the copies were numbered, or the source has made notes on the paper. In the case of very secret (usually government) documents, there may be tiny differences between copies which the untrained eye would not spot, but which experts can use to identify the source. Destroying or altering documents once an order for delivery up has been made is contempt of court, so, if it looks as though a situation might end up in court, it may be best to destroy the document before that happens.

A court can also order the media to identify the source of the leak, but this power is limited by the protection given to sources under the Contempt of Court Act 1981 (see Chapter 21).

Account of profits

The nature of stories built on confidential information means that they are often the kind that sell newspapers and magazines. Therefore, if a breach of confidence is found, and the publishers have made money as a result of it, they can be ordered to give an account of profits to the claimant, which means an amount of money based on the profits they have made from the story (it is an alternative to damages, not an addition).

Law in practice Confidentiality and defamation

Stories based on confidential information can also raise a dilemma with regard to defamation. Documents can be forged, sources may be wrong or bear a grudge and, by their nature, these kinds of stories will often leave you at risk of a defamation claim if they turn out not to be true. In this situation, journalists are often concerned that, if they go to the subject of the story to check the facts, and that person or organisation realises the story is based on confidential information, the story may be stopped by an injunction for breach of confidence. Rod Dadak, Head of Defamation at solicitors Lewis Silkin, has this advice:

- If you go ahead and use confidential information without checking the facts, you are taking a big risk. Judges don't look at these issues from a journalist's point of view, and they disapprove of any failure to give the subject of a story a chance to see the allegations and put their side.
- If possible, try to get confirmation of the facts from other sources, so that you can then check with the subject without revealing that you have the confidential material.
- It's worth bearing in mind that the Article 10 rules on injunctions (see p. 314) are making it harder for claimants to get pre-publication injunctions where material is in the public interest, so the risk of an injunction may not be as high as you think.

KEY POINTS

Breach of confidence

A claim for breach of confidence must prove:

- the information 'has the necessary quality of confidence';
- it was obtained in circumstances which impose an obligation of confidence; and
- it was or is intended to be used in an unauthorised way.

Confidential information includes:

- trade secrets and commercial ideas;
- information about an individual's health or private life;
- company finances.

Photographs can count as confidential information, and may be more likely to do so than words which convey the same facts.

Situations which may create an obligation of confidence include:

- employer–employee relationships;
- employment by the Government;
- exchange of documents in a court case;
- where circumstances suggest confidentiality is expected;
- in exceptional cases, where confidentiality is the only way to protect individuals associated with high-profile crimes from serious harm.

If an obligation of confidence exists with regard to information, it covers anyone who uses the information without authorisation, if they know it was obtained under an obligation of confidentiality.

Remedies

Publishing without consent is usually enough to prove unauthorised use.

A successful claimant may win:

- an injunction (permanent or temporary);
- damages;
- an order for delivery up;
- an account of profits.

TEST YOUR KNOWLEDGE

1 What are the three elements of a traditional breach of confidence action?

2 A well-known author is about to publish the final instalment of a series of novels, and there has been a lot of publicity about how the story will end. You get a call from someone who works at the book's printers, and says he can tell you what happens on the last page. Can you use the information?

3 You work on a trade magazine for the construction industry, and have recently written about a new process which can halve the time it takes for cement to dry. After publication, you are sent what seems to be an internal memo from the company concerned, in which one of their technical staff suggests there may be a possibility that the substance used in the process can cause cancer. You do not know who sent the memo. Can you use the information?

4 You work on a celebrity magazine. A well-known film star holds a birthday party for his wife, to which 1,000 guests are invited. No press are invited, and the couple have hired a security firm to keep out anyone without an invitation. After the party, one of the security guards offers you pictures taken with a secret camera. Can you use them?

5 You receive a press release stating that a local company is about to make 100 of its workers redundant; the press officer confirms the figures, and you run the story. It turns out that the press officer is one of the people on the list to be made redundant, and has released information which was supposed to be kept secret for another two weeks, as an act of revenge. Are you in breach of confidence?

ONLINE RESOURCES

Venables and Thompson v *News Group Newspapers and Others* can be read at:
http://www.bailii.org/ew/cases/EWHC/QB/2001/32.html

Privacy

From the phone hacking scandal and the Leveson Inquiry, to the seemingly endless stream of cases involving footballers and other celebrities, the law of privacy never seems to be out of the headlines for long. So it might surprise you to know that privacy claims as we know them today have a relatively short history in English law, having been created in the 2004 case of ***Campbell* v *MGN*.** As a result, the rules on privacy claims are still developing, and it can still be difficult to predict when a claim will succeed, but in this chapter, we look at some of the factors which the courts take into consideration.

As with breach of confidence (see the previous chapter), it is worth knowing that in a privacy case, the claimant is usually seeking to get an injunction to prevent material being published in the first place. If possible, they will want a permanent injunction, but in many cases an interim injunction, which is designed to prevent publication until the case can be heard in court, can do the same job, because if publication can be put off for long enough, the story will become stale and never be used anyway.

ELEMENTS OF A PRIVACY CLAIM

Technically, there is no such thing as a privacy claim in English law, but this name has come to be used for claims based on principles set down in ***Campbell* v *MGN*** (2004), a case where model Naomi Campbell sued the *Daily Mirror* over stories about her being a recovering drug addict and attending Narcotics Anonymous (NA) meetings. In that case, the House of Lords created a new form of claim which they called 'misuse of private information'. It was loosely based on the old breach of confidence claim, but also influenced by the Human Rights Act 1998, which enshrines in English law the rights to privacy, and to freedom of expression. It has now come to be the main form of claim used when people – usually, though not always, celebrities and public figures – want to prevent publication of stories about them or pictures of them.

In ***Campbell,*** the House of Lords said that to decide whether to grant a claim for misuse of private information, a court had to use a two-stage test:

- Does the claimant have a reasonable expectation of privacy with respect to the information or material disclosed? If they do,
- Is the claimant's right to privacy more important, in all the circumstances, than the defendant's right to freedom of expression?

Reasonable expectation of privacy

In deciding whether the claimant had a reasonable expectation of privacy, the courts take account of a wide range of factors. In *Murray* v *Express Newspapers* (2008), the Court of Appeal said:

> As we see it, the question whether there is a reasonable expectation of privacy is a broad one, which takes account of all the circumstances of the case. They include the attributes of the claimant, the nature of the activity in which the claimant was engaged, the place at which it was happening, the nature and purpose of the intrusion, the absence of consent and whether it was known or could be inferred, the effect on the claimant and the circumstances in which and the purposes for which the information came into the hands of the publisher.

The following are some of the factors which have been important in decided cases.

Attributes of and effect on the claimant

What the courts are looking at here is really the effect that publication of the material would have on the claimant, given his or her personality and situation.

In ***Campbell***, Lord Hope suggested that the courts ask: 'whether disclosure of the information about the individual ('A') would give substantial offence to A, assuming that A was placed in similar circumstances and was a person of ordinary sensibilities . . . The mind that has to be examined is that, not of the reader in general, but of the person who is affected by the publicity'. A key factor in allowing the claim was that, as a former drug addict who was trying to beat her addiction, Ms Campbell was vulnerable. Publishing photos of her at the door of her NA meeting could make her fear she was being stalked by photographers, and make her less likely to continue attending meetings, which could threaten her recovery.

In ***Terry* v *Person Unknown*** (2010), the footballer John Terry attempted to get an injunction preventing publication of any stories about the fact that he was having an affair with the ex-girlfriend of another England team member. In refusing to continue the injunction Mr Terry had obtained, Mr Justice Tugendhat said that the personality and circumstances of the claimant were relevant: 'the less sensitive the information is considered by the applicant to be, and the more robust the personality of the applicant . . . the less a court may find a need to interfere with freedom of expression by means of an injunction.' In this case, he judged that the information was not especially intrusive, and that John Terry appeared to have 'a very robust personality, as one might expect of a leading professional sportsman'. There was no real suggestion that he was likely to be caused personal distress by the revelations, and it appeared that the real reason for the action was to protect his commercial interests.

The nature of the activity

The courts have drawn a distinction between private activities, which are more likely to create a legitimate expectation of privacy, and public activities, which will not.

In ***Campbell***, the *Mirror*'s stories detailed how often Ms Campbell went to NA meetings, and what was likely to happen there. The House of Lords found that this was the equivalent of revealing the details of someone's medical treatment, which had always been considered confidential, and there was a legitimate expectation of privacy regarding such details.

In ***The Author of a Blog* v *Times Newspapers Limited*** (2009), the court ruled that an anonymous blogger did not have a legitimate expectation of privacy regarding his identity, because blogging was a public activity. The claimant was a serving police constable, who at the time wrote a blog about his police work under the pseudonym 'Night Jack'. *The Times* had worked out his real name from things he had said in the blog, and he sought an interim injunction preventing them from publishing any information that would or might lead to his identification, claiming this was misuse of private information. In considering whether he had a reasonable expectation of privacy, Eady J said that the fact that bloggers may take steps to disguise their identity was not sufficient reason to prevent those who work it out from revealing it.

Where a story or pictures concern someone involved in sexual activity, there will be a legitimate expectation of privacy, providing the activity involves consenting adults.

In *Jagger* v *Darling* (2005), the model Elizabeth Jagger was awarded an injunction preventing further publication of CCTV images, which showed her and her boyfriend 'engaging in sexual activities' inside the closed door of a nightclub. The court said this was a situation where there was clearly a legitimate expectation of privacy.

In ***Mosley* v *News Group Newspapers*** (2008), the claimant was Max Mosley, President of the FIA, which runs Formula 1 motor racing. He had been secretly filmed at a sadomasochistic orgy with five prostitutes, and the *News of the World* published the story. Mr Justice Eady upheld Mr Mosley's claim for misuse of personal information, stating that public figures were entitled to a personal life, and people's sex lives were 'essentially their own business'. He said that there would usually be a reasonable expectation of privacy with regard to sexual activity, especially if it was on private property and between consenting adults, regardless of whether some of them were paid to join in.

However, although there will usually be a reasonable expectation of privacy with regard to details about sexual activity, the same does not necessarily apply to merely revealing that two people are in a sexual relationship with each other.

In ***Terry* v *Person Unknown*** (2010), where footballer John Terry sought a permanent injunction preventing publication of any stories about the fact that he was having an affair, Justice Tugenhat said there was a difference between publishing intrusive details and/or photographs concerning a sexual relationship, and merely publishing the fact that the relationship was going on. He said that if John Terry could have shown that there was a real threat that intrusive details or pictures might be published, he would have been entitled to an injunction preventing that publication, because he would be likely to have been able to prove at trial that the publication was misuse of private information. But the fact that there might be publication of the fact that the relationship existed was not sufficient to justify an injunction.

Photographs and video

A number of cases have been very clear about the fact that photographs, especially if taken covertly, will be considered more intrusive than words alone. However, there is still a certain amount of uncertainty over exactly what kinds of photos are protected by a legitimate expectation of privacy, and which are not. In ***Campbell,*** Baroness Hale said that there was no expectation of privacy with regard to pictures of someone, famous or not, going about their ordinary business in a public place, or as she put it, 'popping out for a pint of milk'. Such pictures could only ever convey trivial information, such as what the person chose to wear when doing the shopping, and trivial information had never been protected by the law of confidence. However, this principle has to be considered in the light of two European Court of Human Rights cases brought by Princess Caroline of Monaco (which we'll look at in the next section), where the ECHR said that public figures could have a right to prevent publication of pictures showing them going about their daily business, where the pictures did not contribute to a 'debate of general interest'. The Princess Caroline cases were decided after the ***Campbell*** case, so at the moment, the English courts are largely following the House of Lords decision in ***Campbell,*** but if a case were to come before the Supreme Court now, they might well fall into line with the ECHR's view that even such ordinary information and pictures should be protected, unless there is something about them that informs public debate on an important subject. Nor do we have a clear ruling on how far covert filming or photography can legally go, especially when people are in a place that might be considered private, such as a remote beach. This is because when claims about such activity have been made, the press have usually settled and paid damages, which means there has been little opportunity for the court to make rulings. The following cases, however, offer some guidelines.

In ***Campbell***, the House of Lords held that there was a legitimate expectation of privacy regarding the photos taken of Ms Campbell at the door of the place where her NA meeting was held. Even though the pictures were taken on a public street, the situation was such that their publication could add to the potential harm to Ms Campbell by making her think she was being followed by photographers and betrayed by whoever told them where the meeting was. This might discourage her from continuing with the meetings.

In ***Sir Elton John*** v ***Associated Newspapers*** (2006), the case involved pictures of Elton John walking from his car as he arrived home. He complained that publication invaded his privacy because the photos appeared to show that his baldness was returning (Sir Elton famously had a hair transplant many years ago). Refusing his claim for an injunction, Mr Justice Eady said that the pictures did not convey any kind of private information. They were in the same category as a shot of someone 'popping out for a pint of milk', which Baroness Hale had said created no expectation of privacy.

In ***Peck*** v ***UK*** (2003), the ECHR ruled that there had been a 'serious interference' with the claimant's rights under Article 8, after the BBC broadcast footage of his suicide attempt, which had been captured on a local authority's CCTV cameras. The film was used in a programme about the use of CCTV, the point of it being to show that the cameras had effectively saved the man's life by enabling help to get to him. The claim was brought before the misuse of private information claim was developed in ***Campbell***, but the result would almost certainly be the same under that type of claim, because of the principle that film or pictures are so much more intrusive than words. Newspapers routinely report on suicides without infringing Article 8, but using the film was a different matter.

Children and photographs

It appears that children may have a reasonable expectation of privacy in situations where an adult might not, such as where they are photographed doing ordinary everyday things.

In ***Murray*** v ***Express Newspapers plc and Another*** (2008), the author J.K. Rowling sued over pictures taken of her toddler son, David, by a hidden photographer using a long lens, when the family were out walking along a street in Edinburgh. The Court of Appeal said that the rule that there was no legitimate expectation of privacy for pictures of someone doing ordinary things in a public place might not apply to children. There was no guarantee of privacy just because the claimant was a child, and the courts would need to balance the right to privacy against the right to freedom of expression, but in principle, the courts should protect children from intrusive media attention, at least to the extent of holding that there could be a reasonable expectation that a child would not be targeted for photographs taken for publication, without consent, and which the photographer knew would be objected to. The Court of Appeal's finding also emphasised that David's parents had always tried to keep him out of the public eye; it is not clear whether the situation might be different if the claimants were parents who had happily used their children for publicity purposes, but then objected to particular photographs or disclosures.

In ***Weller*** v ***Associated Newspapers*** (2014), the *Daily Mail* was ordered to pay £10,000 damages after publishing unpixellated pictures of singer Paul Weller's children on a family day out. Mr Justice Dingemans said that showing their faces and the emotions they expressed on a normal family day out was an invasion of the children's Article 8 right to privacy, and there was no public interest factor to set in the balance against that.

However, the fact that a claimant is a child will not always mean that they have an expectation of privacy regarding information about them.

In ***AAA* v *Associated Newspapers*** (2012), the claimant was a young child. She had been born as the result of an affair between her mother and a well-known politician, who was married at the time, and who was already known to have fathered a previous child in an extramarital affair. Shortly after the child was born, the politician appointed her mother to a job. It was not publicly known that the child was his daughter, but there was evidence that her mother had dropped hints about it, including to people she did not know, at a party, and that as a result there had been gossip and speculation that went further than her personal circle of friends. The *Mail* and *The Mail on Sunday* had published stories speculating that the politician was her father, as well as pictures of the child, and her mother sought an injunction to prevent further publication. As regards the story itself, the judge said that there was a legitimate expectation of privacy, but this had been compromised by her mother's willingness to divulge the secret to others. She agreed with the *Mail* that there was a public interest in publishing the story, because the fact that a high-profile politician who already had one child as a result of an affair had done it again suggested that recklessness was part of his character, and therefore relevant to his fitness for public office. As a result, publication of the story was justified. Publication of the pictures, however, was not, because there was no public interest in people actually seeing the child. The judge said that using the photo would only have been justified if there had been 'exceptional public interest' reasons to do so. The claimant was awarded £15,000 damages.

Where the information comes from

The way in which information was obtained is relevant, as it has always been in the traditional breach of confidence action.

In ***McKennitt* v *Ash*** (2006), the claimant, Ms McKennitt, was a successful Canadian folk singer, and the defendant, Ms Ash, had been a close friend of hers. Ms Ash wrote a book about going on tour with Ms McKennitt, which discussed, among other things, Ms McKennitt's personal and sexual relationships; her personal feelings, including her reaction to the death of her fiancé some years earlier; her health and diet; and her emotional vulnerability. In the book, Ms Ash said that it was because of her close friendship with Ms McKennitt that she was able to present such a revealing portrait of the singer. In the High Court, Eady J said that the fact that they had a close friendship was a reason why Ms McKennitt had a reasonable expectation that conversations between them, about personal matters, would stay private. He ordered an injunction banning further publication, along with £5,000 damages. This finding was supported by the Court of Appeal.

In ***Lord Browne of Madingley* v *Associated Newspapers*** (2007), the then chief executive of BP sought an injunction to prevent his ex-boyfriend, Jeff Chevalier from publicising their relationship, and revealing details about Lord Browne's discussions about BP strategy with a third party, his misuse of BP resources for Mr Chevalier's benefit, and the fact that he had shared confidential information about the company with Mr Chevalier. Mr Justice Eady said that it was not the subject matter of the revelations that would decide whether they were protected, but the circumstances in which they were conveyed. The information about Lord Browne's discussions on BP's strategy was only learned by Mr Chevalier because of their relationship, and so there was a reasonable expectation of privacy for this. However, Lord Browne had chosen to appear in public with Mr Chevalier at parties and functions, and so the fact of their relationship could not be regarded as private. Nor could the information about the misuse of company resources, because it was not something Mr Chevalier learned about in circumstances of confidence. Regarding the sharing of confidential information with Mr Chevalier, the judge said that the paper was not seeking to reveal what the information was, only the fact that it had been shared, and there was no legitimate expectation of privacy regarding that fact.

Information in the public domain

Where information is already 'in the public domain', and generally known about, there will be no expectation of privacy, because there is nothing left for the law to protect.

In ***Mosley* v *News Group Newspapers*** (2008), the case involving stories about the President of Formula 1 taking part in orgies with prostitutes, the newspaper had posted its video evidence on its website, where it attracted 1.4 million hits. The video was initially removed at Mr Mosley's request but when the paper decided to put it back up, he sought an injunction to stop it. Mr Justice Eady agreed that the film clearly impacted on the claimant's right to privacy, and that there was no legitimate public interest in showing it, but refused the injunction on the grounds that, since the video had been viewed so widely, there could be no reasonable expectation of privacy with regard to it, and no privacy left to be protected.

In ***Trimingham* v *Associated Newspapers*** (2012), the partner of MP Chris Huhne complained about stories in the *Daily Mail* which mentioned the fact that she was bisexual and had previously been in a civil partnership with a woman. Tugendhat J said there could be no legitimate expectation of privacy regarding these issues, as Ms Trimingham was open about her sexuality, and a civil partnership was a public event.

In ***Heather Mills* v *The Sun*** (2001), model and campaigner Heather Mills applied for an injunction to prevent the *Sun* publishing the address of a new home she had bought near Hove in West Sussex. The court refused, on the grounds that it was already widely known that she lived in the area, and in a well-populated town like Hove, it would be impossible for her to keep her address secret anyway.

However, the courts have been quite clear that the fact that a group – even quite a large group – of people know about something, does not necessarily mean it is in the public domain.

In ***HRH Prince of Wales* v *Associated Newspapers*** (2006), the case was brought by Prince Charles, after *The Mail on Sunday* published extracts from journals he had kept. The diaries contained no personal information, but detailed his thoughts and views as he went about his official engagements, including his view of Chinese officials as 'appalling old waxworks'. He routinely sent copies to between 20 and 70 friends and acquaintances, and the newspaper said this meant their content was already in the public domain. The court disagreed, saying they were only ever circulated privately, to specific people, and this did not amount to being in the public domain. Quoting from the judgment in **Douglas** v **Hello**, Mr Justice Blackburne said:

> Information will be confidential if it is available to one person (or a group of people) and not generally available to others, provided that the person (or group) who possesses the information does not intend that it should become available to others.

In ***ETK* v *News Group Newspapers*** (2011), the Court of Appeal granted an injunction preventing reporting of a story involving a married man in the entertainment industry who had been having an affair with a colleague. The newspaper argued that there was no reasonable expectation of privacy, because the affair had become common knowledge at the company where the two worked. The Court disagreed, saying that the fact that people who worked with them knew about the affair did not mean the information was in the public domain. The claimant was reasonably entitled to expect his colleagues to treat the information as confidential, whether they knew about the affair from their own observations of how the couple behaved, or had heard gossip, or had been told, in confidence, by one of the couple. Therefore, there was a legitimate expectation of privacy.

In ***Green Corns Ltd* v *Claverley*** (2005), the claimants were a company which provides residential care for children referred to it by local authorities. They had chosen four houses in the Wolverhampton area to use as homes, and the *Wolverhampton Express and Star* reported this, publishing the addresses of the homes and describing the children who were likely to be sent there as 'yobs' and 'sex offenders'. After demonstrations were held outside the houses, Green Corns sought an injunction against further publication of addresses. The paper argued that they were in the public domain: neighbours would know which houses were being used, and anyone could find out the information by searching through the Land Registry. The court disagreed: by combining the addresses with comments on the disabilities and characteristics of the children, the paper would essentially be creating new information beyond that which was in the public domain.

Even if parts of a story are in the public domain, there can still be a legitimate expectation of privacy which prevents further revelations on the same subject.

In ***McKennitt*** v ***Ash***, the case of Canadian folk singer and the book written by her friend (or by then, ex-friend), the book gave a detailed picture of how devastated Ms McKennitt had been by the death of her fiancé in a sailing accident. Ms McKennitt had in the past given interviews about her fiancé's death, as part of a campaign to prevent similar accidents, and Ms Ash claimed that this meant the matter was in the public domain. Ms KcKennitt said that she disliked personal publicity, and would only give interviews on restricted subjects; with regard to her fiancé's death, she had only said enough in interviews as was necessary to get across the message about safety at sea. The court supported her argument, saying that there was a clear difference between what was in the public domain as the result of a carefully measured interview, and the eight pages of the book in which Ms Ash described her friend's 'pitifully grief-stricken reaction' to the death in close-up detail. Where a case involved personal information, the fact that the information had been revealed to one group of readers did not mean that fresh revelations to different groups could not cause grief or distress. For this kind of information, protection should only be lost where the information is so generally accessible that it can no longer be considered confidential.

In ***CTB*** v ***Newsgroup*** (2012), footballer Ryan Giggs sought to suppress reports of his affair with *Big Brother* contestant Imogen Thomas. In the press, the story had been reported but without saying who Ms Thomas had had an affair with, and Mr Giggs got an injunction preventing his identification. This resulted in a nationwide guessing game played out on the internet, and, before long, anyone who wanted to find out could do so very easily online. Newsgroup went to court to try to get the injunction lifted, on the basis that the information was now in the public domain, but the court held that the injunction should remain in place, because there was likely to be other information that could be published about the affair, and because 'wall to wall coverage' in the papers was likely to be more intrusive and distressing than the mere availability of the information on the internet for those who wanted to find it (the injunction was eventually lifted, much later, after Mr Giggs and Ms Thomas came to an agreement that she would not reveal any details of the affair; in fact, as it turned out, it was not her who had leaked the story in the first place).

Privacy versus freedom of expression

If the court finds that there is a legitimate expectation of privacy regarding the information (or photographs), the next stage is to weigh the claimant's right to privacy against the defendant's right to freedom of expression. In ***Campbell***, the House of Lords said that, as a part of this process, the court should take into account the justifications put forward for interfering with each right, and apply a test of proportionality. The question to ask was whether the benefit of suppressing the information outweighs the benefit of publishing it. Exactly what factors a court will take into account when deciding this varies from case to case, but, essentially, what the courts are asking is whether there is a public interest in publishing the material that outweighs the claimant's right to privacy. These are some of the issues that have been brought into that argument.

Does the material contribute to a debate of general interest?

A key factor that can tip the scales in favour of publication is if the material complained of is relevant to some kind of important debate or discussion. This can be the case even where the story merely reveals something about someone's private life, if that story adds something to the debate.

In *Rio Ferdinand* v *MGN Newspapers* (2011), footballer Rio Ferdinand sued over a story about an affair he had had. In balancing Mr Ferdinand's right to privacy against the newspaper's right to freedom of expression, Mr Justice Nicol looked first at the effect of the story itself, and found that it did not 'excessively intrude . . . into the claimant's private life'. A picture used with the story showed Mr Ferdinand and the woman concerned in a hotel room, but both of them were fully clothed, they were not embracing or kissing, and the photo had obviously been taken by someone who they both knew was there, so there was no serious intrusion there either. On the other side of the scales, there was a genuine public interest in publishing the story, because Rio Ferdinand had recently been appointed captain of the England team, and there had been some debate about whether he was suitable for a job that made him a role model for young boys, because in the past, he had had a 'wild image' and had admitted to being unfaithful to his then partner, now his wife. The story from which the case arose clearly contributed to this debate, especially as Mr Ferdinand had made deliberate attempts to portray himself as a reformed character. The judge concluded that publication should be allowed.

In *The Author of a Blog* v *Times Newspapers Limited* (2009), the case of the anonymous blog by a police officer (see p. 318), *The Times* argued that there was a public interest in revealing the blogger's identity, given that in the blog, he was revealing information gained during police investigations, which was against police conduct rules. In addition, they argued, the public was entitled to know the blogger's identity, in order to assess how far they should believe what they read on such an important issue. The claimant argued that the public interest was in his favour, because he was contributing to a debate of general interest, which he could only do anonymously, and, in addition, if he was identified, he would be disciplined and this would affect his right to freedom of expression. Eady J said that it was not the court's job to protect the claimant from disciplinary action. If the claimant was contributing to a debate of general interest, then *The Times'* story about him would be doing the same. He therefore refused to order an injunction, on the grounds that even if, at trial, it was found that the claimant did have a right to privacy regarding his identity, this was likely to be outweighed by the public interest in a police officer having made these communications.

In *Axel Springer* v *Germany* (2012), the ECHR held that there was a general public interest in reports of criminal proceedings. The case concerned publication by a German magazine of reports that a well-known German actor had been arrested at the Munich Beer Festival and found guilty of possessing cocaine. The German courts had banned publication of the actor's name in connection with the crime, and the ECHR held that this was an unjustified interference with the right to freedom of expression, because the public had an interest in being informed about criminal cases; the story stuck largely to the facts of the matter and did not contain information about the actor's private life, and the information was obtained from reliable sources, including the police. It did not matter that the story was one which was only reported because the defendant was a celebrity.

In *Hutcheson* v *News Group* (2011), the Court of Appeal dismissed a privacy claim by the father-in-law of chef Gordon Ramsey. Chris Hutcheson was attempting to prevent the press from reporting that he had fathered two children with his mistress. He had for some time been involved in a very public dispute with Gordon Ramsey over his sacking as Chief Executive of the chef's company, and had made attacks in the press on the way his son-in-law ran the company, and suggested that Gordon Ramsey was responsible for a breakdown in relations between Gordon Ramsey's wife and her parents. The Court of Appeal found that this was the main reason why the story should not be protected by an injunction. Although there was no particular public interest in the fact that Mr Hutcheson had a secret second family, given than he was not someone who was a public figure, the allegations he had made about Mr Ramsey meant that the 'second family' story could be seen as showing another side to that dispute. The judge said Mr Hutcheson could not use the courts to prevent Mr Ramsey responding to the allegations, using the full facts.

Correcting a false image or impression

Where a celebrity or public figure has set out to create a particular public image for themselves, and a story shows that image to be false, there may be a public interest in publishing the story that outweighs the subject's right to privacy.

In ***Campbell***, the House of Lords held that there was public interest in the *Mirror* revealing that Naomi Campbell was a drug addict, given that, during her career, she had frequently said that many models had problems with drugs, but she did not.

In 2005, David and Victoria Beckham failed to get an injunction preventing their nanny from revealing details of their relationship, even though her employment contract contained a confidentiality clause. The court accepted the paper's argument that the revelations were in the public interest, because the couple presented themselves as blissfully happily married, and the nanny's revelations suggested that this impression was false.

In ***Rio Ferdinand*** v ***MGN Ltd*** (2011), the fact that the footballer had presented himself as a reformed character who no longer played around with other women was a factor in the court deciding that his right to privacy was outweighed by the newspaper's right to freedom of expression.

In ***Mosley***, Mr Justice Eady confirmed that publication might have been in the public interest if the information corrected a false image put about by the claimant. This might be the case, for example, if he had promoted himself as someone who was opposed to sex outside marriage. But that was not the situation here, so there was no public interest in publishing the story.

In 2012, former England football manager Steve McClaren was denied an injunction to prevent the *Sun* reporting that he had had an affair. The fact that he had presented himself as happily married, being photographed with his wife when he was appointed to the England manager's job, meant there was a public interest in revealing that this image was false, especially given the high-profile nature of his job.

However, it appears that stories revealing that a celebrity is not what they claim to be will only be justified in the public interest when they reveal serious discrepancies between the public image and the celebrity's real behaviour, and not trivial differences.

In ***McKennitt*** v ***Ash*** (see above), the author claimed that the personal values Ms McKennitt presented herself as holding were not always reflected in her behaviour, and her book corrected this false impression. Mr Justice Eady rejected this argument, and said that, while revelations of serious misbehaviour by a celebrity might be justified in the public interest, relatively trivial matters would not:

> the mere fact that a celebrity falls short from time to time, like everyone else, could not possibly justify exposure, in the supposed public interest, of every peccadillo or foible cropping up in everyday life.

The public interest and celebrities

In the past, the courts were very clear that there is a distinction between subjects that are a matter of public interest, and subjects that the public are interested in. That meant that, as a general rule, where stories about the private lives of celebrities did not contribute to a debate of general interest, or correct a misleading impression, their right to privacy would outweigh the media's right to freedom of expression.

In ***Mosley* v *News Group Newspapers*** (2008), the case involving the President of Formula 1 motor racing and his sadomasochistic orgy, the paper claimed that the orgy had had a 'Nazi theme'. They said there was a public interest in knowing that a man in the claimant's public position was indulging in sado-masochistic sex with prostitutes, and doing so within a Nazi-themed setting. Mr Justice Eady found that, on the facts, there was no truth in the allegations of Nazi overtones. That being the case, he said that there was no public interest in revealing the fact that someone in the claimant's position was taking part in sadomaso-chistic orgies which did not go so far as to break any criminal law. If the claimant had been involved in mock-ing the Holocaust in such a way as to call into question his role in an organisation to which he was accountable, the defence could apply, but here there was no evidence of this.

However, after a key decision by the European Court of Human Rights, there has been a shift in this approach.

In ***Von Hannover* v *Germany*** (2012) Princess Caroline of Monaco brought a case concerning the publication by several German magazines of a picture story about her and her family on holiday. The German courts had granted an injunction against some of the coverage, but allowed publication of a story about the health of the princess's father, and the fact that she had gone on holiday while he was ill. The ECHR said the German courts were justified in refusing an injunction, partly because the prince's health was a mat-ter of public interest, but also, crucially, because the princess was a 'public figure'. They went on to define this quite broadly, stating that:

> Public figures are persons holding public office and/or using public resources and, more broadly speaking, all those who play a role in public life, whether in politics, the economy, the social sphere, sport or in any other domain.

This widened the previous approach to the question of who was or was not a public figure, and it appears the UK courts are following suit.

In ***Spelman* v *Express Newspapers*** (2012), the then Environment Secretary Caroline Spelman had obtained an interim injunction preventing publication of a story about her teenage son, who is an international rugby player, and was seeking to continue it. The story was about him taking drugs that were banned under anti-doping rules, when recovering from an injury. The judge refused to continue the injunc-tion, partly because as an international rugby player, Mr Spelman could be considered a public figure.

In ***McClaren* v *News Group Newspapers*** (2012), the former England football manager Steve McClaren tried to prevent publication of a story about a sexual relationship he had had. The judge rejected the application. He agreed that there was a reasonable expectation of privacy regarding sexual relationships, but said that this was outweighed by the fact that Mr McClaren was a public figure who had held positions of responsibility, and from whom it was reasonable for the public to expect a higher standard of behaviuor.

In ***RocknRoll* v *Newsgroup Newspapers Ltd*** (2013), the court held that being married to a celebrity did not make their spouse a public figure in their own right. The case was brought by the husband of actress Kate Winslet, who secured an injunction to prevent the *Sun* publishing semi-naked photos of him at a party. The court said that Mr RocknRoll had briefly become 'something of a public figure' as a result of his marriage, and it was inevitable that pictures would be published of the couple together. But this did not justify him being treated as a public figure in his own right.

The right to tell

Privacy cases often involve weighing the claimant's right to privacy against the media's right to freedom of expression. But where a story involves two people, there may be a second set of clashing rights to consider: the party wanting to tell the story's right to freedom of expression, against the right to privacy of the party wanting to keep it secret. The courts then have to weigh up one party's right to freedom of expression regarding their own story, against the other's right to privacy. In general, the position seems to be that the person wanting to tell their story can only do so if they can do it without infringing the other person's privacy. However, the decided cases have all been ones where there was no real public interest in telling the story; the balance might be struck differently in a case where there was.

In ***McKennitt* v *Ash*** (see above), part of Ms Ash's claim was that the story was not just Ms McKennitt's but hers as well, because she was a friend of Ms McKennitt and had been involved in a lot of the incidents in the book. She said her right to freedom of expression meant she should be free to tell that story. The court found that if a person wants to publish information about their relationship with someone else, and that information is of a kind that would normally create an expectation of privacy, the material published has to be shaped in such a way as to protect the other person's privacy. Mr Justice Eady commented that: 'It does not follow that, because one can reveal one's own private life, that one can also expose confidential matters in respect of which others are entitled to protection if their consent is not forthcoming.'

In ***CTB* v *Newsgroup*** (2012), where footballer Ryan Giggs sought to suppress reports of his affair with *Big Brother* contestant Imogen Thomas, the court said that Miss Thomas was free to exercise her Article 10 right by selling her life story, but only in so far as she could do so without intruding on the privacy rights of others.

Necessity of the information

As we saw above, the balancing act between the right to privacy and the right to freedom of expression requires the courts to look at proportionality: is the amount of interference with one right proportionate to the importance of allowing the other? They may therefore find that, while a story overall is of sufficient public interest to allow publication, certain details should be left out because they are unnecessary to that purpose.

In ***Green Corns* v *Claverley*** (see above), the case involving publication of the addresses of homes for children in local authority care, the paper argued that it was in the public interest for there to be public debate over how such children were cared for. The court agreed that these were issues of public interest, but said that preventing publication of the addresses did not prevent the debate.

Privacy and court cases

As we saw elsewhere on court reporting, individuals involved in court cases, either directly or indirectly, will often try to use the law to protect their privacy. In most cases they will try to use the laws which specifically apply to court reporting, but it is perhaps not surprising that attempts would be made to use the developing law of privacy where reporting restrictions do not offer protection. However, the courts have not been willing to go along with this kind of application.

In ***PNM* v *Times Newspapers*** (2014), a man who had been arrested but not charged in a child sex abuse case tried and failed to use privacy laws to prevent *The Times* from naming him. The man was one of several arrested in connection with child trafficking, but was not charged along with the others. A child witness in the case had named him, but then failed to identify him, and he successfully sought a s4(2) order (see Chapter 8) to prevent his name being reported when the other men were tried, arguing that this would prejudice his trial if he was ever charged. When the s4(2) order was discontinued because proceedings against him were no longer pending, he applied for an injunction, arguing that naming him would breach his right to privacy. The court refused, saying that there was a public interest in court proceedings being reported openly, which outweighed his right to privacy.

Using pictures

The issue of how the competing rights to privacy and freedom of expression should be balanced with regard to pictures of well-known people has been examined in two ECHR cases, which the English courts should take into account.

In ***Von Hannover* v *Germany*** (2004), Princess Caroline of Monaco had tried to sue certain newspapers in the German courts, complaining that she was constantly followed and photographed by paparazzi, even when she was doing ordinary things like shopping or taking her children to school. The German courts refused her claim, saying that, as a public figure, she had to accept that the public had a legitimate interest in knowing about even her ordinary daily life. She took her case to the European Court of Human Rights (ECHR), claiming that German law did not protect her right to privacy under Article 8 of the European Convention on Human Rights. The ECHR upheld her claim. They said that the key question when balancing the rights of privacy and freedom of expression was whether the material published contributed to 'a debate of general interest'. If it did, the right of freedom of expression was more likely to win out, but if it did not, the right of privacy was likely to have more importance. In this case, it said, the pictures made no real contribution to a debate of general interest. There was no legitimate public interest in seeing pictures of Princess Caroline when she was not performing her official role, so her right of privacy should take priority over the media's right to freedom of expression.

In ***Von Hannover* v *Germany*** (2012), also brought by Princess Caroline, the ECHR clarified when pictures of someone going about their ordinary business would be considered to contribute to a 'debate of general interest'. The case involved photos in German magazines of the Princess and her family on a skiing holiday. The German courts granted an injunction over two of the pictures, but allowed publication of a third one, which showed Princess Caroline and her husband taking a walk during the holiday, and was accompanied by a story about the poor health of her father, Prince Rainier, and a headline which pointed out that the Princess had gone on holiday while her father was ill. The German courts found that the Prince's health was a matter of public interest and the press was entitled to report the way in which his children were reconciling their family obligations with their need for a private life, including the wish to go on holiday. There was a sufficiently close link between this subject matter and the photograph to justify its publication. They went on to say that, where a story on a matter of public interest was just used as a pretext for publication of a photo, the photo would not be a contribution on a matter of public interest and there would be no justification for allowing the public interest in publication to win out over the subject's right to privacy. The ECHR approved this approach, and also noted other factors in favour of allowing publication: that the Princess and her husband were public figures, that the photos were not taken surreptitiously or secretly, and that their content was not offensive in any way. As a result, the Court said, the decision to allow publication had struck the right balance between freedom of expression and the right to a private life.

In ***Von Hannover* v *Germany (No 3)*** (2013), the ECHR rejected another claim by Princess Caroline over pictures of her private life. She tried to secure an injunction to prevent further publication of photos of her and her husband on holiday, which were shown with a story about celebrities who rent out their holiday villas. The ECHR upheld the German national courts' finding that the story was about a matter of general interest, and the picture contained nothing that violated any privacy rights. The article did not contain any details about the Princess's private life, and so it could not be said that it was just a pretext for publishing the photo, or that the link between them was contrived.

Using material from the public and social media

It has become increasingly common for all sections of the media to use content that comes not from journalists or professional photographers, but from the public: someone who happens to be on the scene of an incident and captures video or photos on their phone will often have material that is more newsworthy than anything else. However, when using this kind of material, it is important to be aware of issues of privacy. A member of the public who has filmed or photographed an accident or incident will not be aware that showing people involved without their consent may be a breach of both privacy laws and the ethical rules of IPSO and Ofcom, but if you use the material, you could be sued/and or found to be in breach, so you need to apply the same care to this kind of material as you would to anything you had produced yourself.

Care also needs to be applied when using pictures or other material from social media sites such as Facebook, Twitter and Flikr; the fact that you can physically access this material does not necessarily mean you can or should use it. Publishing photos of someone in a situation where there is a legitimate expectation of privacy, even if those photos have already been published to that person's friends on Facebook, could put you at risk of a claim for misuse of personal information (remember that there can be a legitimate expectation of privacy even where material has been published to a group of people – see the Prince Charles case, p. 306).

Ethical considerations also apply here. Guidance from the PCC (which is very likely to be echoed by IPSO) suggests that when deciding whether using pictures from social media in a news story will infringe someone's privacy, relevant considerations include whether the image is of a personal nature, whether access to it was limited (for example by restricting its publication to friends on Facebook), whether the person shown uploaded it themselves, and whether there is a public interest in using it. Even if the picture has been uploaded by the person concerned, and published on social media without restrictions, whether it is ethical to use it will depend on the context. For example, if the subject of the picture is a murder or accident victim, you could well be in breach of the Code provisions on intrusion into shock and grief if you use an inappropriate shot – such as one of the victim drunk, or in a silly pose – in a report of the death.

REMEDIES IN PRIVACY ACTIONS

As we saw at the beginning of this chapter, the main remedy in a privacy action is an injunction, but where information has already been published, the claimant may also get damages.

Injunctions

Claimants can apply for an injunction to prevent publication in the first place, or to prevent further publication if the material has already been published. In either case, the injunction may be an interim one – which is designed to put the situation on hold until the issue is tried – or a permanent one – which is issued if a claimant proves their case at trial (in some cases an interim injunction will be issued before trial, and then if the claimant wins, it becomes a permanent one).

In practice, as explained at the beginning of this chapter, an interim injunction can often effectively kill a story without the defendant needing to prove their case at trial. A further problem is that they can be issued at very short notice (judges will do this over the phone, even at night), and it is not unusual for an injunction to be ordered just before a paper goes to press, or even after printing has started. On the other hand, in many cases, if the media can successfully fight off an interim injunction, the claimant will not bother taking the matter to trial, because to do so would only give even more publicity to the information.

When considering either type of injunction, the Human Rights Act makes it clear that the courts must take into account its potential effect on press freedom. Section 12 of the Act states that if a court is asked to give any order which could affect freedom of expression, with regard to journalistic material, they must take into account the importance of the right to freedom of expression, and must consider the extent to which the material concerned is already in the public domain, and any public interest in publication.

Although this merely recognises defences which exist in English law, it makes it clear that the possibility of such defences applying must be considered even in the application for an interim injunction, and not just at trial. The court also has to consider 'any relevant privacy code'. This means that, if a case involves the press, the courts are likely to look at whether, during work on the story, the journalists have behaved in accordance with the Editor's Code, while in cases involving broadcast, they will look at the Ofcom Code or the BBC's own codes of practice. The overall effect of these provisions, as accepted by the Court of Appeal in ***Douglas***, is that the courts must assess the merits of the case before they allow publication to be suppressed.

Special rules for interim injunctions

As we saw earlier (in Chapter 16), an injunction which prevents material being published in the first place is viewed as a serious restriction on freedom of expression, and, although the courts are more willing to grant such injunctions in confidentiality cases than defamation ones, they still have to take into account some extra restrictions which the Human Rights Act puts on such injunctions. Section 12 provides that injunctions which restrain publication before trial should only be granted where the claimant can show that they are 'likely' to prove a breach of confidence if the case goes to trial. In ***Cream Holdings* v *Banerjee*** (2004), the House of Lords said this meant that in most cases an interim injunction should only be ordered if the claimant could prove that it was more likely than not that they would win at trial. However, an injunction might also be granted in exceptional situations where the claimant could not prove they were likely to win, but where the consequences of disclosing the information would be especially serious for them.

In addition, s12 provides that a court should not grant an injunction unless:

- the journalist is present;
- the claimant has taken all practical steps to notify the journalist; or
- there are compelling reasons why the journalist should not be notified.

In practice, these restrictions are sometimes not difficult to get round; in the ***Douglas*** case (see above), the initial temporary injunction was granted over the phone, late at night, after *OK!* said that they had tried to contact the editor of *Hello!*, but the only person available at their offices at that time of night was a security guard. However, there are signs that the courts are now taking a stricter approach to this issue.

In ***Terry* v *Person Unknown*** (2010), Mr Justice Tugendhat refused to continue an injunction preventing publication of footballer John Terry's affair, partly on the grounds that he could not assess whether publication was in the public interest, because the media had not been told of the application and so were not there to argue for the public interest defence. The claim was made against a 'Person Unknown' who the claimant alleged was leaking details of the affair, and, when an interim injunction was ordered while the judge considered the case, the claimant made the national press aware of the injunction. This meant that they were also bound by it (see below), and reporting of the affair was therefore restricted. In deciding not to renew the injunction, the judge said it was clear that the order was really intended to be used against the media, and stressed that, when someone intended an injunction to cover the media, the media should be notified so that they could have a realistic opportunity of putting forward arguments against the injunction or its terms.

As with defamation cases (see Chapter 16), a claimant seeking an injunction to prevent publication before trial must also prove that their loss could not be equally well compensated by damages. In cases that are genuinely about privacy, this will not be difficult, because clearly no amount of money can make information secret again. But the courts are alert to the fact that some privacy claims have a more financial motive, and, in these cases, damages can be considered adequate.

In *Terry v Person Unknown* (2010), Mr Justice Tugendhat said it was clear that the claimant would not be caused personal distress by the revelations he was seeking to ban, but instead was concerned about the effect that damage to his reputation might have on his sponsorship deals. Therefore damages would be a sufficient remedy, and an injunction was not appropriate. The judge also pointed out that the claim appeared to have been framed as misuse of private information in an attempt to get round the rules on injunctions for defamation cases, where injunctions will not normally be granted if the defendant is likely to plead justification (the old name for the truth defence). But it was in reality a defamation claim, and had to be treated like one.

The party seeking an interim injunction has to give what is called a cross-undertaking in damages, which means that if the matter goes to trial, and the court holds that there was no breach of confidence, the claimant has to pay damages to the defendant, and may have to pay costs as well.

Extent of injunctions

If a court imposes an injunction preventing publication, that injunction applies to all media organisations which know about the injunction, and not just the newspaper named in the case.

In the long-running *Spycatcher* litigation (see above), the *Sunday Times* first published information from Peter Wright's book, and the Government successfully secured an injunction preventing them from publishing further material. When other papers then published material from the book, they were held in contempt of court, because, the court said, the purpose of the injunction was to prevent publication and they had frustrated that purpose. This ruling was later confirmed by the House of Lords.

An injunction imposed by an English court does not prevent publication in another country, including Scotland (though a claimant can go to court in Scotland and ask for a similar order, called an interdict).

Super injunctions and anonymised injunctions

In some cases, an injunction may be so widely drafted that it not only prevents publication of the material concerned, but also bans the media from mentioning that action has been taken to prevent publication. This type of injunction has become known as a super injunction, and it means that the claimant can not only prevent the press from reporting on them, but also prevent them from reporting that that person is trying to gag the press. Publishing details of a super injunction is a contempt of court.

In practice, super-injunctions are not commonly used, but anonymised injunctions are more common in privacy cases. In this type of injunction, the claimant, and sometimes, though not always, the defendant, are not named, but referred to by randomly chosen initials. Where this kind of injunction applies, the press can report that the injunction exists, and report any details of the story which are not restricted by the injunction, but cannot name anyone who is anonymised in the injunction. Again, breach of these terms is contempt of court.

There has been some concern that the courts had become too willing to grant both super-injunctions and anonymised injunctions, and in ***JIH* v *News Group Newspapers*** (2011), the Master of the Rolls, Lord Neuberger, set out the factors that courts should take into account in cases where individuals attempt to prevent the press from reporting that they are seeking a privacy order. The case was brought by a well-known sportsman who wanted to prevent both reporting on his private life, and reporting of the fact that he was seeking a gagging order. Lord Neuberger said that, as a general rule, parties to a case are named in court documents, and there is no general exception to this rule just because the case involves private matters. Nor did the fact that a claimant was a celebrity entitle them to any special treatment. Where a court was asked to conceal the identity of one or more parties, it should closely scrutinise the application, and decide whether any restraint on publicity is necessary, by looking at whether there is sufficient public interest in publication to justify any curtailment of the parties' rights to privacy and respect for family life. They should also consider whether there is any less restrictive way of achieving the same effect.

CLAIMS UNDER THE PROTECTION FROM HARASSMENT ACT 1997

The Protection from Harassment Act 1997 was introduced to deal with stalkers, and creates two criminal offences. The first, defined in s1, is committed where someone pursues a course of conduct which amounts of harassment of another, and they know or ought to know it amounts to harassment. It can be punished with six months' imprisonment or a fine. The second, more serious offence, defined in s4, is committed where someone puts another in fear of violence on at least two occasions, and knows or ought to know they are doing so. It carries a maximum sentence of five years' imprisonment or a fine.

The Act also allows a civil claim for damages or an injunction against anyone committing harassment as defined in the Act, whether or not they have been charged with one of the criminal offences.

It was always clear that this Act might also be used against journalists who use tactics like persistent doorstepping, or photographers who pursue celebrities to an unreasonable degree. What was not predicted was that the Act might be used against the media on the grounds of what it published, but in fact two attempts have been made to do this. However, it is clear from both the cases that in any harassment case that was based on a publication the courts would have to consider the effect on freedom of expression, and in the Trimingham case, below, Mr Justice Tugendhat said that a course of conduct involving journalistic publication could not amount to harassment under the Act unless it was so unreasonable that there was a pressing social need to sanction it, and it was proportionate to do so. This is clearly quite a high bar, and the ***Trimingham*** case especially makes it clear that what Mr Justice Tugendhat called 'insults and other offensive matter' will not in itself be enough to justify sanctions under the Act.

In ***Thomas* v *News Group Newspapers Ltd*** (2002), the *Sun* carried a story about an incident which took place in a police station. A Somali asylum seeker came into the station asking for directions to an asylum centre, and after the woman left, Ms Thomas, who was a clerk at the police station, overheard another officer making a joke which she considered to be racist. She complained, and the officer was demoted. The *Sun*'s initial story referred to Ms Thomas as 'a black clerk', and the paper then published several readers' letters criticising her. A second article then invited readers to give their views on the decision to discipline the officer who made the joke, and the paper then published a number of readers' letters criticising Ms Thomas. As a result, she received hate mail, and became afraid to go to work. She brought a case against the *Sun* under the Protection from Harassment Act. The paper tried to have the claim struck out but the Court of Appeal held that Ms Thomas had an arguable case, and the newspaper would have to show that its conduct was reasonable. The court said that where a harassment case involved publication, the test would be whether publishing material that was likely to cause someone distress was an abuse of the freedom of the press.

In ***Trimingham* v *Associated Newspapers*** (2012), the partner of MP Chris Huhne sued over a number of articles in the *Daily Mail*, which, among other things, referred to her as 'a comedy lesbian from central casting', implied she was ugly and looked like a man, constantly mentioned her sexuality, and went into great detail about her previous relationships and sex life. In refusing her claim, Mr Justice Tugendhat held that, although the material did include insults and offensive matter, it did not amount to harassment.

What the codes say **Privacy**

The Editor's Code of Practice used by IPSO includes the following provisions on privacy:

- 'Everyone is entitled to respect for his or her private and family life, home, health and correspondence, including digital communications.'
- 'Editors will be expected to justify intrusions into any individual's private life without consent. Account will be taken of the complainant's own public disclosures of information.'
- 'It is unacceptable to photograph individuals in private places without their consent.' The Code explains that "private places" can be public or private property, where there is 'a reasonable expectation of privacy.'

In ***McCartney* v *Hello!***, the PCC upheld a complaint by Paul McCartney over pictures published of him and two of his children lighting a candle in a cathedral in memory of his wife Linda, who had recently died. The PCC said the cathedral was a clear example of a place where there was a reasonable expectation of privacy.

- Young people should be free to complete their time at school without unnece1ssary intrusion.
- A child under 16 must not be interviewed or photographed on issues involving their own or another child's welfare unless a custodial parent or similarly responsible adult consents. The PCC has, however, made it clear that parental consent for photographing a child can be assumed in contexts where the child is in a crowd or public place and the picture is 'innocuous'.

In ***Quigley* v *Zoo*** (June 23, 2006), the PCC rejected a complaint from a man who was photographed with his ten-year-old daughter at a football match at Old Trafford. Both the child and her father were shown making offensive gestures, and the photo was published

in *Zoo* magazine in a report on bigotry among football crowds. The man claimed his daughter's face should have been pixellated (which other papers had done) but the PCC said this was not necessary because the photo was taken in a public place and the story did not concern the child's welfare.

Editors will always need a strong public interest reason to infringe a child's privacy, and even where there is a strong public interest in the story itself, it may still be necessary to conceal the identity of any children involved.

In ***Mrs Laura Gaddis* v *Hamilton Advertiser*** (July 30, 2007), the PCC criticised the *Advertiser* for publishing, on its website, footage of disruptive behaviour in a classroom, which was filmed by one of the children in the class to show how the behaviour was disrupting her education. The PCC agreed with the newspaper that it was in the public interest to show the film, but said the paper should have concealed the faces of the children shown.

- Pupils must not be approached or photographed at school without the permission of the school authorities.
- Minors must not be paid for material involving children's welfare, nor parents or guardians for material about their children or wards, unless it is clearly in the child's interest.
- Editors must not use the fame, notoriety or position of a parent or guardian as sole justification for publishing details of a child's private life.

The above provisions are subject to the public interest exemption (see p. 384).

The Ofcom Code of Practice has a number of provisions on privacy. In some cases (stated below) an invasion of privacy will be allowed if it is 'warranted'. The Code explains that warranted means that the broadcaster must be able to explain why the actions were justified in the particular case. Invasions of privacy may be justified, for example, where they are in the public interest, but the broadcaster would have to explain why the public interest outweights the right of privacy. Examples of the public interest would be stories revealing or detecting crime, protecting public health or safety, exposing misleading claims made by individuals or organisations, or revealing incompetence that affects the public.

The Ofcom provisions on privacy are:

- 'Any infringement of privacy in programmes, or in connection with obtaining material included in programmes, must be warranted.'
- Legitimate expectations of privacy will vary according to the place and nature of the information, activity or condition in question, the extent to which it is in the public domain (if at all) and whether the individual concerned is already in the public eye. There may be circumstances where people can expect privacy even in a public place. Some activities and conditions may be of such a private nature that filming or recording, even in a public place, could involve an infringement of privacy. People under investigation or in the public eye, and their immediate family and friends, retain the right to a private life, although private behaviour can raise issues of legitimate public interest.

- The location of a person's home or family should not be revealed without their consent, unless warranted.
- Broadcasters should recognise that people who are caught up in newsworthy events still have a right to privacy, unless it is warranted to infringe it. This applies both when reporting current events, and for later programmes looking at those events.
- Broadcasters should ensure that words, pictures or actions filmed or recorded in public places are not so private that their inclusion in a programme should require consent from the people featured, unless broadcast without consent is warranted. As examples, Ofcom's guidance on the Code suggests that situations where people can expect a degree of privacy even in a public place might be where someone has a disfiguring medical condition, or cases of suicide attempts.
- Any material which infringes privacy should only be used with the person's informed consent, or where it is warranted, as defined above (callers to phone-in shows are considered to have given consent by the act of phoning in).
- If a person or organisation's privacy is being infringed, and they ask for filming or recording to stop, the programme maker should normally comply with their request, unless continuing is warranted.
- When filming or recording takes place inside the premises of an organisation, institution or other agency, permission should be obtained from the relevant authority, unless it is warranted to go ahead without permission. In sensitive places, such as hospitals, ambulances, schools, prisons or police stations, separate consent should be obtained from anyone in a sensitive situation, before filming and again before broadcast, unless not obtaining consent is warranted. It is not normally necessary to get consent from employees or members of the public whose appearance is incidental.
- It is not normally necessary to get consent from employees or members of the public whose appearance is incidental.
- The means of obtaining material must be proportionate in the circumstances, and particularly to the subject matter of the programme. This simply means that tactics that might be appropriate in a programme that, for example, uncovers serious wrongdoing, might not be allowed in a less publicly important story.
- Broadcasters should ensure that the re-use of material, whether their own or someone else's does not involve an unwarranted infringement of privacy.
- Doorstepping for factual programmes should not take place unless it has not been possible to request an interview, the request has been refused, or there is reason to believe that the investigation will be frustrated if the subject is approached openly, and doorstepping is warranted in the circumstances. The Code defines doorstepping as filming or recording an interview or attempt at an interview, or announcing that a phone call is being filmed or recorded for broadcast, without prior warning (you might do this, for example, if you wanted to put allegations of wrongdoing to someone by catching them at home). This does not include vox pops, and the Code also says that broadcasters can normally interview, film or record people in public places, without prior warning.

→

- Broadcasters can record telephone conversations where they have identified themselves and the purpose of the call, and explained that it may be broadcast (if that applies), unless it is warranted not to do so. If it only becomes clear later than that the call may be broadcast, consent must be obtained, unless not getting it is warranted.
- Material obtained by surreptitious filming or recording should not be used unless it is warranted. This includes material obtained by using long lenses or recording devices; by leaving a camera or recorder unattended on private property, without the informed consent of the owner of the property; by taping a phone conversation without telling the other person; or by deliberately continuing to record when the subject believes you have stopped.
- Broadcasters should not film, record, or use footage or tape of, people involved in an emergency, accident victims, or anyone suffering a personal tragedy, where to do so would be an infringement of privacy, unless it is warranted or the people concerned have given informed consent. This applies whether the events are in a public place or not.
- People who are distressed should not be pressurised to give interviews or otherwise take part in a programme, unless this is warranted.
- Broadcasters should take care not to broadcast the names of anyone who has died, or been involved in an accident or violent crime, unless they are sure that the next of kin have already been told, or unless it is warranted.
- When covering past events that have caused trauma to individuals (including crime), broadcasters should try to reduce the potential distress to victims and/or relatives, unless not doing so is warranted. As far as possible, surviving victims and/or close relatives of victims should be told when such programmes are made and broadcast.
- Broadcasters should take special care not to infringe the privacy of people under 16, and should recognise that the fact that they do not lost their right to privacy because their parents may be famous, or because newsworthy events have happened at their school.
- Where a programme features someone under 16 in such a way that their privacy is infringed, consent should be obtained from the person themselves, if possible, and also from their parent, guardian, or someone over 18 who is in loco parentis, unless the subject is trivial, the person's participation is minor, or the invasion of privacy is warranted.
- People under 16 should not be questioned about personal matters without the consent of their parent, guardian, or someone over 18 who is in loco parentis, unless it is warranted to do so without consent.
- People who are over 18, but vulnerable in some way should not be questioned about personal matters without the consent of someone over 18 who has primary responsibility for their care, unless it is warranted to do so without consent. As examples of vulnerable adults, the Code cites the bereaved, people with learning difficulties, people with mental problems or dementia, and people who are traumatised, sick or terminally ill.

KEY POINTS

Privacy claims

Privacy claims involve a two-stage test.

- Does the claimant have a reasonable expectation of privacy? And if so,
- Is their right to privacy more important in the circumstances than the defendant's right to freedom of expression?

In deciding whether there is a reasonable expectation of privacy, the courts look at all the circumstances.

- the attributes of the claimant and the likely effect of publication on them;
- the type of activity mentioned – private activities are more likely to be protected;
- use of photos or video – these may be considered more intrusive than words conveying the same information;
- whether children are involved;
- where the information comes from;
- whether and how far the material is already in the public domain.

In balancing the right of privacy against the right of freedom of expression, the courts will look at whether there is a public interest in publication which outweighs the right to privacy. Relevant factors include:

- whether the material contributes to a general debate;
- whether it corrects a false impression;
- whether particular details are necessary in the public interest.

Remedies

The main remedy for a privacy claims is an injunction, and special rules apply to the use of pre-trial injunctions.

Where information is already published, damages may be claimed.

TEST YOUR KNOWLEDGE

1 What is the test for a privacy, or misuse of private information claim?

2 Which of the following make it more likely that there will be a legitimate expectation of privacy?

(a) The story reveals intimate details of a sexual relationship.

(b) The story involves a celebrity who has been convicted of crime.

(c) The story includes details of someone's medical treatment.

3 Billy Brash is a Premier League footballer whose public image is that of a clean-cut family man, and who has made a lot of money through appearing in advertisements with his wife and their two photogenic children. You find out that he has been having an affair with a well-known TV presenter. He goes to court to get an injunction preventing publication of the story. What arguments can you make to persuade the court that the injunction should not be granted?

ONLINE RESOURCES

Campbell v *MGN* can be read at:
www.bailii.org/eu/cases/ECHR/2012/228.html

Details of complaints about invasion of privacy under the PCC Code and their outcome can be read at: www.pcc.org.uk. Details of old cases are still on the PCC website, but new adjudications will appear on the IPSO one at: www.ipso.co.uk

Chapter 20 Trespass, harassment and unethical behaviour

We have looked at situations where the media might be said to invade privacy because of what they publish (see Chapter 19). However, there are also situations where people feel their privacy has been invaded by the way the media behaves when gathering information or pictures for a story. The most topical example is of course phone hacking, but problems can also be caused by more traditional methods of gathering information, such as doorstepping. In this chapter, we look at the law on trespass (which means being on someone's land or property without permission), harassment (which can be a criminal offence), and phone tapping and hacking. We also include some other criminal offences which cover unethical behaviour while newsgathering: bribery, misconduct in public office and perverting the course of justice.

As well as the legal provisions regarding these issues, they are also covered in the codes of practice used by IPSO and Ofcom. In many cases, people will turn to these rather than legal action (because it is easier and costs them nothing), so it is important to be aware of their provisions in this area.

TRESPASS

There are clearly many cases when in order to get a story – or even a comment for one – journalists go onto other people's property without an invitation. In such situations, it is not uncommon for the unwilling interviewee to threaten to have reporters 'done' for trespass, but in fact trespass is a civil, rather than a criminal offence.

Trespass is committed by 'unlawful interference' with someone else's land (land includes buildings, such as someone's house or office) or their property. 'Unlawful interference' can be as little as going onto the land without permission, or staying there after being asked to leave, and it also applies where you have permission to be on the land, but while there, you do something which goes beyond what you have permission to do. For example, if someone agrees to let you into their house and answer a few questions, you might commit trespass if, while they are out of the room, you search a drawer or go and wander about upstairs. If you gain entry to somewhere by deception (e.g. by claiming you are someone else), then you will be considered to have entered the land without permission, even if the owner asks you in.

It is, therefore, fairly easy to commit trespass, but it is not common for journalists to be sued for it, simply because the law offers a few useful remedies in these situations. Trespass is not (with one exception, discussed below) a criminal offence but a civil wrong, so you will not find yourself arrested and escorted off the premises simply for trespassing. The police can help the landowner to use reasonable force to get you off the premises, but they are not obliged to.

The landowner can go to court to get an injunction to stop you trespassing again, but, unless you are following the same story over a long period of time, this clearly offers them no practical help, especially as the courts have shown themselves to be very reluctant to prevent publication of material gained through trespass. A landowner can also sue for damages, but, unless you have actually caused damage to their land, these will not amount to much. However, if a journalist had behaved extremely badly during a trespass, for example by forcing their way into someone's home, or searching through private property, a court might show its disapproval by ordering exemplary damages, which means an additional sum designed to punish a defendant who has behaved very badly.

Only the landowner or the person who is in 'immediate possession' of the land can sue for trespass. This would include, for example, the tenant of a house or office, but not someone who is a guest or visitor.

In ***Kaye*** v ***Robertson*** (1991), the case involving the actor 'interviewed' in his hospital bed (see p. 280), Mr Kaye could not sue for trespass, as he was effectively only a guest or visitor.

Trespass to land can only be committed by going onto land, or throwing or putting something on it; it cannot be committed, for example, by standing in a public place (or somewhere you have permission to be) and photographing someone on private land, or standing outside someone's front garden and waiting for them to leave the house (though where a large group of journalists and/or photographers gather, the police can use powers under the Highways Act 1980 to move them on).

In ***Bernstein*** v ***Skyviews and General Ltd*** (1978), Lord Bernstein, then chairman of Granada TV, went to court to try to get damages from a company which took photos of his house using aerial photography. As the plane was never less than several hundred feet above the land, the court held that there was no trespass.

As stated above, there is one criminal offence related to trespass: aggravated trespass under the Criminal Justice and Public Order Act 1994. It is committed by entering land where a lawful activity is taking place, and doing anything intended to disrupt or obstruct that activity. The offence is intended to deal with situations such as protests and hunt sabotage and, as journalists are likely to be present at such events, there is a possibility that they could be accused of the offence, for which the penalty is up to three months' imprisonment or a fine. Section 69 of the Act allows a senior police officer to order any person involved in aggravated trespass to leave the property, and failing to do so, or returning within three months, is an offence. However, there is a defence to this section, which applies where someone has a 'reasonable excuse' to stay, and it is arguable that this could apply to a journalist or photographer reporting the incident.

HARASSMENT

The Protection from Harassment Act 1997 was designed to deal with the problem of stalkers, but the definition of the Act is wide enough to include journalistic practices such as persistent doorstepping, chasing people to get a quote or a photo, or persistent phone calls; celebrities including Sienna Miller, Lily Allen and the late Amy Winehouse have all managed to get injunctions against the press by using the Act.

The Act creates two criminal offences, and also allows a victim of harassment under the Act to sue in the civil courts, for damages and/or an injunction. A civil case can be brought even if the defendant has not been charged with a criminal offence under the Act.

The first of the two criminal offences, defined in s1, is committed where someone:

- pursues a course of conduct which amounts to harassment of another; and
- knows or ought to know that that course of conduct amounts to harassment.

The Act does not specifically define harassment; the only explanation given, in s7, is that it includes behaviour which alarms the victim or causes them distress. This would seem to cover more than just physical violence or threats and might, for example, include doorstepping, constant phone calls or photographers chasing someone in the street, but, as so far very few cases have been reported, we do not know for certain exactly what might qualify as harassment, nor how severe the distress or alarm would need to be. The behaviour must take place as part of a 'course of conduct', which is defined as something which happens on at least two occasions. This offence can be punished with up to six months' imprisonment and/or a fine.

The second, more serious offence, defined in s4, is committed when someone puts another person in fear of violence on at least two occasions, and they know or ought to know they are putting that person in fear of violence. It is punishable by up to five years' imprisonment and/or a fine.

If someone is convicted of either of the offences, a court can, in addition to punishing them, impose a restraining order to prevent the harassment being repeated. There is a defence to both offences if the person said to have harassed the claimant can show that, in the circumstances, their behaviour was reasonable, or was for the purposes of preventing or detecting crime.

INTERCEPTING CALLS, POST OR EMAILS

Intercepting someone's phone calls, email or post is a serious criminal offence. Section 1 of the Regulation of Investigatory Powers Act 2000 makes it illegal to intercept any communication in a public or private telecommunications system, or any public postal system. Intercepting is defined as modifying or interfering with the system or its operation, or monitoring transmissions, so as to make communications available to someone who is not the intended recipient. A number of journalists have been charged under the Act in connection with the phone hacking scandal.

Intercepting someone's communications is also a clear breach of privacy, and hundreds of victims of phone hacking have sued or are suing News International, with damages generally being settled at around £30,000–£50,000, though some have been much higher.

The Act does not prohibit straightforward taping of a phone call, for example, if you are interviewing someone, unless the tape will be passed on to someone else or broadcast (in which case you would need their consent to the taping). However, it is considered ethical to inform someone if you are taping them.

The Computer Misuse Act 1990 makes it an offence to get unauthorised access to a computer with the intention of:

- accessing any program or information on it;
- committing or facilitating the commission of an offence;
- impairing the computer to hinder or prevent access to information or programs on it;
- impairing or intending to impair the operation of any program or the reliability of date.

As far as journalists are concerned, this clearly covers hacking into someone's emails or files. There is no public interest defence, but as with the other offences in this chapter, it appears that the CPS will take into account whether there is a public interest element to the story a journalist is sourcing information for, when deciding whether to prosecute.

In 2013, the CPS announced that it would not be prosecuting a Sky News journalist who hacked into the emails of a man who had committed insurance fraud by staging his own death and disappearing to South America.

Listening to police radio messages

The Wireless Telegraphy Act 1949 bans the unauthorised use of 'wireless apparatus' with intent to obtain information about the contents of any message, and also disclosure of such information. This means it is an offence to listen in to police messages in the hope of getting information about an investigation.

What the codes say Harassment, trespass and eavesdropping

The Editors' Code of Practice used by IPSO states that journalists must not:

- engage in intimidation, harassment or in persistent pursuit;
- persist in questioning, telephoning or photographing individuals once asked to stop;
- remain on someone's property after being asked to leave;
- follow people;
- seek to obtain or publish material acquired by using hidden cameras or clandestine listening devices; or by intercepting private or mobile telephone calls, messages or emails; or by the unauthorised removal of documents or photographs; or by accessing digitally held private information without consent.

If requested, journalists should identify themselves and who they represent.

Editors should take care not to use material acquired through the kind of behaviour referred to above.

The Ofcom Broadcasting Code provides that:

- Where someone whose privacy is being infringed asks for filming/recording/broadcasting to stop, it should stop, unless continuing is warranted.
- Doorstepping should not take place unless an interview has been requested and refused, a request is impossible, or there is good reason to believe that an investigation will be frustrated if the subject is approached openly.
- People who are distressed should not be pressurised to give interviews.
- The means of gathering material should be proportionate to the circumstances and the subject matter of the programme.

Broadcasters can record telephone calls between the broadcaster and the other party if they have, from the outset of the call, identified themselves, explained the purpose of the call and that the call is being recorded for possible broadcast (if that is the case), unless it is warranted not to do one or more of these practices. If at a later stage it becomes clear that a call that has been recorded will be broadcast (but this was not explained to the other party at the time of the call), then the broadcaster must obtain consent before broadcast from the other party, unless it is warranted not to do so.

Bribery

It is not unusual for journalists to pay for information from sources, and in many cases, not unethical or illegal either. However, there are some circumstances in which payment to a source could be an offence under the Bribery Act 2010. The Act makes it an offence to offer, promise or give someone a financial or other advantage to induce them 'improperly to perform a relevant function or activity', to reward them for improper performance, or to do so knowing or believing that accepting the money or other advantage would in itself amount to improper performance.

The person bribed need not be a public official. The Act covers bribery of anyone involved in the following, as long as they are expected to do the relevant thing in good faith, impartially or in a position of trust:

- any function of a public nature;
- any activity connected with a business, trade or profession;
- things done in the course of employment;
- activities performed by or on behalf of a body or organisation.

Bear in mind that, in general, most employees will be considered to be in a position of trust within their employment; a payment to a junior secretary who has access to private information on their boss could be as much a risk as one to a government official.

The relevant activity need not be performed in the UK, or have any connection with the UK, and the offence can be committed regardless of whether the person bribed is the person who performs the relevant activity. It also applies whether the offer is made directly, or through a third party.

It is also an offence under the Act to bribe a foreign public official, with the intent to influence them in their public capacity and obtain or keep business or a business advantage.

The Act contains penalties of up to 10 years in prison and an unlimited fine. There is no public interest defence, nor any special rules for journalists, but the CPS is likely to consider whether the story was in the public interest when deciding whether to prosecute.

Misconduct in a Public Office

This is a serious offence, with a maximum sentence of life imprisonment, and is committed when a public official wilfully neglects to perform their duty, or commits some misconduct, which amounts an abuse of the public's trust in them, and they have no reasonable justification for it. As far as the media is concerned, this is most likely to involve an official disclosing information to the press, either for money or other reasons. Although it is the official who would be charged with misconduct, the journalist who receives the information can be charged with conspiracy to commit the offence, or aiding and abetting.

The Serious Crime Act 2007

This Act makes it an offence intentionally to encourage or assist in committing an offence, or doing something in the belief that an offence will be committed. It would apply, for example, to a journalist who employed a private investigator to obtain someone's private information by illegal means, or paid a computer hacker to get into someone's emails.

KEY POINTS

Trespass

Trespass can committed by:

- entering someone's land (or building) without permission;
- staying when asked to leave;
- doing something you have no permission to do.

Harassment

The Protection from Harassment Act 1997 creates two offences:

- pursuing a course of conduct which amounts to harassment of another;
- putting someone in fear of violence on at least two occasions.

The Act also creates a civil right to sue for harassment.

Intercepting phone calls and emails

The Regulation of Investigatory Powers Act 2000 makes it an offence to intercept phone calls, emails or post.

The Misuse of Computers Act covers computer hacking.

Bribery

The Bribery Act makes it an offence to bribe someone, in certain circumstances, and paying for information can be covered by it.

Misconduct in a public office

Journalists can be convicted of conspiracy to commit this offence if they gain information from a public official, in circumstances which amount to a betrayal of the public's trust.

The Serious Crime Act

This applies where someone else commits a crime on behalf of a journalist, such as a private investigator or computer hacker; the journalist can be prosecuted too.

TEST YOUR KNOWLEDGE

1 Who can sue for trespass?

2 You are reporting a case in which a child was murdered, and want to get an interview with her parents. In which of these situations might you commit trespass:

(a) You wait outside the front gate of her house for her parents to come out. They ask you to leave, but you stay where you are.

(b) The father agrees to an interview and invites you in. You ask to use the toilet, so that you can have a look at the child's bedroom and describe it in your story.

(c) You stand opposite the house and look through the window, so that you can describe the parents in your story.

3 What is the definition of harassment under the Protection from Harassment Act 1997?

4 What can you use as a defence if sued for harassment?

5 You are a reporter on a celebrity magazine. Your cousin works at an exclusive cosmetic surgery clinic, where many celebrities go. Every now and then, she tells you who's visited, and what they had done, and you pay her for the information. Have you committed an offence under the Bribery Act?

ONLINE RESOURCES

The Protection from Harassment Act 1997 can be read at:
www.legislation.gov.uk/ukpga/1997/40/contents

The Regulation of Investigatory Powers Act 2000 can be read at:
www.legislation.gov.uk/ukpga/2000/23/contents

Thomas v *News Group Newspapers* can be read at:
www.freebeagles.org/caselaw/CL_hs_Thomas_full.html

Protecting sources and source material

Many of the most important stories the media carry involve publishing information which someone else does not want to be known: allegations of crime or corruption in high places, for example, or facts which suggest an individual or organisation has lied to or misled the public. In many such cases, the information on which the story is based will come from a source who is only willing to provide it on the understanding that they will remain anonymous. Sometimes this is because their position simply makes it awkward for them to be seen to have talked to the press; often it is because they risk losing their job, or even being prosecuted if they are revealed as the source of the information.

Whatever the reason, it is a basic rule of journalistic ethics, laid down in the ethical codes used by the NUJ, IPSO and Ofcom, that a journalist who agrees to keep a source's identity confidential should honour that promise. The reason for this is not only fairness to that particular source, but also a wider public interest: if sources could not trust the media to protect their identity, an enormous amount of information that the public ought to know would never be revealed.

English media law recognises that the public interest in some circumstances will protect the journalist's right to keep their sources secret, and this is backed up by decisions made at the European Court of Human Rights. However, this protection is far from absolute, so a journalist needs to know under what circumstances they can be ordered to reveal their sources.

A related issue covered in this chapter pertains to when you can be forced to hand over to the police (and certain other organisations) research material that you use in your work, and when they can search for it themselves, or even intercept your emails. There is some special protection for journalistic material in this context, particularly if it is confidential, but, again, this protection is limited.

There are four main legal provisions under which a journalist can be required to reveal their sources, or allow access to their research material:

- the Contempt of Court Act 1981;
- the Police and Criminal Evidence Act 1984 (PACE);
- the Official Secrets Acts;
- the Terrorism Act 2000.

In addition, there are other acts which give investigative powers to the police and other agencies with regard to specific types of offence.

THE CONTEMPT OF COURT ACT 1981

The Contempt of Court Act details when a journalist can be ordered by a court (or some kinds of tribunal) to disclose a source or information which would reveal a source.

Usually, if a person refuses to answer a question put to them in court, they will be in contempt of court. However, if the person is a journalist, and the answer to the question would reveal the source of a story, the Contempt of Court Act provides that a refusal to answer will not be contempt of court, except in three situations. These situations are where the court is satisfied that disclosure is necessary for one of the following reasons:

- in the interests of national security;
- in the interests of justice;
- for the prevention of crime or disorder.

On the face of it, this sounds like fairly strong protection for the media, but unfortunately the way in which the courts have interpreted the three categories means that there are in fact a wide range of situations in which disclosure may be ordered. Of course, even where one of the three conditions referred to above applies, the court cannot physically compel you to disclose your source, but if you fail to do so when ordered to, you can be found in contempt of court and fined or even sent to prison.

The European Court has ruled the protection of sources is part of the Article 10 right to freedom of expression, and in a number of recent cases has ruled that attempts to force journalists to reveal their sources were unlawful. This attitude should increasingly influence the English courts.

Interests of national security

Case law suggests that where national security is involved to any degree, the courts are likely to decide that disclosure is necessary; in fact in *X Ltd* v *Morgan Grampian* (1991), the court stated that the decision would be 'almost automatic':

In *Secretary of State for Defence* v *Guardian Newspapers* (1985), the *Guardian* published a confidential memo from the Secretary of State for Defence, regarding the arrival of cruise missiles in Britain. The Government went to court to get the document back, and the paper realised that returning it would enable the Ministry of Defence to identify the civil servant, Sarah Tisdall, who had leaked it. The *Guardian* argued that it was protected by s10 of the Contempt of Court Act, because the information in the document did not actually threaten national security. However, the Government claimed that the return of the document was necessary, because, even if the revelation in question did not endanger national security, the interests of national security demanded that civil servants who had access to confidential information and were willing to leak it should be identified. It argued that such a person might well leak something more dangerous next time. The House of Lords accepted this argument and ordered disclosure; the *Guardian* complied and Ms Tisdall was sentenced to six months' imprisonment.

Interests of justice

This is perhaps the most grey area in the legislation, and a category which has proved to be much wider than the media would like. At one time it was assumed that this category would only apply where disclosure of the source was vital to court proceedings which were already under way, or at least planned. However, in the key case of *X Ltd* v *Morgan Grampian* (1991), the facts of which are stated below, the courts gave the term a considerably wider definition. Disclosure, the court said, could be considered necessary in the interests of justice where it was necessary to enable someone to 'exercise important legal rights and to protect themselves from serious legal wrongs'.

In deciding whether this was the case, the court said that the relevant issues were:

- **The nature of the information obtained from the source.** The greater the legitimate public interest in the information, the more likely a court would be to allow protection of the source.
- **The way in which the source obtained the information.** A court would be more likely to protect a source who has got hold of the information legitimately, whereas if it was stolen or otherwise obtained illegally (which would include in breach of confidence – see Chapter 18), there would need to be a strong public interest in publication to persuade the court to allow the source to be kept secret. There would, however, still be cases where sources should be protected even though they had obtained information illegally: the court gave the example of a source acting to expose wrongdoing.

As a result, the 'interests of justice' category is capable of being a worryingly wide one, and it can be difficult to predict the results in individual cases.

In ***X Ltd*** v ***Morgan Grampian*** (1991), a then trainee reporter, Bill Goodwin, was working for the trade magazine *The Engineer* when he received a call from a source telling him that a company called Tetra was in financial difficulties. He called Tetra to get its reaction to the information, which alerted it to the fact that his source must have had access to a confidential company document, a copy of which had recently gone missing. Tetra applied for an injunction to prevent publication of the story; when that was granted, it then applied for an order requiring Mr Goodwin to disclose his source. Mr Goodwin claimed the protection of s10, but Tetra argued that disclosure was necessary 'in the interests of justice', because it would enable it to bring proceedings to get the document back. The case went all the way to the House of Lords, which decided in favour of Tetra. Bill Goodwin refused to disclose the source and was fined £5,000 for contempt of court. However, he took his case to the European Court of Human Rights and won (***Goodwin*** v ***United Kingdom*** (1996)). The court ruled that forcing him to disclose his source was a breach of the Article 10 right to freedom of expression, and that failing to give adequate protection to sources undermined the role of the press as a public watchdog. The public interest in protecting Goodwin's source outweighed Tetra's interest in identifying that person.

In ***Camelot Group Plc*** v ***Centaur Communications Ltd*** (1999), an employee of Camelot, which runs the National Lottery, sent the magazine *Marketing Week* a copy of the company's draft accounts, a week before they were due to be made public. The magazine ran a story based on the leaked material, which put the company directors in a bad light, and Camelot went to court to try to make the magazine give them the documents. This would have identified the source, so the magazine refused. The Court of Appeal supported Camelot's claim, ordering that the documents should be handed back because the disloyal employee posed an 'ongoing threat' to Camelot, and its interest in identifying that person outweighed the public interest in protecting sources.

In ***Ashworth Security Hospital*** v ***MGN Ltd*** (2002), the *Mirror* got hold of details about the medical treatment of Ian Brady, the notorious 'Moors murderer', who killed several children during the 1960s. Brady was in Ashworth Security Hospital, and was on hunger strike at the time in protest against his treatment there. The story revealed details of the way in which the hospital was dealing with the hunger strike, including force-feeding Brady. The paper had got the information from a journalist who had been paid for it; the paper did not know where he had got it from. The hospital went to court to get the *Mirror* to divulge its source, but the paper argued that to do so would reveal who the journalist's source was. Like Bill Goodwin's case, the matter went all the way to the House of Lords and, once again, it ruled that the source should be disclosed, because it was in the interests of justice that someone leaking confidential information from hospital records should be identified and punished by the hospital, in order to prevent further leaks from that person and deter others from doing the same. The journalist, a freelance called Robin Ackroyd, then came forward and identified himself voluntarily, but refused to divulge his source.

The hospital then took Ackroyd to court, but in ***Ackroyd*** v ***Mersey NHS Trust*** (2006), the High Court refused to order him to reveal his sources. The judge said that although the hospital had a legitimate interest in discovering the source, this was outweighed by the public interest in journalists protecting their sources. On the evidence, the judge said, Mr Ackroyd was a responsible journalist whose purpose was to act in the public interest, and, over the time since the case was first examined, it had become clear that the original source had not been acting for financial reasons. In addition, the extent of material leaked was less than originally claimed, security procedures had been tightened, and there had been no further significant leaks. Taken together, these factors meant that the court could find no 'pressing social need' to order disclosure of the source. The decision of the High Court was upheld by the Court of Appeal (***Mersey Care NHS Trust*** v ***Ackroyd*** (2007)).

In ***Interbrew*** v ***Financial Times*** (2002), stories had been published about the brewery company Interbrew, which led to a fall in its share price. The stories turned out to be based on false information and a forged document, and the company took several newspapers to court to try to find out the source of it. The Court of Appeal ordered disclosure, stating that this was in the interests of justice because the fact that the document was forged made it clear that the source had intended to cause problems for the company. The newspapers involved tried to appeal to the House of Lords, but were refused permission, so took their case to the European Court of Human Rights. In ***Case of Financial Times Ltd and Others*** v ***UK*** (2009), it found that the orders made by the Court of Appeal were a breach of the newspapers' right to freedom of expression. The Court said that the fact that a source might be acting in bad faith should not be decisive in determining whether a disclosure order should be made. It might be a factor, but it had to be weighed against the importance of freedom of expression, and, in this case, there was no certainty about what the source's motivation was, anyway. The Court also considered the argument put forward in the Court of Appeal that a disclosure order would help Interbrew stop further leaks, and that this benefit outweighed the public interest in protecting sources. It said that stopping further leaks could only justify a disclosure order in exceptional circumstances, where prevention of leaks could not be achieved by less invasive methods, and where the risk of further leaks was sufficiently serious. That was not the situation here.

In 1996, a journalist for *The Journal* in Newcastle was taken to court by the local police over a story which alleged that local crime figures had been presented in a misleading way. However, the High Court refused to force the reporter to reveal her sources, stating that her story had raised a question of 'considerable public importance', and this outweighed the police argument that the source should be revealed in the 'interests of justice'.

In ***The Assistant Deputy Coroner for Inner West London*** v ***Channel 4*** (2007), the coroner conducting the inquest into the deaths of Princess Diana and Dodi Fayed ordered Channel 4 to identify two confidential sources. The sources had been used in a documentary about the accident that killed the couple, and Mr Justice Eady said that it was highly likely that their information would 'help to complete the picture' for the coroner. That objective justified setting aside confidentiality for the sources.

In 2004, freelance investigative journalist Graham Smith managed to get a request for his sources withdrawn, with support from the NUJ legal department. He had been covering the story of the mysterious sinking of a trawler for some years, and one of his stories involved evidence from an anonymous former naval officer. When the Government launched an inquiry into the sinking, he sent the statement to the inquiry, which then asked for all his documents, recordings and notes. Backed by NUJ lawyers, Mr Smith refused and the request was eventually withdrawn.

In 2009, journalist Suzanne Breen won a long-running battle over protection of sources with the police in Northern Ireland. She had been ordered by the police to reveal information about her interviews with two Real IRA members over the murder of two British soldiers. She argued that her life would be in danger if she revealed the information. The court agreed, pointing out that the threat would exist as soon as she handed over the information, and could go on for many years. The judge said that there was a public interest in finding out who committed the murders, but this was outweighed by a journalist's right to life under the Human Rights Act.

The courts have, in two cases, suggested that they will be less likely to order disclosure in cases where claimants have turned straight to legal action, without making their own attempts to discover the source of information. The reasoning seems to be that if there is some other way of finding the source, it cannot be said to be 'necessary' to order disclosure by the media.

In 1994, the top-security Broadmoor Hospital went to court to try to force a news agency to reveal its source for reports that two convicted killers had escaped while on day trips. The court declined to make the order, because the hospital had not made any attempt to investigate the leak for itself.

In *John* v *Express Newspapers plc* (2000), the Court of Appeal refused to order Express Newspapers to divulge the source of a confidential document about the singer Elton John's financial affairs, partly because he had not made sufficient efforts to find out the source of the leak before going to court.

Prevention of crime

Obvious examples of cases where disclosure is necessary for the 'prevention of crime' might be those where, for example, identifying a source would help the police stop that person or someone else from committing a planned crime. In practice, the courts have given the category a wider meaning, and in ***X Ltd* v *Morgan Grampian*** (1991), it was stated that disclosure in these cases, as in those involving national security, disclosure should be 'almost automatic'.

In *Re an Inquiry under the Company Securities (Insider Dealing) Act 1985* (1988), a journalist for the *Independent* was questioned by inspectors from the Department of Trade, who were investigating suspected insider dealing, resulting from leaks from government departments. The reporter had written stories which suggested he had sources in those departments, but he refused to reveal them. The inspectors were using disclosure powers granted under the Financial Services Act 1986, which does not give any protection to journalists' sources, but as it allows anyone who refuses to reveal information to be treated as though they were in contempt of court, the House of Lords ruled that s10 of the Contempt of Court Act should be considered.

The House of Lords found that the reporter was not protected by s10, because disclosure was 'necessary for the prevention of crime'. It had been argued that this category could only apply if revealing the source was necessary in order to prevent further insider dealing, but the House of Lords held that the meaning was wider than this. In this case, they said, the job of the inspectors was not just to prevent further insider dealing by the same people, but also to investigate the case so that measures could be taken to deter insider trading generally. The identity of the source was 'necessary' for that process to take place, and that process would prevent crime.

PACE – INFORMATION REQUIRED BY THE POLICE

In some circumstances, the police can demand access to information or material which they believe will assist in an investigation. This may include material which identifies sources, but it can also extend to just about any kind of material used in journalistic work. For example, the courts have frequently ordered the media to hand over footage and/or photographs of violent demonstrations. This has led to a belief among some groups that the press are on the side of the police, which can put photographers and reporters at risk, and clearly, taking photographs at such events becomes more difficult when the subjects know that the pictures might end up being used as evidence against them. Similarly, it is more difficult to make credible promises of confidentiality to a source in situations where the police have power to access material which could identify sources.

In ***Sanoma Uitgevers BV* v *Netherlands*** (2010), the European Court of Human Rights stressed the importance of protecting journalistic sources, ruling against Dutch prosecutors for requiring a publisher to hand over identifying photos to the police.

Answering police questions

With the exceptions of investigations related to terrorism and breaches of the Official Secrets Acts (see below), the law does not oblige anyone, including journalists, to answer questions put to them by the police. It is often believed (sometimes even by the police) that refusing to answer questions amounts to the offence of obstructing the police in their duties, but this is not the case. The Police Act 1996 defines this offence as 'wilfully' obstructing an officer, and in the key case of ***Rice* v *Connolly*** (1966), the High Court stated that to do something 'wilfully' meant to do it without legal excuse. In this country, it explained, we may have a moral and social duty to help the police, but there is no legal duty to do so, and so there is legal excuse for refusing to answer a police officer's questions. Although ***Rice*** was decided before the Police Act 1966 was passed, similar wording was in use before; the case remains good law and was referred to, for example, in ***Ashworth* v *MGN*** (see p. 332). Note, however, that this does not extend to giving false or misleading information. This means that if the police want access to information that you have, they have to go to court to get it, usually under powers granted in the Police and Criminal Evidence Act 1984 (PACE). These only apply, however, to records and documents, and not to information which is not in any recorded form, such as the name of a source which you have not written down.

Police search and seizure powers

The Police and Criminal Evidence Act 1984 (PACE) is the main piece of legislation governing police powers of search and seizure. It sets out special rules for police access to journalistic material, which are stricter than those which apply to most other material (e.g. the police must apply to a circuit judge for access to journalistic material, rather than to a magistrate, as they do for most other material).

PACE defines 'journalistic material' as records or documents 'acquired or created for the purposes of journalism' and held in the possession of the person who acquired or created it for those purposes. This can include research material as well as actual copy.

PACE divides journalistic material into two different categories:

- **Excluded material** is defined as material which is held under an 'undertaking, restriction or obligation of confidence'. This would include any material which has been given to a journalist on the understanding that its source was not revealed. The requirement of confidentiality must have existed from the time when the material was acquired or created.
- **Special procedure material** is all other (non-confidential) journalistic material.

If the police wish to obtain material in either of these categories, they have to apply to a circuit judge, usually for a production order which requires the holder of the material to hand it over (though in some circumstances they can apply for a search warrant instead – see below). A production order should only be granted if the police can satisfy the requirements set out in Schedule 1 of PACE. The person or company who holds the material must be told about the application, and can put their arguments against it to the judge.

For excluded material an order should only be granted if the police can show that:

- there are reasonable grounds for believing that excluded material exists on the premises;
- a search warrant would have been granted under any legislation which existed before PACE.

There are very few pre-PACE provisions which would allow the police to obtain or search for excluded material so, in practice, journalists will only rarely be obliged to give up this kind of material. Two exceptions, however, are where the material has been stolen, as the Theft Act 1968 provides for such material to be seized (or searched for), or where the material relates to offences under the Official Secrets Acts.

For special procedure material, an order should only be granted if there are reasonable grounds for believing that:

- a serious offence has been committed;
- there is special procedure material on the premises;
- the material is likely to be of substantial value to the investigation of the offence;
- the material is likely to be admissible evidence; and other ways of obtaining the material have either failed, or not been tried because they were bound to fail;
- it is in the public interest for the order to be granted.

In the past, the courts have had a tendency to accept that the public interest lies more in helping the police to solve crime than in protecting freedom of expression, and there have been a number of cases where production orders were given even though the police had provided very little evidence that the material required would be of substantial use. In recent cases, however, the approach seems to be changing.

In ***Bright* v *Central Criminal Court*** (2001), the police applied for a production order regarding correspondence between a newspaper reporter and David Shayler, an ex-employee of MI5 who had made a number of allegations of wrongdoing against the Security Services, and who had fled to France to avoid charges under the Official Secrets Act. The order was initially granted, but then overturned by the Divisional Court, which emphasised the importance of free speech, particularly with regard to allegations that, might be embarrassing or inconvenient to public authorities. The court stated that, where the media was conducting a genuine investigation into 'corrupt or reprehensible activities by a public authority', the courts should only allow access to their material where there was 'compelling evidence' that this would be in the public interest, and the material was genuinely relevant. That was not the case here.

In ***R (on the application of BSkyB, the BBC, Hardcash Productions Ltd and Jason Parkinson)* v *Chelmsford Crown Court*** (2012), the High Court quashed production orders which would have forced media organisations to hand over film of controversial evictions from a travellers' site in Essex. Mr Justice Eady said the value of the footage to the police in tracing people involved in disorder was clear, but that had to be balanced against the level of interference with the media's right to freedom of expression.

There was convincing evidence that forcing the media to hand over film from this kind of event meant that public trust in them as neutral observers would be reduced, and that would compromise their ability to report. In order to outweigh those arguments, the police would need clear and specific evidence to show why orders were justified, and, here they did not.

If a media organisation or journalist refuses to comply with a production order, the police can apply to a circuit judge for a search warrant; they can also do this instead of applying for a production order. The holder of the material does not have to be told of the application for a search warrant, and, even if they are told, or find out, they have no right to put their case against a warrant to the judge.

To get a search warrant (whether for excluded or special procedure material), the police must show that the Schedule 1 conditions which would be necessary for a production order (see above) are satisfied, and in addition, that *one* of the following four conditions applies:

- it is not practicable to communicate with anyone who is entitled to grant entry to the premises;
- it is not practicable to communicate with anyone who is entitled to grant access to the material;
- the material contains information which is subject to a restriction on disclosure or obligation of secrecy imposed by statute (an example would be material which the Official Secrets Act 1989 makes it an offence to disclose – see Chapter 26) and is likely to be disclosed in a way that breaches that legislation if the warrant is not granted; or
- serving notice of an order might seriously prejudice the investigation.

If the police enter premises with such a warrant, they can remove additional material not covered by that warrant without going back to court.

In 1987, the police used these powers to get a warrant to search the offices of the *New Statesman* after it published an article by the investigative journalist Duncan Campbell about Zircon, a £500-million spy satellite that the Government was said to have concealed from Parliament. They were able to get a warrant because the offices were thought to have contained material which was subject to the Official Secrets Act.

Warrants under PACE have to be issued for specific premises, but the Serious Organised Crime and Police Act 2005 introduced an 'all premises' warrant, which allows the police to search any premises occupied or controlled by the person named in the warrant. This could potentially mean that one warrant could cover not just a journalist's office, but their home as well. Before ordering such a warrant, the judge must be satisfied that it is not reasonably practical for the police to list all the premises they might need to search, and that there are reasonable grounds for searching premises not specified in the application.

Law in practice Dealing with documents

Once a media organisation or journalists has been served with notice that the police are applying for a production order, it becomes a potential contempt of court to destroy, hide or alter the material concerned. Before notice is served, however, this does not apply, so any journalist who thinks such an application might be made would be well advised to dispose of any unnecessary material in advance (e.g. in the cases concerning film and photography of demonstrations, much of the material demanded was unpublished extra footage and pictures, which could have been destroyed).

In *R (on the application of British Sky Broadcasting Ltd) v the Commissioner of Police of the Metropolis* (2014), the Supreme Court ruled that media organisations asked to hand over documents under PACE must be given access to all the evidence supporting the claim.

THE OFFICIAL SECRETS ACTS

Official Secrets legislation (see Chapter 26) provides extensive powers of investigation to the police. Section 6 of the Official Secrets Act 1920 (as amended by the Official Secrets Act 1939) states that, where the chief officer of police has reasonable grounds for suspecting that an offence under s1 of the Act (these are spying offences) has been committed and that a person can supply information about the offence, the chief of police can authorise a senior police officer to require that person to reveal the relevant information. Before doing this, the chief of police must usually get the Secretary of State's permission, but, in cases of 'great emergency', can go ahead without it.

It is a criminal offence to refuse to comply, or knowingly supply false information, and the provision applies to journalists and journalistic information just as to everyone else; there is no special protection.

Section 9 of the Official Secrets Act 1911 provides that, with a warrant from a magistrate, the police can enter any premises named in the warrant, at any time, and can use force to get in if they need to. They can search the premises and anyone there, and take any material which is evidence of an offence under the Act. In cases of emergency, the police need not even get a warrant: a superintendent can issue a written order which has the same effect.

Section 8 of the Official Secrets Act 1989 provides that, if someone is in possession of documents or articles containing information which has been disclosed by a government employee, entrusted to someone in confidence by a government employee, or entrusted in confidence to other states or international organisations, it is a criminal offence not to hand over that information to a government official if asked to do so.

THE TERRORISM ACT 2000

Anti-terrorism legislation creates some widely drawn offences concerning cooperation with police inquiries into terrorism, with perhaps the most significant development being that, where terrorist offences are concerned, the rule that no one is obliged to help the police with their enquiries does not apply.

These are the offences which are most likely to affect the media in their work:

- Section 38b of the Terrorism Act 2000 (as amended by the Anti-Terrorism, Crime and Security Act 2001) makes it a serious offence to withhold information concerning suspected terrorist offences, and the offence can be committed not just by refusing to answer questions if asked, but also by failing to offer the information voluntarily, even if you are not asked for it and the police do not know you have it. The section states that it is an offence not to disclose to the police, as soon as reasonably practical, information which you know or believe might be of 'material assistance' in:
  - preventing someone from committing an act of terrorism; or
  - bringing about the apprehension, prosecution or conviction of someone in the UK, for committing, preparing or instigating an act of terrorism.

There is a defence where the person in possession of the information has a 'reasonable excuse' for not disclosing it (which is not defined in the Act). There is no special defence relating to the media. The maximum sentence for this offence is five years in prison.

- A similar provision in s19 makes it an offence to withhold information about people who are involved in funding terrorism. It states that where someone, through their trade, profession, business or employment, acquires information that leads them to believe or suspect that someone else has committed an offence concerning the financing of terrorism, the person who has the information will commit an offence if they do not disclose their suspicion, and the information which prompts it, to the police as soon as reasonably practicable. Again, 'reasonable excuse' is a defence, but there is no specific media defence. The maximum sentence is five years' imprisonment.
- Section 58 makes it an offence to collect, record or possess information (including photographs) which is likely to be useful to someone preparing or committing an act of terrorism. The only defence in the Act is to prove reasonable excuse for collecting, recording or possessing the material. The maximum sentence is 10 years' imprisonment.
- Section 39(1) makes it an offence for someone who knows, or has reasonable cause to suspect, that a terrorism investigation is being or will be conducted, to disclose anything which is likely to prejudice the investigation, or interfere with material likely to be relevant to it. Disclosure here could include publication.
- Section 39(2) applies when someone knows or has reasonable cause to suspect that information has been disclosed under s19 (see above), and discloses to another information which could interfere with any resulting investigation, or interferes with material which could be relevant to that investigation. For both s39 offences, there is a defence where the person did not know or have reason to suspect that a terrorist investigation was likely to be affected, or where there is reasonable excuse for the disclosure or interference.

The police have extensive investigatory powers in relation to offences of terrorism, which are contained in Schedule 5 of the 2000 Act. In addition to general powers to enter and search premises, search anyone in them, and seize and retain relevant material, paragraph 5 of Schedule 5 provides that the police can apply to a circuit judge for an order giving them access to journalistic material, in both the excluded and special procedure categories defined by PACE (see p. 335).

The application has to relate to specific material, or material of a specific description, and the judge must believe that the person the order is made against has the material in their possession, custody or control. The order can require a person to hand over, or give the police access to, such material within seven days (or the judge can decide on a different period). If the person is not in possession of the material, they can be required to disclose, to the best of their knowledge, its location, again, within seven days.

Where a judge makes an order giving access to journalistic material, he or she can also order any person who appears to be entitled to grant entry to the relevant premises to allow the police to enter the premises and access the material. This order can only be granted if the judge is satisfied that:

- the material is excluded or special procedure material (see p. 335);
- it does not include material subject to legal privilege (see the Glossary);

- the order is being sought for the purposes of a terrorist investigation;
- there are reasonable grounds for believing that the material is likely to be of substantial value to a terrorist investigation, either by itself or with other material;
- there are reasonable grounds for believing that it is in the public interest that the material should be produced or access given to it, taking into account the potential benefit to the terrorism investigation, and the circumstances in which the material is held.

Anyone who is ordered to hand over or make available material, or who has had material taken by the police under a warrant, can then be required to explain that material under paragraph 13 of Schedule 5. It is an offence, with a maximum sentence of two years, to give a false or misleading explanation.

In 2008, freelance journalist Shiv Malik was ordered to give the police research material, including notes and tape recordings, which he had gathered while working on a book on terrorism. However, he fought the order and, in a judicial review hearing, was able to get the amount of material to be handed over reduced. The original order required him to supply all the original source material for his book, which included interviews with a suspected terrorist, Hassan Butt, but the judicial review hearing found that this was too wide. It was held that he could supply copies rather than originals, that he need only give police material relating to Hassan Butt, rather than all the material gathered for the book, and that he could blank out parts of that material that would identify sources other than Butt. In resisting the police's demands for the material, Shiv Malik could potentially have been committing an offence under the Terrorism Act s19, but the Greater Manchester Police said he would not be prosecuted.

Additional provisions for Northern Ireland

Three additional important provisions for the media in the Terrorism Act 2000 apply to Northern Ireland only. Paragraphs 19–21 respectively allow the Secretary of State for Northern Ireland to issue orders:

- giving any police officer an authority equivalent to a search warrant, in respect of specific premises;
- requiring any person to produce or allow access to special procedure material or excluded material;
- requiring any person to provide an explanation of material seized as a result of actions taken under the two above provisions.

OTHER LEGISLATION

In addition to the legislation discussed above, there are statutes which provide powers to order disclosure of information on specific matters, or powers of search and seizure. These are some of the most important as regards the media's areas of work.

The Financial Services Act 1986 gives inspectors from the Department for Business, Innovation and Skills powers to summon people for questioning about any matter relating to their inquiries (which are usually into allegations of financial misconduct). Failure to attend without a reasonable excuse is an offence.

The Serious Organised Crime and Police Act 2005 gives the police, the Serious Organised Crime Agency, and officers of HM Revenue & Customs powers to issue a 'disclosure notice' to anyone they believe has information relating to investigation of one of the offences listed under the Act, which is likely to be of substantial value to the investigation. The notice can require the person to answer questions, supply information or hand over documents. It does not, however, apply to excluded material as defined by PACE.

The Criminal Justice Act 1987 permits the director of the Serious Fraud Office to order anyone whom he or she believes has information relevant to an investigation, to answer questions, provide information or supply documents. Refusing to do so is an offence, which can result in a prison sentence.

The Police Act 1997 allows police investigating serious crime to break into premises and plant bugs, where the chief constable thinks that this is necessary because evidence gained is likely to be of substantial value in the prevention or detection of serious crime, and the purpose cannot be achieved any other way. However, where the material sought is 'confidential journalistic material', the police must get the approval of a commissioner (one of a specially appointed group of sitting or former High Court judges) first or, in urgent cases, as soon as possible afterwards. Serious crime in this context includes any offence involving violence, or substantial financial gain, or carried out by a large group of people.

The Regulation of Investigatory Powers Act 2000 allows the Home Secretary to issue a warrant allowing specified officials of the police, security services and Revenue & Customs to intercept emails, where they are satisfied that this would be proportionate to the purpose for which the warrant is sought, and the warrant is necessary for any of the following reasons:

- in the interests of national security;
- for the purpose of preventing or detecting serious crime;
- for the purpose of safeguarding the economic well-being of the UK;
- for the purpose of giving effect to the provisions of any international agreement on mutual assistance.

When considering requests for warrants, the Home Secretary must also look at whether the same information could be obtained in another way. The warrant can be issued secretly, and there is no way of finding out whether you are the subject of one (in fact your internet service provider, who would have to facilitate the intercepting, is not allowed to tell you).

The Act also provides for the police, Revenue & Customs and the intelligence services to have access to 'communications data', which does not include the content of emails, but does cover information such as phone numbers called, addresses emails have been sent to, and the time and date of calls/emails. Access to communications data is less restricted than access to the content of communications, and can be allowed for a wide variety of purposes, including in the interests of public safety, to prevent death or injury, to assess or collect any tax or duty, and for any other purpose specified by the Secretary of State. If you encrypt your email messages, you can be ordered to reveal the encryption code, and if you are ordered to reveal the code, it is an offence to tell anyone that you have done so.

As this edition was being written, concerns began to be raised at the frequency with which the police were using powers under RIPA to discover the sources of press stories, and thereby undermine the usual protection for sources described elsewhere (in Chapter 20). The practice was criticised not only by journalists but also by a former Lord Chancellor, Lord Falconer. A report into the issue by the surveillance watchdog, the Interception of Communications Commissioner's Office, was expected to be published at some point during 2015.

Protection of sources under human rights legislation

Protection of sources falls with the Article 10 right to freedom of expression under the Human Rights Act and, as we saw earlier, the European Court of Human Rights found in ***Goodwin*** (see p. 344) that English law failed to give adequate protection and was a breach of the Article 10 right. Two recent ECHR cases have confirmed the importance of protection of journalistic sources under human rights law.

In *Tillack* v *Belgium* (2007), the claimant was a journalist who had been writing stories about fraud within the EU Commission, based on leaked information. The EU anti-fraud department alleged that he had bribed his source (which Mr Tillack denied), and his home was raided by Belgian police in an attempt to discover who the source was. The ECHR found that the raid breached Mr Tillack's right to receive and impart information under Article 10. It said that the right of journalists to protect their sources was not merely a privilege that could be overridden because the sources might be unlawful, and on the facts of the case, the police had insufficient justification for breaching Article 10 rights in this way.

Voskuil* v *Netherlands (2007), was brought by a Dutch journalist who had been jailed for 30 days after refusing to reveal his sources to the Amsterdam Court of Appeal. The Dutch court said that the information was necessary in the interests of justice, but the European Court of Human Rights again emphasised the importance of protection of sources for a free press, and held that Mr Voskuil's Article 10 rights had been violated, not least because his refusal to reveal his sources had not actually impeded the court's ability to do justice in the case.

There are some signs that these cases are beginning to have more of an influence on the British courts, though apparently not on the police.

In 2008, a court threw out a case against a journalist for the *Milton Keynes Citizen* after an 18-month investigation in which she was arrested, strip-searched and told she could go to prison for life. The case involved the alleged leaking of confidential information to her from a local police officer. The police officer was charged with misconduct in public office, which carries a potential life sentence, and the journalist with aiding and abetting the offence. The charges against both of them were dropped when the court threw out the case, saying that the police investigation had been a breach of the Article 10 protection for sources.

What the codes say **Protecting sources**

The Editors' Code of Practice used by IPSO states that:

- Journalists have a moral obligation to protect confidential sources of information.

In *A Man* v *Lancashire Telegraph* (Oct 31, 2007), the PCC upheld a complaint regarding protection of sources after a man spoke to the paper on condition that he was not identified. The story was about possible plans to close the local mortuary, and the man was one of two employees there. The story referred to him as a worker at the mortuary, which meant it was very easy for his boss to identify him as the person who had spoken to the paper, and he was sacked. The reporter did not know he was one of only two employees, but the PCC said they should have checked with him before describing him as a worker there.

The Ofcom Broadcasting Code provides that:

- Guarantees given to contributors, for example relating to the content of a programme, confidentiality or anonymity, should normally be honoured.

KEY POINTS

Contempt of Court Act 1981

Refusal to reveal a source is not contempt of court, except where disclosure is necessary:

- in the interests of national security;
- in the interests of justice;
- for the prevention of crime or disorder.

Information required by the police

Refusing to answer police questions is not an offence (except in terrorism and official secrets cases).

Court orders to give material to the police are made:

- for excluded material (confidential) only if a search warrant could have been issued pre-PACE;
- for special procedure material (non-confidential) if six grounds are satisfied.

The Official Secrets Acts

- Refusing to give information about an espionage offence is an offence.
- The police can search premises and seize potential evidence, with a warrant.
- Refusing to hand over certain types of leaked documents is an offence.

The Terrorism Act 2000

It is an offence to:

- withhold information about suspect terrorist offences, or information, acquired through work or business, about the funding of terrorism;
- collect, record or possess information likely to be useful in terrorism;
- disclose anything likely to prejudice a terrorism investigation.

Other legislation

Other legislation providing investigative powers that can be used against the media includes:

- the Financial Services Act 1986;
- the Serious Organised Crime and Police Act 2005;
- the Criminal Justice Act 1987;
- the Police Act 1997;
- the Regulation of Investigatory Powers Act 2000.

TEST YOUR KNOWLEDGE

1 In which three situations does the Contempt of Court Act 1981 require a journalist to reveal their sources, or risk being in contempt?

2 In which of these situations might a court order that you should reveal your source?

(a) You have published a story about the temper tantrums of a well-known celebrity, based on information given to you by her chauffeur.

(b) You are sent a secret document detailing plans to buy new nuclear missiles and publish a story based on information in the document. You do not know who sent it.

(c) You publish details of plans by an animal rights group to kidnap the son of a high-profile model, known for her support of the fur trade. Your information comes from someone within the organisation.

3 You have recently published a story about alleged corruption within the local police force. Two police officers turn up at your workplace and ask you to tell them where you got the information from. Do you have to tell them?

4 What are the two types of journalistic material defined under PACE? How do police powers with regard to them differ?

5 You are researching a story about alleged sexual harassment of female police officers in your local force, comprising sexist remarks and jokes. You put the allegations to a senior officer, who asks you to hand over your evidence, threatening to get a production order if you do not. What should you do?

6 You have recently conducted an interview with a member of an extremist group, which is suspected to be involved with terrorism. The police ask to see your notes; in what circumstances can you be forced to hand them over?

ONLINE RESOURCES

The full text of *Ashworth* v *MGN* can be read at:
www.parliament.the-stationery-office.co.uk/pa/ld200102/ldjudgmt/jd020627/ash-1.htm

The Terrorism Act 2000 can be read at:
www.legislation.gov.uk/ukpga/2000/11/contents

News stories about protection of sources are covered on the website of the Campaign for Press and Broadcasting freedom, at:
www.cpbf.org.uk

Reports on the state of the law on protection of sources in the UK and other countries can be found on the European Federation of Journalists website, at:
www.ifj-europe.org/default.asp?Issue=EFJsources&Language=EN

Chapter 22 Data protection

The increasing use of computers over the past couple of decades has made it easy for organisations to hold a vast amount of information about individuals, to access and use that information, and to pass it on to others. As a result, legislation was passed to regulate the accumulation, storage and use of this information, and the current situation is governed by the Data Protection Act 1998. It creates rights for people who are the subject of stored information, and duties for those who hold the information.

Trainee journalists are often surprised to find out that they need to know about the Data Protection Act, which at first glance would seem to have more to do with the work of marketing departments and companies which send out junk mail. But in fact the Act affects the work of the media in two important ways:

- Media organisations themselves (from the biggest newspaper company to the individual freelance journalist working from home) collect, store and use information on individuals, and this fact gives them responsibilities under the Act. The Act provides for the media to be exempt from most of these responsibilities in certain situations, but these are limited.
- Organisations approached by the media for information will often use the Act as a reason to refuse disclosure. Sometimes they will be correct to do so, but in many cases the refusal is the result of a misunderstanding of the Act, or the Act is deliberately wrongly used as a reason to keep information secret. A good understanding of the legislation is the best way to deal with these situations.

The Act is overseen by the Information Commissioner, the same official who oversees the Freedom of Information Act (see Chapter 29).

As this book was going to press, the Office of the Information Commissioner published a useful guide on the application of the Data Protection Act to the press. The Guide can be found in the Sector Guides section of the ICO website, www.ico.org.uk.

INFORMATION COVERED BY THE ACT

The Data Protection Act 1998 applies to what it calls 'personal data'. In normal language, we might use 'personal data' to mean the kind of information which could prove embarrassing if disclosed, but the Act defines it much more widely than this. It uses a two-part definition, detailing what 'data' is, and which data is 'personal'.

Data is essentially any information held on computer, or in a non-computerised filing system where information is organised in such a way as to make specific information relating to a particular person readily accessible. This means that, for example, information written on a piece of paper in a pile on your desk with lots of other randomly assorted pieces of paper would not be covered, and probably nor would interview notes in a notebook which covered lots of different stories in no particular order. However, if you filed the information so that you could easily access information about a particular person, the information held that way would be subject to the provisions of the Act. In practice, of course, most of us now keep information on our computers, and this is all covered by the Act.

In ***Campbell* v *MGN*** (2002) it was established that photographs could be classified as data for the purposes of the Act. This approach was confirmed in ***Douglas* v *Hello!*** (2005). The facts of both cases are discussed below.

Personal data is defined under the Act as information relating to a particular person, held in the above ways, from which that person can be identified, either from that piece of information alone, or in combination with other information which the holder has or is likely to get. It includes not just factual details about the person, but any expression of opinion about them, or any suggestion of anyone's intentions with regard to that person. In the case of ***Durant* v *Financial Services Authority (Disclosure of Information)*** (2003), the Court of Appeal clarified this definition, stating that it essentially meant 'biographical' information, which affects someone's privacy in relation to their personal or family life, business or profession. Merely mentioning someone in a document did not make that document 'personal data'. This means that notes of an interview with someone for a human interest story or personal profile, for example, would clearly be 'personal data', and so would a contacts list with people's names and phone numbers. On the other hand, incidental mention of a person's name in a document which did not relate in any way to their privacy would not qualify as 'personal data'.

There is also a special category of 'sensitive personal data', which is defined as information which relates to any of the following details about a person:

- race or ethnic origin;
- political views;
- religious beliefs or beliefs of a similar nature;
- membership of a trade union;
- physical or mental health or condition;
- sex life;
- having committed or being alleged to have committed any offence;
- legal proceedings related to the commission or alleged commission of an offence by the person, the result of such proceedings and any sentence passed.

Sensitive personal data is subject to stricter rules about when and how it can be processed than other forms of information (see below).

In ***Campbell* v *MGN*** (2002), the model Naomi Campbell brought a claim against the *Mirror* regarding publication of information and photographs concerning her treatment for drug addiction. The case is most often discussed in the context of privacy and breach of confidence (see Chapters 18 and 19), but Ms Campbell also said that the paper's use of the information breached the Data Protection Act. In this context the High Court found that the information published could be classified as sensitive personal data, as it referred to her health, and this finding was not disturbed by the two later appeals in the case.

Terminology

There are three other terms which are worth explaining before we look at the provisions of the Act:

- **Data subject** means the person the information is about (in this chapter, the word 'subject' is used to mean the data subject).
- **Data controller** is the term used for the person or organisation which holds the information (defined as whoever 'determines the purposes for which and the manner in which' personal data is processed).
- **Processing** is widely defined, but in practice covers just about anything that a journalist would be likely to do with information, including obtaining it, recording it, holding it, looking at it, using it or disclosing it to anyone else.

MEDIA DUTIES UNDER THE ACT

As explained above, media organisations all process personal data, which makes them data controllers. Data controllers have three main obligations under the Act:

- to register their status as a data controller;
- to comply with the Act when processing personal data;
- to act in accordance with the rights the Act provides for the subjects of personal data.

As stated above, in some cases, the media are exempt from some of these duties, and these exemptions are discussed elsewhere (at p. 351).

Registration

All data controllers are required to register with the Office of the Information Commissioner and each data controller must supply their name and address, and details of the purposes for which they process data, the category of people they hold information on, and the kind of information held. These details need not be especially precise: for example, the Information Commissioner's Office suggests that for the media, the stated purpose should be:

> Processing by the data controller of any journalistic, literary or artistic material, made or intended to be made available to the public or a section of the public.

This information is published on the Information Commissioner's public register of data controllers. Data controllers also have to provide a security statement detailing measures taken to protect against unlawful use of the data by others; this is not made public.

There is no journalistic exemption from the obligation to register, and failure to do so is a criminal offence.

Law in practice Freelances and data protection

Journalists who work for a company will be covered by the company's registration under the Act, but if you are freelance, and you process data, the law requires you to register personally as a data controller. This can be done online at the website of the Information Commissioner's Office (see *Online resources* at the end of this chapter), and there is a charge. In 2008, a freelance photographer was fined £300 and ordered to pay £500 in costs after failing to register despite several reminders from the ICO.

Processing personal data

The Act sets out eight principles which should be followed when data is processed. Data must be:

1 processed fairly and lawfully;

2 processed for limited purposes;

3 adequate, relevant and not excessive;

4 accurate and up to date;

5 kept no longer than necessary;

6 processed in accordance with the data subject's rights;

7 kept with an appropriate degree of security;

8 not transferred outside the European Economic Area (EEA), except to countries which have adequate protection for the data subject. (The EEA comprises the EU, plus Iceland, Liechtenstein and Norway.)

In order for data to be fairly processed, at least one of a number of conditions have to be met. The conditions are laid out in Schedule 2 of the Act, and those most likely to apply in situations where information is processed by the media are:

- The subject has consented to the processing.
- Processing is necessary for the performance of a contract with the subject (e.g. many publications use contracts when organising an interview with a celebrity or the subject of a human interest story, though in these cases there will be consent as well).
- Processing is necessary in order to pursue the legitimate interests of the data controller or third parties. The media might argue, for example, that processing certain data is necessary in order for it to pursue its legitimate interests of publishing journalistic material. This provision will not apply where pursuing the defendant's legitimate interests unjustifiably prejudices the interests of the subject (see the ***Douglas*** case, below).

The fact that one of these conditions has been met does not, however, necessarily mean that the data has been processed fairly and lawfully. They are minimum standards, and it is quite possible for a data controller to meet one of these conditions and yet still deal with the information in a way which is unfair or unlawful. The Act makes it clear, for example, that if information is obtained by deception, including where the subject is deceived about the purpose to which it will be put, any subsequent processing of it cannot be considered fair.

In *Douglas* v *Hello!* (2005), the court considered the claims of film stars Catherine Zeta-Jones and Michael Douglas that publication of unauthorised photos of their wedding represented a breach of the Act's provisions on fair and lawful processing. The High Court found that the fact that the pictures were obtained surreptitiously (the photographer sneaked in to the wedding and took the pictures secretly) meant that the processing could not be fair. In addition, it was clear that none of the conditions in Schedule 2 had been satisfied. The only potentially arguable condition was that the use of the photos was necessary in order for *Hello!* to pursue its legitimate interests, but the court held that this was not applicable because publication would unjustifiably prejudice the interests of the couple.

Processing sensitive personal data

Processing of data which fulfils the definition of 'sensitive personal data', as explained above, can only be fair and lawful if at least one of the conditions listed in Schedule 2 are met, plus at least one of a list of extra conditions listed in Schedule 3 to the Act, or in the Data Protection (Processing of Sensitive Personal Data) Order 2000. The conditions most likely to be of use where the media are processing information are:

- The subject has given their explicit consent.
- The information has been deliberately made public by the subject.
- The processing is in the public interest, is necessary for the detection or prevention of any unlawful act (or failure to act), and has to be carried out without the subject's consent being sought, in order not to prejudice that purpose.
- The processing is in the public interest, and is necessary for the discharge of any function which is designed to protect the public from dishonesty, malpractice, incompetence, seriously improper conduct, or mismanagement of or failure in services provided by any organisation, and has to be carried out without the subject's consent being sought, in order not to prejudice that purpose.
- Disclosure of the information is for the purposes of journalism, with a view to publication, and is in the public interest, and is in connection with:
  - the commission or alleged commission of any unlawful act;
  - alleged or proven dishonesty, malpractice, seriously improper conduct, incompetence or unfitness of any person; or
  - alleged or proven mismanagement of or failure in services provided by any organisation.

(The first two conditions come from Schedule 2; the rest are contained in the 2000 Order.)

Rights of the data subject

The Act gives data subjects a series of rights; some of these have no relevance to the work of journalists, but the following may:

- The right to access: Data subjects are entitled to find out what information about them is being processed by or on behalf of a specific data controller. They have to pay the data controller a fee (currently no more than £10), and the information must be provided within 40 days.
- The right to prevent processing: Anyone can ask a data controller to stop (or not start) processing data relating to them if it is causing, or could cause, unwarranted substantial

damage to the data subject or someone else. The data controller has 21 days to respond, and can either agree to comply, or argue that the request is unjustified. In the latter case, the subject can go to court to apply for an order.

- The right to rectification or destruction: If personal data is inaccurate, or contains expressions of opinion based on inaccurate data, the subject can apply to a court to order the data controller to rectify or destroy the data.
- The right to compensation: If a media organisation breaches any provision of the Act and a person suffers loss and/or distress as a result, the organisation can be liable to pay compensation (though so far this does not seem to offer a way for people to prise huge payouts from the media; Catherine Zeta-Jones and Michael Douglas were only awarded £50 for their claim under the Act). It is a defence in this situation to prove that the organisation has taken all reasonable care.
- The right to an assessment: Anyone who believes personal data on them has been processed in ways that breach the Act can ask the Information Commissioner to make an assessment. If the Commissioner agrees, and the matter cannot be settled voluntarily, the Commissioner can serve an enforcement notice.

The Criminal Justice and Immigration Act 2008 gives the Information Commissioner the power to fine data controllers who intentionally or recklessly disclose personal data, or who repeatedly and negligently allow such information to be disclosed.

EXEMPTIONS FOR THE MEDIA

Having read the provisions detailed above, it will be obvious that there are many situations in which the media cannot comply with the Data Protection Act and still do their jobs effectively. For example, no form of investigative journalism would be possible if reporters had to tell the subjects of their stories every bit of information that they held on them, and the subject had to consent before the material could even be looked at, let alone published. Recognising this, s32 of the Act contains a special exemption for material (including sensitive personal data) that is processed for journalistic purposes, which allows the media to lawfully breach some provisions of the Act.

However, the exemption does not apply automatically in every situation where information is processed for journalistic purposes. It will only apply where all three of the following conditions are satisfied:

- the processing is undertaken with a view to publication of journalistic or literary material (these are not defined in the Act);
- the data controller reasonably believes that, having regard to the special importance of the public interest in freedom of expression, publication would be in the public interest;
- the data controller reasonably believes that, in all the circumstances, it is impossible to comply with the provision in question.

In deciding whether publication is in the public interest, the Act states that the Information Commission can take into account the publisher's compliance with any relevant code of practice (examples would be the Ofcom codes for broadcast journalists, and the Editors Code for print media).

If (and only if) these conditions are satisfied, the media need not comply with any of the following provisions:

- all of the provisions on fair and lawful processing, except the seventh, which requires safe storage of information;
- the requirement to allow data subjects access to the information held on them;
- the requirement to stop (or not start) processing information where it is causing or could cause the subject damage or distress;
- the requirement to rectify or delete inaccurate data or expressions of opinion based on inaccurate data.

In addition, if someone goes to court to try get an order giving them access to information held on them by the media, or to stop or prevent processing of that information, and the media organisation claims they are covered by the journalistic exemption, the proceedings can be 'stayed' (meaning suspended, so that no order can be given), while the Commissioner decides whether or not the exemption conditions are satisfied. This only applies if the information concerned has not yet been published. Without this provision, someone being investigated by the press could use the Act to find out what information was held on them, and then prevent it being reported by claiming that disclosure would cause them distress or damage.

In ***Douglas*** v ***Hello!*** (2005), the court roundly rejected the magazine's claim to the exemption, because it was impossible to establish any public interest reason for publishing the photographs. Mr Justice Lindsay commented that the fact that the public would be interested in the pictures 'is not to be confused with there being a public interest'.

In ***Campbell*** v ***MGN***, the Court of Appeal held that the journalistic exemption did apply, because the *Mirror* could demonstrate that there was a public interest in publication of the story: Ms Campbell had lied when she previously denied having a drug problem, and the story was correcting the false impression those denials gave. The Court of Appeal also specifically stated (overturning a ruling given in the High Court) that the exemption applied both before and after publication of the story. Although Ms Campbell then appealed to the House of Lords and won her case, the House of Lords' decision was based purely on the issues of breach of confidence and privacy, and the Data Protection Act claim was not discussed. This would seem to suggest that the Court of Appeal's view on the application of the defence still applies, but we will not know this for sure until it is tested again in the courts.

In ***Stone*** v ***South East Coast Strategic Health Authority*** (2006), a convicted murderer called Michael Stone tried to use the Data Protection Act to prevent publication of a report into his treatment for mental health problems and drug abuse. Mr Stone was undergoing the treatment at the time, in 1996, when he attacked Lin Russell and her daughters Megan and Josie, killing Lin and Megan and leaving Josie seriously injured. An independent inquiry was ordered to try to find out if there was anything that could have been done to prevent the killing, and Mr Stone cooperated with the inquiry, but objected to the report being made public on the grounds that it would divulge his private medical details. However, the High Court found that there was a clear public interest in publishing the report in full.

The Criminal Justice and Immigration Act 2008 creates a new defence for journalists to an offence under the Data Protection Act of unlawfully obtaining personal data. An individual has a defence if he or she can show that they acted with a view to the publication of journalistic, literary or artistic material, and in the reasonable belief that it was in the public interest to obtain or disclose the information.

Law in practice Data protection and broadcasting

It is not unusual for the subjects of investigative programmes to demand to see rushes, claiming that the Data Protection Act gives them the right to do so. In most cases, this kind of material will fall within the journalistic exemption, so there should be no requirement to let the subject see anything before the programme is broadcast. Where such a request is made, it is sensible to get legal advice.

Protecting sources

The right of access to information could potentially be a route for people to find out who has supplied information to the media. Take, for example, a situation where an employee tells a paper about misconduct by a senior member of management in the firm where they work. If the senior manager learns that they are being investigated, they could make a request for the information held by the paper, from which they could very probably work out who the source was.

However, some protection against this scenario is provided by s7(4) of the Act, which provides that where access to information cannot be given without disclosing information relating to another individual, from which that individual can be identified, the data controller need not comply with the request unless that person gives consent, or it is reasonable in all the circumstances to do so without consent. In deciding whether or not compliance is reasonable without consent, the data controller can take into account any duty of confidentiality owed to the person who supplied the information, and any express refusal of consent by that person.

The journalist may nevertheless be obliged to give the subject access to as much of the material is possible without divulging the source's identity, for example by withholding names and other identifying details.

INVESTIGATION AND ENFORCEMENT

The Act provides for the Information Commissioner to issue enforcement notices, requiring people or organisations who are in breach of the Act to comply with it. This provision is backed up with powers of entry and inspection for which a warrant from a judge is required. However, a warrant should not be granted if the data controller claims that the data concerned is being processed for the purposes of journalism, until the Commissioner has determined whether the journalistic exemption applies.

Where a data controller claims the journalistic exemption, an enforcement notice cannot be issued until the Information Commissioner has assessed whether the exemption applies, and a court has given leave for the enforcement notice to be issued. A court should only give this leave where it is satisfied that the Information Commissioner has reason to suspect that the breach of the Act is of substantial public importance.

Failure to abide by an enforcement notice, or persistent breaches of the Act, can be prosecuted as a criminal offence, punishable with a fine of up to £5,000.

PROBLEMS WITH GATHERING INFORMATION

So far we have looked at the implications of the Act when media organisations act as data controllers, but, as mentioned in the introduction to this chapter, the Act also has an impact on journalists' research activities, in that organisations may, rightly or wrongly, use it as a reason not to reveal information. The Newspaper Society's 2004 Press Freedom Survey found widespread concern about the way in which the Act was used to stifle news-gathering, with 43 editors naming it as the single greatest obstacle to reporting. As well as deliberate misuse of the Act to avoid answering difficult questions, editors complained that, in many organisations, the Act was misunderstood, or used as an excuse when officials simply could not be bothered to collate the information required.

Local authorities, hospitals and councils were all mentioned as problem areas, but the two areas where most difficulty seems to be caused are the police, particularly with regard to information about crime and accident victims; and schools, many of which seem to believe (wrongly) that the Act absolutely prevents them from revealing the names of children photographed by the press at events such as sports days. Both these areas have now been addressed by guidelines, which are discussed below; a good knowledge of these may help reporters get the information they need.

In general terms, though, the best defence against obstructive and unnecessary use of the Act is to have a thorough knowledge of its provisions, and to be able to explain them when you believe a refusal of disclosure is based on a misunderstanding.

Law in practice Challenging use of the Data Protection Act

As the Newspaper Society's 2004 Press Freedom Survey shows, the Data Protection Act is widely misunderstood, and organisations will often cite it as a reason for refusing information in situations where the Act does not actually prevent the information being released. If you suspect this to be the case, it can be useful to ask them to explain why they think the Act prevents disclosure, as you may be able to clarify the misunderstanding.

For example, organisations will often refuse to reveal the name or contact details of an individual because they do not have the subject's consent to do so, but the Act does not say that they may not ask for that consent. In some cases, of course, the subject will not give consent, but often organisations will refuse to put you in touch with someone even in the most innocuous of circumstances when the subject would actually be quite happy to be contacted. In that case explaining that the Act allows them to ask for the person's consent may solve the problem.

The Information Commissioner also issues Good Practice Notes and other guidelines from time to time, to help correct situations where the Act appears to have been misinterpreted; new ones are published on the Office of the Information Commissioner's website (see *Online resources* at the end of this chapter).

Information from the police

The Association of Chief Police Officers (ACPO) has a Code of Practice on data protection, and its Media Advisory Group has produced further guidelines covering the effect of the Data

Protection Act on the release of information to the media (see *Online resources* at the end of this chapter). The guidelines specifically state that 'the Police Service should be supportive of a free flow of information to the media', as well as ensuring that people's rights under the Act are respected. To assist officers in striking the right balance, the guidelines make these specific points:

- The Act provides for situations in which personal information can be released without the subject's consent, where that would be in the public interest. Whether a particular situation falls within this category must be assessed on a case-by-case basis; the guidelines give the example of a major accident involving a large number of casualties, where it would be in the public interest to give out information about the victims without having to wait and get consent from them or their next of kin, in order to minimise public alarm and distress. ACPO's Code of Practice on Data Protection gives a further example, stating that information may be disclosed without consent where it is the public interest because police are appealing for witnesses.
- In general, however, personal details of victims, witnesses or anyone who is next of kin to a victim should not be released to the media without that person's consent. Before deciding how to publicise a crime or accident, the police should ask for the views of the victim, witnesses or next of kin, and, where juveniles are involved, it would be good practice to consult the parents or guardians, even though this is not specifically required by the Act. However, personal details can be released to the media even if the subject says they do not want them to be, if the police feel that, in the specific case, there is an 'exceptional reason' to do so.
- The Act does not give victims the right to prevent any details of the incident from being released, as long as doing so does not make it possible to identify them.
- When someone's consent is sought for release of information, the question should be put in a balanced way (the suggested wording is 'We often find it helpful in our enquiries to pass on someone's details to the media. Do you object if we do that in your case?'). In other words, the police should not aim to discourage people from having their details released.
- Where victims of crime agree to have their details released, but to do so might make them vulnerable to further crime, the police are justified in refusing to release the details (the guidelines give the example of an elderly person living alone). In this situation, police officers should explain the reason for the refusal, so that journalists who happen to find out the victim's name another way will take this issue into account when deciding whether to publish it.
- The guidelines also address situations where journalists ask the police for further details on stories they have obtained from other sources, but the subject of the information has not consented to its release. In this situation, the police should consider whether releasing the information would provide an opportunity to correct inaccuracies or speculation. They should not volunteer the name of anyone who is under investigation but has not been charged, but if the media already has the name, the police can confirm it.
- In some cases, the victim of an accident may subsequently be charged with a crime (e.g. where a stolen car is involved in a crash). In such situations, if an arrest is imminent, the identity of the person should not be released, even if they consent to it, until they have been charged. If it turns out that no charge is brought, the identity can be released then. Where the person is a juvenile, their identity should not be disclosed even after they are charged.

In 2009, the Information Commissioner ruled that the Data Protection Act does not prevent police forces from disclosing the names of escaped prisoners who are on the run. After it was revealed that around 1,000 convicted criminals were at large after escaping from custody, some police forces refused to name escapees in their areas, saying this was illegal under the Act. The Information Commissioner's office told the Press Association that this was incorrect. It recognised that the police might have good operational reasons not to release names (for example, where this would make it more difficult to catch escapees) but said there was nothing in the Act which prevented release of this information.

Information from schools

Twenty-five of the editors surveyed for the Newspaper Society's 2004 Press Freedom Survey said schools were refusing either to allow press photography of school events at all, or more commonly allowed photography but then claimed that the Data Protection Act prevented them from supplying the names of the children in the photo. This was the case even though the pictures were often taken for stories which celebrated the school's achievements. Many schools were also reluctant to release exam results to the press. Other organisations dealing with children, such as sports clubs, were also imposing restrictions on photography and/or caption information. As one editor quoted in the survey commented: 'These restrictions are hampering local newspapers reporting on the many positive stories, and preventing a whole generation of children from being proud to appear in their local newspaper.'

In answer to these criticisms (and also to press stories that even parents were being prevented from taking pictures at school events), the Information Commissioner produced a Good Practice Note on the subject (see *Online resources* at the end of this chapter). It states that as long as the school agrees to the press taking photographs, and the parents are informed that photos taken may be used in the press, there is no breach of the Act in allowing photographers to take pictures in school or at school events. As far as information for captions is concerned, the Department for Education and Skills has released guidance on this, which contains advice from the Information Commissioner. It states that schools can simply ask parents whether they mind the information being released, and, if this consent is given, schools can give out the information without breaching the Act.

With regard to exam results, guidelines from the Information Commissioner explain that, under the Act, schools have to inform parents and pupils about the data they process. This is usually done at the start of a child's time in the school, using a template form produced by the Office of the Information Commissioner, and, on this form, the purposes for which data may be used includes disclosure to the press. As well as being given this form, parents should also be told that they can object to publication. If this has been done, there is no problem with releasing results to the press, and no need to get further consent (unless a particular child or parent has objected, which the school will know about).

Law in practice School photography

One of the few editors in the Newspaper Society's 2004 Press Freedom Survey who reported no problems with getting caption information for school photos explained that schools in the local area sought blanket permission from parents at the start of each school year, so that there was no need to do so every time a photographer attended a school event. Far from refusing consent, parents were usually more anxious to make sure their children were not left out. It may therefore be useful for local papers to suggest this course of action to schools in their area.

OBTAINING INFORMATION FROM OTHERS

What is the situation where a journalist obtains information from someone else, and that person's disclosure is in breach of the Act? Section 55 of the Data Protection Act 1998 makes it an offence to knowingly or recklessly, without the consent of the data controller, obtain, disclose or procure the disclosure of personal data or the information in it. There is a defence where the person procuring, obtaining or disclosing the information believed doing so was justified in the public interest. The offences are not imprisonable, but, if prosecuted in the Crown Court, can lead to an unlimited fine.

KEY POINTS

Information covered by the Act

The Act covers personal data, defined as information held on computer or in a filing system, from which an individual can be identified.

Media duties under the Act

Media organisations and journalists who process personal data must:

- register with the Information Commissioner;
- process data fairly and lawfully, in accordance with the eight principles stated in the Act;
- comply with others' rights under the Act.

Stricter rules apply to 'sensitive personal data' covering issues such as race, political views, health or religious beliefs.

Exemptions for the media

The media can be exempt from most of the Act's provisions, but only where it can prove that:

- data was processed for the purpose of publication;
- publication was in the public interest;
- it was impossible to comply with the Act.

Investigation and enforcement

The Information Commissioner has powers of investigation and enforcement, but use of these against the media is restricted.

Problems with gathering information

The Act is often used to deny the press information. This can be challenged by:

- knowledge of the Act;
- understanding guidelines from the Information Commissioner;
- understanding guidelines issued by ACPO, for information from the police.

Obtaining information from others

Knowingly or recklessly obtaining, disclosing or procuring personal data without the consent of the data controller is an offence.

TEST YOUR KNOWLEDGE

1 What do these terms mean:
   (a) data controller
   (b) data subject
   (c) processing?

2 Which of these falls within the definition of 'personal data' under the Data Protection Act?
   (a) Photographs of individuals held on computer.
   (b) Hand-written notes from interviews with individuals, stored in paper files labelled with each interviewee's name.
   (c) Notes of interviews for a series of personal profiles, typed up and held on computer.
   (d) Business cards of regular contacts, stored in a card index.
   (e) A box full of press cuttings, unsorted.
   (f) Files of press cuttings, sorted into files on different people.

3 You are holding information about a celebrity, which details their mental health problems. What is the minimum you have to do to make sure you process this information in compliance with the Data Protection Act?

4 You are researching a story about a local businessman paying bribes to council officials. The businessman submits a written request, citing the Act and requiring you to disclose the information you hold about him. Do you have to comply?

5 You are researching a story about the marital difficulties of a very well-known actor. He submits a written request, citing the Act and requiring you to disclose the information you hold about him. Do you have to comply?

6 You and a photographer visit a local school to report on a carol concert. Photographs are taken, but when you call to get information for the picture captions, you are told that the Data Protection Act prevents the school disclosing the name of any pupil. Is this true?

ONLINE RESOURCES

The Data Protection Act 1998 can be read at:
http://www.legislation.gov.uk/ukpga/1998/29/contents

The Office of the Information Commissioner's website is at:
www.ico.org.uk

The Association of Chief Police Officers Media Advisory Group Code of Practice on Data Protection can be read at:
http://www.acpo.presscentre.com/imagelibrary/downloadMedia.ashx?MediaDetailsID=238

The Freedom of Information Centre website contains articles by journalist Mark Watts, on illegal information gathering by the media, at:
www.foiacentre.com

Chapter 23 Copyright

The law of copyright is part of a branch of law known as intellectual property, and gives those who create something – from a magazine article, to a novel or a piece of music – the power to protect the work they have done from being copied or used by other people. If you own the copyright on something, the law states that others cannot copy it or use it as if it were their own work, without your permission. So if, for example, you hold the copyright on a feature which has been published in a magazine, and it is then reproduced without permission on an unrelated website, you could sue for damages.

There are two reasons why a journalist needs to know about copyright: first, because in some instances you will own the copyright on your own work; and second, because you will often want to quote other people's words or use other people's work during your research, and you need to know how far the law allows you to do this.

Most of the English law on copyright comes from the Copyright, Designs and Patents Act 1988.

WORKS PROTECTED BY COPYRIGHT

The Copyright, Designs and Patents Act 1988 states that copyright applies to three types of work:

- original literary, dramatic, musical or artistic works;
- sound recordings, films or broadcasts;
- the typographical arrangements of published editions.

If a piece of work does not fall into one of these categories, it is not protected by copyright.

Literary, dramatic, musical and artistic works

The key requirement here is that work must be original. However, this does not mean it has to be strikingly imaginative, unusual or new, simply that it is the copyright holder's own work and not merely copied from something else.

In *Independent Television Publications Ltd* v *Time Out Ltd* (1984), a court found that the programme listings carried by the *TV Times* could be counted as an original literary work, because, although they were only a compilation of information from different sources, some work and effort had been put in to compiling and organising the information. (Television companies are now obliged under the Broadcasting Act 1990 to supply listings to any publisher that wants them, but they still retain copyright and can charge for the listings.)

In ***Ladbroke (Football) Ltd*** v ***William Hill (Football) UK Ltd*** (1964) the court found that football fixture lists were protected by copyright, which was owned by the Football Association.

The fact that two pieces of work may be very similar does not mean that they cannot both be subject to copyright, so long as the similarity is accidental and not the result of copying.

The two types of work in this category that are most relevant to journalists are literary and artistic works. Literary works are defined in s3(1) as: 'any work, other than a dramatic or musical work, which is written, spoken or sung'. 'Literary' in this context really means capable of being written down; it does not mean that the work has to have any literary merit or be capable of being considered 'literature', or even that it has to comprise words. Common examples are books, newspaper and magazine features and stories, interviews, speeches and song lyrics, but the category also includes computer programs, databases and tables: so the South East Trains timetable is protected by copyright in exactly the same way as the latest Booker Prize-winning novel.

However, there must be some sort of substance to the work: slogans and catchphrases are too brief to be covered by copyright. (They can be registered as trademarks if the originator wants to protect them, but copyright does not arise automatically as it would for an article or book.)

Artistic works include photographs, maps, graphics and drawings, and, again, there is no need for any great creative merit; even a very simple sketch may be covered. However, there must be some tangible item as a result of the work.

In ***Kenrick & Co*** v ***Lawrence & Co*** (1890) a simple drawing of a voting paper and a hand making a pencilled cross against the name of a candidate was held to be covered by copyright. However, as it was so simple, it was only protected against exact or near-exact copies; a slightly different picture with the hand in a different position was not a breach of copyright.

In ***Creation Records Ltd*** v ***News Group Newspapers*** (1997), the band Oasis was involved in a photo shoot at a country hotel. The pictures had been set up with the band members positioned around a pool, and a Rolls-Royce apparently rising out of the water. A photographer for the *Sun* got a room in the hotel, and from the window, was able to photograph the scene. The record company which had organised the shoot tried to sue for breach of copyright, arguing that the arrangement of the scene itself (even before any photos were taken) constituted an artistic work, comparable to a collage. The court disagreed; the scene was too impermanent to amount to an artistic work (it was, however, protected by the law on confidentiality; see Chapter 18).

In 2001, the AA was sued by the map-maker, Ordnance Survey, after the AA used Ordnance Survey maps as the basis for producing its own maps. Ordnance Survey was able to prove the plagiarism, because it had deliberately put tiny mistakes in its own maps, and these were reproduced in the AA material. The case was settled out of court, with the AA paying £20 million.

Sound recordings, films and broadcasts

Sound recordings include any recording of sounds, regardless of how it is made. Film covers any recording of a moving image. Broadcast is defined as an electronic transmission of images, sounds and information to the public, but does not include internet transmission unless it is a concurrent transmission of a live event, or part of a programme service transmitted at scheduled times, or a transmission that also takes place at the same time by other means. The Act specifically provides that taking a photograph of a TV screen while a programme is broadcast (sometimes known as a 'screen grab') can be a breach of copyright.

Typographical arrangements

This category covers the way in which a printed page is laid out and protects against unauthorised photocopying.

Copyright and ideas

Section 3(2) of the 1988 Act provides that, in order to be covered by copyright, literary, dramatic and musical works have to be recorded in a tangible form, such as writing or a tape recording. This means that mere ideas which have not been put into a permanent form will not be protected by copyright, and nor will words which have been spoken but not recorded or written down. The main implication of this for journalists comes in the area of commissioning. If, for example, a freelance writer suggests a feature idea to a magazine, that idea is not protected by copyright, and an unscrupulous commissioning editor may be able simply to take it and give it to another writer, or produce the feature in-house (in this situation, however, there will sometimes be protection from the law of confidentiality – see Chapter 18).

In ***IPC Media Ltd*** v ***Highbury Leisure Publishing*** (2004), IPC sued rival publisher Highbury, alleging that its new magazine *Home* infringed IPC copyright on its title *Ideal Home*. IPC alleged that *Home* copied *Ideal Home*'s design, pointing out the similarities between the two title's cover formats, inside layouts and subject matter of features. The court rejected the claim, saying that all the features and techniques mentioned were commonly used throughout the magazine industry, and that, in a highly competitive market, it was inevitable that designers would use similar tricks and techniques, and subject matter would coincide. The similarities IPC had pointed to were really at the level of ideas, themes and styles, which copyright law did not protect.

In ***Baigent*** v ***Random House*** (2006), two of the three authors of a book called *The Holy Blood and The Holy Grail* sued the publisher of the best-selling novel *The Da Vinci Code*. The claimants' book was a non-fiction work, advancing the theory that Jesus married Mary Magdalene and had children. *The Da Vinci Code* uses this theory as the basis for a thriller, in which the hero tries to find evidence that would prove it to be true, while those who want to keep it secret try to stop him. The author of *The Da Vinci Code* admitted that *The Holy Blood* had been used as part of his background research, and had one of his characters refer to it in the book. The claimants argued that he had breached their copyright by copying the 'central theme' of their book. The court rejected this argument, saying that there had been no copying of a central theme, and that, even if there had been, that central theme was essentially a collection of ideas, and, as such, could not be protected by copyright. Only the expression of those ideas could be copyrighted, and the court found no evidence of substantial copying of the text.

News and information

Because of the requirement that copyright material has to have some tangible form, news and information are not covered by copyright, only the words used to express them in a particular news story. This means that, if you uncover a scoop about, for example, a local politician having an affair, the actual story that you write about it will be copyright, but other papers can still report the facts in different words, even if the only information they have comes from your story and they would not otherwise have known about it. Equally, of course, you can do the same with stories in rival papers.

However, this does not amount to a wholesale licence to lift stories from other publications. Where the lifting goes beyond the basic facts, and reproduces a substantial amount of either the original writer's words, or quotations used in the original piece, without acknowledging that they came from the copyright holder, there may be a breach of copyright.

In ***Express Newspapers plc* v *News (UK) Ltd*** (1990), the *Daily Express* sued the *Today* newspaper for breach of copyright, after *Today* ran a story about Pamela Bordes, who at the time was in the news for being what the tabloids like to call a 'high class call girl'. The *Express* had had the story as an exclusive in its first edition, and the facts and quotes were lifted by *Today* for its second edition. *Today* then counter-sued the *Express* for lifting one of its stories on the Royal family. In both cases, the judge refused to accept that publishing the facts of the stories was a breach of copyright. He pointed out that it was (and still is) standard practice for newspapers to pick up stories from each other and rewrite them, and said that to accept that this practice was a breach of copyright would allow individual newspapers to claim a monopoly in particular news stories, which would not be in the public interest. However, both newspapers were liable for breach of copyright for reproducing the other's quotes, because getting the quotes in the first place demanded skill and effort and was therefore work which could be protected.

In ***Walter* v *Steinkopf*** (1892), Rudyard Kipling had been writing news dispatches for *The Times*, and a paper called the *St James Evening Gazette* began regularly printing substantial parts of them in its own coverage. *The Times* sued. The court confirmed that there was no copyright in news itself, but that there was copyright in the way that news was expressed in a story. It observed that the *Gazette* had used large amounts of copy from *The Times*, had done so regularly and deliberately, and had not made any effort to rewrite the reports at all; what the *Gazette* had done was described as 'a mechanical operation with scissors and paste'. The *Gazette* was taking advantage of someone else's labour at no cost to itself and, the court held, what it had done amounted to breach of copyright.

In ***Walter* v *Lane*** (1900), a *Times* reporter was granted damages after a rival newspaper copied word for word a speech which he had taken down in shorthand and used in a news story. As with ***Walter* v *Steinkopf***, what appeared to influence the court was that the *Times* reporter had used skill and effort in taking the speech down in shorthand, whereas the other paper was getting something for nothing. (Obviously, had the rival paper's reporter attended the speech, they could have made their own notes and used those without breaching *The Times*' copyright.)

As some of the judgments above point out, it is in the public interest that news is reported as widely as possible, and Parliament specifically recognised this when passing the 1988 Act, which creates a special defence which, within limits, can allow use of copyright material (such as quotes) in reporting current events, provided the copyright holder is acknowledged (see below).

Speeches and interviews

A speech which has previously been written down is covered by copyright, because it exists in a tangible form before it is spoken; the copyright belongs to the speaker. Someone who records that speech (on sound or film) would own the copyright to the recorded words, so both the person who wrote the speech, and the person who recorded it could sue for breach of copyright.

Where a speaker talks off the cuff, or gives an interview, there is no copyright in their words until they are written down or recorded by someone else (such as a reporter), whether with or without the speaker's permission. Where a journalist makes an accurate note or recording of words spoken off the cuff or in an interview, the copyright for the words belongs to the speaker, but the journalist will own the copyright to the tape or notes. A defence under the 1988 Act allows words recorded in these circumstances to be used for reporting current events, or in a broadcast or cable programme, without the speaker's permission (see p. 369).

What does copyright protect?

Protected	Not protected
Original literary, dramatic, musical and artistic works, including almost anything written down in words, plus photos, maps and drawings	Ideas (though these may be protected by confidentiality; see Chapter 18)
Sound recordings, films and broadcasts	Facts
Typographical arrangements	News and information

Official information

Documents published by or on behalf of the Government are covered by what is called Crown copyright, so they cannot simply be copied or reproduced without permission. In most cases, where the media wants to publish extracts from a government document which is publicly available, a licence is issued allowing publication of small amounts of material without charge. However, there are some categories where Crown copyright is waived. Copying material which by law must be available to public inspection is not usually a breach of copyright.

Reporting words spoken or read during parliamentary or court proceedings is not an infringement of copyright.

Myths and misconceptions Establishing copyright

✗ *To get copyright, you have to mark your work with the © symbol and post it to yourself.*

The copyright on a piece of work comes into existence as soon as the work is created, and gives the holder (usually, though not always, the creator of the work) the right to sue anyone who uses the work unlawfully. It is often believed that in order to establish the copyright to a work, you have to mark it with the copyright symbol and/or post it to yourself or someone else so that the date of creation is confirmed. This is not the case. Copyright comes into existence automatically when a work is created, and does not need to be registered in any way; nor does the work have to be published in order for copyright to exist. The posting technique can be useful as a way to prove the date that copyright arose, in case of a dispute later, but the copyright will exist anyway.

OWNERSHIP OF COPYRIGHT

The 1988 Act provides that the first owner of any work is the person who creates it, unless the work is created in the course of employment. In that case, unless you have agreed otherwise in your employment contract, the employer owns the copyright. So, for example, if you are on the staff of a magazine or newspaper, your employer will usually own the copyright to everything you write as part of your job, and can use it for any purpose. A freelance journalist, on the other hand, owns the copyright to all their work, unless they agree otherwise with the company that commissions it.

Once the work is created, the copyright holder can transfer ownership to someone else. For example, when magazines and papers commission a freelance to write for them, they quite often buy the copyright to that article from the freelance as part of the deal. This then enables them to sell on the work to other publications, or use it online, if they wish to, without paying any more money to the freelance, or asking their permission. This is often called buying 'all rights'. Freelances can, of course, refuse to work on this basis and negotiate to keep the copyright, simply allowing the work to be used on a one-off basis (or to allow further use, but be paid for it).

If a reader sends a letter to a newspaper and does not state that it is not to be published, they are effectively giving permission to publish that letter (in legal terms, this is issuing a licence – see below). However, the writer of the letter retains copyright in it.

Ownership of photographs

If a photograph was taken after the 1988 Act came into force on 31 July 1989, the original copyright belongs to the person who takes the photo; this applies as much to a family snapshot as to a picture taken by a famous photographer. For photos taken before the Act came into force, copyright belongs to the person who commissioned them, so in the case of a wedding photo, for example, it would usually be the couple themselves or one of them.

In addition to the copyright issue, privacy rights attach to pictures commissioned for 'private and domestic purposes' (see p. 376).

Law in practice Using photos

Caution should be exercised when illustrating stories about ordinary people with school, college or wedding photographs, or any other pictures which have been taken by a professional photographer. People are often happy to hand these over to a reporter, but in fact they may not own the copyright, even if they paid for the photograph; in most cases it remains with the photographer, whose permission should be sought before publishing. Similarly, it can be risky to lift pictures from social networking websites such as Facebook, if you do not know who owns the copyright.

Transferring copyright

Someone who owns copyright in a work can give (or more commonly, sell) all or part of that right to someone else in one of two ways:

- assignment;
- licence.

Assignment

Assigning copyright is the equivalent to selling it, or part of it. For example, as stated above, many publishers buy copyright as part of the deal when they commission a feature. In that case, the writer is assigning the copyright to the publisher, who can then use the feature as many times as it wants to, and can also sell it to other publishers; effectively, the feature becomes the publisher's property. Assignment of copyright must be in writing to be legally binding. In some large publishing companies, regular freelances are asked to sign a form stating that all commissions are on an all rights basis unless otherwise agreed; in others, a commissioning form is sent out when each job is ordered.

Licence

A licence is a way of giving someone permission to use the work in a particular way or for a particular length of time. If, for example, a freelance writer only grants a licence – for example, the right to publish the article once in a particular magazine – the copyright remains with the writer and if the publisher wants to use the piece elsewhere or again it must get permission. A licence granting exclusive use of material must be in writing to be legally binding (and in fact it is good practice to get any agreement involving copyright in writing).

Law in practice **Commissioning work**

If you commission work – whether copy or photographs – from someone else, and you (or your company) may at some point want to use that work for something other than the original use, you need to agree this with the freelance, either at the time of commissioning or when you want to reuse the material. If, for example, you commission someone to write a feature for your magazine, that does not give you the right to put it on your website as well, unless you agree that with the freelance in advance. Similarly, if you commission a photographer to take pictures for a particular feature, you do not automatically have the right to use them on a later occasion, even in the same magazine. Many large publishing companies, particularly magazine companies, now use printed commissioning forms, which are sent out to the freelance, confirming the rights that have been bought; this is a useful way to make sure both sides are clear on what is being bought. To have legal effect, however, the freelance needs to be informed of the terms at the time the commission is agreed; sending a form after the job is done is not legally binding, although it is common practice in many companies.

INFRINGING COPYRIGHT

There are several ways in which copyright can be infringed, but, for journalistic purposes, the most important is copying, which includes reproducing all or part of someone else's work as though it were your own work, or publishing it without permission, even if you acknowledge it as the copyright holder's work (there are, however, some situations in which this is permitted; see p. 368).

In order to count as an infringement of copyright, the 1988 Act provides that there must be use of a 'substantial part' of the original work. There is no set rule on what proportion of a work will be considered substantial, but the quality of what is reproduced (in terms of its importance to the original work) can be as important as the quantity.

In ***PCR Ltd* v *Dow Jones Telerate Ltd*** (1998) a business reporter used information from a private report on the world cocoa market, including sets of figures, in an article of her own. Although the amount of information used was not large, it included more or less all the significant points in the market report, and, as a result, her article was held to be a breach of copyright.

In ***Infopaq International A/S* v *Danske Dagblades Forening*** (2010), the European Court of Justice found that using an 11-word extract from a newspaper article could be a breach of copyright if the work had sufficient originality.

In ***Newspaper Licensing Agency Ltd* v *Meltwater Holding BV*** (2010), the High Court stated that copying a headline could be breach of copyright, because of the skill and expertise that went into writing them. The case also confirmed that the test of whether copying involved a 'substantial' part of a work related to the quality of what was stolen, not the quantity

Exact copies are obviously a breach of copyright, while taking a set of facts from a story and expressing them in a completely different way is not. In between the two, however, lies a grey area. The basic test is whether the person doing the second piece of work has contributed a significant degree of work and skill over and above that already in the original work so, obviously, just changing the odd word in a feature and then reproducing it is very likely to be a breach of copyright. If, however, the original work is genuinely only the basis, and significant skill and effort has gone into the second piece of work, the courts are less likely to find a breach. The amount of effort and skill which went into the original work is also a factor; as the case of ***Kenrick* v *Lawrence*** (see earlier), about the drawing of a hand, shows, less protection is given when the original work itself requires little skill.

In ***Warwick Film Productions* v *Eisinger*** (1969), the courts were asked to decide whether the compiler of one anthology of quotations had breached the copyright of another, published earlier. Although some of the quotations were the same, the court found that the material had been arranged differently, and used with material from other sources. This involved a sufficient degree of work to ensure that there was no breach of copyright.

Myths and misconceptions Copyright and the internet

✗ ***You can use words and pictures you find on the internet because they're in the public domain.***

It is often assumed that it is quite safe to reuse any material you find on the internet, because it is already available for anyone to see. This is absolutely not the case. Material on the internet is covered by the same copyright protection as any other form of media, and you can be sued if the copyright owner finds out that you have used their words or pictures. This includes pictures on social networking sites.

Parodies

In 2014, new provisions were added to the Copyright, Design and Patents Act 1988, which state that limited amounts of an original work can be used for the purposes of parody, without the copyright owner's permission. The amount used must fall within the terms of the fair dealing defence, so it would not be possible to use the whole of a particular work.

Parodies can cause problems with the moral right of protection against false attribution of authorship (see p. 376).

Embargoes

When a copyright holder gives permission for their material to be used (in legal terms, issues a licence – see p. 366), they may put certain conditions on that use, such as an embargo, which states that the material cannot be used before a stated date. If this is ignored, the resulting publication may be a breach of copyright.

In 1992, the *Sun* published the Queen's Christmas message two days before Christmas. It is usual practice for the message to be issued to all national papers before Christmas, with an embargo prohibiting publication until after the Queen's broadcast on Christmas Day, and this happened as usual, but the *Sun* ignored the embargo. The Queen began an action for breach of copyright, and the case was settled out of court with the paper agreeing to pay a substantial sum to charity.

Length of copyright

Before the 1988 Act, copyright could last for ever, but now the Act lays down limits for how long copyright in different types of work lasts. When these periods come to an end, the work goes out of copyright, and is said to be 'in the public domain'. It can then can be used by anyone, in any way, without charge.

The table below shows the lengths of copyright for different types of work, under the Act. However, it only applies to works created since the Act was passed; older works may be subject to different time periods, and specialist legal advice may need to be sought regarding these.

Work	Length of copyright
Literary, dramatic, musical and artistic works	70 years from the end of the calendar year in which the author/composer/artist dies.
Sound recordings	50 years from the end of the calendar year in which they were made.
Broadcast	50 years from the end of the calendar year in which it was made.
Film	70 years from the end of the calendar year which sees the death of the last among the principal director, screenplay writer, writer of the dialogue or composer of music created especially for the film.
Published editions (layouts, design and so on – see p. 362)	25 years from the end of the calendar year in which it was first published.

DEFENCES

The Copyright, Designs and Patents Act 1988 allows some use of copyright-protected works without permission from the copyright owner, and these can provide defences to an action for breach of copyright. The five which are most relevant to the media are:

- fair dealing;
- incidental inclusion;
- reproduction of speeches and interviews;
- public interest;
- acquiescence.

Fair dealing (news and review)

This allows parts of copyright works to be quoted, reproduced or used for the purposes of criticism or review, or in the course of reporting current events. This means that if you are writing a review of a book, for example, you can quote parts of it word for word, while in reporting a news story, a broadcaster could use parts of another channel's broadcast, in both cases without getting the copyright holder's consent. The defence applies where:

- the material is used for the purpose of criticism or review; or in reporting current events;
- the copyright holder receives 'sufficient acknowledgement' (though this is not always necessary for TV and film clips; see below);
- the amount of material used is fair;
- the material used has already been made available to the public.

In broadcasting, the fair dealing defence is often known as 'news and review', though in practice a case of fair dealing will almost always apply to either news or review, not both, and it is important to know that the rules differ depending on which you are covering.

In 2014, the Government amended the 1988 Act, extending the fair dealing defence to cover the use of short quotations for any purpose, not just news and reviews. The change means that short quotations (but not long extracts) can be used without getting the copyright holder's permission, so long as the source is acknowledged and the number of words used falls within the fair dealing rules.

What material can be used?

The defence of fair dealing applies to written or spoken words, to film clips and 'artistic works'. This means that, for example, if a celebrity hits the news, BBC news could use excerpts from an ITN interview with that person, and newspapers can quote from each other's stories. As well as material from other publishers and TV companies, the defence can allow the media to use other copyright material, such as government and local authority reports and private papers (though they must have been made available to the public; see below).

Material used for criticism and review

Clearly this covers specific reviews of the work concerned, but it is wider than this, covering situations where copyright material is used to illustrate the theme of a feature or programme.

In *Pro Sieben Media AG* v *Carlton UK Television Ltd* (1999), Pro Sieben, a German TV company, had the rights to a TV interview with Mandy Allwood, a British woman who had hit the news when she was pregnant with octuplets. It used the interview on a daily news programme. Carlton then used clips of the same interview in a programme of its own, about chequebook journalism, and this was found to be within the limits of fair dealing, since Mandy Allwood had been paid by newspapers for her story (see later for more details on this case).

In *Time Warner Entertainments Co* v *Channel Four* (1994), Channel 4 made a TV programme about the fact that the film *A Clockwork Orange* had been withdrawn from public showings because of the violence in it. Using clips from the film in the programme was covered by the defence of fair dealing (see later for more details on this case).

Material used for reporting current events

The fair dealing defence also allows broadcasters and newspapers to use each other's material where it is fair to do so for the purpose of reporting current events. This means that, for example, if one TV company has footage of a key event in the news, others can use clips from it to illustrate the story, and where one newspaper has broken a story, others can use excerpts from it. As with reviews, the copyright holder should be given sufficient acknowledgement, but this is waived for sound recordings, film or broadcasts where it would be impossible 'for reasons of practicality or otherwise' to acknowledge the copyright holder.

The Act does not define current events, and there seems to be no set time limit on whether an issue will be considered current; it is clear, however, that the defence is not limited to coverage of events happening at or just before the time of reporting.

In *Hyde Park Residence Ltd* v *Yelland* (2000) the Court of Appeal considered whether a story about the relationship between Princess Diana and Dodi Fayed could count as reporting current events, considering that they had both been dead for a year when it was published. The court held that it could, taking into account the fact that news stories about the relationship had continued appearing since the car crash which killed the couple, and that Dodi's father had recently issued press statements about it (though the case failed for other reasons; see later).

In *Ashdown* v *Telegraph Group* (2001), the Court of Appeal held that a story about a meeting between Tony Blair and Paddy Ashdown, then leader of the Liberal Democrats, could be considered reporting of current events, even though the meeting had taken place a couple of years earlier. The issue, the court said, was whether the report in question was informing the public about 'matters of current concern' (the defence in fact failed on other grounds).

The requirement for the reporting to be of current events only applies to the report which uses the copyright material; the material itself need not be a report of current events. For example, where a celebrity hits the headlines, fair dealing would allow use of excerpts from an old interview with that person.

Using photographs

The use of photographs is covered by the fair dealing defence when they are used for criticism and review, but not where they are used in reporting current events. If one paper holds the copyright on a particular photograph, others cannot publish it and then use the defence of fair dealing in reporting current events, even if they acknowledge where it came from.

In *Banier* v *News Group Newspapers* (1997), the case concerned stories about Princess Caroline of Monaco, who was suffering from alopecia (hair loss). Pictures of her had been taken by a French photographer, and several papers had bought permission to use the pictures from him. The *Sun* did not seek permission, but printed some of the pictures anyway. The paper claimed that it intended to negotiate a licence fee after publication, and that it was common practice to print without permission and pay afterwards where a story needed to be published quickly in order to remain newsworthy. The court rejected this argument, stating the publication was unlawful. It ordered an injunction and awarded damages to the photographer.

It is important to be aware that a newspaper or magazine may hold copyright to photos even if it has not taken or commissioned them. Where an ordinary person is involved in a high-profile news story, a paper may pay relatives or friends for the copyright to family snaps, which means that other papers will be breaching copyright if they publish them.

Stills taken from TV or film do not count as photographs for the purpose of fair dealing, and their use can therefore be covered by the defence.

In *Fraser-Woodward* v *BBC* (2005), a photographic agency sued the BBC for showing its photographs, without permission, in a programme about the tabloid press. The pictures were seen in shots of the pages of newspapers. Mr Justice Mann ruled that they were used for the purpose of criticism of the practices of the tabloid press and therefore could fall within the defence.

Sufficient acknowledgement

To be covered by fair dealing, the review must contain 'sufficient acknowledgement' of the copyright work. This means that it must be clear who the copyright holder of the work is, unless it is published anonymously or is not published, and it is impossible to find out the copyright owner by reasonable inquiry. The acknowledgement must identify the source properly, so words such as 'a book on the subject says' or 'an academic report stated' would not be sufficient. However, as long as the source is clearly identified, it is not necessary to thank them for use of the material.

In the *Pro Sieben* case mentioned above, the clips carried the Pro Sieben logo in one corner of the screen, and it was suggested that this could not count as 'sufficient acknowledgement' because the symbol was meaningless to most UK viewers. However, the Court of Appeal held that this was irrelevant; the symbol was the way in which the company habitually identified itself, and therefore amounted to sufficient acknowledgement.

Fairness

The courts will look at whether the usage of material was 'fair', but it is important to realise that fairness here relates to the amount of material used, not the way in which it was used. There is no problem, for example, with using quotes in a book review even if the review concludes that the book is terrible. The issue of fairness is simply whether the amount of material used was reasonable, given the purpose of the work it was used in; if the amount used is excessive for that purpose, the defence will not apply. There is no set amount of copyright material that can be used in this way, but it must not amount to 'illegitimate exploitation' of the work. The courts will also consider whether the purpose could have been achieved without using the copyright material, and whether the use of the material had a commercial impact on the copyright holder, for example if it represented competition to the original work.

In the 'Clockwork Orange' case referred to above, the TV programme used 12 clips from the film, which it was found amounted to around 8 per cent of its length, and 40 per cent of the TV programme. It acknowledged the film company as copyright holders. However, the film company claimed that fair dealing could not apply because in selecting only violent scenes, Channel 4 had misrepresented the film. The Court of Appeal held that the fact that the clips were unrepresentative of the work was not relevant, as long as the purpose of using them was genuinely criticism or review. The main issue was the amount of material used, and the court ruled that it was within the limits of fair dealing, so the defence applied.

In ***BBC* v *British Satellite Broadcasting Ltd*** (1992), British Satellite Broadcasting (BSB) had paid a lot of money for rights to show World Cup matches played in 1990, and owned the copyright for those broadcasts. The BBC showed clips from them in its news broadcasts, and was sued by BSB. The court held that the usage was fair, even though the clips comprised the most important parts of each match, and also held that sports reports were included within the definition of current events. (As a result of this decision, most UK TV companies made a voluntary agreement setting out when and how clips from other broadcasters' sports coverage could be used.)

In the *Pro Sieben* case (see earlier), the fact that the extract used was just 30 seconds out of an original nine-minute interview contributed to the court's finding that Carlton was covered by the fair dealing defence. The court was also swayed by the fact that the Carlton's documentary did not represent any commercial competition to Pro Sieben.

In ***Hyde Park Residence Ltd* v *Yelland*** (2000) (see p. 370) the story about Princess Diana and Dodi Fayed was illustrated with stills taken from security cameras at Villa Windsor, a house in Paris. Mr Fayed's father had claimed the couple were engaged and had viewed the house as a possible marital home. The *Sun*'s story sought to disprove this by demonstrating that Dodi and the Princess had only spent half an hour there, hence the use of the security cameras. The Court of Appeal held that the paper could have conveyed this information adequately without using the copyright material and, in any case, the length of the couple's stay at the house did not prove whether or not they planned to marry.

In *Ashdown* v *Telegraph Group* (2001) (see p. 370), the court was influenced by the fact that the use of the leaked document had a commercial value to the paper, in attracting more readers, and also had a potentially adverse impact on the economic interests of Mr Ashdown, the copyright holder, because it might diminish the value of his memoirs, which he intended to publish at some point.

Defendants often argue that, if material was obtained in an underhand way, use of it cannot be fair. The courts, however, draw a distinction between unauthorised obtaining of material and actual stealing.

In the 'Clockwork Orange' case, Channel 4 had gone abroad to get a copy of the film (which was banned in the UK) rather than going through the copyright holders, and the copyright holders claimed that this meant the usage could not be fair. However, the court stated that the way in which material was obtained would seldom, if ever, be relevant to the issue of fair dealing.

In the *Hyde Park* case, the court specifically mentioned the fact that the security film had been stolen as one of the reasons why fair dealing did not apply.

Available to the public

The work concerned must be one which has been made available to the public. Essentially, this means that the defence will not cover use of a copyright work which has become available by means of a leak. For example, when the sixth episode in the Harry Potter saga was published in 2005, some copies were stolen before publication. If a newspaper had quoted from one, it would not have been covered by the defence of fair dealing.

In the past, the courts have held that material could be considered to be 'available to the public' without actually being published in the normal sense of the word: the fact that it has been seen, legitimately, by a number of people may be sufficient. However, the Copyright and Related Rights Regulations 2003 state that the fair dealing defence will not apply to material used for criticism or review, which has been made available by an 'unauthorised act'. This does not apply to material used for reporting current events.

In *Sun Printers Ltd* v *Westminster Press* (1982) the court held that a company memo which had been sent to top executives and union officials could be said to be available to the public for the purposes of the fair dealing defence.

In *Fraser* v *Evans* (1969), a secret document written for the Greek Government was leaked to the *Sunday Times*. The paper wanted to use quotes from the report in a story about its contents, and the Court of Appeal agreed that it had an arguable defence of fair dealing, even though only very few people had seen the report. The Court pointed out, however, that the defence was arguable in the case of publishing extracts, but said that an injunction might have been granted if the paper had wanted to publish the whole report.

Law in practice Fair dealing in broadcasting

If you are working in TV, your broadcasting company is likely to have made agreements with other broadcasters to use or not use their footage, so there may be occasions when fair dealing would seem to allow you to use footage but an agreement is in place which prevents that. Make sure that you are aware of these arrangements, as well as the requirements of the fair dealing defence.

Incidental inclusion

Section 31 of the 1988 Act provides a defence where copyright material is used 'incidentally' in an artistic work, sound recording, film, broadcast or cable programme. Take, for example, a news clip of a reporter walking down a high street. In just a few seconds of film, the reporter might walk past store logos and advertising billboards, while music might be heard from shops or even passing cars, all of which would be covered by copyright. Without the incidental use defence, all these would have to be cleared for copyright use.

'Incidental' is not defined in the Act, but the defence is considered to apply to any brief inclusion of copyright material that is not deliberate, and would be hard to avoid. Examples might include a glimpse of a TV programme if a TV is on in the background of a shot, a billboard or store logo briefly visible as a reporter walks by, magazine covers briefly seen in a shop, or background music playing where you are filming (but not background music which you add to the film, however briefly). On the other hand, if something like a poster is deliberately included in a film, or commented on, copyright clearance would usually be necessary.

Spoken words

The Act acknowledges that once spoken words are recorded (on tape, film or in writing), copyright applies, and belongs to the person who said the words. However, s58 provides that where the media records spoken words (in writing or otherwise), for the purpose of reporting current events, broadcasting or including in a cable programme service, they can then use the material recorded, provided five conditions are met:

- the record was made directly from the speech or interview, not taken from a previous recording;
- the speaker has not said that a recording should not be made;
- the words themselves do not breach any existing copyright;
- the speaker has not prohibited the use that is made of the words, before they were recorded;
- the person who has lawful possession of the record (e.g. the person who made the notes) consents to the use made of the words.

This basically means that, when reporting current events, you are permitted to use any spoken words, unless the speaker has specifically said that they do not want them noted down and/or published. This applies regardless of whether the words are spoken in public or not.

Public interest

The 1988 Act does not specify a defence of public interest, but the courts have recognised over the years that there are situations where the subject of a report, story or programme is important enough to override the protection of copyright.

In ***Lion Laboratories* v *Evans*** (1985), a court allowed publication of copyright material about a machine used to test whether motorists were above the drink-driving limit; the material suggested that the device might not be completely accurate. The *Daily Express* successfully raised the public interest defence, and this use of the defence was specifically approved by the Court of Appeal in ***Hyde Park Residence Ltd* v *Yelland*** (2001).

In *Hyde Park Residence Ltd* v *Yelland* (2001) (see p. 370), the *Sun* claimed that it was covered by the public interest defence, because the issue of whether the mother of the future King of England had planned to remarry was a matter of public interest. The court acknowledged that the events surrounding Princess Diana's death were a matter of public importance, but said there was nothing about the stills themselves that justified removing copyright protection from them.

Acquiescence

Where the owner of copyright knows that their work is being used, and allows this to go on without complaint, they may find it difficult to make a claim for breach later on.

In *Film Investors Overseas Services SA* v *Home Video Channel Ltd* (1996), the copyright holder on a collection of porn films had granted a licence for their use to the Home Video Channel. However, the use made of the films went further than the licence allowed; the copyright holders were aware of this from early 1993, but did nothing about it. The court held that, where a copyright holder is aware of a breach and does not complain, it has effectively consented to the use and so has no claim.

Innocent infringement

This is not strictly speaking a defence, but can affect the remedy claimed. If a breach of copyright is committed, but the publisher or broadcaster did not know, or have any reason to suspect that the work was subject to copyright, the copyright owner can claim an account of profits (see below), but not damages. This could apply, for example, where a publisher wrongly believed that material was out of copyright.

REMEDIES FOR BREACH OF COPYRIGHT

Breach of copyright is a criminal offence, but, in practice, prosecutions are only brought in cases of large-scale pirating, for example of DVDs. For the media, the risk is more one of being sued. A successful claim will be dealt with by one or more of the following remedies:

- interim injunctions, which are granted before publication, and prevent it going ahead (the Human Rights Act limits the situations where these can be used);
- permanent injunctions, which prevent further publication;
- an order to hand all the relevant material back to the copyright owner, or to destroy it;
- damages;
- account of profits.

An award will often include both an injunction and damages, or an injunction and an account of profits; however, damages and account of profits are alternatives, and are not both ordered in the same case.

If damages are awarded, the amount will depend on the circumstances of the case. In some situations, a court will consider that it is only necessary to compensate the copyright holder for their financial loss, in which case what are called 'infringement damages' will be ordered, which normally amount to the price the publisher would have had to pay if use of the copyright material had been agreed in advance. However, a court can also impose what are called 'flagrant damages', where it believes the justice of the case demands this. These are higher damages, aimed at marking the court's disapproval of the defendant's conduct, and deterring them (and others) from breaching copyright again. They might be ordered, for example, where a copyright holder has refused permission to publish their work, and the defendant has gone ahead and published it anyway, or in a situation where the copyright holder would never have given permission and so was not asked.

In ***Williams* v *Settle*** (1960) a photographer sold some wedding photographs to the media after the bride's father-in-law was murdered. She would never have given permission for this, and under the law as it was at this time, she owned the copyright because she had paid for the photos. The court ordered flagrant damages of £1,000 against the newspaper which published them.

In ***Nottinghamshire Healthcare NHS Trust* v *News Group Newspapers*** (2002), the *Sun* published a photograph taken from the medical records of a convicted killer, who was being kept in a secure mental hospital; the picture was used to illustrate a story about the killer being let out on day release. The NHS Trust sued for breach of copyright, and the court awarded flagrant damages of £10,000.

In 2005, photographer Chris Tofalos accepted damages of £45,000, after English Basketball, the sport's regulating body, used his pictures without authorisation on over 200 occasions.

Instead of damages, a claimant may ask for account of profits, which means that, instead of claiming the amount that they lost through the breach of copyright, they base their claim on the amount that the defendant has made as a result of using the material. This is most often done in cases concerning books, as with newspapers, magazines and broadcast programmes, it is clearly very difficult to assess the amount of profit which can be attributed to use of the copyright material.

MORAL AND PRIVACY RIGHTS

While copyright is essentially about the economic value of a person's work, moral rights address the fact that the kind of work which is protected by copyright tends to involve a certain amount of creativity and self-expression, and, for that reason, the people who produce it usually want to be acknowledged for it, and to have some say in how it is used or altered. The Copyright, Designs and Patents Act 1988 therefore includes rules about people being credited for the work they produce, which is called the right of paternity, and about what is done with the work after completion, called the right of integrity.

For journalists, these rights are very limited, as we shall see, but it is still important to know about them, as often journalists assume they have moral rights over work when in fact they do not. You need to know both what your rights over your own work are, and, if you commission work from others, what rules cover your use of that work.

The Act also creates moral rights which protect against use of some private photos, and false attribution of authorship. With all these rights, do not be deceived by the term 'moral rights'; they may sound like no more than rules which nice people abide by, but they are legal rights like any others, and breach of them can result in a claim for damages and/or an injunction.

Right of paternity

The 1988 Act provides that the creator of a literary, dramatic, artistic or musical work has the right to be identified as its author. Unlike copyright, though, this right does not arise automatically, and must be 'asserted' by a statement from the creator of the work. (This is the reason why many books contain a statement that 'The author has asserted her moral right . . . ') Photographers and journalists are not covered by this provision, and so there is no automatic right to a byline in newspapers or magazines.

Where copyright work is used in a situation covered by the fair dealing defence, it is not necessary to identify the author of the work concerned, unless they are the copyright holder.

Right of integrity

Under the 1988 Act, the author of a literary, dramatic, artistic or musical work has the automatic right not to have that work undergo 'unjustified modification', and any changes made to the work have to be 'reasonable in the circumstances and not prejudicial to the honour or reputation' of the author. As with the right of paternity, however, work produced for newspapers and magazines is exempt from this provision, so photographers and journalists have no right under the Act to object to a feature being rewritten, or a picture cropped in a way they do not like.

False attribution of authorship

Elsewhere (in Chapter 16), we saw that saying something untrue about a person could not lead to liability for libel unless the statement damaged their reputation; the fact that it was untrue is not enough in itself. However, there is one situation where publishing a false statement, even if not defamatory, can break the law, and that is what is called false attribution of authorship. It applies where words are published in such a way as to suggest that a particular person said or wrote them, when that is not the case. It could apply, for example, to making up quotations, or to substantially rewriting an article which gives the writer's personal opinion.

In *Moore* v *News of the World* (1972), the *News of the World* interviewed the writer Dorothy Squires, and, on the basis of that, published an article which it said she had written. Ms Squires said she had not used the words that the paper printed, and the court awarded her £100 in damages.

In *Clark* v *Associated Newspapers Ltd* (1998), the publishers of the London *Evening Standard* were sued over a piece which was written as a parody of the diaries published by MP Alan Clark. The piece carried the name of its author, Peter Bradshaw, and it was explained in the heading that this was an imaginary entry in Mr Clark's diary. The court said that the rule of false attribution did not prevent publication of parodies like this, but that, to stay within the law, the publisher had to make it very clear that the article was a parody and not the real thing. This had not been made sufficiently clear in this case, where the overall impression given was that this was Mr Clark's work.

In 1988, Godfrey Cannon, a nutrition expert, was awarded substantial damages after the *Today* newspaper falsely attributed authorship of an article to him. The paper had commissioned him to write an article, but did not use the copy he supplied, and instead printed another piece with his name on it, which contained views with which Mr Cannon completely disagreed.

Unlike the rights of paternity and integrity, the right not to have authorship falsely attributed does apply to journalists, and to material used in newspapers and magazines.

Unauthorised use of pictures

As well as moral rights for the creators of copyright work, the Act provides that, where someone has commissioned pictures for 'private and domestic purposes' (such as wedding photos, for example), they have a moral right not to have copies issued to the public, which includes the press, even if the person issuing the picture owns the copyright. This means that even if you get hold of someone's wedding picture via the photographer who took it, and the photographer consents to its use, publishing the photo may be in breach of the rights of the person who commissioned the photography in the first place (usually the couple).

KEY POINTS

Works protected

Copyright protects:

- original literary, dramatic, musical and artistic works;
- sound recordings, films and broadcasts;
- typographical arrangements.

Establishing copyright

Copyright comes into existence when works are created; it does not have to be registered.

Ownership

Copyright is owned by the creator of the work or their employer, but can be assigned to others.

Infringing copyright

Copyright is breached by copying a substantial part of it, or breaking the conditions of a licence.

Defences

There are five defences:

- Fair dealing permits fair use of published material for reporting current events or in criticism or review, with acknowledgment.
- Incidental inclusion allows use that is incidental, such as part of a background.
- Public interest allows use where the material is such that copyright protection would be against the policy of the law.
- Speech can be reproduced in reporting current events.
- Acquiescence applies where the copyright holder knows of the breach and takes no action.

Remedies

Any of three remedies may be ordered:

- injunctions, temporary or permanent;
- damages;
- account of profits.

Moral and privacy rights

The 1988 Act also gives moral rights and a privacy right:

- the right of paternity, which is the right to be identified as author of a work; this does not apply to journalists or photographers;
- the right of integrity, which protects against 'unjustified modification' of work; this does not apply to work for magazines and newspapers;
- the right not to be falsely identified as the author of published words;
- the right for someone who has commissioned private photographs not to have them released to the public.

TEST YOUR KNOWLEDGE

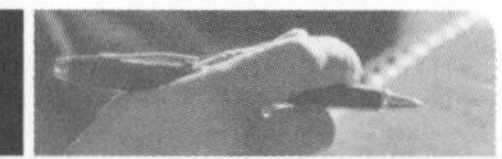

1 Which of these is likely to be a breach of copyright?

(a) You need a map to illustrate a feature, so your designer finds one in a book, then redraws it, using different colours and typefaces.

(b) You are writing a feature on reality TV, and, to illustrate it, you use a screen grab from a popular reality show.

(c) You work on a magazine for the building industry, and one of your rival titles features an interview with an important architect. You use the quotes given in the feature, but with completely different copy.

(d) You work on a woman's magazine, and a rival title does a feature on women who leave their children. You think this a really interesting idea, so you cover the same subject in your magazine.

(e) You attend a speech given by a local businessman. Before he begins his speech, he says that he does not wish any of his words to be reported in the press. The speech turns out to reveal that he is planning to close a local factory, which is an important employer in the area, so you write a news story, quoting from his speech.

(f) You are reporting a story about a young girl who has gone missing, and her parents give you a school photograph, which you publish.

(g) You work on a local weekly paper and receive the text of a very newsworthy speech by a local politician, which is under an embargo until the following week. Your rival paper comes out earlier in the week than you, so if you respect the embargo, they will get the story first. You publish the speech.

(h) You report a court case, in which one witness gives a long answer about the scientific explanation behind a particular piece of evidence. You print the answer verbatim.

2 You are on the staff of a magazine. Who owns the copyright on the stories you produce?

3 What does selling 'all rights' mean?

4 Who owns the original copyright on photographs?

5 What are the four elements of the defence of fair dealing?

6 In which of these situations could you be in breach of copyright, or of a moral right provided by the 1988 Act:

(a) You are a features editor and you receive a feature which you do not think is up to scratch, so you completely rewrite it, leave out some of the case histories, and add a new one which you have found yourself.

(b) You commission a photographer to do a fashion shoot on raincoats. Six months after using the pictures in the fashion feature, you need a picture to illustrate a piece on the weather, so you use one of the fashion shots.

(c) A local politician has been exposed as having an affair with his secretary. You publish a humorous piece, presented as the secretary's diary.

(d) You are reporting on a murder case which has just finished, and a local wedding photographer rings to say she took the defendant's wedding photos and is willing to supply copies for a fee. You agree, and publish one of the pictures.

ONLINE RESOURCES

The Copyright, Designs and Patents Act 1988 can be found at:
www.legislation.gov.uk/ukpga/1988/48/contents

The UK Patent Office (responsible for intellectual property in the UK) has a useful guide to copyright law at:
www.intellectual-property.gov.uk

The National Union of Journalists has useful practical advice on copyright for commissioning editors and freelance journalists at:
www.nuj.org.uk/inner.php?docid=56

Section 5 CODES OF PRACTICE AND ETHICS

So far in this book, we have looked at the rules of law which affect the way journalists do their jobs. But in addition to those legal rules, the work of journalists is also governed by Codes of Practice, which set down ethical principles about the way we do our jobs, and what we write and broadcast. Although these codes do not have the force of law, there can be sanctions for breaking them, and most respectable employers will expect you to abide by them. In addition, in some cases, the law allows a court to take into account whether the provisions of any relevant code of practice were followed.

Until recently, print journalism was overseen by the Press Complaints Commission (PCC), but after the phone hacking scandal and other issues over press behaviour, there were calls for a new body to take on this role. After much debate, we now have a new organisation, the Independent Press Standards Organisation (IPSO), which began operating while this edition was in production. Initially at least, it will continue to use the Editors Code of Practice formerly used by the PCC, so the standards and principles print journalists are expected to work to will not change, but the new organisation will have slightly different powers to punish breaches of the Code, which are explained in Chapter 24. Another key difference is that almost all major publishers agreed to be overseen by the PCC, but significant publishers have chosen not to be part of the IPSO scheme.

Broadcast journalism is regulated by Ofcom, and largely works to the Ofcom Broadcasting Code, though there are some areas where the BBC uses its own code.

Both the PCC and the Ofcom codes are included on the law syllabus of the NCTJ Diploma in Journalism, so you need a good knowledge of them if you are taking this exam. In this section, we look at how these two codes work, and you will find the full text of both codes in Appendices 1 and 2.

IPSO and the Editors' Code of Practice of the Press Complaints Commission

The Independent Press Standards Organisation regulates newspaper and magazine journalism (and journalism on the websites of newspapers and magazines) in two main ways. Firstly, it oversees the industry's code of practice, which for the time being is still the Editors' Code of Practice formerly used by the Press Complaints Commission (and usually known as the PCC Code), which sets out ethical principles that journalists should work to, both in the way we go about our work, and what we publish. Secondly, it provides a means of redress for people who are affected by breaches of the Code; they can complain to IPSO, which will investigate and adjudicate on the issue, and can impose financial penalties on a publisher.

The way in which IPSO works is described as self-regulation, in that publishers are not forced by law to work to the PCC Code, but instead voluntarily agree to do so, and to abide by its adjudications when the Code is breached. This differs from the situation in some other countries, where the work of newspapers and the print media is subject to state controls, which may cover who can own or run a publication, and set down rules about how they operate. In this country, anyone can own or run a publication (subject to rules designed to prevent one organisation having a monopoly on news media), and as long as they keep within the laws on contempt of court, defamation and so on, print publications are largely free to write what they like: they can take sides on topical issues, support one political party over another, or criticise public organisations and elected bodies and individuals. This differs from broadcast media, where, as we will see later (in Chapter 25), media organisations are required to be impartial and unbiased.

Most major publishers have agreed to be regulated by IPSO, but Guardian Newspapers, the Independent and Independent on Sunday, the London Evening Standard and the Financial Times have all chosen not to join, and instead to deal with complaints themselves.

COMPLAINTS TO IPSO

IPSO only handles complaints which may amount to breaches of the Editors' Code; it does not consider complaints relating to taste or decency, which are not covered in the Code, nor contractual issues. Complaints may relate to journalists' behaviour when covering a story and/or to what was published. Complaints must be brought within four months of the behaviour or the publication, but where material remains accessible online, complaints may be accepted for up to 12 months. People can also complain before material is published, or while harassment or persistent questioning is still going on. IPSO has no power to prevent either the publication or the behaviour, but can issue a 'private advisory notice' to alert the publication to a possible breach of the Code.

Complaints about matters of factual inaccuracy can be made by the person or organisation the inaccuracy relates to, and sometimes by third parties (this might mean, for example, a pressure group), if IPSO considers that appropriate. Other types of complaint can be made by the person or organisation affected or, where the issue is significant and taking up a complaint is in the public interest, by 'representative groups'.

Complainants need not have taken the matter up with the publication first, as they had to under the PCC, and if they have done so, they can complain to IPSO at any point if they feel the publication is not handling the matter appropriately, need advice or the complaint is not resolved. IPSO will not consider complaints which are already the subject of legal proceedings.

If IPSO decides that a complaint may involve a breach of the Code, it will write to the relevant editor and ask for them to deal directly with the complainant, with the aim of achieving a speedy settlement of the issue. If the matter is not resolved within 28 days (and in some cases before this), IPSO takes over the complaint, asks for a response, and decides whether there has been a breach.

If there is a breach, IPSO can require the publication to publish a report of its adjudication and, if appropriate, a correction, and it can say how big the piece should be and where it should go. In cases of persistent bad behaviour, it can impose a fine of up to £1 million.

THE EDITORS' CODE OF PRACTICE

The Code of Practice contains 16 clauses which set out standards on a range of issues, including accuracy, privacy, stories involving children, crime reporting, financial journalism, protection of sources, and press behaviour in sensitive situations such as at hospitals, and after suicides.

Some clauses in the Code are absolute, in that journalists are expected to abide by them even where they think there might be good reason not to. However, a number are covered by a public interest exception, which means that the Code allows that they can justifiably be breached, where it is in the public interest to do so (these provisions are all marked with an asterisk in the Code; see Appendix 1). The public interest exception can cover both the way a journalist goes about researching a story and what they eventually publish.

The Code states that situations where the public interest exception will apply (but are not limited to) include:

- where the breach involves detecting or exposing crime or serious impropriety;
- where the breach involves protecting public health and safety;
- where the breach involves preventing the public from being misled by an individual or organisation's conduct or words.

The Code also points out that there is a public interest in freedom of expression itself.

An editor faced with a complaint who wants to use the public interest exception will have to be able to show that they 'reasonably believed that publication, or journalistic activity undertaken with a view to publication, would be in the public interest and how, and with whom, that was established at the time'. They will usually also need to show that what was done or published was proportionate to the public interest in the story.

Although the public interest exception can apply to stories involving children, the Code makes it clear that in such cases it will be necessary to show an 'exceptional' public interest if the breach is to be considered justified.

Many of the Code's provisions are covered in the chapters of this book which deal with the subject areas where they apply, but in this chapter, we will look at those which have general application to most areas of work, need more explanation or have not been mentioned elsewhere. We include in this section some PCC adjudications on complaints; although the PCC is no longer operating, the Code remains the same and so these are still likely to be useful guidance.

Accuracy and opportunity to reply

This is a key provision of the Code: year after year, the majority of complaints to the PCC involved inaccurate reporting. Clause 1 states that:

- 'The Press must take care not to publish inaccurate, misleading or distorted information, including pictures' and
- 'The Press, while free to be partisan, must distinguish clearly between comment, conjecture and fact.'

In ***Adam Sheppard* v *Daily Star*** (September 27, 2010), the PCC ruled that the *Daily Star* had breached clause 1, in a story about new toilets in a Rochdale shopping centre. The report claimed that the council had used taxpayers' money to install 'Muslim-only squat hole loos', but the PCC found that the toilets could not accurately be described as 'Muslim-only', and had not been paid for by the council.

Where a significant inaccuracy, misleading statement or distortion has been published, the Code requires editors to print a correction 'promptly and with due prominence' and, where appropriate, with an apology. Clause 2 also requires editors to give a fair opportunity to reply to inaccuracies when one is 'reasonably called for'.

The public interest exception does not apply to these provisions.

Intrusion into grief and shock, and coverage of suicides

Journalists are very often required to cover stories where those involved have been injured or bereaved, or for a number of other reasons are suffering terrible grief or shock, and the Code requires that such people are treated sensitively. Clause 5 provides that:

- 'In cases involving personal grief or shock, enquiries and approaches must be made with sympathy and discretion and publication handled sensitively. This should not restrict the right to report legal proceedings, such as inquests.'

Where this issue has come up in complaints, PCC adjudications have said that stories about violent or accidental deaths should not include graphic details about what happened, where this could add to the distress of relatives. Great care is also needed in the use of pictures.

In ***Kirkland* v *Wiltshire Gazette*** (23 April 2008), the PCC criticised the *Gazette* for using a picture of a woman who had been involved in a road accident, while she was still at the scene and being treated by paramedics. The woman was not named and the picture only showed part of her face, but the number plate of her car was clearly visible, so anyone who knew her well would recognise her. The PCC said that the media had a duty to publish stories about serious accidents, but, when doing so, they had to handle things sensitively and respect the feelings of those involved and their families. In this case, they criticised the fact that the picture was published online very shortly after the accident, when relatives might not have been informed, or, if they were, would be in a state of shock. The PCC said that the media had to exercise caution when considering showing images that relate to a person's health or medical treatment, even if taken in public places. There might be a public interest justification for showing such images when reporting on a large-scale and unusual event such as a terrorist attack or a natural disaster, but a relatively routine event such as a road accident did not have enough of a public interest justification to outweigh the right to privacy of an individual who was injured and receiving medical treatment, especially while their condition was still uncertain.

Journalists also need to take care to make sure relatives have been informed about a death before either talking to them or publishing the identity of the dead person.

In ***Oliver*** v ***Manchester Evening News*** (1998), the PCC criticised the newspaper for using on their website a picture of a road crash in which the accident victim could be identified, at a time when relatives might not yet have been informed, or might still be in a state of shock.

PCC adjudications have also criticised the use of pictures of funerals which have been taken without the family's consent.

However, the PCC has said that in cases of serious and large-scale incidents, such as terrorist attacks and natural disasters, it may be permissible to show pictures of the aftermath, including showing identifiable victims without their consent, because there is such a high degree of public interest in reporting this type of event.

Reports of suicides require particularly careful handling. Not only must you abide by the provisions on cases involving grief and shock when talking to the relatives, but you also need to be aware of a second provision in clause 5, which provides that:

- When reporting suicide, care should be taken to avoid excessive detail about the method used.'

The reason for this provision is that research has shown that reading about suicides can help prompt others to take their own lives.

In ***A Woman*** v ***The News (Portsmouth)*** (28 January 2010), the PCC ruled that the newspaper's report of an inquest into a suicide breached clause 5, because it said which brand of anti-depressant pills the woman had taken, and suggested how many had been taken by stating how many were left in the pack.

The public interest exception does not apply to these provisions.

Reporting in hospitals and on health and medical treatment

Reporting on accidents and violent crime, among other things, will sometimes require that journalists interview hospital patients and staff. The Code makes it clear that this may require sensitive and responsible handling. Clause 8 provides that:

- 'Journalists must identify themselves and obtain permission from a responsible executive before entering non-public areas of hospitals or similar institutions to pursue enquiries' and
- 'The restrictions on intruding into privacy are particularly relevant to enquiries about individuals in hospitals or similar institutions.' (The restrictions on intruding into privacy are listed in Chapter 19.)

Reporting crime

The Code contains a number of provisions on reporting crime, covering the process of newsgathering, and payments to people involved in crime stories, either as witnesses or those who have committed crime. Clause 9 provides that:

- Relatives or friends of persons convicted or accused of crime should not generally be identified without their consent, unless they are genuinely relevant to the story.

- Particular regard should be paid to the potentially vulnerable position of children who witness, or are victims of, crime. This should not restrict the right to report legal proceedings.

Regarding payments to witnesses, clause 15 provides that:

- No payment or offer of payment to a witness – or any person who may reasonably be expected to be called as a witness – should be made in any case once proceedings are active as defined by the Contempt of Court Act 1981.
- This prohibition lasts until the suspect has been freed unconditionally by police without charge or bail or the proceedings are otherwise discontinued; or has entered a guilty plea to the court; or, in the event of a not guilty plea, the court has announced its verdict.
- Where proceedings are not yet active but are likely and foreseeable, editors must not make or offer payment to any person who may reasonably be expected to be called as a witness, unless the information concerned ought demonstrably to be published in the public interest and there is an overriding need to make or promise payment for this to be done; and all reasonable steps have been taken to ensure no financial dealings influence the evidence those witnesses give. In no circumstances should such payment be conditional on the outcome of a trial.
- Any payment or offer of payment made to a person later cited to give evidence in proceedings must be disclosed to the prosecution and defence. The witness must be advised of this requirement.

The second two of these provisions (but not the first two) are covered by the public interest exemption. Payments to witnesses can also be a contempt of court (as we saw in Chapter 6).

The Code also covers payment to convicted or self-confessed criminals. Clause 16 states that:

- Payment or offers of payment for stories, pictures or information, which seek to exploit a particular crime or to glorify or glamorise crime in general, must not be made directly or via agents to convicted or confessed criminals or to their associates – who may include family, friends and colleagues.
- Editors invoking the public interest to justify payment or offers would need to demonstrate that there was good reason to believe the public interest would be served. If, despite payment, no public interest emerged, then the material should not be published.

The reasoning behind these provisions is that it is seen as undesirable for criminals to profit from their own wrongdoing. However, clause 16 is covered by the public interest exemption, so there are situations where it is permitted to pay a criminal for information.

Obtaining information by deception and clandestine devices

Obviously, as a journalist, there will be times where people will not wish to tell you what you want to know, and the only way to get that information may be to lie or misrepresent who you are and why you want to know, or to use techniques like secret cameras or tapes, or intercepting calls or messages. Clause 10 of the Code lays down the principles on use of such tactics.

The basic principle is that the use of deception, subterfuge and clandestine devices is not allowed, unless their use is in the public interest. Clause 10 states that:

- The press must not seek to obtain or publish material acquired by using hidden cameras or clandestine listening devices; or by intercepting private or mobile telephone calls, messages or emails; or by the unauthorised removal of documents or photographs; or by accessing digitally held private information without consent.

- Engaging in misrepresentation or subterfuge, including by agents or intermediaries, can generally be justified only in the public interest and then only when the material cannot be obtained by other means.

This effectively means that journalists should usually be open and honest about what they are doing when researching a story, including telling anyone they speak to as part of their research that they are a journalist; it is not enough only to mention it if you are asked. Filming, photography or recording must be done openly, and hacking into emails, voicemails or other communications is not allowed. Recording interviews that you do over the phone, however, is not a breach of clause 10, even if you do not tell the other person you are taping the conversation.

However, clause 10 is covered by the public interest exemption, so any or all of these tactics may be allowed under the Code, if an editor can show that there was a sufficient public interest in their use, and the information cannot be obtained without them.

In *Mrs Jean Bellfield* v *Daily Mirror* (23 July 2009), the PCC rejected a complaint alleging breach of clause 10, because, although the reporter had used a degree of deception, the story was in the public interest. The complaint was made by the mother of Levi Bellfield, who at the time was in prison after being convicted of murdering two women, and was later convicted of the murder of a schoolgirl, Milly Dowler. The *Mirror*'s reporter asked Bellfield's family to organise an interview with him, claiming it was to help him with his appeal; in fact the reporter wanted to ask about events related to Milly Dowler's murder, of which Bellfield was already suspected. The PCC said the interview had brought out significant new information about Milly's murder, and the public interest in revealing this information justified the deception.

In order for the use of deception and/or clandestine devices to be justified in the public interest, there needs to be a specific and serious allegation to be investigated, and clear grounds for such an investigation. The PCC has made it clear that the Code does not allow for the use of these tactics in 'fishing expeditions', where journalists set out to find a story that may or may not exist.

In *Liberal Democrat Party* v *Daily Telegraph* (10 May 2011), the PCC ruled that the *Telegraph* were in breach of clause 10, after the paper ran an undercover investigation to gather evidence that some Ministers were misleading the public by pretending to agree with certain policies of the Conservative–Liberal Democrat coalition government, when in fact they held different views. The reporters attended Ministers' constituency surgeries, pretending to be constituents and secretly recording the conversations, in the hope that the Ministers would express views that were out of line with official policies (which some of them did). The PCC said the investigation breached clause 10 because the paper had had no prior evidence that the Ministers had expressed dissenting views, and what evidence it did have was not enough to justify secret taping.

Discriminatory and pejorative material

Clause 12 of the Code covers the publication of material which mentions someone's race, colour, religion, gender, sexual orientation, physical or mental illness or disability. It provides that:

- 'The press must avoid prejudicial or pejorative reference to an individual's race, colour, religion, gender, sexual orientation or to any physical or mental illness or disability' and

- 'Details of an individual's race, colour, religion, sexual orientation, physical or mental illness or disability must be avoided unless genuinely relevant to the story.'

It has to be said that this particular provision seems to be largely ignored by much of the tabloid press and, at times, the broadsheets too, but nevertheless, it does exist.

In *Clare Balding* v *Sunday Times* (17 September 2010), the PCC ruled that the paper was in breach of clause 12 over a TV review of a programme called *Britain by Bike*, presented by Clare Balding. Ms Balding is gay, and the TV reviewer described her as 'a dyke on a bike'. The PCC said that the use of the word 'dyke' was pejorative, demeaning and gratuitous, and the *Sunday Times* should have apologised at the first opportunity.

Clause 12 is not covered by the public interest exemption.

Financial journalism

Journalists who write about financial matters sometimes learn details about companies that they could use to make money, for example by buying shares in companies about to do something which is likely to raise their share prices. They may also have the opportunity to affect the value of investments they already hold, by what they write about them. Clause 13 of the Code prohibits journalists from making personal financial gains in this way. It provides that:

- 'Even where the law does not prohibit it, journalists must not use for their own profit financial information they receive in advance of its general publication, nor should they pass such information to others.'
- They must not write about shares or securities in whose performance they know that they or their close families have a significant financial interest without disclosing the interest to the editor or financial editor.'
- 'They must not buy or sell, either directly or through nominees or agents, shares or securities about which they have written recently or about which they intend to write in the near future.'

Clause 13 is not covered by the public interest exemption.

KEY POINTS

IPSO sets ethical standards for the print media, through the Editors' Code of Practice, and deals with complaints from the public.

The Code contains 16 clauses. Some are absolute, and others are covered by a public interest exemption.

The Code covers:

- accuracy and opportunity to reply;
- intrusion into grief and shock;
- reporting in hospitals;
- reporting crime;
- use of deception and clandestine devices;
- discriminatory and pejorative material;
- financial journalism.

(Other topics are covered elsewhere in this book.)

TEST YOUR KNOWLEDGE

1 In which of these jobs would you be expected to abide by the Editors' Code of Practice of the PCC, as used by IPSO?
   (a) reporter on a local paper;
   (b) feature writer on a women's magazine;
   (c) editor of an independent website;
   (d) editor of the website of a national newspaper;
   (e) reporter on a local radio station.

2 What powers does IPSO have to deal with a breach of the Code?

3 You are reporting on a court case where the defendant is 15. What provisions of the Code do you need to be aware of?

4 A reader complains that a report you wrote about him was seriously misleading and inaccurate. What does the Code require you to do?

ONLINE RESOURCES

The PCC website is still available, and gives useful guidance on how the Code should be interpreted, and the results of its adjudications, at:
www.pcc.org.uk

Details of how IPSO works can be found on its website
www.ipso.co.uk

Chapter 25

The Ofcom Code

Ethical standards in TV and radio journalism are covered by the Broadcasting Code issued by Ofcom, the body which regulates broadcasting in the UK, usually known as the Ofcom Code. The Ofcom Code works in a different way to the Editors' Code of Practice used by IPSO. The Editors' Code is a self-regulation scheme, under which the media agree to work to certain ethical standards, and accept adjudications by IPSO where those standards are breached. Broadcasting, however, is subject to state regulation, of which the Ofcom Code is a part. This means that broadcasters must have a licence to operate, and are subject to requirements that are not placed on print media, including rules on impartiality on politics and social issues. If a broadcaster breaches Ofcom rules, it can face serious fines and even potentially lose its licence to broadcast.

The reason for the difference between the treatment of print and broadcast media is that TV and radio have always been considered to carry risks that print media does not, or at least not to the same extent. The impact of moving pictures and sound, and the fact that they can be broadcast immediately, means their effect can be stronger and more direct than that of printed text and photos, so they are thought to have greater potential to offend, persuade, intrude into privacy or incite responses than print media. In addition, until very recently broadcasting took place over analogue wavelengths, of which there was only a limited number, so some kind of regulator was needed to decide who the wavelengths should be allocated to and, by imposing strict standards, ensure that the best use was made of them.

Neither of these arguments really carries much weight now, as the internet has allowed print media to use film on the websites, and to carry news almost as it happens, and the switch to digital transmission means there is no longer such a tight restriction on the number of channels. However, given current disapproval of the way the print press has behaved under self-regulation, there is no prospect of state regulation being removed from broadcasting.

In addition to the Ofcom Code, BBC journalists are covered by the BBC's own Editorial Guidelines, overseen by the BBC Board of Governors (see *Online resources* at the end of this chapter).

THE OFCOM BROADCASTING CODE

The Code was published on 25 May 2005, and came into force on 25 July 2005. It replaces six previous codes issued by the organisations which regulated broadcasting before Ofcom was created: the Broadcasting Standards Commission, the Independent Television Commission and the Radio Authority. Programmes broadcast before 25 July 2005 are covered by the relevant previous codes, but, where a programme was originally shown before that date, and is repeated after it, the new Code applies to the repeat(s), as well as to all new programmes shown after that date.

The Code covers all UK broadcasters, but some of the sections do not apply to the BBC, and for BBC journalists those sections are replaced by the BBC's own editorial guidelines.

The role of Ofcom

Ofcom was created under the Communications Act 2003, and, as well as broadcasting, it regulates a number of other areas, including phone, postal and broadband services. It is independent of government and accountable to Parliament.

In terms of broadcasting, Ofcom's main roles are to grant licences to broadcast (which involves examining what programming the organisation is planning to present, and whether they are a 'fit and proper' holder of a licence), setting standards for programme content, which are detailed in the Ofcom Code, and dealing with complaints about breaches of those standards.

Complaints to Ofcom

Any member of the public can complain to Ofcom about the content of a television or radio programme or, where someone was in the programme, the way the programme's makers have gone about putting together that content. Ofcom only deals with complaints about programmes once they have been broadcast; it has no remit to prevent initial broadcast, or to intervene in the making of a programme. It also only handles complaints that relate to issues covered by the Code. Where a particular issue is covered by both the Ofcom Code and the BBC's own code of practice, complaints about the BBC relating to that issue are handled under the BBC code, and not by Ofcom (these are detailed in the text below). Web content published by broadcast organisations is not covered by the Code, and Ofcom will not take up complaints about online material.

Ofcom will investigate the complaint, and if a breach is found, can order any of the following sanctions:

- Forbid repeat broadcast of a programme.
- Order the broadcaster to broadcast a correction, or a statement of Ofcom's findings in a specified format.
- Impose a fine of up to £250,000 or five per cent of the broadcaster's 'qualifying revenue', which is a specific proportion of its income (the BBC and the Welsh channel S4C can only be fined up to £250,000). In 2008, Ofcom fined ITV over £5 million for persistent breaches of the Code which involved misleading viewers about phone-in competitions.
- Shorten or even revoke a company's licence to broadcast (this does not apply to the BBC, S4C and Channel 4, because they are public service broadcasters). This only happens if breaches are serious and persistent, and in fact Ofcom has never yet revoked a licence.
- Find that the matter is resolved and no further action is needed. This will only happen where the breach was hard to avoid or accidental, and the company has taken any necessary precautions to make sure it does not happen again (see the Radio Sheffield case, below).

PROVISIONS OF THE CODE

Issues covered by the Code include:

- protecting the under-18s;
- harm and offence;
- crime;
- religion;

- impartiality and accuracy;
- elections and referendums;
- fairness;
- privacy;
- sponsorship;
- commercial references.

Not all the provisions in the Code will have direct relevance to the daily work of journalists; the following sections discuss only those that do.

Protecting the under-18s

This section covers both the effect of broadcasting content on the under-18s, and the treatment of under-18s by broadcasters. Key provisions include the following:

- The under-18s must be protected from content which could seriously impair their physical, moral or emotional development, and the under-15s from content which is unsuitable for them. In this context, TV companies must respect the 9 p.m. 'watershed', and radio broadcasters must take particular care over what is broadcast at times when children are likely to be listening, such as at breakfast time. Clear information should be given about content likely to distress children if broadcast on radio at these times, or before the watershed on TV.
- When reporting sexual offences involving under-18s (whether as defendants, victims or witnesses, in the criminal, civil or family courts), broadcasters should take care not to breach inadvertently any statutory rules preventing identification, for example by broadcasting details which could lead to identification when pieced together with material from elsewhere.
- When covering any pre-trial investigation into an alleged criminal offence, broadcasters should pay particular regard to the vulnerable position of any victim, witness or defendant who is not yet adult, before publishing their name, address, school, college, place of work, or any picture of them.
- Violence, dangerous behaviour, offensive language and sexual content should not be shown before the watershed or when children are likely to be listening, unless justified by the context.

Harm and offence

This section is a mixed bag of provisions, ranging from rules about the use of flashing lights which could trigger epilepsy attacks, to preventing audiences from being put into a trance by a TV hypnotist. Those most relevant to journalists include the following:

- TV programmes must meet 'generally accepted standards' of protection for the public against harmful and offensive material. If offensive material is used, it must be justified by its context.
- Factual programmes or items should not 'materially mislead' viewers or listeners.
- Methods of suicide or self-harm should not be included unless justified editorially and by their context.
- If simulated news is broadcast (e.g. in a documentary), broadcasters must make sure the audience is not misled into thinking they are watching actual news.

In 2006, Ofcom examined a complaint against BBC Radio Sheffield after a caller to a phone-in on football used highly offensive language about a particular player. The radio station agreed that the language was unacceptable, but said that the caller had not shown any sign that he might be abusive when talking to the production team before being put on air, that it regularly warned callers to avoid strong language, and that the presenter had closed down the call quickly, apologised to listeners and made it clear that the station found the caller's words unacceptable. Ofcom agreed that it was very difficult for the station to have anticipated the incident, and acknowledged that it had taken further steps to prevent a repeat. Ofcom held that the matter was resolved.

In 2007, STV was the subject of a complaint about archive CCTV footage of extreme violence, used during a report on new police powers to tackle anti-social behaviour with on-the-spot fines. Violence is among the potentially offensive material that must be justified by its context. Ofcom found that the level of violence shown was not justified by the context of the story, which was about more minor anti-social behaviour. STV accepted this and so Ofcom considered the issue resolved.

In 2008, the BBC was the subject of 31 complaints regarding a news broadcast which showed an incident in Jerusalem, where a Palestinian man rammed cars and buses with a bulldozer, killing three people. The footage showed the man being pursued and then shot dead by an Israeli soldier. Ofcom said that showing someone at the point of death causes offence to many people, and requires exceptional justification. However, Ofcom took account of the fact that the programme was after 10 p.m. and the report did forewarn viewers of what they were about to see, and that there was a public interest in the matter. Given that the BBC had itself decided that showing the footage was inappropriate, and had put a statement saying that on its website, Ofcom considered the matter resolved.

In 2010, the TV channel Al Jazeera was found in breach over a news report which featured film of Nigerian police officers apparently carrying out extra-judicial killings. The footage, which was shown just after the watershed, showed men being forced to lie on the ground, and then shot. It was possible to see their bodies moving after the first shots were fired into them. Ofcom said that the film was extremely disturbing and graphic, and its usage therefore had to be justified by its context. Images showing the point of death could be broadcast, but would require very strong justification and extreme care. They noted that the story was one of serious public interest, and was reported seriously and not sensationalised, on a channel where the audience was predominantly adult. The presenter had warned viewers about the disturbing nature of the footage before it was shown. However, it was shown only just after the watershed, when viewers might expect not to see the most upsetting kinds of images. In deciding that the channel was in breach, Ofcom took particular note of the length of the clip, the fact that the killings were shown in long, unedited shots and at close range, the depiction of extremely ruthless behaviour by the police, and the fact that the victims were not fighting back against their captors, and two were on crutches. They said that the sheer length and the graphic nature of the images went beyond accepted standards and were not justified by the context.

Crime

This section deals with material which could encourage crime or lead to disorder.

- Descriptions or demonstrations which could show how to commit crime should not be used unless editorially justified.
- Convicted or self-confessed criminals must not be paid or promised payment of any kind for interviews or other programme contributions concerning their criminal activities, except where the payment would be in the public interest.
- No payment should be made to anyone who is or is likely to be a witness in criminal proceedings, while those proceedings are active, nor should any payment be suggested or made dependent on the result of a trial. Loss of earnings and expenses can, however, be reimbursed.

- Where future criminal proceedings are foreseeable, no payment should be made to anyone who might reasonably be expected to be a witness, unless there is a clear public interest in that person giving information (such as for the purposes of investigating crime), and the information could not be obtained without the payment.
- Broadcasters must 'use their best endeavours' to ensure they do not broadcast anything which could endanger lives, or compromise attempts to deal with a kidnapping or a hostage situation.

Religion

This section covers 'religious programmes', but as this is defined as 'a programme which deals with matters of religion as the central subject, or a significant part, of the programme', it would appear that it could equally well apply to, for example, a documentary about the Catholic Church or Islam, as to *Songs of Praise* or the *Morning Service*. The main provision applicable in a documentary context would be that the views of people who belong to a particular religion or religious denomination must not be subject to 'abusive treatment'.

Impartiality and accuracy

This is an important section for journalists, as it specifically covers news. (This section does not apply to the BBC, but the BBC's own guidelines contain provisions on impartiality and accuracy; see *Online resources* at the end of this chapter.) The section provides that:

- News 'in whatever form', must be reported with 'due accuracy' and presented with 'due impartiality'. Impartiality is defined as not favouring one side or the other, but the Code makes it clear that 'due impartiality' means a level of impartiality that is appropriate to the programme in question, and the subject. It does not require that each side is given exactly equal airtime, or that every argument has to be represented.
- Significant errors should be corrected promptly, on air, and at an appropriate time (i.e. so that people who saw or heard the mistake are also likely to see or hear the correction).
- No news programme should use a politician as an interviewer, newsreader or reporter, unless editorially justified. In that case, the politician's political allegiance must be stated.

Special rules apply to coverage of 'matters of political or industrial controversy, and matters relating to current public policy'. Matters of political or industrial controversy are defined as political or industrial matters on which politicians, industry and/or the media are 'in debate'. Matters relating to current public policy are policies under discussion, or already adopted by local, regional or national Government, or bodies which make policy on their behalf, such as quangos. Where coverage relates to any of these issues:

- Programmes must not include expressions of the broadcaster's own opinion (unless they are speaking in a court of law or a legislative forum). The exception to this rule is where the matter under discussion concerns the provision of programme services.
- Due impartiality must be observed. However, this need not be done in a single programme, but can be achieved by the combined effect of a series of programmes. 'Series' in this context includes not just the usual meaning of the word in broadcasting terms but also, for example, a cluster or season of programmes on the same subject, or two programmes, such as a drama and a documentary, covering the same issue. To gain this protection, however, it should be made clear on air that the programmes are linked.

- Views and facts must not be misrepresented, and should be presented 'with due weight over appropriate timeframes'.
- If a presenter or reporter has a personal interest which could call into question the due impartiality of the programme, this should be made clear to viewers.
- Presenters and reporters (other than those on news programmes), and chairs of discussion programmes can put forward their own points of view, but these must be balanced with adequate representation of other views, either in the same programme or in the series as a whole.
- Presenters who appear regularly must not use this advantage in such a way as to compromise the requirement for due impartiality.
- Phone-in presenters must encourage alternative views.
- 'Personal view' programmes must be indicated as such from the outset. The Code defines such programmes as those which 'present a particular view or perspective', ranging from the highly partial views of campaigners on a particular issue, to the opinion of a journalist, author or academic with experience or knowledge of a particular subject. The requirement that the nature of such programmes should be made clear is described as a minimum standard, and in some cases it may be necessary to do more than that to ensure a programme does not breach the impartiality requirements (the Code does not suggest what these extra measures might be).
- On local radio, local digital sound services and radio licensable content services, a further rule prohibits programmes from giving 'undue prominence' to the views of particular persons or bodies on these subjects. 'Undue prominence' is defined as 'a significant imbalance of views' in a station's coverage of an issue as a whole over a relevant period of time.

Two extra rules apply where coverage concerns matters of political or industrial controversy, or matters relating to current policy, which are of national or international significance, or which carry a similar weight of importance within a smaller broadcast area. Where programmes concern these kinds of issues:

- 'An appropriately wide range' of views must be presented, and given due weight, either in a single programme or across a range of clearly linked programmes.
- Views and facts must not be misrepresented.

This means, among other things, that TV and radio stations are not free to campaign on issues in the way that print media can. If, for example, a new motorway is being planned in a particular area, the local paper can campaign for or against it, publishing features which only put one side of the argument, and encouraging readers to sign a petition or write to their MP. The local radio station or TV news programme, however, could not do any of this; they can cover the issue, but they must put both sides of the story, and cannot be seen to take sides.

In 2005, the satellite channel Bloomberg TV was found to have breached the Code provisions on impartiality. During the 2005 general election, it broadcast live coverage of the launch of the Labour Party's 'Business Manifesto', followed by in-depth interviews with Tony Blair and two other members of the party. No other political party was featured. Bloomberg argued that the interviews had not been uncritical, and that other parties had been invited to take part, but declined. Ofcom, however, found that no other political party had been featured in this depth at any point in the campaign, and held that Bloomberg was in breach of the Code. It was ordered to broadcast the Ofcom finding three times.

In 2008, Channel 4 was the subject of 12 complaints about impartiality regarding the programme *The Court of Ken*, about Ken Livingstone's record as Mayor of London, including the congestion charge and a controversial agreement made with the President of Venezuela. It was presented by a journalist who had been critical of Mr Livingstone before. Ofcom agreed that the subjects included were matters of political controversy and so required the programme to be impartial, and to make clear any personal interest of the presenter. Ofcom noted that the programme was the result of the production team's investigations, and not a personal view authored by the presenter; in any case, it was made clear that he was someone who had once supported the mayor and now did not. It also pointed out that the programme included a number of viewpoints, both critical and supportive, of the congestion charge, and included the mayor's own explanation of the Venezuela deal. It therefore concluded there was no breach of the impartiality rule.

In 2008, Talksport Radio was found in breach of the impartiality rules after the MP George Galloway, while presenting one of its shows, made a number of criticisms on air of another politician. Announcing his intention to stand as MP for a London constituency, he criticised the constituency's current MP, and his record of voting in Parliament. Ofcom found that this was a serious breach of the Code, especially given that the other MP was given no opportunity to respond. It considered sanctions but decided against them because this was the first time a complaint about impartiality had been made against Talksport.

Elections and referenda

This section covers broadcasts during an 'election period' or 'referendum period'. (This section does not apply to the BBC, but the BBC's own guidelines contain provisions on reporting elections; see *Online resources* at the end of this chapter.) The Code defines the start of these periods as follows:

- for a general election or Scottish Parliament election, when Parliament or the Scottish Parliament is dissolved;
- for parliamentary by-elections, when the writ is issued, or on any earlier date published in the *London Gazette*;
- for by-elections to the Scottish Parliament, when the vacancy occurs;
- for the Welsh National Assembly, the Northern Ireland Assembly, the London Assembly and local government elections, on the last date for publication of notices of the election;
- for referenda held under the Northern Ireland Act 1998, when the draft of an Order is laid before Parliament;
- for other referenda, at the time stated in the Act which authorises the referendum.

In all cases, the period ends when the polls close.

During an election or referendum period, these rules apply:

- During a referendum period, coverage must give due weight to 'designated organisations'. These are organisations which the Electoral Commission designates as the lead campaigners for one of the possible outcomes. Broadcasters must also consider giving appropriate cover-age to other 'permitted participants'; these are organisations that have registered with the Electoral Commission, which allows them to spend more than £10,000 on their campaign, but obliges them to comply with the Commission's regulations.
- Candidates in UK elections, or representatives of 'permitted participants' in a referendum must not act as newsreaders, presenters or interviewers in any type of programme.
- Appearances of candidates in UK elections, or representatives of 'permitted participants', on non-political programmes can go ahead if they were planned before the election period, but new appearances should not be arranged after the period starts.

- Reports or discussions about a particular constituency or electoral area must observe due impartiality, and candidates representing parties with significant previous electoral support or evidence of significant current support must be invited to take part, as must independents with significant support. If one candidate agrees to take part, the candidates from other major parties in that area should then be invited to do so as well. (In either circumstance, if one or more candidates refuse or cannot take part, the item/programme can still go ahead.)
- Any report or discussion of a constituency or electoral area must include a list of all the candidates, giving their first and last names, and the party they represent (or stating that they are independent). For larger regional elections (e.g. to the Scottish Parliament, European Parliament or London Assembly), the list need not mention every candidate in a region by name, just the parties and the names of any independent candidates. If a radio item is broadcast more than once on the same day, the list need not be repeated, but listeners/viewers should be told where they can find out this information (e.g. on a website).
- If a candidate takes part in a programme on any subject, he or she should not be allowed to make points about the constituency or electoral area, unless other candidates will be given a similar opportunity.
- All discussion and analysis of issues related to the election or referendum must end when the polling stations open.
- The results of opinion polls must not be broadcast on polling day, until the polls close.

In 2010, Bangla TV was found to be in breach of the Code, because of a programme it broadcast during a General Election Campaign. The programme, *Election 2010*, featured representatives from the Labour and Conservative Parties, talking about their opposition to a proposed mayoral referendum. Ofcom found that the channel was in breach because the Labour Party representative was a candidate, and was talking about his proposed constituency, but the representative for the Conservatives was not a candidate in that constituency, and the channel had not invited the other candidates for the constituency to take part either.

Radio station Clyde 1 was found in breach of the code in 2010, concerning a programme broadcast on the day of a General Election, while the polls were still open. Two radio presenters discussed who they were voting for, and one joked about who certain high-profile football players would vote for, saying that it would definitely be the Labour Party. Ofcom received complaints that the discussion had expressed support for the Labour Party, in breach of the rule that all discussion of election issues should stop once polls open. Although it acknowledged that the discussion was meant to be light-hearted, Ofcom said this was a clear breach of the rules on election broadcasting.

Fairness

This section deals with the way in which broadcasting companies treat the people who are directly affected by programmes, such as those mentioned, shown or interviewed. The overall rule of the section is that broadcasters must avoid unjust or unfair treatment of individuals in programmes, and it sets out practices which should be followed in this respect. Failing to follow any of these practices will only be a breach of the Code if it results in unfairness to an individual or organisation. However, the Code points out that it cannot prescribe a set of practices that, if followed, would absolutely prevent all unfairness, and so a company may be in breach of the rule on fairness even if it has followed all the specified breaches, if it is nevertheless unfair or injust in some other way.

The practices to be followed are:

- Broadcasters and programme makers should be fair in their dealings with potential contributors to programmes, though there may be exceptional cases where they are justified in not being fair.
- Anyone invited to take part in a programme (unless the subject is trivial and/or their role very minor) should be informed, at an appropriate stage, about:
  - the nature, subject and purpose of the programme;
  - why he or she has been asked to contribute;
  - when and where the programme will be broadcast;
  - what kind of contribution he/she is expected to make (e.g. whether an interview or discussion, live or recorded);
  - the areas of questioning, if appropriate, and the nature of other contributions;
  - any significant changes to the programme during the process of making it, which might affect the individual's decision to participate, and/or cause material unfairness;
  - the nature of the individual's contractual rights, and those of the programme maker/broadcaster;
  - whether the participant will be able to have changes made to the programme if he/she is to be shown a preview.

If, having been given all this information, a person or organisation consents to take part in a programme, that consent is known as informed consent (see Privacy below). It may, however, be fair to withhold some or all of this information when it is justified in the public interest, or because of other provisions in this section.

- If a contributor is under 16, permission should be obtained from a parent, guardian or other person over 18 who is *in loco parentis*. Contributors who are under 16 should not be asked for their views on matters which it is not within their capacity to answer properly without this consent.
- If a person over 16 is not in a position to give consent, it should be sought from someone aged 18 or over who has primary responsibility for that person's care. Contributors in this position should not be asked for their views on matters which it is not within their capacity to answer properly without this consent.
- If a programme is edited, contributions should be represented fairly.
- If contributors are given any kind of guarantee (e.g. of anonymity or confidentiality, or relating to the content of a programme), these promises should normally be honoured.
- If material produced for one programme is later reused in another (whether by the same company or a different one), the broadcaster should make sure this reuse does not create unfairness.
- Before broadcasting a factual programme, broadcasters should ensure that material facts have not been presented, disregarded or left out in such a way as to be unfair to an individual or organisation, and if someone has been left out in circumstances which could cause unfairness, that party should be offered a chance to contribute.
- No programme should present facts, events, people or organisations in a way that is unfair to any individual or organisation.

- If a programme makes allegations of wrongdoing or incompetence, or any other serious allegations, the subject of the allegations should normally be given an 'appropriate and timely' chance to respond.
- If someone is asked to contribute to a programme, but chooses not to appear or give a comment, the programme should state this, and give that person's explanation (if any), if it would be unfair not to do so.
- Where a person or organisation chooses not to take part in a programme, and it is appropriate for the programme to include that person's or organisation's view, this must be done fairly.

The section also contains a set of rules on 'Deception, set-ups and wind-up calls', which states that broadcasters and programme makers should not normally obtain information, sound, film or consent to contribute to a programme through deception, which includes surreptitious filming or recording. However, there are three situations where the Code says it may be legitimate to use material obtained through deception or misrepresentation, without the subject's consent:

- where it is in the public interest to do so, and the material could not be obtained in any other way;
- where the subject is not clearly identifiable;
- where the subject is a person in the public eye. However, in this case, unless there is also a public interest justification, this material should not be used where it would result in unjustified public ridicule or personal distress.

In 2005, a *Dispatches* programme was the subject of a complaint about fairness from a company featured in it. The programme concerned parking charges, and contained allegations about incompetence and unfairness in the way these charges were imposed. One of the companies criticised in the programme, Capita, complained that, although it had provided a statement in response, it was not given an adequate chance to prepare this, because it was only made aware of the allegations two weeks before broadcast, and was not allowed to preview the programme. Ofcom rejected this part of the complaint, as Channel 4 had provided full information about the programme and the allegations made, and was not obliged to allow previewing of the film; given the nature of the allegations, two weeks was enough time to respond. Capita also complained that the response it supplied was not included, and that no explanation was given for this. It appeared that this was because Channel 4 had refused to broadcast the full statement, and therefore Capita had withdrawn it rather than have part of it broadcast. Ofcom found that even so, Channel 4 remained aware of Capita's position on the allegations, and should have represented it fairly. In addition, failing to supply any explanation for the lack of a statement could have given a negative impression of Capita, given that statements from the two other companies mentioned were included. Therefore, in these two respects Channel 4 had been unfair and was in breach of the Code.

In 2005, Ofcom upheld a complaint from drugs company Novartis about a Channel 4 programme concerning its leukaemia drug, Glivec. The company had been contacted several months before the broadcast and told that it would be given the opportunity to comment, but it was then only given the chance to answer detailed questions a month before the programme was shown. Ofcom found that it had been treated unfairly. The discrepancy between the time considered fair for a response here, and the time considered fair in the Capita case (above), illustrates that there is no set time limit; it will depend on the nature of the allegations.

In 2010, Sky News was cleared of breaching Ofcom rules during a live interview with Peter Andre where questions about his children caused him to break down and cry. As readers of the magazines *Heat* and *OK!*

will know, Peter Andre was married to and had two children with model and businesswoman Katie Price, and was a devoted stepfather to her son from a former relationship. After their divorce, she married again, to a cagefighter and would-be film star called Alex Reid, and the interview took place shortly after this. As well as asking about his ex-wife's remarriage and its possible impact on their children, presenter Kay Burley asked how he might feel if Alex Reid said he wanted to adopt his children. Almost 900 viewers complained about the 'intrusive manner' of the interview, but Ofcom said there was no breach of the rules. They pointed out that Peter Andre had considerable experience of dealing with the media, he had agreed to appear knowing that his ex-wife's remarriage was in the news and likely to be mentioned, and the interviewer expressed concern about his well-being and did not press him for a response.

Privacy

This section works in a similar way to the previous one, with a basic rule and a set of practices to be followed. Failing to follow one or more of the practices will only be a breach of the Code where it results in an unwarranted invasion of privacy, but, as with the previous section, following the practices is not a guarantee that a broadcaster will not be found in breach, if it has in some other way committed an unwarranted invasion of privacy. The Code recognises that in some situations – particularly emergencies – there may be difficult decisions to be made on the spot about whether privacy is being infringed. It also acknowledges that there is a clear public interest in such situations being reported, and promises that Ofcom will take both factors into account when judging complaints about privacy.

The basic rule stated in this section is that any infringement of privacy, whether it is a result of the process of making a programme, or of the content of a programme, must be 'warranted'. The Code explains that in order for an invasion of privacy to be warranted, the programme maker must be able to justify it, in the particular circumstances of the case. If the justification offered is in the public interest, the broadcaster must be able to show that this outweighs the right to privacy. Examples of the public interest, the Code says, would be where the invasion of privacy is justified in the cause of revealing or detecting crime, protecting public health or safety, exposing misleading claims or revealing incompetence that affects the public.

The practices to be followed are:

- The location of a person's home or family should not be revealed without his/her consent, unless warranted.
- Broadcasters should recognise that people who are caught up in newsworthy events still have a right to privacy, unless it is warranted to infringe it. This applies both when reporting current events, and for later programmes looking at those events.
- Broadcasters should ensure that words, pictures or actions filmed or recorded in public places are not so private that their inclusion in a programme should require consent from the people featured, unless broadcast without consent is warranted.
- Any material which infringes privacy should only be used with the person's informed consent, or where it is warranted (callers to phone-in shows are considered to have given consent by the act of phoning in).
- If a person's or organisation's privacy is being infringed, and they ask for filming or recording to stop, the programme maker should normally comply with the request, unless continuing is warranted.
- When filming or recording takes place inside the premises of an organisation, institution or other agency, permission should be obtained from the relevant authority, unless it is

warranted to go ahead without permission. Where filming takes place in a sensitive place, such as a school, hospital, ambulance, prison or police station, and involves someone in a sensitive situation, consent should be obtained both for filming and then again for broadcast, unless not doing so is warranted. Where a child is being filmed and will be identifiable, this double consent should be obtained both from the institution where the filming takes place, and the child's parent. It is not normally necessary to get consent from employees or members of the public whose appearance is incidental.

- Material obtained by surreptitious filming or recording should not be used unless it is warranted. This includes material obtained by using long lenses or recording devices; by leaving a camera or recorder unattended on private property, without the informed consent of the owner of the property; by taping a phone conversation without telling the other person; or by deliberately continuing to record when the subject believes you have stopped.
- Broadcasters should not film, record, or use footage or tape of people involved in an emergency, accident victims, or anyone suffering a personal tragedy, where to do so would be an infringement of privacy, unless it is warranted or the people concerned have given informed consent. This applies whether the events are in a public place or not.
- People who are distressed should not be pressurised to give interviews or otherwise take part in a programme, unless this is warranted.
- Broadcasters should take care not to broadcast the names of anyone who has died, or been involved in an accident or violent crime, unless they are sure that the next of kin have already been told or unless it is warranted.
- When covering past events that have caused trauma to individuals (including crime), broadcasters should try to reduce the potential distress to victims and/or relatives, unless not doing so is warranted. As far as possible, surviving victims and/or close relatives of victims should be told when such programmes are made and broadcast.
- Broadcasters should take special care not to infringe the privacy of people under 16, and should recognise the fact that they do not lose their right to privacy because their parents may be famous, or because newsworthy events have happened at their school.
- Where a programme features someone under 16 in such a way that his/her privacy is infringed, consent should be obtained from that person, if possible, and from his/her parent, guardian, or someone over 18 who is *in loco parentis,* unless the subject is trivial, the person's participation is minor, or the invasion of privacy is warranted.
- People under 16 should not be questioned about personal matters without the consent of their parent, guardian, or someone over 18 who *is in loco parentis,* unless it is warranted to do so without consent.
- People who are over 18, but vulnerable in some way, should not be questioned about personal matters without the consent of someone over 18 who has primary responsibility for their care, unless it is warranted to do so without consent. As examples of vulnerable adults, the Code cites the bereaved, people with learning difficulties, people with mental problems or dementia, and people who are traumatised, sick or terminally ill.

In 2006, satellite channel ATN Bangla was the subject of a complaint about footage of a minibus crash in Bangladesh, which included shots of dead bodies and an interview with a distressed child, who was filmed identifying her parents' bodies. Ofcom found that the footage of dead bodies, while disturbing, was 'not overly graphic in the context of a valid news report about such an horrific accident'. The shots were either at medium distance, or, where they were closer, were partly obscured by electronic blurring techniques, which Ofcom said lessened the impact, with the result that there was no breach of the Code. Ofcom was not able to judge the footage concerning the child as ATN Bangla could not supply a copy; this failure was itself a breach of the Code, which provides that broadcasters must keep copies for specified lengths of time (these vary depending on the type of broadcaster, and are detailed on the Ofcom website).

In 2004, a Mrs Josephine Merrick, a descendant of the 'Elephant Man' Joseph Merrick, complained that her privacy had been invaded by a programme which showed her name, and her husband's and daughter's, on a family tree diagram. The programme was examining the possible cause of Joseph Merrick's deformities, and, in particular, whether there was any genetic basis for them. Ofcom found that there had been no invasion of privacy, because the family tree was shown so briefly that it was unlikely that she could be identified from it. In addition, there was a clear public interest in showing that descendants had nothing to fear from their genetic inheritance.

In 2007, the BBC was the subject of a complaint from a woman shown in a family photograph, in a programme featuring her uncle. The programme was about the parole system, and featured Mr Mukhtar Hussain who was serving his nineteenth year of a life sentence for the murder of his brother's wife in 1987. The programme included a wedding photograph of Mr Hussain's sister, Ms Soraya Ali, who was also convicted of the murder, and the photograph also featured Mr Hussain's niece and Ms Ali's daughter, Ms Tasneem Southern. Ms Southern complained that her privacy was unwarrantably infringed in the broadcast of the programme in that: the photograph was shown in the programme without her knowledge or consent; and she was not told about the programme before its broadcast. The BBC argued that it would have been impossible for anyone who was not already aware of Ms Southern's connection with the murder case to link her to the events being discussed in the programme and the prospect of anyone but the principal participants being identified was so remote that there was no need to seek consent of others (including Ms Southern) who appeared in it. Ofcom found that, while the circumstances surrounding this case were personally distressing to Ms Southern, she did not have a legitimate expectation of privacy in relation to the broadcast of a photograph which was freely provided to the programme makers by the owner, and in which Ms Southern was shown only briefly and in passing, without any reference to her or her relationship to those featured in the programme. Therefore, there was no infringement of her privacy.

In 2007, Channel 4 was the subject of a complaint from the mother of a girl featured in a documentary about falling standards in British schools. Covertly recorded footage showed the girl throwing a pencil and responding 'No' to a question from the teacher, but her face was pixellated. Her mother complained that her daughter was treated unfairly in that she was secretly filmed and the material was broadcast without consent, she was not given an opportunity to respond to the material before broadcast, and that she was recognised despite the pixelation. Ofcom found that the programme was of significant public interest in exposing failures in the secondary education system, and had to show examples of persistent low-level misbehaviour in the classroom in order to expose how the education system was failing the children. In light of this, and of the appropriate measures taken to obscure Ms V's daughter's identity, and having taken account of the particular vulnerabilities of children, Ofcom did not find that inclusion of the footage of Ms V's daughter resulted in unfairness to her, nor that her privacy was unwarrantably infringed in either the making or broadcast of the programme.

In 2008, Ofcom rejected complaints about a BBC programme, *Whistleblower: Childcare*, which showed the results of an undercover investigation into standards at a nursery. The programme showed film of children at the nursery, with their faces obscured to protect their identities, in order to reveal the problems there, including broken glass in the garden and power tools left unattended where children could get to them. Parents of the children shown complained, but Ofcom held that showing the film was justified in view of the public interest in revealing such serious failings, and that as the children's faces were concealed their privacy had not been infringed.

Sponsorship

The main relevant provision here is that news programmes may not be sponsored. The Code includes within this category news bulletins and news desk presentations on radio, and news and current affairs programmes on television. Current affairs programmes are defined as those carrying explanation and analysis of current events and issues.

Commercial references

This section provides that broadcasters must maintain editorial control over their programmes and ensure that advertising and programme content are kept separate. The main provisions which could potentially affect journalists are:

- Undue prominence should not be given to a product or service in any programme. 'Undue prominence' is defined as the presence of a product in a programme where there is no editorial justification for it, or the manner in which it is referred to.
- Advertising must not appear within programmes, unless editorially justified.
- Wherever possible, the broadcast of charity appeals, over a period of time, should benefit a broad range of charities.

Bauer Media was found to be in breach of the Code in 2008 regarding an item on a news bulletin on the Clyde 1 radio station, about the fact that the station's flagship sports programme had a new sponsor. The bulletin announced that the sponsorship deal had been struck, and then interviewed the managing director of the firm sponsoring the programme. Ofcom found that this was in breach of the rule on giving undue prominence to a product or service.

COMPLAINTS UNDER THE CODE

Complaints about privacy or fairness can only be brought by 'persons affected', or someone who they authorise to make a complaint. 'Persons affected' are defined as:

- a person who took part in the programme and may have been the subject of the alleged unfairness;
- a person who has a 'sufficiently direct interest' in the subject matter of the alleged unfairness;
- a person whose privacy may have been invaded, either by the content of a programme or the process of making it.

'Person' in this sense can include a company or other organisation. In exceptional cases, a relative or someone else who is closely connected can bring a complaint without the affected person's authorisation (e.g. if the person is a child).

Other complaints can be brought by anyone, and investigations can also be instigated by Ofcom itself. While it does not have to investigate every complaint, Ofcom is obliged to look into complaints where the complainant raises evidence that there is a case to answer. During investigations, broadcasters are given the chance to respond to the allegations made.

KEY POINTS

The Ofcom Broadcasting Code

The Code covers all UK broadcasters, but only certain sections apply to the BBC; those that do not apply are replaced by the BBC's own guidelines.

Breaches of the Code can only lead to sanctions after broadcast; it is not used to ban or censor programmes in advance.

Sanctions for breach include:

- fines;
- prevention of repeat broadcast;
- broadcasting corrections;
- cutting short or revoking a licence.

Protecting the under-18s

Restrictions apply to:

- broadcasts containing sex, violence, offensive language and other content which could be damaging or unsuitable;
- reporting crime involving the under-18s, especially sexual offences.

Harm and offence

Under the Code, broadcasters:

- must not 'materially mislead';
- must meet 'generally accepted standards';
- should not include details of self-harm or suicide unless justified;
- should not use simulated newscasts in a misleading way.

Crime

Restrictions apply to:

- payment to criminals and witnesses;
- descriptions of how to commit crime;
- material which could endanger lives, especially in hostage or kidnap situations.

Religion

Programmes dealing with religion must not subject religious views to 'abusive treatment'.

Impartiality and accuracy

News must be reported with 'due accuracy' and 'due impartiality'.

Elections and referendums

Regulations apply to ensure that no one party is favoured by a broadcaster's coverage during elections and referendums.

Fairness

People interviewed, shown or mentioned in programmes should usually be:

- given full information about the programme;
- fairly represented;
- given a fair chance to respond to detrimental allegations.

Privacy

Invasions of privacy must be warranted, and special rules apply to:

- home and family details;
- people in newsworthy events;
- surreptitious filming and recording;
- people affected by past traumatic events;
- children and vulnerable people.

Sponsorship

News and current affairs programmes may not be sponsored.

Commercial references

- Products and services must not be given undue prominence.
- Advertising should not be shown in programmes.
- Charity appeals should benefit a range of organisations.

Complaints under the Code

Complaints about privacy and fairness must be brought by someone affected or their representative; others can be brought by anyone or instigated by Ofcom.

TEST YOUR KNOWLEDGE

1. What powers does Ofcom have to censor programmes before transmission?
2. You are covering a story about identity theft, and you have an interview with a former fraudster, who explains exactly how she goes about getting the information needed to set up a bank loan in someone else's name. Would broadcasting the interview breach the Ofcom Code?
3. You work for a local radio station, and report a dispute between two local organisations. One of them rings up complaining that you only used two short quotes from him, whereas his opponent was heard for approximately twice as long. Does he have a case under the Ofcom Code?
4. How does the Code define 'matters of political and industrial controversy'?

5 You work for a local TV station and are reporting on the possible closure of a local school. The local council says it has to be closed because of falling numbers, but parents are opposing the plan. Your child attends the school. Can you report the story without breaching the Code?

6 When does the 'election period' for a local government election begin? When does it end?

7 What information does the Code require contributors to a radio or TV programme to be given?

8 In what situations does the Code allow film or sound obtained by deception to be broadcast?

ONLINE RESOURCES

The Ofcom Code is published in full, along with reports of adjudicated cases, at:
www.ofcom.org.uk

The BBC Editorial Guidelines can be read at:
www.bbc.co.uk/guidelines/editorialguidelines/advice/

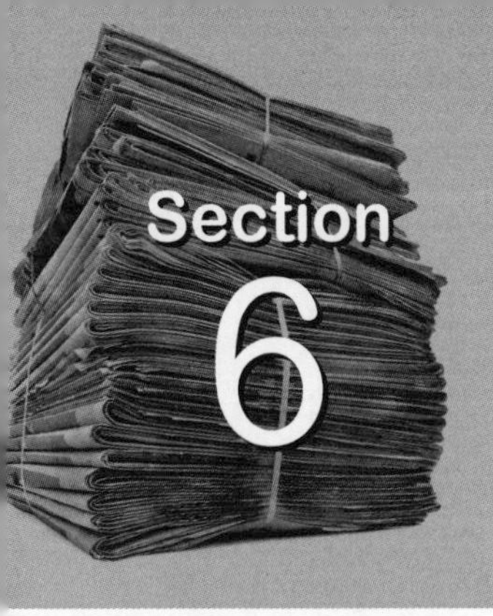

REPORTING GOVERNMENT AND BUSINESS

As the title suggests, this section deals with laws which apply specifically to writing about government and other public bodies, and about businesses. The law dealt with in these chapters is of two different kinds: as well as restrictions on what the press can write, these chapters also cover laws which help journalists, because they oblige organisations to make certain types of information available to the public.

Chapter 26 covers the law on publishing particular types of government information, such as material relating to national security or defence, while Chapter 27 explains the law on press access to the decision-making meetings of local government, and also details other laws under which local public bodies must make information public. During elections, laws come into play which restrict what can be written about candidates and the election, and these are covered in Chapter 28.

Chapter 29 covers the Freedom of Information Act 2000, which provides a right to access information from a wide range of public bodies. The chapter explains how journalists can use the legislation, and how to proceed if a request for information is refused.

Finally, Chapter 30 covers laws which relate specifically to writing about businesses. It contains details of the kinds of information which certain types of company must, by law, make public, and where to find it. It also covers the law on insolvency, a key area for any journalist who covers a specific industry or business in general.

Chapter 26 Official secrets

Certain types of official information, such as material related to issues such as defence and national security, are subject to stringent laws which make it a criminal offence not just to publish that information, but in some cases even to receive it. The reason for such strict protection is that it is considered necessary to keep such information secret because it could be useful to enemies of the UK, whether these might be other states or terrorists. In practice, however, governments have frequently tried (sometimes successfully) to keep such information secret even when its disclosure poses no real threat, and could even be considered to be in the public interest.

The main restrictions are contained in two Acts: the Official Secrets Act 1911 and the Official Secrets Act 1989. Although prosecutions of journalists under the Acts are rare, they can happen. In addition, the Acts criminalise many situations in which official information is passed to journalists, which means protection of sources is very important in these cases (the law on this issue is covered in Chapter 21).

THE OFFICIAL SECRETS ACT 1911

Section 1 of the Act makes it an offence if:

> any person for any purpose prejudicial to the safety or interests of the state –
>
> (a) Approaches, inspects, passes over or is in the neighbourhood of or enters any prohibited place [this is defined in the Act, and essentially covers any government or military building, any site concerned with essential services such as gas or electricity, and anywhere related to communications, such as railways and roads]; or
>
> (b) Makes any sketch, plan, model or note which is calculated to be or might be or is intended to be or could be directly or indirectly useful to an enemy; or
>
> (c) Obtains, collects, records or publishes, or communicates to any other person any secret official code word or password, or any sketch, plan, model, article or note, or other document or information which is calculated to be or might be or is intended to be directly or indirectly useful to the enemy.

A person convicted of doing any of these things could be liable to up to 14 years in prison.

For the media, the most likely source of problems comes from s1(c) of the Act, but in practice the case below is the only one in which a journalist has been prosecuted under s1 in over 50 years.

In 1978, two journalists who had interviewed an ex-soldier about what the source described as security 'scandals' were prosecuted under the Act, in what became known as the 'ABC case' after the initials of the defendants. However, the judge criticised the prosecution as 'oppressive', pointing to the fact that the Act required that a defendant had acted 'for any purpose prejudicial to the safety or interests of the state'. The government had suggested that the intention to publish the information in a magazine was sufficient to meet this requirement, but the judge found that the words meant that the Act was really intended to deal with people who were in league with a foreign power. Although he did not rule out use of s1 against the media, he said that it should be reserved for cases where there was an accusation of collusion with a foreign power and, as a result, the Attorney-General withdrew that part of the prosecution.

OFFICIAL SECRETS ACT 1989

The 1911 Act originally had a s2, which concerned the publication or receipt of pretty much any official information. It was so widely drawn that it effectively made it an offence to publish even the most harmless and trivial details of government activity, such as the brand of paperclips used in the Foreign Office, or whether the apple pie in the Department of Employment canteen was served with cream or custard. It was widely criticised, and eventually the then government passed the 1989 Act, which abolished s2 of the 1911 Act, and replaced it with a series of specific offences related to particular types of information. The Act is quite complicated and creates a number of different offences relating to different types of information, disclosed by different types of government employee, so the sections below can only be a summary of the provisions, but will give you a basic understanding of the kind of behaviour that is prohibited.

Offences of disclosure

The 1989 Act makes it an offence for anyone who is or has been employed by the Crown (which covers the armed services, the Civil Service and Ministers), and government contractors to disclose information in relation to:

- security and intelligence (s1);
- defence (s2);
- international relations (s3);
- crime (s4);
- details of government phone tapping, interception of mail, or other communications (s4);
- information on security, intelligence, defence or international relations, which has been communicated in confidence to other states or international organisations (s6).

By narrowing the law down to these specific categories, the Act makes it plain that material will not be protected by the Official Secrets Act merely because it is secret and comes from the government; it must fall within one of these classes.

In 2000, a former MI5 agent called David Shayler wrote about the activities of the security services in *The Mail on Sunday*, alleging, among other things, that MI5 kept secret files on a number of Labour MPs. He was convicted under s1 and s4 of the 1989 Act, and sentenced to six months' imprisonment.

Myths and misconceptions Leaks in the public interest

✘ *There is a defence if leaked material concerns a matter of public interest.*

It is often assumed that there must be a public interest defence for government employees who leak information which it is in the public's interest to know. The Act, however, contains no such defence for this offence, and in the *Shayler* case, the House of Lords confirmed that it did not exist.

The offences created by ss1–4 and s6 mean that, if a source employed by, or under contract to, the Crown passes information in one of these categories to you, they could be convicted under the Act. Protecting your sources obviously then becomes an issue in this situation (see Chapter 21). However, there is a further implication for journalists in this section of the Act, in that it is also possible for a journalist to be charged with aiding and abetting, or inciting, these offences if, for example, the source has been paid for the information, or helped or encouraged to get or disclose it. This could be the case even if, in the event, the material was never published.

Offences concerning publication

Section 5 of the Act makes it an offence for any person to disclose (which includes publishing) without lawful authority:

- any information, document or other material that falls within the categories detailed in ss1–4 (see above); and
- which has been disclosed without authorisation by a Crown employee or government contractor; or
- which has been disclosed without authorisation by someone to whom the information was properly entrusted, in confidence, by a Crown employee or government contractor; or
- which has been disclosed by a Crown employee or government contractor; in circumstances where it was intended to be kept confidential.

In addition to proving the above facts, if the information is covered by ss1–3 of the Act, the prosecution also has to prove that:

- the disclosure was damaging to the public interest; and
- the person disclosing it knew, or had reasonable cause to know, that it was protected information under the Act, that the disclosure was unauthorised and that its publication was damaging.

The issue of whether a disclosure was damaging to the public interest is to be judged on the facts of the case, and would be a question for a jury to decide if a person was prosecuted. Note that this provision is not the same as a public interest defence. A public interest defence would allow the press to avoid conviction if it could be shown that it had published material which it was to the public's benefit to know; but under the 1989 Act this defence is not available, and so it makes no difference that a publication might disclose, for example, government wrongdoing or incompetence. The reference to the public interest in s5 simply means that there will be no liability for revelations that are harmless (e.g. because the information is trivial, or does not reveal any real secret).

Section 6 makes it an offence to disclose, without lawful authorisation, information on security, intelligence, defence or international relations, which has been communicated in confidence to other states, or international organisations. Again, the disclosure must be damaging, and the person disclosing it must know, or have reason to know it was damaging, and to know that the material was obtained in circumstances prohibited by the Act. However, this section contains a defence which is not applicable to the other classes of information, which states that there will be no offence if the information or material has previously been made available to the public with the authority of the nation or organisation concerned, or if the person making the disclosure is a member of that organisation.

Penalties and prosecutions

The maximum sentence under the 1989 Act is two years' imprisonment. Prosecutions under the 1989 Act can only be brought with the consent of the Attorney-General, or, in the case of information relating to crime, with the consent of the Director of Public Prosecutions. Although there have been some attempts to prosecute journalists, none has so far resulted in a conviction, probably because in political terms no government wants to be seen to be trying to suppress press freedom. However, sources who have supplied information to the press have been successfully convicted.

In 1998, journalist and defence expert Tony Geraghty wrote a book called *The Irish War*, which discussed surveillance techniques used in Northern Ireland. Although the Government knew about the book, and made no attempt to prevent its publication, shortly after it was published Mr Geraghty was arrested and his home searched. However, a year later, the Attorney-General discontinued the prosecution, without giving a reason.

In 1999, an officer in the Royal Navy was sentenced to 12 months in prison for leaking information about a possible biological weapon attack by Iraq to the *Sun*. The paper paid him £10,000, and ran the story, but no one from the *Sun* was prosecuted.

In 1997, a former MI6 officer was sent to prison for a year, for sending a synopsis of a book about his work to a publisher.

Investigation powers

Although prosecutions of journalists under the Official Secrets Acts are rare, the special investigatory powers provided to the police under the Acts can bring their own problems for the media, even if no charge is brought. If the police suspect that a crime under the Acts has been committed, or is about to be committed, and can prove reasonable grounds for that suspicion, a magistrate can authorise a warrant entitling them to search premises and seize evidence. In an emergency, where the police believe that the interests of the state demand immediate action, a police superintendent can sign the warrant.

Under the usual law on search and seizure for investigating crime (see p. 336), material which is held in confidence for the purposes of journalism is called 'excluded material' and cannot usually be seized. However, in exceptional circumstances, such material can be seized with a warrant from a circuit judge, and the Police and Criminal Evidence Act 1984 allows police to get such a warrant where an offence under the Official Secrets Acts is suspected. They can also get a warrant to seize what is called 'special procedure material', which includes material for journalistic purposes that is not within the category of 'excluded material' (this would include, for example, pictures or documents that had not been received under circumstances of confidentiality).

Journalists can be questioned in court about the sources of information protected under the Acts. The Contempt of Court Act 1981 places some limits on this questioning, because of the importance of journalists protecting their sources (see Chapter 21); however, this does not apply when national security is at issue.

Official secrets and breach of confidence

Using the Official Secrets Act is not the only way to suppress publication of official secrets; in some cases, the Government will instead use the law on breach of confidence, which concerns disclosure of information that was obtained in circumstances of confidentiality. (This is discussed in Chapter 18.)

DEFENCE ADVISORY NOTICES

Defence Advisory Notices (usually referred to as DA Notices) are part of a system which allows the Government of the day to warn the press in advance that publishing information on certain subjects is considered to be damaging to the national interest, or likely to put lives at risk. A DA Notice is not a legally enforceable order, but a request that the press do not publish information on the matters listed, without first seeking advice from the DA Notice Secretary, who can be contacted at any time.

The notices are issued by the Defence, Press and Broadcasting Advisory Committee (DPBAC), which is made up of representatives from the Foreign Office, Ministry of Defence, the Home Office and the media, and meets twice a year. They are sent to newspaper editors and to their equivalents in the broadcasting sector, and also posted at the DPBAC website (see *Online resources* at the end of this chapter).

Currently there are five DA Notices in place, which cover defence and security issues. DA Notice 3, for example, concerns weapons, and requests that information is not published on issues such as the design of nuclear weapons and the technology behind them; security arrangements for their transport and storage; or the design details, capabilities or areas of vulnerability of non-nuclear weapons.

According to the Committee's website, the idea of the system is not to censor information, but to promote negotiation between the Government and the media, so that as much as possible of a story can be published without revealing genuinely secret and harmful information. Breach of a DA Notice is not a criminal offence, and the DA Notice system does not have any sanctions of its own; however, there is clearly potential for overlap between the issues cited in DA Notices, and the sort of material which is protected from disclosure by the Official Secrets Acts and the law on breach of confidence, and legal action can be taken using these routes. According to the website, this should not happen as a result of discussions with the DA Notice Secretary, which are confidential, but the media law experts, Robertson and Nicol, suggest that it may be unwise to trust this assertion. They cite a 1985 case in which a publisher submitted an advance copy of a book, assuming that it would receive useful guidance on making sure that it contained no harmful material, and instead found itself on the receiving end of an injunction, which meant that the book could never be published.

Law in practice DA Notices

The DA Notice system encourages journalists to contact the DA Notice Secretary before publishing anything covered by a DA Notice and, in some cases, discussions with the Secretary may mean that, rather than abandoning a story, you can find an approach that tells the story without revealing harmful information. The Secretary can be contacted at any time; contact details are published on the DA Notice website (see *Online resources*, at the end of this chapter).

KEY POINTS

The Official Secrets Act 1911

It is an offence, for a purpose prejudicial to the safety or interests of the state, to:

- be in or near a prohibited place;
- make a sketch, plan or note that could be useful to an enemy;
- obtain or publish anything that could be useful to an enemy.

The Official Secrets Act 1989

It is an offence for government employees and contractors to disclose information on:

- security and intelligence;
- defence;
- international relations;
- crime;
- interception and phone tapping;
- confidential information given to other nations or international organisations.

It is also an offence to publish information in these categories, if unlawfully disclosed by a government employee or contractor.

The Act also gives police wide powers of search, seizure and arrest.

Governments also use breach of confidence laws to stop leaks of information.

Defence Advisory Notices

The DA Notice system is a voluntary system for protecting information which could harm the national interest or put lives at risk.

TEST YOUR KNOWLEDGE

1 List the six categories of information that are protected under the Official Secrets Act 1989.

2 Which of these situations could mean you are guilty of an offence under the Official Secrets Acts?

(a) A computer consultant working for a company which is installing new systems for the Ministry of Defence gives you a document detailing weaknesses in the system that could expose it to hackers. You publish a story based on the document.

(b) A civil servant gives you a secret document, which should only have been seen by top NHS officials, that details plans to halve the number of intensive care departments in hospitals. You publish a story revealing the plans.

(c) A former member of the security services contacts you with a story about phone taps on well-known public figures. Your paper pays £10,000 for the evidence, but in the end decides not to run the story.

3 You have been working on a story given to you by a top civil servant, about problems with security at a naval base. Before the story can be published, the police arrive at your office, and state that you are suspected of being about to commit an offence under the Official Secrets Act 1989. What powers do they have with regard to:

(a) your research material;

(b) you.

ONLINE RESOURCES

The website of the Defence, Press and Broadcasting Advisory Committee, with details of how the DA Notice system works, and current DA Notices, is at:
www.dnotice.org.uk

The full text of the Official Secrets Act 1989 is at:
www.legislation.gov.uk/ukpga/1989/6/contents

Details of some high-profile cases brought under official secrets legislation can be read at:
news.bbc.co.uk/1/hi/uk/216868.stm

News stories about the effect of official secrets legislation on the media are featured on the website of the Campaign for Press and Broadcasting Freedom, at:
www.cpbf.org.uk

Reporting local government

The decisions made by local authorities, from the London Assembly right down to the smallest parish council, can have important implications for local communities, and are a rich source of stories for local – and sometimes national – papers and broadcasters. In this chapter we look at the rules on access to council meetings and documents, including the resources available for investigating the standards of behaviour of council members. In 2014, the Government passed new regulations which make it clear that local government meetings should, as a general rule, be open and accessible to both the press and the public, and that it should be possible to report them using social media, as well as the traditional methods.

THE BASIC RULES ON REPORTING LOCAL GOVERNMENT MEETINGS

The new guidelines are called the Openness of Local Government Bodies Regulations 2014. They cover:

- district councils;
- English county councils;
- London borough councils;
- the London Assembly (Greater London Authority)
- the Common Council of the City of London when meeting in its capacity as a local authority or police authority;
- the London Fire and Emergency Planning Authority;
- any joint authority established under Part 4 of the Local Government Act 1985;
- economic prosperity boards;
- combined authorities;
- any fire and rescue authority in England constituted by a scheme under s2 of the Fire and Rescue Services Act 2004, or a scheme to which s4 of that Act applies;
- the National Park Authorities for England's National Parks;
- the Broads Authority;
- a Council of the Isles of Scilly;
- any parish council or parish committee.

The rules also cover meetings of any committee, sub-committee or joint committee of one of the above bodies.

The Regulations state that all meetings of the bodies listed must be open to the press and public, except in specific circumstances (these vary slightly between different types of authority, and we will look at the details later in this chapter). Neither the entire body nor any of its committees can decide to meet in private unless they have a legal right to do so.

If a meeting of one of the bodies listed is in public, you can also take photographs, film or record the proceedings, Tweet from them and report on them via traditional or social media. You can comment on the meeting as it proceeds via any written medium (such as Twitter or text) but you cannot provide an oral commentary during it because of the potential for disruption (before or after the meeting is fine). Anyone acting in a disruptive manner can be excluded from the meeting. The guidelines say this covers anything which disrupts the conduct of a meeting or impedes others from seeing, hearing or filming the proceedings, including, for example, moving outside the designated public area, making excessive noise in recording or setting up equipment, using intrusive lighting or flash photography, or asking for statements to be repeated for recording purposes.

You do not need to ask permission to report, either beforehand or at the time, but the guidelines to the Regulations advise that it is sensible to let local government staff know in advance if you want to film or record, so that they can make any necessary arrangements to make that possible. The Regulations only require them to provide 'reasonable facilities' for reporting, but the guidelines say this should include space to hear and see the meeting, seats and ideally a desk.

Some local government bodies have their own regulations, called Standing Orders, which may prohibit recording, or activities like tweeting. The guidelines stress that, nevertheless, such bodies have a legal duty to follow the Regulations, and recommend that they waive the relevant provisions in their Standing Orders and then take steps to update those orders.

The guidelines also state that the Department for Communities and Local Government 'would discourage any system which vetted journalists or restricted reporting to approved journalists. Councils should support freedom of the press . . . and not seek to restrict those who may write critical comments'.

In many cases, a council will have a legal right to discuss certain matters in private, and they may include those matters on the agenda with others. They can only exclude the press and public while the relevant matters are being discussed, and not for the entire meeting. For this reason, such matters are often left till last, to save having to send people out and then let them in again.

ACCESS TO LOCAL GOVERNMENT MEETINGS

This section applies to meetings of most bodies covered by the 2014 Regulations, with the exceptions of meetings of a local council's executive, and meetings of parish and town councils, which are dealt with later. The 2014 Regulations state that:

- Meetings must be held in public, except in certain clearly-defined situations (see below).
- The council must give notice of a public meeting at least five clear days before it takes place, publishing the information at its offices and on its website where practicable.

- The agenda must be published, along with any background paper. If an item is added within five days of the meeting, a revised agenda and background papers must be published as soon as the item is added.
- The council can exclude from the agenda any material likely to be discussed in private (see below for when this is allowed).
- On request (and usually on payment of the cost of postage or transmission), the council must supply journalists with a copy of the agenda and background material.

Meetings in private

Meetings must be held in private where the presence of the public is likely to result in the council breaching a legal duty to third parties to keep certain information confidential. A council can also decide to hold a meeting in private where exempt information would otherwise be likely to be disclosed, but it does not have to.

The chairman can also exclude anyone where necessary to maintain order or prevent misbehaviour at a meeting.

Confidential information is defined as information which:

- has been supplied by a government department, under an obligation not to disclose it to the public; or
- which is prohibited from being disclosed, either by law or by a court order.

Exempt information covers a range of types of information, including:

- information relating to any individual;
- information likely to reveal the identity of any individual;
- information relating to the financial or business affairs of any particular person (including the authority holding the information), unless it is information required to be registered under the Companies Acts, the Friendly Societies Acts 1974 and 1992, the Industrial and Provident Societies Acts 1965 to 1978, the Building Societies Act 1986 or the Charities Act 2011;
- information relating to actual or planned consultations or negotiations, on any labour relations matter between the council or a Minister of the Crown, and the council's employees or officers;
- information which could be covered by legal professional privilege in the event of legal proceedings;
- information revealing that the authority proposes to give someone notice of a legal requirement it is imposing on them, or proposes to make any order or direction under the law;
- information relating to any action taken or to be taken in connection with the prevention, investigation or prosecution of crime.

Information falling into one of the above categories is not exempt if it relates to proposed development for which the authority may grant itself planning permission under regulation 3 of the Town and Country Planning General Regulations 1992.

The categories of exempt information are subject to a backstop provision, that the information is only exempt if the public interest in maintaining the exemption outweighs the public interest in disclosing the information.

Law in practice Exempt information

The categories of exempt information under the Local Government Acts are wider than the categories of information which councils can refuse to disclose under the Freedom of Information Act. This means that if a council excludes the press while it is discussing exempt information, you may be able to get access to the information by making a request under the Freedom of Information Act 2000 (see Chapter 29).

If a council has a legal right to hold a certain meeting in private, it need not give notice that it is going to do so. However, if part of a public meeting is to be private, the council must say so when giving notice of that meeting.

The rules detailed above only apply when the council members are meeting formally as the council; there is no right of access to informal briefing meetings for councillors, or when councillors meet as members of a political group.

Information on council decisions

If you cannot attend a council meeting, you can still find out what was decided there. After a public meeting, the council must make available for public inspection copies of the minutes, the agenda, any report relating to a subject discussed in public, any background papers to reports, and a summary of the proceedings, where applicable. All these documents must be available for six years, apart from background papers which must be available for four years.

Access to meetings of a council's executive

Some councils have a decision-making body called the executive, which consists of an elected mayor or leader, and a number of councillors. In these cases, certain types of decision can be taken by the executive, by various types of committee under it, or by individual councillors or officers (the council will have local rules which state who can take which decisions). The rules on access to meetings of a council's executive are contained in the Local Authorities (Executive Arrangements) (Meetings and Access to Information) (England) Regulations 2012. These state that:

- Meetings of the executive must be held in public, except in certain clearly-defined situations (see below).
- The council must give notice of a public meeting of the executive at least five clear days before it takes place, publishing the information at its offices and on its website where practicable.
- The agenda must be published, along with any background paper, and no item can be added to the agenda unless it is available for public inspection five clear days before the meeting, and if an item is added, a revised agenda, public report and background papers must be published as soon as the item is added.
- The council can exclude from the agenda any material likely to be discussed in private.
- On request (and usually on payment of the cost of postage or transmission), the council should supply journalists with a copy of the agenda, any reports to be discussed, any other

material necessary to indicate the nature of the items on the agenda, and, if the relevant officer agrees, a copy of any other document supplied to members of the executive in connection with the relevant item on the agenda.

Executive meetings in private

The Regulations require an executive meeting to be held in private where:

- the presence of the public is likely to result in the council breaching a legal duty to third parties to keep certain information confidential; or
- a lawful power is used to exclude the public in order to maintain order or prevent misbehaviour at the meeting.

A meeting can also be closed to the press and public if the executive decides that exempt information would otherwise be likely to be disclosed. This is a discretionary power: the executive does not have to sit in private to discuss exempt information (see above for the definitions of confidential and exempt information).

If an executive meeting is to be held in private, the council must usually give 28 days' notice, and say why the press and public are excluded. Anyone can then make representations as to why the meeting should not be held in private, and the backstop provision on public interest referred to above can be a useful weapon when doing this. If the council decides to go ahead with the private meeting, it must give notice again, five days before, and include details of any representations against that, and its response. This is in itself can be a news story.

A private meeting can only be held without the 28 days' notice if the Chairman of the Overview and Scrutiny Committee, the Council Chairman or Vice-Chairman agree it cannot be delayed, and then the council must publish its reasons for this. Otherwise, the meeting must be held in public.

The rules above only apply when the executive meets as a decision-making body to exercise its statutory responsibilities; there is no right of access to informal briefing meetings for councillors, or where the members of the executive meet as members of a particular political group.

Notice of key decisions

In addition to the rules about giving notice of meetings detailed above, special rules apply where a meeting is going to take what is called a key decision. These tend to be the more important decisions, and are defined in the Local Authorities (Executive Arrangements) (Meetings and Access to Information) (England) Regulations 2012 as decisions which are likely:

- to result in the authority incurring expenditure or making savings which are significant, having regard to its budget for that service or function; or
- to be significant in terms of its effects on communities living or working in an area comprising two or more wards or electoral divisions within the authority's boundaries.

At least 28 days before a meeting where a key decision is to be taken, the authority must publish, at its offices and on its website, a document which states:

- that a key decision is going to be taken, and when;
- what it is about;

- who is taking the decision;
- a list of documents given to the decision maker to consider, where to get copies of them and how.

Where this procedure cannot be followed, for example for reasons of urgency, the council has to get permission from the Chairman of the Overview and Scrutiny Committee, the Council Chairman or Vice-Chairman, and publish the reasons why the usual procedure could not be followed.

Information from executive meetings

If you are unable to attend an executive meeting, you can still find out what happened. The executive must record:

- the decision and date;
- the reasons for it;
- any other options considered and reasons for rejecting them;
- details of any conflicts of interest affecting an executive member of the decision-making body.

This record must be available for public inspection for six years (four for background papers).

Access to meetings of parish and town councils

This section applies to parish and town councils, and the Council of the Isles of Scilly. Like the other types of body described in this chapter, they must all hold their meetings in public, except in limited circumstances. They must give three clear days' notice of meetings, except for parish meetings which require seven days' notice. They are encouraged, but not obliged, to place copies of the agenda and background material at their offices and on their websites.

Meetings in private

These bodies can meet in private if they decide to by resolution, because confidential matters are to be discussed, or for other reasons where publicity would be prejudicial to the public interest. The guidelines to the 2014 Regulations suggest these criteria would cover meetings involving discussion of the conduct of employees, negotiation of contracts or terms of tenders, or the early stages of a legal dispute, but this list is not exhaustive.

The chairman can also exclude anyone to maintain order or prevent disruption.

Information about decisions

Parish and town councils must make a copy of the minutes available for public inspection after a public meeting.

Bodies not covered by the Regulations

The Regulations cover all the major local government bodies, but not, for example, local groups such as neighbourhood forums and Local Enterprise Partnerships. However, the guidelines to the Regulations state that all public bodies 'should adopt maximum openness and transparency', and groups not covered should 'allow the same filming, audio-recording, taking of photographs, tweeting and blogging as applied to local government bodies, particularly if they are in receipt of public funds'.

Access to meetings in Wales

In councils operating executive arrangements in Wales, meetings must be held in public unless:

- the nature of the matters to be discussed make it likely that confidential information would be disclosed if the public were present;
- the council passes a resolution excluding the public because exempt information is to be discussed (the categories of exempt information in Wales contain additional categories – see *Online resources* at the end of the chapter).

Exclusion from council meetings

As we have seen, councils can exclude the public where exempt information is being discussed. According to the media law experts, Geoffrey Robertson and Andrew Nicol (see *Media Law*, p. 619), this provision is sometimes used to cover up matters that might embarrass the authority or an official, rather than being used in the public interest. As a result, they suggest that journalists should challenge use of the secrecy provisions, and ask that the press be allowed to stay, even if the public have to be excluded.

A case which can be used in support of this argument is ***R* v *Liverpool City Council, ex p Liverpool Taxi Fleet Operators Association*** (1975). It concerned a council meeting to discuss raising the number of local taxi licences, where a number of taxi drivers and others wanted to attend and have their say. The room was too small for all of them, so the council ruled that the public would be excluded, but the press could stay. The decision was challenged in court, but the Divisional Court held that it was reasonable, partly because the council had not deliberately chosen too small a room, but also because it had allowed the press to stay. This suggests that the decision was acceptable because it was not a deliberate attempt to avoid publicity, which in turn implies that, if such an attempt was made, it could be successfully challenged.

Defamation and other restrictions on reporting

Public meetings of local authorities and their committees are covered by qualified privilege, so it is safe to report anything said during them, so long as you make sure you are within the rules of that defence (see Chapter 16). Qualified privilege also covers fair and accurate copies or extracts of any material issued by a local authority for the information of the public, or of any register or other document which is required by law to be open to public inspection.

Remember, though, that this protection does not extend to everything said by local councillors – only what they say in public meetings or the specified classes of document. Local councils cannot, as a body, sue for libel, but individual councillors can (see Chapter 15).

Reports of council activity may also be covered by the new defences of honest opinion and reporting on a matter of public interest.

The 2014 guidelines encourage local government bodies to adopt a policy on the filming of members of the public, and particularly children, the vulnerable and anyone who actively objects to being filmed, to protect their privacy without undermining the transparency of the meeting. It is worth asking your local council whether it has such a policy, so you know what you should and should not film.

ACCESS TO LOCAL GOVERNMENT RECORDS

All local authorities are covered by the Freedom of Information Act 2000 (the operation of which is discussed in Chapter 29). In addition, there are other legal provisions which require them to make specified types of information available to the public.

General information

The Local Government Transparency Code sets out minimum levels of information that every local council should publish. These include:

- spending transactions of over £500;
- salaries of senior staff;
- organisational charts;
- contracts;
- the location of public land and assets.

The Code applies to all local authorities, including parish councils, which have annual income or expenditure (whichever is higher) of over £200,000.

Accounts

Section 15 of the Audit Commission Act 1998 provides a right for 'any person interested' to see a local authority's accounts and 'all books, deeds, contracts, bills, vouchers and receipts relating to them' for 20 working days before the council's annual audit (this also applies to fire, police and civil defence authorities). Copies must be supplied if requested (there may be a charge for this). There is some debate about whether journalists qualify as a 'person interested', but it is clear that if the journalist is on the local electoral roll they will qualify, so, as long as there is someone on the staff who lives in the area, access should be feasible. Alternatively, if your employer is based in the area and pays business rates to the relevant council, a representative of that company will count as an interested person.

In *R (HTV Ltd)* v *Bristol City Council* (2004), HTV successfully applied for judicial review after Bristol City Council refused access to its accounts. HTV was making a documentary about complaints against a local landlord who was housing vulnerable people referred by the local authority. HTV argued that 'a person interested' had to include the media. The court rejected this line, but found that, because the company had offices in Bristol and paid business rates, it had a sufficient interest to be given access to the accounts.

In ***Veolia ES Nottinghamshire Ltd*** v ***Nottinghamshire County Council*** (2009), the High Court clarified what kinds of documents are covered by the Act. Veolia were a waste management company who wanted to prevent the local press seeing documents relating to a contract between them and the council. They argued that the Act only covered documents which were specifically mentioned in the council's annual Statement of Accounts. The High Court rejected this argument, and said that the term 'accounts' in the Act covered all accountancy records arising from the council's day-to-day activities during the relevant financial year. As long as there was a 'nexus' between the document requested and the council's accounts, it was covered by the Act.

The case of ***Hillingdon LBC*** v ***Paulsson*** (1977) establishes that the right of access exists even in relation to documents described as confidential, with the exception of personal information about staff in connection with their employment. Nor can councils refuse to disclose documents, or conceal parts of them, because they may reveal matters of commercial confidentiality (for example, the amount paid to private companies for services). In the ***Veolia*** case, mentioned above, Veolia wished to conceal certain information in the documents requested, on the grounds that it was commercially sensitive and their business interests could be damaged by revealing it. Mr Justice Cranston firmly rejected this argument, stating that there was no provision in the Act for keeping information secret on the grounds of commercial confidentiality.

It is not necessary to specify the exact document you want; you can ask to see a complete class of documents (such as all contracts), and the request can only be refused if the amount of paperwork would be of an unmanageable size (***Evans* v *Lloyd*** (1962)). However, if you know you want a particular document that qualifies for inspection under the Act, the council must give you that. In ***Northampton Borough Council ex parte Oliver*** (1987), the local council argued that it was sufficient to give a reporter a summary of income and expenditure, but the court held that the Act required them to supply the actual document requested.

Councils do not always welcome journalists using the Act with open arms, but they cannot avoid its provisions: refusing a request for a copy of any document covered by the Act or obstructing lawful access to the records is a criminal offence. The 20-day period must be advertised by the council, usually on its website and in a local paper.

The Act also allows local electors, at any time of the year, to see a council's statement of account (the document prepared by the auditor which shows income and expenditure for the preceding year). Many authorities now post this on their websites. In addition, the Local Government Act 1972 provides a right for local electors to see all orders for payment by a council, and the Local Authorities (Members' Allowances) Regulations 1991 allow local electors to see details of allowances and expenses claimed by councillors.

Law in practice **Investigating council expenditure**

The Audit Commission Act is a very useful back-up to the Freedom of Information Act, and has been used by both local and national press to bring to light examples of wasteful or unjustified spending by local councils. Bear in mind that it entitles you to see actual documents, so you can use it to get hold of councillors' expense claims, PFI (Public Finance Initiative) contracts, invoices from firms offering services to the council which your readers may or may not feel are justified, such as PR and marketing consultants, legal bills relating to any court cases the council is involved in, and bills relating to the production of any newspapers or magazines the council publishes.

Planning and development

Applications for planning permission have to be open to public inspection, and there are also public registers of enforcement notices (issued when work is done without planning permission) and breach of condition notices (issued when work does not comply with planning permission conditions).

Local councils also have a duty to carry out strategic planning for their area, and their draft plans must be open to public inspection, along with the supporting documentation.

In the case of some large construction projects (such as roads or airports), it may be necessary for Parliament to pass a private Bill to make the work possible (see p. 4). The text of such Bills has to be lodged with the local authority, along with detailed plans of the proposed development. These documents must be available to the public for inspection and copying.

Under the Localism Act 2011, all local councils have to set up a register of interests, where councillors must disclose any interests which could have a bearing on the decisions they make or the policies they support. This register has to be available for public inspection. The interests that must be declared include any of the following, held by the councillor or their spouse or civil partner:

- any paid employment, trade, profession or vocation;
- any payment or financial benefits made towards expenses as a councillor or election costs, including sponsorship by trade unions;
- any ongoing contract for goods or services between the local authority and the councillor or a body in which they have a financial interest;
- any beneficial interest in land within the council's boundaries, or licence to occupy land there for a month or more;
- any tenancy between the council and a body in which the councillor has a beneficial interest;
- shares in any body that has a business or land within the council boundaries, within certain financial limits.

The main interest in the register for journalists is, of course, to be able to spot when a councillor has failed to disclose a conflict of interest regarding a specific matter of council business. Each council is required to set up a Code of Conduct, which will set down rules that, among other things, state when councillors should declare a personal interest in a specific subject under discussion, and when they should withdraw from the discussion completely. If you work on a local paper, it is worth making yourself familiar with this code, and checking the register of interests when important decisions are being made, so you can spot if the rules are not followed.

OTHER LOCAL PUBLIC BODIES

Most local public bodies are subject to the provisions of the Freedom of Information Act 2000 (see Chapter 29), but additional provisions on access to information apply to certain important types of local body.

Schools

Legislation imposes a number of duties on schools with regard to publicly available information:

- All schools (state and private) must make available details of their exam results, rates of truancy, numbers of pupils staying on after 16, admission arrangements and policies, and appeal procedures for refusal of admission (Education Acts 1996 and 1997).
- The governing bodies of every county, controlled or maintained school must keep a written statement of their position on policy matters, which the head teacher must make available to any interested person (Education (No. 2) Act 1986).

- The governing bodies of grant-maintained schools must make an annual report available to the public.
- Meetings of school-governing bodies can be open to the public, but do not have to be; however, in most cases their minutes must be open to inspection (Education (School Information) Regulations 1998).

Social services departments

Local social services departments must produce an annual Children Services Plan, detailing how they intend to develop services for children with disabilities over the coming year. The report is available to the public.

Magistrates' courts committees

Magistrates' courts committees must hold a meeting in public at least once a year, and the minutes of their meetings must be available for inspection (confidential information can be excluded from the minutes, but this must be made clear, and a reason given).

NHS Trusts and health authorities

Health authorities have to publish annual statistics on waiting times for each area of medicine, numbers of complaints and the time taken to deal with them, and performance relative to national and local standards established by the Department of Health.

Access to meetings of health authorities and NHS Trusts is covered by the Public Bodies (Admissions to Meetings) Act 1960 (see above), and a circular from the Department of Health, issued in 1998 (Health Service Circular 1998/207) (see *Online resources* at the end of this chapter) makes it clear that both the public and press should be allowed into meetings as far as possible, and that meetings should only be held in private where the business being discussed creates a risk of real harm to individuals if discussed in public.

KEY POINTS

Access to meetings

The general rule is that local authorities must meet in public, and the press is free to report on their meetings. Live recording, filming and use of social media are permitted.

Authorities must meet in private when discussing confidential information, and may do so when discussing exempt information.

Agendas and background material should be available in advance.

Reporting decisions

Information on decisions by local authorities should be made public after meetings.

Access to other information

There are statutory rights of access to a wide range of local government information, including accounts, planning applications and decisions, and expenditure.

Other organisations

Duties to make information public also apply to:

- schools;
- social services departments;
- magistrates' courts committees;
- NHS Trusts and health authorities.

TEST YOUR KNOWLEDGE

1 What is the definition of a 'key decision' under the Local Government Act 2000?

2 Which types of council does the 2000 Act apply to?

3 In what circumstances can the public be excluded from a local council cabinet meeting?

4 In what circumstances can the public be excluded from a parish council meeting?

5 You want to report on a meeting of your local county council, but are told that the meeting will discuss exempt information. What arguments could you use to gain access to the meeting?

6 During a meeting of your local council, one of the councillors accuses another of corruption. The chairman forbids her from saying any more, but when you ring the councillor later, she gives you all the details behind her allegations. What is the position on using the information, with regard to defamation?

7 Who has the right of access to local council accounts under the Audit Commission Act 1998?

ONLINE RESOURCES

The Local Government (Access to Information) (Variation) Order 2006 can be read at:
www.legislation.gov.uk/uksi/2006/88/contents/made

The Local Government Act 2000 can be read at:
http://www.legislation.gov.uk/ukpga/2000/22/contents

The Local Government Association website is at:
www.local.gov.uk

The Orchard News Bureau website has examples of the kind of story that can be investigated through use of the laws described in this chapter:
www.orchardnews.com

Reporting elections

The reporting of elections – whether local, national or European – is governed by special rules, under the Representation of the People Acts, and the European Parliamentary Elections Act 1978. The reason for this legislation is to ensure that the press is not able to mislead voters and unfairly influence election results, as could happen if, for example, a major newspaper published an untrue and damaging story about a candidate just before polling day.

It is important to be aware that the law of defamation also applies to coverage of elections – see below. In addition, broadcasters are subject to extra provisions (which are explained in Chapter 25).

OFFENCES RELATED TO ELECTION REPORTING

The Representation of the People Acts and the European Parliamentary Elections Act 1978 create four main offences with regard to press reporting of elections:

- making false statements about candidates;
- falsely reporting a candidate's withdrawal;
- publishing exit polls before voting ends;
- publishing unauthorised advertisements.

False statements about candidates

Section 106 of the Representation of the People Act 1983 makes it an offence to publish any false statement about an election candidate, before or during an election. In such a case, the prosecution need to prove four elements:

- the statement was one of fact, not opinion;
- the words referred to the character or behaviour of the candidate concerned;
- the statement was made with the purpose of damaging the candidate's chances in the election;
- the statement was untrue.

Fact or opinion?

To fall within the offence, the statement made must be presented as a statement of fact; mere expression of an opinion is not enough. In each case, the judge will decide whether the statement is one of fact or comment, and clearly there will be times when the distinction is a difficult one to see.

In *Ellis* v *National Union of Conservative and Constitutional Associations* (1900), describing someone as a 'radical traitor' was deemed an expression of opinion.

In *Pirbhai* v *DPP* (1995), a leaflet which said of the politician Jack Straw that he 'hates Muslims' was considered to be presenting those words as a statement of fact, because nothing in the leaflet qualified the statement or indicated that it was merely the writer's opinion. As it was found to be false, the offence had been committed.

Referring to character

The false statement must refer to the candidate's 'personal conduct or character'; statements about someone's political beliefs or performance as a politician do not fall within the offence.

In *Burns* v *Associated Newspapers* (1925), a newspaper described the leader of the Labour Party as a Communist, on the eve of an election. The courts refused to issue an injunction against the paper, on the grounds that the claim concerned political allegiance and not personal behaviour.

In 1998, a journalist was prosecuted under the Act for falsely claiming, on a website, that a particular candidate was homosexual. In this case the Act could apply because the allegation referred to the candidate's personal behaviour, not his political beliefs.

The statement does not have to be in any way defamatory; merely making a false accusation about the candidate's character or conduct is enough. This is because a false statement which might not be defamatory can still have an effect on someone's political prospects: for example, to say that someone does not recycle their rubbish would not be defamatory, but it would clearly have the potential to influence voters if the person spoken of was a Green Party candidate. If the statement happens to be true, there is no problem, of course.

Purpose of the statement

The statement must be made with the intention of damaging the candidate's chances in the election. This is effectively judged on the content of the statement itself, and whether it appears to have been calculated to influence voters against the candidate. The statement does not have to be proved to have caused actual damage to the candidate's chances (which in any case would probably be impossible to prove).

Falsity

The candidate does not have to prove categorically that the statement is false; according to the leading media lawyers, Geoffrey Robertson and Andrew Nicol, in their book *Media Law*, an affidavit (see the Glossary) from the candidate stating that the words are false will be enough (but see *Defences*, below).

When does the Act apply?

The Act refers specifically to 'candidates' and, according to Robertson and Nicol, this means it only applies after an election campaign has formally started, since before then there are technically no candidates. There may of course be people who everyone knows will stand (including those currently in the seats to be voted for), but, until the election campaign has formally begun, they are not candidates. Parliamentary elections begin with the dissolution of Parliament, the announcement that the Government intends to dissolve Parliament, or the issue of a by-election writ. Local election campaigns run from five weeks before polling date or from publication of notice of the election.

Defences

There is one defence available, where the person who made or published the statement can show that they had reasonable grounds for believing the words were true.

Penalties

The courts can issue an injunction preventing publication or further publication of the false statement. An injunction preventing publication will not normally be granted if the publisher of the statement says that they believe they have reasonable grounds for believing the statement is true. The maker or publisher of the statement, if convicted of the offence, can be fined and disqualified from voting for up to five years.

False statements about withdrawal

Section 75 of the Representation of the People Act 1983 makes it an offence knowingly to publish a false statement that a candidate has withdrawn from an election, in order to benefit another candidate.

Exit polls

Under the Representation of the People Act 2000, it is an offence to publish any results of an exit poll before the official polls close. An exit poll is defined as any forecast about the result of an election or statement about the way that voters have voted, where the forecast or statement is, or seems to be, based on information supplied by voters, after voting. The reasoning behind this is that publishing such results could dissuade people from bothering to vote, if they see that their favoured party already has a good lead. Anyone who publishes such a poll before official polls have closed can be fined up to £5,000.

In 2004, the European Parliament elections were, in some areas, run using all-postal ballots. On the day of the election, *The Times* published an opinion poll which had asked people in the all-postal areas how they had voted. The Electoral Commission (an independent organisation which regulates UK elections) complained that this amounted to an exit poll and should not have been published. The issue was not tested in the courts, but may have to be in the future, as the use of postal ballots increases.

Unauthorised advertisements

Paid advertisements for or about a particular election candidate may only be published with the authorisation of the candidate concerned, or their agent. This is the case whether the advertisement praises or attacks a particular candidate, and publishing an unauthorised advertisement is an offence. The measure only applies to paid advertisements: there is nothing to stop a publication praising or attacking a candidate in its editorial space (so long as the coverage does not amount to a false statement as described above, or to defamation).

What the codes say Reporting elections

Broadcasters are subject to extra provisions when reporting elections, under the Ofcom Code. The following are the main points (and the guidelines are more fully explained at p. 397).

- Coverage must give due weight to 'designated organisations' (usually the main campaigners).
- Candidates must not act as newsreaders, presenters or interviewers in any type of programme.
- Reports or discussions about a particular constituency or electoral area must observe due impartiality.
- Any report or discussion of a constituency or electoral area must include a list of all the candidates, giving their first and last names, and the party they represent (or stating that they are independent).
- If a candidate takes part in a programme on any subject, he or she should not be allowed to make points about the constituency or electoral area, unless other candidates will be given a similar opportunity.
- All discussion and analysis of issues related to the election or referendum must end when the polling stations open.
- The results of opinion polls must not be broadcast on polling day, until the polls close.

OTHER LEGAL CONSIDERATIONS

When reporting elections, you also need to bear in mind the law on defamation and incitement to racial hatred.

Defamation and elections

Defamation law (as explained in Chapter 15) applies to election candidates just as it does to anyone else. Journalists often assume that reports of remarks made by election candidates must be automatically covered by absolute privilege, just as remarks made in Parliament are, but this is not the case. Section 10 of the Defamation Act 1952, states that:

> A defamatory statement published by or on behalf of a candidate in any election to a local government authority to the Scottish Parliament or to Parliament shall not be deemed to be published on a privileged occasion on the ground that it is material to a question in issue in the election, whether or not the person by whom it is published is qualified to vote at the election.

This means that you can be sued for reporting remarks made by one candidate about another, as well as making (and publishing) defamatory remarks yourself. However, in ***Culnane* v *Morris*** (2005), the High Court held that s10 did not mean that statements made by an election candidate could never be covered by qualified privilege. The judge held that the provision merely meant that the fact that a statement was 'material to a question in issue in the election' did not by itself mean privilege applied. Where a statement fell within the requirements of the common law defence of qualified privilege (see p. 271), the defence could apply.

Honest opinion may apply to remarks made by election candidates, under the normal rules of the defence (see p. 253), as can the new defence of reporting on a matter of public interest.

Race relations law

If you are reporting speeches or literature from extremist candidates, or public meetings held by them, it is important to be aware of the provisions of the Public Order Act 1986, regarding incitement to racial hatred, and of the new offence of inciting religious hatred (see Chapter 31).

Law in practice Covering election meetings

During election campaigns, public places such as schools have to be made available to candidates, so that they can hold public meetings to publicise their campaigns. This being the case, Robertson and Nicol suggest that there can be no legitimate reason for excluding the press from such meetings, and any reporter who is asked to leave should point out that the meeting is a public one and insist on their right to stay. If ejected, say Robertson and Nicol, a reporter could sue for assault.

KEY POINTS

Offences related to election reporting

There are four statutory offences:

- false statements about candidates;
- false reporting of withdrawal;
- publishing exit polls before voting ends;
- unauthorised advertisements.

Other legal considerations

Reporters also need to consider:

- defamation law – statements made by or on behalf of election candidates are not covered by privilege;
- laws on racial and religious hatred.

TEST YOUR KNOWLEDGE

1 Making a false statement about an election candidate is an offence under the Representation of the People Act 1983. What are the four elements of this offence?

2 Assuming all the following statements are false and all the people mentioned are election candidates, which of the statements could amount to an offence under the Act?
   (a) John Black is a complete womaniser and unfit for public office.
   (b) Mary Brown was a member of the Communist Party at university.
   (c) Jane White is a lesbian.
   (d) Terry Green may be a Tory, but his real sympathies lie with the National Front.

3 It is widely thought that a general election will be called in May. Your local MP has already announced his intention to stand again, despite a number of recent scandals about him being made public. During April, you write a stinging criticism of him, arguing that his performance has been abysmal, and voters would be crazy to vote him in again. Two of the accusations you made against him are untrue. Have you committed an offence under s160 of the Representation of the People Act 1983? Are there any other legal problems you should worry about?

4 On the morning of a local election, you do a vox pop in the local shopping centre, asking people whom they have voted for. When can you publish the material?

ONLINE RESOURCES

The Electoral Commission has a media handbook covering local elections, which can be downloaded at: www.electoralcommission.org.uk

Chapter 29 Freedom of information

Most of the chapters in this book concern laws which restrict the material you can publish; by contrast, this chapter explains an area of the law which can help you in your job. Freedom of information (FOI) legislation gives both the press and the public the right to see information about the workings of government and public authorities, and can provide a rich source of stories.

In Sweden, FOI rights have existed for centuries, while the USA has had FOI legislation since the 1960s, and Canada, Australia and New Zealand since the early 1980s. In the UK, however, right up until the end of the twentieth century, there was a culture of secrecy about government information, and public records, even on the most trivial of subjects, generally remained closed to both public and press for 30 years after they were produced.

In 2000, however, the Government passed the Freedom of Information Act, which introduces a general right for the public to see official information held by the government and public authorities, subject to exceptions for certain types of information. Although there have been numerous complaints about public bodies being slow to release information (or refusing to do so at all), the Act has allowed the press to uncover a vast amount of information which would once have been kept secret (see below).

THE FREEDOM OF INFORMATION ACT 2000

The Act came into force on 1 January 2005, but it applies to all records held by public authorities, regardless of whether they were created before or after that date. It gives any person (not just UK citizens or UK residents) the right to request access to all types of recorded information from a public authority in England, Wales or Northern Ireland (a separate, rather more media-friendly Act applies to Scotland). The provisions apply to the press just as they do to everyone else; journalists have the same rights, but no extra ones.

The right of access has two elements:

- the right to be told whether a particular piece of information exists (e.g. you might want to know whether statistics are kept on a particular subject); and
- the right to be given that piece of information.

The Act exempts certain categories of information from the right of access, and also lists a further set of categories to which access need only be granted if it is in the public interest to do so. Authorities can also refuse to fulfil a request for information if the cost of doing so is above a specified limit. Outside these categories, however, if a piece of information exists in recorded form, the public authority must release it, even if doing so might reveal information that the authority would prefer not to make public (e.g. if it would embarrass officials).

The legislation imposes duties on public authorities to make their information easy to access. It also creates an appeal procedure, by which someone whose request has been turned down can have it reviewed by the Information Commissioner, an independent watchdog set up to oversee the working of the Act and, after that, by the independent Information Tribunal.

Public bodies covered by the Act

The Act covers around 100,000 different public authorities, both national and local, including all government departments, the Houses of Parliament, all local authorities, the NHS, schools, the armed forces and the police, plus a vast number of individual organisations ranging from the Civil Aviation Authority to the Potato Council. A full list of the bodies covered can be found in Schedule 1 of the Act (see *Online resources* at the end of this chapter), and is updated monthly. The only public bodies specifically excluded from the Act are MI5, MI6 and Government Communications Headquarters (GCHQ).

As well as the public bodies listed in Schedule 1, the Act also covers companies which are wholly owned by any public body on that list. In addition, the Act allows for the Secretary of State to designate private organisations as public bodies for the purposes of certain aspects of their work, which would mean that there was a right of access to information on that work. This power might be used, for example, to designate a private company contracted to deal with social security claims, or a private hospital which was being paid to treat NHS patients.

Types of information

The Act provides access to all types of recorded information, including written documents, letters, memos, emails, computer records, audio and video cassettes, microfiche, maps, photographs and handwritten notes. This can even include information sent from a public official's private email account: in 2012, the Information Commissioner's Office confirmed that this included emails and texts sent by Government ministers and their officials, even if they came from their private accounts, as long as they contained details about Government business. If the information you want has been recorded somewhere, you should be allowed access to it (unless one of the exemptions allowed under the Act applies).

In 2005, the *Sunday Herald* used the Act's Scottish counterpart to prove that the leader of the Scottish Conservatives, David McLetchie, was claiming expenses for taxis used on private business, including trips to the dentist. The *Herald*'s Scottish Political Editor Paul Hutcheon was able, after a long fight, to get access to the politician's taxi receipts, which were initially refused, but later ordered to be released by the Scottish Information Commissioner. The resulting stories eventually led to McLetchie's resignation.

In 2006, journalist Malcolm Prior used the Act to uncover a catalogue of errors by local councils concerning planning permission for mobile phone masts. A legal loophole allows companies to assume that planning permission for masts below 15 m high has been granted if they do not get a response to their planning application within 56 days. FOI requests to 41 local councils found that 68 applications had gone through because of mistakes, such as sending out mail by second class post instead of first, using the wrong date stamp and calculating deadlines incorrectly.

In 2006, the *Guardian* used the Act to obtain documents held by West Yorkshire police, showing that the serial killer Peter Sutcliffe (known as the Yorkshire Ripper) probably attacked many more victims than the public was told.

In 2006, the BBC used FOI requests to reveal, among other things, that an average of one prisoner per day was absconding from Britain's open prisons, that UK hospitals were each charging patients up to £1.5 million per year for parking, and that the UK secretly sold plutonium to Israel during the 1960s.

If the piece of information you want does not exist in any recorded form, the public body is not obliged to create it: so, for example, if you want to know the number of times your local hospital ward is cleaned each week, and the hospital does not collect this information, you cannot insist on it being put together for you. Although the Act gives a right to the information you ask for (if it exists), this does not necessarily mean that you will be allowed to see the record from which the information comes.

What if the information you want has been deleted from a computer system, but could be retrieved? In 2005, the Information Tribunal considered such a case, and decided that there might be situations where the authority could be expected to try to retrieve the information. Where the information was merely in a computer's recycling bin, or was deleted from the original machine but held on the back-up tape, it could be considered as material the authority still held, and should therefore be supplied. Where retrieving the information demanded specialist skills, an authority might still be expected to do so, depending on how much that process would cost; if the cost of retrieval would go over the standard cost limit (see below), the request can be refused.

The Act includes access to personal information, but where such information concerns people other than the person making the request, it will only be released where to do so would not breach the Data Protection Act 1998 or the Human Rights Act 1998.

Publication schemes

The Act requires public bodies to produce what it calls a publication scheme, which specifies the classes of information it intends to publish, what form the information will be published in, and whether it will be available free of charge or subject to a fee. In most cases, details of the publication scheme will be published on the organisation's website, and, before making a request under the Act, it is obviously sensible to check first whether the information is available through the publication scheme, which will be a quicker way of getting it than making an FOI request. The fact that a certain piece of information is not included in the publication scheme does not, however, mean it is not available, only that it is not published as a matter of course.

Exemptions under the Act

Although the general principle of the Act is that information should be made available, it lists a number of situations, known as exemptions, in which a public authority can refuse to supply information.

There are two classes of exemptions:

- absolute exemptions;
- qualified exemptions.

In addition, s14 of the Act gives authorities the right to refuse 'vexatious' requests; this is not defined in the Act, but the government website which explains the Act (see *Online resources* at the end of this chapter) suggests that it would apply to requests designed to disrupt the authority's work. In addition, where an authority has complied with a request for a particular person, s14 allows it to refuse a subsequent request by the same person for the same, or 'substantially similar', information unless a reasonable time has elapsed since the previous request.

Absolute exemptions

Where information is covered by one of the absolute exemptions listed in the Act, a public authority is not obliged to allow access to it, nor even to confirm or deny whether it exists. The absolute exemptions cover the following.

Information already accessible: Section 21 gives authorities the right to refuse to supply information which is 'reasonably accessible' to the applicant in another way. Information will be considered 'reasonably accessible' if a public authority would be obliged by any other law to give it to the public on request, regardless of whether or not the public is required to pay for such access. For example, the information contained on anyone's birth certificate can be obtained on request by paying a fee, so it is not possible to use the Freedom of Information Act to obtain the same information from another source which might supply it free of charge.

Information which is given voluntarily to the public on request, for a fee, can also be considered 'reasonably accessible', but only if it is made available under the relevant authority's publication scheme (see below), and the charges are in accordance with this scheme. Material which is simply made available for inspection does not count as being 'reasonably accessible'.

Security matters: Section 23 exempts information which refers to any of a list of organisations dealing with security matters, including MI5, MI6, the SAS and Government Communications Headquarters.

Court records: Section 32 exempts information which is only held in a document:

- created by a court for the purpose of its proceedings;
- served on or by the relevant authority for the purpose of court proceedings;
- filed with or in the custody of a court;
- created or held by someone conducting an inquiry or arbitration, for the purposes of those proceedings.

Parliamentary privilege: Section 34 provides an exemption where to disclose the information requested would infringe parliamentary privilege. A certificate to that effect, signed by the Speaker of the House of Commons or the Clerk of the Parliaments, is to be taken as conclusive proof that the exemption is necessary.

Conduct of public affairs: Section 36 exempts information held by the House of Commons or House of Lords, where 'in the reasonable opinion of a qualified person' disclosure could:

- prejudice the operation of collective ministerial responsibility (this is the convention by which ministers publicly support decisions made by the Cabinet, regardless of their personal views);
- prejudice the work of the Executive Committee of the Northern Ireland Assembly or the National Assembly for Wales;
- inhibit the free and frank provision of advice, or exchange of views for the purposes of deliberation;
- prejudice the effective conduct of public affairs in any other way.

The 'qualified person' will be the Speaker in relation to information held by the House of Commons, and the Clerk of the Parliaments for information held by the House of Lords.

Section 36 also applies to information held by government departments, but in this case it is subject to the public interest qualification (see below).

The senior Royals: An amendment passed in 2010 gives public bodies an absolute exemption from releasing information relating to the Queen, Prince Charles and Prince William (the other Royals are covered by a qualified exemption).

Qualified exemptions

Where information falls under one of the following qualified exemptions, the authority which holds it can refuse to disclose it, but, before making this decision, it must consider whether disclosure would be in the public interest. This means that it has to balance the public interest in disclosure against the public interest in keeping the information secret; if the public interest in disclosure is stronger, the information should be supplied. The Act does not define 'public interest', but the Information Commissioner has issued guidance on how the test should be applied (see *The public interest test* box below).

If the authority concludes that the public interest would be better served by refusing to disclose the information, it must give the applicant its reasons, unless doing that would effectively result in disclosing the information. It can also refuse to confirm or deny whether the information even exists.

The categories of qualified exemption are as follows.

Information intended for publication: Section 22 exempts information which the relevant authority intends to publish in the future if, in the circumstances, it is reasonable to refuse access until the date of publication, even if that date is not yet decided. The exemption only applies if the authority had already planned to publish the material when the request was made.

National security: Section 24 allows authorities to refuse access to information where it is necessary for the purpose of safeguarding national security. A certificate signed by a Cabinet Minister, the Attorney-General, the Advocate General for Scotland or the Attorney-General for Northern Ireland saying that this exemption should apply is regarded as conclusive proof that it is necessary.

Defence: Section 26 states that information is exempt from the Act if its disclosure is likely to prejudice the defence of this country or any colony, or compromise the effectiveness of our armed forces or any forces 'cooperating' with them.

International relations: Section 27 provides that authorities need not disclose information which could prejudice:

- relations between the UK and another state, or any international organisation or international court;
- UK interests abroad;
- the promotion or protection of UK interests abroad.

Section 27 also exempts from the Act confidential information obtained from another state, or an international court or organisation.

Domestic relations: Section 28 exempts information which could prejudice relations between any of the following:

- the UK government;
- the Scottish Administration;
- the Executive Committee of the Northern Ireland Assembly;
- the National Assembly for Wales.

Economic interests: Section 29 exempts information which could prejudice:

- the economic interests of the UK;
- the financial interests of the government, the Scottish Administration, the Executive Committee of the Northern Ireland Assembly or the National Assembly for Wales.

Criminal investigations and proceedings: Section 30 exempts information held for the purpose of a criminal investigation or criminal proceedings.

Law enforcement: Section 31 exempts information which could prejudice specified aspects of law enforcement, including:

- prevention or detection of crime;
- offenders being caught or prosecuted;
- the administration of justice;
- tax assessment or collection;
- operation of immigration controls;
- security and order in prisons.

It also exempts information concerning the relevant authority exercising its functions for a stated list of purposes, including:

- investigating accidents;
- securing health and safety at work;
- protecting charities from mismanagement;
- investigating improper or illegal conduct.

Auditing: Under s33, a public authority which has the job of auditing other public authorities, or otherwise examining the way in which they use their resources, can refuse access to information which could prejudice that role.

Formation of government policy: Section 35 provides an exemption for information held by a government department, or the National Assembly for Wales, that relates to:

- the development of government policy;
- ministerial communications;
- advice provided by or requested from any of the law officers;
- the operation of any ministerial private office.

Conduct of public affairs: Section 36 exempts information held by public authorities where 'in the reasonable opinion of a qualified person' disclosure could:

- prejudice the operation of collective ministerial responsibility (this is the convention by which ministers publicly support decisions made by the Cabinet, regardless of their personal views);
- prejudice the work of the Executive Committee of the Northern Ireland Assembly or the National Assembly for Wales;
- inhibit the free and frank provision of advice, or exchange of views for the purposes of deliberation;
- prejudice the effective conduct of public affairs in any other way.

The 'qualified person' will vary according to which authority is holding the information, but will be a senior person within that organisation.

Communications with royalty: Section 37 exempts information relating to communications with the Royal family or the Royal Household, or to the award of honours.

Health and safety: Section 38 exempts information which, if revealed, could threaten the physical or mental health or safety of any person.

Environmental information: Certain types of environmental information is already subject to its own rules on disclosure under a separate Convention, and s39 exempts such information from the provisions of the Freedom of Information Act (see p. 447 for more detail about accessing environmental information).

Personal information: Section 40 exempts disclosure of personal information about any individual – including the person making the request – where that disclosure would breach the Data Protection Act 1998.

Legal professional privilege: Section 42 exempts information which is covered by legal professional privilege, which means documents containing legal advice which pass between a lawyer and their client, and documents produced for the purposes of litigation.

Commercial interests: Section 43 exempts information which amounts to a trade secret, or could prejudice anyone's commercial interests, including those of the organisation which holds the information.

The public interest test

As we have seen, certain categories of information need only be revealed if it is in the public interest to do so. The Information Commissioner's Office has produced a guidance note, *Freedom of Information Act Awareness Guidance No. 3*, explaining how it expects the public interest test to be operated, and it is well worth familiarising yourself with this advice, as it can be used to challenge authorities which operate the test incorrectly. The guidance gives the following advice:

- The right to get access to information, and the right to know whether the information exists are two separate rights. This means that the fact that it is not in the public interest to release the information itself does not necessarily mean that it is not in the public interest to say whether it even exists (though sometimes that may be the case).
- The 'public interest' is quite simply something which serves the interests of the public. The guidance gives the following examples of situations where there is likely to be a strong public interest in disclosure:

- Where it would further understanding of and participation in public debate about current issues. This would be the case, for example, where disclosure would allow a more informed public debate about something which the Government or a local authority was considering doing.
- Where it would promote accountability and transparency with regard to the decisions public bodies take, and/or the way they spend public money. For example, where the private sector is used to deliver publicly funded services, it is likely to be in the public interest to disclose information which ensures greater competition and better value for money. Disclosing details about gifts to or expenses claimed by public officials is also likely to be in the public interest, according to the guidance.
- Where it would help individuals and companies to understand decisions made by public authorities that affect them, and in some cases, to challenge those decisions.
- Where it would bring to light information affecting public health or safety. An example would be where prompt disclosure of information might contribute to the prevention of accidents or disease.
- The fact that something is interesting to the public will not necessarily mean that disclosing it is in the public interest; there has to be some benefit to the public which outweighs the benefits to the public of withholding the information.
- There is a clear distinction between the public interest in withholding information, and private interests in doing so, and only the public interest justifies refusing an FOI request. For example, there is obviously a public interest in not revealing details which would compromise the country's ability to defend itself. However, where disclosure would reveal corruption or incompetence, or would simply embarrass the authority or someone working in it, the interests protected by non-disclosure would be private ones, and authorities should not take these kinds of issues into account when deciding whether information should be released in response to an FOI request. In some cases, private and public interests might coincide, but only the public interest should be a factor in the decision.
- The fact that information might be too complicated for the applicant to understand is not a valid reason for refusing an FOI request. Nor is the fact that disclosure might mislead the public because the information does not give the complete picture (e.g. if the information reveals a policy recommendation that was never actually followed). In both cases, according to the Commissioner, the solution is to provide explanation or set the information in its context, not to suppress it.

Applying for information

A request under the Act must be made in writing, but it need not be on any particular form, even if the organisation has produced one, and the Freedom of Information Act website specifically states that it can be done by email. The request should state clearly what information is required, and give the name of the applicant and an address for correspondence; it is not, however, necessary to identify yourself as a member of the press.

You can also specify what form you want the information in: you can ask, for example, for a summary of it, or copies of a specific document, and can specify whether you want it provided in paper or electronic form. The Act requires the authority, as far as possible, to accommodate such requests.

The authority you apply to should reply as soon as possible, but in any case not later than 20 days after receiving the request. Section 16 of the Act places a duty on public authorities to assist and advise applicants, so if they do not understand the request, they should contact you for clarification. The reply should either:

- tell you that the authority does not hold the information you want;
- supply the information;
- refuse the application, and give reasons for doing so (a refusal should cite which exemption the information falls under);
- state that the information may be subject to one of the public interest exemptions, and that the authority is extending the time limit in order to consider this issue.

If a fee is payable (see below), the authority must let you know before going ahead with supplying the information; when they do this, the 20-day period is suspended until the fee is paid, when it begins again.

Delay in considering public interest exemptions is one of the biggest difficulties with using the Act for journalistic purposes. In this situation, the Act only requires authorities to release the information within a 'reasonable' time, which in practice means they can (and sometimes do) go on extending the time limit for months. This can be a useful delaying tactic as, in many cases, the story will eventually stop being newsworthy (but see below for advice on speeding the process up).

Law in practice Using the information

The Act does not lay down any restrictions on using the information supplied through it, so you do not need permission to publish the results of your application. However, the document in which the information is found may be subject to copyright, and the Act does not lift this, so checks may need to be made before publishing direct copies of such documents.

It is also important to be aware of the risk of defamation when using information obtained under the FOI Act. In letters, emails and internal memos, people may well say things about other individuals or organisations that could be defamatory, so you need to make sure that if you publish these statements you are covered by a defence (see Chapter 16).

Challenging refusals

If your request is refused, in most cases the organisation concerned will have a procedure for challenging this, and details of that procedure should be supplied when you are notified of the refusal. If the request is still refused after using that procedure, you can apply to the Information Commissioner's Office, an independent review body, which can look at it again, and if it agrees that the decision was wrong, order the public authority to release the information. However, the Commissioner's Office has become notorious for delay, and in practice this step will only be worth taking if the story you are chasing will still be newsworthy in several months' time.

Where the information in question is held by a department of central government, and the Commissioner has ordered it to be released on public interest grounds, the Cabinet Minister in charge of that department can veto the Information Commissioner's order, and the veto can only be challenged by judicial review (see p. 206). No other public body can refuse the Information Commissioner's order, and a Minister's veto cannot be extended to information held by any body other than its own department.

If the Information Commissioner does not order the information to be released, there is a final right of appeal to the independent Information Tribunal. This right also applies to an authority who has been ordered by the Commissioner to release requested information; it can go to the tribunal to try to get that decision reversed. It is also possible to seek judicial review (see p. 206), if you believe that the Commissioner or the Tribunal has misinterpreted the Act.

In 2000, *Which?* magazine requested details from local councils of restaurant hygiene inspections made at events such as the Ideal Home Show and the Cheltenham Festival. One of the councils, Hammersmith and Fulham in London, refused the request, but after appealing to the Information Commissioner, the magazine was given access to the information. The Information Commissioner said it was in the public interest to release this kind of information, and there was no good reason not to: well-run restaurants had nothing to lose from public scrutiny.

In 2005, the Information Commissioner ordered Corby Borough Council to reveal information on how much it had paid to a temporary finance officer. The Council had claimed an exemption under s40, claiming that the information was personal, and releasing it would breach the Data Protection Act 1998, and that disclosure would cause damage and distress to the employee concerned. The Information Commissioner rejected these claims. The ruling pointed out that there had been controversy over the way in which the officer was appointed, because it was known that he had been paid a significantly higher rate than was usual (although the salary was known, the FOI request was for the total amount paid, including various allowances). It said that the payment made to senior council officials was a matter of legitimate public interest, and such officials had to be prepared for a certain degree of public scrutiny, which was part of the process of holding them accountable for their actions. The officer could not, therefore, have expected the information to remain confidential, and prejudice to his interests was therefore not a sufficient reason to refuse disclosure.

In 2006, the *Guardian* was successful in getting the Ministry of Defence to reveal the names of 500 arms sales officials. The Ministry had initially refused to supply the information, claiming that disclosure would lead to the officials being harassed by peace campaigners. The *Guardian* had to take its case to the Information Commissioner, who found that there was no evidence that disclosure would result in a threat to the officials' safety.

Costs

Authorities are allowed to charge for providing information requested under the Act. If the information falls within the authority's publication scheme, the scheme will give details of any charges. For other information, the Act states that:

- Information which costs an authority up to £450 to answer (or £600 for information held by central government) should be provided free.
- If your request will cost the authority more than this, it can refuse to answer it, or can answer it and charge anything from no fee up to the full cost of the work involved.

Law in practice Using the Freedom of Information Act

Journalist and campaigner Heather Brooke runs courses for journalists on how to use the FOI Act effectively and it was her work which led to the 2009 MPs' expenses scandal coming to light. She offers these tips:

- The key to successful searches is being as precise as possible. 'Journalists often imagine they can go on a big fishing expedition, order all an authority's records for the past ten years and then trawl through and find a big story. But that kind of request will instantly be refused on cost grounds, so you need to narrow it down.'
- Most larger authorities now have a person designated to handle FOI requests, whose name can be found on their websites or by calling the organisation. Try to develop a relationship with the FOI officer at any public authority you deal with regularly. They can help you make your requests more precise, by giving you information on what records they hold, and how the information in them is broken down. 'For example, I wanted to find out some statistics going back across five years, and the FOI officer I dealt with was able to tell me that they'd only held that information electronically for part of that time, and searching through the paper records would go over the cost limit. By narrowing my search to the records they held electronically, I avoided having the request refused, and still got enough information for a really good story.'
- Section 16 of the Act gives authorities a duty to assist people requesting information, so if an authority is not very forthcoming about how it holds information, it can help to remind it politely of s16.
- If you are unable to narrow your request down, you can avoid a rejection on cost grounds by breaking it up, and making separate, smaller searches. So instead of asking for a certain figure going back over ten years, for example, you could make separate requests for smaller chunks of time. You can also break information up by geographical area, or ask for all the correspondence relating to one person, and then make another request relating to another person. The Act does allow authorities to aggregate costs, so if you make a lot of searches over a short period, they can add them together and reject them on cost grounds. In practice, no one seems to be doing this, but, if it looks as though it might be a problem, either space your requests out (a space of two months prevents aggregation), or get colleagues to submit requests in their names. 'In theory, you could even use a false name, but that could cause problems if your request is refused and you have to go through the process of challenging it.'
- If the information you want is not held centrally, check whether it is held regionally. For example, people often want to find out information about the police as a whole, but there is surprisingly little information held that way, However, if you make a separate request to each police force, you might get the same information that way.
- The Act is not only useful for investigating individual stories; it can also be used to open up whole categories of information which will be useful for everyday news-gathering. For example, once you have successfully requested information from a food safety inspection, you know you can go back and get that kind of information every time you write a relevant story, because the precedent is established.
- Delay is the biggest problem with using the Act, but there are ways to speed things up. When an authority extends the 20-day period on a request to consider whether disclosure is in the public interest, it has to have a set of criteria by which it measures the public interest, so, as soon as you are notified of the extension, write and ask to be informed of the criteria by which it is deciding the question. 'Firstly, it shows that you are serious and you know your rights, and secondly, you'll often find that they'll mention criteria which aren't allowed under the Act, such as embarrassment to officials, which you can obviously then challenge.'
- The Information Commissioner has signed a memo of understanding with the Department of Constitutional Affairs stating that he would give requesters updates on the progress of their requests every 28 days, so it's worth writing and asking for those. The Commissioner has also said that he will make more effort to recognise that some types of information are perishable, so stress the importance of timeliness to your story.

Alternatives to FOI requests

The fact that a request for information made under the Freedom of Information Act is legally refused does not necessarily mean that the information is not available. In a case brought before the Supreme Court in 2014 (***Kennedy* v *Charity Commission***), the Supreme Court held that the Charity Commission had been correct in an interpretation of the FOI Act that meant the Act exempted it from releasing certain information to a journalist in response to an FOI request. However, the Court said that the Charities Act 2003 gave the Commission power to disclose that same information, and the principles of transparency and accountability contained in that Act meant there was a very strong argument that it should do so. If the Commisson decided not to, it would be possible to bring a case for judicial review of that decision, and the courts would be mindful of the importance of the press being able to cover issues of serious public interest. What this means is that where you are covering issues of public interest involving public bodies there may well be other ways to get the information you need, even if a FOI request cannot succeed.

ENVIRONMENTAL INFORMATION

As we saw earlier, information about the environment is covered by one of the FOI Act exemptions, but this does not mean it is inaccessible. The reason for the exemption is that access to this type of information is covered by a separate set of Regulations, which work in a similar way to the FOI Act, and in fact give greater access because they cover more organisations and contain fewer exemptions. The Environmental Information Regulations 2004 were passed to put into effect an EU Directive, and create a right of access to information about the environment held by public bodies as well as private companies which carry out a public function, such as water, electricity and gas suppliers. As with the FOI Act, the Regulations are enforced by the Information Commissioner.

Information covered

The Regulations apply to environmental information which is held in some recorded form, which includes anything written down, drawn, recorded on tape or kept in the form of a computer file. 'Environmental' is defined as covering:

- the 'state of the elements of the environment', including air, water, soil, landscape, natural sites, biological diversity and its components, including genetically modified components, and the interaction between these various elements;
- factors which are likely to affect the elements of the environment, such as noise, energy, radiation or waste;
- measures likely to affect the elements of the environment, including legislation, policies and plans, and cost–benefit analyses used to assess such measures;
- reports on the implementation of environmental legislation;
- the state of human health and safety, including contamination of the food chain and conditions of human life; and cultural sites and built structures as far as they are affected by the state of the elements of the environment.

Making a request

Requests for information can be made orally or in writing (including by email), although the Information Commissioner's Office recommends that a written note of oral requests is kept. They can be made to any employee of the relevant organisation but, as with FOI, most bodies covered by the Regulations have designated a specific person to deal with such queries. The Regulations impose a duty to assist people wanting information, so, if your request is too general, the organisation should come back to you and ask for it to be narrowed down.

Requests must be responded to as soon as possible, and within 20 days at most, unless they involve a particularly large amount of information or are very complex. In that case, the deadline can be extended by another 20 days. If the organisation does not hold the information you want, but knows or believes that another body does, it should either pass on your request, or tell you where it believes the information is held.

Exemptions

The Regulations allow organisations to reject requests for certain types of information, but only where doing so would be in the public interest; there are no absolute exemptions as in the FOI Act.

The categories are:

- personal information where disclosure would breach the Data Protection Act;
- 'manifestly unreasonable' requests (guidance from the Information Commissioners suggests this covers requests designed to disrupt the work of the authority, or which would be so expensive that the cost outweighs the public interest in disclosure);
- requests which are too general (but before rejecting such requests, the body must try to help the requester narrow them down);
- unfinished or incomplete information;
- internal communications;
- information which, if disclosed, would adversely affect:
  - international relations;
  - national security;
  - defence;
  - public safety;
  - the course of justice;
  - a person's ability to get a fair trial;
  - the ability of a public body to conduct a criminal or disciplinary enquiry;
  - intellectual property rights;
  - the confidentiality of proceedings of any public body, where confidentiality is provided by law;
  - confidentiality of commercial or industrial information;
  - the interests of the person supplying the information;
  - protection of the environment.

(The last four categories do not apply where the information sought concerns emissions.)

The public interest test works in the same way as for the FOI Act, and the Information Commissioner's guidance stresses that, even where information falls within the above categories, it can only be withheld if the public interest in keeping it secret outweighs the public interest in disclosure.

Challenging refusals

If a request is rejected, you can challenge this through the relevant body's appeal procedure. If the information is still not released, you can appeal to the Information Commissioner and the Information Tribunal, as for FOI requests.

Charges

Public authorities cannot charge for access to any public registers or list of environmental information, nor for allowing someone to inspect a particular record at a place of the authority's choice. For other requests (such as supplying a copy or summary of a particular record) they can make a reasonable charge. Charges should be published in advance.

KEY POINTS

The Freedom of Information Act

The act applies to all information held by public authorities.

It gives any person the right to:

- be told whether requested information exists; and
- be given that information.

Exemptions

There are two categories of exempted information:

- absolute exemptions – information covered can be withheld;
- qualified exemptions – information can be withheld if it is in the public interest to do so.

Challenging refusals

There are four ways to challenge refused requests:

- the authority's own procedure;
- the Information Commissioner;
- the Information Tribunal;
- judicial review.

Environmental information

The Environmental Information Regulations provide a right of access to environmental information held by public bodies and private companies carrying out public functions.

Types of information

'Environmental information' includes information on:

- the state of air, water, soil, landscape and biological diversity;
- noise, energy, radiation and waste;
- legislation and policies which affect the environment;

- human health and safety;
- cultural sites and buildings as affected by the state of the environment.

Exemptions

Sixteen classes of information can be withheld if doing so would be in the public interest.

Challenging refusals

Routes for challenge are the same as for FOI requests.

TEST YOUR KNOWLEDGE

1 How long does a public body have to deal with an FOI request?

2 You apply to your local council for details of the price paid for the rather spectacular floral displays it has placed outside the town hall. Your request is refused, on the grounds that the material is covered by a qualified exemption. Can you challenge the refusal and, if so, how?

3 You ask your local hospital for details of expenses claimed by senior managers over the past year. Which of these reasons is grounds under the Act for refusing a request for information?

(a) The information cannot be revealed because the officials concerned regard their expenses as private.

(b) Putting together the information would cost £200, and the public body believes this is not a good use of its budget.

(c) The hospital considers that all expenses claimed are fair and reasonable, and chooses to make no comment on your story.

(d) The public would not understand the nature of the expenses claimed, and might be misled.

(e) The hospital will not release the figures unless you agree to include corresponding figures from other hospitals, so as to put the sums in context.

4 Which bodies are covered by the Environmental Information Regulations 2004?

5 Your local authority has recently switched to a new company for collecting waste in the area, after going through a process of tendering. You apply to see the contract between them, but the council says it is exempt from the Environmental Information Regulations because disclosure would adversely affect commercial confidentiality. Can you challenge the refusal and, if so, how?

WWW ONLINE RESOURCES

The Freedom of Information Act 2000 can be read at:
www.legislation.gov.uk/ukpga/2000/36/contents

Schedule 1 of the Act, incorporating regular updates, can be found at:
www.legislation.gov.uk/ukpga/2000/36/schedule/1

The Office of the Information Commissioner has a website at:
www.ico.org.uk

The Campaign for Freedom of Information website includes a user guide to the Act, and over 500 examples of press stories based on disclosures made under it:
www.cfoi.org.uk

Chapter 30 Writing about business

If you are one of the hundreds of journalists who work for trade magazines, you will spend most of your time writing about businesses, as will many newspaper journalists. In this area the law offers both opportunities and problems. On the plus side, the law obliges companies to make public a considerable amount of information about themselves, and knowing your way around these sources is an essential tool for a business journalist. On the minus side, companies, especially big ones, tend to employ expensive lawyers, which means they are often prone to threaten legal action if they do not like something you write. Obviously that does not mean you should never write anything that might upset a company, but you do need to be absolutely certain of your legal ground. In addition to this chapter, therefore, business reporters need to make sure they are very familiar with the law on defamation (covered in Chapters 15 and 16) and breach of confidence (in Chapter 18).

This chapter also covers the various types of insolvency proceedings. As these usually (though not always) involve the failure of a company, they are an area where inaccurate reports can cause real problems, so a business reporter needs to have a good understanding of the types of proceeding and their implications.

THE LAW ON BUSINESS INFORMATION

English law recognises several different types of business, and the type of information which must legally be made available to the public varies with each type of business.

Limited companies (also known as incorporated firms) are a legal concept, which is used as a way of giving what is called 'legal personality' to a group of people who are running a business together. Having legal personality means that an organisation has a legal existence which is separate from the people who make it up, and can make contracts, own property, and sue or be sued in its own name.

In addition, a limited company has what is called limited liability, which essentially means that any debts run up by the company are legally the responsibility of the company, and not of the individuals who run or own the company. The practical result of this is that, if the company fails, the individuals who own the company can only lose the amount of money they have invested in the company; they cannot be sued personally or have any of their own assets taken, even if the company does not have enough money to pay its debts. New limited companies are formed by registering with the Companies' Registrar (usually known as Companies House, this is not, as often believed, a specific building, but an agency of the Department of Trade and Industry which has centres in London and Cardiff). In exchange for the benefits of limited liability, they have to submit to strict rules about the way they are set up and operated, including disclosing certain information for public inspection. The idea behind making this information available is that it allows the public to make informed decisions about companies that they may wish to invest in or do business with (see below), but it can also be very helpful to journalists.

Limited companies can be private or public, the main difference being that public companies can raise money by selling shares in the company to the public in general. A company which has 'plc' after its name is a public company.

Sole traders are the simplest type of business, and consist of one person in business by themselves. There are no legal requirements for setting up as a sole trader, beyond the fact that the sole trader must register as self-employed with Revenue & Customs so that they can be properly taxed. A sole trader has what is called unlimited liability, which means that any debts incurred in the course of trading are the sole trader's personal responsibility. If they go out of business owing money, their creditors may have a claim on the sole trader's assets and personal possessions, just as they would if the debts had been run up for personal purposes. Sole traders are not required to publish any information about their business, so the only real way to get useful information, other than from the sole trader themselves, is from clients or suppliers.

Partnerships work in a similar way to sole trading, but involve two or more people in business together. Like sole traders, they can simply set up and trade, without needing to register with Companies House, but the Business Names Act 1985 requires that the names of partners must be open to public inspection at the partnership's main place of business. In most cases partners will also draw up a legal document called a Partnership Agreement, which details who owns what and who does what, but this is not required to be open to public inspection. In some cases, both or all the partners share the work of the partnership, but it is also possible to have sleeping partners, whose role is to put money into the business, rather than to take part in the work it does. Partners usually have unlimited liability, and each one of them is personally liable for all the debts of the partnership.

Limited liability partnerships are a relatively new form of business, created in the Limited Liability Act 2000. They allow partners to benefit from limited liability, very much as the directors of limited companies do, and are subject to many of the same formalities as limited companies regarding setting up and operating. The main difference is that the partners have more freedom to decide (and change) their rights and responsibilities within the partnership than directors of a limited company do.

INFORMATION ON LIMITED COMPANIES

As mentioned above, limited companies are subject to a number of legal provisions covering the way they operate, many of which require them to make particular types of information available to the public and/or shareholders.

Law in practice Company information

The information which, by law, limited companies have to make available can be a useful source of stories, or at least leads, for journalists who write about business and business people. The information will be kept either at the relevant company's registered office or by Companies House. Information held by Companies House can be accessed online (though there is a small charge for all but the most basic information about a company), as well as at its centres in London and Cardiff (see *Online resources* at the end of this chapter).

Initial documentation

When a new limited company is set up, it must register with Companies House and lodge four documents: the Memorandum of Association, the Articles of Association, Form 10 and Form 12. These are as follows:

- The Memorandum of Association details the company name, the initial shareholders, whether the registered office is in England, Wales or Scotland, and the purpose of the company (this need not be at all precise; Companies House advises that vague wording such as 'to carry on business as a general commercial company' is adequate).
- The Articles of Association state how the company will be run, including the respective powers of the directors, managing director and shareholders, the arrangements for meetings between shareholders and the board, and the rules on selling shares in the company. (In some firms, for example, there may be a rule that shares can only be sold with the consent of the rest of the board, and/or that members of the board get first refusal on shares to be sold; in this way, the directors can keep control of the ownership of the company.) Companies can draw up their own Articles or simply elect to state that they will adopt a model system devised by Companies House.
- Form 10 gives details of the first director(s), the company secretary and the intended address of the registered office. As well as their names and office addresses, the company's directors must give their date of birth, occupation and details of other directorships they have held within the past five years.
- Form 12 is a statement that the directors have complied with all the legal formalities.

Ownership and finance

Under the Companies Act 1985, every shareholder's interest must be registered, and this register is open to public inspection at the company's registered office. The Companies Act 2006 provides that anyone wanting to inspect a company's register must declare his or her purpose for doing so, and the company can apply to a court for an order to prevent the inspection if it is for an 'improper purpose'. This provision is intended for use against, for example, animal rights activists seeking to harass shareholders of firms involved in animal experimentation; during Parliamentary debate the Government said it was not intended to prevent legitimate investigative journalism.

Company directors have to register all the shares they hold in their company, and the prices paid when they are bought or sold. This includes holdings through nominees, or by directors' spouses or children, or in a parent or subsidiary company. They also have to register any increase or decrease in their holdings. The company must inform one of the Regulated Information Services, which are firms approved by the FSA for making such information public, and are listed on the FSA website (see *Online resources* at the end of this chapter).

Information on directors

In addition to information on their holdings in a company, directors have to submit certain other details to public and/or shareholder scrutiny. Copies of a director's contract of service with the company have to be made available to shareholders, and companies quoted on the London Stock Exchange must, under its rules, make service contracts available for public inspection at their registered offices, and for at least 15 minutes before its Annual General Meeting.

The documentation must include details of the directors' salaries and other remuneration, any provisions for early retirement, and any compensation to be paid for ending directors' contracts. The chairman's earnings also have to be stated in the annual accounts.

If a director has a financial interest in contracts their company has made, or if the company has made a loan or any other credit transaction to a director, that must be disclosed in the company's annual accounts. Companies also have to list any directorships which their directors hold in other companies, or have held over the past five years. This information must be available to public inspection.

These requirements can, with some clever digging, yield some very interesting stories. Robertson and Nicol cite the examples of one service contract which revealed that a particular director was required to take his wife along on every overseas trip, and a set of accounts which disclosed that a company had loaned a director £140,000 to buy a £200,000 house, allowing him to pay just £23 a week to live there. Because directors' home addresses also had to be disclosed at the time, a *New Statesman* journalist was able not just to report the story but also to get a photo of the rather luxurious residence.

A new provision in the Companies Act 2006, which came into force in October 2009, provides that directors no longer need to disclose their home addresses. However, the 5 million addresses already on the register will not be removed.

Law in practice **Ownership of buildings**

Sometimes it can be useful to find out whether a business, or one of its directors, owns a particular building or piece of land. For the vast majority of buildings and land in the UK, this information has to be registered with the Land Registry when land is bought or sold, and then becomes publicly available (only land which has not changed hands since 1925 is not included in the Register). The information held includes the price paid, and details of what are called 'restrictive covenants' on the property, which may limit what can be done there. These details can be accessed via the Land Registry website (see *Online resources* at the end of this chapter), on payment of a small fee. The usual way to search is by looking up individual properties. If you want to find out all the property that a company owns, there is also an index which can be searched this way, but only at the discretion of the registrar. It is not usually possible to search for property owned by an individual in this way.

Accounts

Limited companies have to prepare annual accounts, which are sent to Companies House and can be inspected by the public. All but the smallest companies must have their accounts checked by auditors, whose job is to verify, for the benefit of shareholders, that the picture painted in the accounts is true.

Companies planning to issue shares to the public also have to make available information documenting their recent performance, and expectations for the future.

Annual general meetings

All public limited companies must hold an Annual General Meeting (AGM) of their members (some private companies also do so, but do not have to). In most cases, annual general meetings are fairly bland, stage-managed events, with little important discussion, but, in situations where it is known there are problems with a company, they can be much more useful to journalists. The meetings include a vote on the directors' remuneration, which shareholders may use to show their displeasure at the company's performance: in 2002, for example, the Prudential was forced to backtrack on its planned executive pay scheme after shareholders refused to support it.

AGMs must also provide an opportunity for shareholders to question directors, and this too can provide some useful copy. As well as 'ordinary' shareholders showing their displeasure at the way a company is performing, question-and-answer sessions may feature representatives of pressure groups, who can gain access to the meeting by buying just one share.

Companies are not obliged to admit the press to AGMs, though many do. If press access is denied, buying one share in the company turns you into a shareholder with a right to attend; alternatively, a shareholder can nominate someone to attend in their place (known as a proxy), and, if shareholders want publicity for something they feel is going wrong at the company, you may be able to get one to let you attend as their proxy. AGMs of public (but not private) companies are covered by qualified privilege under the Defamation Act 1996 (see p. 259), as is publication of fair and accurate extracts from any document that the board of the public company makes available to its members, or any document circulated to the members of a public company which concerns the appointment, resignation, retirement or dismissal of the company's directors. The events at an AGM of a public company will usually be a matter of public interest, so the defence of fair comment may also apply.

What the codes say **Financial journalism**

The Editors' Code of Practice used by IPSO contains three provisions for journalists writing about business:

- Journalists who receive financial information before it is generally published must not use it for their own profit, nor pass it to others.
- Journalists must not write about shares or securities which they know they or their close families have a significant financial interest in, without disclosing the interest to their editor or financial editor.
- Journalists must not buy or sell shares or securities which they have recently written about or intend to write about in the near future.

INSOLVENCY PROCEEDINGS

The idea of insolvency proceedings is that a person or company who cannot pay their debts can have their assets fairly shared among their creditors and, after a period, have any remaining debts cancelled. This can be done voluntarily or at the request of a creditor. An individual who becomes insolvent is described as going bankrupt, while for companies or partnerships the term used is going into liquidation. There is also a way of winding up a company which occurs for reasons other than being unable to pay debts (and often involves no fault or failure), which is called members voluntary liquidation (see below).

Bankruptcy

Bankruptcy proceedings begin with the filing of a petition for a bankruptcy order. This can be done by the person who is going bankrupt (known as the debtor), or one of the people or companies they owe money to (known as creditors), either at the High Court in London or the county court nearest where the debtor works or lives. The debtor must owe at least £750 in unsecured debts. A petition from a creditor can be refused if the debtor has already made an offer and it has been unreasonably refused.

Where a debtor has assets worth over £2,000, and debts of £20,000 or less, the district judge can make an interim bankruptcy order and refer the case to a licenced insolvency practitioner, who will try to make voluntary payment agreements with the creditors, so that the debtor can avoid bankruptcy. This is called an individual voluntary arrangement.

If the bankruptcy order goes ahead, the person is legally bankrupt from the time the order is made. Legal control of all the debtor's property is then taken over by the Official Receiver (an officer of the court) or a licensed insolvency practitioner (the latter being most likely in cases where there is a good chance of the creditors getting a large proportion of what they are owed). This person is known as the trustee in bankruptcy. Notice of the bankruptcy is advertised in the *London Gazette* and in a local or national newspaper (sometimes both).

The official then examines the debtor's assets and liabilities, which must be laid out in a statement within 21 days. A creditors' meeting may then be held to inform creditors of the full situation. The Official Receiver can allow journalists into a creditors meeting, but is not obliged to do so.

If the debtor does not cooperate fully with the Official Receiver, a public examination in bankruptcy (often referred to as the PE or bankruptcy court) can be held, which takes place before a district judge. It can also be held at the request of at least 50 per cent of the creditors. Anyone, including the press, may attend, and fair and accurate reports of a public examination are protected by absolute privilege.

In 2008, former pop star Kerry Katona tried to have the press banned from her bankruptcy hearing, but failed. Her lawyer argued that she was having personal problems, that further press attention would be detrimental to her health, and that the media interest was 'purely gossip related'. The Deputy Registrar refused to ban the press, saying that there was no medical evidence to suggest a risk to Ms Katona's health.

The public examination is designed to satisfy the court that it has full information on the debtor's financial situation, and to clarify why they have been unable to pay their debts, including an assessment of whether the situation involves any criminal offence. It also considers whether any assets of the debtor which have been transferred to someone else should be recovered; any transaction from the past two years can be declared void, unless it is a standard trading transaction. This period can be extended to 10 years, if it can be proved that transfers were made in order to deprive creditors of money.

The information divulged will usually include:

- the debtor's liabilities (debts);
- the debtor's assets;
- whether there are secured creditors (often banks or building societies, these will be creditors who loaned money against security, for example via a mortgage).

From this you can build up a picture of the scale of the bankruptcy (i.e. how much of the money will not be paid back), who will be affected by it and to what degree. After the costs of bankruptcy are accounted for, secured creditors are generally the first to be paid, since they have the right to be paid from the sale of the property used as security. Assuming there is some money left, the group with next claim on it are what are called 'preferential creditors'. This group now mostly comprises employees of the bankrupt person. Unsecured creditors are only paid if there is money left over after these two groups have been paid.

What it means to be bankrupt

An individual going through the bankruptcy process must declare all assets to the Official Receiver, right down to their household goods and clothes. The Official Receiver then decides what they can keep – usually just clothes and household necessities, and equipment or vehicles needed for work. Everything else that the bankrupt owned comes under the legal control of the Official Receiver and can be sold to pay the creditors. If the bankrupt still has an income, deductions can be made from it, though they must be left with enough to meet their family's normal domestic needs.

A person who is bankrupt must disclose this fact if applying for a bank account or credit of more than £500; not doing so is a criminal offence. The bankrupt can still trade as a self-employed person, but is not allowed to trade under a different name from that which they were made bankrupt under, unless they tell everyone they do business with that this is the case. Bankrupts are barred from acting as company directors, and from some professions, but are no longer automatically banned from holding public offices such as MP, local councillor or magistrate.

The names of people who are currently bankrupt are held on a register which is open to the public (see *Online resources* at the end of this chapter).

How does bankruptcy end?

Bankruptcy is usually imposed for a year, after which the bankrupt is automatically discharged. This releases bankrupts from their former debts (except any arising from fraud), and the restrictions of bankruptcy. It can happen earlier if the Official Receiver finishes his investigations earlier and files a notice with the court. If the debts and bankruptcy costs are paid before the date of discharge, the bankruptcy can be lifted immediately. The discharge can be postponed if the Official Receiver considers that the person has not carried out their duties under the bankruptcy order.

If, during his enquiries, the Official Receiver concludes that the individual has been dishonest before or during the bankruptcy, or is otherwise to blame for their situation, the Official Receiver can apply to the court for a Bankruptcy Restrictions Order, which keeps the individual under the bankruptcy restrictions for a longer than usual period, which can be up to 15 years. Alternatively the individual can agree to such restrictions by giving a bankruptcy restrictions undertaking, which means the matter does not have to go before the court.

Liquidation proceedings

Liquidation means the closure of a company. It can take place because the company cannot meet its debts, but this is not always the case, so it is important to know the difference between the following three types of liquidation:

Members voluntary liquidation: This takes place when the directors of a solvent company decide to close it down. An example might be where the directors of a small family firm are all retiring. A liquidator is appointed, but creditors do not have to be notified. This procedure can only be used where the company is able to pay its debts within 12 months; if the liquidator finds this not to be the case, the procedure becomes a creditors voluntary liquidation.

Creditors voluntary liquidation: Despite the name, this procedure is initiated by the directors of a company, rather than the creditors, because the company cannot meet its debts or its assets are worth less than its liabilities. The procedure can only go forward if company shareholders with 75 per cent of the shares agree to it. They appoint a liquidator, who will then meet the creditors to examine why the situation has arisen and assess the assets and liabilities. Only after these meetings have been held can the company be said to be in liquidation.

Compulsory liquidation: In this case, the liquidation is initiated by a creditor, who petitions the court to wind up the debtor company on the grounds that it cannot meet its debts (technically, compulsory liquidation can also arise because a company has failed to file its statutory report, or hold its statutory set-up meeting, has suspended or not even started doing business, or does not have the number of members required by law; however, most cases are concerned with insolvency). If the court grants a winding-up order, the Official Receiver then takes over the company, closes it down, and supervises the distribution of assets to the creditors.

OTHER PROCEEDINGS FOR COMPANIES IN TROUBLE

There are other routes which a company facing insolvency may take, and if you write about businesses, it is essential to know the difference between them.

Administration: This process is used as an alternative to liquidation, where either the directors of a failing company or its creditors believe it can either continue as a going concern, or be sold for more than would be raised from going into receivership. Either the company directors, or a creditor, can apply to the court for an administration order.

If the court is satisfied that the business cannot pay its debts (or is likely to become unable to), an insolvency practitioner is appointed as administrator, either to sell the company or put into effect a rescue plan. The effect is to give the business a breathing space: while the company is in administration, the creditors cannot take legal action to wind up the company or appoint a receiver. The process is known as being 'in administration'.

Receivership: The process of administrative receivership (usually known as being 'in receivership') is not a court process, and takes place when a major creditor (usually a bank) appoints an insolvency practitioner as receiver, to recover money owed to it. The receiver does not make payments to unsecured creditors.

Voluntary agreements: A company in trouble may be able to avoid liquidation by applying to the court to make a corporate voluntary arrangement. If the court agrees, it will make an interim order, which has the effect of suspending all proceedings by creditors against the company. A liquidator prepares a proposal for repayment, which is put to the creditors; if 75 per cent of them (calculated by the value of their debts) agree to it, the agreement is binding on all other creditors who know about it. If the creditors do not agree, the interim order lapses and the creditors can take legal proceedings.

Law in practice Defamation and insolvency

Clearly, neither businesses nor individuals take kindly to being reported as being in financial difficulties, so reporting insolvency can easily land you in trouble with the libel lawyers if you are not careful. These are some of the traps to watch out for:

- Saying that someone is bankrupt when they are not is defamatory. You should never describe someone as bankrupt until a bankruptcy order has been made, even if one has been filed. Unless the debtor has themselves filed for bankruptcy, it is unwise to report that an order has been applied for at all; if it is refused (e.g. if the creditor has rejected an offer from the debtor which the court feels was reasonable), the debtor may sue on the basis that you were implying they were bankrupt.
- A public examination in bankruptcy is a court proceeding which is covered by absolute privilege. This is not, however, the case with a creditors meeting, so, if any possibly defamatory allegations are made at such a meeting (as they often will be when angry creditors are involved), you need to be sure that you are covered by another defence, such as justification, if you report them.
- The distinction between members voluntary liquidation and creditors voluntary liquidation is very important. A members voluntary liquidation does not generally involve any fault or failure on the part of a company, so if you describe a firm going through this process using the wrong term, you are saying (falsely) that it cannot pay its debts, which is obviously defamatory.
- Technically, a company going into administration reflects less badly on its management than going into liquidation, since there is still some value left in it. Whether this distinction would be enough to found a libel action if you used the wrong term is unclear, but it is safest (and obviously better practice) to make sure you clarify which type of proceedings is involved before you report a story. Certainly the terms are not, as some reporters assume, interchangeable.

KEY POINTS

The law on business information

There are four main types of business under English law, each covered by different rules on the information they must publish:

- limited companies;
- sole traders;
- partnerships;
- limited liability partnerships.

Information on limited companies

Limited companies have a legal duty to make public:

- documentation created when a company is started;
- details of shareholders;
- information about directors, including their remuneration package;
- annual accounts.

Insolvency proceedings

Insolvency proceedings (except for members voluntary liquidation) occur when an individual or company cannot pay their debts.

- bankruptcy applies to individuals;
- liquidation applies to companies.

Other proceedings for companies in trouble

There are three other routes:

- administration, where a failing company may still have a future as a business;
- receivership, where a major creditor appoints an insolvency practitioner to recover money owed to it;
- voluntary agreements, where court proceedings are suspended while a failing company and its creditors try to make their own agreement regarding payment.

TEST YOUR KNOWLEDGE

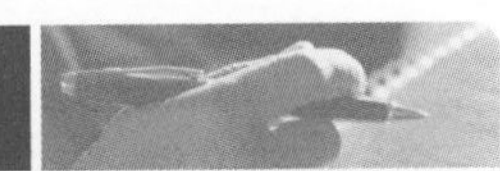

1 What are the four main types of company recognised in English law?

2 You are writing about a limited company, and want to find out if its directors have been linked to any other companies. What information is publicly available and where would you find it?

3 You want to attend the Annual General Meeting of a public company in the industry you write about, but you are told that the press is not invited. What can you do?

4 What is the difference between bankruptcy and insolvency?

5 What is a Bankruptcy Restrictions Order?

6 A local company has gone into members voluntary liquidation. Which of these sentences is it safe to use when writing the story?

(a) Anderson Brothers have gone into members voluntary liquidation.

(b) Anderson Brothers have gone bust.

(c) Anderson Brothers have gone into liquidation.

(d) Anderson Brothers have gone into compulsory liquidation.

(e) Anderson Brothers have gone into receivership.

7 You suspect that a local businessman may have been disqualified from holding directorships. How can you check?

ONLINE RESOURCES

Companies House has a website where you can access information on limited companies:
www.companieshouse.gov.uk

The Land Registry website is at:
www.gov.uk/government/organisations/land-registry

The Insolvency Service website is at:
https://www.gov.uk/government/organisations/insolvency-service

RACE, RELIGION AND PUBLIC ORDER

This section covers legal restrictions on publishing material which, broadly speaking, has the potential to stir up hatred, extreme offence or disorder. It includes details of the Public Order Act, which makes it an offence to publish certain types of material which could stir up racial hatred, and the newer legislation against stirring up religious hatred.

Chapter 31 Race and religion

Legislation against stirring up racial hatred has existed for several decades, and, though its main target is those who publish words (or pictures) with the intention of causing racial hatred, the wording of the legislation also makes it possible for journalists reporting such words to be guilty of an offence, which is why you need to know about it. Until 2006, similar protection was not available for religious groups which were not also racially defined (so Jews and Sikhs, for example, were covered by the legislation, but Muslims, Catholics and Buddhists were not).

The previous government was keen to introduce new legislation in this area, and, after a long parliamentary struggle, passed the Racial and Religious Hatred Act 2006. However, widespread opposition to the legislation meant the government's initial Bill was very much watered down in the Lords, and the resulting Act does not offer the same degree of protection as that regarding racial hatred. Until 2008, the common law offence of blasphemy made it a criminal offence to attack the beliefs of the Church of England. This law was abolished under the Criminal Justice and Immigration Act 2008.

INCITEMENT TO RACIAL HATRED

The law on inciting racial hatred is contained in the Public Order Act 1986. This states that it is an offence to do any of the following with the intention of stirring up racial hatred, or in circumstances where racial hatred is likely to be stirred up:

- use threatening, abusive or insulting language or display abusive or insulting written material;
- publish or distribute abusive or insulting written material, perform plays, distribute or present visual images or sounds, or produce a programme containing abusive or insulting written material;
- possess written material or recordings of images or sounds that are threatening, abusive or insulting, with a view to displaying or publishing them (this provision does not make it an offence to receive unsolicited racist material, or keep it, for example as background research, as long as you do not plan to publish it).

The Public Order Act 1986 was amended by s164 of the Broadcasting Act 1990, so that the offence can also be committed by broadcasting a TV or radio programme. The broadcaster, the programme maker and the person shown or heard using the threatening, abusive or insulting language can all be prosecuted.

Racial hatred

Section 17 of the Public Order Act 1986 defines 'racial hatred' as 'hatred against a group of citizens in Great Britain defined by reference to colour, race, nationality (including citizenship) or ethnic or national origins'.

Intention and circumstances

The offence can be committed with two different states of mind:

- where the defendant deliberately stirs up racial hatred;
- where the defendant does not have this intention, but does any of the prohibited acts in circumstances where racial hatred is likely to be stirred up.

The latter provision means that a publication could potentially be guilty of the offence if it reports, for example, inflammatory speeches given or leaflets issued by a politician with racist views. It was also made clear, during the process of the Bill that became the Act, that publishing readers' letters which use threatening, abusive or insulting words may be an offence. The Home Office stated that if such letters were published, merely including other letters putting the opposing view, or adding an editorial comment to that effect, would not necessarily be enough to avoid committing the offence. However, if a court was called upon to decide such a case, it would (the Home Office said) look at the whole context of the publication and not just the offending words in isolation.

This somewhat inconclusive position has the potential to make it difficult for the media to examine the issue of racism, since it is impossible to expose racist statements to public criticism if you cannot repeat them or show them being made. However, some support for the media's position has come from a decision of the European Court of Human Rights, in ***Jersild* v *Denmark*** (1995). The case was brought by Danish broadcasters, who had produced a documentary discussing the issue of growing racial hatred among the country's young people. The programme included interviews with racists, in which they put forward their views. The broadcasters were not seeking to promote those views, only to report on the fact that they seemed to be held by an increasing number of young people, but they were prosecuted and convicted under Denmark's anti-racism laws (as were the people interviewed). They brought an action against the Danish Government on the grounds that their right to freedom of expression had been breached, and the Government argued that, within the programme, they should have included opposing views, or in some other way refuted the statements made. The Court of Human Rights disagreed. It said that the interviewees were not protected by Article 10 because of the nature of the statements they made, and so their convictions were not a breach of the right to freedom of expression. However, the broadcasters were merely showing the statements in the context of a serious investigation into an important issue, and to convict them for doing this was a serious violation of Article 10.

This suggests that if a TV programme or press report shows or repeats words which would be caught by the Act, as part of a serious examination of a subject of public interest, prosecuting the media for incitement to racial hatred would be a breach of Article 10.

In 2004, the Crown Prosecution Service (CPS) announced it would not be prosecuting the broadcaster Robert Kilroy Silk over an article in which he criticised Arab states. The CPS said that the offence of incitement to racial hatred had not been committed, because there was no evidence that Mr Kilroy Silk intended to stir up racial hatred against Arabs; his purpose had been to criticise the regimes in particular countries. Nor were the words 'likely' to stir up racial hatred. The CPS said that in this context, 'likely' meant more than 'liable to'; it had to be shown that the probable result of the words would be to create extreme dislike of a racial group, to such an extent that public order could be affected. As the article had previously been published a year earlier without complaint, it did not appear likely that the second publication would have this effect.

Threatening, abusive or insulting

These words carry their ordinary, everyday meaning; there is no special definition and in each case, it is for the court to decide whether the words used were threatening, abusive or insulting. However, decided cases have made it clear that to justify a conviction, the words need to be more than merely rude or unpleasant.

In 2006, Mizanur Rahman was convicted of stirring up racial hatred for carrying placards calling for non-Muslims to be 'annihilated' and 'beheaded', during a demonstration about the publication in Denmark of cartoons of the prophet Mohammed.

Law in practice Reporting racist remarks

When reporting inflammatory racist remarks made by someone, it will often be safer to paraphrase them, rather than quoting directly, so that the words you publish are not themselves 'threatening, abusive or insulting'.

Defences

Section 19(2) of the Public Order Act 1986 provides a defence where the person accused of the offence is not shown to have intended to stir up racial hatred, and was unaware and did not suspect or have reason to suspect, that the material concerned was threatening, abusive or insulting.

In addition, the Act does not apply to words used in a fair, accurate and contemporaneous report of public proceedings in a court or tribunal, or fair and accurate reports of proceedings in Parliament.

Prosecutions

Prosecutions can only be brought with the consent of the Attorney-General. In 1987, the Attorney-General said that, if asked to consider a prosecution concerning the media, he would take into account the type of publication and its circulation and potential readership, and any special circumstances which existed at the time and might have influence on the effect of the published material.

All the offences mentioned above can result in a sentence of up to two years' imprisonment and/or a fine.

RELIGIOUS HATRED

The Racial and Religious Hatred Act 2006 makes it an offence to do any of the following with the intention of stirring up religious hatred:

- use threatening words or behaviour, or display any threatening material;
- publish or distribute written material which is threatening to the public or a section of the public;

- distribute, show or play a recording of sounds or images which are threatening;
- possess written material or recordings which are threatening, with a view to it being shown, published, displayed, distributed, played or included in a programme service (defined in the Broadcasting Act 1990 as any television or radio service).

Note that the words must be threatening; in contrast to the law on racial hatred, insulting or abusive words are not enough. In addition, the acts must be committed 'with the intention of stirring up religious hatred', rather than, as with racial hatred, in circumstances where it is likely to be stirred up; this gives better protection to responsible media reports of views held by others.

The 2006 Act defines religious hatred as 'hatred against a group of persons defined by religious belief or lack of religious belief'. This is potentially a very wide definition, since 'religious belief' would appear to extend further than actual membership of a recognised religion.

Defences

The 2006 Act provides a potentially wide defence to protect freedom of expression, stating that:

> Nothing in this Part shall be read or given effect in a way which prohibits or restricts discussion, criticism or expressions of antipathy, dislike, ridicule, insult or abuse of particular religions or the beliefs or practices of their adherents, or of any other belief system or the beliefs or practices of its adherents, or proselytising or urging adherents of a different religion or belief system to cease practising their religion or belief system.

This was added as a response to critics of the Bill, who argued that the planned legislation was an unjustified interference with freedom of speech, and would prevent everything from reasoned discussion of religious issues to jokes about religion.

The 2006 Act does not apply to words used in a fair, accurate and contemporaneous report of public proceedings in a court or tribunal, or fair and accurate reports of proceedings in Parliament.

Investigation and prosecutions

Prosecutions can only be brought with the consent of the Attorney-General. A successful prosecution carries a sentence of up to seven years in prison and/or a fine.

What the codes say Race and religion

The Editors' Code of Practice used by IPSO provides that:

- the press must avoid prejudicial or pejorative reference to an individual's race, colour or religion;
- details of an individual's race, colour or religion should not be given unless genuinely relevant to the story.

The Ofcom Broadcasting Code states that:

- the views of people who belong to a particular religion must not be subject to abusive treatment.

KEY POINTS

Racial hatred

It is an offence to use, possess, distribute or publish threatening, abusive or insulting words, sounds of pictures with the intention of stirring up racial hatred, or in circumstances where racial hatred is likely to be stirred up.

There is a defence for anyone who did not intend to stir up racial hatred, and had no reason to suspect the relevant material was abusive, threatening or insulting.

Religious hatred

It is an offence to use, publish, show or display material which is threatening, with the intention of stirring up religious hatred. The offence is not supposed to restrict criticism or discussion of religion.

A defence protects criticism which is not threatening.

Exceptions

Neither offence applies to fair, accurate and (for court reports) contemporaneous court or Parliamentary reports.

Investigation and prosecution

Both offences carry search powers for the police; neither can be prosecuted without the Attorney-General's consent.

TEST YOUR KNOWLEDGE

1 To which of these groups does the law on inciting racial hatred apply:
 (a) Black people
 (b) Asians
 (c) Italians
 (d) Jews
 (e) Catholics
 (f) Welsh people?

2 You attend a public meeting in which your local MP makes a speech, which is extremely abusive about Asian people in the area. Can you report what he says?

3 The same MP repeats his allegations in Parliament. Can you report them?

4 You are attending a court case in which the accused is charged with a racially motivated attack. While being cross-examined, he launches into a tirade of racist language and threats against the family of his victim. Can you report this?

5 How is 'religious hatred' defined in the Racial and Religious Hatred Act 2006?

ONLINE RESOURCES

The Racial and Religious Hatred Act 2006 can be read at:
www.legislation.gov.uk/ukpga/2006/1/contents

Jersild v *Denmark* can be read at:
www.worldlii.org/eu/cases/ECHR/1994/33.html

PHOTOGRAPHY

This section deals with the law as it applies to photographers and photo-journalists. As we saw earlier, photos can give rise to claims in defamation, privacy and breach of copyright, but there are also specific laws about when and where photographs can be taken, which are covered in this section.

Photography

Much of the law already explained in this book applies to photographers as well as those who write the words that go with their pictures. However, there are some restrictions which apply specifically to photographers and photo-journalists, and they are the subject of this chapter. Photographers should also make sure they are familiar with the law on harassment (Chapter 20); defamation (Chapter 15); and the Data Protection Act (Chapter 22).

PRIVATE PROPERTY

Being on someone else's land without their permission, or refusing to leave when asked to, is trespass (see Chapter 20). Trespass is also committed by any 'interference' with land, which could include, for example, climbing onto a fence to get a view into someone's garden, even if no damage is done. There is no law against standing outside a private place and taking photographs, unless the pictures taken stray into the area of confidentiality (see below).

If you are on someone's land (which includes being in their house, shop or office) with their permission, there is no general law against taking photographs, but the person in control of the land (usually the owner or tenant) can impose conditions on what you will be allowed to do there. This means that they have the right to ban the taking of photographs, and if you ignore this and take them, you then commit trespass, because you are acting outside your permission to be on the land.

This rule applies even in private places which are open to the general public (such as stately homes or shops). Even if there is no general ban on taking photographs on the property which applies to everyone, the land owner or tenant can require an individual photographer to stop taking pictures, and/or order them to leave. They can also use reasonable force if a trespasser refuses to leave; however, this would not permit, for example, physically attacking a photographer. In some cases, a landowner or tenant (or more often, employees such as security guards) may demand that film is handed over, but they have no legal right which backs up such a demand. Neither film nor cameras can be legally confiscated, or damaged, even if the photographer is trespassing.

There are remedies which can be ordered against a person who is liable for trespass (see Chapter 20). It is theoretically possible that a court could issue an injunction preventing publication of photographs obtained by trespassing, but in practice this is unlikely.

Photographs taken in a private place may, however, be caught by the law of confidentiality. The law on this issue is currently in a slightly uncertain state (see Chapter 18), but in cases such as ***Campbell* v *MGN*** (2004) (see p. 304), it was stated that the question to be asked was whether the person photographed had 'a reasonable expectation of privacy'. The same would apply if the person taking the photograph was outside the private place, but the subject of the photograph was in the private place.

PUBLIC PLACES

There is no general law that prevents the press (or anyone else) from taking photographs in a public place. However, there have been concerns about cases where police officers have tried to prevent photographers and photo-journalists from taking pictures in situations where it is perfectly legal to do so. In response to this problem, the Association of Chief Police Officers have issued guidelines explaining how the police should deal with press photographers, and, in 2007, these guidelines were adopted by all UK police forces. They state that:

- Members of the media do not need a permit to take photographs or film in public places.
- The press have a duty to report on many of the incidents that the police deal with, and the police should help them do this duty where it does not conflict with their own.
- Where cordons have to be put in place, it is good practice to give the media a good vantage place from which to operate.
- The police have no legal or moral responsibility to restrict or prevent the media from taking photographs or filming incidents.
- Once images are recorded, the police have no power to delete or confiscate them without a court order, even if they may contain damaging or useful evidence.
- It is for editors to decide what is published or broadcast, not the police.
- If someone who is distressed or bereaved asks the police to intervene to prevent the press photographing or filming them, the police can pass on the request, but cannot force the press to stop filming or photographing.
- It is not usually possible to give journalists access to the scene of an incident during the early stages of an investigation, because of the demands of evidence gathering, but requests for access should be passed to the Senior Investigating Officer, who should allow access as soon as practicable.

The guidelines suggest that if journalists feel they are being prevented from doing their job by the police, they should show the guidelines to the officer concerned, and if that does not solve the problem, they should speak to a senior officer or a police press officer if one is at the scene.

Official secrets and terrorism provisions

The Official Secrets Act bans photography in a 'prohibited place', which includes:

- defence establishments;
- all factories, dockyards, ships and aircraft which belong to the Crown;
- any place where munitions are stored;
- any place which belongs to the Civil Aviation Authority;
- any telecommunications office owned by a public telecommunications operator;
- any place belonging to the Crown, or any railway, road, waterway, or gas, electricity or water works, which has been designated a 'prohibited place' by order of the Secretary of State.

The ban only applies to photographs which could be 'useful to an enemy' and are 'taken for a purpose prejudicial to the interests of the state', but photographers who are found in sensitive areas may find themselves quite closely questioned about what they are doing and why.

Section 58 of the Terrorism Act 2000 makes it an offence to take or possess a 'record of information' likely to be useful to a person committing or preparing an act of terrorism; a photograph can count as such a record. The Terrorism Act gives police wide powers to stop and search anyone who they reasonably suspect of an offence under the Act (see Chapter 21). These powers have been regularly used by police against photographers taking pictures in public areas, especially in central London.

In July 2009, the Metropolitan Police issued new guidelines for photographers, which stated that police officers had the right to view any images taken in public, under the Terrorism Act 2000. After complaints from the NUJ, the guidelines have now been revised, and make it clear that police only have the right to view such images where they suspect the photographer to be involved in terrorism.

The Metropolitan Police have also said that police officers should not use the anti-terrorism powers to stop people taking photographs in public places. *Media Law* reported in January 2010 that Assistant Commissioner John Yates had sent a message to all officers in December 2009, reminding them that there is no restriction on people taking photographs of public buildings and spaces, and photographers should not be stopped and searched without a valid reason.

Privacy

It is still unclear how far taking pictures of someone in a public place can be seen as a breach of confidence, or more accurately, the version of confidentiality which is described as 'misuse of private information' (in Chapter 17). In ***Campbell* v *MGN*** (2004) (see p. 304), the House of Lords said that a picture taken in a public place might be a misuse of private information where it showed a person in a particularly humiliating position, and the ***Princess Caroline*** case states that public figures such as celebrities have a right not to be photographed when going about their private business. The 2006 case involving Elton John (see p. 303), however, suggests this does not prevent photography of activities that are not of a personal nature, as long as there is no harassment of the subject.

What the codes say **Photography**

In addition to the legal restrictions detailed above, the Editors' Code of Practice used by IPSO has a number of things to say about photography:

- Photographs of individuals on private property should not be taken without permission.
- The use of long lens cameras to take pictures of people on private property is unacceptable.
- Children should not be photographed in relation to issues involving their welfare (or that of another child) without permission from a parent or 'similarly responsible adult'.
- Children should not be photographed at school without permission from the school authorities.
- The press should not obtain or publish material that is the result of using hidden cameras.

Courts

The Contempt of Court Act 1981 makes it a criminal offence to take any photograph within the 'precinct' of a court, and a further offence to publish such a picture, both offences punishable with a fine of up to £1,000. However, the Act does not define where the precincts of the court begin and end, and, although taking pictures within a court building is clearly off limits, different courts apply different rules to, for example, pictures taken of people coming out of the door of a court, but still on court land. It is best to check with the individual court as to its policy before taking pictures outside the building. It is, however, permissible to take pictures of people leaving court, once both you and they are outside in the street.

As explained in the chapter on contempt of court, some tribunals are considered courts for the purposes of the Act, in which case photographs may not be taken within their 'precincts'. Again, it is sensible to check with the tribunal itself before taking pictures.

Even when it is legal to take a picture in connection with a court case, there may be restrictions on publishing it. This issue is dealt with in more detail in the chapters on reporting the courts, but the main restrictions are:

- Photographs of the victim of a sexual offence may not be published during that person's lifetime, if to do so would be likely to lead the public to identify the person as the victim of a sexual offence (see p. 133).
- People under 16 who are involved in youth court proceedings may not be identified, unless the court gives permission by lifting the statutory restrictions (see p. 149). This applies to victims and witnesses as well as defendants.
- In some cases, the courts may make discretionary orders preventing identification of certain witnesses or victims in a case. Publishing a photograph of that person will usually breach this order (see p. 140).
- No photograph of a defendant in a criminal case should be published if to do so would create a risk of serious prejudice to the court proceedings (see p. 73).

Obstruction and public order

Section 137 of the Highways Act 1980 states that an offence is committed when anyone 'without lawful authority or excuse, in any way wilfully obstructs the free passage along a highway'. For the purposes of the Act, 'highway' includes pavements as well as roads, so there is clearly potential in many situations for photographers to commit this offence.

The offence is potentially quite a wide one, and it can be difficult to pin down exactly what will amount to obstruction; simply standing on the pavement to take a photograph would usually not be, whereas a crowd of photographers blocking the road outside someone's house probably would be, but there are clearly many situations in between these two extremes.

Usually, if the police believe the highway is being obstructed, they will simply ask photographers to move on. However, a photographer who refuses to go, or continues to cause an obstruction, can be arrested.

Photographers may also run the risk of being arrested for obstructing the police in the execution of their duty, under s51 of the Police Act 1964. This is another very wide offence, and can be committed by doing anything which prevents the police from doing their job.

In 2007, a Nottingham photographer was convicted of obstructing the police after a police officer asked him to stop taking pictures of armed police officers in a public place, and he politely refused. He was given a nine-month conditional discharge and ordered to pay £400 costs. An agreement between Nottinghamshire police and the NUJ had provided that the police had no right to arrest someone for taking photographs.

A situation which has caused particular problems for photographers is that of riots and demonstrations. In this situation, photographers have been arrested for breach of the peace, or under the Public Order Act 1986, which allows the police to arrest anyone behaving in a way that is 'likely to cause harassment, alarm or distress'. In several cases, photographers have been arrested, held for long enough to miss their news deadlines, and then had charges against them dropped; clearly, it is better to avoid being arrested in the first place if you can.

Photographing the police

Section 58a of the Counter-Terrorism Act 2008 makes it an offence to photograph police officers if the pictures could be useful to terrorists. There is a defence if you can show that you had 'reasonable excuse' for taking the picture. In June 2009, Lord Carlile, who at that time had responsibility for keeping anti-terrorism legislation under review, emphasised that this provision was not a complete ban on photographing the police. He said that taking pictures of the police remained legal, except where the resulting pictures could be used to help terrorists, and warned the police not to misuse the power provided in the 2008 Act. Any police officer who used or threatened force in the context of preventing legitimate photography of police activities could, he said, 'run the real risk of being prosecuted themselves for one or more of several possible criminal and disciplinary offences'.

COPYRIGHT AND CONFIDENTIALITY

Taking a photograph of something that is protected by copyright can be a breach of that copyright. A common example arises in connection with human interest stories, where, rather than hand over precious original photographs, people may allow a photographer to shoot a direct copy of them. This is fine if the person who allows the photographer to do this actually owns the copyright, but in many cases (e.g. wedding or school photographs) they do not. Taking the photograph and publishing it will be a breach of copyright. The same applies to, for example, taking a photograph of an artwork, or a montage of headlines from other publications, unless the copyright holder(s) give permission.

Taking your own photograph of, for example, a scene that appears in someone else's picture will not be a breach of copyright. However, in some circumstances this may be a breach of confidentiality.

In the 1997 case of ***Creation Records*** v ***News Group Newspapers***, a photo shoot was organised for the cover of an Oasis album. Heavy security was in place around the set, but a press photographer managed to get in, and surruptitiously took some pictures, which were (not surprisingly) similar to the one that was chosen for the album cover. The record company sued, and the court found that publication was a breach of confidence.

In ***Douglas*** v ***Hello!*** (2005) the film stars Catherine Zeta-Jones and Michael Douglas sued *Hello!* magazine for publishing photographs of their wedding, taken secretly by a photographer who had sneaked in. The Court of Appeal said that the right of celebrities to sell pictures of themselves was comparable to a trade secret, and was therefore protected by the law of confidentiality in the same way as the recipe for a soft drink, for example, would be.

(For a more detailed explanation of the law on copyright and confidentiality, see Chapters 23 and 18.)

KEY POINTS

Private land

Entering and/or taking pictures without permission may be trespass and/or breach of confidence.

Public places

Permission may be needed; breaches of the Official Secrets Acts and Terrorism Acts are possible.

Courts

Photography within the precincts is banned; publication of pictures related to court cases may be restricted.

Public order

Photographers can be arrested for breach of the peace, obstruction of the highway and obstruction of the police.

Copyright and confidentiality

- Photographing a copyright work may be breach of copyright.
- Photographing a scene can be a breach of confidence.

TEST YOUR KNOWLEDGE

1 You are reporting a story about a local man who has built a huge extension on his house, without getting planning permission. You are standing on the pavement outside the house, taking pictures of the extension, when the owner comes out and demands that you hand over your film. What are his legal rights?

2 You spot a well-known celebrity buying haemorrhoid cream in a shop, and manage to snatch a photo before the security guard escorts you from the premises. Can you publish the photo?

3 You work for a local paper, which is currently reporting a very high-profile rape case. You realise that the victim is someone whom you photographed for an earlier, unrelated story. Can you publish that picture?

4 You are sent to photograph a family whose son has been killed in a hit-and-run accident. They do not want to hand over any pictures of their son, in case they are lost, but suggest that you photograph his old school photos. Can you do this?

5 A local stately home is hosting a birthday party for a major pop star; the press have been banned from the venue, but your sister is a waitress there, and offers to sneak in a camera and take some pictures for you. What legal issues do you need to consider?

ONLINE RESOURCES

The Editorial Photographers UK and Ireland (EPUK) website has useful advice on copyright issues at: www.epuk.org

The Editors' Code of Practice, and adjudications relating to photographs, can be read at: www.pcc.org.uk. Details of old cases are still on the PCC website, but new adjudications will appear on the IPSO one at: www.ipso.co.uk

Appendix 1
Editors' Code of Practice of the PCC

The Press Complaints Commission has been replaced by the Independent Press Standards Organisation, but it will continue to use the Code of Practice previously used by the PCC. The latest version came into effect on 1 January 2011 (it was ratified by the PCC in October 2010). Clauses marked* are covered by exceptions relating to the public interest.

THE CODE

All members of the press have a duty to maintain the highest professional standards. The Code, which includes this preamble and the public interest exceptions below, sets the benchmark for those ethical standards, protecting both the rights of the individual and the public's right to know. It is the cornerstone of the system of self-regulation to which the industry has made a binding commitment.

It is essential that an agreed code be honoured not only to the letter but in the full spirit. It should not be interpreted so narrowly as to compromise its commitment to respect the rights of the individual, nor so broadly that it constitutes an unnecessary interference with freedom of expression or prevents publication in the public interest.

It is the responsibility of editors and publishers to apply the Code to editorial material in both printed and online versions of publications. They should take care to ensure it is observed rigorously by all editorial staff and external contributors, including non-journalists, in printed and online versions of publications.

Editors should co-operate swiftly with the Independent Press Standards Organisation CIC (the 'Regulator') in the resolution of complaints. Any publication judged to have breached the Code must publish the adjudication in full and with due prominence agreed by the Regulator, including headline reference to the Regulator.

1 Accuracy

(i) The Press must take care not to publish inaccurate, misleading or distorted information, including pictures.

(ii) A significant inaccuracy, misleading statement or distortion once recognised must be corrected, promptly and with due prominence, and – where appropriate – an apology published. In cases involving the Commission, prominence should be agreed with the PCC in advance.

(iii) The Press, whilst free to be partisan, must distinguish clearly between comment, conjecture and fact.

(iv) A publication must report fairly and accurately the outcome of an action for defamation to which it has been a party, unless an agreed settlement states otherwise, or an agreed statement is published.

2 Opportunity to reply

A fair opportunity for reply to inaccuracies must be given when reasonably called for.

3 *Privacy

(i) Everyone is entitled to respect for his or her private and family life, home, health and correspondence, including digital communications.
(ii) Editors will be expected to justify intrusions into any individual's private life without consent. Account will be taken of the complainant's own public disclosures of information.
(iii) It is unacceptable to photograph individuals in private places without their consent.

Note – Private places are public or private property where there is a reasonable expectation of privacy.

4 *Harassment

(i) Journalists must not engage in intimidation, harassment or persistent pursuit.
(ii) They must not persist in questioning, telephoning, pursuing or photographing individuals once asked to desist; nor remain on their property when asked to leave and must not follow them. If requested, they must identify themselves and whom they represent.
(iii) Editors must ensure these principles are observed by those working for them and take care not to use non-compliant material from other sources.

5 Intrusion into grief or shock

(i) In cases involving personal grief or shock, enquiries and approaches must be made with sympathy and discretion and publication handled sensitively. This should not restrict the right to report legal proceedings, such as inquests.
(*ii) When reporting suicide, care should be taken to avoid excessive detail about the method used.

6 *Children

(i) Young people should be free to complete their time at school without unnecessary intrusion.
(ii) A child under 16 must not be interviewed or photographed on issues involving their own or another child's welfare unless a custodial parent or similarly responsible adult consents.
(iii) Pupils must not be approached or photographed at school without the permission of the school authorities.
(iv) Minors must not be paid for material involving children's welfare, nor parents or guardians for material about their children or wards, unless it is clearly in the child's interest.
(v) Editors must not use the fame, notoriety or position of a parent or guardian as sole justification for publishing details of a child's private life.

7 *Children in sex cases

1 The press must not, even if legally free to do so, identify children under 16 who are victims or witnesses in cases involving sex offences.

2 In any press report of a case involving a sexual offence against a child –

 (i) The child must not be identified.
 (ii) The adult may be identified.
 (iii) The word 'incest' must not be used where a child victim might be identified.
 (iv) Care must be taken that nothing in the report implies the relationship between the accused and the child.

8 *Hospitals

(i) Journalists must identify themselves and obtain permission from a responsible executive before entering non-public areas of hospitals or similar institutions to pursue enquiries.
(ii) The restrictions on intruding into privacy are particularly relevant to enquiries about individuals in hospitals or similar institutions.

9 *Reporting of crime

(i) Relatives or friends of persons convicted or accused of crime should not generally be identified without their consent, unless they are genuinely relevant to the story.
(ii) Particular regard should be paid to the potentially vulnerable position of children who witness, or are victims of, crime. This should not restrict the right to report legal proceedings.

10 *Clandestine devices and subterfuge

(i) The press must not seek to obtain or publish material acquired by using hidden cameras or clandestine listening devices; or by intercepting private or mobile telephone calls, messages or emails; or by the unauthorised removal of documents or photographs; or by accessing digitally held private information without consent.
(ii) Engaging in misrepresentation or subterfuge, including by agents or intermediaries, can generally be justified only in the public interest and then only when the material cannot be obtained by other means.

11 Victims of sexual assault

The press must not identify victims of sexual assault or publish material likely to contribute to such identification unless there is adequate justification and they are legally free to do so.

12 Discrimination

(i) The press must avoid prejudicial or pejorative reference to an individual's race, colour, religion, gender, sex, sexual orientation or to any physical or mental illness or disability.
(ii) Details of an individual's race, colour, religion, sexual orientation, physical or mental illness or disability must be avoided unless genuinely relevant to the story.

13 Financial journalism

(i) Even where the law does not prohibit it, journalists must not use for their own profit financial information they receive in advance of its general publication, nor should they pass such information to others.
(ii) They must not write about shares or securities in whose performance they know that they or their close families have a significant financial interest without disclosing the interest to the editor or financial editor.
(iii) They must not buy or sell, either directly or through nominees or agents, shares or securities about which they have written recently or about which they intend to write in the near future.

14 Confidential sources

Journalists have a moral obligation to protect confidential sources of information.

15 Witness payments in criminal trials

(i) No payment or offer of payment to a witness – or any person who may reasonably be expected to be called as a witness – should be made in any case once proceedings are active as defined by the Contempt of Court Act 1981.

This prohibition lasts until the suspect has been freed unconditionally by police without charge or bail or the proceedings are otherwise discontinued; or has entered a guilty plea to the court; or, in the event of a not guilty plea, the court has announced its verdict.

(*ii) Where proceedings are not yet active but are likely and foreseeable, editors must not make or offer payment to any person who may reasonably be expected to be called as a witness, unless the information concerned ought demonstrably to be published in the public interest and there is an over-riding need to make or promise payment for this to be done; and all reasonable steps have been taken to ensure no financial dealings influence the evidence those witnesses give. In no circumstances should such payment be conditional on the outcome of a trial.

(*iii) Any payment or offer of payment made to a person later cited to give evidence in proceedings must be disclosed to the prosecution and defence. The witness must be advised of this requirement.

16 *Payment to criminals

(i) Payment or offers of payment for stories, pictures or information, which seek to exploit a particular crime or to glorify or glamorise crime in general, must not be made directly or via agents to convicted or confessed criminals or to their associates – who may include family, friends and colleagues.

(ii) Editors invoking the public interest to justify payment or offers would need to demonstrate that there was good reason to believe the public interest would be served. If, despite payment, no public interest emerged, then the material should not be published.

*THE PUBLIC INTEREST

1. The public interest includes, but is not confined to:
   (i) Detecting or exposing crime or serious impropriety.
   (ii) Protecting public health and safety.
   (iii) Preventing the public from being misled by an action or statement of an individual or organisation.
2. There is a public interest in freedom of expression itself.
3. Whenever the public interest is invoked, the Regulator will require editors to demonstrate fully that they reasonably believed that publication, or journalistic activity undertaken with a view to publication, would be in the public interest and how, and with whom, that was established at the time.
4. The Regulator will consider the extent to which material is already in the public domain, or will become so.
5. In cases involving children under 16, editors must demonstrate an exceptional public interest to override the normally paramount interest of the child.

END

This Code incorporates changes taking effect from 1 January 2012. For later changes, refer to the IPSO website.

Source: Editors' Code of Practice Committee. The Code is published by the Press Standards Board of Finance Ltd, 21 Lansdowne Crescent, Edinburgh, EH12 5EH.

Appendix 2
The Ofcom Broadcasting Code

SECTION 1: PROTECTING THE UNDER-EIGHTEENS

Relevant legislation includes, in particular, sections 3(4)(h) and 319(2)(a) and (f) of the Communications Act 2003, Article 27 of the Audiovisual Media Services andArticle 10 of the European Convention on Human Rights.)

This section must be read in conjunction with Section Two: Harm and Offence.

Principle

To ensure that people under eighteen are protected.

Rules

Scheduling and content information

1.1 Material that might seriously impair the physical, mental or moral development of people under eighteen must not be broadcast.

1.2 In the provision of services, broadcasters must take all reasonable steps to protect people under eighteen. For television services, this is in addition to their obligations resulting from the Audiovisual Media Services Directive (in particular, Article 27, see Appendix 2).

1.3 Children must also be protected by appropriate scheduling from material that is unsuitable for them.

Meaning of "children":
Children are people under the age of fifteen years.

Meaning of "appropriate scheduling":
Appropriate scheduling should be judged according to:

- the nature of the content;
- the likely number and age range of children in the audience, taking into account school time, weekends and holidays;
- the start time and finish time of the programme;
- the nature of the channel or station and the particular programme; and
- the likely expectations of the audience for a particular channel or station at a particular time and on a particular day.

1.4 Television broadcasters must observe the watershed.

Meaning of "the watershed":
The watershed only applies to television. The watershed is at 2100. Material unsuitable for children should not, in general, be shown before 2100 or after 0530.

On premium subscription film services which are not protected as set out in Rule 1.24, the watershed is at 2000. There is no watershed on premium subscription film services or pay per view services which are protected as set out in Rules 1.24 and 1.25 respectively.

1.5 Radio broadcasters must have particular regard to times when children are particularly likely to be listening.

Meaning of "when children are particularly likely to be listening":
This phrase particularly refers to the school run and breakfast time, but might include other times.

1.6 The transition to more adult material must not be unduly abrupt at the watershed (in the case of television)or after the time when children are particularly likely to be listening (in the case of radio). For television, the strongest material should appear later in the schedule.

1.7 For television programmes broadcast before the watershed, or for radio programmes broadcast when children are particularly likely to be listening, clear information about content that may distress some children should be given, if appropriate, to the audience (taking into account the context).

(For the meaning of "context" see Section Two: Harm and Offence.)

The coverage of sexual and other offences in the UK involving under-eighteens

1.8 Where statutory or other legal restrictions apply preventing personal identification, broadcasters should also be particularly careful not to provide clues which may lead to the identification of those who are not yet adult (the defining age may differ in different parts of the UK) and who are, or might be, involved as a victim, witness, defendant or other perpetrator in the case of sexual offences featured in criminal, civil or family court proceedings:
- by reporting limited information which may be pieced together withother information available elsewhere, for example in newspaper reports (the 'jigsaw effect');
- inadvertently, for example by describing an offence as "incest"; or
- in any other indirect way.

(Note: Broadcasters should be aware that there may be statutory reporting restrictions that apply even if a court has not specifically made an order to that effect.)

1.9 When covering any pre-trial investigation into an alleged criminal offence in the UK, broadcasters should pay particular regard to the potentially vulnerable position of any person who is not yet adult who is involved as a witness or victim, before broadcasting their name, address, identity of school or other educational establishment, place of work, or any still or moving picture of them. Particular justification is also required for the broadcast of such material relating to the identity of any person who is not yet adult who is involved in the defence as a defendant or potential defendant.

Drugs, smoking, solvents and alcohol

1.10 The use of illegal drugs, the abuse of drugs, smoking, solvent abuse and the misuse of alcohol:
- must not be featured in programmes made primarily for children unless there is strong editorial justification;

- must generally be avoided and in any case must not be condoned, encouraged or glamorised in other programmes broadcast before the watershed (in the case of television), or when children are particularly likely to be listening (in the case of radio), unless there is editorial justification;
- must not be condoned, encouraged or glamorised in other programmes likely to be widely seen or heard by under-eighteens unless there is editorial justification.

Violence and dangerous behaviour

1.11 Violence, its after-effects and descriptions of violence, whether verbal or physical, must be appropriately limited in programmes broadcast before the watershed (in the case of television)or when children are particularly likely to be listening (in the case of radio) and must also be justified by the context.

1.12 Violence, whether verbal or physical, that is easily imitable by children in a manner that is harmful or dangerous:
- must not be featured in programmes made primarily for children unless there is strong editorial justification.
- must not be broadcast before the watershed (in the case of television) or when children are particularly likely to be listening (in the case of radio), unless there is editorial justification.

1.13 Dangerous behaviour, or the portrayal of dangerous behaviour, that is likely to be easily imitable by children in a manner that is harmful:
- must not be featured in programmes made primarily for children unless there is strong editorial justification;
- must not be broadcast before the watershed(in the case of television)or when children are particularly likely to be listening (in the case of radio), unless there is editorial justification.

(Regarding Rules 1.11 to 1.13 see Rules 2.4 and 2.5 in Section Two: Harm and Offence.)

Offensive language

1.14 The most offensive language must not be broadcast before the watershed (in the case of television)or when children are particularly likely to be listening (in the case of radio).

1.15 Offensive language must not be used in programmes made for younger children except in the most exceptional circumstances.

1.16 Offensive language must not be broadcast before the watershed (in the case of television), or when children are particularly likely to be listening (in the case of radio), unless it is justified by the context. In any event, frequent use of such language must be avoided before the watershed.(Regarding Rules 1.14 to 1.16 see Rule 2.3 in Section Two: Harm and Offence.)

Sexual material

1.17 Material equivalent to the British Board of Film Classification ("BBFC") R18-rating must not be broadcast at any time.

1.18 'Adult sex material' – material that contains images and/or language of a strong sexual nature which is broadcast for the primary purpose of sexual arousal or stimulation – must not be broadcast at any time other than between 2200 and 0530 on premium subscription services and pay per view/night services which operate with mandatory restricted access.

In addition, measures must be in place to ensure that the subscriber is an adult.

Meaning of "mandatory restricted access":

Mandatory restricted access means there is a PIN protected system (or other equivalent protection) which cannot be removed by the user, that restricts access solely to those authorised to view.

1.19 Broadcasters must ensure that material broadcast after the watershed which contains images and/or language of a strong or explicit sexual nature, but is not 'adult sex material' as defined in Rule 1.18 above, is justified by the context.

(See Rules 1.6 and 1.18 and Rule 2.3 in Section Two: Harm and Offence which includes meaning of "context".)

1.20 Representations of sexual intercourse must not occur before the watershed (in the case of television) or when children are particularly likely to be listening (in the case of radio), unless there is a serious educational purpose. Any discussion on, or portrayal of, sexual behaviour must be editorially justified if included before the watershed, or when children are particularly likely to be listening, and must be appropriately limited.

Nudity

1.21 Nudity before the watershed must be justified by the context.

Films, premium subscription film services, pay per view services

1.22 No film refused classification by the British Board of Film Classification (BBFC) may be broadcast unless it has subsequently been classified or the BBFC has confirmed that it would not be rejected according to the standards currently operating. Also, no film cut as a condition of classification by the BBFC may be transmitted in a version which includes the cut material unless:

- the BBFC has confirmed that the material was cut to allow the film to pass at a lower category; or
- the BBFC has confirmed that the film would not be subject to compulsory cuts according to the standards currently operating.

1.23 BBFC 18-rated films or their equivalent must not be broadcast before 2100 on any service (except for pay per view services), and even then they may be unsuitable for broadcast at that time.

1.24 Premium subscription film services may broadcast up to BBFC 15-rated films or their equivalent, at any time of day provided that mandatory restricted access is in place pre-2000 and post-0530.

In addition, those security systems which are in place to protect children must be clearly explained to all subscribers.

(See meaning of "mandatory restricted access" under Rule 1.18 above.)

1.25 Pay per view services may broadcast up to BBFC 18-rated films or their equivalent, at any time of day provided that mandatory restricted access is in place pre-2100 and post-0530.

In addition:

- information must be provided about programme content that will assist adultsto assess its suitability for children;
- there must be a detailed billing system for subscribers which clearly itemisesall viewing including viewing times and dates; and

- those security systems which are in place to protect children must be clearly explained to all subscribers.

(See meaning of "mandatory restricted access" under Rule 1.18 above.)

1.26 BBFC R18-rated films must not be broadcast.

Exorcism, the occult and the paranormal

1.27 Demonstrations of exorcisms, occult practices and the paranormal (which purport to be real), must not be shown before the watershed (in the case of television) or when children are particularly likely to be listening (in the case of radio). Paranormal practices which are for entertainment purposes must not be broadcast when significant numbers of children may be expected to be watching, or are particularly likely to be listening. (This rule does not apply to drama, film or comedy.)(See Rules 2.6 to 2.8 in Section Two: Harm and Offence and Rule 4.7 in Section Four: Religion.)

The involvement of people under eighteen in programmes

1.28 Due care must be taken over the physical and emotional welfare and the dignity of people under eighteen who take part or are otherwise involved in programmes. This is irrespective of any consent given by the participant or by a parent, guardian or other person over the age of eighteen in loco parentis.

1.29 People under eighteen must not be caused unnecessary distress or anxiety by their involvement in programmes or by the broadcast of those programmes.

1.30 Prizes aimed at children must be appropriate to the age range of both the target audience and the participants.(See Rule 2.16 in Section Two: Harm and Offence.)

SECTION 2: HARM AND OFFENCE

(Relevant legislation includes, in particular, sections 3(4)(g) and (l) and 319(2)(a), (f) and (l) of the Communications Act 2003, and Articles 10 and 14 of the European Convention on Human Rights.)

This section must be read in conjunction with Section One: Protecting the Under-Eighteens. The rules in this section are designed not only to provide adequate protection for adults but also to protect people under eighteen.

Principle

To ensure that generally accepted standards are applied to the content of television and radio services so as to provide adequate protection for members of the public from the inclusion in such services of harmful and/or offensive material.

Rules

Generally Accepted Standards

2.1 Generally accepted standards must be applied to the contents of television and radio services so as to provide adequate protection for members of the public from the inclusion in such services of harmful and/or offensive material.

2.2 Factual programmes or items or portrayals of factual matters must not materially mislead the audience.(Note to Rule 2.2: News is regulated under Section Five of the Code.)

2.3 In applying generally accepted standards broadcasters must ensure that material which may cause offence is justified by the context (see meaning of "context" below). Such material may include, but is not limited to, offensive language, violence, sex, sexual violence, humiliation, distress, violation of human dignity, discriminatory treatment or language (for example on the grounds of age, disability, gender, race, religion, beliefs and sexual orientation). Appropriate information should also be broadcast where it would assist in avoiding or minimising offence.

Meaning of "context":
Context includes (but is not limited to):

- the editorial content of the programme, programmes or series;
- the service on which the material is broadcast;
- the time of broadcast;
- what other programmes are scheduled before and after the programme or programmes concerned;
- the degree of harm or offence likely to be caused by the inclusion of any particular sort of material in programmes generally or programmes of a particular description;
- the likely size and composition of the potential audience and likely expectation of the audience;
- the extent to which the nature of the content can be brought to the attention of the potential audience for example by giving information; and
- the effect of the material on viewers or listeners who may come across it unawares.

Violence, dangerous behaviour, and suicide

2.4 Programmes must not include material (whether in individual programmes or in programmes taken together) which, taking into account the context, condones or glamorises violent, dangerous or seriously antisocial behaviour and is likely to encourage others to copy such behaviour. (See Rules 1.11 to 1.13 in Section One: Protecting the Under-Eighteens.)

2.5 Methods of suicide and self-harm must not be included in programmes except where they are editorially justified and are also justified by the context. (See Rule 1.13 in Section One: Protecting the Under-Eighteens.)

Exorcism, the occult and the paranormal

2.6 Demonstrations of exorcism, the occult, the paranormal, divination, or practices related to any of these that purport to be real (as opposed to entertainment) must be treated with due objectivity. (See Rule 1.27 in Section One: Protecting the Under-Eighteens, concerning scheduling restrictions.)

2.7 If a demonstration of exorcism, the occult, the paranormal, divination, or practices related to any of these is for entertainment purposes, this must be made clear to viewers and listeners.

2.8 Demonstrations of exorcism, the occult, the paranormal, divination, or practices related to any of these (whether such demonstrations purport to be real or are for entertainment purposes) must not contain life-changing advice directed at individuals. (Religious programmes are exempt from this rule but must, in any event, comply with the provisions in Section Four: Religion. Films, dramas and fiction generally are not bound by this rule.)

Meaning of "life-changing":
Life-changing advice includes direct advice for individuals upon which they could reasonably act or rely about health, finance, employment or relationships.

Hypnotic and other techniques, simulated news and photosensitive epilepsy

2.9 When broadcasting material featuring demonstrations of hypnotic techniques, broadcasters must exercise a proper degree of responsibility in order to prevent hypnosis and/or adverse reactions in viewers and listeners. The hypnotist must not broadcast his/her full verbal routine or be shown performing straight to camera

2.10 Simulated news (for example in drama or in documentaries) must be broadcast in such a way that there is no reasonable possibility of the audience being misled into believing that they are listening to, or watching, actual news.

2.11 Broadcasters must not use techniques which exploit the possibility of conveying a message to viewers or listeners, or of otherwise influencing their minds without their being aware, or fully aware, of what has occurred.

2.12 Television broadcasters must take precautions to maintain a low level of risk to viewers who have photosensitive epilepsy. Where it is not reasonably practicable to follow the Ofcom guidance (see the Ofcom website), and where broadcasters can demonstrate that the broadcasting of flashing lights and/or patterns is editorially justified, viewers should be given an adequate verbal and also, if appropriate, text warning at the start of the programme or programme item.

Broadcast competitions and voting

2.13 Broadcast competitions and voting must be conducted fairly.

2.14 Broadcasters must ensure that viewers and listeners are not materially misled about any broadcast competition or voting.

2.15 Broadcasters must draw up rules for a broadcast competition or vote. These rules must be clear and appropriately made known In particular, significant conditions that may affect a viewer's or listener's decision to participate must be stated at the time an invitation to participate is broadcast.

2.16 Broadcast competition prizes must be described accurately.

(See also Rule 1.30 in Section One: Protecting the Under-Eighteens, which concerns the provision of appropriate prizes for children.)

Note:
For broadcast competitions and voting that involve the use of premium rate telephonyservices (PRS), television broadcasters should also refer to Rules 9.26 to 9.30. Radiobroadcasters should refer to Rules 10.9 to 10.10.

Meaning of "broadcast competition":
A competition or free prize draw featured in a programme in which viewers or listeners are invited to enter by any means for the opportunity to win a prize.

Meaning of "voting":
Features in a programme in which viewers or listeners are invited to register a vote by any means to decide or influence, at any stage, the outcome of a contest.

SECTION 3: CRIME

(Relevant legislation includes, in particular, sections 3(4)(j) and 319(2)(b) of the Communications Act 2003, Article6 of the Audiovisual Media Services Directive, and Article 10 of the European Convention on Human Rights.)

Principle

To ensure that material likely to encourage or incite the commission of crime or to lead to disorder is not included in television or radio services.

Rules

3.1 Material likely to encourage or incite the commission of crime or to lead to disorder must not be included in television or radio services.

3.2 Descriptions or demonstrations of criminal techniques which contain essential details which could enable the commission of crime must not be broadcast unless editorially justified.

3.3 No payment, promise of payment, or payment in kind, may be made to convicted or confessed criminals whether directly or indirectly for a programme contribution by the criminal (or any other person) relating to his/her crime/s. The only exception is where it is in the public interest.

3.4 While criminal proceedings are active, no payment or promise of payment may be made, directly or indirectly, to any witness or any person who may reasonably be expected to be called as a witness. Nor should any payment be suggested or made dependent on the outcome of the trial. Only actual expenditure or loss of earnings necessarily incurred during the making of a programme contribution may be reimbursed.

3.5 Where criminal proceedings are likely and foreseeable, payments should not be made to people who might reasonably be expected to be witnesses unless there is a clear public interest, such as investigating crime or serious wrongdoing, and the payment is necessary to elicit the information. Where such a payment is made it will be appropriate to disclose the payment to both defence and prosecution if the person becomes a witness in any subsequent trial.

3.6 Broadcasters must use their best endeavours so as not to broadcast material that could endanger lives or prejudice the success of attempts to deal with a hijack or kidnapping.

SECTION 4: RELIGION

(Relevant legislation includes, in particular, sections 319(2)(e) and 319(6) of the Communications Act 2003, and Articles 9, 10 and 14 of the European Convention on Human Rights.)

The rules in this section apply to religious programmes.

Principles

To ensure that broadcasters exercise the proper degree of responsibility with respect to the content of programmes which are religious programmes.

To ensure that religious programmes do not involve any improper exploitation of any susceptibilities of the audience for such a programme.

To ensure that religious programmes do not involve any abusive treatment of the religious views and beliefs of those belonging to a particular religion or religious denomination.

Rules

4.1 Broadcasters must exercise the proper degree of responsibility with respect to the content of programmes which are religious programmes.

Meaning of a "religious programme":
A religious programme is a programme which deals with matters of religion as the central subject, or as a significant part, of the programme.

4.2 The religious views and beliefs of those belonging to a particular religion or religious denomination must not be subject to abusive treatment.

4.3 Where a religion or religious denomination is the subject, or one of the subjects, of a religious programme, then the identity of the religion and/or denomination must be clear to the audience.

4.4 Religious programmes must not seek to promote religious views or beliefs by stealth.

4.5 Religious programmes on television services must not seek recruits. This does not apply to specialist religious television services. Religious programmes on radio services may seek recruits.

Meaning of "seek recruits":
Seek recruits means directly appealing to audience members to join a religion or religious denomination.

4.6 Religious programmes must not improperly exploit any susceptibilities of the audience.

(Regarding charity appeals in programming and appeals for funds by broadcasters, television broad casters should refer to Rules 9.33 and 9.34, and 9.36 and 9.39.Radio broadcasters should refer to Rules 10.11 and 10.12.

4.7 Religious programmes that contain claims that a living person (or group) has special powers or abilities must treat such claims with due objectivity and must not broadcast such claims when significant numbers of children may be expected to be watching (in the case of television), or when children are particularly likely to be listening (in the case of radio).

SECTION 5: DUE IMPARTIALITY AND DUE ACCURACY AND UNDUE PROMINENCE OF VIEWS AND OPINIONS

Relevant legislation includes, in particular, sections 319(2)(c) and (d), 319(8) and section 320 of the Communications Act 2003, and Article 10 of the European Convention on Human Rights.)

This section of the Code does not apply to BBC services funded by the licence fee, which are regulated on these matters by the BBC Trust.

Principles

To ensure that news, in whatever form, is reported with due accuracy and presented with due impartiality.

To ensure that the special impartiality requirements of the Act are complied with.

Rules

Meaning of "due impartiality":
"Due" is an important qualification to the concept of impartiality. Impartiality itself means not favouring one side over another. "Due" means adequate or appropriate to the subject and nature of the programme. So "due impartiality" does not mean an equal division of time has to be given to every view, or that every argument and every facet of every argument has to be represented. The approach to due impartiality may vary according to the nature of the subject, the type of programme and channel, the likely expectation of the audience as to content, and the extent to which the content and approach is signalled to the audience. Context, as defined in Section Two: Harm and Offence of the Code, is important.

Due impartiality and due accuracy in news

5.1 News, in whatever form, must be reported with due accuracy and presented with due impartiality.
5.2 Significant mistakes in news should normally be acknowledged and corrected on air quickly. Corrections should be appropriately scheduled.
5.3 No politician may be used as a newsreader, interviewer or reporter in any news programmes unless, exceptionally, it is editorially justified. In that case, the political allegiance of that person must be made clear to the audience.

Special impartiality requirements: news and other programmes

Matters of political or industrial controversy and matters relating to current public policy

Meaning of "matters of political or industrial controversy and matters relating to current public policy":
Matters of political or industrial controversy are political or industrial issues onwhich politicians, industry and/or the media are in debate. Matters relating to current public policy need not be the subject of debate but relate to a policy under discussion or already decided by a local, regional or national government or by bodies mandated by those public bodies to make policy on their behalf, for example non-governmental organisations, relevant European institutions, etc.

The exclusion of views or opinions

(Rule 5.4 applies to television and radio services except restricted services.)

5.4 Programmes in the services (listed above) must exclude all expressions of the views and opinions of the person providing the service on matters of political and industrial controversy and matters relating to current public policy (unless that person is speaking in a legislative forum or in a court of law). Views and opinions relating to the provision of programme services are also excluded from this requirement.

The preservation of due impartiality

(Rules 5.5 to 5.12 apply to television programme services, teletext services, national radio and national digital sound programme services.)

5.5 Due impartiality on matters of political or industrial controversy and matters relating to current public policy must be preserved on the part of any person providing a service (listed above). This may be achieved within a programme or over a series of programmes taken as a whole.

Meaning of "series of programmes taken as a whole":
This means more than one programme in the same service, editorially linked, dealing with the same or related issues within an appropriate period and aimed at a like audience. A series can include, for example, a strand, or two programmes (such as a drama and a debate about the drama) or a 'cluster' or 'season' of programmes on the same subject.

5.6 The broadcast of editorially linked programmes dealing with the same subject matter (as part of a series in which the broadcaster aims to achieve due impartiality) should normally be made clear to the audience on air.

5.7 Views and facts must not be misrepresented. Views must also be presented with due weight over appropriate timeframes.

5.8 Any personal interest of a reporter or presenter, which would call into question the due impartiality of the programme, must be made clear to the audience.

5.9 Presenters and reporters (with the exception of news presenters and reporters in news programmes), presenters of "personal view" or "authored" programmes or items, and chairs of discussion programmes may express their own views on matters of political or industrial controversy or matters relating to current public policy. However, alternative viewpoints must be adequately represented either in the programme, or in a series of programmes taken as a whole. Additionally, presenters must not use the advantage of regular appearances to promote their views in a way that compromises the requirement for due impartiality. Presenter phone-ins must encourage and must not exclude alternative views.

5.10 A personal view or authored programme or item must be clearly signalled to the audience at the outset. This is a minimum requirement and may not be sufficient in all circumstances. (Personality phone-in hosts on radio are exempted from this provision unless their personal view status is unclear.)

Meaning of "personal view" and "authored":
"Personal view" programmes are programmes presenting a particular view or perspective. Personal view programmes can range from the outright expression of highly partial views, for example by a person who is a member of a lobby group and is campaigning on the subject, to the considered "authored" opinion of a journalist, commentator or academic, with professional expertise or a specialism in an area which enables her or him to express opinions which are not necessarily mainstream.

Matters of major political or industrial controversy and major matters relating to current public policy

5.11 In addition to the rules above, due impartiality must be preserved on matters of major political and industrial controversy and major matters relating to current public policy by the person providing a service (listed above) in each programme or in clearly linked and timely programmes.

Meaning of "matters of major political or industrial controversy and major matters relating to current public policy":
These will vary according to events but are generally matters of political or industrial controversy or matters of current public policy which are of national, and often international, importance, or are of similar significance within a smaller broadcast area.

5.12 In dealing with matters of major political and industrial controversy and major matters relating to current public policy an appropriately wide range of significant views must be included and given due weight in each programme or in clearly linked and timely programmes. Views and facts must not be misrepresented.

The prevention of undue prominence of views and opinions on matters of political or industrial controversy and matters relating to current public policy

(Rule 5.13 applies to local radio services (including community radio services), local digital sound programme services (including community digital sound programme services) and radio licensable content services.)

5.13 Broadcasters should not give undue prominence to the views and opinions of particular persons or bodies on matters of political or industrial controversy and matters relating to current public policy in all the programmes included in any service (listed above) taken as a whole.

Meaning of "undue prominence of views and opinions":
Undue prominence is a significant imbalance of views aired within coverage of matters of political or industrial controversy or matters relating to current public policy.

Meaning of "programmes included in any serviceTaken as a whole":
Programmes included in any service taken as a whole means all programming on a service dealing with the same or related issues within an appropriate period.

SECTION 6: ELECTIONS AND REFERENDUMS

(Relevant legislation includes, in particular, sections 319(2)(c) and 320 of the Communications Act 2003, and Article 10 of the European Convention on Human Rights. Broadcasters should also have regard to relevant sections of the Representation of the People Act 1983 (as amended) ("RPA") see in particular sections 66A, 92 and 93 (which is amended by section 144 of the Political Parties, Elections and Referendums Act 2000).)

This section of the Code does not apply to BBC services funded by the licence fee, which are regulated on these matters by the BBC Trust.

Rules made under section 333 of the Communications Act 2003 (regarding party election broadcasts, party political broadcasts and referendum campaign broadcasts) and paragraph 18 of Schedule 12 are contained in Ofcom Rules on Party Political and Referendum Broadcasts on the Ofcom website. However, such broadcasts are also required to comply with the relevant provisions of this Code, for example the provisions regarding harm and offence notwithstanding that the content is normally the responsibility of the relevant political parties.

Principle

To ensure that the special impartiality requirements in the Communications Act 2003 and other legislation relating to broadcasting on elections and referendums, are applied at the time of elections and referendums.

Rules

Programmes at the time of elections and referendums

6.1 The rules in Section Five, in particular the rules relating to matters of major political or industrial controversy and major matters relating to current public policy, apply to the coverage of elections and referendums.

Programmes at the time of elections and referendums in the UK

The remainder of this section only applies during the actual election or referendum period which is defined below.

Meaning of "election":
For the purpose of this section elections include a parliamentary general election, parliamentary by-election, local government election, mayoral election, Police and Crime Commissioner election, Scottish Parliament election, Welsh, Northern Ireland and London Assembly elections, and European parliamentary election.

Meaning of "referendum":
For the purpose of this section a referendum (to which the Political Parties,Elections and Referendums Act 2000 applies) includes a UK-wide, national or regional referendum but does not extend to a local referendum.

6.2 Due weight must be given to the coverage of major parties during the election period. Broadcasters must also consider giving appropriate coverage to other parties and independent candidates with significant views and perspectives.

Meaning of "major party":
At present major parties for each nation in the United Kingdom are defined in theOfcom List of Major Parties.

Meaning of "election period":
For a parliamentary general election, this period begins with the announcement of the dissolution of Parliament. For a parliamentary by-election, this period begins with the issuing of a writ or on such earlier date as is notified in the London Gazette. For the Scottish Parliament elections and National Assembly for Wales elections, the period begins with the dissolution of the Scottish Parliament or the National Assembly for Wales as appropriate or, in the case of a by-election, with the date of the occurrence of a vacancy. For the Northern Ireland Assembly, the London Assembly and for local government elections, it is the last date for publication of notices of the election. For European parliamentary elections, it is the last date for publication of the notice of election, which is 25 days before the election. In all cases the period ends with the close of the poll.

Meaning of "candidate":
Candidate has the meaning given to it in section 93 of the Representation of the People Act 1983 (as amended) and means a candidate standing nominated at the election or included in a list of candidates submitted in connection with it.

6.3 Due weight must be given to designated organisations in coverage during the referendum period. Broadcasters must also consider giving appropriate coverage to other permitted participants with significant views and perspectives.

Meaning of "designated organisation" and "permitted participants":
Designated organisations and permitted participants are those that are designated by the Electoral Commission.

Meaning of "referendum period":
For referendums different periods may apply. A referendum held under the Northern Ireland Act 1998 (as amended) begins when the draft of an Order is laid before Parliament for approval by each House. In the case of a referendum held under other Acts, the time at which a referendum period commences is given in the individual Acts. In the case of an Order before

Parliament, the time will be given in that Order. In all cases the period ends with the close of the poll.

6.4 Discussion and analysis of election and referendum issues must finish when the poll opens. (This refers to the opening of actual polling stations. This rule does not apply to any poll conducted entirely by post.)

6.5 Broadcasters may not publish the results of any opinion poll on polling day itself until the election or referendum poll closes. (For European Parliamentary elections, this applies until all polls throughout the European Union have closed.)

6.6 Candidates in UK elections, and representatives of permitted participants in UK referendums, must not act as news presenters, interviewers or presenters of any type of programme during the election period.

6.7 Appearances by candidates (in UK elections) or representatives (of permitted participants in UK referendums) in non-political programmes that were planned or scheduled before the election or referendum period may continue, but no new appearances should be arranged and broadcast during the period.

Constituency coverage and electoral area coverage in elections

(Rules 6.8 to 6.13 will only apply to S4C if S4C has adopted them under the RPA as its Code of Practice.)

6.8 Due impartiality must be strictly maintained in a constituency report or discussion and in an electoral area report or discussion.

Meaning of "electoral area":
Electoral area (for example electoral division, borough ward or other area) is the local government equivalent to the parliamentary term "constituency".

6.9 If a candidate takes part in an item about his/her particular constituency, or electoral area, then candidates of each of the major parties must be offered the opportunity to take part. (However, if they refuse or are unable to participate, the item may nevertheless go ahead.)

6.10 In addition to Rule 6.9, broadcasters must offer the opportunity to take part in constituency or electoral area reports and discussions, to all candidates within the constituency or electoral area representing parties with previous significant electoral support or where there is evidence of significant current support. This also applies to independent candidates. (However, if a candidate refuses or is unable to participate, the item may nevertheless go ahead.)

6.11 Any constituency or electoral area report or discussion after the close of nominations must include a list of all candidates standing, giving first names, surnames and the name of the party they represent or, if they are standing independently, the fact that they are an independent candidate. This must be conveyed in sound and/or vision. Where a constituency report on a radio service is repeated on several occasions in the same day, the full list need only be broadcast on one occasion. If, in subsequent repeats on that day, the constituency report does not give the full list of candidates, the audience should be directed to an appropriate website or other information source listing all candidates and giving the information set out above.

6.12 Where a candidate is taking part in a programme on any matter, after the election has been called, s/he must not be given the opportunity to make constituency points, or electoral area points about the constituency or electoral area in which s/he is standing, when no other candidates will be given a similar opportunity.

6.13 If coverage is given to wider election regions, for example in elections to the Scottish Parliament, Welsh Assembly, Northern Ireland Assembly, London Assembly or European Parliament, then Rules 6.8 to 6.12 apply in offering participation to candidates. In these instances, all parties who have a candidate in the appropriate region should be listed in sound and/or vision, but it is not necessary to list candidates individually. However, any independent candidate who is not standing on a party list must be named. Where a report on a radio service is repeated on several occasions in the same day, the full list need only be broadcast on one occasion If, in subsequent repeats on that day, the constituency report does not give the full list of candidates, the audience should be directed to an appropriate website or other information source listing all candidates and giving the information set out above.

SECTION 7: FAIRNESS

(Relevant legislation includes, in particular, sections 3(2)(f) and 326 of the Communications Act 2003 and sections 107(1) and 130 of the Broadcasting Act 1996 (as amended), Article 28 of the Audiovisual Media Services Directive and Article 10 of the European Convention on Human Rights.)

Foreword

This section and the following section on privacy are different from other sections of the Code. They apply to how broadcasters treat the individuals or organisations directly affected by programmes, rather than to what the general public sees and/or hears as viewers and listeners.

As well as containing a principle and a rule this section contains "practices to be followed" by broadcasters when dealing with individuals or organisations participating in or otherwise directly affected by programmes as broadcast. Following these practices will not necessarily avoid a breach of this section of the Code (Rule 7.1). However, failure to follow these practises will only constitute a breach where it results in unfairness to an individual or organisation in the programme. Importantly, the Code does not and cannot seek to set out all the "practices to be followed" in order to avoid unfair treatment.

The following provisions in the next section on privacy are also relevant to this section:

- the explanation of public interest that appears in the meaning of "warranted" under Rule 8.1 in Section Eight: Privacy;
- the meaning of surreptitious filming or recording that appears under "practices to be followed" 8.13 in Section Eight: Privacy.

Principle

To ensure that broadcasters avoid unjust or unfair treatment of individuals or organisations in programmes.

Rule

7.1 Broadcasters must avoid unjust or unfair treatment of individuals or organisations in programmes.

Practices to be followed (7.2 to 7.14 below)

Dealing fairly with contributors and obtaining informed consent

7.2 Broadcasters and programme makers should normally be fair in their dealings with potential contributors to programmes unless, exceptionally, it is justified to do otherwise.

7.3 Where a person is invited to make a contribution to a programme (except when the subject matter is trivial or their participation minor) they should normally, at an appropriate stage:

- be told the nature and purpose of the programme, what the programme is about and be given a clear explanation of why they were asked to contribute and when (if known) and where it is likely to be first broadcast;
- be told what kind of contribution they are expected to make, for example live, pre-recorded, interview, discussion, edited, unedited, etc.;
- be informed about the areas of questioning and, wherever possible, the nature of other likely contributions;
- be made aware of any significant changes to the programme as it develops which might reasonably affect their original consent to participate, and which might cause material unfairness;
- be told the nature of their contractual rights and obligations and those of the programme maker and broadcaster in relation to their contribution; and
- be given clear information, if offered an opportunity to preview the programme, about whether they will be able to effect any changes to it.

Taking these measures is likely to result in the consent that is given being 'informed consent' (referred to in this section and the rest of the Code as "consent").

It may be fair to withhold all or some of this information where it is justified in the public interest or under other provisions of this section of the Code.

7.4 If a contributor is under sixteen, consent should normally be obtained from a parent or guardian, or other person of eighteen or over in loco parentis. In particular, persons under sixteen should not be asked for views on matters likely to be beyond their capacity to answer properly without such consent.

7.5 In the case of persons over sixteen who are not in a position to give consent, a person of eighteen or over with primary responsibility for their care should normally give it on their behalf. In particular, persons not in a position to give consent should not be asked for views on matters likely to be beyond their capacity to answer properly without such consent.

7.6 When a programme is edited, contributions should be represented fairly.

7.7 Guarantees given to contributors, for example relating to the content of a programme, confidentiality or anonymity, should normally be honoured.

7.8 Broadcasters should ensure that the re-use of material, i.e. use of material originally filmed or recorded for one purpose and then used in a programme for another purpose or used in a later or different programme, does not create unfairness. This applies both to material obtained from others and the broadcaster's own material.

Opportunity to contribute and proper consideration of facts

7.9 Before broadcasting a factual programme, including programmes examining past events, broadcasters should take reasonable care to satisfy themselves that:

- material facts have not been presented, disregarded or omitted in a way that is unfair to an individual or organisation; and
- anyone whose omission could be unfair to an individual or organisation has been offered an opportunity to contribute.

7.10 Programmes such as dramas and factually-based dramas should not portray facts, events, individuals or organisations in a way which is unfair to an individual or organisation.

7.11 If a programme alleges wrongdoing or incompetence or makes other significant allegations, those concerned should normally be given an appropriate and timely opportunity to respond.

7.12 Where a person approached to contribute to a programme chooses to make no comment or refuses to appear in a broadcast, the broadcast should make clear that the individual concerned has chosen not to appear and should give their explanation if it would be unfair not to do so.

7.13 Where it is appropriate to represent the views of a person or organisation that is not participating in the programme, this must be done in a fair manner.

Deception, set-ups and 'wind-up' calls

7.14 Broadcasters or programme makers should not normally obtain or seek information, audio, pictures or an agreement to contribute through misrepresentation or deception. (Deception includes surreptitious filming or recording.) However:

- it may be warranted to use material obtained through misrepresentation or deception without consent if it is in the public interest and cannot reasonably be obtained by other means;
- where there is no adequate public interest justification, for example some unsolicited wind-up calls or entertainment set-ups, consent should be obtained from the individual and/or organisation concerned before the material is broadcast;
- if the individual and/or organisation is/are not identifiable in the programme then consent for broadcast will not be required;
- material involving celebrities and those in the public eye can be used without consent for broadcast, but it should not be used without a public interest justification if it is likely to result in unjustified public ridicule or personal distress. (Normally, therefore such contributions should be pre-recorded.)

(See "practices to be followed" 8.11 to 8.15 in Section Eight: Privacy.)

SECTION 8: PRIVACY

(Relevant legislation includes, in particular, sections 3(2)(f) and 326 of the Communications Act 2003, sections 107(1) and 130 of the Broadcasting Act 1996 (as amended), and Articles 8 and 10 of the European Convention on Human Rights.)

Foreword

This section and the preceding section on fairness are different from other sections of the Code. They apply to how broadcasters treat the individuals or organisations directly affected by programmes, rather than to what the general public sees and/or hears as viewers and listeners.

As well as containing a principle and a rule this section contains "practices to be followed" by broadcasters when dealing with individuals or organisations participating or otherwise directly affected by programmes, or in the making of programmes. Following these practices will not necessarily avoid a breach of this section of the Code (Rule 8.1). However, failure to follow these practises will only constitute a breach where itresults in an unwarranted infringement of privacy. Importantly, the Code does not and cannot seek to set out all the "practices to be followed" in order to avoid an unwarranted infringement of privacy.

The Broadcasting Act 1996 (as amended) requires Ofcom to consider complaints about unwarranted infringement of privacy in a programme or in connection with the obtaining of material included in a programme. This may call for some difficult on-the-spot judgments about whether privacy is unwarrantably infringed by filming or recording, especially when reporting on emergency situations ("practices to be followed" 8.5 to 8.8 and 8.16 to 8.19). We recognise there may be a strong public interest in reporting on an emergency situation as it occurs and we understand there may be pressures on broadcasters at the scene of a disaster or emergency that may make it difficult to judge at the time whether filming or recording is an unwarrantable infringement of privacy. These are factors Ofcom will take into account when adjudicating on complaints.

Where consent is referred to in Section Eight it refers to informed consent.

Please see "practice to be followed" 7.3 in Section Seven: Fairness.

Principle

To ensure that broadcasters avoid any unwarranted infringement of privacy in programmes and in connection with obtaining material included in programmes.

Rule

8.1 Any infringement of privacy in programmes, or in connection with obtaining material included in programmes, must be warranted.

Meaning of "warranted":

In this section "warranted" has a particular meaning. It means that where broadcasters wish to justify an infringement of privacy as warranted, they should be able to demonstrate why in the particular circumstances of the case, it is warranted. If the reason is that it is in the public interest, then the broadcaster should be able to demonstrate that the public interest outweighs the right to privacy. Examples of public interest would include revealing or detecting crime, protecting public health or safety, exposing misleading claims made by individuals or organisations or disclosing incompetence that affects the public.

Practices to be followed (8.2 to 8.22)

Private lives, public places and legitimate expectation of privacy

Meaning of "legitimate expectation of privacy":

Legitimate expectations of privacy will vary according to the place and nature of the information, activity or condition in question, the extent to which it is in the public domain (if at all) and whether the individual concerned is already in the public eye. There may be circumstances where people can reasonably expect privacy even in a public place. Some activities and conditions may be of such a private nature that filming or recording, even in a public place, could involve an infringement of privacy. People under investigation or in the public eye, and their immediate family and friends, retain the right to a private life, although private behaviour can raise issues of legitimate public interest.

8.2 Information which discloses the location of a person's home or family should not be revealed without permission, unless it is warranted.

8.3 When people are caught up in events which are covered by the news they still have a right to privacy in both the making and the broadcast of a programme, unless it is warranted to infringe it. This applies both to the time when these events are taking place and to any later programmes that revisit those events.

8.4 Broadcasters should ensure that words, images or actions filmed or recorded in, or broa-dcast from, a public place, are not so private that prior consent is required before broadcast from the individual or organisation concerned, unless broadcasting without their consent is warranted.

Consent

8.5 Any infringement of privacy in the making of a programme should be with the person's and/or organisation's consent or be otherwise warranted.

8.6 If the broadcast of a programme would infringe the privacy of a person or organisation, consent should be obtained before the relevant material is broadcast, unless the infringement of privacy is warranted. (Callers to phone-in shows are deemed to have given consent to the broadcast of their contribution.)

8.7 If an individual or organisation's privacy is being infringed, and they ask that the filming, recording or live broadcast be stopped, the broadcaster should do so, unless it is warranted to continue.

8.8 When filming or recording in institutions, organisations or other agencies, permission should be obtained from the relevant authority or management, unless it is warranted to film or record without permission. Individual consent of employees or others whose appearance is incidental or where they are essentially anonymous members of the general public will not normally be required.

- However, in potentially sensitive places such as ambulances, hospitals, schools, prisons or police stations, separate consent should normally be obtained before filming or recording and for broadcast from those in sensitive situations (unless not obtaining consent is warranted). If the individual will not be identifiable in the programme then separate consent for broadcast will not be required.

Gathering information, sound or images and the re-use of material

8.9 The means of obtaining material must be proportionate in all the circumstances and in particular to the subject matter of the programme.

8.10 Broadcasters should ensure that the re-use of material, i.e. use of material originally filmed or recorded for one purpose and then used in a programme for another purpose or used in a later or different programme, does not create an unwarranted infringement of privacy. This applies both to material obtained from others and the broadcaster's own material.

8.11 Doorstepping for factual programmes should not take place unless a request for an interview has been refused or it has not been possible to request an interview, or there is good reason to believe that an investigation will be frustrated if the subject is approached openly, and it is warranted to doorstep. However, normally broadcasters may, without prior warning interview, film or record people in the news when in public places. (See "practice to be followed" 8.15).

Meaning of "doorstepping":

Doorstepping is the filming or recording of an interview or attempted interview with someone, or announcing that a call is being filmed or recorded for broadcast purposes, without any prior warning. It does not, however, include vox-pops (sampling the views of random members of the public).

8.12 Broadcasters can record telephone calls between the broadcaster and the other party if they have, from the outset of the call, identified themselves, explained the purpose of the call and that the call is being recorded for possible broadcast (if that is the case) unless it is warranted not to do one or more of these practices. If at a later stage it becomes clear that a call that has been recorded will be broadcast (but this was not explained to the other party at the time of the call) then the broadcaster must obtain consent before broadcast from the other party, unless it is warranted not to do so.

(See "practices to be followed" 7.14 and 8.13 to 8.15.)

8.13 Surreptitious filming or recording should only be used where it is warranted. Normally, it will only be warranted if:

- there is prima facie evidence of a story in the public interest; and
- there are reasonable grounds to suspect that further material evidence could be obtained; and
- it is necessary to the credibility and authenticity of the programme.

(See "practices to be followed" 7.14, 8.12, 8.14 and 8.15.)

Meaning of "surreptitious filming or recording":
Surreptitious filming or recording includes the use of long lenses or recording devices, as well as leaving an unattended camera or recording device on private property without the full and informed consent of the occupiers or their agent. It may also include recording telephone conversations without the knowledge of the other party, or deliberately continuing a recording when the other party thinks that it has come to an end.

8.14 Material gained by surreptitious filming and recording should only be broadcast when it is warranted. (See also "practices to be followed" 7.14 and 8.12 to 8.13 and 8.15.)

8.15 Surreptitious filming or recording, doorstepping or recorded wind-up' calls to obtain material for entertainment purposes may be warranted if it is intrinsic to the entertainment and does not amount to a significant infringement of privacy such as to cause significant annoyance, distress or embarrassment. The resulting material should not be broadcast without the consent of those involved. However if the individual and/or organisation is not identifiable in the programme then consent for broadcast will not be required. (See "practices to be followed" 7.14 and 8.11 to 8.14.)

Suffering and distress

8.16 Broadcasters should not take or broadcast footage or audio of people caught up in emergencies, victims of accidents or those suffering a personal tragedy, even in a public place, where that results in an infringement of privacy, unless it is warranted or the people concerned have given consent.

8.17 People in a state of distress should not be put under pressure to take part in a programme or provide interviews, unless it is warranted.

8.18 Broadcasters should take care not to reveal the identity of a person who has died or of victims of accidents or violent crimes, unless and until it is clear that the next of kin have been informed of the event or unless it is warranted.

8.19 Broadcasters should try to reduce the potential distress to victims and/or relatives when making or broadcasting programmes intended to examine past events that involve trauma to individuals (including crime) unless it is warranted to do otherwise. This applies to dramatic reconstructions and factual dramas, as well as factual programmes.

- In particular, so far as is reasonably practicable, surviving victims and/or the immediate families of those whose experience is to feature in a programme, should be informed of the plans for the programme and its intended broadcast, even if the events or material to be broadcast have been in the public domain in the past.

People under sixteen and vulnerable people

8.20 Broadcasters should pay particular attention to the privacy of people under sixteen. They do not lose their rights to privacy because, for example, of the fame or notoriety of their parents or because of events in their schools.

8.21 Where a programme features an individual under sixteen or a vulnerable person in a way that infringes privacy, consent must be obtained from:

- a parent, guardian or other person of eighteen or over in loco parentis; and
- wherever possible, the individual concerned;
- unless the subject matter is trivial or uncontroversial and the participation minor, or it is warranted to proceed without consent.

8.22 Persons under sixteen and vulnerable people should not be questioned about private matters without the consent of a parent, guardian or other person of eighteen or over in loco parentis (in the case of persons under sixteen), or a person with primary responsibility for their care (in the case of a vulnerable person), unless it is warranted to proceed without consent.

Meaning of "vulnerable people":
This varies, but may include those with learning difficulties, those with mental health problems, the bereaved, people with brain damage or forms of dementia, people who have been traumatised or who are sick or terminally ill.

SECTION 9: COMMERCIAL REFERENCES IN TELEVISION PROGRAMMING

(Relevant legislation includes, in particular, sections 319(2)(fa), (i) and (j) and 319(4) (a), (c), (e) and (f), section 321(1) and (4) and section 324(3) of the Communications Act 2003; section 202 of the Broadcasting Act 1990 (paragraph 3 in Part 1 of Schedule 2), Articles 9, 10, 11, and Chapter VII (Articles 19 to 26) of the Audiovisual Media Services Directive; regulation 3(4)(d) of the Consumer Protection From Unfair Trading Regulations 2008; section 21(1) of the Financial Services and Markets Act 2000; paragraph 3 of the Investment Recommendation (Media) Regulations Act 2005; and Article 10 of the European Convention on Human Rights).

This section of the Code covers all commercial references that feature **within television programming.** Section Ten of the Code concerns radio only.

Commercial references on the two media are subject to varying legislative requirements. Therefore where similar terminology is used in Sections Nine and Ten of the Code, it does not necessarily have the same meaning. Broadcasters should refer to the specific meanings provided in each section.

Note:
This section of the Code contains **a set of principles and general, overarching rules** that apply to all commercial references in television programming. It also contains **specific rules** for different types of commercial references (e.g. product placement, programme-related material, sponsorship).

The rules ensure that the principles of editorial independence; distinction between advertising and editorial content; transparency of commercial arrangements; and consumer protection are maintained.

This section does not apply to BBC services funded by the licence fee, with the exception of the relevant product placement rules (see the additional note on the BBC that accompanies the product placement rules).

Meaning of "programming":
All broadcast content except spot advertising and teleshopping. Programmes, trailers, cross-promotions and sponsorship credits are all forms of programming.

Meaning of "commercial reference":
Any visual or audio reference within programming to a product, service or trade mark (whether related to a commercial or non-commercial organisation).

Meaning of "trade mark":
In relation to a business, includes any image (such as a logo) or sound commonly associated with that business or its products or services.

Principles

To ensure that broadcasters maintain editorial independence and control over programming (editorial independence).

To ensure that there is distinction between editorial content and advertising (distinction).

To protect audiences from surreptitious advertising (transparency).

To ensure that audiences are protected from the risk of financial harm (consumer protection).

To ensure that unsuitable sponsorship is prevented (unsuitable sponsorship).

Rules

General rules

Note:
Rules 9.1 to 9.5 apply to all commercial references included within television programming. They reflect the fact that the inclusion of commercial references in television programming creates a particular risk that the key principles may be, or appear to be, undermined.

9.1 Broadcasters must maintain independent editorial control over programming.
9.2 Broadcasters must ensure that editorial content is distinct from advertising.

Note:
For the definition of "advertising", see Ofcom's Code on the scheduling of television advertising ("COSTA").

9.3 Surreptitious advertising is prohibited.

Meaning of "surreptitious advertising":
Surreptitious advertising involves a reference to a product, service or trade mark within a programme, where such a reference is intended by the broadcaster to serve as advertising and this is not made clear to the audience. Such advertising is likely to be considered intentional if it occurs in return for payment or other valuable consideration to the broadcaster or producer.

9.4 Products, services and trade marks must not be promoted in programming.

Note:
For specific exemptions to this rule, see rules on premium rate services (Rules 9.26 to 9.30) and rules on programme-related material (Rules 9.31 and 9.32).

9.5 No undue prominence may be given in programming to a product, service or trade mark. Undue prominence may result from:
- the presence of, or reference to, a product, service or trade mark in programming where there is no editorial justification; or
- the manner in which a product, service or trade mark appears or is referred to in programming.

Product placement (and prop placement)

Broadcasters should note that the meanings set out below are statutory definitions included in UK legislation (unless indicated otherwise, the Communications Act 2003, as amended).

Meaning of "product placement":
The inclusion in a programme of, or of a reference to, a product, service or trade mark where the inclusion is for a commercial purpose, and is in return for the making of any payment, or the giving of other valuable consideration, to any relevant provider or any person connected with a relevant provider, and is not prop placement.

Meaning of "prop placement":
The inclusion in a programme of, or of a reference to, a product, service or trade mark where the provision of the product, service or trade mark has no significant value, and no relevant provider, or person connected with a relevant provider, has received any payment or other valuable consideration in relation to its inclusion in, or the reference to it in, the programme, disregarding the costs saved by including the product, service or trade mark, or a reference to it, in the programme.

Prop placement involving the supply of products or services that are of "significant value" will be treated as product placement and must comply with Rules 9.6 to 9.14.

Meaning of "significant value":
A residual value that is more than trivial.

Meaning of "residual value":
Any monetary or other economic value in the hands of the relevant provider other than the cost saving of including the product, service or trade mark, or a reference to it, in a programme.

Meaning of "relevant provider":
The provider of the television programme service in which the programme is included or the producer of the programme.

Meaning of "connected person":
Connected person has the same meaning as it has in section 202 of the Broadcasting Act 1990 (paragraph 3 in Part 1 of Schedule 2). The full definition is reproduced in Appendix 1 of the Code (Relevant UK Legislation). In summary, the following persons are connected

with a particular person (person' includes an individual as well as a body corporate and other incorporated and unincorporated legal entities):

(a) a person who controls that person;
(b) an associate of that person or of the person in (a); and
(c) a body which is controlled by that person or an associate of that person.

Control and associate have the meanings set out in paragraph 1, Part 1, Schedule 2 of the 1990 Act. The full definition is reproduced in Appendix 1 of the Code (Relevant UK Legislation).

Notes:

1) The BBC is prohibited from accepting most types of commercial revenue in relation to services funded by the licence fee. However, the Act's product placement requirements apply to programmes the BBC acquires or those produced/commissioned by its commercial services or any connected entities. The Code rules required by the Act apply to the BBC in those respects.
2) The following rules also apply to paid-for references to products, services or trade marks that are included in a programme for a non-commercial purpose.
3) The rules do not permit the inclusion in programmes of paid-for references to other interests of third party funders (e.g. their aims, objectives or beliefs). Broadcasters should also refer to Rule 9.1 and Section Five of the Code.

Rules 9.6 to 9.11 apply to all programmes

9.6 Product placement is prohibited except in the following programme genres:

a) films;
b) series made for television (or other audiovisual media services);
c) sports programmes; and
d) light entertainment programmes.

Meaning of "films":
Includes films made for cinema and films (including single dramas and single documentaries) made for television or other audiovisual media services.

"Series made for television (or other audiovisual media services)" includes serials.

9.7 Programmes that fall within the permitted genres must not contain product placement if they are:

a) news programmes; or
b) children's programmes.

Meaning of a "children's programme":
In this context a children's programme is "a programme made for a television programme service or an on-demand programme service, and for viewing primarily by persons under the age of sixteen".

9.8 Product placement must not influence the content and scheduling of a programme in a way that affects the responsibility and editorial independence of the broadcaster.

Note:
There must always be sufficient editorial justification for the inclusion of product placement in programmes. In particular, editorial content must not be created or distorted so that it becomes a vehicle for the purpose of featuring placed products, services or trade marks.

9.9 References to placed products, services and trade marks must not be promotional.

9.10 References to placed products, services and trade marks must not be unduly prominent.

Note:
Broadcasters should refer to the guidance accompanying Section Nine of the Code for further information on how to apply Rules 9.9 and 9.10.

9.11 The product placement of the following products, services or trade marks is prohibited:
- a) cigarettes or other tobacco products;
- b) placement by or on behalf of an undertaking whose principal activity is the manufacture or sale of cigarettes or other tobacco products; or
- c) prescription-only medicines.

In addition to Rules 9.6 to 9.11, Rules 9.12 to 9.13 also apply to product placement included in all programmes produced under UK jurisdiction:

Meaning of "programmes produced under UK jurisdiction":"programmes produced under UK jurisdiction" means any programme produced or commissioned by either:
- a) the provider of the television programme service or any person connected with that provider (except in the case of a film made for cinema); or
- b) any other person with a view to its first showing taking place in a television programme service under the jurisdiction of the United Kingdom (for the purposes of the AVMS Directive).

9.12 Product placement is not permitted in the following:
- a) religious programmes;
- b) consumer advice programmes; or
- c) current affairs programmes.

Meaning of "current affairs programme":
A current affairs programme is one that contains explanation and/or analysis of current events and issues, including material dealing with political or industrial controversy or with current public policy.

9.13 The product placement of the following is prohibited:
- a) alcoholic drinks;
- b) foods or drinks high in fat, salt or sugar ("HFSS");
- c) gambling;
- d) infant formula (baby milk), including follow-on formula;
- e) all medicinal products
- f) electronic or smokeless cigarettes, cigarette lighters, cigarette papers, or pipes intended for smoking; or
- g) any product, service or trade mark that is not allowed to be advertised on television.

Note:
HFSS food and drink products are defined by the nutrient profiling scheme which was devised by the UK's Food Standards Agency for use by Ofcom. This can be found at: http://food.gov.uk/healthiereating/advertisingtochildren/nutlab/nutprofmod

In addition to Rules 9.6 to 9.13, Rule 9.14 also applies to programmes (including films made for cinema) produced or commissioned by the provider of the television programme service or any person connected with that provider:

9.14 Product placement must be signalled clearly, by means of a universal neutral logo, as follows:

a) at the beginning of the programme in which the placement appears;
b) when the programme recommences after commercial breaks; and
c) at the end of the programme.

Note:
The universal neutral logo is defined by the criteria set out in Annex 1 to the guidance accompanying Section Nine of the Code.

Acquired programmes and signalling:
When a broadcaster acquires a programme containing product placement (i.e. the broadcaster has not produced or commissioned the programme, and it has not been produced or commissioned by a connected person), there is no signalling requirement. However, please note that such programmes must comply with any other relevant Code rules.

If a broadcaster acquires a programme from a third party on the condition that product placement within the programme will be broadcast (subject to compliance with relevant rules), the requirements of Rule 9.3 (surreptitious advertising) should be noted. In such circumstances, Ofcom expects broadcasters to ensure that audiences are made aware that the programme includes product placement.

Sponsorship

Meaning of "sponsored programming":
Sponsored programming (which may include a programme, channel, programme segment or block of programmes) is programming that has had some or all of its costs met by a sponsor. It includes advertiser-funded programmes.

Meaning of "sponsor":
Any public or private undertaking or individual (other than a broadcaster or programme producer) who is funding the programming with a view to promoting its products, services, trade marks and/or its activities.

Meaning of "sponsor reference":
Any reference to the sponsor's products, services or trade marks.

Meaning of "costs":
Any part of the costs connected to the production or broadcast of the programming.

Note:
1) The rules seek to ensure editorial independence is preserved and a distinction is maintained between editorial and advertising. They also aim to protect against unsuitable sponsorship, and to ensure that sponsorship arrangements adhere to the principle of transparency.
2) With the exception of the sponsorship credits, any reference to a sponsor that appears in a sponsored programme as a result of a commercial arrangement with the broadcaster, the programme maker or a connected person will be treated as product placement and must comply with Rules 9.6 to 9.14.

Content that may not be sponsored

9.15 News and current affairs programmes must not be sponsored.

Meaning of "current affairs programme":
See meaning under Rule 9.12.

Prohibited and restricted sponsors

9.16 Programming (including a channel) may not be sponsored by any sponsor that is prohibited from advertising on television.

9.17 Sponsorship must comply with both the content and scheduling rules that apply to television advertising.

Content of sponsored output

9.18 A sponsor must not influence the content and/or scheduling of a channel or programming in such a way as to impair the responsibility and editorial independence of the broadcaster.

Note:

This rule should be read in conjunction with Rules 9.1 to 9.5.

Sponsorship arrangements should not lead to the creation or distortion of editorial content so that it becomes a vehicle for the purpose of promoting the sponsor or its interests.

There are limited circumstances in which a sponsor (or its products, services or trade marks) may be referred to during a programme it is sponsoring as a result of a commercial arrangement with the broadcaster or programme-maker. For example, in the case of a product placement arrangement (see Rules 9.6 to 9.14) or when the sponsorship arrangement is identified (see Rules 9.19 to 9.25).

Where an incidental reference to the sponsor (i.e. a reference that does not result from a commercial arrangement between the sponsor and the broadcaster and/or programme maker or a connected person) appears in a sponsored programme, it must comply with Rules 9.1 to 9.5.

Sponsorship credits

9.19 Sponsorship must be clearly identified by means of sponsorship credits. These must make clear:

a) the identity of the sponsor by reference to its name or trade mark; and

b) the association between the sponsor and the sponsored content.

9.20 For sponsored programmes, credits must be broadcast at the beginning and/or during and/or end of the programme.

Note:

Credits may also be broadcast entering and/or leaving a commercial break during the sponsored programme.

For other sponsored content (e.g. channels) sponsorship credits should be broadcast at appropriate points during the schedule to ensure audiences understand that the content is sponsored.

9.21 Sponsorship credits must be distinct from editorial content.

9.22 Sponsorship credits must be distinct from advertising. In particular:

a) Sponsorship credits broadcast around sponsored programmes must not contain advertising messages or calls to action. Credits must not encourage the purchase or rental of the products or services of the sponsor or a third party. The focus of the credit must be the sponsorship arrangement itself. Such credits may include explicit reference to the sponsor's products, services or trade marks for the sole purpose of helping to identify the sponsor and/or the sponsorship arrangement.

b) Sponsorship credits broadcast during programmes must not be unduly prominent. Such credits must consist of a brief, neutral visual or verbal statement identifying the sponsorship arrangement. This can be accompanied by only a graphic of the name, logo, or any other distinctive symbol of the sponsor. The content of the graphic must be static and must contain no advertising messages, calls to action or any other information about the sponsor, its products, services or trade marks.

9.23 Where a sponsor is prohibited from product placing in the programme it is sponsoring, sponsorship credits may not be shown during the sponsored programme.

9.24 Where a sponsorship credit is included in a programme trail, the credit must remain brief and secondary.

9.25 Programme-related material may be sponsored and the sponsor may be credited when details of how to obtain the material are given. Any credit must be brief and secondary, and must be separate from any credit for the programme sponsor.

Premium rate telephony services (PRS)

Note:
In this section, premium rate telephony services (PRS) are those regulated by PhonepayPlus.

9.26 Where a broadcaster invites viewers to take part in or otherwise interact with its programmes, it may only charge for such participation or interaction by means of premium rate telephone services or other telephony services based on similar revenue-sharing arrangements.

9.27 Premium rate telephony services will normally be regarded as products or services, and must therefore not appear in programmes, except where:

a) they enable viewers to participate directly in or otherwise contribute directly to the editorial content of the programme; or
b) they fall within the meaning of programme-related material.

Note:
Each of the above exceptions is subject to the undue prominence rule.

9.28 Where a premium rate telephony service is featured in a programme, the primary purpose of the programme must continue to be clearly editorial. Promotion of the featured premium rate service must be clearly subsidiary to that primary purpose.

9.29 Any use of premium rate telephone numbers must comply with the Code of Practice issued by PhonepayPlus.

9.30 The cost to viewers for using premium rate telephony services must be made clear to them and broadcast as appropriate.

Note:
Licensees should refer to the guidance for further details on the application of this rule, as well as guidance to relevant associated rules (see in particular, the guidance to Rules 2.13 to 2.16).

Programme-related material (PRM)

Meaning of "programme-related material": Programme-related material consists of products or services that are both directly derivedfrom a programme and specifically intended to allow viewers to benefit fully from, or tointeract with, that programme.

Notes:

1) Broadcasters may refer to the availability of programme-related material without such references counting towards the amount of advertising they are permitted to transmit (as specified in Ofcom's Code on the scheduling of television advertising ("COSTA"). The following rules support the key principle of editorial independence by ensuring that references to programme-related material are made primarily for editorial and not advertising reasons.
2) Programme-related material may be sponsored (see Rule 9.25).

9.31 Programme-related material may be promoted only during or around the programme from which it is directly derived and only where it is editorially justified.

Note:
Broadcasters should refer to the statutory definition of product placement (see meanings and rules preceding Rule 9.6). Where the inclusion of references during programmes to PRM could meet the definition of product placement, the promotion of such material should be kept distinct from editorial content to avoid issues being raised under Rule 9.9.

Likewise, where the PRM involves the promotion to the audience of the availability of products or services in return for payment, it is possible that this could meet the definition of television advertising (see COSTA). Therefore, such promotions should be kept distinct from editorial content (see Rule 9.2).

9.32 The broadcaster must retain responsibility for ensuring the appropriateness of promoting programme-related material.

Cross-promotions

Note:
The cross-promotion of programmes, channels and other broadcasting-related services is covered by specific rules contained in the Cross-promotion Code. This is included as an Appendix to the Broadcasting Code.

Broadcasters should note that cross-promotions should also comply with all relevant requirements of the Broadcasting Code and, in particular, Rules 9.1 to 9.5.

Charity appeals

Note:
Charity appeals are allowed in programming only if they are broadcast free of charge.

The following rules recognise that while charities differ from purely commercial entities, there is still a potential risk that the audience may suffer financial harm as a result of such appeals (consumer protection). Further, many charities operate in competition with one another and the rules therefore aim to ensure that charity appeals benefit a range of charities. Where appropriate, broadcasters must also pay particular attention to Section Five of the Code (Due Impartiality).

9.33 Charity appeals that are broadcast free of charge are allowed in programming provided that the broadcaster has taken reasonable steps to satisfy itself that:

a) the organisation concerned can produce satisfactory evidence of charitable status, or, in the case of an emergency appeal, that a responsible public fund has been set up to deal with it; and
b) the organisation concerned is not prohibited from advertising on television.

9.34 Where possible, the broadcast of charity appeals, either individually or taken together over time, should benefit a wide range of charities.

Financial promotions and investment recommendations

Meaning of "financial promotion":
A financial promotion is an invitation or inducement to engage in investment activity (in accordance with section 21(1) of the Financial Services and Markets Act 2000 (Restrictions on financial promotion).

Meaning of an "investment recommendation":
An investment recommendation occurs when someone directly recommends a particular investment decision, for example, buying or selling a particular share or underwriting a particular share offer.

Note:
The rules applying to such promotions and recommendations reflect the particular risk that such references could result in financial harm to the audience (consumer protection), and the resulting need for editorial independence and transparency to be maintained and protected.

9.35 When broadcasting financial promotions and investment recommendations broadcasters must comply with the relevant provisions in Appendix 4 to this Code.

Appeals for funds for programming or services

Note:
During programming, broadcasters may broadcast appeals for donations to make editorial content or fund their service.

Rules 9.36 to 9.39 reflect the potential for financial harm when broadcasters appeal for funds from viewers (consumer protection) and ensure editorial independence, transparency, and distinction between advertising and editorial content are maintained.

9.36 Viewers must be told the purpose of the appeal and how much it raises.
9.37 All donations must be separately accounted for and used for the purpose for which they were donated.
9.38 Broadcasters must not offer any additional benefits or other incentives to donors.
9.39 Appeals for funds for programming or services must not be given undue prominence in relation to the overall output of the service.

SECTION 10: COMMERCIAL COMMUNICATIONS IN RADIO PROGRAMMING

(Relevant legislation includes, in particular, sections 319(2)(f), (i) and (j), 319(4)(e) and (f) and 321 of the Communications Act 2003, regulation 3(4)(d) of the Consumer Protection From Unfair Trading Regulations 2008, section 21(1) of the Financial Services and Markets Act 2000, paragraph 3 of the Investment Recommendation (Media) Regulations Act 2005, and Article 10 of the European Convention on Human Rights).

This section of the Code does not apply to BBC services funded by the licence fee, which are regulated on these matters by the BBC Trust.

This section of the Code applies to radio only. Code Section Nine (Commercial References in Television Programming) applies to television only.

Radio and television are subject to different legislative requirements and terminology is therefore specific to radio in this Code section.

Principle

To ensure the transparency of commercial communications as a means to secure consumer protection.

Rules

General Rules

10.1 Programming that is subject to, or associated with, a commercial arrangement must be appropriately signalled, so as to ensure that the commercial arrangement is transparent to listeners.

10.2 Spot advertisements must be clearly separated from programming.

10.3 No commercial reference, or material that implies a commercial arrangement, is permitted in or around news bulletins or news desk presentations.

This rule does not apply to:

- reference to a news supplier for the purpose of identifying that supplier as a news source;
- specialist factual strands that are not news bulletins or news desk presentations, but may be featured in or around such programming;
- the use of premium rate services (e.g. for station/broadcaster surveys); and
- references that promote the station/broadcaster's own products and/or services (e.g. the programme/station/broadcaster's website or a station/broadcaster's event).

10.4 No commercial reference, or material that implies a commercial arrangement, is permitted on radio services primarily aimed at children or in children's programming included in any service.

This rule does not apply to:

- credits for third party association with either programming or broadcast competition prize donation;
- the use of premium rate services (e.g. for broadcast competition entry); and
- references that promote the station/broadcaster's own products and/or services (e.g. the programme/station/broadcaster's website or a station/broadcaster's event).

10.5 No commercial arrangement that involves payment, or the provision of some other valuable consideration, to the broadcaster may influence the selection or rotation of music for broadcast.

10.6 No programming may be subject to a commercial arrangement with a third party that is prohibited from advertising on radio.

10.7 Commercial references in programming must comply with the advertising content and scheduling rules that apply to radio broadcasting.

10.8 Commercial references that require confirmation or substantiation prior to broadcast must be cleared for broadcast in the same way as advertisements.

Programming

Programming comprises all broadcast material other than spot advertisements.

Spot advertisements

Spot advertisements comprise advertising broadcast in commercial breaks.

Commercial arrangement

A commercial arrangement is a contract, or any other formal understanding, between a broadcaster (or any agent or employee of the broadcaster) and a third party (or third parties).

Examples of a commercial arrangement include programming sponsorship, competition prize donation and premium rate service provision. Programming that is subject to a commercial arrangement will therefore generally include payment and/or the provision of some other valuable consideration in return for a commercial reference (whether promotional or not).

Commercial reference

For the purposes of this section of the Code, a commercial reference is a reference in programming to a brand, trademark, product and/or service that:

- is subject to a commercial arrangement; or
- promotes the station/broadcaster's own products or services.

Transparency

Listeners should know when material is broadcast in return for payment or other valuable consideration. Signalling is the means by which transparency is achieved.

Transparency of a commercial arrangement should be achieved through the appropriate signalling of a brand, trademark, product and/or service of a third party (or third parties) that has paid for broadcast exposure by, for example: including a sponsorship credit; reference to the donor of a prize; the promotion of a premium rate number for listener interaction in programming.

Signalling

Broadcasters are required to give, at appropriate times, clear information within programming, to inform listeners of any commercial arrangement affecting that programming.

Appropriate signalling is therefore essential in complying with Rule 10.1. There are four aspects to consider when assessing what signalling is appropriate, to ensure compliance:

- Wording this must be clear, to ensure immediate transparency of the commercial arrangement;
- Positioning transparency of the commercial arrangement generally requires signalling at the outset of each instance of broadcast material subject to it;
- Frequency longer output that is subject to a commercial arrangement may require signalling at appropriate intervals;
- Identity (of the third party) transparency of the commercial arrangement requires the third party's relevant title to be stated on air.

Broadcasters should ensure that broadcast material appearing either to be a station campaign or to provide any independent assessment of products/services is genuinely independent and not subject to a commercial arrangement. Signalling commercial references in, for example, consumer advice/affairs programming therefore requires particular care, as it is essential that the broadcast of paid-for promotions of goods and services is not presumed to be independent observation/comment.

Specialist factual strands

Specialist factual strands in or around news bulletins or news desk presentations might include, for example,travel, sport, finance and weather.

Factual programming, including matters of political or industrial controversy and matters relating to current public policy
Broadcasters should note that all programming must comply with Section Five of the Code. Commercial references broadcast under such an arrangement are also subject to Section 7 of The Broadcasting Committee of Advertising Practice UK Code of Broadcast Advertising. In addition, broadcasters are reminded that Rule 2.2 applies to **all** factual programming (i.e. factual items must not materially mislead the audience).

Commercial references that require confirmation or substantiation
Examples include, but are not limited to: complex factual claims (including those that are capable of objective substantiation); market leadership claims; special offer prices; comparisons with competitors; superlative claims; claims and offers involving significant limitations and exclusions; "free" claims; testimonials; endorsements; and claims that may be of particular interest to children.

Premium rate and similar services

10.9 Any use of premium rate telephony services in programming must comply with the Code of Practice and any additional broadcast-related requirements issued by PhonepayPlus.

10.10 The cost to listeners for using premium rate telephony services, or other services based on similar revenue-sharing arrangements, must be made clear to them and broadcast as appropriate.

Charity appeals

10.11 Fund-raising activity broadcast on behalf of a charity (or emergency appeal) is only permitted if:

- it is broadcast free of charge;
- it does not contain any commercial reference that is subject to a commercial arrangement with the relevant charity (or emergency appeal); and
- the broadcaster has taken reasonable steps to satisfy itself that:
  - the organisation concerned can produce satisfactory evidence of charitable status, or, in the case of an emergency appeal, that a responsible public fund has been set up to deal with it; and
  - the organisation concerned is not prohibited from advertising on radio.

Appeals for funds for programming or services

10.12 Broadcasters may broadcast appeals for donations to make programming or fund their service. Listeners must be told the purpose of the appeal and how much it raises. All donations must be separately accounted for and used for the purpose for which they were donated.

Financial promotions and investment recommendations

10.13 When broadcasting financial promotions and investment recommendations broadcasters must comply with the relevant provisions in Appendix 4 to this Code.

Financial promotion

A financial promotion is an invitation or inducement to engage in investment activity (in accordance with section 21(1) of the Financial Services and Markets Act 2000 (Restrictions on financial promotion)).

Investment recommendation

An investment recommendation occurs when someone directly recommends a particular investment decision, for example, buying or selling a particular share or underwriting a particular share offer.

Appendix 3
Defamation Act 1996

SCHEDULE 1

QUALIFIED PRIVILEGE

PART I

STATEMENTS HAVING QUALIFIED PRIVILEGE WITHOUT EXPLANATION OR CONTRADICTION

1. A fair and accurate report of proceedings in public of a legislature anywhere in the world.

2. A fair and accurate report of proceedings in public before a court anywhere in the world.

3. A fair and accurate report of proceedings in public of a person appointed to hold a public inquiry by a government or legislature anywhere in the world.

4. A fair and accurate report of proceedings in public anywhere in the world of an international organisation or an international conference.

5. A fair and accurate copy of or extract from any register or other document required by law to be open to public inspection.

6. A notice or advertisement published by or on the authority of a court, or of a judge or officer of a court, anywhere in the world.

7. A fair and accurate copy of or extract from matter published by or on the authority of a government or legislature anywhere in the world.

8. A fair and accurate copy of or extract from matter published anywhere in the world by an international organisation or an international conference.

PART II

STATEMENTS PRIVILEGED SUBJECT TO EXPLANATION OR CONTRADICTION

9. (1) A fair and accurate copy of or extract from a notice or other matter issued for the information of the public by or on behalf of—
   (a) a legislature in any member State or the European Parliament;
   (b) the government of any member State, or any authority performing governmental functions in any member State or part of a member State, or the European Commission;
   (c) an international organisation or international conference.

   (2) In this paragraph "governmental functions" includes police functions.

9. (1) A fair and accurate copy of, extract from or summary of a notice or other matter issued for the information of the public by or on behalf of—

(a) a legislature or government anywhere in the world;

(b) an authority anywhere in the world performing governmental functions;

(c) an international organisation or international conference.

(2) In this paragraph "governmental functions" includes police functions.

10. A fair and accurate copy of or extract from a document made available by a court in any member State or the European Court of Justice (or any court attached to that court), or by a judge or officer of any such court.

[10. A fair and accurate copy of, extract from or summary of a document made available by a court anywhere in the world, or by a judge or officer of such a court.]

11. (1) A fair and accurate report of proceedings at any public meeting or sitting in the United Kingdom of—

(a) a local authority [, local authority committee or in the case of a local authority which are operating executive arrangements the executive of that authority or a committee of that executive];

(b) a justice or justices of the peace acting otherwise than as a court exercising judicial authority;

(c) a commission, tribunal, committee or person appointed for the purposes of any inquiry by any statutory provision, by Her Majesty or by a Minister of the Crown [a member of the Scottish Executive] [the Welsh Ministers or the Counsel General to the Welsh Assembly Government] or a Northern Ireland Department;

(d) a person appointed by a local authority to hold a local inquiry in pursuance of any statutory provision;

(e) any other tribunal, board, committee or body constituted by or under, and exercising functions under, any statutory provision.

[(1A) In the case of a local authority which are operating executive arrangements, a fair and accurate record of any decision made by any member of the executive where that record is required to be made and available for public inspection by virtue of section 22 of the Local Government Act 2000 or of any provision in regulations made under that section.]

(2) — [In sub-paragraphs (1)(a) and (1A)—

"executive" and "executive arrangements" have the same meaning as in Part II of the Local Government Act 2000;]

"local authority" means—

(a) in relation to England and Wales, a principal council within the meaning of the M1Local Government Act 1972, any body falling within any paragraph of section 100J(1) of that Act or an authority or body to which the M2Public Bodies (Admission to Meetings) Act 1960 applies,

(b) in relation to Scotland, a council constituted under section 2 of the M3Local Government etc. (Scotland) Act 1994 or an authority or body to which the Public Bodies (Admission to Meetings) Act 1960 applies,

(c) in relation to Northern Ireland, any authority or body to which sections 23 to 27 of the M4Local Government Act (Northern Ireland) 1972 apply; and

"local authority committee" means any committee of a local authority or of local authorities, and includes—

(a) any committee or sub-committee in relation to which sections 100A to 100D of the Local Government Act 1972 apply by virtue of section 100E of that Act (whether or not also by virtue of section 100J of that Act), and

(b) any committee or sub-committee in relation to which sections 50A to 50D of the Local Government (Scotland) Act 1973 apply by virtue of section 50E of that Act.

(3) A fair and accurate report of any corresponding proceedings in any of the Channel Islands or the Isle of Man or in another member State.

[11A A fair and accurate report of proceedings at a press conference held anywhere in the world for the discussion of a matter of public interest.]

12. (1) A fair and accurate report of proceedings at any public meeting held in a member State.

(2) In this paragraph a "public meeting" means a meeting bona fide and lawfully held for a lawful purpose and for the furtherance or discussion of a matter of public concern, whether admission to the meeting is general or restricted.

12. (1) A fair and accurate report of proceedings at any public meeting held anywhere in the world.

(2) In this paragraph a "public meeting" means a meeting bona fide and lawfully held for a lawful purpose and for the furtherance or discussion of a matter of public interest, whether admission to the meeting is general or restricted.]

13. (1) A fair and accurate report of proceedings at a general meeting of a UK public company.

(2) A fair and accurate copy of or extract from any document circulated to members of a UK public company—

(a) by or with the authority of the board of directors of the company,

(b) by the auditors of the company, or

(c) by any member of the company in pursuance of a right conferred by any statutory provision.

(3) A fair and accurate copy of or extract from any document circulated to members of a UK public company which relates to the appointment, resignation, retirement or dismissal of directors of the company.

(4) In this paragraph "UK public company" means—

(a) a public company within the meaning of [section 4(2) of the Companies Act 2006], or

(b) a body corporate incorporated by or registered under any other statutory provision, or by Royal Charter, or formed in pursuance of letters patent.

(5) A fair and accurate report of proceedings at any corresponding meeting of, or copy of or extract from any corresponding document circulated to members of, a public company formed under the law of any of the Channel Islands or the Isle of Man or of another member State.

[13. (1) A fair and accurate report of proceedings at a general meeting of a listed company.

(2) A fair and accurate copy extract from or summary of any document circulated to members of a listed company—

(a) by or with the authority of the board of directors of the company,

(b) by the auditors of the company, or

(c) by any member of the company in pursuance of a right conferred by any statutory provision.

(3) A fair and accurate copy, extract from or summary of any document circulated to members of a listed company which relates to the appointment, resignation, retirement or dismissal of directors of the company or its auditors.

(4) In this paragraph "listed company" has the same meaning as in Part 12 of the Corporation Tax Act 2009 (see section 1005 of that Act).

. . .]

14. A fair and accurate report of any finding or decision of any of the following descriptions of association, formed in the United Kingdom or another member State, or of any committee or governing body of such an association—

(a) an association formed for the purpose of promoting or encouraging the exercise of or interest in any art, science, religion or learning, and empowered by its constitution to exercise control over or adjudicate on matters of interest or concern to the association, or the actions or conduct of any person subject to such control or adjudication;

(b) an association formed for the purpose of promoting or safeguarding the interests of any trade, business, industry or profession, or of the persons carrying on or engaged in any trade, business, industry or profession, and empowered by its constitution to exercise control over or adjudicate upon matters connected with that trade, business, industry or profession, or the actions or conduct of those persons;

(c) an association formed for the purpose of promoting or safeguarding the interests of a game, sport or pastime to the playing or exercise of which members of the public are invited or admitted, and empowered by its constitution to exercise control over or adjudicate upon persons connected with or taking part in the game, sport or pastime;

(d) an association formed for the purpose of promoting charitable objects or other objects beneficial to the community and empowered by its constitution to exercise control over or to adjudicate on matters of interest or concern to the association, or the actions or conduct of any person subject to such control or adjudication.

14. A fair and accurate report of any finding or decision of any of the following descriptions of association, formed anywhere in the world, or of any committee or governing body of such an association—

    (a) an association formed for the purpose of promoting or encouraging the exercise of or interest in any art, science, religion or learning, and empowered by its constitution to exercise control over or adjudicate on matters of interest or concern to the association, or the actions or conduct of any person subject to such control or adjudication;

    (b) an association formed for the purpose of promoting or safeguarding the interests of any trade, business, industry or profession, or of the persons carrying on or engaged in any trade, business, industry or profession, and empowered by its constitution to exercise control over or adjudicate upon matters connected with that trade, business, industry or profession, or the actions or conduct of those persons;

    (c) an association formed for the purpose of promoting or safeguarding the interests of a game, sport or pastime to the playing or exercise of which members of the public are invited or admitted, and empowered by its constitution to exercise control over or adjudicate upon persons connected with or taking part in the game, sport or pastime;

    (d) an association formed for the purpose of promoting charitable objects or other objects beneficial to the community and empowered by its constitution to exercise control over or to adjudicate on matters of interest or concern to the association, or the actions or conduct of any person subject to such control or adjudication.]

[14A A fair and accurate—

    (a) report of proceedings of a scientific or academic conference held anywhere in the wold, or

    (b) copy of, extract from or summary of matter published by such a conference.]

15. (1) A fair and accurate report of, or copy of or extract from, any adjudication, report, statement or notice issued by a body, officer or other person designated for the purposes of this paragraph—

    (a) [for England and Wales, by order of the Lord Chancellor], and

    (b) for Scotland, by order of the Secretary of State.

    (c) for Northern Ireland, by order of the Department of Justice in Northern Ireland]

    (2) [Subject to sub-paragraph (3)] an order under this paragraph shall be made by statutory instrument which shall be subject to annulment in pursuance of a resolution of either House of Parliament.

    [(3) An order under sub-paragraph (1)(c) shall be made by statutory rule for the purposes of the Statutory Rules (Northern Ireland) Order 1979 and subject to negative resolution within the meaning of section 41(6) of the Interpretation Act (Northern Ireland) 1954.]

[15. (1) A fair and accurate report or summary of, copy of or extract from, any adjudication, report, statement or notice issued by a body, officer or other person designated for the purposes of this paragraph by order of the Lord Chancellor.

. . .

. . .

. . .

(2) An order under this paragraph shall be made by statutory instrument which shall be subject to annulment in pursuance of a resolution of either House of Parliament.

. . .]

PART II
SUPPLEMENTARY PROVISIONS

16. (1) In this Schedule—

"court" includes any tribunal or body exercising the judicial power of the State;

"international conference" means a conference attended by representatives of two or more governments;

"international organisation" means an organisation of which two or more governments are members, and includes any committee or other subordinate body of such an organisation; and

"legislature" includes a local legislature.

(2) References in this Schedule to a member State include any European dependent territory of a member State.

(3) In paragraphs 2 and 6 "court" includes—

(a) the European Court of Justice (or any court attached to that court) and the Court of Auditors of the European Communities,

(b) the European Court of Human Rights,

(c) any international criminal tribunal established by the Security Council of the United Nations or by an international agreement to which the United Kingdom is a party, and

(d) the International Court of Justice and any other judicial or arbitral tribunal deciding matters in dispute between States.

(4) In paragraphs 1, 3 and 7 "legislature" includes the European Parliament.

17. (1) Provision may be made by order identifying—

(a) for the purposes of paragraph 11, the corresponding proceedings referred to in sub-paragraph (3);

(b) for the purposes of paragraph 13, the corresponding meetings and documents referred to in sub-paragraph (5).

(2) An order under this paragraph may be made—

(a) [for England and Wales, by order of the Lord Chancellor], and

(b) for Scotland, by the Secretary of State.

[(c) for Northern Ireland, by order of the Department of Justice in Northern Ireland]

(3) [Subject to sub-paragraph (4)] an order under this paragraph shall be made by statutory instrument which shall be subject to annulment in pursuance of a resolution of either House of Parliament.

[(4) An order under sub-paragraph (2)(c) shall be made by statutory rule for the purposes of the Statutory Rules (Northern Ireland) Order 1979 and subject to negative resolution within the meaning of section 41(6) of the Interpretation Act (Northern Ireland) 1954.]

[16. In this Schedule—

"court" includes—

(a) any tribunal or body established under the law of any country or territory exercising the judicial power of the state;

(b) any international tribunal established by the Security Council of the United Nations or by an international agreement;

(c) any international tribunal deciding matters in dispute between States;

"international conference" means a conference attended by representatives of two or more governments;

"international organisation" means an organisation of which two or more governments are members, and includes any committee or other subordinate body of such an organisation;

"legislature" includes a local legislature; and

"member State" includes any European dependent territory of a member State."

. . .

17. . . .]

Please note, there are a number of prospective changes likely to be made to this schedule, based on sections of the Defamation Act 2013, which are not yet in force at the time of going to press. As such, we have highlighted any of these potential changes immediately below the relevant section in a tinted box. It is recommended that you check the Act yourself when you come to refer to this appendix to find out whether the changes we believe will go ahead are now in force.

Glossary

Acquittal A verdict of not guilty in a criminal case.

Affidavit A written statement which has been sworn on oath by a witness, which can be used as evidence in court.

Appeal A case taken to a higher court by someone who believes the wrong result was reached in the original hearing.

Appellant Person who brings an appeal.

Attorney-General A government minister who acts as the government's main legal advisor. Certain types of crime (such as offences under the Contempt of Court Act – **see Chapter 6**) require consent from the Attorney-General before prosecutions can be brought, and, if this consent is given, the prosecution is brought in the name of the Attorney-General.

Automatic reporting restrictions Reporting restrictions which a statute says apply in particular types of case. These arise in every case of that kind, without the need for a court order, though in some cases a court may order that they be lifted.

Bail The arrangement under which someone charged with a criminal offence can be allowed to remain free of custody until their trial.

Balance of probabilities The standard of proof in civil cases, where the claimant must prove that there is a more than 50 per cent chance that what they say is true (in other words, that it is more likely than not).

Beyond reasonable doubt The standard of proof in criminal cases. The prosecution must prove to the magistrates or jury that it is beyond reasonable doubt that the defendant committed the offence they are charged with.

Bill A written proposal for a new law, which is debated in Parliament.

Case law Law made by the decisions of judges in cases heard in the higher courts, which form precedents to be followed in later cases. Also known as common law.

Caution A formal warning given by the police as an alternative to prosecution; can only be used when an offender admits guilt.

Claimant The person bringing a case in the civil courts.

Committal hearing A hearing in a magistrates' court, to decide whether there is sufficient evidence to send a defendant charged with an either way offence to the Crown Court for trial.

Common law Law made by the decisions of judges in cases heard in the higher courts, which form precedents to be followed in later cases. Also known as case law.

Conditional fee agreement An agreement between solicitor and client in civil cases, under which the client pays nothing if they lose the case, and the solicitor gets an extra fee if they win. Often known as 'no win, no fee'.

Contemporaneous Published as soon as possible after an event (usually a court case).

Count Each one of the criminal charges faced by a defendant.

CPR/Civil Procedure Rules A set of rules covering how civil cases are run, with the aim of making sure both parties are treated fairly, unreasonable delay is avoided and court resources are allocated fairly.

Damages An amount of money which may be awarded by a court to someone who wins a civil case.

Defence **1** A legal provision which allows someone who would otherwise be guilty of a crime or a tort to escape liability, if the circumstances of the defence are met (e.g. justification, fair comment and privilege in defamation). **2** The name given to the lawyers representing a person who is accused of a crime, or a person who is being sued in the civil courts.

Defendant Someone who is being prosecuted in the criminal courts, or sued in the civil courts.

Delegated legislation Legislation that is made as a result of a statute but not contained within the words of the statute itself. A statute will often contain broad powers, and delegated legislation is used to spell out the detailed rules by which those powers are put into action. Also known as secondary legislation.

Director of Public Prosecutions *See* DPP.

Discretionary reporting restrictions Reporting restrictions which a statute allows a court to apply, but does not require as a matter of course. Discretionary restrictions only apply if the court makes an order saying so.

Double jeopardy An ancient rule which prevented someone acquitted of a crime from being charged again for the same offence; no longer an absolute rule in English law.

DPP Director of Public Prosecutions. The DPP is the head of the Crown Prosecution Service, advises the police and makes decisions about the most complex and sensitive cases. Some types of case can only be prosecuted with the DPP's permission.

Either way offence An offence which may be tried in a magistrates' court or the Crown Court. If the defendant does not choose Crown Court trial, magistrates decide whether to try the case themselves or refer it to the Crown Court.

Examining justices Magistrates, when they are holding committal proceedings, sending for trial or proceedings which lead up to these. Magistrates must sit in public when they are sitting as examining justices, except where there are statutory provisions against this, or a public hearing would not be in the interests of justice.

Expert witness Someone who is paid to give evidence in a particular case, because of their expertise in a relevant matter. In a criminal case, for example, expert witnesses may give evidence on the meaning of forensic evidence found in the case. They have a legal duty to give evidence impartially, even though they may be paid by one side or the other.

Family proceedings Hearings related to family matters, including divorce, adoption, and the care, custody, maintenance and paternity of children.

Green Paper A document issued by the Government when it is planning new legislation, setting out basic details of the area of law to be changed, and inviting comment.

In camera Used of court and tribunal hearings to which the public are not admitted, though the press may be. The term 'in private' is usually preferred.

In chambers Used of court and tribunal hearings held somewhere other than in an open court room, but not necessarily closed to public or press.

In private Used of court and tribunal hearings which are closed to the public. In some cases, the press will be allowed in to private hearings, but there may be restrictions on what you can report.

Indictable offence An offence which can only be tried by a Crown Court, with a jury.

Inherent jurisdiction The power which all courts have to control their own proceedings, which can include excluding the public and/or press.

Inherent jurisdiction with regard to minors The power which the High Court has to make decisions on behalf of under-18s.

Injunction A court order, which obliges someone to do or not to do something, either permanently or temporarily. Injunctions against the press usually prevent publication of particular material.

IPSO The Independent Press Standards Organisation, which regulates the conduct of the print media

Jigsaw identification Identification of someone whose identity should be concealed, by disclosure of different bits of information For example, if you report that ten years ago, a man raped a 15-year-old, and you also mention that the man has a stepdaughter aged 25, readers who know the family may be able to piece together the girl's identity.

Journalistic material Material which has been 'acquired or created for the purposes of journalism'. This type of material has a degree of protection from search and seizure by the police.

Judicial review An action brought in the High Court, in which decisions made by official bodies can be reviewed. If the decision has been made unlawfully, or is completely unreasonable, it may be quashed.

Limitation period A time limit set down in law, by which time a particular type of case must be brought. A case brought after the limitation period is said to be out of time or statute-barred, and cannot usually go ahead. In some cases the courts have discretion to extend time limits, though this power is subject to strict rules and used sparingly.

Malice A factor in the defamation defence of qualified privilege; if malice is present, the defence does not apply. In qualified privilege, malice is present where the maker of the statement's motive in making it was personal spite or ill-will, or any other improper motive.

Ofcom The body which regulates broadcasting in the UK It has a Code of Practice for broadcasters, breach of which can lead to fines and even loss of a broadcasting licence.

On remand Held in custody after being charged with a criminal offence, usually until the trial.

Open court A court which is open to the public, including the press (regardless of whether the public or press are actually present).

Open justice principle The principle that court proceedings should wherever possible be held in public, and the press be allowed to report on them freely. There are legal restrictions on this principle, but where possible open justice should prevail.

PACE The Police and Criminal Evidence Act 1984, which covers police procedure and powers during criminal investigations.

Plea The defendant's answer to the charge in a criminal case (i.e. guilty or not guilty).

Pleas in mitigation Arguments made by lawyers for a defendant who has been found (or pleaded) guilty to a crime, designed to give the court reason to treat them more leniently than they otherwise would.

Practice Direction An official document which contains detailed guidance for the courts on a particular issue, and supplements their ordinary rules of procedure.

Precedent A decision made in a legal case, which should be followed in later cases.

Private bill A proposal for legislation put forward by an individual, company or organisation, which affects a local issue such as a big construction project, but does not make general law.

Private prosecution A prosecution brought by a private individual, if the Crown Prosecution Service declines to take a case to court.

Prosecution 1 The process of bringing someone accused of crime before the courts. 2 The lawyers who represent that person.

Quash To declare invalid (usually used of a court order, verdict or sentence).

Rule against prior restraint A traditional principle of English law which states that as far as possible the media should not be censored in advance, but dealt with after publication if material published is unlawful.

Settle out of court To agree a solution to a court case with the other party, without going to court. The majority of civil cases are settled in this way.

Settlement The agreement made between two parties in a civil case, if they decide not to go to court. May include payment of damages and/or other conditions.

Skeleton arguments Written documents which explain the arguments which lawyers in a case plan to make. Issued to both sides and the judge in advance of the hearings. In ***Howell, Harris and May*** (2003), the Court of Appeal said journalists should be given copies on request.

Special measures directions Orders made to protect vulnerable witnesses, such as excluding the public from the court.

Standard of proof How certain the decision maker (magistrates, judge or jury) must be in deciding a case. In criminal cases, they should only convict if they are sure beyond reasonable doubt that the person is guilty. In a civil case, the claimant should only win if their case is proved on a balance of probabilities, meaning that it is more likely than not that their claim is correct.

Sting Used of defamatory remarks, this is the part of the statement which has the defamatory effect. If you write that a man hit his wife last Thursday, the sting of the libel is the allegation that he hit his wife, not the day he did it on.

Striking-out application A preliminary hearing which decides whether, assuming the facts alleged by a party in a case are true, they would have an arguable case in law. In defamation cases, for example, the defendant may apply for the claim to be struck out because the words complained of are not capable of bearing a defamatory meaning.

Sub judice Latin phrase meaning 'under judicial consideration'. Often used to describe legal proceedings that are under way or about to start. It is a myth that 'sub judice' matters cannot be discussed at all in the media.

Summary offence An offence which can only be tried in a magistrates' court. This does not necessarily mean it is a trivial offence.

Summary trial Trial of a summary offence in a magistrates' court.

Tainted trial A trial where there is evidence that someone has tried to affect the outcome by, for example, making threats or offering bribes to jury members.

TICs Offences which a defendant has not been charged with, but is willing to admit to (TIC stands for offences taken into consideration).

Tort A type of wrongdoing that is dealt with by the civil courts, rather than the criminal legal system.

Trial bundle A package of documents that details the legal arguments that each side intends to put forward, and includes witness statements and other written evidence.

Ward of court A person under 18 who, as a result of a legal order, is under the care of the Family Division of the High Court.

Young person Someone who is under 18.

Youth court A branch of the magistrates' courts, which deals with cases involving defendants aged under 18. The term describes a type of hearing, rather than a place.

Further reading

Section 1 Law and the legal system

Berlins, M. and Dyer, C. (2000) *The Law Machine.* Penguin.
Bradley, A and Ewing, K. (2010) *Constitutional and Administrative Law* Part I (15th edn). Pearson.
Elliott, C. and Quinn, F. (2014) *English Legal System* (15th edn). Pearson.
Elliott, C. and Quinn, F. (2014) *Criminal Law* (10th edn). Pearson.
Elliott, C. and Quinn, F. (2010) *Tort Law* (7th edn). Pearson.

Section 2 Writing about the courts

Banks, D. and Hanna, M. (2014) *McNae's Essential Law for Journalists,* Part 1 (24th edn). Oxford University Press.
Bonnington, A., Clive, E., McInnes, R. and McKain, B. (2010) *Scots Law for Journalists.* W. Green.
Media Lawyer newsletter, published bi-monthly by Tom Welsh, 3 Broom Close, Broughton-in-Furness, Cumbria LA20 6JG.
Robertson, G. and Nicol, A. (2008) *Media Law* (5th edn), Chapters 7, 8 and 9. Penguin.

Section 3 Defamation and malicious falsehood

Cain, N., Duodo, K. and Price, D. (2009) *Defamation; Procedure and Practice* (4th edn). Sweet and Maxwell.
Crone, T. (2002) *Law and the Media* (4th edn), Chapter 1. Focal Press.
Mason, P. and Smith, D. (1998) *Magazine Law: a Practical Guide,* Chapters 2, 3, 5, 6 and 7. Routledge.
Milo, D. (2008) *Defamation and Freedom of Speech.* Oxford University Press.
Robertson, G. (1999) *The Justice Game.* Vintage.
Robertson, G. and Nicol, A. (2008) *Media Law* (5th edn), Chapter 3. Penguin.

Section 4 Privacy, confidentiality and copyright

Frost, C. (2011) Journalism Ethics and Regulation. Longman.
Rozenberg, J. (2004) Privacy and the Press. Oxford University Press.
Tomlinson, H. (2002) Privacy and the Media: The Developing Law. Matrix Chambers.
Tugendhat, M. and Christie, I. (2006) The Law of Privacy and the Media. Oxford University Press.

Section 5 Codes of practice

Frost, C. (2011) Journalism Ethics and Regulation. Longman.
Hudson, G. and Rowlands, S. (2012) The Broadcast Journalism Handbook. Pearson.

Section 6 Reporting government and business

Brooke, H. (2007) Your Right to Know: A Citizen's Guide to the Freedom of Information Act (2nd edn). Pluto Press.
Morrison, J. (2009) Public Affairs for Journalists. Oxford University Press.
Pilger, J. (2005) Tell Me No Lies: Investigative Journalism and Its Triumphs. Vintage.
Robertson, G. and Nicol, A. (2008) Media Law (5th edn), Chapter 12. Penguin.
Thurlow, R. (1994) The Secret State. Blackwell.

Section 7 Race, religion and public order

Fenwick, H. and Phillipson, G. (2006) *Media Freedom under the Human Rights Act,* Part 3. LexisNexis UK.
Robertson, G. and Nicol, A. (2008) *Media Law* (5th edn), Chapter 4. Penguin.

Section 8 Photography

Cassell, D. (1989) *The Photographer and the Law.* BFP Books.

Index

AA *see* Automobile Association
abduction 166
ABH *see* actual bodily harm
abortion 183
absence of jury 75, 114
absolute discharge 31
absolute exemptions 439–40
  accessible information 439
  conduct of public affairs 439–40
  court records 439
  Parliamentary privilege 439
  security matters 439
  senior Royals 440
absolute privilege 93, 257–9
  accuracy 258
  contemporaneity 258–9
  fairness 257–8
abusive language 467
access to civil courts 106–7
  applications for injunctions 107
  closed material procedures 107
  housing cases 107
access to court documents 172–3
access to courts 97–112
  general rule on access 97–9
  restrictions on access 100–110
  summary 110–111
access to criminal courts 101–6
  information from prosecution 105–6
  names and addresses 106
  obtaining information 103–5
  restrictions on 102–3
  rules for excluding press 103
access to documents in inquest 191
access to family proceedings 167–73
  access to court documents 172–3
  exclusion from courts 170–72
  hearings 'in camera' 169–70
  hearings not open to press 169
  opposing press exclusion 172
access to local government meetings 419–24
  access to meetings of executive 421–2
  access to parish/town council meetings 423
  bodies not covered by regulations 423–4
  defamation/other restrictions on
    reporting 424
  exclusion from council meetings 424
  executive meetings in private 422
  information on council decisions 421
  information from executive meetings 423
  meetings in private 420–21
  notice of key decisions 422–3
access to local government records 425–7
  accounts 425–6
  general information 425
  planning and development 426–7
access to meetings of council executive 421–2
access to parish/town council meetings 423
accessible information 439
accord 271–2
account of profits 298, 375
accounts 425–6, 455
accreditation 168
accuracy 258, 385, 395–7, 480, 492–5
  principles of Ofcom code 492
  rules of Ofcom code 493–5
accurate contemporary reports 80, 93
ACPO *see* Association of Chief Police Officers
acquiescence 374
acquired programmes 509
acquittal 27, 31–4, 66, 89–90, 143–5
  appeals against 33–4, 143–5
active proceedings 65–8, 84
  appeals 68
  civil proceedings 67–8
  criminal proceedings 65–7
acts of Parliament 3–5
  stages 4–5
actual bodily harm 37
actus reus 35

adjournment 129, 189
adjusting impressions 309
administration 459
administration of justice offences 68
administrative convenience 170
adoption 169, 177–8
adult sex material 486–7
affidavits 253
aggravated damages 274
aggravated burglary 38
AGMs *see* annual general meetings
Ahmad, Babar 56
AIDS 288, 295
Aitken, Jonathan 248, 251, 253
Al Jazeera 394
allegations 229–30, 258
Allen, Lily 324
Allitt, Beverly 229–30
Allo, Allo 280
allocation cases 46, 127–9
allowing death of a vulnerable adult 36
Allwood, Mandy 369
ancillary relief hearing 169, 207
André, Peter 219, 400–401
annoyance 161
annual general meetings 455–6
annulment 166
anonymised injunctions 315–16
anonymity orders 121–3, 145, 151–2
answering police questions 335
anti-Semitism 232–3
anti-social behaviour 160–62, 394
  provisions against 160–62
anti-social behaviour orders 160–61, 209
  see also criminal behaviour orders
apologies 271
appeals 31–4, 58
  against acquittal 33–4
  by defendant 31–3
  in civil cases 47–9
  second appeals to Court of Appeal 33
appeals against acquittal 143–5
  anonymity for teachers 145
  appeals on new evidence 144
  extradition hearings 145
  referrals on points of law 144–5
  stopped trials 144
  tainted trials 144
appeals by way of case stated 32–3
appeals from county courts 48
appeals from Court of Appeal 34
appeals from High Court 48
appeals for funds 513, 516
appeals on new evidence 144
appeals to Crown Court 32–3
appeals to tribunals 198
application for injunction 107
application for planning permission 426–7
application of Representation of the People Act
    1983 431–2
applications for bail 129
applications for dismissal 132
applying for information 443–4
applying to original court 205–6
appropriate scheduling 484
appropriation 38
Archer, Jeffrey 250–51
archive material 240, 268–9
The Argus 209
Armstrong, Lance 251
arraignment pre-trial 25–6
arrests 66
artistic works: copyright on 360–61
ASBOs *see* anti-social behaviour orders
Ashdown, Paddy 370, 372
assault occasioning ABH 37
assaults 36–7
assertions of fact 73, 254
assignment 365–6
assisting police 102
Association of Chief Police Officers
    354, 474
associations 241
assuming guilt 75
assuming outcome of preliminary issues 76
attending court 160
attorney-general 15
attributes of claimant 302
auditing 441
Author of a Blog v Times Newspapers Limited
    (2009) 302–3, 308
Automobile Association 361
availability to public 372
avoiding justice 151
avoiding liquidation 459–60

background of character 72–3
background material 84, 127–8
Bagshaw, Roderick 216, 242
bail 22–3, 25, 129
balance of probabilities 44, 249
balancing relevant factors 77–8
ban in interests of justice 120–22
  in connection with proceedings 121
  risk to person claiming anonymity 121–2
ban on photographing police 477

Banbury Guardian 155
Bangla TV 398, 402
bankruptcy 457–8
  how it ends 458
  scale of 457–8
  what it means 458
Barot, Dhiren 117
barristers 13–14
basic rules on reporting local government meetings 418–19
basis of opinion 254–5
Bauer Media 404
BBC 56, 70–71, 179, 196, 227, 232, 269, 282, 291, 296, 370–71
BBC Breakfast 241
Beckham, David 309
Beckham, Victoria 218, 249–50, 309
being in charge of a vehicle while unfit 39
Bell, Mary 292
Bellfield, Levi 73, 388
Benefits Street 221
Big Brother 223
bigamy 236
bill stage of statute 4
Bin Laden, Osama 230
binding over orders 30–31
Birmingham Mail 115
Birmingham Post 76
Birmingham Six 228
blackmail 38, 102, 156, 208
Blair, Tony 119, 276, 294, 370, 396
blanket bans 181
bleeping 235
Bloody Sunday 201
Bloomberg TV 396
BNP *see* British National Party
bodies not covered by official secrets regulations 423–4
  in Wales 424
Bordes, Pamela 363
Bota Sot 271
Bovril 231
Bradshaw, Peter 376
Brady, Ian 332
Brainteaser 225
Branson, Richard 254
breach of confidence 287–300, 415
  defences to claim 294–7
  elements of claim 287–93
  and official secrets 415
  remedies for 297–8
  summary 298–9
breach of contract 50
breaches of CBOs 162
breaches of convention 53
breaking embargoes on court judgments 90
Breen, Suzanne 334
bribery 110, 327
Britain by Bike 389
British Broadcasting Corporation *see* BBC
British National Party 268
British Sky Broadcasting 219
broadcast competitions 490
broadcasting 108, 225–7, 272–4, 353, 361
  and context 225–7
  copyright on 361
  and data protection 353
  from court 108
  live broadcast defence 272–4
  see also context; juxtaposition
Broadmoor Hospital 334
Brooke, Heather 446
Bulger, James 56, 292
Bunn, Robert 291
burglary 38, 81
Burrell, Michael 116
Burton Mail 234
business information: law on 452–3
Butt, Hassan 340
by-laws 5

Campbell, Duncan 337
Campbell, Naomi 301, 347
Cannon, Godfrey 376
Capita 400
careless driving 39
Carr, Jimmy 240
Carr, Maxine 292
case law 6, 97
cases under Children Act 1989 175–6
causing death of a child 36
causing death through dangerous driving 39
causing death through drink 39
causing offence 488–90
causing sexual activity 37–8
CBOs *see* criminal behaviour orders
celebrities 58, 309–310
  see also public interest
challenging refusals 444–5, 449
challenging reporting restrictions 204–211
  challenging orders 205–210
  preventing restrictions 204–5
  summary 210
challenging s11 orders 122
challenging s39 orders 158

challenging use of Data Protection Act 354
chambers 99
Chancery Division 43
changes over time 222
  see also defamation
Channel 4 79, 221, 269, 290, 295, 333, 369, 396, 400–403
Channel 5 92, 225, 250
character attacks 262, 431
charges 449
charity appeals 512–13, 516
Charity Commission 447
checking information 264
Cheltenham Festival 445
Chevalier, Jeff 305
Chick, David 117
child witnesses in sex offences 102
children 37–8, 132–3, 149–65, 304–5, 481
  and photographs 304–5
  reporting restrictions re 149–65
  sexual offences against 37–8, 102, 132–3, 159–60, 481
  transfer of sexual cases 132–3
circuit judges 14
circulation of publication 71
circumstances of offence 73
civil case appeals 47–9
civil courts 43–52, 108–110
  access to 106–7
  county courts 44–5
  High Court 43–4
  obtaining information from 108–110
  procedure of 43–52
civil jurisdiction of magistrates' courts 49
civil law 11
civil litigation procedure 44–7
  allocating the case 46
  making the claim 45
  pre-trial procedure 46
  procedure to trial 46–7
civil partnerships 177
Civil Procedure Rules 45, 88, 98, 106–9, 244
civil proceedings 67–8
claiming anonymity 121–2
claims for breach of confidence 287–93
  confidential information 288–9
  obligation of confidence 289–93
  unauthorised use 293
claims under Protection from Harassment Act 1887 316–20
clandestine devices 387–8, 482
Clockwork Orange 369, 371–2
closed material procedures 103, 107
Codes of Practice and ethics 381–408
  IPSO and Editors' Code of Practice 383–90
  Ofcom Code 391–407
Cole, Andrew 219
Cole, Ashley 235
Cole, Cheryl 220
College of Policing 21
commercial communications in radio programming 513–17
  principles of Ofcom code 514
  rules of Ofcom code 514–17
commercial interests 442
commercial references in TV programming 404, 504–513
  principles of Ofcom code 505
  rules of Ofcom code 505–513
commissioning work 366
committals for sentencing 129
committee stage of statute 5
common assault 37
common civil claims 49–50
  breach of contract 50
  negligence 50
  nuisance 50
  trespass 50
common crimes 35–9
  assaults 36–7
  homicide offences 35–6
  offences related to motor vehicles 39
  sexual offences against adults 37
  sexual offences against children 37–8
  theft/fraud 38–9
common problems with contempt 93
communications with royalty 442
community sentence 30
Companies House 452–5
company information 453
compensation orders 30
compensatory damages 274
complainants in later proceedings 137
complaints to IPSO 383–4
complaints to Ofcom 392
complaints under Ofcom code 404
compulsory liquidation 459
'concerned in proceedings' 155–6, 209
conciliation 169
concurrent sentences 29–30
conditional discharge 31
conduct of public affairs 439–40, 442
confidential circumstances 292
confidential information 288–9, 420, 482
  old information 289
  photographs 289

confidentiality 285–380
  breach of confidence 287–300
  copyright 360–79
  data protection 346–59
  and photography 477–8
  privacy 301–322
  protecting sources and source material 330–45
  trespass, harassment, unethical behaviour 323–9
confiscation orders 30
connected persons 506
connection with proceedings 121
consecutive sentences 29–30
consent 248, 502
consideration of public interest 118
  orders made for other purposes 118
  scope of s4(2) orders 118
constituency coverage 497
contemporaneity 258–9
contempt of court 63–96, 196
  and inquests 191
  intentional contempt 82–5
  other types of contempt 86–91
  publications prejudicial to fair trial 64
  sanctions for contempt 91–3
  'strict liability' contempt 64–82
  summary 94–5
  and tribunals 196
Contempt of Court Act 1981 64–6, 75–82, 86–8, 113–14, 331–4, 476
  interests of justice 331–4
  interests of national security 331
  prevention of crime 334
  reporting restrictions under 113–14
  where orders may be heard 114
contempt in Scotland 84–5
contemptuous damages 275
content of report 71–7
  assertions of fact 73
  assuming guilt 75
  assuming outcome of preliminary issues 76
  circumstances of offence 73
  criticism of decision to prosecute 71
  defendant's background 72
  guilty pleas to other charges 74
  inaccurate reporting 77
  interfering in proceedings 77
  interviewing witnesses 76–7
  involvement in other proceedings 74
  photographs/description 73–4
  previous convictions 71–2
  proceedings without jury 75
  protected documents/information 76
  speculating about damages 76
  undermining witnesses 77
  vilifying suspects 75–6
content of sponsored output 510
contents of Editors' Code of Practice 480–83
  accuracy 480
  children 488
  children in sex cases 488
  clandestine devices 482
  confidential sources 482
  discrimination 482
  financial journalism 482
  harassment 481
  hospitals 482
  intrusion into grief or shock 481
  opportunity to reply 480
  payment to criminals 483
  privacy 481
  reporting crime 482
  victims of sexual assault 482
  witness payment 483
context 226
  and broadcasting 226–7
  importance of 226
  and the internet 227
contradictions 261
copyright 360–79
  defences 368–74
  infringement of 366–8
  moral and privacy rights 375–7
  ownership of 364–6
  and photography 477–8
  remedies for breach of 374–5
  summary 377–8
  works protected by 360–64
Cornwell, Charlotte 253
coroner's officer 194
corporations 241
correcting false image 309
corrections 272
corruption 236
costs 45, 445–6
council decisions 421
council executive 421–2
counsel *see* barristers
Country Life 219
county courts 44–5, 48
  appeals from 48
court exclusion 170–72
court information 105
Court of Protection 183–4
court records 439

court report corrections 272
court rules 98
court system 12–13
Courting Disaster 290
coverage of children subject to s39 orders 156
coverage of copyright 364
coverage of Ofcom Broadcasting Code 391–2
  complaints to Ofcom 392
  role of Ofcom 392
coverage of suicides 385–6
covering election meetings 434
CPR *see* Civil Procedure Rules
CPS *see* Crown Prosecution Service
crediting sponsorship 510
creditors voluntary liquidation 459
crime 491
  principles of Ofcom code 491
  rules of Ofcom code 491
crime prevention 334
crime reporting 386–7, 482
criminal behaviour orders 28, 161–2
  reporting 161–2
  reporting breaches 162
criminal cases and reporting restrictions 126–48
  appeals against acquittal 143–5
  hearings before trial 126–33
  pleas in mitigation 139–40
  protecting vulnerable witnesses 140–43
  rape and sexual offences 133–9
  summary 146
Criminal Cases Review Committee 32–3
criminal courts 18–41, 101–6
  access to 101–6
  procedure of 18–41
criminal justice procedure 19–28
  hearings before a trial 24–6
  investigating crime 19–23
  procedure to trial 26–7
  prosecution 23–4
  sentencing 28
criminal law 11
Criminal Procedure Rules 103–5, 113
criminal proceedings 65–7, 190, 441
  in contempt cases 65–7
  in inquest 190
criminal proceedings in inquest 65–7, 190
criticism of decision to prosecute 71
criticism material 369
Cronin, John 85
cross-promotions 512
cross-undertaking 315
Crossman, Richard 289
Crown Court 19, 25–6, 32–3
  pre-trial hearings 25–6
  types of appeal from 32–3
  youth court cases 152
Crown Prosecution Service 15, 23–6, 71, 100, 102, 249, 466
Croydon Advertiser 150
current event reporting 369–70
current proceedings 117
current public policy 494–5
custom 8–9

DA notices *see* defence advisory notices
Da Vinci Code 91, 362
Dadak, Rod 225, 233, 243–4, 252, 277, 298
Daily Express 81–2, 182, 236, 251, 363, 373
Daily Express Today 78
Daily Mail 70–73, 78–81, 88, 174, 181, 218–20, 236, 241, 249–50, 304–6, 317
Daily Mirror 72–3, 218, 220–21, 295, 301, 332, 347, 352, 388
Daily Record 85
Daily Star 74, 78, 218–19
Daily Telegraph 218, 234, 254, 388
Dallas 253
damage to reputation 213–84
  defamation 215–46
  defences and remedies for defamation 247–79
  malicious falsehood 280–83
damages 76, 274–5
  aggravated damages 274
  compensatory damages 274
  contemptuous damages 275
  exemplary damages 275
  nominal damages 275
  speculation about 76
damaging admissions 272
Dando, Jill 220
dangerous behaviour 393, 486, 489
dangerous driving 39
data; definition of 346–7
data controller 348
data protection 346–59
  exemptions for media 351–3
  information covered by the Data Protection Act 1998 346–8
  media duties under the Act 348–51
  obtaining information from others 357
  problems with gathering information 354–6
  summary 357–8
data subject 348

Dawkins, Marvin 115, 120
de Beke, Anton 219
dealing with documents 337
debate of general interest 308, 312
debt repayment 44
deception 387–8, 400, 500
decisions on injunctions 57
deeming order necessary 115–16
defamation 196–7, 215–46, 424, 433–4
  in elections 433–4
  elements of 216
  and inquests 191
  meaning of 'defamatory' 216–33
  and other restrictions on reporting 424
  publication 238–41
  referring to claimant 233–8
  slander 243–4
  summary 244–5
  and tribunals 215–46
defamatory apologies 272
defaming a group 237–8
defence advisory notices 415–16
defence of the country *see* national security
defence limits 259
defences against strict liability 79–81
  discussion of public affairs 80–81
  fair and accurate contemporary reports 80
  innocent publication 79–80
defences for contempt 93
defences for defamation 93, 247–79
  remedies 274–7
  summary 277–8
  types of 247–74
defences for incitement of racial hatred 467
defences for religious hatred 468
defences to breach of copyright 368–74
  acquiescence 374
  fair dealing 368–72
  incidental inclusion 373
  innocent infringement 374
  public interest 373–4
  spoken words 373
defences to claim for breach of confidence
    294–7
  information in public domain 294
  public interest 294–7
defendant appeals 31–3
  from Crown Court 32–3
  from magistrates' courts 32
defendant assisting police 102
defendant's character 72–3
defendants in multiple trials 103
deferred sentence 30
defining malicious falsehood 280–82
  financial loss 281–2
  malicious publication 281
  untrue statements 280–81
definition of strict liability 65
definition of trespass 323–4
delegated legislation 5–6
deliberate prejudice 82–3
delivery up 297–8
Dempster, Nigel 88
Denmark 364, 466
Department of Constitutional Affairs 201
Deripaska, Oleg 250
derogation 54–5
descriptions 73–4
design of tribunals 195–7
  contempt of court 196
  defamation 196–7
  reporting restrictions 197
designated organisations 433
Desmond, Richard 251–2
Diana Princess of Wales 171, 333, 370–71
diminished responsibility 36
Director of Public Prosecutions 15, 24,
    33, 414
disclosure 331–2, 334, 412–13
discretionary reporting restrictions 179–80
discrimination 482
discriminatory material 388–9
discussion of public affairs 80–81
dismissal 132
Dispatches 400
distress 320, 503–4
district judges 14
divorce 176–7
DNA 144–5
documents relating to court cases 291
domestic relations 441
doorstepping 316, 319–20, 502–3
Dorset Echo 154
double jeopardy 33–4
Douglas, Michael 289, 297, 350–51, 477
Dowler, Milly 72, 141, 388
Down's Syndrome 80–81
DPP *see* Director of Public Prosecutions
dramatic works: copyright on 360–61
dramatising trials on TV 27, 79
drink driving 39
driving without insurance 39
dropping hints 234–5
  see also defamation
drug use 22–3, 485–6
due impartiality 395–7, 492–5

principles of Ofcom code 492
rules of Ofcom code 493–5

Earl Spencer 171
Eastenders 218
Eastern Daily Press 155
EATs *see* employment appeal tribunals
eavesdropping 326
see also harassment; trespass
ECHR *see* European Convention on Human Rights
economic interests 441
ECtHR *see* European Court of Human Rights
Editors' Code of Practice of the PCC 297, 326, 383–90, 480–83
accuracy/opportunity to reply 384
contents 480–83
discriminatory/pejorative material 388–9
financial journalism 389
intrusion/coverage of suicide 385–6
obtaining information by deception 387–8
public interest 483
reporting crime 386–7
reporting in hospital/medical treatment 386
see also Independent Press Standards Organisation
Edmonds, Noel 218
effect on claimant 302
effect of claimant's existing reputation 222–3
effect of s49 150
either way offences 18, 24–5
Election 2010 398
election reporting 430–35
offences relating to 430–33
other legal considerations 433–4
summary 434
elections 397–8, 495–8
principles of Ofcom code 495
and referendum 397–8
rules of Ofcom code 495–8
Electoral Commission 397
elements of defamation 216
elements of privacy claim 301–313
privacy vs freedom of expression 307–313
reasonable expectation of privacy 302–7
'Elephant Man' 403
Elstein, David 293
emailing from court 108
embargoes 90, 367–8
breaking on court judgments 90
employer–employee relationships 290
employment appeal tribunals 198
employment tribunals 197–201
appeals 198
procedure 197–8
reporting employment tribunals 198–9
reporting restrictions 199–201
encouraging crime 394–5
end of bankruptcy 458
ending pre-trial hearing restrictions 131
ending restrictions 129
ending s39 order 158–9
enforcement of Data Protection Act 1998 353
enforcing contempt laws 85
Engineer magazine 288, 332
English court system 12–13
environmental information 442, 447–9
challenging refusals 449
charges 449
exemptions 448
information covered 447
making a request 447–8
epilepsy 393
Epsom Guardian 155
equity 9
establishing copyright 364
ethics *see* Codes of Practice and ethics
EU law 6–8
European Convention on Human Rights 9, 53–5
applying rights 55
protected rights 54–5
European Court of Human Rights 53–4, 303–4, 310–312, 335, 342, 466
European courts 8
European Parliament 432
evidence of sexual history 103
excluded material 335–6
exclusion from council meetings 424
exclusion from court 170–72
notice of proposed exclusion 171–2
exclusivity 366
executive meetings in private 422
exemplary damages 275
exempt information 420–21
exemptions for media 352–3
protecting sources 353
exemptions under FOI 2000 438–43, 448
absolute exemptions 439–40
qualified exemptions 439–40
existing reputation 222–3
see also defamation
exit polls 432
exorcism 488–90

expectation of privacy 302–7, 501–2
  attributes of and effect on claimant 302
  children photographs 304–5
  information in public domain 306–7
  nature of activity 302–3
  photographs/video 303–4
  where information comes from 305
expert witnesses 174–5
explanation 261
extent of injunctions 315
extra-judicial killing 394
extradition hearings 145

face of court contempt 86
Facebook 313, 365
factors posing risk of prejudice 128
Fagin, Michael 81
failing to comply with court order 87–8
failure to provide specimen 39
fair contemporary reports 80, 93
fair dealing 368–72
  availability to public 372
  fairness 371–2
  material for criticism and review 369
  material for reporting current events 367–70
  material that may be used 369
  sufficient acknowledgement 370–71
  using photographs 370
fair trial, right to 58
fairness 257–8, 371–2, 398–401, 498–500
  principles of Ofcom code 498
  rules of Ofcom code 498–500
false attribution of authorship 367, 376
false statements about electoral candidates 430–32
  application of Representation of the People Act 1983 431–2
  defences 432
  fact or opinion 430–31
  falsity 431
  penalties 432
  purpose of statement 431
  referring to characters 431
false statements about withdrawal 432
falsity 431
Family Court 166–87
  reporting in 166–87
Family Division 43
family proceedings before magistrates 176
family proceedings not involving children 181
fast track cases 46–7
Fathers4Justice 117
Fayed, Dodi 333, 370–71
Ferdinand, Rio 308
fiddling expenses 131
filming outside court 87
films: copyright on 361
financial dispute resolution hearings 159
financial journalism 389, 456, 482
financial loss 281–2
financial promotions 513, 517
financing limited company 454
fines 30
first reading of statute 4
fishing expeditions 388
fixed sentences 29
flagrant damages 374–5
following invalid orders 209–210
food hygiene 35
Foot Anstey 103, 122, 150, 152, 158, 206
Football Association 361
formation of government policy 441
forms of defamation 216
fraud 38–9
freedom of expression 55–8, 307–313
  correcting false impression 309
  and court cases 311
  debate of general interest 308–9
  necessity of information 311
  protection against injunction 57–8
  public interest and celebrities 309–310
  right to tell 310–311
  using material from public/social media 312–13
  using pictures 312
  vs privacy 307–313
freedom of information 436–51
  environmental information 447–9
  Freedom of Information Act 2000 436–47
  summary 449–50
freelances 346, 349, 364–5
  and data protection 346
  and freedom of information 349
frustrating court orders addressed to others 88

gagging orders 93, 316
Galloway, George 254, 293, 397
gang rape 74
Garraway, Kate 219
Gascoigne, Paul 220
gathering information 354–6, 502–3
GBH *see* grievous bodily harm
Geldof, Peaches 272
general information on local government records 425
general reporting restrictions 113–25, 173–84

in family court matters 173–84
other reporting restrictions 123–4
postponing publication 114–18
preventing publication 119–22
summary 124
under Contempt of Court Act 1981 113–14
general rules on court access 97–9
types of hearing 98–9
George, Barry 220
Geraghty, Tony 414
Giggs, Ryan 307, 311
Gillick, Victoria 227
Glivec 400
Gloucester Citizen 128
Goldsmith, Sir James 273
good behaviour 31
Goodfellas 256
Goodwin, Bill 332
government employees 290–91
government legal officers 15
government policy, formation of 441
government stories, public interest in 296–7
Granada Television 293
Greene, Martha 276
grief 385–6
grievous bodily harm 37
Grobbelaar, Bruce 266, 275
grounds for challenge 207–9
Guardian 88, 109–110, 233, 248, 251, 270, 291, 331, 437, 445
guilty pleas 26, 74

habeas corpus 21
habitual conduct 229
see also defamation
Hain, Peter 86
Hamilton, Neil 249
handling complaints 243–4
handling goods 39
Hansard 255
harassment 323–9, 481
see also trespass
Hargey, Taj 217
harm and offence 393–4, 488–90
principle 488
rules 488–90
HarperCollins 270
Harry Potter and the Half-Blood Prince 288
Have I got News for You 70
health authorities 428
health and safety 442
hearing an inquest 188–9
hearings before trial: restrictions on 126–33
applications to dismiss 132
bail applications 129
hearings in magistrates' court 127–9
pre-trial hearings 129
preparatory hearings 131–2
transfer of sexual offence cases involving children 132–3
hearings in chambers 84
hearings 'in camera' 169–70
Heat magazine 222, 400–401
Hello! magazine 289, 297, 314, 317, 477
helping police with their inquiries 66
Hendrix, Jimi 222
High Court 43–4, 48, 167
anonymity in 123
appeals from 48
inherent jurisdiction 123–4, 167
High Court judges 14
HM Revenue & Customs 11, 341
Holby City 192
holding injunction 57
Holy Blood and the Holy Grail 362
homicide offences 35–6
homosexuality 217, 431
honest opinion 253–7
basis of opinion 254–5
privileged material 255–6
statement must be 253–4
types of statement covered 256–7
hospital reporting 386, 482
House of Floris 236
House of Lords 5
housing cases 107
how law is made 3–10
sources of law 3–9
summary 9–10
Hughes, Paul 141
Huhne, Chris 306, 317
human rights 53–60, 342–3
European Convention and Human Rights Act 53–5
and media law 55–8
and protection of sources 342–3
summary 58–9
Huntley, Ian 182, 292
hypnosis 490

Ideal Home 362
Ideal Home Exhibition 445
ideas 362
see also copyright
identifying adults 182
identifying correct person 106

identifying jurors 89
identifying sources 251
identity parades 74
illegality 49
imminent proceedings 82, 114, 117
impartiality 395–7
implication 224
implied reference 235
implying habitual conduct 229
importance of context 226
importance of good conduct 270–71
imprisonment 29–30
  consecutive/concurrent sentence 29–30
  length of sentence 29
  life sentence 29
  suspended/deferred sentence 30
impropriety 384
'in camera' hearings 169–70
inaccurate reporting 77
incest cases 139
incidental inclusion 373
incidental prejudice 81
incidental prevention of identifying adults 182
incitement of racial hatred 463–70
incorporated firms *see* limited companies
indecent assault 135
Independent Press Standards Organisation 383–90
  complaints to 383–4
  Editors' Code of Practice 384–9
  summary 389
Independent on Sunday 237
indictable offences 18, 25
individuals 241
infanticide 36
inflicting GBH 37
information after case is over 110
information on council decisions 421, 423–4
information covered by Data Protection Act 1996 346–8
information covered by FOI 2000 447
information from executive meetings 423
information from police 21–2, 93, 354–6
information from prosecution 105–6
information from schools 356, 427
information intended for publication 440
information on limited companies 453–6
  accounts 455
  annual general meetings 455–6
  information on directors 454–5
  initial documentation 454
  ownership/finance 454
information on limited company directors 454–5
information in public domain 294, 306–7
information required by police 334–8
  answering police questions 335
  powers of search and seizure 335–8
infringing copyright 366–8
  embargoes 367–8
  length of copyright 368
  parodies 367
infringing privacy 401–3
inherent jurisdiction 100, 123–4, 167
  see also High Court
initial documentation on limited company 454
initial reports 84
injunctions 57–8, 107, 161, 275–7, 313–16
  affecting wards of court 178–9
  application for 107
  extent of injunctions 315
  interim injunctions 314–415
  preventing nuisance and annoyance 161
  preventing publication 57
  protection against 57–8
  super injunctions 315–16
innocent dissemination 272–4
innocent infringement of copyright 374
innocent publication 65, 79–80
innuendo 223–4
  see also defamation
inquests 188–94
  media attendance 190–93
  procedure 188–90
  summary 193
inquiries 195–203
  see also tribunals
insolvency proceedings 456–60
  bankruptcy 457–8
  liquidation proceedings 458–9
insufficient prominence 272, 385
insulting language 467
integrity 376
intellectual property 360, 448
  see also copyright
intention to incite racial hatred 466
intentional contempt 82–5
  contempt in Scottish cases 84–5
  intention 82–3
  proceedings pending or imminent 82
intercepting communications 325–7, 412
  bribery 327
  listening to police messages 326

Interception of Communications Commission 341–2
interests of justice 120–22, 331–4
interests of national security 331
interference with land *see* trespass
interfering in proceedings 77
interfering with witnesses 89–90
interim injunctions 314–15
interlocutory hearings 108
international relations 440
international treaties 8
the internet 78–9, 227, 239–40, 367
  and contempt 78–9
  and copyright 367
  and publication 239–40
interpretation of legislation 53–4
interviewing witnesses 76–7
interviews 363–4
  see also copyright
intrusion into grief 385–6, 481
invalid orders 209–210
investigating council expenditure 426
investigating crime 19–23
  bail 22–3
  police questioning 21–2
  pre-arrest powers 20
investigating jury deliberations 88–9
investigation anonymity order 142
investigation of religious persecution 468
investigation under Data Protection Act 1998 353
investigations 66, 229–30, 414–15
  and arrests 66
  powers 414–15
investment recommendations 513, 517
involuntary manslaughter 36
involvement in other proceedings 74
IPNAs 161
  reporting 161
  see also injunctions
Irish News 256
The Irish War 414
irrationality 49
Islam, Yusuf 219
issuing s39 order 158

Jaffa, Tony 103, 122, 150, 152, 158, 206
Jefferies, Chris 75–6, 85
jigsaw identification 137, 159–60
John, Elton 304, 334, 475
Johnson, Andy 24
jokes 232–3
journalistic material 335–8
joyriding 39
JPs *see* justices of the peace
JSB *see* Judicial Studies Board
judges 14–15
judicial precedent 6
judicial proceedings 282
judicial review 49, 206–7
Judicial Studies Board 104, 155, 158, 207, 209
justice 120–22, 331–4
justices of the peace 14–15
justification 216
  see also truth
juxtaposition 224–5
  and broadcasting 225
  see also defamation

Katona, Kerry 457
Kaye, Gorden 280–82, 324
Keays, Sara 254
Kensington and Chelsea Borough Council 179
Kent Messenger 119, 134
Khashoggi, Soraya 276
Kiam, Victor 274
Kidman, Nicole 217, 276
kidnapping 73
Kilroy Silk, Robert 466
Kipling, Rudyard 363
Knights, Geoff 72, 77, 85
KPMG Peat Marwick 297

Labour Party 396
Lancashire Evening Post 135
Lancashire Evening Telegraph 154
law on business information 452–3
law enforcement 441
Lawrence, Stephen 87, 201
lawyers 13–14
The Lawyer 91
leaks 372, 413
  see also public interest
leapfrog procedure 49
leave and licence 248
Leeds Weekly News 266
Legal Aid 25, 120, 144
legal considerations when reporting elections 433–4
  defamation 433–4
  race relations law 436
legal professional privilege 442
legal system 1–60
  civil courts and procedure 43–52
  criminal courts and procedure 18–42
  how law is made 3–10
  human rights and English law 53–60
  organisation of 11–17

length of copyright 368
Lennon, John 294
Lewis Silkin 233, 243–4, 252, 277, 298
libel claims 93, 240–43, 248
'libel tourism' 242–3
licence 366
Liddle, Ron 87
lifting reporting restrictions 181–2
lifting restrictions 128–9
lifting s49 restrictions 151–2
lifting Sexual Offences restrictions 136
limited companies 452–6
  information on 453–6
limited liability partnerships 453
limits of defence 259
liquidation 458–9
listening to police radio messages 326
literary works: copyright on 360–61
live broadcast defence 272–4
Liverpool Echo 154, 297
Living Marxism 215
Livingstone, Ken 396–7
local authorities 242
local government reporting 418–29
  access to meetings 419–24
  access to records 425–7
  basic rules on 418–19
  other local public bodies 427–8
  summary 428–9
Local Government Transparency Code 425
location of trial 71
loco parentis 180, 320, 399, 402, 488, 499, 504
London Evening Standard 72, 249, 255, 257
London Gazette 457
London Stock Exchange 454
Lord Chancellor 15
Lord and Lady Justices of Appeal 14
loss of control 35–6
Love It! 223
Loyalist Volunteer Force 72
Lugano Convention 243

McBride, Nicholas 216, 242
McCann, Madeleine 219–20
McCartney, Paul 317
McClaren, Steve 309–310
McFadden, Brian 222
McGill, Anthony 219
Mackenzie friend 47
McLetchie, David 437
magistrates *see* justices of the peace
magistrates' courts 18–19, 32, 49, 428
  appeals from 49
  committees 428
  Crown Court 19
  family proceedings before 176
  pre-trial hearings 24–5, 130
  routes of appeal from 32
  sending for trial 127–9
magistrates' error 32
Mail on Sunday 89, 218, 276, 294, 305–6, 412
main remedies for defamation 274–7
  damages 274–5
  injunctions 275–7
Major, John 228, 295
making civil claims 45
making law 3–10
making orders 114
making a request 447–8
malice 263
malice aforethought 35–6
malicious falsehood 280–83
  definition 280–82
  summary 282–3
malicious publications 281
malicious wounding 57
Malik, Shiv 340
mandatory restricted access 487
manslaughter 22–3, 35–6
Marie Claire 135
Marketing Week 332
Master of the Rolls 14, 117, 121, 316
Materazzi, Marco 219
material contributing to debate of general
    interest 308
material for defence 369
material difference 238
material referred to in court 109
Maxwell, Lisa 218
Maxwell, Robert 70, 116, 294
meaning of 'allegedly' 228
meaning of bankruptcy 458
media attendance in Family Court 173–84
  adoption cases 177–8
  cases under Children Act 1989 175–6
  Court of Protection 183–4
  discretionary reporting restrictions 179–80
  divorce cases 176–7
  family proceedings before magistrates 176
  family proceedings not involving children
    181
  general reporting restrictions 173–5
  incidental prevention of identifying adults
    182
  lifting reporting restrictions 181–2
  rules not yet in force 183

using information about family cases 182–3
wardship cases 178–9
media duties under Data Protection Act 1996 348–51
processing personal data 349–50
processing sensitive personal data 350
registration 348–9
rights of data subject 350–51
Media Law 424, 431, 475
media law and human rights 55–8
freedom of expression 55–8
right to fair trial 58
right to respect for private and family life 58
Media Lawyer 106–7, 183
media position 293
media representation 57
mediation 169
medical treatment reporting 386
meetings of local government 418–24
access to 419–24
basic rules on reporting 418–19
meetings in private 420, 423
members voluntary liquidation 458–9
mens rea 35
mental health orders 30
mentioning other details 127
Merrick, Josephine 403
MI5 88, 336, 412
MI6 414
Miller, Sienna 324
Milton Keynes Citizen 342
Ministry of Defence 331
Ministry of Justice 173, 190
misconduct in public office 327, 342
Serious Crime Act 2007 327
misuse of alcohol 485–6
misuse of private information 301
Mitchell and Forbes (1998) 222
mitigation 139–40
money laundering 262
'Moors Murderers' 332
moral rights in copyright issues 375–7
false attribution of authorship 376
right of integrity 376
right to paternity 375–6
unauthorised use of pictures 376–7
MORI polls 273
Moss, Kate 222, 250
motor vehicle offences 39
mugging 67
multi-track cases 46–7
multiple publications 78–9
contempt and the internet 78–9
Munchausen's Syndrome by Proxy 174–5
Munich Beer Festival 308
murder 35
musical works: copyright on 360–61
My Country, Right or Wrong 291
Myskow, Nina 253

NA *see* Narcotics Anonymous
names and addresses 106, 258
naming dead children 155
naming and shaming 151
Narcotics Anonymous 301–4
narrative verdict 189
national emergency 5
National Lottery 236, 254, 332
national security 98, 331, 440
nature of activity 302–3
necessity of information 311, 332
necessity of order 115–16
Neeson, Liam 228
negligence 50
Neighbours 226
neutral reports of disputes 268
new evidence 33, 144, 251–3
new legislation 54
New Statesman 337, 454
Newcastle Journal 333
News at Ten 79
news and information 362–3, 368–72
see also copyright; fair dealing
News International 325
News of the World 70, 80, 219–20, 223, 226, 235, 238, 249–50, 253, 288, 293–4, 303, 376
Newspaper Society 356
NHS trusts 428
Nicol, Andrew 90, 415, 424, 431, 434, 455
'Night Jack' 302–3
no win no fee agreements 45
nominal damages 275
Northern Echo 78, 136, 397
Northern Ireland 56, 72, 87, 102, 139, 150, 153, 215, 260, 340, 439–42
conduct of public affairs 439
terrorism provisions for 340
not 'concerned in proceedings' 155–6
orders attempting to cover other proceedings 156
other coverage of children subject to s39 orders 156
not guilty pleas 26–7
notice of key decisions 422–3
notice of proposed press exclusion 171–2

notice of s4(2) and s11 orders 122
challenging s11 orders 122
Novartis 400
nudity 487
nuisance 50, 161

obligation of confidence 289–93
confidential circumstances 292
documents relating to court cases 291
employer–employee relationships 290
government employees 290–91
people at risk of harm 292–3
position of media 293
Observer 88
obstruction 476–7
obtaining information by deception 387–8
obtaining information from civil courts 108–110
information when case is over 110
material referred to in court 109
obtaining information from criminal courts 103–205
obtaining information from others 347
occult practices 488–90
Ofcom Broadcasting Code 296, 318–20, 326, 391–407, 484–517
commercial communications in radio programming 513–17
commercial references in TV programming 504–513
complaints under 404
crime 491
due impartiality/undue prominence 492–5
elections/referendum 495–8
fairness 498–500
harm and offence 488–90
history of 391–2
privacy 500–504
protecting the under-18s 484–8
provisions of 392–404
religion 491–2
summary 405–6
offences covered by Sexual Offences restrictions 134–5
offences related to election reporting 430–33
exit polls 432
false statements about candidates 430–32
false statements about withdrawal 432
unauthorised advertisements 432–3
offences to be taken into consideration 28
offensive language 393–4, 486
offer of amends 269
Office of the Information Commissioner 346, 348, 353–4, 356, 437, 440–49
official information 261, 364
Official Receiver 457–8
official secrets 411–17, 474–5
defence advisory notices 415–16
Official Secrets Act 1911 411–12
Official Secrets Act 1989 412–15
and photography 474–5
summary 416
Old Bailey 12, 79
old information 289
one-off inquiries 201
open court 98
opinion based on privileged material 255–6
opportunity to reply 480
opposing press exclusion 172
order for delivery up 297–8
orders attempting to cover other proceedings 156
orders in council 5
orders made for other purposes 118
Ordnance Survey 361
organisation of legal system 11–17
court system 12–13
people in the legal system 13–15
summary 15–16
types of law 11–12
origins of defamation 216–33
changes over time 222
context and broadcasting 226–7
context and the internet 227
defamation and truth 221
effect of claimant's existing reputation 222–3
implying habitual conduct 229
importance of context 226
innuendo 223–4
juxtaposition 224–5
other people's words 227–8
pictures 224
previous convictions 231
product stories 231–2
reporting investigations 229–30
reporting rumour 228
requirement for serious harm 220–21
settlements in defamation cases 218–20
spoofs, jokes 232–3
Osborne, Ozzy 219
O'Sullivan, Ronnie 72
other courts in which s49 restrictions apply 152
youth court cases sent to Crown Court 152
other legislation relating to police 340–43
other local public bodies 427–8
magistrates' courts committees 428

NHS trusts and health authorities 428
schools 427–8
social services departments 428
other people's words 227–8
see also defamation
other proceedings for companies in trouble 459–60
other reporting restrictions 123–4
anonymity orders in High Court 123
High Court's inherent jurisdiction 123–4
other restrictions in sexual offence cases 138–9
ownership of buildings 455
ownership of copyright 364–6
photographs 365
transferring copyright 365–6
ownership of limited company 454
Oxford Mail 122

Packer, Kerry 234
paedophilia 141, 155
paranormal practices 488–90
Parker, Chris 218, 244
Parkinson, Michael 220, 241
Parliamentary privilege 439
parody 367
Parole Board 29
partnerships 453
pay per view services 487–8
payment into court 76
payment to criminals 483
peer-reviewed statements 262–3
pejorative material 388–9
penalties 414, 432
pending proceedings 82, 114, 117
penetration 37
people at risk of harm 292–3
people in the legal system 13–15
government legal officers 15
judges 14–15
lawyers 13–14
personal data 346–7
definition of 347
personal information 442, 448
Petters, Lee 225
Phoenix Nights 269
phone tapping 412
photo-journalism *see* photography
photography 86–7, 289, 303–4, 370, 471–9
copyright and confidentiality 477–8
ownership 365
private property 473
public places 474–7
summary 478
photosensitive epilepsy 490
pictures 84, 224, 312
protecting privacy 312
see also defamation; photography
pirating 374
pixellating 74, 235, 403
planning and development matters 426–7
pleading guilty to other charges 74
pleas in mitigation 139–40
Plymouth Evening Herald 118, 150
points of law referrals 144–5
police appeals 66
Police Federation 234
police information 93
police questioning 21–2, 335
police radio messages 326
Police Review 238
political parties 242
pornography 226, 374
position of media 293
postponement orders 117–18
postponing publication 114–18
powers of arrest 20
powers of investigation 414–15
powers of search and seizure 335–8
powers to restrict access 100–101
practicality 369–70
pre-action protocol 244
pre-arrest powers 20
pre-trial civil procedure 46
pre-trial criminal hearings 24–5
either way offences 24–5
indictable offences 25
summary offences 24
pre-trial hearings 24–6, 130–31
bail applications 25
in the Crown Court 25–6, 130–31
end of restrictions 131
in the magistrates' courts 24–5, 130
precedent 6, 49, 54
precincts of court 476
preferential creditors 458
premium rate telephony services 511, 516
preparatory hearings 131–2
preservation of due impartiality 493–4
Press Association 106, 115, 117–21, 136, 156, 192
press attendance at inquests 190–93
access to documents 191
inquest and contempt of court 191
inquest and defamation 191
reporting restrictions 191–3
press bench 106

Press Complaints Commission 57, 134
Press Freedom Survey 2004 354, 356
Press Gazette 150
preventing distress 208
preventing publication 92–3, 119–22
preventing restrictions 204–5
prevention of crime 334
prevention of publication injunction 57
previous convictions 28, 71–2, 231
  see also defamation
Price, Katie 219, 401
Prince Charles 306, 313
Princess Caroline of Monaco 303, 310, 312, 370, 475
Prior, Malcolm 437
prior restraint 57
privacy 301–322, 401–3, 475, 481, 500–504
  claims under Protection from Harassment Act 1997 316–20
  elements of claim 301–313
  and photography 475
  principles of Ofcom code 501
  remedies to action 313–16
  rules of Ofcom code 501–4
  summary 321
  vs freedom of expression 307–313
privacy rights in copyright issues 375–7
  see also moral rights in copyright issues
private bills 4
private hearings 98–9
private law 11–12
private lives 501–2
private members' bills 4
private property photography 473
private prosecutions 11, 24, 83
privilege 93
privileged material 255–6
PRM *see* programme-related material
Pro-Life 80
problems with gathering information 354–6
  information from police 354–6
  information from schools 356
procedure of civil courts 43–52
  appeals in civil cases 47–9
  civil litigation procedure 45–7
  common civil claims 49–50
  summary 51
  types of civil court 43–5
procedure of criminal courts 18–41
  appeals, retrials 31–4
  common crimes 35–9
  criminal cases 18
  criminal justice procedure 19–28
  magistrates' courts 18–19
  summary 40–41
  types of sentence 28–31
procedure of inquests 188–90
  criminal proceedings/public inquiries 190
  hearing 188–9
  verdicts 189–90
procedure in tribunals 197–8
proceedings closed to press 169
proceedings of Parliament 262
proceedings without jury 75, 114
Proceeds of Crime Act 2002 129
processing personal data 348–50
  sensitive data 250
product placement 506
product stories 231–2
  see also defamation
programme-related material 511–12
prohibited places 474–5
prohibited sponsors 510
proportionality 55
prosecution 23–4, 414, 467–8
  private prosecution 24–6
Prosecutor Fiscal 84
protected documents 76
protecting adult defendants 156–8
protecting against libel 276
protecting sources 342
protecting under-18s 393, 484–8, 504
  principle 484
  rules 484–8
protecting vulnerable witnesses 140–43
  Coroners and Justice Act 2009 142–3
  Serious Organised Crime and Police Act 143, 2005
  Youth Justice and Criminal Evidence Act 1999 140–42
protection against injunction 57–8
  decisions on injunction 57
  injunctions preventing publication 57–8
  media representation 57
protection of sources 330–45, 353
  Contempt of Court Act 1981 331–4
  Official Secrets Acts 338
  other legislation 340–43
  PACE: information required by the police 334–8
  summary 343–4
  Terrorism Act 2000 338–40
proving implications 250–51
proving truth 249

provisions against anti-social behaviour
160–62
CBOs 161–2
IPNAs 161
provisions not yet in force 162, 182
provisions of Ofcom code 392–404
commercial references 404
crime 394–5
elections and referendum 397–8
fairness 398–401
harm and offence 393–4
impartiality and accuracy 395–7
privacy 401–3
protecting under-18s 393
religion 395
sponsorship 404
PRS *see* premium rate telephony services
psychological trauma 155
public affairs, conduct of 439–40, 442
public bills 4
public bodies covered by FOI 2000 437
public domain 294, 306–7
information in 306–7
Public Finance Initiative 426
public inquiries 190, 201
inquest 190
one-off inquiries 201
reporting 201
public interest 118, 263–8, 296–7, 309–310, 373–4, 386, 413, 483
celebrities and 309–310
consideration of 118
in government stories 296–7
public interest defence 268–9, 327
public interest test 442–3
public law 11–12
public office misconduct 327
public order 463–70, 476–7
and obstruction 476–7
race and religion 463–70
publication of defamation 238–41
archive material after a libel claim 240
libels in more than one publication 240–41
publication and the internet 239–40
publication on matter of public interest 263–8
Reynolds criteria 264–5
publication schemes 438
publications prejudicial to fair trial 64
publishing interviews 76
publishing jury deliberations 88–9
purpose of statement 431
qualified exemptions 440–43
auditing 441
commercial interests 442
communication with royalty 442
conduct of public affairs 442
criminal investigations 441
defence 440
domestic relations 441
economic interests 441
environmental information 442
formation of government policy 441
health and safety 442
information intended for publication 440
international relations 440
law enforcement 441
legal professional privilege 442
national security 440
personal information 442
qualified privilege 93, 259–72, 518–24
accord and satisfaction 271–2
importance of good conduct 270–71
judicial proceedings 262
malice 263
neutral reports of disputes 268
offer of amends 269
peer-reviewed statements 262–3
proceedings of Parliament 262
public interest defence and archived material 268–9
publication on matter of public interest 263–8
reply to character attacks 262
statements subject to contradiction 518–23
statements without explanation 518
supplementary provision 523–4
under Defamation Act 1996 259–61
using defence 269–70
quashing conviction 32, 144
Queen Elizabeth II 368
Queen's Bench Division 15, 32, 43–4, 49, 68
Queen's Counsel 14

race relations law 434
race and religion 465–70
incitement to racial hatred 465–7
religious hatred 467–8
summary 469
racial hatred 465–7
racism 467
Radio Sheffield 394
Rahman, Mizanur 467
Ramsey, Gordon 256, 308–9
Ramsey's Kitchen Nightmares 256

rape 22–3, 37, 74, 133–9
  jigsaw identification 137
  lifting restrictions 136
  offences covered by restrictions 134–5
  rape complainants in later proceedings 137
  restrictions in 133–9
  scope of restrictions 135–6
readers' letters 233
reasonable expectation of privacy 302–7, 473–4, 501–2
receivership 459
reconstructions 105
recorders 14
records of local government 425–7
  access to 425–7
reference to client 233–8
  defaming a group 237–8
  dropping hints 234–5
  implied reference 235
  pixellating, bleeping 235
  unintended reference 235–7
referendum 397–8, 495–8
  see also elections
referral to Criminal Cases Review Committee 32–3
referrals on points of law 144–5
referring to character 431
registration of status as data controller 348–9
religion 395, 465–70, 491–2
  principles of Ofcom Broadcasting Code 491–2
  rules of Ofcom Broadcasting Code 492
  see also race and religion
religious hatred 467–8
  defences 468
  investigation and prosecutions 468
remedies for breach of confidence 297–8
  account of profits 298
  order for delivery up 297–8
remedies for breach of copyright 374–5
remedies for defamation 247–79
  see also defences for defamation
remedies in private action 313–16
  injunctions 313–16
removal of risk by order 117
repeat actions 274
reply to character attacks 262
report stage of statute 5
reporting after an arrest 67
reporting breaches of CBOs 162
reporting CBOs 161–2
reporting current events 369–70
reporting elections 433
reporting employment tribunals 198
reporting Family Court matters 166–87
  access to family proceedings 167–73
  media attendance in Family Court 173–84
  summary 184–6
  work of Family Court 166–7
reporting government and business 409–462
  freedom of information 436–51
  official secrets 411–17
  reporting elections 430–35
  reporting local government 418–29
  writing about business 452–62
reporting hearings heard in private 90–91
reporting inquests 188–94
  restrictions 191–3
reporting inquiries 201
reporting investigations 66, 229–30
reporting IPNAs 161
reporting pre-trial hearings 133
reporting proceedings 261
reporting racist remarks 467
reporting restrictions 113–65, 197, 199–201
  in criminal cases 126–48
  in employment tribunals 199–201
  general 113–25
  re children 149–65
  in tribunals 197
reporting restrictions re children 149–65
  children in adult courts 152–60
  provisions against anti-social behaviour 160–62
  provisions not yet in force 162
  summary 163
  youth court cases 149–52
reporting rumours 228
reporting tribunals and inquiries 195–203
reputation 272
requirement for serious harm 220–21
  see also defamation
residual impact 77
residual value 506
respect for private/family life, right to 58
restricted sponsors 510
restrictions on access to criminal courts 102–3
  cases under Official Secrets Act 103
  child witnesses in sex offences 102
  closed material procedure 103
  defendants assisting the police 102
  evidence of sexual history 103

special measures directions 102
youth court proceedings 102
restrictions on court access 100–110
access to civil courts 106–7
access to criminal courts 101–6
broadcasting and use of social media from court 108
general powers to restrict access 100–101
obtaining information from civil courts 108–110
restrictions in rape offences 133–9
jigsaw identification 137
lifting 136
offences covered 134–5
other restrictions 138–9
rape complainants in later proceedings 137
scope of 135–6
special rules in incest cases 139
restrictions in sexual offences 133–9
jigsaw identification 137
lifting 136
offences covered 134–5
other restrictions 138–9
rape complainants in later proceedings 137
scope of 135–6
special rules in incest cases 139
retrials 31–4
appeals against acquittal 33–4
see also appeals
reversal of acquittal 33–4
appeals by way of case stated 33
appeals from Court of Appeal 34
new evidence 33
sentence review 34
stopped trials 34
witness intimidation 33
review material 369
Reynolds, Albert 265
Reynolds criteria 263–8
Richardson, Natasha 228
Richmond and Twickenham Times 154
right of paternity 375–6
right to fair trial 58
right to reply 385
right to respect for private/family life 58
right to tell 310–311
rights of data subject 350–51
risk of incurring costs 209
risks to person claiming anonymity 121–2
robbery 35, 38
Robertson, Geoffrey 90, 415, 424, 431, 434, 455
Rock Follies 288
role of Ofcom 392
Rolls-Royce 253, 289
Ronaldo, Cristiano 220
Rooney, Colleen 156, 241
Rooney, Wayne 156, 241
routes of appeal from magistrates' court 32
by way of case stated 33
magistrate error 33
referral to Criminal Cases Review Commission 33
to Crown Court 32
Rowling, J.K 288, 304
Royal Assent 5
Royal Courts of Justice 43
Royal family 306, 313, 368, 440–42
Prince Charles 306, 313
Queen Elizabeth II 368
Royal Navy 414
rules for excluding press from criminal courts 103
rumours 228
see also defamation

s159 appeals 207–9
St James Evening Gazette 363
same-sex orgies 235
sanctions for contempt 91–3
preventing publication 92–3
satisfaction 271–2
scale of bankruptcy 457–8
scandalising a judge 86
Scarborough Evening News 139
school information 356, 427–8
school photography 356
scope of s4(2) orders 118
scope of Sexual Offences restrictions 135–6
scope of strict liability contempt 81–2
Scotland 63, 84–5, 315, 397–8, 440–42
contempt in 84–5
'Scott Affair' 230, 234
Scott, Norman 230, 234
SCPO *see* serious crime prevention order
search and seizure powers 335–8
second appeal to Court of Appeal 33
second reading of statute 4
section 4(2) order 114–18
consideration of public interest 118
current/imminent/pending proceedings 117
necessary order 115–16
order must remove risk 117
postponement for specific time 117–18
risk must be substantial 116–17
substantial risk of prejudice 115
see also Contempt of Court Act 1981

section 11 order 119–22
  ban necessary in interests of justice 120–22
  name or matter must be withheld in court 119
  notice of s4(2) and s11 orders 122
  see also Contempt of Court Act 1981
secured creditors 458
security matters 439
security scandals 412
self-defence 55
sending for trial 127–9
sensitive data processing 250
sentence review 34
sentencing 28, 129, 258
serious crime prevention order 31
Serious Fraud Office 19, 291
serious harm 220–21
serious interference 304
serious offences 258
serious prejudice 68–77, 114–17
set-ups 400, 500
settlements 44, 218–20
  in defamation cases 218–20
sexism 219
sexual activity 37–8
sexual offences 37–8, 133–9
  against adults 37
  against children 37–8, 159–60, 481
  restrictions in 133–9
sexual offences prevention order 121
sexual orientation 388–9
Shayler, David 336, 412–13
Shipman, Harold 229–30
shock 385–6, 481
simulations 393–4
Singh, Simon 254
skeleton arguments 109, 172
Sky News 326, 400
slander 243–4
small claims track 46–7
Smith, Graham 333–4
Smith, Will 219
So Solid Crew 115
social media 312–13
social services departments 428
sole traders 453
soliciting information 88–9
solicitor-general 15
solicitors 13–14
SOPO *see* sexual offences prevention order
sound recordings: copyright on 361
source material protection 330–45
  see also protection of sources
sources of information 264, 305, 332
sources of law 3–9
  case law 6
  delegated legislation 5–6
  EU law 6–8
  statute 3–5
sources protection under human rights legislation 342–3
special measures directions 102
special procedure material 335–6
special rules in incest cases 139
special rules for interim injunctions 314–15
Spectator 87
speculation about damages 76
speeches 363–4
  see also copyright
spoken words 373
sponsorship 404, 509
spoofs 232–3
  see also defamation
spot advertisements 514
Spycatcher 288, 291, 294, 296, 315
Squires, Dorothy 376
stalking 316
standard of proof 44
Star magazine 218–19
statement of opinion 253–4
Stationery Trade News 225, 272
status of information 264
statute 3–5, 97–8
statutory instruments 5
stealing 38
stipendiary magistrates 69
stopped trials 34, 144
stories about ordinary people 242
stories involving children 180
Straw, Jack 431
strict liability contempt 64–82
  active proceedings 65–8
  balancing relevant factors 77–8
  defences 79–81
  definition 65
  multiple publications 78–9
  scope of 81–2
  substantial risk of serious prejudice 68–77
Strictly Come Dancing 219
striking out 67, 276–7
sub judice proceedings 83, 93
subbing errors 225
subpoenas 252
substantial risk of serious prejudice 68–77, 114–17
  circulation of publication 71

content of report 71–7
timing of publication 70–71
trial location 71
who case is tried by 69
substantial truth 249–50
subterfuge 482
suffering 503–4
sufficient acknowledgement 370–71
suicide 36, 304, 319, 385–6, 489
suicide bombing 117, 257
suicide pact 36
suing for defamation 241–3
'libel tourism' 242–3
summary offences 18, 24
summons 65
Sun Printers 294–5
Sunday Business 71
Sunday Express 141, 217
Sunday Herald 437
Sunday Life 73, 228
Sunday Mirror 70, 72, 219, 236
Sunday People 56, 222
Sunday Sport 280, 282
Sunday Telegraph 228, 240
Sunday Times 230, 291, 295–7, 315, 372, 389
Sunday World 72
Sunderland Echo 134
The Sun 71–4, 83–5, 128, 182, 228–30, 266, 306, 370–71, 375
super injunctions 315–16
Supreme Court justices 14
surreptitious filming 503, 506
surveillance 341–2
suspended sentence 30
Sutcliffe, Peter 437
system of appeals in civil cases 47–9
from civil jurisdiction of magistrates' courts 49
from county courts 48
from High Court 48–9
judicial review 49

tainted trials 144
Take a Break magazine 220
taking notes in court 107
taking photographs in public places 474–7
courts 476
obstruction and public order 476–7
official secrets and terrorism provisions 474–5
photographing police 477
privacy 475
tape recording 86–7
tariff sentences 29
Taylforth, Gillian 72, 77, 85, 248
teachers' anonymity 145
terrorism 103
terrorism and photography 474–5
terrorism provisions for Northern Ireland 340
Terry, John 302–3, 314–15
test of public interest 442–3
Tetra 288, 332
texting from court 108
Thalidomide 291
Thatcher, Margaret 295
theft 35, 38–9, 75
third reading of statute 5
Thorpe, Jeremy 230
threatening language 467
TICs *see* offences to be taken into consideration
time limits 274
timed postponement orders 117–18
The Times 251, 311, 363, 432
timing of publication 70
Tisdall, Sarah 331
Titbits 224
Today 179, 281, 363
Tofalos, Chris 375
Top Gear 232, 282
tort 44, 50
Tort Law 216
tracing suspects 151
trade marks 505
trade unions 242
trafficking 135
transfer of sexual offence cases 132–3
transferring copyright 365–6
assignment 365–6
licence 366
transparency 515
trespass 50, 323–9
definition 323–4
harassment 324–5
intercepting calls, post, emails 325–7
misconduct in public office 327
summary 328
trial by newspaper 70
trial procedure 26–7
guilty pleas 26
not guilty pleas 26–7
tribunals 195–203
employment tribunals 197–201
public inquiries 201
reporting tribunals 195–7
summary 202

truth 221, 248–53
  identifying sources 251
  new evidence 251–3
  proving implications 250–51
  proving truth 249
  substantial truth 249–50
  see also defamation
TV Times 360
tweeting from court 108
Twitter 313, 419
TWOC *see* joyriding
types of appeal from Crown Court 32–3
  by way of case stated 33
  referral to Criminal Cases Review Commission 33
  to Court of Appeal 33–4
types of challenge to orders 205–210
  applying to original court 205–6
  following invalid orders 209–210
  judicial review 206–7
  risk of incurring costs 209
  section 159 appeals 207–9
types of civil trial 46–7
types of contempt 86–91
  breaking embargoes on court judgments 90
  contempt in the face of court 86
  failing to comply with court order 87–8
  frustrating court orders addressed to others 88
  identifying jurors 89
  interfering with witnesses 89–90
  investigating/publishing jury deliberations 88–9
  reporting hearings heard in private 90–91
  scandalising a judge 86
  tape recording and photographs 86–7
  using documents disclosed during proceedings 88
types of defence for defamation 247–74
  absolute privilege 257–9
  consent 248
  honest opinion 253–7
  innocent dissemination 272–4
  qualified privilege 259–72
  time limits and repeat actions 274
  truth 248–53
types of hearing 98–9
types of information 437–8
types of law 11–12
  criminal and civil law 11
  public and private law 11–12
types of sentence 28–31
  absolute/conditional discharges 31
  binding over orders 30–31
  community sentences 30
  compensation/confiscation orders 30
  fines 30
  imprisonment 29–30
  mental health orders 30
  serious crime prevention orders 31
types of statement covered by honest opinion 256–7
typographical arrangements 362
  copyright and ideas 363

Ulster Television 58
ulterior motives 80
unauthorised advertisements 432–3
unauthorised use of material 293
unauthorised use of pictures 376–7
undermining witnesses 77
undue prominence 404, 492–5
  of opinions 492–5
  principles of Ofcom code 492–5
  rules of Ofcom code 493–5
unethical behaviour 323–9
  see also trespass
unfairness 49
unincorporated organisations 242
unintended reference 235–7
unintentional disobedience 87–8
United Nations 257
unjustified modification 376
unlawful interference 323
  see also trespass
unlawful killing 189
unlawful publication 413–14
unsecured creditors 458
untrue statements 221, 280–81
unwarranted demand with menaces 38
  see also blackmail
urgency 264
using defence 269–70
using documents disclosed during proceedings 88
using Freedom of Information Act 2000 446
using information about family cases 182–3
using law to protect privacy 311

using photographs 365
using truth defence 252

verdicts 189–90, 258
in inquests 189–90
very young children 155
victims of sexual offences 37–8, 133–9, 482
videos 303–4
vilification of suspects 75–6
violence 393–4, 486, 489
voluntary liquidation 458–60
voluntary manslaughter 35–6
vulnerable witnesses 140–43
protection of 140–43

Wales 397, 424, 439–42
access to meetings 424
conduct of public affairs 439
Wall Street Journal 239
wardship 167, 178–9, 292
injunctions affecting wards of court 178–9
Warrington Guardian 100
Waterman, Hannah 218
watershed 393–4, 484, 486
Watford Observer 294–5
Weller, Paul 304–5
West, Fred 69, 128
West, Rosemary 69
Western Gazette 154
what copyright protects 364
where orders may be used 114
Which? 445
Whistleblower: Childcare 403–4
whistleblowing 290
who tries a case 69
wife-swapping 270–71
'wind-up' calls 400, 500
Winehouse, Amy 324
Winslet, Kate 310
withholding names and addresses in court 119
witness anonymity order 142
witness intimidation 33, 114
witness payment 90, 483
witness protection 121
Wolverhampton Express and Star 306–7
Woman's Own 276
Worcester Evening News 155
work of Family Court 166–7
wardship 167
works protected by copyright 360–64
literary/artistic works 360–61
news and information 362–3
official information 364
sound recordings 361
speeches/interviews 363–4
typographical arrangements 362
World Cup 371
World Trade Center 230
wounding with intent 37
Wright, Peter 15, 88, 291, 315
writing about business 452–62
information on limited companies 453–6
insolvency proceedings 456–9
law on business information 452–3
other proceedings for companies in trouble 459–60
summary 460–61
writing about courts 61–212
access to courts 97–112
challenging reporting restrictions 204–211
contempt of court 63–96
general reporting restrictions 113–25
reporting the Family Court 166–87
reporting inquests 188–94
reporting restrictions in criminal cases 126–48
reporting restrictions re children 149–65
reporting tribunals and inquiries 195–203

Yachting World 230
Yaquib, Waseem 224
Yeates, Joanna 75
'Yorkshire Ripper' 437
young defendants in adult courts 152–60
child victims of sex offences 159–60
children 'not concerned in proceedings' 155–6
ending s39 order 158–9
issuing s39 orders 158
naming dead children 155
protecting adult defendants 156–8
very young children 155
youth court cases 102–3, 149–52
effect of s49 150
lifting s49 restrictions 151–2
other courts in which s49 restrictions apply 152

Zeta-Jones, Catherine 289, 297, 350–51, 477
Zircon 337